PRINCIPLES OF POLISH CRIMINAL PROCEDURE

Little is available in English on the procedural aspects of the Polish criminal justice system and the tenets of its criminal process. This authoritative new work addresses this gap, setting out an analysis of the founding principles, its main phases and of those systemic and structural components which inform it. Taking an applied, practical approach, it surveys the process from beginning to end. Pre-trial, trial, post-trial, questions of evidence and remedies are all clearly addressed. The authors, two acknowledged experts in the field, also explore the role of more general rule of law/standards of law questions that are currently impacting on the law and its interpretation. Comparative criminal lawyers will welcome this important new work.

Volume 22 in the series Studies in International and Comparative Criminal Law

Studies in International and Comparative Criminal Law
General Editor: Michael Bohlander

Criminal law had long been regarded as the preserve of national legal systems, and comparative research in criminal law for a long time had something of an academic ivory tower quality. However, in the past 15 years it has been transformed into an increasingly, and moreover practically, relevant subject of study for international and comparative lawyers. This can be attributed to numerous factors, such as the establishment of ad hoc international criminal tribunals and the International Criminal Court, as well as to developments within the EU, the UN and other international organisations. There is a myriad of initiatives related to tackling terrorism, money laundering, organised crime, people trafficking and the drugs trade, and the international 'war' on terror. Criminal law is being used to address global or regional problems, often across the borders of fundamentally different legal systems, only one of which is the traditional divide between common and civil law approaches. It is therefore no longer solely a matter for domestic lawyers. The need exists for a global approach which encompasses comparative and international law.

Responding to this development this new series will include books on a wide range of topics, including studies of international law, EU law, the work of specific international tribunals, and comparative studies of national systems of criminal law. Given that the different systems to a large extent operate based on the idiosyncracies of the peoples and states that have created them, the series will also welcome pertinent historical, criminological and socio-legal research into these issues.

Recent titles in this series:

The Construction of Guilt in China: An Empirical Account of Routine Chinese Injustice
Yu Mou

The Amicus Curiae in International Criminal Justice
Sarah Williams, Hannah Woolaver and Emma Palmer

Principles of German Criminal Procedure, Second Edition
Michael Bohlander

Principles of Chinese Criminal Procedure
Liling Yue

Principles of Indonesian Criminal Law
Topo Santoso

Principles of Polish Criminal Procedure
Jarosław Zagrodnik and Kazimierz Zgryzek

Principles of Polish Criminal Procedure

Jarosław Zagrodnik
and
Kazimierz Zgryzek

•HART•
OXFORD • LONDON • NEW YORK • NEW DELHI • SYDNEY

HART PUBLISHING

Bloomsbury Publishing Plc

Kemp House, Chawley Park, Cumnor Hill, Oxford, OX2 9PH, UK

1385 Broadway, New York, NY 10018, USA

29 Earlsfort Terrace, Dublin 2, Ireland

First published in Great Britain 2023

A catalogue record for this book is available from the British Library.

A catalogue record for this book is available from the Library of Congress.

Library of Congress Control Number: 2023944926

ISBN: HB: 978-1-50995-077-5
ePDF: 978-1-50995-079-9
ePub: 978-1-50995-078-2

Typeset by Compuscript Ltd, Shannon
Printed and bound in Great Britain

PREFACE

I am pleased to present the first book devoted to a comprehensive outline of Polish criminal procedure for English-speaking readers. It includes a presentation of the conceptual assumptions, the basic rules and procedural tools, the main procedural actors and the fundamental components of the process in criminal cases. It is my hope that the book will not only allow the reader to become familiar with the specifics of Polish criminal procedure in theoretical and practical terms, but will also become a reference platform for comparative analyses and play a role in the development of the science of comparative criminal procedural law. The book, in its conceptual and theoretical structure, is integrally inscribed in the ideological assumptions of the rule of law, democratic legal order and in the material and procedural aspects of justice. Therefore, it is not devoid of critical remarks as to how these assumptions are realised in current Polish regulation of penal procedural law. I am the author of the introduction and five of the eight chapters. Three chapters concerning the System of Principal Procedural Rules; Proceedings before the Court of First Instance; and Evidence, were prepared together with Professor Kazimierz Zgryzek. At this point, I would like to express my great thanks to the Professor for agreeing to participate in the preparation of the book and enriching the monograph in our jointly prepared chapters with his knowledge and experience.

This book would not have been written were it not for the inspiration, commitment and great kindness of Professor Michael Bohlander. I hereby express my gratitude to Professor Bohlander. I also hope that the content of the book will meet his expectations.

I would like to express my gratitude to Hart Publishing both for the honour of publishing this monograph and for their great support in giving the book its final shape, both in terms of content and layout.

Finally, my deepest thanks go to the most important persons to me, my parents and my son Timothy for their understanding of my work and ongoing support, without which the preparation of the text of the book would not have been possible.

Jarosław Zagrodnik

CONTENTS

Introduction: The Purpose of the Book

In explaining the title of this book, which is a part of a series of studies on legal systems,[1] it should be emphasised that the book presents an outline of Polish criminal procedure. The aim of the book is not to present in a detailed and comprehensive way all the solutions, institutions and mechanisms of criminal procedural law that might fall under this title, but to analyse and emphasise those that make it possible to explain the structure of the Polish criminal process, to present its main actors and their procedural roles, key procedural actions (decisions) as well as basic means of procedural coercion that intersect deeply with the sphere of civil liberties and rights. The extensive and constantly evolving legal regulation of international cooperation in criminal matters, as well as the regulation of compensation issues in a criminal trial, remain beyond the scope of this work. Only the problem of prosecuting certain crimes privately has been outlined.

Due to the assumptions adopted and presented above, the book concentrates on presenting particular legal solutions and their basic characteristics, taking into account the achievements of the doctrine of penal procedural law and the court judicature. Theoretical considerations, therefore, recede into the background and are limited to the most controversial issues, especially those concerning legal constructions that raise objections from the perspective of their compliance with the standards of human rights and freedoms set out in the Polish constitution and the European Court for Human Rights. Some deeper reflections accompany a critical analysis of the inquisitorial model of the trial in the current legal state.

To those more familiar with common law legal culture, the Polish criminal trial, based strictly on the provisions of the Criminal Procedure Code (CPC), which set a rigid legal framework for the activities of procedural authorities, including the courts administering the justice, as well as the activities of other procedural participants, may seem to be overly formalistic. Within this framework, there is no possibility of resorting to a certain flexibility and freedom in the pursuit of justice in individual cases, characteristic of the common law system, based on recourse to what is referred to as common sense.[2] The indicated binding and, at the same time, limiting of the procedural organs, as well as of other participants of the process, by rigid procedural rules, strongly referencing Germanic legal culture, is shown in its full form in the following chapters of this book.

The fundamental law concerning criminal trials is the aforementioned CPC, within the framework of which the provisions of substantive criminal law, contained mainly in

[1] M Bohlander, *Principles of German Criminal Procedure* (Oxford, Hart Publishing, 2021).
[2] ibid 2.

the Criminal Code (the basic act defining types of crimes), are implemented. The penal-procedural matter is also reflected in constitutional acts concerning courts (ie the Law on the Common Court System and the Supreme Court Act and certain other acts of 20 December 2019).

In practical terms, the interpretation of provisions of the criminal procedural law is significantly influenced by constitutional standards, which will be discussed later. At this point it should be emphasised that this influence may result from the jurisprudence of the Constitutional Tribunal concerning the compliance of the provisions of the CPC with the Constitution of the Republic of Poland, or it may be based on the direct application of the provisions of the Constitution of the Republic of Poland by common courts, or on the pro-constitutional interpretation of penal procedural norms. The provisions of the European Convention for the Protection of Human Rights and Fundamental Freedoms (ECHR) and the case law of the European Court of Human Rights (ECtHR) have an analogous impact on the process of applying the provisions of the CPC.[3] It should be added that the judgments of the Court, apart from their binding character resulting from their issuance in a specific case against Poland as a state party to the ECHR, also affect the process of application in other cases by setting out the proper direction of interpretation of the provisions of the Convention, which should be respected at the national level and reflected in the pro-conventional interpretation of the provisions of the CPC.[4] This view is consistent with the position expressed years ago by the then independent Constitutional Tribunal, according to which the courts bound by the Convention should, in the course of applying the law, refer to the principles and methods of interpretation leading to results that are in harmony with the standards set out in ECtHR judgments.[5]

Polish Materials Used

The framework of this book and its main goal of outlining Polish criminal procedure have determined that the literature sources should be limited to the most important monographs, commentaries and textbooks. The source material of the book is significantly supplemented by references to the jurisprudence of courts, especially the Supreme Court, whose decisions significantly influence the application of penal procedural law by common courts subject to its supervision. To avoid misunderstandings, it should be noted that in the Polish legal order the *stare decisis* rule does not apply, but common courts in practice respect the views of the Supreme Court in interpreting binding provisions. These courts are absolutely bound by the view of the Supreme Court if it was contained in a resolution of this Court adopted in response to a legal question referred to it by the appellate court ruling on a given case, aimed at resolving a legal issue requiring a fundamental interpretation of the law (Article 441 § 1 CPC). In other

[3] See J Zagrodnik, *Proces karny* (Warsaw, Wolters Kluwer, 2021) 53.

[4] M Wąsek-Wiaderek, in *System Prawa Karnego Procesowego*, ed P Hofmański, vol 3, 2, *Zasady procesu karnego*, red P Wiliński (Warszaw, 2014) 1352 and n.

[5] Constitutional Court Judgment – 11 December 2012, K 37/11, OTK-A 2012/11, pos 133; Constitutional Court Judgment – 19 July 2011, K 11/10, OTK-A 2011/6, pos. 60.

cases, the binding character of common courts to the views of the Supreme Court in the matter of interpretation of the applicable regulations is indirect and based mainly on *sui generis* prognostic motivation, consisting in the fact that a common court has to take into account the fact that basing a decision on a view different from that presented by the Supreme Court will lead to its being challenged, if not in the appellate court, which in turn will take into account the interpretative standpoint of the Supreme Court, then as a result of filing a cassation appeal to the Supreme Court.[6] This applies in particular to those views of the Supreme Court which have the force of a legal principle, ie which are formulated in a resolution adopted by the full composition of that Court, a composition of the combined Chambers or a composition of the full Chamber, or in a ruling issued by a bench of seven judges which has decided to give its resolution the force of a legal principle (Article 87 § 1 Supreme Court Act). Such rules are binding on all formations of the Supreme Court, unless a departure from the legal principle is made by the relevant composition of that Court (Article 88 Supreme Court Act).

Historical Development

The book does not include a description of the historical development of the criminal trial process in Poland, as it is not necessary for the realisation of the underlying premise. Historical references are consequently sporadic and constitute only a background for a better understanding of the legal solutions and mechanisms in force, especially when viewed from the conceptual perspective.

[6] See J Kasiński, *Meritum Postępowanie Karne* (Warsaw, Wolters Kluwer, 2019) 27.

1

Basic Concepts

The Model of the Polish Criminal Trial

Despite the passage of more than three decades since 1989 when Poland regained full independence and freed itself from Soviet influence, it has not yet been possible to establish a model criminal trial which fully meets the challenges of the present day and above all the standards of a democratic state governed by the rule of law, particularly in terms of guaranteeing the protection of the rights and freedoms of citizens involved in the operation/action of a complex procedural machinery.[1] Progressive changes in criminal procedural law made between 2013 and 2015[2] were essentially annihilated in 2016 on a *ratione imperii* basis as a direct result of right-wing groups coming to power. Under the slogan 'the desire to guarantee the implementation of the principle of truth' in criminal proceedings, changes have been made to criminal procedural law, setting it back in terms of development and in essence marking a return to the model solutions that are deeply rooted in the past, in the patterns of thought developed in the largely authoritarian *entourage* of 1944–1989, under the aegis of the police state, only to undergo a kind of 'facelift' in the spirit of the democratic rule of law in the original version of the 1997 CPC.[3] These changes brought about a de facto strengthening of the inquisitorial elements in the area of the regulation of the course of criminal proceedings, in particular with regard to the main trial, and a significant expansion of the procedural authority of the public prosecutor (eg in new provisions of Article 168b and Article 237 and amended provisions of Article 328 § 2 and Article 524 § 3 CPC) and its advantage over other procedural

[1] See J Zagrodnik, *Model interakcji postępowania przygotowawczego oraz postępowania głównego w procesie karnym* (Warsaw, Wolters Kluwer, 2013) 1–41.

[2] The core of these changes was a reshaping of the trial model that was subordinated, on the one hand, to increasing the scope for applying solutions that allow the consensual conclusion of criminal trials, and on the other hand, to striving to ensure the actual adversarial nature of the trial in contentious cases which requires to be examined in the main trial, while at the same time strengthening the reformatory (exploratory) aspect of sentencing in the appeal instance. The reconstruction of the judicial process in this spirit meant the actual empowerment of the parties at the final trial and the expansion of procedural guarantees, eg by opening up the way to obtain a judicial review, eg by opening the way to obtain, in the court proceedings, the assistance of a defence counsel or an official representative without having to prove their incapacity or by explicitly excluding the taking and use of evidence obtained for the purposes of the criminal proceeding by means of a prohibited act as defined in Art 1 § 1 CC of the Act of 6.06.1997 – Penal Code (Art 168a CPC in its original wording).

[3] Zagrodnik (n 1) 504.

parties in judicial proceedings (eg amended Article 55 § 4 and added Article 396a CPC), while at the same time lowering the guarantee standard of criminal trials.[4]

It should be pointed that outlining the current shape of the Polish criminal trial model requires considering how it is shaped in the pre-trial (preparatory) proceedings and the main proceedings (judicial proceedings).

Regarding the preparatory proceedings, it should be emphasised first of all that its purpose is not only to allow the prosecutor to verify the grounds for the indictment (or other main complaint) or otherwise discontinue the proceedings. According to Article 297 § 1(5) CPC, the objective of the preparatory procedure is collecting, securing and preserving evidence for the court – to the extent necessary. This combination of tasks, which offers wide-ranging possibilities for clarifying the case during the pre-trial proceedings (Article 297 § 1(4) CPC), in fact exemplifies the superiority of the pre-trial proceedings over the main proceedings, particularly the main trial, in terms of clarifying the case and gathering evidence. An extreme manifestation of this superiority is the reduction of the evidentiary proceedings at the main trial to, in essence, a review of the validity of the findings of the pre-trial proceedings, which often simply consists of the judge repeating the findings of the first stage of the process. That there is no added value in this, as far as the knowledge (cognitive) process of the main trial is concerned, seems almost self-evident and needs no proof. At the same time, this raises the danger of basing a judgment on evidence that is tainted by an accusatory bias of the prosecuting authorities and, consequently, on factual findings that only take into account the interests of one of the actors, namely the public prosecutor. This calls into question the optimal guarantee of the rights of defence of the accused in the judicial proceedings.

There are two forms of pre-trial procedures: principal investigation and simplified investigation. These two forms of investigation do not differ, either in their internal structure or in their tasks. For each of them, within their structural order, it is possible to distinguish between an *in rem phase*, ie so-called anonymous prosecution (of the case), and an *in personam phase*, ie so-called real criminal prosecution (against the person). In each of these forms, the pre-trial procedure is a non-judicial procedure. The police are the main body that conducts the proceedings which performs evidentiary activities in the pre-trial proceedings. In what constitutes the predominant form of simplified investigation, the police are the primary body conducting the pre-trial proceedings (*argumentum* ex Article 325 a § 1 CPC). Although the prosecutor is the main body in the principal investigation (Article 311 § 1 CPC), in practice, it is the police who carry out most procedural acts in this proceedings, given the widely used possibility to make a full or partial response or to entrust specific procedural acts to them (Article 311 § 2 CPC). Regardless of who conducts the preparatory proceedings and who carries out the individual acts of taking evidence, a wide range of evidence gathered at the first stage of the criminal proceedings can, and in practical terms

[4] S. Waltoś, 'Circulus vitiosus polskiej procedury karnej' in S Steinborn and K Woźniewski (eds), *Proces karny w dobie przemian. Zagadnienia ogólne* (Wydawnictwo Uniwersytetu Gdańskiego, Gdańsk, 2018) 28–32; J Zagrodnik, 'Model procesu karnego status quo i status futurus – kilka refleksji na temat dwóch rzeczywistości, nie tylko normatywnych' in *W pogoni za rzetelnym procesem karnym. Księga dedykowana Profesorowi Stanisławowi Waltosiowi* (Warsaw, Wolters Kluwer, 2022) 120 and n.

does, flow into the main trial. The presented picture of a principal investigation and a simplified investigation, proving that there are no substantial differences between these forms of pre-trial proceedings, undoubtedly puts a question mark on the sense of their normative separation.[5]

Against the background of the regulation of court proceedings, a distinction can be made between consensual procedural processes, generally involving a motion for a judgment of conviction to be issued in a session (Article 335 §§ 1 and 2 in connection with Article 343 CPC), voluntary surrender of responsibility (Articles 338a and 343a CPC) or a motion for the conditional discontinuance of the proceedings (Articles 338a and 343a CPC), and the trial of the case at the main proceedings (main trial).[6] Having regard to what has been said about the pre-trial proceedings, it should be pointed out that the distinguished courses of court proceedings are not interrelated to the distinction between the two forms of investigation. In other words, each of the specified court proceedings may be preceded by both a principal investigation and a simplified investigation. For each of them, the range of evidentiary activities (clarification of the case and preserving evidence) carried out in the preparatory proceedings is essentially the same. Basically, as an exception is made for the so-called a motion for a judgment of conviction to be issued in a session that is based on an accused's plea guilty that opens the way for the omission of further procedural acts in the pre-trial proceedings (Article 335 § 1, first sentence CPC). A similar connection between the scope of the clarification of the case and the course of the judicial proceedings is distinctly missing in relation to the main hearing (main trial). One would expect in this case that the priority of the main hearing over the clarification of the case in the pre-trial stage would be clearly established.[7]

The consensual model of the court proceeding consists in substantive adjudication by the court at a session (*posiedzenie wyrokowe*) on the basis of the investigation file, ie the evidence collected under the conditions of the inquisition. It is based on the filing with the court of one of the aforementioned motions which is filed instead of the indictment or attached to it. These motions are the expression of an agreement between the prosecution and the defence to settle the subject of the trial. Their consideration implies the acceptance of this agreement and the proposed outcome by the court. However, the court retains the right to modify these motions subject to the approval of the parties. The conclusion of a criminal trial by deciding on its subject at the session results, on the one hand, in a conciliatory resolution of the dispute arising from the commission of a criminal offence, and, on the other hand, in the speeding up of the criminal trial by avoiding the often lengthy evidence procedure. *De lege ferenda*, a comprehensive regulation of the consensual course of judicial proceedings and its close connection with the regulation of the pre-trial phase would be desirable. It would also be expected that the possibility of a consensual end of criminal proceedings will

[5] See S Waltoś, *A może jednolita forma postępowania przygotowawczego?* in M Rogacka-Rzewnicka, H Gajewska-Kraczkowska and BT Bieńkowska (eds), *Wokół gwarancji współczesnego procesu karnego. Księga jubileuszowa Profesora Piotra Kruszyńskiego* (Warsaw, Wolters Kluwer, 2015) 479–82.

[6] Zagrodnik (n 1) 506.

[7] Zagrodnik (n 1) 287–300; see also L Schaff, *Zakres i formy postępowania przygotowawczego* (Warsaw, Wydawnictwo PWN, 1961) 160ff.

be extended so that this will eventually be the case in at least 80 per cent of the cases submitted to the court.

In terms of the second model of the judicial proceedings, the model structure of the main hearing is of crucial importance. In this respect, it should be stated at the outset that the main hearing is entirely inquisitorial in nature.[8] It is characterised by the 'hyperactivity' (*hiperaktywność*) of the court and the presiding judge during the taking of evidence. Several factors determine this. First of all, in principle, is the unlimited evidentiary initiative of the court and its obligation to clarify *ex officio* all circumstances important to the determination of the case (*argumentation ex* Article 168 in conjunction with Article 2 § 2 and Article 366 § 1 CPC). No less important is the practical imposition on the court of a proactive attitude to the clarification of the case and the taking of evidence at the main hearing supported by the systemic exemption of the public prosecutor from responsibility for the 'success' of the prosecution – the outcome of the trial. Without such responsibility, the public prosecutor may be generally passive during the main hearing. Moreover, in the vast majority of cases, such as those where the pre-trial stage ends in the form of a simplified investigation, the public prosecutor does not have to be present at the trial at all (Article 46 § 2, first sentence CPC). This means, in essence, by virtue of the aforementioned obligations incumbent on the court, that the burden of proof is reversed to the court and the court takes steps that constitute the exercise of the function of prosecution. When juxtaposed with this solution that the participation of the accused at the main hearing is in principle his prerogative (Article 374 § 1 CPC) and hence he/she does not have to be present at the trial, we see a picture of a main hearing in which the court remains the only active and present actor during the evidential process. It seems obvious that under such conditions there can be no question at all of an adversarial process at the main trial – not only in its developed form, taking the shape of a genuine legal dispute between equal parties before a court, based on evidence conducted before that body as an impartial arbiter deciding the dispute, but also in its partial form, namely a main hearing involving the taking of evidence with the participation of the parties. In the light of the comments made, it can be said that the main trial is a forum for examining a case with the participation of the parties only possible in the evidentiary hearing, in any case subordinated to the dominant role of the court, which consists mainly – due to the principle of the presumption of innocence – in taking actions that make up the implementation of the function of the prosecution in a criminal trial.[9]

It should be also pointed out that de facto the passivity of the public prosecutor, the real transfer of the burden of proof to the court and the 'hyperactivity' of this body during the evidentiary procedure would not have been possible had it not been for the fact that the court has unlimited access to the pre-trial files, allowing it to get an idea of the evidentiary steps to be taken, in particular the questions that need to be asked

[8] See T Grzegorczyk, 'Model polskiego procesu karnego po 14 kwietnia 2016 r' in A Lach (ed), *Postępowanie karne po nowelizacji z dnia 11 marca 2016 r* (Warszaw, Wolters Kluwer, 2017) 17; J. Zagrodnik, 'Model postępowania dowodowego na rozprawie głównej w świetle najnowszych propozycji nowelizacji KPK', in R Olszewski (ed), *Artes serviunt vitae sapentia imperat. Proces karny sensu largo. Rzeczywistość i wyzwania. Księga jubileuszowa Profesora Tomasza Grzegorczyka z okazji 70 urodzin* (Warszaw, 2019) 223.

[9] Grzegorczyk (n 8) 17; Zagrodnik (n 8) 223.

of the prosecution witnesses. With such access, the court proceeds to hear the case under according to the investigation file, tainted by the accusatory bias of the criminal prosecuting authorities.[10] There is no mechanism to counterbalance this suggestion or to prevent such suggestion. There are thus insufficient guarantees that the court will maintain the distance from the case that is necessary to ensure an impartial judgment, free from the power of suggestion resulting from a reading of the investigation files. In addition, there is wide scope for the evidence in the investigation file to be used as part of the consideration of the case at trial and, as a result, to have a real impact on the evidential basis for the sentence, although this is most often carried out by the prosecuting authority under conditions of investigative and secrecy, ie without the involvement of the parties and their professional representatives.

Regarding the status quo of the main hearing outlined above, it can be concluded that because of the position of the presiding judge and the court in this forum – which negates the fundamental division of procedural functions between charge, defence and adjudication – the significant influence of the evidence collected during the investigation on the examination and determination of the case by the court, and the lack of real guarantees that the evidence will be taken at the main hearing with the active participation of the parties, there is currently no possibility for an independent court to decide the case and play its role as an impartial arbiter, based on a dispute between equal parties, according to evidence placed directly before this authority which allows the use of the dialectics of the cognitive process to reconstruct the course of events relevant to criminal law.[11] Taking the view that this possibility, involving a completely adversarial trial, is the optimal method to achieve substantive and procedural justice in cases of factual and legal complexity that come before the court, one should definitely advocate its introduction into the Polish legal order. There are strong arguments in favour of such a solution for guarantee reasons, in particular for empowering the accused during the evidentiary procedure at the trial and thus ensuring that he has a real possibility to exercise his rights of defence and to enter into a substantive defence against the prosecutor. Ensuring in this way the implementation of the adversarial principle in criminal trials, in its developed form, should be accompanied by more extensive changes in criminal procedural law, fully subject to the principles of a democratic state under the rule of law, taking into account the constitutional standards and treaty obligations of the Republic of Poland and guarantees the protection of human rights and freedoms, corresponding to a humane approach tailored for the twenty-first century. The framework and nature of this chapter do not allow for a detailed presentation of the proposals for such amendments, and some of these deserve a broader discussion and analysis, from both a theoretical and a practical point of view.[12]

[10] Zagrodnik (n 1) 180–85.

[11] Zagrodnik (n 4) 125–26.

[12] These proposals were recently outlined in the publication, entitled: 'Model of Criminal Trial Status Quo and Status Futurus – Some Reflections on Two Realities, Not Only Normative', in *Pursuit of a Reliable Criminal Trial. Księga dedykowana Professorowi Stanisławowi Waltosiowi* (Warszaw, 2022) 120 and next.

Subject Matter and Purposes of Criminal Proceedings

The subject matter of criminal proceedings is not uniformly understood in the Polish literature.

Against the background of the preventive and resocialising model of criminal law binding in Poland, a theory developed which envisaged explaining the subject matter of a trial by means of the term *ius puniendi*.[13] According to this theory, the subject matter of a criminal process is a claim that the state has against the offender (*ius puniendi*). The content of this claim is the power of the state to impose penalties and other measures in response to the crime committed. At present, this theory does not find acceptance in Polish criminal procedural law, mainly because it links the subject of the trial with the existence of a criminal-material relationship or, more simply, with the fact that an crime has been committed. In questioning this connection, it is pointed out that under the theory put forward, the subject matter of the criminal process would in fact depend on the commission of the crime. It would therefore exist in those cases where, as a result of the criminal trial, the fact of the crime would be established. While such cases predominate in practical terms, there are also situations where a criminal trial results in a discontinuance or acquittal as a consequence of a finding of no crime. If one were to adhere to the theory of *ius puniendi*, one would have to assume that in the situations mentioned above, the criminal trial lacked a subject from the outset.[14]

On the basis of the criticism of the theory of *ius puniendi*[15] outlined above, a now widely accepted understanding of the subject of a criminal trial has crystallised, which considers it is that which the trial is subordinate to, and which is to be determined and resolved by it.[16] To clarify this thought it is assumed, following Cieślak, that the main subject of a criminal trial boils down to the question of the legal responsibility of a convicted person for an crime that has been charged (or attributed) to them.[17] This issue raises the following questions: whether a crime has been committed at all and who committed it, in what form, and what legal consequences they are to bear for it.[18] The subject matter of the trial is therefore not the mere fact that a crime has been committed, since the examination of the relevant facts does not constitute an aim in itself but only an intermediate objective that serves to determine liability and the extent of the liability. Without in any way questioning this precise understanding of the subject matter of the criminal trial in the Polish doctrine of criminal procedure, it must be pointed out that, sometimes with some simplification, the subject matter is nevertheless identified with the criminal offence itself.

[13] S Śliwiński, *Polski proces karny przed sądem powszechnym. Zasady ogólne* (Warsaw, Gebethner i Wolff, 1961) 19 et seq.

[14] K Marszał, *Proces karny. Zagadnienia ogólne* (Katowice, Volumen, 2013) 14–15.

[15] L Lisiakiewicz, '"Ius puniendi" czy metafizyka', PiP 1963/8–9, p. 220; and W Daszkiewicz, *Prawo karne procesowe. Zagadnienia ogólne* (Poznań, Branta, 2000) 19.

[16] L Schaff, 'Wszczęcie postępowania karnego. Problematyka podstawy i przedmiotu procesu', PiP 1959/2, 257.

[17] M Cieślak, *Polska procedura karna* (Warsaw, PWN, 1971) 47–48; Daszkiewicz (n 15) 19–20.

[18] ibid. We can find such idea in English doctrine of criminal process – see A Ashworth and M Redmayne, *The Criminal Process* (Oxford, Oxford University Press, 2005) 19.

The term of the subject matter of a criminal trial is closely related to the determination of the main purpose of this trial, because this purpose is to decide the subject matter of the criminal process.[19] However, not every ruling on the substance of a criminal trial achieves its objective, namely that the ruling embodies justice in the substantive sense, and is therefore in that sense just. Substantive justice is thus a 'measure' of how a ruling in the subject of a criminal trial (ie, the end result of the criminal trial) is assessed in terms of achieving the aim of the trial. At the criminal procedural law level, 'substantive justice' is closely linked to the procedural justice. This last term should be identified with the procedure that provides the highest degree of probability of achieving a substantively just result (achieving substantive justice). A just procedure in this sense creates a presumption of a just ruling of the subject matter of the criminal process.[20]

Substantive justice and procedural justice are two complementary conceptual categories of justice.[21] The assumption of the achievement of substantive justice in the criminal process leads directly to *sui generis* an 'order' for the establishment (construction) of institutions and procedural mechanisms, allowing the achievement of this purpose. One can find support for this order in the normative framework, in Article 2 § 1 CPC, according to which the purpose of the CPC is to establish rules of criminal procedure which ensure that:

1. the perpetrator of a criminal crime is detected and held criminally liable and that no person who has not been proven guilty bears such liability;
2. by a correct application of measures provided for in the criminal law, and by the disclosure of circumstances conducive to committing a criminal crime, the tasks of criminal procedure be fulfilled not only in combating crime but also in preventing it, as well as in consolidating the rule of law and the principles of community life;
3. legally protected interests of the injured be secured and that, at the same time, the dignity of the injured be preserved;
4. resolution of the case be achieved within a reasonable time.

The directives guiding the criminal justice process, highlighted above in points 1 and 2, constitute the principle of an adequate penal response (*zasadę trafnej reakcji karnej*). This principle reflects the coupling of the overarching aim of the criminal justice process and the demand for substantive justice.[22]

Against the background of the above, and in order to avoid any misunderstanding, it must be pointed out that the aim of a criminal trial is not to establish the truth in the classical sense as the reconstruction of objective reality. Truth in this sense is not and cannot be an end in itself. Nor is it a measure of substantive justice. This becomes clear when one considers that a materially fair outcome of a criminal trial cannot be excluded even though the truth has not been established in the trial. And conversely, there

[19] Marszał (n 14) 14–15.
[20] K Marszał and J Zagrodnik, in J Zagrodnik (ed), *Proces karny* (Warsaw, Wolters Kluwer, 2021) 29–35.
[21] See W Lang, 'Prawo procesowe a prawo materialne. Wzajemne relacje', in W Czapliński (ed), *Prawo w XXI wieku. Księga pamiątkowa 50-lecia Instytutu Nauk Prawnych Polskiej Akademii Nauk* (Warszaw, Scholar, 2006) 429 et seq.
[22] M Cieślak, *Nieważność orzeczeń w procesie karnym PRL* (Warsaw 1965) 5.

is a possibility that a decision on the subject matter of a criminal trial lacks material justice although it is the result of the discovery of the truth in the criminal trial. This leads to the conclusion that the directive that the decision should be constituted by the findings of fact and thus aim at restoring objective reality in a criminal proceeding (Article 2 § 2 CPC) must be seen only in the context of maximising the probability of achieving a materially fair decision on the merits of the criminal proceedings.[23]

The findings so far have concerned the main purpose of the criminal trial. In addition to the main goal, one can distinguish partial goals which are to be achieved at different stages of the trial and which are synchronised with the main purpose. In the case of pre-trial proceedings, these objectives are set out in Article 297 CPC, which is outlined in chapter five. The purpose of the appeal proceedings is to correct defective rulings.

Sources of Criminal Procedural Law

In criminal procedural law, the term 'source of law' is used in the normative sense. In this sense, a source of law is a formalised act of state authority that establishes the provisions of applicable law.[24] Sources of criminal procedural law are sources of universally binding law in the Republic of Poland. These include, in accordance with Article 87 (1) of the Constitution of the Republic of Poland, the constitution, statutes, ratified international agreements and regulations. The condition precedent for the coming into force of statutes, regulations and enactments of local law shall be the promulgation thereof (Article 88 para 1 Polish Constitution).

The main sources of criminal procedural law are outlined in the following subsections.

The Constitution of the Republic of Poland

At the constitutional level the limits and at least the basic conditions of state interference in the sphere of rights and freedoms of the individual in the conditions of the criminal trial are primarily determined. On the same grounds the system and fundamental principles of the functioning of the administration of justice as one of the forms of the state's activities are regulated – this allows for the conclusion that the acts regulating the matter of the criminal trial are in fact the concretisation of the constitutional norms pertaining to this matter (eg in terms of regulating the legal situation of the individual and the forms and principles of the operation of courts), thus becoming a part of constitutional law *sensu largo*.[25] The Constitution of the Republic of Poland contains many provisions relating directly to the criminal trial, eg provisions

[23] Marszał and Zagrodnik (n 20) 36.
[24] Marszał (n 14) 40; T Grzegorczyk and J Tylman, *Polskie postępowanie karne* (Warsaw, LexisNexis, 2014) 62.
[25] S Waltoś, 'Konstytucja a proces karny', in S Waltoś (ed), *Konstytucyjne podstawy wymiaru sprawiedliwości w sprawach karnych. Kraków 16–18.06.1988. Materiały z konferencji naukowej* (Warsaw, PWN, 1989) 68; S. Wiliński, *Proces karny w świetle Konstytucji* (Warsaw, Wolters Kluwer, 2011) 21–22.

concerning the deprivation or restriction of liberty (Article 41), the right to a court (Article 45 para 1, Article 77 para 2), the presumption of innocence (Article 42 para 3), the right to a defence (Article 42 para 2), the audience of hearings (Article 45 para 2), the two-instance course of proceedings before a court (Article 176). The influence of the Polish constitution on the criminal trial is particularly important in the guarantee dimension. It is connected with the fact that the establishment of the foundations of the criminal procedural regulation on constitutional grounds means at the same time, from the negative side, the setting of impassable limits for legislative activity. The Constitution of the Republic of Poland constitutes a *sui generis* anchor that maintains the criminal procedural law system in a position that guarantees its stability within the scope of its core components, which are strictly connected with defining the relations between the state and the citizens at the highest normative level. The Constitution should also ensure, within the indicated scope, at least a relative immunity to waves of legislative activity in the area of penal procedural law, which are often manifestations of penal populism, threatening fundamental civil rights and freedoms, as well as standards of fair proceedings.[26]

European Convention on Human Rights

The ECHR constitutes an international agreement signed by the Member States of the Council of Europe on 4 November 1950, and ratified by the Republic of Poland on 19 January 1993; its rank in the hierarchy of sources of criminal procedural law is determined by the fact that it refers to the freedoms, rights and duties of citizens set out in the Constitution of the Republic of Poland, as well as to proceedings before the courts, ie a matter which currently requires ratification with the prior consent of the Sejm expressed in a statute. This determines – pursuant to Article 91(2) in conjunction with Article 241 of the Polish constitution – the precedence of the Convention as an international agreement over internal (domestic) statutes; such an international agreement ratified shall have precedence over statutes if an agreement cannot be reconciled with the provisions of such statutes.

Criminal Procedure Code

The CPC is a basic law containing provisions regulating the objectives of a criminal trial, the conditions of its admissibility, the entities participating in it, the activities aimed at achieving this objective and the course of the trial.

Criminal Code

The Criminal Code (CC) regulates the conditions of criminal responsibility for a crime, the penalties, punitive measures and other measures of criminal reaction

[26] J Zagrodnik, in Zagrodnik (n 20) 56.

(eg probationary measures) applied in connection with its commission, and the directives and principles of penalty assessment (CC General Part regulations 1–116), and also defines the basic types of criminal acts as crimes (CC Special Part regulations 117–363). The CC also regulates such issues as prescription (Articles 101–105 CC) or expungement of sentences (Articles 106–108 CC). The provisions of the General Part of the CC apply to other statutes providing for criminal liability, unless these statutes explicitly provide otherwise (Article 116 CC).

Law on the System of Common Courts (LSCC)

The Law on the System of Common Courts (LSCC) is the law that regulates the organisational structure of common courts, their tasks and bodies, and the rights and duties of judges.

Supreme Court Act

The Supreme Court Act (SCA) determines the structure of the Supreme Court, the organs of that court, the jurisdiction of the various chambers of the Supreme Court, and the rights and obligations of the judges of that court.

The last two Acts belong to a broader group of so-called system acts, which also includes Act – Law on the Prosecutor's Office, the Law on the Bar and the Act on the Police. These Acts regulate the organisational structure, organs, and tasks of the Prosecutor's Office, the self-government of solicitors and legal advisers, the police, as well as the rights and duties of prosecutors, solicitors, legal advisers and police officers. Acts relating to the subject matter of the criminal process also include, among others, the Act on Crown Witnesses. It is also worth noting that Polish law regulates separately the matter of penal fiscal law, ie the law in cases involving fiscal crimes and fiscal transgressions. Regulations concerning these matters are contained in the Penal Fiscal Code. The problem of execution of penalties, penal measures and other means of penal reaction, as well as execution of, for example, temporary arrest, is regulated in the Executive Penal Code.

Acts of a lower rank than a statute, which may be the source of criminal procedural law, shall be executive acts in the form of regulations. Regulations shall be issued on the basis of specific authorisation contained in, and for the purpose of implementation of, statutes by the organs specified in the constitution. The authorisation shall specify the organ appropriate to issue a regulation and the scope of matters to be regulated as well as guidelines concerning the provisions of such act (Article 92 (2) Constitution). In the case of criminal procedural law, the minister of justice is most often authorised to issue regulations. The regulations cannot lead to limiting the scope of rights of the litigants or serve to regulate the basis for the use of coercive measures.[27]

[27] Marszał (n 14) 41.

In the Polish legal system, the sources of criminal procedural law are neither custom nor judicial decisions (precedents) nor the views of the criminal procedural doctrine. This does not mean that court decisions, especially those of the Supreme Court, or doctrinal views are completely irrelevant to the penal procedural sphere. They play an important role at the level of interpreting the applicable regulations in the process of applying the law.[28]

Procedural Grounds

The construction of procedural grounds is the foundation of the criminal trial.[29] The importance of this construction is fully revealed in the background to the definition of procedural grounds, which emphasises their essential nature. Respecting the content of Article 17 § 1 CPC, we concur with the view prevailing in the Polish literature, according to which procedural grounds are factual and legal conditions, which, in accordance with the aforementioned provision (Article 17 § 1 CPC), determine the legal admissibility of a criminal trial.[30] In this sense, they are conditions for the existence of a criminal trial – they condition the initiation and conduct of a criminal trial. Article 17 § 1 CPC defines them from the negative side: the occurrence of one of the circumstances specified in this provision creates a procedural obstacle that precludes the commencement or continuation of a criminal trial.[31] This provision states that proceedings shall not be instituted, or shall be discontinued, when:

1. the act was not committed or there are no sufficient grounds to suspect that it was committed;
2. the act does not have the features of a prohibited act, or when it is acknowledged by the CPC that the perpetrator has not committed a criminal offence;
3. the act inflicts a minor social harm;
4. it has been established under the CPC that the perpetrator is not subject to penalty;
5. the accused is deceased;
6. the prescribed statute of limitations has lapsed;
7. criminal proceedings concerning the same act committed by the same person have been finally concluded or, if previously instituted, are still pending;
8. the perpetrator is not subject to jurisdiction of the Polish criminal courts;
9. no complaint has been filed by the authorised prosecution counsel;

[28] See S Waltoś and P Hofmański, *Proces karny. Zarys systemu* (Warsaw, Wolters Kluwer, 2016) 142–46.

[29] It is worth noting that this construction was taken from the science of German criminal procedure, the creator of which is regarded to be A von Kries (see 'Die Prezessvoraussetzungen des Reichsstrafprozesses' [1885] no 5 *Zeitschrift für Gesamte Strafrechtswissenschaft* 1 et seq). He transferred the constructional assumptions of procedural grounds adopted at the level of civil procedure by O Bülow, in *Die Lehre von den Prozesseinreden und die Prozessvoraussetzungen* (Giessen, 1868) 5 et seq. J Goldschmidt, in *Der Prozess als Rechtslage* (Berlin, 1925), made an important contribution to the development of the concept of procedural grounds on the grounds of criminal procedure.

[30] L Schaff, *Proces karny Polski Ludowej* (Warsaw, Wydawnictwo Prawnicze, 1953) 223 and n; M Cieślak, 'O przesłankach procesowych w polskim postępowaniu karnym' (1969) 12 *PiP* 960; Marszał (n 14) 143; Waltoś and Hofmański (n 28) 469; Grzegorczyk and Tylman (n 24) 175–76.

[31] Grzegorczyk and Tylman (n 24) 178.

10. there is no permission obtained for prosecuting or no motion to prosecute from an authorised person, unless otherwise provided in the CPC;
11. other circumstances precluding such proceedings occur.

The distinguished procedural grounds can be classified in various ways, using different criteria that enable their more complete characterisation.

Taking into account the scope of action of procedural grounds, ie whether they act in the course of the entire trial, within the scope of the main procedural stream, or, for example, only in one of the procedural stages, the following types of grounds can be distinguished:

1. occurring only in the proceedings before the court, eg the complaint of the authorised accuser;
2. relating to both pre-trial and trial proceedings – these grounds are the most numerous; they include, for example, the statute of limitations for criminal offences, lack of a request for prosecution, and lack of the constituent elements of a prohibited act;
3. acting only in executive proceedings, eg the prescription of execution of a sentence (Article 103 CC).[32]

Taking into account the permanence of a procedural obstacle, the consequences connected with it, caused by the existence of a procedural ground set forth in Article 17 § 1 CPC, grounds may be divided into absolute and relative ones.[33] Absolute grounds constitute conditions for admissibility of proceedings in any procedural setting. A procedural obstacle resulting from an absolute procedural ground excludes the possibility of commencing and continuing a criminal trial both at the time of its determination and in the future, as it is impossible to change the procedural arrangement in such a way that would open the way for conducting a criminal trial despite the state of affairs creating the obstacle. Procedural grounds of this nature may include, for example, the expiration of the statute of limitations for the crime. The ending of the time period after which a criminal offence ceases to be punishable is of a final nature; there is no possibility of a reversal in time or a turning back of time, which would neutralise the ending of the indicated time period and make it possible to initiate or continue a criminal trial. Relative grounds, on the other hand, condition the admissibility of a trial only in a specific procedural setting. This means that a procedural obstacle arising from such a circumstances does not preclude the possibility of a trial against the same person for the same act in a changed procedural setting. An example of such a premise is a complaint by an authorised accuser. The filing of a complaint by an unauthorised prosecutor causes the trial (a criminal trial in the judicial stage) to be discontinued. However, it is possible to change the procedural arrangement in which the trial is inadmissible, by again filing a successful complaint by the authorised accuser, opening the possibility of proceeding against the same person for the same act, provided, of course, that the statute of limitations for the crime has not expired.

[32] Cieślak (n 17) 408; Marszał (n 14) 143.
[33] Cieślak (n 17) 409–10; Marszał (n 14) 146.

Taking into account the nature of the condition that creates a procedural obstacle, in particular the connection with substantive criminal law, it is possible to distinguish:

1. strictly procedural (purely procedural) grounds;
2. grounds anchored in substantive criminal law;
3. states of a factual nature, forming the factual premise of the criminal trial, provided for in (1), namely:
   (a) the act was not commited;
   (b) lack of sufficient grounds to suspect that it was committed; this premise coincide with the grounds for initiating pre-trial proceedings.[34]

Against the background of this division, it should be clearly emphasised that procedural grounds are always a procedural phenomenon. This does not change the fact that some of them are clearly connected with substantive criminal law, on the basis of which they are conditions for criminal liability, eg insignificant social harm of the act or lack of the elements of a prohibited act. It is important that the procedural criminal law binds the admissibility or inadmissibility of a criminal process to them.

Although for the purposes of this book we will confine ourselves to the illustrated divisions of procedural grounds, it must be emphasized that their listing in Article 17 § 1 CPC is not comprehensive. This follows unequivocally from the content of Article 17 § 1 point 11 CPC, which provides for the qualification in the category of procedural obstacles of conditions excluding criminal prosecution other than those listed in points 1–10 of this provision. An example of such a condition may be abolition, provided for in amnesty laws.

Verification of the admissibility of a criminal trial through the prism of procedural obstacles is the duty of the procedural authorities.[35] This obligation extends to the entire proceedings and follows not only from the content of Article 17 § 1 CPC, but also, for example, from Article 339 § 3(1) CPC concerning preliminary examination of the case before it is referred to the main hearing, and from Article 439 § 1(9) CPC defining procedural defects consisting in ruling despite the existence of procedural obstacles specified therein and applicable in appeal proceedings and – in connection with Articles 523, 539a § 3 and 542 § 3 CPC – in extraordinary appeal proceedings. Determination of the existence of a procedural obstacle prior to the commencement of a criminal trial shall result in a refusal to commence the trial. If such determination occurs in the course of a criminal trial, the trial shall, as a rule, be discontinued.[36] In pre-trial proceedings and in judicial proceedings until the commencement of judicial examination, the ruling in this regard takes the form of a decision. After the institution of judicial examination, the court shall render a judgment about discontinuance of the proceedings (Article 414 § 1, first sentence). An exception applies to the circumstances described in Article 17 § 1 points 1 and 2. If these are found, the court shall render a judgment of acquittal, unless the perpetrator was in a condition of insanity at the time they committed the act.

[34] See Cieślak (n 17) 411–13; Marszał (n 14) 146–47; Waltoś and Hofmański (n 28) 472–83.
[35] Marszał (n 14) 148.
[36] If the court finds that it lacks jurisdiction, it shall not discontinue the proceedings, but it shall refer the case to a court of competent jurisdiction or to another body (Art 35 § 1).

The Criminal Trial Process

A criminal trial is a social phenomenon that undergoes dynamic development and has a beginning, a course and an end.[37] In the course of criminal proceedings, which for the most part concern the issue of criminal responsibility for the committed crime in the most general terms, the following procedural stages can be distinguished, taking into account the functions they perform.

There is no unanimity in criminal trial doctrine as to whether appellate proceedings can be considered as a separate procedural stage.[38] Its distinctiveness is supported by the fact that appellate proceedings primarily perform the control function in relation to the ruling issued in the first instance. Within the framework of the distinct procedural stages one can distinguish smaller separate sections, namely procedural phases, and then further, even smaller stages, in the form of sub-phases of the criminal trial.[39] The most important procedural phases and sub-phases are discussed further within the framework of a discussion of the course of the criminal trial in individual stages, leading to a final resolution of the issue of criminal responsibility.

The first three fundamental procedural stages, in which exploratory activities aimed at the correct determination of the issue of criminal responsibility are undertaken, determine the field of action of the interaction between the procedural entities. This interaction is driving force is the activity of procedural subjects. Referring the concept of interaction to the mutual relations between these subjects, we can say that the interaction is based on opposition or cooperation. Contradictions are revealed along the line of relations between the prosecution and the defence. These give a dialectical dimension to procedural cognition (the cognitive process in criminal proceedings), which refers to a thought pattern that provides – in its simplest formulation – a transition from a thesis through an antithesis to a synthesis, which should be combined with the enrichment of the state of knowledge about a criminally relevant event, which the settlement of criminal liability is supposed to concern.[40] Cooperation as another manifestation of interaction between procedural subjects which becomes apparent primarily at the level of relations between criminal prosecution authorities (the prosecution) and the court. An example of this in pre-trial proceedings can be the use of provisional detention by the court at the request of the prosecutor.

Interaction can also be considered a feature of the criminal trial, having in mind the system of interrelations between the various procedural stages, which is reflected in the model formation of the course of the criminal trial during these stages. In this sense, in connection with the cognisance of the case, the interaction occurring between the pre-trial proceedings and the main proceedings is of fundamental importance in the criminal trial.[41]

[37] See Cieślak (n 17) 53–54; Marszał (n 14) 492; Waltoś and Hofmański (n 28) 487–88.
[38] See Cieślak (n 17) 54–55; Marszał (n 14) 493.
[39] Cieślak (n 17) 53–54.
[40] See in German doctrine: J Meyer, *Dialektik im Strafprozess* (J.C.B.Mohr (Paul Siebeck, Tubingen, 1965) 45; see also Zagrodnik (n 1) 36–40.
[41] Zagrodnik (n 1) passim.

Terminological Issues

A significant difficulty when it comes to an attempt to present the Polish criminal process in an international, Anglophone dimension results from a specific net of procedural terms, which is reflected on the grounds of criminal procedural regulation. At this point we can only show this specificity in a few aspects, namely the terminology corresponding to different forms of procedural decisions, types of procedural time limits and selected features of procedural actions. In the following chapters we will elucidate various aspects of the procedural status of the person against whom the actions of criminal prosecution are directed (the accused *sensu largissimo*), evidentiary actions (explanations of the accused, testimonies of witnesses) and appeal measures.

Types of Procedural Decisions

Procedural decisions are imperative statements of the will of the bodies that direct the criminal process, which are binding on the parties and other participants in the proceedings.[42] The name 'procedural decision' is an umbrella term covering two groups of procedural decisions, namely rulings and orders.

Rulings are the most important procedural decisions. They do not constitute a uniform category. They are divided primarily into judgments and decisions (Article 93 § 1 CPC). Rulings also include resolutions issued by the Supreme Court in response to a question from an appellate court concerning the clarification of a legal issue requiring a fundamental interpretation of a statute (Article 441 § 3 CPC).

In pre-trial proceedings, a ruling may only take the form of a decision. At this procedural stage, decisions shall be issued by a public prosecutor and another authorised body (eg the police), and in cases provided for in the CPC, by the court (Article 93 § 3 CPC). In some cases, a decision issued by a non-prosecutorial criminal prosecution body, eg the police, requires the approval of the public prosecutor in order to be effective. This applies, for example, to a decision refusing to initiate or discontinue pre-trial proceedings (Article 325e § 2 CPC). Until approval, the police decision remains incomplete, as it has no procedural effect. Upon approval, the decision is treated as if it had been issued by the prosecutor.[43]

In court proceedings, a decision may take the form of a judgment or a decision. It follows from Article 93 § 1 that unless the CPC requires a judgment, the court shall issue a decision. In light of this regulation, it is important to determine the cases in which it is necessary for the court to issue a judgment. Two groups of such cases can be identified. First, the court shall issue a judgment when it decides on the subject matter of the trial, ie on the guilt or innocence of a certain person (when it decides on the criminal responsibility of a certain person). This follows indirectly from

[42] Cieślak (n 17) 51; Marszał (n 14) 288; Waltoś and Hofmański (n 28) 46.

[43] A Gaberle, *Umorzenie postępowania przygotowawczego w polskim procesie karnym* (Warsaw, Wydawnictwo Prawnicze, 1972) 53; J Zagrodnik, *Instytucja skargi subsydiarnej w procesie karnym* (Warsaw, CH Beck, 2005) 149.

Article 42(3) of the Polish constitution, which provides that everyone shall be presumed innocent of a charge until their guilt is determined by the final judgment of a court. The judgment deciding the subject of the trial may be, in its content, a judgment of conviction, acquittal or conditional discontinuance of criminal proceedings. The second of the indicated groups of cases concerns the establishment of one of the procedural grounds (procedural obstacles) described somewhat above, set forth in Article 17 § 1 CPC. The form of the ruling that corresponds to this establishment is determined by the state of progress of the criminal trial. Upon commencement of judicial examination, the court shall render a judgment deciding upon such discontinuance of the proceedings. If, however, it transpires that the circumstances (procedural obstacles) described in Article 17 § 1(1) and (2) CPC have occurred, the court shall render a judgment of acquittal, unless the perpetrator was in a condition of insanity at the time they committed the act. In the latter case, a judgment discontinuing the proceedings shall be rendered (Article 414 § 1 CPC).[44] Apart from the cases described above, court rulings take the form of decisions.

Exceptionally, in situations provided for in the CPC, decisions may also be issued by a court clerk (*referendarz*) (Article 93a § 1 CPC). Such decisions are declaratory in nature, confirming a certain state of affairs, eg when the court clerk (*referendarz*) discontinues proceedings following the prosecutor's abandonment of the charge in question (eg Article 57 § 2, Article 60 § 4 CPC).[45]

Next to the rulings, the second group of procedural decisions are – as established above – orders. These are usually issued in cases of minor importance.[46] Sometimes, however, they can directly affect the course of a criminal trial, eg in the case of an order refusing to accept a complaint against a decision to discontinue criminal proceedings or refusing to accept an appeal against a judgment. The issuance of the aforementioned orders results in the decisions appealed against becoming final and, consequently, in the termination of the criminal trial. In court proceedings, whether a procedural decision should take the form of a decision or an order is determined by the status of the authority authorised to issue it. If it is up to the court to issue a decision, a ruling is always required. The use of the verb 'to order' in relation to the court does not therefore mean that it can issue an order.[47] A decision takes the form of an order if the president of the court, the chairman of a division, the presiding judge of a panel of judges, or an authorised judge is authorised to issue the decision (Article 93 § 2 CPC). In cases defined in the CPC, a court clerk may issue orders (Article 93a § 1 CPC). For example, a court clerk may issue an order for the appointment of a public defender (Article 81 § 1 CPC). In pre-trial proceedings, orders are issued by the prosecutor or other authorised body (Article 93 § 3 CPC). Decisions of law enforcement agencies take this form if it does not follow from the provisions of the CPC that the resolution of a particular issue should take the form of a decision.

The diversity of forms of procedural decisions translates to a significant extent into a diversity of means of appeal for their control. Judgments may be appealed against

[44] Marszał (n 14) 307–08.
[45] Zagrodnik, in Zagrodnik (n 20) 185–86.
[46] Waltoś and Hofmański (n 28) 47.
[47] Marszał (n 14) 314.

by way of an appeal. Decisions and orders may be appealed against by means of a complaint.[48] Apart from that, orders issued by the presiding judge at the main trial may be contested before the adjudicative panel, unless the rulings are issued by one judge (Article 373 CPC). If the order of the presiding judge is contested, a ruling must be issued by the court. Decisions and orders issued by a court clerk are subject to objection. Should an objection be filed, the decision or order shall cease to be valid (Article 93a § 3 CPC). As a consequence of the filing of an objection, the decision must be issued – depending on whether it takes the form of an order or a decision – by the court clerk or the court.[49]

Characteristics of Procedural Actions

Looking at procedural actions from the perspective of compliance with the law and the legal consequences of failure to comply with this requirement, the following features can be distinguished: admissibility, effectiveness, defectiveness, validity and legitimacy.[50]

Admissibility of a procedural act is connected with the legal possibility of performing the act in the light of the CPC regulations.[51] An action that is not prohibited by these provisions is admissible. Taking a different perspective, procedural acts that are prohibited by the provisions of the law are considered inadmissible. 'Prohibition' may result from an express prohibition to perform a certain action or from a lack of entitlement, which may be established by inference *a contrario* based on the scope of the entitlement granted by law to perform an action of a certain type (eg the scope of the entitlement to file a complaint set forth in Article 459 § 1 and § 2 CPC).[52]

An effective procedural act takes place when the act produces the effects intended by the acting party, as specified in the CPC provisions. As a rule, the ineffectiveness of an action is a consequence of the failure to fulfil all the conditions of a given action that determine its effectiveness.[53] It is assumed that ineffectiveness is the property of an inadmissible action performed by a litigant or its representative. It can be concluded on this basis that admissibility and effectiveness are attributes of a procedural action taken by a party or its representative which are necessary for the action to have procedural effects provided for in the CPC regulations.

The defectiveness of a procedural action is characterized by actions performed not in accordance with the requirements arising from the provisions of the CPC.[54] A defect in an action may be reformed (cured). Reform means healing (correction) of the defective action with retroactive effect. Reformed action is treated as if it was correct from the beginning (the defect of this action is treated as null and void). Remedial effects may result from the force of law (eg in connection with an amendment to the act as a result

[48] See ch 8.
[49] D Świecki, in D Świecki (ed), *Meritum Postępowanie karne*, (Warsaw, Wolters Kluwer, 2019) 948.
[50] Marszał (n 14) 291 et seq; Grzegorczyk and Tylman (n 24) 388–95; Waltoś and Hofmański (n 28) 50–63.
[51] Grzegorczyk and Tylman (n 24) 389.
[52] Marszał (n 14) 291–92.
[53] Grzegorczyk and Tylman (n 24) 391–92.
[54] Grzegorczyk and Tylman (n 24) 389; see also Waltoś and Hofmański (n 28) 54–56.

of which a previous defective action loses its significance) or from the initiative of the parties or another participant of the process (eg as a result of supplementing deficiencies of the pleading, or repetition of the action by the procedural body). Conversion of an act should be distinguished from reform. The conversion consists in producing, by means of one act, effects characteristic not only of the act itself, but also of another act. A prime example of the conversion of an action is the filing of an appeal against a judgment within the seven-day period provided for filing a motion for a written statement of reasons for the judgment, which produces the effect proper to the said motion, even though it was not filed (Article 423 § 1 CPC).[55]

Justification and unfoundedness are features of procedural actions related to their substantive assessment.[56] For example, the unfoundedness of an action may result in the discontinuance of a criminal trial in the phase preceding the main hearing when it concerns the indictment (charge) and is of a manifest nature (Article 339 § 3 (2) CPC).

Invalidity provides a criterion for evaluating procedural acts adopted on the basis of a theoretical concept, the main idea of which is that in the case of particularly serious violations of law, an act should be considered invalid from the moment of its execution (*ex tunc*).[57] This concept is not reflected in the current CPC, which means that actions affected by even the most serious violations of law remain valid in the eyes of the law.

An important feature of actions taking the form of judgments is validity, which is a measure of the stability of these procedural decisions. Validity means the state in which a decision is final, ie when it constitutes the 'last word' in a criminal trial. Two types of validity should be considered: formal validity and substantive validity.[58] Formal validity means the state of unchallengeability of a decision by means of an ordinary appeal measures, ruling out the continuation of a given criminal trial. Substantive validity is in a sense an effect of formal validity. This effect can only be associated with rulings ending proceedings against a specific person for a specific act. The essence of substantive validity is the *ne bis in idem* prohibition. As long as a substantively valid judgment is in force, it prohibits instituting or continuing proceedings against a designated person for a specific act.[59] Revocation of a final judgment shall cause the prohibition arising from substantive validity to cease.

Procedural Time Limits

Procedural time limits serve primarily to ensure the efficient conduct of a criminal trial.[60] The CPC uses the word 'term' in several senses.

First, this term serves to define a period of time, distinguished by its beginning and end, in which a certain action can be taken, eg an appeal filed (Article 445 § 1 CPC),

[55] Marszał (n 14) 293–94; Grzegorczyk and Tylman (n 24) 389–91.
[56] Grzegorczyk and Tylman (n 24) 392; see also Waltoś and Hofmański (n 28) 57–58.
[57] Grzegorczyk and Tylman (n 24) 395.
[58] Marszał (n 14) 321–22.
[59] ibid 324.
[60] Grzegorczyk and Tylman (n 24) 420; Waltoś and Hofmański (n 28) 63.

a cassation appeal made against a defendant (Article 524 § 3 CPC) or for filing the expert opinion.

Secondly, the term 'time limit' refers to the designation of the final moment in the course of a criminal trial at which, at the latest, an act may be performed, eg by indicating the moment when the judicial examination is opened or closed (Articles 12 § 3, 41 § 2, 54 § 1 CPC).

Thirdly, the CPC provides for time limits for the use of coercive measures, defining the temporal framework for the admissibility of their use, such as the time limits for provisional detention set out in Article 263 CPC.

Fourthly and finally, the term 'time limit' is used in the context of the time of commencement and sometimes continuation of the trial (eg Articles 353 § 1 and 2, 402 § 1, 404 § 2 CPC).[61]

The first of the above meanings of 'time limit' is of fundamental importance and will be discussed in more detail.

Time limits in this sense may be statutory time limits, if they are specified in the provisions of a statute, and may be set by the procedural authority, if it is up to this authority to determine the time within which a certain action should be performed, eg preparation of an opinion.[62]

Statutory time limits are the most commonly encountered type, and can be classified in various ways. At the most general level, one can distinguish between decisive and non-decisive terms, also referred to as instructional or orderly terms. The criterion allowing for a distinction between these two categories is whether the lapse of a given time limit produces procedural effects, particularly the inability to effectively perform a given action after the deadline.[63] Such effects occur in the case of the first category of statutory time limits. Time limits falling into the second category (instructional time limits) do not entail procedural consequences if they are exceeded, and the procedural act for which they are provided may be effectively performed after the expiry of the time limit. As a rule, they are addressed to the procedural authorities[64] and are intended to stimulate their efficient operation. Their violation can have extraprocedural consequences, namely in the area of disciplinary liability, if the failure to meet a deadline is the fault of a particular authority. Examples of these time limits are deadlines for providing a statement of reasons for decisions (Article 98 § 2 CPC) and statement of reason for judgments (Article 423 § 1 CPC) or the deadline for investigations (Article 307 § 1 CPC).

Decisive time limits can be further classified by distinguishing:

1. final time limits (*terminy zawite*);
2. preclusion time limits (*terminy prekluzyjne*);
3. other decisive time limits.[65]

[61] Marszał (n 14) 296–97.
[62] ibid 297.
[63] ibid 297–98; Grzegorczyk and Tylman (n 24) 426.
[64] As an exception, instructional time limits may be addressed to the parties. An example of such a deadline is the seven-day deadline that is provided in Art 338 § 1 for submitting motions to take evidence, which runs from the time the indictment is served on the accused. Failure to submit such motions within the indicated time limit shall not preclude their later submission during the proceedings.
[65] Marszał (n 14) 297.

A procedural action effected after the final time limit has passed shall be without legal effect. The time limits for lodging appeal measures are final, as shall also be time limits recognised as such under the CPC (Article 122 § 2 CPC). This is also the nature of time limits that are intended to have final effect, even though the CPC does not expressly recognise them as final (Article 120 § 2 CPC). Time limits that fall into this group are subject to reinstatement under conditions that are further specified.

Preclusion periods are characterised, similarly to final time limits, by the fact that a procedural act performed after the deadline is ineffective.[66] They differ from final time limits in that they cannot be reinstated. Thus they can be said to be more categoric (decisive). The preclusionary character of a deadline (its non-reversibility) is determined by the normative context, from which it must follow that in the case of a given deadline there is no possibility of performing an action after its expiration.[67] An example of a preclusionary time limit is the one-month time limit for an auxiliary prosecutor to file a subsidiary indictment in place of the public prosecutor (Article 55 § 1 CPC).

A subgroup of other decisive time limits consists of deadlines whose violation entails certain procedural consequences but does not render a procedural act ineffective.[68] The effect of exceeding them is, for example, the obligation to conduct the trial from the beginning, which arises if the time limit for the interruption in a trial (42 days) or if the time limit of adjournment of the rendering of a judgment (14 days) are exceeded (Articles 402 § 3 and 411 § 1 and 2 CPC).

The time limits are calculated according to the rules set out in Article 123 CPC. In accordance with this provision, the day from which a time limit is being calculated shall not be included in the time limit (§ 1). This means that where a time limit is calculated from the day on which an order is published, the day on which that publication takes place shall not be included. If a time limit is defined in weeks, months or years, the time limit shall lapse on the day of the week or month corresponding to the commencement of such a time limit; if a given month has no such day, then the time limit shall lapse on the last day of such a month. Where a time limit ends on a day statutorily recognised as a non-working day or on a Saturday, the action may be undertaken on the next day that is not a non-working day or a Saturday (§ 3). Article 127a CPC provides for the suspension of the time limit for a party to proceedings if a procedural action, in order to be valid, has to be conducted by a defence counsel or an attorney. This suspension lasts until the petition for legal assistance in this scope is examined. If a defence counsel or attorney is appointed ex officio, the time limit for conducting the action by the appointed legal representative shall be calculated as of the date of serving on them the decision or order on the appointment.

It should be emphasised that a pleading filed mistakenly with a court, public prosecutor, body of the police or another investigative body lacking jurisdiction in the matter prior to the lapse of the time limit shall be treated as one properly filed (Article 125 CPC).[69] The filing does not have to be made directly to a specific procedural body. The time limit is also observed if, before its expiry, for example a letter was posted

[66] Grzegorczyk and Tylman (n 24) 424–25.
[67] ibid 424.
[68] Marszał (n 14) 298.
[69] Supreme Court Decision, 27 April 2011, III KZ 16/11, Lex no 1144101.

at an office of an entity delivering correspondence in the European Union or at a Polish consular office (Article 124 CPC).

As has already been determined above, a final time limit can be reinstated. Reinstating a final time limit has a restitutionary effect, as it results in an act performed after expiration of a time limit being deemed to have been performed in compliance with the time limit.[70] The conditions of reinstating a final time limit are set forth in Article 126 CPC, which provides that if a failure to meet the final time limit took place for reasons beyond the control of a party, the party may, within seven days from the day on which the obstacle has been removed or expired, submit a petition to have the time limit reinstated, at the same time effecting the action which was to be effected within the previously applicable time limit; the same provision shall apply to persons who are not parties to the proceedings. Reasons beyond the control of the party or the person who is not party to the proceedings are obstacles for which they are not responsible.[71] In practical terms, justifying the occurrence of an obstacle independent of the entity filing a motion requesting a reinstatement of a time limit consists in proving due diligence, which is tantamount to denying the existence of circumstances in the light of which the failure to observe a time limit could be treated as a sign of recklessness or negligence. An application for restoration of a final time limit shall be made before the authority before which a given act should have been performed within the time limit. Such a motion shall not stop the execution of the ruling, although the body with which it has been filed or a body appointed to examine the appeal measure may suspend the execution of the ruling; a refusal to suspend shall not require a statement of reasons (Article 127 CPC). The decision on reinstatement shall take the form of a decision (Article 126 § 2 CPC). A refusal to reinstate a time limit may be contested (Article 126 § 3 CPC), whereas a decision to reinstate a time limit is not subject to complain. It may, however, be subject to review in the appellate instance. If it is established that the appeal has been accepted as a result of an unjustified reinstatement of the time limit, the appellate authority shall leave it unheard (Article 430 § 1 CPC).[72] This decision may be contested before another equivalent panel of an appellate court, unless it has been issued by the Supreme Court (Article 430 § 2 CPC).

Form of Procedural Actions

In terms of the form of procedural actions, two types of interdependence are revealed in relation to the previously established main purpose of a criminal trial, namely the correct – ie the one that corresponds to the idea of substantive justice – settlement of the issue of criminal responsibility of a given person for the act he/she is charged with. On the one hand, from the perspective of achieving this goal, the form of procedural actions cannot constitute a superior value.[73] On the other hand, the forms of procedural

[70] Marszał (n 14) 300.

[71] See P Hofmański, E Sadzik and K Zgryzek, *Kodeks postępowania karnego. Komentarz* (Warsaw, CH Beck, 2004) vol I, 592–93.

[72] ibid 596.

[73] S Śliwiński, *Proces karny. Zasady ogólne* (Warsaw, Gebethner i Wolff, 1948) 420.

acts specified in the binding regulations are subordinated to the fact that the criminal trial constitutes a compact sequence of acts, leading in an optimal way to the realisation of its main goal.[74]

For a main hearing, the principle of holding an oral hearing applies (Article 365 CPC). However, it should not be overlooked that actions taken during the trial are at the same time recorded in writing (Article 143 § 1(11) CPC) and are sometimes recorded by means of video and sound recording equipment (Article 147 § 2b CPC). This should not be seen as a sign of excessive procedural formalism. It is dictated by reasons of legal certainty and serves to record in the case file as precisely as possible the content of the statements made, especially evidentiary statements, which constitute the basis for the factual findings underlying the judgment.[75] The written form of procedural actions is obligatory if it clear follows from applicable regulation.[76] The group of actions that deserve to be distinguished are appeal measures, ordinary and extraordinary, which need to be made in writing (Article 428 § 1 in connection with Articles 518, 539–40 and 545 CPC). To the extent that the CPC does not require a specific form of procedural actions, the parties and other entities entitled to take part in the procedural action have the right to choose the form of their motions and other statements, and they may do this in writing or orally into the minutes (Article 116 CPC).

A procedural action performed in writing must meet the general requirements for a pleading, which – pursuant to Article 119 § 1 CPC – include:

1. designation of the body to which it is addressed and of the case to which it relates;
2. an indication and the address of the person filing the pleading, as well as – in the first pleading filed in the case – the telephone number, the fax number and the email address, or a statement on their non-possession;
3. the contents of the motion or statement, with a statement of reasons thereof, if needed;
4. the date and the signature of the person filing such a pleading.

If a person is unable to sign, eg because of a hand injury, another person authorised by them shall sign for them and indicate the reasons for doing so (Article 119 § 2 CPC). The general conditions of a pleading are sometimes supplemented by special provisions which provide for additional requirements to be met by a pleading of a certain type.[77] Referring again to the example of appeal measures, it may be noted that it is incumbent on each applicant to indicate the contested decision or finding, ie to define the limits of the complaint, and to state what he/she demands, ie to formulate the appeal request (Article 427 § 1 CPC).

Pursuant to Article 120 § 1 CPC, if a pleading does not meet the formal requirements set forth in Article 119 or in special provisions, and the nature of the defect prevents further processing of the pleading or the defect consists in failure to pay the applicable fees or to submit an authorisation to undertake a procedural action, the person who filed that pleading shall be requested to remedy the defect within seven

[74] Cieślak (n 17) 226.
[75] ibid 227.
[76] Marszał (n 14) 294.
[77] ibid 295.

days. The existence of such a defect prevents further processing of the pleading, making it substantially impossible to examine its merits.[78] The absence of the signature of the person filing the pleading may be regarded as such a defect.[79] It does not include, for example, failure to provide the opposing parties with a sufficient number of copies of the pleading because that is a technical defect which does not affect the ability to respond to the substance of the pleading lodged.[80] If the defect in the pleading is remedied within the time limit specified above, the pleading shall take effect from the day on which it is filed. If the defect is not corrected within the prescribed time limit, the pleading shall be considered null and void, and the person filing it shall be advised thereof upon being served the summons (Article 120 § 2 CPC).

An example of mitigation of excessive procedural formalism is the standard according to which the significance of a procedural action shall be evaluated pursuant to the contents of the statement filed (Article 118 § 1 CPC). An erroneous designation of a procedural action and, in particular, of an appeal measure shall not deprive such an action of its legal significance (Article 118 § 2 CPC). It follows from the cited provisions that in terms of effective performance of a procedural action it is not its correct designation that matters, but the actual content of the statement making up the action.[81] Thus, for example, if the defendant files in timely fashion a pleading marked as a complaint against a judgment served upon him/her with a statement of reasons, it should be treated as an appeal initiating an appellate control of the judgment.

[78] Supreme Court Decision, 20 April 2017, II KZ 8/17, Lex no 2281252; see Hofmański et al (n 72) 592–93 (2004).

[79] Supreme Court Decision, 23 October 2013, IV KZ 55/13, Lex no 1412343.

[80] Supreme Court Decision, 8 November 2000, II KZ 120/00, OSNKW 2001, no 1–2, pos 11; J Zagrodnik, *Obrońca i pełnomocnik w procesie karnym i karnym skarbowym* (Warsaw, Wolters Kluwer, 2020) 471.

[81] See, for example, Supreme Court Judgment, 1 April 2003 r, III KKN 155/01, Lex no 77454; Supreme Court Decision 13 January 2004, III KZ 60/03, Lex no 185581.

2

The System of Principal Procedural Rules

Introduction

The construction of principles appears within individual disciplines of law; it is particularly important in the disciplines of procedural law, especially in criminal procedural law.[1]

The importance of the principles of criminal procedure is supported by historical justification, as well as the scientific values of their construction. The conciseness of the formulation of these principles undoubtedly favours the process of teaching criminal law. Moreover, it also helps to formulate interpretation directives in practice.

The term 'principle' is not unambiguously understood. In the literature, the term 'principle' is understood in two senses. On the one hand, it is regarded as a directive that defines a standard of an ideal character. Such a postulate sets the direction of essential solutions for the model of a criminal trial. It is also understood as a principle in the abstract sense. On the other hand, in order for a principle to be binding it requires reference to a designated system of criminal procedural law in a given state, for only then can it become a binding norm; as a result we can speak of a procedural principle in the concrete sense.

Distinguishing procedural rules always requires using a criterion that allows one to distinguish among the legal norms of a given system of criminal procedural law those that can be classified as rules that have a fundamental character. However, which norm has such a character depends on the position of the author. Often in such a case the criterion of superiority of legal norms is used; at other times the criterion of the social importance of a given norm is used.

The principles of the process are undoubtedly the models for shaping the subject of the normalization in the form of an obligation and thus in the form of a directive. In the following paragraphs we will talk about principles in the concrete sense.

The criminal process principle is a legal norm which can be clearly stated as a principle in the binding regulations or can be interpreted from them. The decisive factor in this regard appear to be the subject of the regulation, in other words, what the norm refers to. Placement of a given norm in a specific legal act or in the system

[1] M Cieślak, *Polska procedura karna. Podstawowe założenia teoretyczne, Dzieła wybrane* (Wydawnictwo Uniwersytetu Jagiellońskiego, Kraków, 2011) vol II, 157 et seq; K Marszał, S Stachowiak and K. Zgryzek, *Proces karny* (Katowice, Volumen, 2003) see also Grzegorczyk and Tylman (n 24), Polskie postępowanie karne (Wolters Kluwer, Warszawa, 2016).

of a specific criminal procedural law may also be significant. Some of the norms that are defined as the principles of the criminal process may be formulated in an alternative form, and for this reason it is possible to distinguish opposing principles of the criminal process. But sometimes the legislator constructs a particular norm in such a way that it is possible to indicate exceptions to the accepted rule, but these are permissible only in a situation when the legislator explicitly provides for such an exception. In such cases their 'wider' interpretation is inadmisssible, because such an interpretation could undermine the meaning of the principle itself. In a doctrine we can also find a division of rules into a dominant principle and a supplementary principle, and finally, into a codified principle, if it has been directly included in the provisions of penal procedural law, and an uncodified principle that is a synthesis resulting from a specific group of provisions.[2]

Constitutional Principles

Due to the fact that criminal procedural law is a repressive law, because it is constructed in such a way that in case of violation of the criminal law, a system of repression against the perpetrator of a crime can be activated, the constitutional principles determining the foundations of criminal law and criminal procedure are of fundamental importance in this branch of law. Such principles are sometimes referred to in the doctrine as the systemic and organisational principles.

The constitutional rules include the principle of judicial administration of justice, as well as the right to a court, impartiality, independence of judges, collegiality of courts, and finally the participation of a social factor.

The principle of judicial administration of justice is a constitutional principle because Article 175 (1) (Polish Constitution (PC) indicates that this administration of justice is exercised in Poland by: the Supreme Court, common courts, administrative courts and military courts. The common courts include district courts which have jurisdiction over all cases if not exercised in the first instance by regional courts and appellate courts; the latter adjudicate only in the second instance. The administrative court system consists of provincial administrative courts and the Supreme Administrative Court, which rules only as a court of second instance. The military courts are composed of garrison courts and of military regional courts, and the decisions passed by military regional courts may be appealed to the Supreme Court of the Republic of Poland. It must be emphasised that in Poland the only bodies that exercise the administration of justice are the courts mentioned in the provision of the PC described above. These courts have a monopoly in this respect and no other organ can exercise the administration of justice consisting of resolving disputes, ie conflict situations. In addition, in the field of criminal procedure, the administration of justice consists of making a binding decision, by application of the law as to the criminal liability of a particular person prosecuted for the act with which he/she is charged.

[2] A Murzynowski, *Istota i zasady procesu karnego* (Warsaw, Wydawnictwo PWN, 1994).

The fundamental premise of a democratic state under the rule of law is the principle of the right to a court.[3] Importantly, this principle is also confirmed by constitutional norms, since Article 45 section 1 PC states that 'Everyone shall have the right to a fair and public hearing of his case, without undue delay, before a competent, impartial and independent court.' This directive is reflected in the provisions of the international law, such as international conventions ratified by Poland: the ECHR (Article 6 section 1) and the International Covenant on Civil and Political Rights (Article 14 section 1). The constitutional right is a 'source of obligation' on the part of the state. The state is obliged to establish certain legal regulations of a systemic and procedural nature, which ensure that an individual can have his/her case heard in proceedings complying with constitutional standards. It follows from the cited provision that everyone has the right to initiate specific proceedings before an independent and impartial court, while the state is obliged to shape the judicial procedure in such a way as to make it consistent with the requirements of justice and public, and everyone has the right to a court judgment, ie to obtain a binding decision by the court.

The provision of Article 45 (1) of the PC also implies a directive imposing an obligation on the court to maintain an impartial attitude towards the participants in the trial and the case. Thus, what follows from this provision is the prohibition of partiality, ie favouring one of the parties and referring with disfavour to the other, as well as bias and directional attitude to the case. This directive applies to all bodies conducting proceedings, and therefore not only to the court. The guarantee of maintaining impartiality derives from the regulation of evidence proceedings that preserves the impartiality of procedural organs, not only of the court, but also of other state organs.[4]

Similarly, the principle of judicial independence has been elevated to constitutional status (Article 178 (1) CPC).[5] It is closely linked to the principle of independence of the judiciary, and its abolition or restriction leads inevitably to the collapse of the judiciary. All solutions, whether legislative or factual, that undermine judicial independence undermine the foundations of a democratic state under the rule of law. Judicial independence implies the prohibition of any influence on a judge as to the direction of consideration of a case and the content of his or her ruling, independence in resolving any doubts that may arise as to the legal and factual status, independence in making any rulings, and, finally, the absence of criminal or disciplinary liability for rulings made in accordance with one's conscience, within the limits of their own discretion of and on the basis of the provisions of acts. The constitution and acts set out detailed conditions that the judiciary must meet to preserve judicial independence; these conditions are referred to as constitutional and process guarantees of judicial independence.

[3] B Czechowicz, 'Ukształtowanie i realizacja prawa do sądu i rzetelnego procesu sądowego w Polsce', in B Kmieciak and K Stępniak (eds), *Prawa człowieka i ich ochrona z okazji 70. rocznicy uchwalenia Powszechnej Deklaracji Praw Człowieka* (Warsaw, Think & Make, 2018).

[4] J Kociubiński, 'Dostęp do niezawisłego i bezstronnego sądu jako element prawa do rzetelnego procesu karnego w orzecznictwie Europejskiego Trybunału Praw Człowieka', in L Boguni and P Mikłaszewicz (eds), *Nowa kodyfikacja prawa karnego, Niezależność sądów i niezawisłość sędziów w kontekście zasady rządów prawa – zasadniczy element funkcjonowania UE w świetle orzecznictwa TSUE*, PiP 2018, no 3, 40 et seq.

[5] See A Sakowicz, 'Niezależność sądów i niezawisłość sędziów w Polsce w świetle standardu konstytucyjnego, konwencyjnego oraz unijnego. Uwagi na tle zmian przeprowadzonych w l. 2016–2018', in C Kuleszy and A Sakowicz (eds), *Ewolucja polskiego wymiaru sprawiedliwości w l. 2013–2018 w świetle standardów rzetelnego procesu* (Białystok, Wydawnictwo Temida 2, 2019).

One of the guarantees of judicial independence is the principle of judicial collegiality.[6] This principle applies only to courts, because in preliminary proceedings the trial is conducted by a authority comprising a single person. Unfortunately, the current systemic solutions, which prefer one-person adjudication, also in criminal cases, significantly negate this collegiality of adjudication. In too many cases, court proceedings are conducted by one judge; this does not foster reflection and does not provoke discussion on rulings, as was the case before the significant expansion of one-person adjudication. It seems that the justification for the introduction of one-person adjudication cannot be based on issues of a financial nature or restrictions on the recruitment of lay judges to the courts.[7]

The last of the constitutional rules that should be presented here is the principle of social factor participation in the criminal trial.[8] This principle, too, has its constitutional source, but the provision of Article 182 of the PC resolves this issue not so much laconically, as without indicating what such participation of citizens in the administration of justice means. It is assumed that this participation takes three forms: participation of citizens in the composition of the adjudicating court (lay judges, jury), participation of entities representing the public interest (social representative) and access of the public to the hearings (main trials) held in public. The constitution, as mentioned above, does not prescribe anything in this respect, delegating the entire regulation to the statute. Unfortunately, the first form of social participation in adjudicating panels, as indicated here, experiences significant limitations; in criminal trials the rule is one-person adjudication, ie without the participation of lay judges. This is not conducive to social control over the courts, nor does it protect against sometimes arbitrary decisions. Apparently, one should expect an increase in the participation of lay judges in adjudication, at least in first-instance proceedings.

Theoretically, the participation of citizens in adjudication can take two forms: in juries and as a lay judge. In the first case, the jury decides on the guilt or innocence of the accused, while the decision on the legal classification of the act and the punishment is made by the professional judge. In the second case, the lay judge is both a judge of law and a judge of fact; the lay judge is therefore an equal member of the adjudicating court, equivalent to a professional judge. Lay judges are members of the court of first instance, since panels of second instance are always professional panels and therefore composed exclusively of professional judges.

Principles that Relate to the Initiation of a Criminal Trial

The group of principles related to the initiation of a criminal trial includes the principle of prosecution ex officio (otherwise known as the principle of officialdom), the principle of mandatory prosecution (principle of the legalism) and the accusatory principle.

[6] See G Artymiak, 'Udział czynnika społecznego w wymiarze sprawiedliwości w sprawach karnych i kolegialność orzekania – zasada czy wyjątek?' (1996) 19 *RZN*.

[7] See J Zagrodnik, 'Garść refleksji w sprawie kolegialności składu sądu wyrokującego w pierwszej instancji 527', in M Rogacka-Rzewnicka and H Gajewska-Kraczkowska (eds), *Istota i zasady procesu karnego 25 lat później. Księga poświęcona pamięci Profesora Andrzeja Murzynowskiego* (Warsaw, Wolters Kluwer, 2020) 527–40.

[8] See A Murzynowski, 'Udział ławników w orzecznictwie sądów karnych' (1987) 2 *Ławnik Ludowy* 4 et seq.

The principle of prosecution ex officio is based on the assumpton that if the state has determined the legal order, it is also the duty of the state to protect this order. In connection with the method of prosecution, a distinction should be made between offences prosecuted ex officio (public prosecution) and those prosecuted privately. Public prosecutions are connected with the state's monopoly on the protection of legal order. A crime prosecuted by public indictment (prosecuted ex officio) is prosecuted irrespective of the will and conduct of the injury person or other authorised entity, and even sometimes against their will. In such cases, the interest of the state in prosecuting crimes prevails over the interest of the injury person. In only a few cases does the state refrain from prosecuting a crime that violates a specific legal interest of the injury person and makes the prosecution of such a crime dependent on the will of that person.[9]

The principle indicated herein refers not only to the initiation of proceedings, but also to the proceedings themselves, from their initiation to their final conclusion. It also needs to be emphasised that should a law enforcement agency receive information that a crime has been commited, it may not refrain from prosecuting the crime and wait for the injury person to report that the crime has been committed.

The very principle of prosecution ex officio is normalised in the provision of Article 9 § 1 CPC.[10] It follows that if an offence is not prosecuted by privately, it is prosecuted ex officio. The provisions of substantive criminal law must therefore clearly specify the mode of prosecution of a given offence: if the mode has not been shaped as prosecuted by public indictment (ex officio), prosecution shall only take place when an accusation is made by an entitled entity (the injured person). In some cases, prosecution of a crime ex officio may be conditional upon fulfilment of a specific condition. This is the so-called conditional ex officio prosecution subject to the permission of a specific state authority, eg a disciplinary court. It is the duty of the prosecutor to seek such permission (Article 13 CPC). Another mode of prosecution is prosecution on motion. It depends on the submission of an appropriate request for prosecution. The form of prosecution on motion is specified (as in the case of offences prosecuted by private prosecution) in the substantive criminal law. The injured person is not obliged to file a motion, as it is their right; they should be instructed about this right as well as about the effects of filing a motion. This mode of prosecution applies to offences prosecuted at the motion of the injured person (eg Article 157 § 5 CC), prosecuted at the motion of the commander of the unit (eg Article 343 § 4 CC), or a social welfare authority or an authority undertaking actions with regard to the maintenance debtor (Article 209 § 2 CC). It must be emphasised that when a motion for prosecution is filed, the proceeding is conducted ex officio (Article 12 § 1, sentence 1 CPC).[11]

[9] S Waltoś and P Hofmański, *Proces karny. Zarys systemu* (Warsaw, 2020) s 287; K Dudka and H Paluszkiewicz, *Postępowanie karne* (Warsaw, 2016) 189; A Murzynowski, 'Udział ławników w orzecznictwie sądów karnych' (1985) *ZN IBPS* no 24; Ł Chojniak and Ł Wiśniewski, 'Ławnicy w postępowaniu karnym – ujęcie historyczne i konstytucyjne' (2013) *WSS* nos 3–4.

[10] A Murzynowski, *Istota i zasady procesu karnego* (Warsaw, Wydawnictwo PWN, 1994) 143–46.

[11] See T Grzegorczyk, 'Wniosek o ściganie w projektach nowej kodyfikacji karnej' (1992) *SpiE* no 46, passim; T Grzegorczyk, 'Cofnięcie wniosku o ściganie w procesie karnym' (1997) *PS* no 1, passim; Z Kwiatkowski, 'Cofnięcie wniosku o ściganie w procesie karnym', in R. Olszewski (ed), *Artes serviunt vitae, sapientia imperat. Proces karny sensu largo. Rzeczywistość i wyzwania. Księga Jubileuszowa Profesora Tomasza Grzegorczyka z okazji 70.urodzin* (Łódź, 2019) 318.

A motion submitted with regard to certain perpetrators of a given offence also concerns co-perpetrators, instigators, aiders and abettors as well as other persons, whose offence remains closely linked to the one of the person indicated in the motion. This results from the principle of subjective indivisibility of the motion for prosecution, about which the petitioner should also be instructed. However, if the offence has been committed by a person who is a very close relative, by blood or affinity, of the person submitting the motion, the request must specify by name the person concerned (Article 12 § 2 CPC). A minor may not file a motion for prosecution. The content of the motion must clearly state the will to prosecute.

Pursuant to Article 12 § 3, sentence 1 CPC, the motion for prosecution may be withdrawn,[12] but in preparatory proceedings this may take place only with the consent of the prosecutor, and in jurisdictional proceedings with the consent of the court up until the conclusion of the judicial examination within the first main trial. In cases where the indictment was brought by a public prosecution counsel, the withdrawal of a motion after the commencement of the judicial examination shall be effective if the public prosecution counsel present at the trial or hearing does not object to this. Refiling of a motion shall not be allowed (Article 12 § 3 sentences 2 and 3 CPC).

It should be added here that prosecution of the injured person's motion may be either absolute or relative. Absolute prosecution on motion takes place when a crime is prosecuted on motion, irrespective of the person of the perpetrator, and therefore in any such case proceedings cannot be instituted if no motion for prosecution has been filed. Prosecution shall not take place unless a request for prosecution is made. Relative prosecution occurs when the principal mode of prosecution is prosecution ex officio and only certain categories of offenders are prosecuted upon application if certain conditions set forth in the law have occurred. As a rule, this will be the closest relationship, by blood or affinity.

An exception to ex officio prosecution is private prosecution. In this case, proceedings for this offence are initiated if a complaint (private indictment) is filed. As soon as the complaint is filed, the injured person becomes a private prosecutor, and the question of supporting the accusation is left to the discretion of the injured person (Article 59 § 1 CPC). However, if there is interference of the prosecutor in the prosecution of these crimes, which may occur if it is necessary to protect the public interest, the mode of prosecution of such a crime transforms from private prosecution to ex officio prosecution (Article 60 §§ 1 and 2 CPC).

The principle of mandatory prosecution (the principle of legalism, *zasada legalizmu*) is a directive obliging the prosecution of crimes prosecuted ex officio. It stems from substantive law and indicates that if a crime has been committed, whoever committed it should bear the consequences. The essence of legalism is therefore the duty to prosecute. The principle of prosecution ex officio indicates the mode of prosecution of a certain type of crime, while the principle of legalism imposes an obligation on the authorities to prosecute crimes prosecuted ex officio. At the core of this principle is the assumption that all are equal before the law.[13]

[12] Grzegorczyk (n 3, 1997).
[13] T Grzegorczyk and J Tylman, *Polskie postępowanie karne* (Warsaw, LexisNexis, 2014) 131.

Its opposite is the principle of opportunism, which leaves it to the procedural authorities whether or not it is expedient to prosecute. For this reason, it is left to the law enforcement authorities to decide whether to institute investigation, independently whether or not a crime has been committed. Opportunism can be proper or improper. The former indicates the abandonment of prosecution because of the need to protect the public interest regardless of the gravity of the crime; the latter justifies the abandonment of prosecution because of the low gravity of the crime (ie the low degree of social harmfulness caused by the act). A manifestation of improper opportunism is refraining from prosecution due to negligible social harm caused the act. In such a case – pursuant to Article 17 § 1 point 3 CPC – the proceedings shall be discontinued, because as follows from Article 1 § 2 CPC, a prohibited act of negligible social harmfulness does not constitute a crime.

As follows from Article 10 CPC,[14] in Polish criminal proceedings the principle of legalism is binding, with exceptions in favour of opportunism. According to this principle, criminal prosecution authorities, ie the prosecutor, the police and other authorities with police powers, are obliged to initiate and conduct investigation, and the public prosecutor is obliged to file and support charges with respect to an act prosecuted ex officio. Closely related to this is the obligation to report (denounce) the commission of a crime: every person who becomes aware of the fact of committing a crime prosecuted ex officio is obliged to make a report in this respect. This obligation applies to the offences specified in Article 240 CC or to offences of a terrorist character and is subject to criminal liability. Other crimes must also be reported.[15] However, this obligation is sanctioned by social responsibility.

The fulfilment of an obligation arising from the principle of legalism is guaranteed by a review of any procedural decisions that obstruct the exercise of justice by the courts. A person or institution that submitted a notification of a criminal offence and was not informed within six weeks about the institution or refusal to institute a principal investigation shall have the right to bring a complaint to the superior public prosecutor or the public prosecutor authorised to supervise the body to which the notice has been submitted (Article 306 § 3 CPC). This is known as a complaint for inaction by a procedural body.

The issue of the prosecutor's obligation to initiate an investigation and bring an indictment in a situation where there are adequate grounds in the evidence gathered during the pre-trial proceedings can be solved in two ways.[16] The first one is referred to as the institution of forcing an indictment (similar to the German process of

[14] P Hofmański (ed), *Kodeks postępowania karnego*, vol I, *Komentarz do artykułów 1–296* (Warsaw, 2011) 119; S. Pawelec, 'Oportunizm ścigania w świetle nowej ustawy o odpwiedzialności podmiotów zbiorowych za czyny zabronione pod groźbą kary', in M Rogalska-Rzewnicka and H Grajewska (eds), *Istota i zasady procesu karnego 25 lat później. Księga poświęcona pamięci Profesora Andrzeja Murzynowskiego* (Warsaw, Wolters Kluwer, 2019) 299–312; D Gruszecka, 'Interes pokrzywdzonego jako uzasadnienie współczesnego oportunizmu. Uwagi na tle art. 59a k.k.', in J Kosowsi, E Kruk and I Nowikowski (eds), *Zasada legalizmu w procesie karnym pod red. B Dudzik* (Lublin, UMCS Lublin, 2015) 47 et seq.

[15] A Kiełtyka, 'Zasada równości wobec prawa w procesie karnym' (2004) *ZN UR*, no 1.

[16] See further: J Zagrodnik, 'Koncepcje kontroli zaniechania ścigania karnego', in A Przyborowska-Klimczak and A Taracha (eds), *Iudicium et Scientia. Księga jubileuszowa Profesora Romualda Kmiecika* (Warsaw, Wolters Kluwer, 2011) 347–69.

Klageerzwingungsverfahren).[17] It consists in the fact that if the court deems the injured person's complaint about the refusal to institute proceedings or its discontinuance to be justified, it sets that decision aside and obliges the prosecutor to file an indictment. The second solution, adopted in the Polish criminal process, consists in the fact that after the appropriate actions have been taken, the injured person obtains the right to file a indictment, called a subsidiary indictment, and then supports such indictment. It should be emphasised that this procedure applies only to crimes prosecuted by public prosecution.[18]

It is also possible for the public prosecutor to withdraw the indictment (Article 14 § 2 CPC).[19] Until the commencement of judicial examination within the first main trial, the withdrawal of the indictment is not subject to the consent of the accused. During judicial examination before a first-instance court, an indictment may be withdrawn only upon the consent of the accused. Filing an indictment against one person for the second time in relation to the same act shall not be admitted. The public prosecutor may withdraw the lodged indictment until the verdict is rendered; this may occur if the results of the proceedings do not confirm the charges of the indictment.

As mentioned above, exceptions to the principle of legalism have been introduced in the form of opportunism;[20] unfortunately, the of these exceptions scope is constantly expanding, which, in the case of the increasingly strong influence of the executive on the administration of justice, is conducive to the erosion of the rule of law. Examples of opportunism are the absorptive discontinuation of the proceedings, the institution of the crown witness, the discontinuation of proceedings against minors, and elaborate procedural agreements.

While the principle of mandatory prosecution applies to each of the stages of the proceedings, ie both preparatory and jurisdictional, the next principle, the accusatory principle,[21] applies only to proceedings before the court. It concerns the attitude of the court to the initiation of proceedings before it. The essence of the accusatory principle comes to the question of whether the court initiates proceedings ex officio (on its own initiative) if there is a need to resolve the issue of criminal responsibility, or whether the proceedings before the court are initiated when an appropriate demand is made by a specific entitled entity.

The choice of the first of the concepts indicated here has different effects on the procedural model. If one accepts the concept of prosecution by the court ex officio, this

[17] E Kruk, *Zasada skargowości w polskim procesie karnym* (Lublin, 2016); H Luettger, 'Der "genuegende Anlass" zur Erhebung der oeffentlichen Klage' (1957) *Goltdammer's Archiv für Straftrecht.*

[18] See further J Zagrodnik, *Instytucja skargi subsydiarnej w procesie karnym* (Warsaw, CH Beck, 2005) passim.

[19] See further: M. Kurowski, 'Cofnięcie aktu oskarżenia przez oskarżyciela publicznego a prawo pokrzywdzonego do sądu', in C Kulesza and A Sakowicz (eds), *Ewolucja polskiego wymiaru sprawiedliwości w latach 2013–2018 w świetle standardów rzetelnego procesu* (Białtystok, Wydawnictwo Temida2, 2019) 643–56; D Świecki, 'Cofnięcie aktu oskarżenia przez oskarżyciela publicznego w postępowaniu karnym skarbowym', in T Grzegorczyk and R Olszewski (eds), *Verba volant, scripta manent. Proces karny, prawo karne skarbowe i prawo wykroczeń po zmianach z lat 2015–2016. Księga pamiątkowa poświęcona Profesor Monice Zbrojewskiej* (Warsaw, Wolters Kluwer, 2017) 461–70.

[20] Pawelec (n 6) 299.

[21] *Skargowy model procesu karnego. Księga ofiarowana Profesorowi Stanisławowi Stachowiakowi pod red zbiór* (Warsaw, Wolters Kluwer, 2008); Murzynowski (n 2) 166.

would mean that the court becomes an entity that concentrates three functions in its hands, ie prosecution, defence and adjudication, thus losing the features of an impartial body. It is therefore difficult to agree with such a solution, which has the characteristics of an inquisitorial process. It was therefore necessary to base the criminal trial on the accusatory principle. The court can conduct proceedings only insofar as an entitled entity files and supports a demand to punish a given person for an act specified in the principal criminal complaint, especially in the indictment. The optimal solution in this respect should reduce the role of the court to that of a silent arbiter, which is best suited to arriving at the truth.

The doctrine divides complaints into basic (principal), staged, conditioning the initiation of a specific stage of proceedings, and incidental, ie one that initiates appropriate proceedings for the issuance of a specific incidental decision.

The complaint rests on two grounds: the factual basis, which describes the act charged against the accused, and the legal basis, which we refer to as the legal classification of the act. The legal basis is secondary to the evidence gathered in the case; because the evidentiary basis may change throughout the proceedings, the legal basis (legal qualification of the act) may also change. If the change in the legal qualification of the act is the result of an error in the legal qualification applied, such a change is referred to as a primary change, but if it is the result of changes in the facts, it is referred to as a secondary change.

It is obvious that after the indictment has been filed, in view of the fact that the act cannot be changed, the act in the judgment must correspond (be identical) to the act in the indictment. Thus, the so-called identity of the act must be preserved, which follows directly from the programmatic function of the indictment.[22] This identity must result from the adopted identity criteria. As Śliwiński has pointed out, in order to speak of the identity of the act, we must define (describe) the factual event in the natural (historical) sense. Since on this basis it is difficult to unambiguously determine whether the act described in the indictment is the one indicated in the verdict, negative criteria are used, so that on their basis the identity of the act could be ruled out. The basic criterion allowing exclusion of the identity of an act is the existence of such differences in the compared descriptions that, according to a sensible and intuitive evaluation, the description of the act in the indictment cannot be regarded as a description of the same factual event. The more differentiating features there are, the easier it is to ascertain the non-identity of the act.

An important role is also played here by the rule of indivisibility of the object of the trial, according to which it is inadmissible to adjudicate on different fragments of the same act in different proceedings. It is also important that a final (validity) judgment concerning a part of the act prohibits trying the same person again for the remaining part of the act.

The subject of the decision may only be the act specified in the indictment. An exception can occur only in the framework of a so-called incidental process, when on the basis of circumstances that came to light during the trial, the prosecutor accuses the

[22] On the function of the indictment, see Chapter 6 for more details.

defendant of an act other than the one included in the indictment; in this case, under other conditions, the prosecutor makes an oral indictment.

It should be pointed out that the court proceedings shall be instituted upon request of a duly authorised prosecution counsel or another authorised entity; the court does not make any procedural decision in this regard (Article 14 § 1 CPC).

Rules Relating to the Evidentiary Proceedings

This group of principles includes: the principle of truth, the principle of directness, the principle of concentration of evidence, and the principle of free evaluation of evidence.

Central place among these principles is the principle of truth.[23] In doctrine, it is incorrectly referred to as the principle of material truth or the principle of objective truth. It should therefore be assumed that we are dealing simply with the principle of truth.

This principle concerns only the facts of the case and not the application of legal regulations. It imposes an obligation on trial authorities to base all decisions in criminal proceedings on factual findings consistent with the actual state of affairs, ie on truthful findings.

This principle is established in Article 2 § 2 CPC, according to which the basis for any kind of decision shall be the constituted by the true findings of fact. This principle is of paramount importance in a criminal procedure,[24] as it is directly related to the objectives of the proceedings. Truth involves making a true statement (a true sentence), ie consistent with the actual state of affairs, in other words, consistent with objective reality. In any procedural decision, the description of the state of facts should be made by means of true sentences, included in the zero/one logical formula. It means that a particular circumstancec under proof may be considered only as true or false.

Procedural authorities have the possibility of knowing phenomena that are consistent with reality, but this depends on the quality of the evidence available to the procedural authority during the proceedings. In this connection, two conditions should be highlighted that determine this knowledge. The first is an objective condition, which means that the evidence should have objective persuasiveness, ie such that on its basis every person should become convinced of the truth of the findings.[25] The second is a subjective condition, which creates a complete internal conviction of the procedural authority as to the truth of the findings of fact. The principle of truth obliges the procedural bodies to actively participate in the proceedings and actively seek, introduce and examine evidence that seeks to clarify all relevant circumstances of the case. This behaviour of

[23] A. Bojańczyk, 'Ustalenia faktyczne dotyczące zdarzeń przyszłych i niepewnych i ustalenia hipotetyczne a zasada in dubio pro reo', in P Hofmański (ed), *Fiat iustitia pereat mundus. Księga jubileuszowa poświęcona Sędziemu Stanisławowi Zabłockiemu z okazji 40. lecia pracy zawodowej* (Warsaw, LexisNexis, 2014) 59–84; P Hofmański, 'Zasada prawdy w postulowanym modelu procesu karnego', in D Kremens and J. Skorupka (eds), *Wrocławskie Seminarium Karnoprocesowe* (Wrocław, Wydawnictwo Uniwersytetu Wrocławskiego, 2013) passim.

[24] Murzynowski (n 2) 113; M Cieślak, (n 17) 258.

[25] J Nelken, 'Uprawdopodobnienie w procesie karnym' (1970) *Nowe Prawo* no 1.

the procedural body, especially the court, is defined by the principle of instructiveness, but this is only one aspect of the principle of truth in a criminal procedure. The so-called 'September amendment' (passed on 27 September 2013), limited the scope of the court's evidentiary activity by shifting it onto the litigants. However, subsequent amendments to the CPC restored the earlier state of law in this respect and broadly empowered the court to actively seek evidence. Thus, if the court can be evidentially active, then when it does so, it loses the attribute of impartiality.[26]

It also needs to be pointed out that truth in a criminal trial cannot be attained by simply any means. Evidence cannot come from an illegal source, although unfortunately Article 168a CPC indicates such a source is admissible.[27] According to this provision, evidence obtained as a result of an infringement of the procedure or the forbidden act referred to in Article 1 § 1 CC does not lose the attribute of evidence.

Another principle concerning evidence in a criminal trial is the principle of directness (*zasada bezpośredniości*). This principle is closely related to the principle of truth and prerequisites its implementation.[28] The principle of directness is one of the principles that is only partially codified, because only one of the directives presented by means of this principle was specified in the CPC.[29] Namely, according to the Article 410 CPC, the court shall base its judgment solely on the basis of all circumstances disclosed at the main trial. Thus, if a specific circumstance was not the object of evidence on the main trial, it cannot be the basis for factual findings. Pursuant to another directive, evidence should be taken directly before the deciding judges, who will allow the court to make observations that will allow for a proper assessment of the evidence taken. It is for this reason that a change in the composition of the court hearing the case is, as a rule, not permitted. Finally, the principle of directness also includes the requirement that the trial authority should primarily use primary evidence, but not eliminate derivative evidence. Therefore, the more derivative the evidence, the greater the chances of distorting the evidentiary basis of the decision.

The Code provides for exceptions to the principle of directness in the form of the possibility to read records from the hearing of the defendant, witness or expert, or to consider these records as read if certain conditions are met (Article 389, 391, 392 and Article 405 §§ 2 and 3 CPC). An even greater scope of deviations from the principle of directness concerns the review proceedings taking place in the second instance.[30]

The principle of concentration of evidence is another directive operating within the rules of evidence. According to this principle, a criminal trial should be a compact sequence of activities and events carried out without undue delay.[31] This is a consequence of the principle of directness and boils down to the requirement that the

[26] See further considerations on the model of the criminal process in chapter 1.

[27] S Pawelec, 'Uwagi na temat dopuszczalności dowodów na tle regulacji art. 168a k.p.k. z perspektywy procesowej oskarżonego', in M Rogalska-Rzewnicka, H Gajewska-Kruczkowska and BT Bieńkowska (eds), *Wokół gwarancji współczesnego procesu karnego. Księga jubileuszowa Profesora Piotra Kruszyńskiego* (Warsaw, Wolters Kluwer, 2015) 370–86.

[28] Waltoś and Hofmański (n 1) 267–68.

[29] K Marszał, *Proces karny. Zagadnienia ogólne* (Katowice, Volumen, 2013) 109.

[30] Waltoś and Hofmański (n 1) 272–73.

[31] Marszał (n 20) 110.

proceedings should be carried out efficiently and that the court should decide on the basis of all the evidence it has been made aware of.[32]

Theoretically speaking, the concentration of evidence, ie the acceleration of proceedings, can take place in two forms – either by means of evidentiary preclusion or by means of the judge's discretionary power. Evidentiary preclusion consists in obliging the parties to submit all facts and evidence known to them on pain of disregarding them at a later date. This way of introducing evidence to the trial is nothing new in the Polish criminal trial, since the CPC of 1928 already mentioned deadlines for taking evidence. The second way makes it possible to take evidence into account as the basis for a decision even if such evidence was not presented by the trial party. For many years, there was a discussion in the doctrine on the introduction of the institution of evidence preclusion to the Polish trial, mostly critical. Finally, in July 2019, a draft of just such a solution was adopted, to which we have to take a critical assessment. The provision of Article 170 CPC was supplemented with a norm allowing dismission of the party's motion for evidence if it was submitted after the expiry of the time limit set by the procedural body, of which the party submitting the motion had been notified. This solution violates the right of the party to shape the evidentiary basis of the settlement and, above all, violates the right of the accused to defence. Admittedly, the added Article 170 §1a CPC provides that a motion cannot be dismiss if the circumstance that is to be proven is of material importance to the determination whether a prohibited act was committed, whether it constitutes a criminal offence and what criminal offence, whether the prohibited act was committed under the conditions referred to in Article 64 or Article 65 CC or whether there are grounds for ordering a stay in a psychiatric hospital pursuant to Article 93g CC, but it does not change the negative assessment of the changes introduced to the CPC.

The concentration of evidence is favoured by the time limits of the investigation. This is obvious, since pre-trial proceedings are designed to collect and secure evidence in the course of these proceedings. In judicial proceedings, the president of the court calls for the accused to submit evidentiary submissions within seven days (Article 338 § 1 CPC). This does not mean that the court will dismiss a later-filed motion to take evidence because the aforementioned time limit is instructional, and the court may, on its own initiative and ex officio, admit evidence that was previously dismissed.[33] The principle of continuity of the trial is in force from the beginning of the trial and implies the invariability of the composition of the court, as only the judge who was present for the entire trial may adjudicate. If the case is likely to last for a longer period of time, the president of the court may appoint an additional judge (an additional lay judge) to the composition and indicate the order in which they will join the composition and take part in deliberations and voting. The rules for appointing and changing the composition of the court were modified by an amendment that took effect on 1 September 2017. The composition of the court may be changed only if it is impossible to hear the case with the existing composition or because of a long-term obstacle that prevents the case from

[32] A Bojańczyk and T Razowski, 'W kwestii optymalnego czasu przerwy i odroczenia' (2009) *CzPKiNP* no 3, 169 et seq.

[33] Supreme Court Decision, 13 September 2016, V KK 77/16, Lex no 2157888.

being heard with the existing composition. The facilitation of ruling despite a change in the composition of the court should be assessed strongly critically.

The principle of free evaluation of evidence[34] is commonly recognised as one of the procedural rules, although there is no lack of opinions about including it among the guarantees for establishing the truth in a criminal trial. It is nevertheless necessary to point out that the problem of evidence evaluation in a criminal proceedings is of great importance for making factual findings in such proceedings.

The doctrine distinguishes between the concept of statutory (legal) evaluation of evidence and the concept of free evaluation of evidence.[35] The statutory evaluation of evidence causes the procedural authority to be constrained by rules in the evaluation of facts (evidence) in a criminal trial. The positive statutory evaluation of evidence consists in stating that the court had to consider a fact (circumstance) as proven if certain state of affairs was ascertained, for example, by two witnesses. According to this rule, if a particular fact (circumstance) was not confirmed by a particular type of evidence (eg by the testimony of two witnesses), it cannot be considered as proven. The concepts mentioned here have only historical significance today.

A free evaluation of evidence means that the trial authority evaluates evidence according to its own conviction, without taking into account the rules of evidence, but nevertheless with due consideration of the principles of sound reasoning, knowledge standards and personal experience (Article 7 CPC). Within the framework of the principle of free evaluation of evidence thus defined, one can distinguish between free, uncontrolled and free, controlled evaluation of evidence.[36] The first of these consists in the fact that the court does not have to present arguments in the scope of its assessment, and thus it does not have to externalise its reasoning in connection with the assessment made, or indicate in the statement of reason the evidence that convinced it to take this or that standpoint. The controlled principle is connected with presenting the argumentation that convinces the court to take a particular stance resulting from the rules for evaluating evidence. In Polish criminal proceedings the principle of a free and controlled evaluation of evidence is binding, although the changes introduced in the CPC in the form of an assumption that the statement of reason should be concise and additionally included on a form (*formularz*) brings the Polish trial closer to a trial in which a free and uncontrolled evaluation of evidence is binding (Article 99a CPC).

The aforementioned evaluation of evidence can be *a priori* or *a posteriori*.[37] *A priori* evaluation is a form of preliminary assessment of evidence and is done before the evidence is admitted to trial, ie before its evidentiary value is examined. *A posteriori* evaluation is a form of evaluation of evidence that has already been taken; this evaluation plays a fundamental role in criminal trials.

As indicated above, a free and controlled evaluation of evidence has been adopted in the Polish criminal trial. Such an evaluation of evidence in a criminal trial refers not only

[34] See, first of all, Z. Świda-Łagiewska, *Zasada swobodnej oceny dowodów w polskim procesie karnym* (Wrocław, Acta Universitatis Wratislaviensis Prawo, 1983) passim.

[35] Marszał (n 20) 112–13.

[36] Waltoś and Hofmański (n 1) 259–60.

[37] ibid 261–62.

to the court, but also to other bodies managing the trial. The fact that this evaluation is free does not mean that it is an arbitrary evaluation.[38] This assessment is externalised in the statement of reason for the ruling, especially the judgment. This statement of reason, as follows from the provision of Article 424 § 1, point 1 CPC, is to be concise,[39] which brings the evaluation made by the authority closer to a free but uncontrolled evaluation. For this reason, the changes introduced to the CPC in this respect should be assessed negatively. Additionally, it was adopted that this statement of reason should be included – as already noted above – on a form,[40] which will automate the process of evidence evaluation, but at the same time will significantly restrict the principle of the accused's right to defence and will make it difficult for the parties to obtain knowledge of the court's evaluation of evidence in order to dispute the ruling issued in their case.

Principles Relating to the Form and Conduct of the Trial

These principles, which are of equal importance to those concerning the taking of evidence, include the principle of a fair trial, the principle of an adversarial process, the principle of an open hearing, the principle of oral argument (proceeding orally), and the principle of speedy proceedings. Undoubtedly, the most important of these is the principle of a fair trial.

The principle of a fair trial[41] is defined differently in the doctrine. Most often it is defined as the right to a fair, just and honest trial. This principle is provided for in Article 14 ICPCR and Article 6(1) ECHR. It is for this reason that this principle constitutes a set of important directives addressed to the procedural authorities, but also to the state organs creating legal norms, because these norms together should meet the conditions set out in the aforementioned legal acts. Such requirements are also provided for in the PC, which in Article 175(1) emphasises that the administration of justice in Poland is carried out by the courts, and thus it is the duty of the courts to decide on the merits of any accusation against a person. It follows, however, that the rule of fair trial is not directly applicable to pre-trial proceedings. It undoubtedly follows from the rules of a fair trial that in the course of criminal proceedings it is necessary to maintain equality of arms, to ensure the accused's right to defence, to have an interpreter under certain

[38] Supreme Court Judgment, 23 July 2003, V KK 375/02, Lex no 80278; Supreme Court Decision, 15 December 2003, IV KZ 48/03, Lex no 185729; Supreme Court Judgment, 7 June 2005, IV KK 29/05, Lex no 199865.

[39] K Zgryzek, 'Zwięzłe uzasadnienie – czy to jeszcze uzasadnienie?', P Hofmański (ed), *Fiat iustitia pereat mundus. Księga jubileuszowa poświęcona Sędziemu Stanisławowi Zabłockiemu z okazji 4o.lecia pracy zawodowej* (Warsaw, LexisNexis, 2014) 663–76.

[40] P Hofmański and S Zabłocki, 'Standaryzacja uzasadnień wyroków sądów pierwszej instancji', in R Olszewski (ed), *Artes serviunt vitae, sapientia imperat. Proces karny sensu largo. Rzeczywistość i wyzwania, Księga jubileuszowa profesora Tomasza Grzegorczyka z okazji 70. urodzin* (Łódź. Wolters Kluwer, 2019) 235–56; M Laskowski, *Uzasadnienie wyroku – rzeczywistość i próby jej zmiany*, J. Kasiński, A. Małolepszy, P. Misztal, R. Olszewski., K. Rydz-Sybilak, D. Świecki (ed.), Artes serviunt vitae sapientia imperat. Proces karny sensu largo. Rzeczywistość i wyzwania. Księga jubileuszowa Profesora Tomasza Grzegorczyka z okazji 70. urodzin (Łódź, Wolter Kluwer 2019) 339–46.

[41] J Skorupki (ed), *Rzetelny proces karny. Materiały konferencji naukowej. Trzebieszowice 7–19 września 2009 r* (Warsaw, W Jasińskiego, 2010) passim.

conditions, to maintain the loyalty of the procedural authorities to each participant in the proceedings, and, lastly, to have a competent court established by law conduct the proceedings and to decide the case within a reasonable time. This increasingly important principle can be treated as a meta-principle, and its element is the directive of loyalty, which prohibits misleading the participants of the proceedings and orders the provision of information not only in situations expressly provided for in the provisions of the CPC, but also in any case where it may be relevant to the participant of the proceedings. This information, pursuant to the provision of Article 16 § 1 CPC, should be provided to the litigant when necessary; however, this need cannot be determined arbitrarily, but should be based on objective criteria.

It also follows from the principle of a fair trial that the trial should be held within a reasonable time; in other words, it should not be protracted. A claim that a trial should be conducted within a reasonable time should be analysed *in concreto*, ie the proceedings in which, in the opinion of a party, the procedural authority committed a delay should be examined. The institution of a complaint for delay is a safeguard against delay.

The adversarial principle (*zasada kontradyktoryjności*)[42] means the directive that a trial should be conducted in the form of a dispute between equal parties before an impartial court. Its opposite is the principle of inquisitorial process. Next to the accusatory principle, the adversarial principle determines the trial model most fully.

For a trial to be called adversarial the following conditions must be fulfilled. In the first place, only parties with equal rights may appear in the trial. Equality of parties means that the parties in dispute enjoy the same procedural rights and are subject to the same obligations. An adversarial process consists in a real conflict between the parties, each of whom should be directly interested in the content of the outcome and have the right to fight with their procedural opponent in order to achieve the best possible resolution of the legal dispute. *Kontradyktoryjność* is based on the existence of a three-party process: the prosecutor, the accused and the court. The latter, since it decides the legal dispute, must be equipped with a position of impartiality. The rights of the parties in the adversarial proceedings include the right to participate in the activities of the proceedings, the right to ask questions and make statements, the right to submit motions (including motions for evidence), the right to be assisted by a person adequately prepared professionally to appear before the court, and, finally, the right to initiate a procedural review of issued decisions.[43]

Since an adversarial process involves a dispute between parties it is undoubtedly of the greatest importance where this dispute takes place, ie at the main hearing (main trial).[44] The order in which the interrogated persons are asked questions is also clearly significant. This order is determined by the provision of Article 370 CPC,

[42] J Skorupka, 'Szkic o sprawiedliwości kontradyktoryjnego procesu karnego', in P Hofmański (ed), *Fiat iustitia pereat mundus. Księga jubileuszowa poświęcona Sędziemu Stanisławowi Zabłockiemu z okazji 40. lecia pracy zawodowej* (Warsaw, LexisNexis, 2014) 501–12.

[43] See also J Zagrodnik, 'Kontradyktoryjność jako wyznacznik formy procesu karnego (rozważania na tle zmiany modelu rozprawy głównej w nowelizacji wrześniowej)' (2014) *Palestra* no 11-12, 20–33.

[44] See further S Lelentala, J Kudrelek and I Nowicka (eds), *Czynności dochodzeniowo-śledcze i działania operacyjne policji a rola sądu w postępowaniu przygotowawczym. Materiały konferencyjne* (Szczytno, 2008) passim.

indicating that the court is the last to ask questions. Unfortunately, this order is often violated in practice.[45]

Preparatory proceedings, unlike court process, are inquisitorial. This is due to the fact that pre-trial proceedings take place in a different forum to that of the judicial trial, in which the participation of the parties has a completely different shape than during the judicial trial. This does not mean that pretrial proceedings are devoid of adversarial elements; These can be seen in the status of the procedural parties – the injured person and the suspect – and in the participation of those parties in the activities of the proceedings, including those requested by the party and those carried out ex officio.

Institutions that allow for consensual resolution of disputes arising out of acts with a lesser degree of social harm also constitute a manifestation of adversarialism. It should be expected that the consensual resolution of disputes both in practice and on the normative plane will be broadened.

With the group of principles concerning the forms and ways of conducting proceedings, we should also include the principle of openness of proceedings, ie open justice (*zasada jawności*). Its importance results from the fact that it is confirmed by constitutional provisions. Article 45 PC provides that everyone has the right to a fair and public hearing of his case; exceptions to the public nature of hearings may be made for reasons of morality, state security, public order or protection of the private life of a party, or other important private interes. Judgments shall be announced publicly.

The principle of open justice in a criminal trial is implemented through two directives.[46] The first of these indicates that the case should be heard in public in front of outsiders. This form of openness is referred to as external openness or the principle of the public participation (principle of publicity). This form of openness of is intended to strengthen the rule of law, because, by participating in the proceedings, the public exercise control over the bodies conducting these proceedings; external openness is a guarantee of the independence and impartiality of the court. The second directive indicates that the parties must not be prevented from participating in the proceedings.[47]

The first of these directives is confirmed in the provisions of the CPC. Article 355 CPC indicates that the trial shall be held in open court. The trial held in public may be attended, persons participating in the proceedings, and others if they are of age, unarmed and not in a state incompatible with the court's dignity, for example, intoxicated (Artricle 356 § 1 and § 3 CPC). The course of trials shall be recorded by means of equipment that records sound or image and sound, unless this is impossible for technical reasons (Article 147 § 2b CPC). If a trial has been made confidential for fear that information classified as 'secret' or 'top secret' might be disclosed, the course of the trial shall not be recorded in the manner specified in § 2b where there is no possibility of ensuring the proper protection of a sound recording or an image and sound recording against unauthorised disclosure (Article 147 § 2c CPC).

[45] See further J Zagrodnik, *Model interakcji postępowania przygotowawczego oraz postępowania głównego w procesie karnym* (Warsaw, Wolters Kluwer, 2013) 31–32.

[46] Marszał (n 20) 119–20.

[47] See further B Wójcicka, *Jawność postępowania karnego w polskim procesie karnym* (Łódź, Acta Universitatis Lodziensis, 1989) passim.

The openness of trials is subject to limitations in certain cases. A trial is conducted in whole or in part in camera if the public nature of the trial might be result in: disturbing public order; offending decency; disclosing circumstances which, due to important state interests, should be kept secret; or infringing an important private interest. These restrictions are also required when questioning a witness about circumstances classified as 'secret' or 'top secret' and information classified as 'restricted' or 'confidential' or secrets connected with their profession or office, as well as in the case of questioning as a witness person, who is obliged to maintain professional confidentiality: notaries, solicitors, legal counsels, tax advisers, physicians, journalists or statisticians and a counsel of the Solicitor's Office of the Republic of Poland (Article 181 § 1 in principio in conjunction with Article 179 and in conjunction with Article 180 CPC and Article 360 § 1 point 1 CPC). This exclusion of openness does not, however, apply to cases where release from secrecy occurred on the basis of certain provisions of the Act of 5 December 1996 on professions of doctors and dentists (Journal of Laws of 2021, item 790, as amended) and the Act of 6 November 2008 on Patient Rights and Patient Ombudsman (Journal of Laws of 2020, item 849, as amended), within the scope provided for by these acts and in the absence of any objection indicated therein (Article 181 § 1 CPC).

The public is also excluded when the trial regards a motion of the public prosecutor for discontinuance of the proceedings due to the insanity of the perpetrator and for applying a protective measure and a case of calumny or insult; however, in the latter case, at the request of the injured, the hearing may be held in public (Article 359 CPC). The court may also exclude the hearing in whole or in part when so requested by the person who filed the motion prosecution (Article 360 § 1 point 3 CPC). Where at least one of the accused is a minor, the court may exclude the hearing in part or in whole. It may also do so during the questioning of a witness who is under fifteen years of age (Article 360 § 1 point 2 CPC). Where the public prosecutor objects to the exclusion of the public from the trial, the trial shall be held in open court (Article 360 § 2 CPC).

The exclusion of the hearing from public view does not deprive participants of the proceedings of their right to participate (Article 361 § 1 CPC). In addition to the person participating in the proceedings, two persons designated by the public prosecution counsel, the subsidiary prosecutor, the private prosecutor and by the accused may participate in the trial. If there is more than one prosecution counsel or more than one accused, each of them may ask for one person to be present in the courtroom where the trial is held (Article 361 § 1 CPC). Persons of trust are excluded from the trial when there is a fear of disclosure of classified information categorized as 'secret' or 'top secret' (Article 361 § 2 CPC). Despite the exclusion of the hearing from public view, the presiding judge may allow specified persons to be present at the trial (Article 361 § 3 CPC).[48]

As of the moment of filing a motion to have a trial held in camera, the trial in the scope of this motion shall take place in camera, provided that the motion is filed by a party or the court deems it advisable (Article 363 CPC). If the trial is held in camera, the presiding judge shall instruct those present about their obligation to keep secret

[48] RA Stefański, 'Tajemnica przesłuchania z wyłączeniem jawności' (2003) *Prok i Pr* no 11, 33 et seq.

the circumstances disclosed during the trial and about the consequences of any failure to do so (Article 362 CPC).

Despite the conduct of a trial in camera, the judgment is always announced in open court, ie in public (Article 364 § 1 CPC). If the entire trial or any part has been held in camera, the judgment may also correspondingly be announced in its entirety or partially in camera (Article 364 § 2 CPC).

The deliberation and voting on a ruling shall be conducted in a closed session (Article 108 § 1 CPC). Exemption from secrecy in this regard is not allowed, and during the deliberation and voting, apart from the adjudicative panel, only the court clerk may be present in the deliberation room (Article 108 § 2 CPC).

In pre-trial proceedings, external openness (the principle of public participation) is not applicable. The aims and tasks of this stage of the proceedings mean that openness to outsiders would make it difficult or even impossible to gather the relevant evidence.

Internal openness in court proceedings is broader than external openness. Even if a trial is held in camera, it takes place with the participation of the parties. According to Article 374 § 1 CPC, the accused has the right to participate in the trial, but the presiding judge or the court may consider the presence of the accused mandatory.

Exceptionally, the accused may be expelled from the courtroom by the presiding judge for a certain period of time if, despite being warned by the presiding judge, they conduct themselves in a manner that disturbs the order of the trial, or is incompatible with the dignity of the court (Article 375 § 1 CPC). In exceptional circumstances, if there is a justified risk that the presence of the accused may have an inhibiting effect on the explanations given by their co-accused or the testimony of a witness or an expert witness, the presiding judge may order too that the accused leave the courtroom for so long as such other person is being questioned (Article 390 § 2 CPC).

Exceptionally, the trial may be continued in the absence of the accused if the accused deliberately renders themselves in a condition that makes them unfit to participate in a trial or session where their presence is deemed mandatory, or having been notified of the date and time of the trial or session, declares that they will not participate in the trial or session, makes it impossible to bring them to the trial or session or, having been notified of it personally, fails to appear at the trial or session without excuse (Article 377 § 1 and § 3 CPC). If the accused has not yet given any explanation to the court, the court may order that he/she be heard by way of legal assistance (under Article 396 § 2 CPC) or consider it sufficient to read out his/her earlier submitted explanations (Article 377 § 4 CPC). Conducting a trial in the absence of the accused whose presence at the trial is mandatory may also take place if the accused, after giving explanations, has arbitrarily, without permission of the presiding judge, left the courtroom (Article 376 § 1 CPC).

The above regulation raises a number of doubts as to its compliance with the Polish constitution.

As a rule, sessions are held in camera; however, parties and persons not being parties, if they demonstrate a legal interest in the decision, have the right to participate in the session where the statute stipulates so, unless their participation is mandatory (Article 96 § 1 CPC). In such cases, the parties and persons not being parties shall be notified of the date of the session. In other cases, the said persons have the right to take part in the session if they appear, unless the statute stipulates otherwise (eg an injunctive judgment is issued at a session without the participation of the parties; Article 500 § 4 CPC).

In pre-trial proceedings, internal openness has been extended compared with the 1969 CPC. The right of the parties to participate in the preparatory proceedings (principle and simplified investigation) is presented in more detail in Chapter 6:[49]

Nowadays, the problem of the audience of the trial acquires particular importance due to the increasing role of the mass media.[50]

In Polish criminal proceedings, in addition to the important principle of publicity, there is also the principle of orality. Its subject is a directive to conduct procedural actions orally. This indicates the significant relationship of this principle with other principles, including in particular the principle of directness. It is obvious that orality promotes the contact of the procedural authority with the evidence gathered in the case. It is also obvious that orality of the trial favours the deformalizing of its course. It also favours the precision of statements and allows them to be controlled, even after a long period of time.

Not every element of criminal proceedings can be oral: some must also be in writing for them to be valid. In this case, the principle of oral argument and the written rule coexist. The principle of oral activities is a codified principle; according to the provision of Article 365 CPC, the trial shall be conducted orally. It should be remembered, however, that actions performed orally require their recording in writing. Preserving of a procedural action takes place in the form of a record. However, some of them may be made both in writing and orally, which in no way affects the validity of such action (eg a motion for evidence may be submitted both orally and in writing). A judgment, for its validity, always takes the dual form of oral and written. On the other hand, an indictment and appeal measures take the written form.

In addition to the principle of oral proceedings and publicity, the principle of speed of proceedings is also binding in Polish criminal proceedings. This is stipulated by the provisions of Article 6 ECHR, as well as Article 45 paragraph 1 PC, which states that criminal proceedings should proceed efficiently without undue delay.[51] This issue is primarily of criminological significance, as the later the subject of the proceedings is decided, the more difficult it becomes to punish the offender fairly. In addition, from the procedural point of view, it often becomes difficult or even impossible to punish the perpetrator after a long period of time from the day the crime was committed. The passage of time is also increasingly conducive to the obliteration of evidence. Thus, in the interests of both the state and the parties, the speedy conduct of proceedings is of vital importance.

The principle of a speedy trial has been expressed in the form of time limits of different natures, which are to guarantee the efficiency and speed of the proceedings. These

[49] See further C Kulesza, 'Udział czynnika społecznego w procesie karnym na tle orzecznictwa sądowego' (2016) *BSP* no 2.

[50] H Gajewska-Kraczkowska, 'Rola środków masowego przekazu w realizacji zasady jawności rozprawy głównej' (1985) *Studia Iuridica* no 3, 86 et seq.

[51] Marszał (n 20) 127.

time limits are addressed both to procedural authorities and to procedural parties.[52] They all aim at speeding up the proceedings.

In a modern criminal trial the lengthiness of proceedings can be described as a nightmare to be fought against. The proceedings should be conducted without undue delay. As it follows, not every delay in conducting proceedings may be described as unjustified. *In concreto*, individual proceedings can be defined as being conducted at an unreasonable time, ie too slowly. Delays in proceedings are in many cases the subject of complaints lodged by parties to the ECHR. The adopted law, which was supposed to prevent unjustified lengthiness, has not become a means to counteract it. As can be seen from the conducted analyses, the changes introduced to the Polish criminal process described as a 'deformation' not only failed to accelerate proceedings, but actually slowed them down.

It seems that there is a need for a thorough remodelling of the system of penal procedural law, which would allow for a division of cases according to their importance into those in which the evidence collected in the course of pre-trial proceedings and not disputed by the accused makes it possible to limit the scope of examination the evidence by the court, and thus to accelerate the proceedings, and those whose importance would make it necessary to thoroughly examine the evidence collected by law enforcement authorities, and thus prolong the proceedings. Such a deformalising of the pre-trial and jurisdictional proceedings may be conducive to efficient and non-protracted proceedings, especially in court.[53]

The following circumstances are exceptions to the principle of speedy proceedings: an interruption in the trial, adjournment of the trial, adjournment of the rendering of a judgment. A comparison of the duration of the individual institutions listed here clearly shows that they are becoming increasingly prolonged. An interruption in the trial, according to the current legal status, may last no longer than forty-two days, although in the original wording of the 1997 CPC it was no longer than thirty-five days, in the legal status determined by the provisions of the 1969 CPC it was twenty-one days, and in the provisions of the 1928 CPC it was (only!) fourteen days. Similar changes apply to any delay in rendering a judgment. Thus, the 1969 CPC provided for a maximum three-day adjournment of the rendering of a judgment, the 1997 CPC set this adjournment limit at seven days, while the 'September amendment' (effective 1 July 2015) extended such adjournment to fourteen days. Unfortunately, practice proves that in most cases the fourteen-day deadline for adjournment of the rendering of judgment is used. Indicated extension of time limits is in contradiction with the demands of speeding up the proceedings contained in the statements expressed by the current authorities.

[52] See further I Nowikowski, *Terminy w kodeksie postępowania karnego* (Lublin, Wydawnictwo Uniwersytetu Marii Skłodowskiej-Curie, 1998).

[53] P Kardas, 'Jeden czy dwa modele procesu karnego? Kilka uwag o paradoksach związanych z nowelizację Kodeksu postępowania karnego w perspektywie funkcji prawa karnego', in P Hofmański (ed), *Fiat iustitia pereat mundus. Księga jubileuszowa poświęcona Sędziemu Stanisławowi Zabłockiemu z okazji 40. lecia pracy zawodowej* (Warsaw, LexisNexis, 2014) 261–82.

Principles Concerning the Position of the Accused in the Criminal Process

The procedural rules discussed above, and among them the rules concerning the conduct of proceedings, make it possible to describe clearly the model of a criminal trial and possible directions of changes in Polish criminal procedures. It is obvious that two further principles – the presumption of innocence and the right to defence – also determine the adopted model.

The principle of the presumption of innocence of the accused is a fundamental directive defining the procedural situation of the accused.[54] This principle is a kind of 'extension' of the presumption of honesty and the rule that no one can be considered a perpetrator of a crime unless this fact is proven in the proceedings conducted against that person.[55]

The presumption of innocence means that the accused is presumed innocent until his or her guilt is legally recognised in accordance with the provisions of the CPC. It may seem that there is a contradiction between the presumption of innocence and the grounds that cause proceedings to be directed against a particular person, ie the grounds that cause a suspect and then an accused to appear in a criminal trial. The prosecuting authority, in order to direct proceedings against a specified person, must have at its disposal appropriate evidence, and it is precisely in spite of this evidence that from the time of the presentation of charges against a specified person, the accused (suspect) enjoys the legal presumption of innocence.

The principle of presumed innocence is a constitutional principle, set out in Article 42(3) PC.[56] It has also been codified in Article 5 § 1 CPC. It is also expressed in Article 6 (2) ECHR. From the fact that a designated person becomes an accused (*sensu largo*), it follows that he should be treated as innocent. In the above-cited provisions, both of domestic law and international law, one common identical element can be found, namely in each of them the term 'shall be presumed innocent' is used. It is in this expression that the essence of the presumption of innocence of the accused lies.

The presumption of innocence may be viewed objectively and subjectively. The difference boils down to the fact that in the objectivist view, the accused should be treated as innocent regardless of the beliefs of the participants of the proceedings, especially the procedural authorities. Only full proof of the accused's guilt can rebut this presumption. The presumption of innocence is defined as the statutory assumption of the innocence of the accused, which includes an injunction directed at the trial authorities to treat the accused as innocent throughout the criminal trial, ie from the time the suspect is charged until the final judgment of conviction for the crime. The subjective understanding of the presumption of innocence means something more. It expresses the demand that, until a final conviction is handed down, the procedural authorities should assume the accused's innocence and treat him accordingly in the

[54] See further P Kruszyński, *Zasada domniemania niewinności w polskim procesie karnym* (Warsaw, Wydawnictwo Uniwersytetu Warszawskiego, 1983) passim.

[55] Marszał (n 20) 131.

[56] P Wiliński, *Proces karny w świetle Konstytucji* (Warsaw, Wolters Kluwer, 2011).

trial. The idea is that the court should not treat the accused as a person guilty of a crime before convicting him.

Two highly significant objections are rightly raised against the subjectivist understanding of the presumption of innocence. First, this position actually amounts to a fiction, since no legal rule is capable of ordering the participants of the proceeding, especially the court, to experience a certain content. No provision is able to prevent the bodies conducting the proceedings from being internally convinced of the guilt of the accused against whom the indictment is brought. Second, this position consequently leads to a relativism of the presumption of innocence, since it requires that the presumption be considered in relation to particular actors and depending on the phase of the criminal process. In this view, there would be some doubt about the operation of the analysed principle in relation to the law enforcement agency that is bringing charges against the suspect.

In order to avoid the disadvantages of looking at the accused through the prism of either an objective or subjective view of the presumption of innocence, a relevant and convincing concept of so-called humanistic scepticism has appeared in the literature, from which two injunctions follow.[57] The first of these is that the procedural authorities and the other participants in the proceedings should relate to the accused and his status in the criminal process in such a way as to show that he/her has not (until the final conclusion of the proceedings) been found guilty. The second requirement is to be critical of the accusation made against the accused by the prosecution. As is pointed out, the procedural authority should be critical of the charge made against the accused, doubting the accuracy of the charge so long as the prosecutor does not convince the court of his/her reasons. It follows that it is not for the court to seek justification for the thesis stated in the indictment, but for the prosecutor to construct the charge in such a way that it is convincing to the doubting court. It should also be pointed out here that it is only in the judgment that the court should reveal its position on the charges against the accused.

Regulated in Article 5 § 1 CPC, the presumption of innocence has been pronounced explicitly. This provision stipulates that an accused shall be presumed innocent until their guilt is proven and recognised in a final judgment. From this perspective, we are dealing with the *in dubio pro reo* rule, which should be distinguished from the *in dubio ne contra reum* rule under the 1969 CPC: Article 3 § 3 CPC 1969 uses the expression 'irremovable doubts must not be resolved to the disadvantage of the accused', while Article 5 § 2 CPC reads that: 'Irremovable doubts shall be resolved in favour of the accused.' Seemingly, the two provisions are identical: in both cases the choice of a situation unfavourable to the accused is excluded. However, there is something more to be said for the current provision, namely that it provides for the selection of a solution that is favourable to the accused and the rejection of a solution that is either unfavourable or indifferent to his/her procedural interest. Article 3 § 3 CPC 1969 stipulated that it was (only) forbidden to choose a solution that was unfavourable to the accused, but this did not preclude a solution that was indifferent from the point of view of the accused.[58]

[57] Waltoś and Hofmański (n 1) 252.

[58] P Kardas, 'Nowe ujęcie zasady in dubio pro reo' (2015) *Palestra* nos 9–10, 7 et seq; R Koper, 'Reguła in dubio pro reo a ochrona interesów pokrzywdzonego w procesie karnym' (2018), *Przegląd Sądowy* no 6, 5 et seq.

Another important element from the point of view of the content of the principle of presumption of innocence should be pointed out here. Namely, an important change to Article 5 § 2 CPC was introduced by the 2013 amendment to Code, the provisions of which were in force from 1 July 2015, and which was unfortunately modified by the March 2016 amendment to the CPC. The amendment of the 2013 CPC captured the rule *in dubio pro reo* impersonally, but using the phrase 'doubts not removed', which meant that it was not for the court to remove them, but for the prosecution to provide the court with convincing evidence of the guilt of the accused. In the amendment to the CPC of March 2016, the term 'unremovable doubts' was again used (following the wording of Article 5 § 2 CPC in force since 1 September 1998), which clearly indicates that again the court – contrary to its impartial role in the trial – should resolve these doubts. Such a return to the previous regulation is undoubtedly a regression.

The presumption of innocence is ended by a finding of guilt of the accused. This occurs in a final judgment of conviction. The presumption of innocence therefore ends not at the moment of the judgment establishing the accused's guilt, but from the moment it becomes validated (final), since otherwise the opposite rule would have to be assumed to apply at second instance.

If the conviction is subsequently reversed by extraordinary means of appellate review (cassation or renewal of judicial proceedings), the presumption of innocence continues to apply. It can therefore be said that the presumption of innocence is excluded as long as the final conviction remains in force. Obviously, the presumption of innocence applies to the convicted person and the act attributed to him or her and is covered by the final and binding conviction.

Under the law, which allowed for conditional discontinuance of proceedings by a court sitting in a session, a doubt arose as to whether conditional discontinuance is a ruling establishing the accused's guilt and precluding the presumption of innocence. Since the conditional discontinuance of proceedings may be ruled by the court only in a judgment, the issue should be clarified in favour of the proposition that a judgment conditionally discontinuing a criminal proceeding is a judgment that the defendant is guilty, thereby precluding the presumption of innocence in the case.

The presumption of innocence operates both inside and outside the criminal process. Its internal function (the internal, procedural aspect) is that the accused is to be treated by the procedural authorities as innocent at every stage of the trial, that is, until the conviction becomes valid. The external function (the extra-trial aspect), on the other hand, is the effect of the principle of the presumption of innocence on any person, institution or organisation that cannot treat the accused as guilty unless that fact is established by a final and binding judgment. Thus, the accused remains protected in terms of his personal rights (Article 24 CC). The external aspect of the presumption of innocence also applies to the mass media. It is forbidden in reports, discussions and publications to prejudge the guilt of the accused before a final and binding judgment is issued by the court. It is also forbidden to use terms such as 'criminal' or 'felon' to describe the accused in the mass media as these indicate that the accused is the perpetrator. This rule is also confirmed by the provision contained in Article 13.1 of the Act of 26 January 1984 – Press Law (Journal of Laws of 2018, item 1914). In addition, the accused is also protected by Article 212 CC.

The presumption of innocence of the accused gives rise to a number of procedural consequences,[59] although there is controversy about some of them, ie whether they are consequences of the presumption of innocence or rather direct independent procedural principles.

The first of these is the requirement to test the guilt of the accused objectively, regardless of the incriminating evidence and the internal conviction of the procedural authority. This requirement applies not only to the court, but also to other procedural authorities, including those conducting or supervising pre-trial proceedings. An accused may be convicted if the evidence establishes the guilt of the accused beyond a reasonable doubt. The principle of the presumption of innocence implies that a conviction must be reasonable and the finding of guilt fully convincing.

The *in dubio pro reo* rule is another undoubted consequence of the principle of the presumption of innocence of the accused. This rule applies only when, despite due diligence on the part of the procedural authority, a given circumstance cannot be explained.

It follows that the procedural authority must exercise maximum care in establishing the evidence, evaluating that evidence and using it as a basis for its findings of fact, which, as discussed above, must be true findings of fact. The procedural authority should demonstrate that it did everything in its power to determine the evidence in the case and to use it as an evidentiary basis for ruling. Therefore, the trial authority cannot just stop at trying to get to the evidence; it must do everything within law to show that, despite its efforts, the evidence could not be established.

In the literature there is a dispute both about the role of rule *in dubio pro reo* in relation to the principle of the presumption of innocence of the accused and about its scope. According to one view, the *in dubio pro reo* rule is a consequence of the presumption of innocence,[60] while according to others, the two principles are equivalent rules.[61] It seems that the first view should be supported. This follows first of all from the essence of both principles. The guilt of the accused can only be established if, on the basis of exhaustively gathered evidence, this guilt can be convincingly established. If irremovable doubts arise, then an additional rule comes into play, namely that existing doubts must be resolved in favour of the accused and possibly lead to his/her acquittal (it should be remembered that this rule cannot be reduced solely to the issue of guilt of the accused). The controversy reported in the doctrine also concerns the question of whether the *in dubio pro reo* rule applies only to doubts about the facts of the case, or whether it appears as an interpretative directive. Since the rule is closely linked to the principle of the presumption of innocence of the accused, and the latter applies only to factual findings of guilt, it follows that the *in dubio pro reo* rule should not extend beyond the scope of the presumption of innocence of the accused, and that it applies after all available evidence has been exhausted. On the other hand, doubts about the content of a legal norm can be fully resolved on the basis of the

[59] Marszał (n 20) 134–36.

[60] Murzynowski (n 2) 258–59; Marszał (n 20) 134–35; P Kruszyński, *Zasada domniemania niewinności w polskim procesie karnym* (Warsaw, Wydawnictwo Uniwersytetu Warszawskiego, 1983) 81 et seq; A Tęcza-Paciorek, *Zasada domniemania niewinności w polskim procesie karnym* (Warsaw, Wolters Kluwer, 2012) 143 et seq.

[61] Waltoś and Hofmański (n 1) 247–58; Grzegorczyk and Tylman (n 5) 132–42.

rules of interpretation and without the need to refer to the rule *in dubio pro reo*. The essence of this rule boils down to the fact that in case of unremovable doubts, a certain version is chosen which is the most favourable for the accused, although it is not excluded that it could have been otherwise, but it has not been possible to establish this definitely.

The consequences of the presumption of innocence concern the formal burden of proof, ie the duty of proof (*onus probandi*), which has been shifted to the trial authorities. In addition, these consequences are not uniformly understood. The discrepancies mainly concern the mutual relationship between the presumption of innocence and *onus probandi*. The literature sometimes points to the need to separate the principle of the burden of proof alongside the presumption of innocence. It seems, however, there is no need for such a distinction. The burden of proof is closely linked to the presumption of innocence. If the accused is protected by the presumption of innocence, then on the opposite side there must be actors proving the guilt of the accused. These entities are the procedural authorities, which is understandable insofar as their behaviour is not dictated by personal interest.[62] And here arises a significant problem of evidentiary activity of the court. The March 2016 reform restored the previous legal status and maintained the laconically worded provision of Article 167 CPC, from which it follows that evidence may be carried out on the initiative of the parties, which is obvious, but also on the initiative of the court (ex officio), and here there is no such obviousness, since the introduction of evidence into the trial will always be associated with a loss of impartiality.[63]

A consequence of the presumption of the accused's innocence is the question of whether it is permissible to apply to him restrictions on his/her freedom that are necessary for the conduct of the trial. This particularly concerns the problem of admissibility of the use of coercive measures, including those that deprive the accused of his/her freedom. In this respect, two solutions are possible. First, it may be assumed that by treating the accused as innocent, one sees the procedural necessity of such a 'secure a proper conduct of the proceedings' when there is sufficient evidence to indicate his/her guilt, although it is not yet proven. Second, a statutory limitation of the principle of presumption of innocence of the accused can be seen in the authorisation of these measures. It seems that the solution to this problem is the second one proposed in the doctrine. The use of provisional detention for the procedural reasons set out in Article 258 § 1 CPC would be justified without the need to see in it a limitation of the principle of presumption of innocence of the accused. However, the use of provisional detention for the reasons set forth in Article 258 §§ 2 and 3 CPC cannot be justified on procedural grounds where the presumption of innocence is in force. This is because

[62] J Skorupka, 'Ciężar dowodu i ciężar dowodzenia w procesie karnym', in T. Grzegorczyk (ed.), *Funkcje procesu karnego. Księga jubileuszowa Profesora Janusza Tylmana* (Warsaw, Wolters Kluwer, 2011) 123–38. See also J Zagrodnik, 'Ciężar dowodu i obowiązek dowodzenia w koncepcji Mariana Cieślaka', in J Skorupka and W Jasiński (eds), *Ciężar dowodu i obowiązek dowodzenia w procesie karnym* (Warsaw, Wolters Kluwer, 2017) 140–73.

[63] See also J Zagrodnik, 'Model postępowania dowodowego na rozprawie głównej w świetle najnowszych propozycji nowelizacji k.p.k.' in R Olszewski, D Świecki, J Kasiński, P Misztal, K Rydz-Sybilak and A Małolepszy (eds), *Artes serviunt vitae sapentia imperat. Proces karny sensu largo. Rzeczywistość i wyzwania, Księga jubileuszowa Profesora Tomasza Grzegorczyka z okazji 70. urodzin* (Warsaw and Łódź, Wolter Kluwer, 2019) ss 222–32.

in such a case the use of a precautionary measure, especially provisional detention, is an anticipation of punishment.

The second principle relating directly to the accused is the principle of the right to defence. The accused is the only subject facing the charge of committing a specific crime, whose procedural position is protected by the right to have protection carried out by a specialised entity, namely the defence counsel. The accused has the right of defence and no one in democratic criminal proceedings may deprive him/her of this right. It should be noted here that whether or not he/she will exercise the right of defence depends solely on him/her, and only in certain cases, due to the situation in which he/she finds him/herself, this right must be realised through a mandatory defence counsel.[64]

The principle of the right to defence is based on humanitarian grounds and is related to the essence of the criminal proceedings, in which the accused is the subject and not the object. Its distinguishing is justified by the special situation of the accused in a criminal proceedings in which he or she is threatened with criminal punishment.

This principle can be expressed in the form of a directive according to which in a criminal proceedings the accused should be provided with the right to defence.[65] This is a constitutional principle, expressed in Article 42(2) PC,[66] which provides that anyone against whom criminal proceedings have been brought shall have the right to defence at all stages of such proceedings. He or she may, in particular, choose counsel or avail him/herself – in accordance with principles specified by statute – of counsel appointed by the court. The source of the right of defence is also Article 6 paragraph 3 ECHR, according to which everyone charged with a criminal offence has at least the right to be informed promptly, in a language which he/she understands and in detail, of the nature and cause of the accusation against him/her; to have adequate time and facilities for the preparation of his/her defence; to defend him/herself in person or through legal assistance of his/her own choosing or, if he/she has not sufficient means to pay for legal assistance, to be given it free when the interests of justice so require; to examine or have examined witnesses against him/her and to obtain the attendance and examination of witnesses on his/her behalf under the same conditions as witnesses against him/her; to have the free assistance of an interpreter if he/she cannot understand or speak the language used in court. The rights indicated are minimum standards that should be observed in domestic law.[67] Ensuring the right of defence is not only about establishing appropriate provisions in the procedural law system, but at the same time ensuring the right conditions so that the rights granted can actually be exercised. Emphasis should therefore be placed on the guarantee nature of the right of defence.

[64] D Gil, 'Prawo do obrony w świetle ostatnich nowelizacji kodeksu postępowania karnego – zagadnienia wybrane' (2016) *Ius Novum* no 4, 120 et seq; J Giezek and P Kardas, 'O etycznych i deontologicznych standardach aktywnej obrony w zmodyfikowanym modelu procedury karnej oraz wiążącej adwokata tajemnicy zawodowej', in J Giezek and P Kardas (eds), *Etyka adwokacka a kontradyktoryjny proces karny* (Warsaw, Wolters Kluwer, 2015) 13–38; J Zagrodnik, 'The Right to the Assistance of the Defense Counsel in the Light of the European Court of Human Rights Case Law' (2022) *Radca Prawny* no 2.

[65] Marszał (n 20) 137.

[66] P Wiliński, *Proces karny w świetle Konstytucji* (Warsaw, Wolters Kluwer, 2011).

[67] See further J Zagrodnik, 'The Right to the Assistance of the Defense Counsel in the Light of the European Court of Human Rights Case Law' (2022) *Radca Prawny* no 2.

The right of defence encompasses all actions taken in the interest of the accused which aim to repel the accusation or to reduce his/her responsibility accordingly, as well as to reduce or abolish any procedural nuisance. The scope of the right of defence from the subjective side includes the right to undertake a number of actions personally by the accused, which is sometimes referred to as material defence, as well as the right to be assisted by a defence counsel, which is sometimes referred to as formal defence. Within the scope of the right to defence are also provisions that order the procedural authorities to take actions also in favour of the accused.

The rights of defence can be divided into two groups. The first group includes rights vested in the accused as a party, while the second group includes rights vested only in the accused as such because of the applying an indictment against the accused and penalty that may be imposed on him or her.[68] The current CPC contains numerous provisions containing rights for parties, including the accused. These were discussed in more detail when the adversarial principle was presented. These provisions include the right to file the motion for evidence, participate in the examining of evidence and appeal against procedural rulings and orders. The rights of the accused alone include the right to be heard, the right to remain silent and the legal protection related to the prohibition *reformationis in peius*. The rights granted to the accused may be exercised but there is no obligation to do so. However, it is necessary to create conditions during the proceeding in which the accused will be able to exercise the rights granted to him/her.

A defence counsel in a criminal trial may be a person entitled to defend cases pursuant to the Act on the Defence Counselling System or the Act on Legal Counsels (Article 82 CPC).

When analysing the principle of the right to defence, one cannot ignore two extremely important changes introduced into the CPC in July 2019. The first concerns the institution of evidence preclusion provided for in Article 170 § 1 point 6 CPC. The provision cited therein places limits on the parties, especially the accused and their defence counsel, for the submission of motion for evidence at a time convenient for the party. This provision allows a motion for evidence to be dismissed only because it was submitted after the time limit set by the procedural authority, of which the requesting party was notified. It is not difficult to imagine a situation where at the very beginning of investigation, the authority conducting these proceedings sets an extremely short time limit for the parties to submit such a motion, thus depriving the party of the right to submit motions for evidence in connection with the developing proceedings. The situation may be even worse in a judicial procedure, where the court, in the initial phase of the judicial process, may set a short time limit for the parties to submit motions for evidence, eliminating the possibility of their later (eg during the speeches of the parties) submission (see comments that were made earlier concerning Article 170 § 1 point 6 CPC).

The second issue relates to the possibility of conducting proceedings in the absence of the accused or his/her counsel. Namely, the court, in particularly justified cases, may conduct evidentiary proceedings despite the absence of these persons, even if they duly explained their absence. Conducting the proceedings in the absence of the

[68] Marszał (n 20) 138–39.

accused or his/her counsel is possible even if there is a justified suspicion that the failure to appear was due to natural disasters or other exceptional reasons. In such a situation, the court may, in particular, examine witnesses who have appeared at the trial, even if the accused has not yet given an explanation (Article 378a CPC). Thus, if the accused did not appear at the main trial because, for example, as a doctor she provided medical assistance to a victim of a traffic accident that she witnessed, or if on the day of the trial due to her father's heart attack she had to go with him to the hospital, the court will be able to continue the evidentiary proceedings. The fact that the accused or defence counsel may in such a situation file a motion for supplementary examination of evidence does not change anything here, because pursuant to Article 378a § 5 CPC in the motion for the supplementary taking of evidence, they shall be obliged to demonstrate that the manner of taking the evidence in their absence violated procedural guarantees, in particular the right to defence.[69]

[69] See further R Ponikowski and J Zagrodnik, in J Skorupka (ed), *Kodeks postępowania karnego. Komentarz* (Warsaw, CH Beck, 2021) 1054–63.

3

Actors in the Criminal Process

Before proceeding to a discussion of the various stages of the trial process, the rules of evidence or the principles of appellate review, it seems useful to present the main participants in the criminal process and give an overview of their procedural roles (procedural situation). Participants in the trial are those taking part in the criminal trial in the role assigned to them by criminal procedural law. From this definition it follows that a participant in a criminal trial can only be an entity whose role in the criminal trial is defined, ie that procedural law imposes certain obligations on this entity or grants certain rights.[1] In a Polish criminal trial, the main procedural participants are:

- courts and judges;
- intra-judicial authorities;
- criminal prosecution authorities;
- the accused (suspect) and his/her defence counsel;
- the injured person and his/her attorney

In addition to these main categories of litigants, a distinction can be made between public interest representatives (eg the Ombudsman), procedural assistants (eg the court reporter, stenographer, translator) and personal evidence sources (eg witnesses).[2]

Courts and Judges

In the Polish criminal justice system, it is generally the courts that carry out the administration of justice by making binding decisions regarding criminal liability for a crime. Apart from the courts, only to a narrower extent, the criminal liability of the President of the Republic of Poland and members of the Council of Ministers falls under the jurisdiction of the State Tribunal (Articles 145(1) and 156(1) PC).[3]

Issues concerning the type of courts adjudicating in criminal cases, the system of courts and the division of competences between them are regulated by the constitution, the so-called judicial acts (the Act on the Supreme Court, the Act on the System of

[1] M Cieślak, *Polska procedura karna* (Warsaw, PWN, 1971) 32; J Zagrodnik, in J Zagrodnik, *Proces karny* (Warsaw, Wolters Kluwer, 2021) 181.

[2] Cieślak (n 1) 32; Zagrodnik (n 1) 181.

[3] T Grzegorczyk and J Tylman, *Polskie postępowanie karne* (Warsaw, LexisNexis, 2014) 205–06; S Waltoś and P Hofmański, *Proces karny. Zarys systemu* (Warsaw, Wolters Kluwer, 2016) 157.

Common Courts and the Act on the System of Military Courts) and the provisions of the CPC. It follows from these regulations that in criminal cases the administration of justice is carried out by common courts, military courts and the Supreme Court.[4]

Pursuant to Article 177 PC, the basic courts deciding criminal cases are common courts. This category of courts includes district courts, regional courts and an appellate courts (Article 1 § 1 Law on the System of Common Courts (PUSP)). Given the two-instance nature of the Polish trial model, it may be noted at this point that cases are heard in the first instance by district and regional courts. At the same time, regional courts are courts of second instance (courts of appeal) from judgments issued by district courts. The appellate courts are courts of second instance (courts of appeal) in relation to the regional courts as courts of first instance.[5]

According to Article 177 *in fine* PC, exceptions to the jurisdiction of common courts relate to matters statutorily reserved to the jurisdiction of other courts. The scope of these exceptions is narrow and includes criminal cases that fall within the competence of military courts.[6] In the first instance, cases are heard by garrison courts or regional military courts (Article 652 CPC). Regional military courts are also courts of second

[4] Grzegorczyk and Tylman (n 3) 205; Waltoś and Hofmański (n 3) 157.

[5] Waltoś and Hofmański (n 3) 160.

[6] According to Arts 647 and 649, the powers of military courts include:

Article 647

§ 1. The rulings of military courts shall extend to cases involving:

1) soldiers in active military service, except for territorial military service performed on a reserve-availability basis, concerning criminal offences:
   a) described in Chapters XXXIX to XLIV of the Criminal Code,
   b) committed against a military authority or against another soldier,
   c) committed during or in connection with official duties, within the military premises or designated area of stationing, involving harm to the army or infringement of duties resulting from the obligation of compulsory military service,
   d) committed abroad, during the use or stationing of the Armed Forces of the Republic of Poland outside the country within the meaning of the Act of 17 December 1998 on the Rules of Use or Stay of Polish Armed Forces outside the Republic of Poland (Journal of Laws of 2014, item 1510 and of 2019, item 1726);
2) military employees – in cases arising out of criminal offences:
   a) defined in Articles 356 to 363 of the Criminal Code in conjunction with Article 317 § 2 of the Code,
   b) committed abroad, during the use or stationing of the Armed Forces of the Republic of Poland outside the country within the meaning of the Act of 17 December 1998 on the Rules of Use or Stay of Polish Armed Forces outside the Republic of Poland;
3) of soldiers of the armed forces of foreign states present in the territory of the Republic of Poland and civilian members of their personnel – in cases arising out of criminal offences committed in connection with their official duties, unless an international agreement to which the Republic of Poland is a party stipulates otherwise.

§ 2. The cases related to criminal offences listed in § 1 shall not cease to be subject to the rulings of military courts even though the soldier has been discharged from active military service or the employment of the civilian employee has ended.

§ 3. If a soldier is discharged from active military service or the employment of a military employee has ended, the case referred to in § 1 (1) (b) or (d), and – if the criminal offence is not related to infringement of duties – in § 1 (2) (b), no later than until the day on which the judicial examination is commenced at the main trial, may be referred by the military court for examination of a common court, provided that this is consistent with the interest of judiciary.

instance, recognising appeals from judgments rendered in the first instance in a garrison court (Article 654 § 3 CPC). In cases subject to first instance in regional military courts, the role of second-instance court (court of appeal) is performed by the Supreme Court (Article 655 § 1.1 CPC).

However, the Supreme Court primarily exercises supervision over common courts and military courts in the area of adjudication (Article 183(1) PC). The Supreme Court's supervision concerns only the sphere of adjudication and is aimed at ensuring the substantive correctness, legality and uniformity of the jurisprudence of the courts and other bodies subject to the Supreme Court's control. Uniformity of jurisprudence is achieved by guaranteeing uniformity of application of the law.[7]

Jurisdiction *Ratione Materiae* and *Ratione Loci*

The concept of jurisdiction serves in this book, on the one hand, to present the courts that are competent to hear a criminal case as a whole, and on the other hand, to define the competence of individual courts to carry out actions that do not constitute a complete hearing of the case. It should be noted here that due to the insignificant practical significance of the jurisdiction of military courts in criminal cases, further discussion will focus on illustrating the jurisdiction of common courts and the Supreme Court.

Jurisdiction *Ratione Materiae*

Within jurisdiction *ratione materiae* we should distinguish, referring to the division commonly recognised in the Polish doctrine of criminal procedure,[8] the competence of courts to examine a case in its entirety in the first instance (jurisdiction at first instance), referred to as subject matter jurisdiction, and the competence to perform actions that do not consist of such an examination of the case in its entirety, referred to as functional jurisdiction.

Jurisdiction at First Instance

Subject matter jurisdiction is the competence of a court to hear a case at first instance. It is a criterion for determining the appropriate level of court within the court hierarchy

§ 4. (repealed).

§ 5. A decision on the referral of a case pursuant to § 3 may be contested.

Article 649

§ 1. If the perpetrator of a criminal offence subject to the rulings of military courts has also committed a criminal offence subject to the rulings of common courts, and these criminal offences are so related to each other that justice shall be better served if they are examined together, they shall be jointly heard by a military court.

§ 2. The provision of § 1 shall apply accordingly to investigations.

[7] Grzegorczyk and Tylman (n 3) 206; Zagrodnik (n 1) 183.

[8] See Waltoś and Hofmański (n 3) 451.

to hear a case at first instance.[9] In the case of common courts, the application of this criterion aims at determining whether a case is to be heard in the first instance by a district court or a regional court. It is therefore a vertical jurisdiction. The rules governing this jurisdiction are an important guarantee of the right to an independent and impartial court and are a manifestation of the rule of law.[10]

As a rule, criminal cases are heard in the first instance by the district court.

An exception to this rule, signifying the competence of the regional court to hear cases in the first instance, concerns cases that by statute have been transferred to the jurisdiction of this court (Article 24 § 1 CPC). These are cases of offences clearly defined by law, which are characterised by a higher gravity than cases falling within the jurisdiction of the district court as a court of first instance. They also usually involve complex factual and legal circumstances.[11] The catalogue of these offences determines the scope of the permanent material jurisdiction of the regional court. Pursuant to Article 25 § 1 CPC, the regional court rules in the first instance on the following crimes:

1. felonies defined in the Criminal Code and in special laws (Article 25 § 1 point 1 CPC);
2. misdemeanours as defined in the Criminal Code and enumerated in Article 25 § 1 point 2 CPC;
3. misdemeanours that by virtue of a special provision belong to the jurisdiction of a regional court (Article 25 § 1 point 3 CPC).

In addition to the permanent material jurisdiction of the regional court, the movable jurisdiction of this court to hear criminal cases in the first instance can be distinguished.[12] It is based on the decision of the appellate court, which, at the request of the district court, may transfer to the regional court as a court of first instance the trial of any criminal case due to the particular gravity or complexity of the case (Article 25 § 2 CPC).

Functional Jurisdiction

Functional jurisdiction means the authorisation of individual courts to perform certain procedural actions that do not involve the overall examination of a criminal case.[13] For cases within the jurisdiction of common courts, one can distinguish the functional jurisdiction of the district court, the regional court, the appellate court and the Supreme Court. It seems neither necessary nor appropriate to list here all activities that fall within the competence of the individual courts adjudicating criminal cases; therefore, below we shall present examples, including the most typical activities that fall within the functional competence of common courts and the Supreme Court.

[9] K Marszał, *Proces karny. Zagadnienia ogólne* (Katowice, Volumen, 2013) 197.

[10] Supreme Court Decision, 12 February 2009, III KO 2/09, Lex no 486164; S Kalinowski, *Polski proces karny* (Warsaw, Wydawnictwo PWN, 1970) 170–71.

[11] P Hofmański, E Sadzik and K Zgryzek, *Kodeks postępowania karnego. Komentarz* (Warsaw, CH Beck, 2004) vol I, 186.

[12] Grzegorczyk and Tylman (n 3) 216.

[13] Waltoś and Hofmański (n 3) 160.

The activities undertaken by the district court, in addition to recognising cases in the first instance, include:

1. any decision on the placement of an accused in pre-trial proceedings for observation in a closed institution (Article 203 § 2 in conjunction with Article 329 § 1 CPC);
2. examining complaints about arrest (Article 246 § 1 and 2 CPC);
3. examination of complaints against certain prosecutor's decisions (eg on precautionary measures (Article 252 § 2 CPC) and on securing property (Article 293 § 2 CPC));
4. applying provisional detention in the course of pre-trial proceedings for up to three months (Article 250 §§ 1 and 2 CPC);
5. providing legal assistance to other courts (Article 396 CPC).

The functional jurisdiction of the regional court includes:

1. determining appeals from judgments and orders issued in the first instance in the regional court (Article 25 § 3 CPC);
2. resolving competence disputes over jurisdiction between district courts (*argumentum* ex Article 38 § 1 CPC);
3. extending pre-trial provisional detention for up to twelve months in cases falling within its subject matter jurisdiction (Article 263 § 2 CPC);
4. issuing a safe conduct (Article 281 CPC);
5. ruling on the renewal of proceedings that have ended with a final decision of a district court (Article 544 § 1 CPC);
6. deciding on the issuance and execution of a European Arrest Warrant (Articles 607a and 607k § 2 CPC).

The functional jurisdiction of the appellate court includes the following activities:

1. recognising appeals from judgments and orders issued in the first instance in the regional court (Article 26 CPC);
2. transferring a case to a regional court for examination in the first instance within the movable subject matter jurisdiction (Article 25 § 2 CPC);
3. resolving competence disputes between regional courts or between district and regional courts (*argumentum ex* Article 38 § 1 CPC);
4. extending provisional detention for more than twelve months in pre-trial proceedings and for more than two years in court proceedings (Article 263 § 4 CPC);
5. ruling on the renewal of proceedings concluded by a final decision of a regional court (Article 544 § 1 CPC).

The functional jurisdiction of the Supreme Court in the course of criminal proceedings in cases subject to the jurisdiction of common courts includes:

1. recognition of cassation appeals;
2. examination of complaints against an appellate court judgment revoking a judgment of the court of the first instance and referring the case for reconsideration (Article 539a CPC);

3. consideration of motions for the renewal proceedings concluded before the Supreme Court or before a court of appeal (Article 547 § 1 CPC);
4. resolving a juridical question requiring a substantial interpretation of the Act, which may be referred to the Supreme Court by the appellate courts (Article 441. CPC).

Jurisdiction *Ratione Loci*

As far as jurisdiction *ratione loci* is concerned, it is of paramount importance whether a criminal case may be heard by a Polish court at all.[14] This issue is not regulated by the provisions of the CPC, but by the provisions of substantive criminal law (CC). Generally speaking, one can say that the domestic jurisdiction of Polish courts is determined by the applicability of Polish substantive criminal law. Conversely, it can be said that if there is no possibility of applying Polish substantive criminal law in a specific case, then at the same time the jurisdiction of Polish courts in the given case would be excluded.[15]

The general rule concerning the application of Polish criminal law is set out in Article 5 CC, which states that:

> The Polish criminal statute applies to a perpetrator who has committed a prohibited act in the territory of the Republic of Poland, as well as on a Polish water-borne or airborne vessel, unless an international agreement to which the Republic of Poland is a party provides otherwise.

This norm is complemented by the regulation contained in Article 115 § 15 CC, according to which:

> A fixed offshore platform anchored directly onto a continental shelf is deemed to be a sea vessel according to this Code.

The place where the offence is committed is defined in Article 6 § 2 CC:

> A prohibited act is deemed to have been committed at the place where the perpetrator has acted or has omitted an action he has been obliged to perform, or where the result constituting an element of a prohibited act has occurred or was to occur according to the perpetrator's intent.

Article 5 CC expresses the principle of territoriality and the principle of the flag as regards the application of Polish substantive criminal law.[16] The scope of application of Polish substantive criminal law arising from these principles, which is connected with committing a crime in the broadly understood territory of the Republic of Poland, is subject to extension under the provisions of Articles 109–14 CC to cases where the place where the crime was committed is outside this territory. On the basis of the indicated provisions, several principles of so-called international criminal law may be distinguished, which define the conditions for the application of Polish substantive criminal law to crimes committed abroad.[17]

[14] See Kalinowski (n 10) 146.
[15] Marszał (n 9) 92.
[16] W Wróbel and A Zoll, *Polskie prawo karne. Część ogólna* (Kraków, Wydawnictwo Znak, 2010) 141–43.
[17] ibid 141–46.

The first of these is the personal (subjective) principle, according to which: 'A Polish criminal statute applies to a Polish citizen who has committed a crime abroad' (Article 109 CC).

According to the next principle, the subjective limited principle,

> A Polish criminal statute applies to an alien who has committed abroad a prohibited act against the interests of the Republic of Poland, a Polish citizen, a Polish juridical person or a Polish organisational entity without a legal personality, and also to an alien who has committed abroad a crime of a terrorist character. (Article 110 § 1 CC)

Moreover:

> A Polish criminal statute applies to an alien who has committed abroad a prohibited act other than provided for in § 1 if the prohibited act is subject to the penalty of deprivation of liberty exceeding 2 years in a Polish criminal statute, and the perpetrator is present in the territory of the Republic of Poland and no extradition order has been issued. (Article 110 § 2 CC)

The application of Polish criminal law in the above-presented cases of crimes committed abroad, whether by a Polish citizen or a foreigner, is not absolute. It depends on the fulfilment of the so-called condition of double criminality resulting from the content of Article 111 § 1 CC. According to this regulation:

> Liability for an act committed abroad is applicable only if this act is also recognised as a crime by the statute being in force in the place of the commission of the act.

This term applies neither to a Polish public officer who has committed a crime abroad in relation to performing his duties, nor to a person who has committed a crime in a place that is not subject to any state authority (Article 111 § 3 CC).

Another rule providing for the application of Polish substantive criminal law to crimes committed abroad is the unlimited object rule expressed in Article 112 CC. According to this regulation:

> Notwithstanding the provisions being in force in the place of the commission of a prohibited act, a Polish criminal statute applies to a Polish citizen or an alien who has committed:
>
> 1) a crime against internal or external security of the Republic of Poland,
> 2) a crime against Polish public offices or public officers or a crime of inveigling a certification of an untruth from a Polish public officer or another person authorised under the Polish law to issue a document,
> 3) a crime against substantive Polish economic interests,
> 4) a crime of false testimony, giving a false statement, opinion or translation, using a document confirming another person's identity, certifying an untruth or a fake document – against a Polish public office,
> 5) a crime from which even an indirect material benefit has been derived in the territory of the Republic of Poland.

The last principle, which extends the scope of application of Polish substantive criminal law beyond cases of commission of a crime in the territory of the Republic of Poland, is the principle of universal repression, which presupposes, notwithstanding the provisions being in force in the place of the commission of a crime, the application of the Polish criminal law to a Polish citizen or an alien who has committed a crime abroad, which the Republic of Poland is obliged to prosecute under an international agreement, or a crime provided for in the Rome Statute of the International Criminal Court, adopted in Rome on 17 July 1998 (2003 Journal of Laws of the Republic of Poland, No 78, item 708 and of 2018, item 1753), and no extradition order has been issued (Article 113 CC). Currently, international agreements oblige prosecution of, among others, crimes of trafficking in human beings, circulation and trafficking in pornographic publications, counterfeiting of money, crimes of genocide, crimes against peace, crimes against humanity, war crimes, sea piracy or drug trafficking.[18]

As a result of establishing on the basis of the presented rules that a specific crime falls within the jurisdiction of a Polish court and determining, using criteria *ratione materiae*, which of the lower or higher courts has subject-matter jurisdiction to hear a case for a given crime, it becomes necessary to determine which of the courts of the same order (subject-matter jurisdiction) has territorial jurisdiction to rule on the specific case. The criteria for territorial jurisdiction lead to the naming of the court with jurisdiction to hear a specific case (eg the District Court of Katowice-Wschód in Katowice).[19]

The basic criterion (criterion of the first degree) for determining local jurisdiction is the place where the crime was committed (*forum delicti commissi*).[20] According to Article 31 § 1 CPC, the court in whose district the crime was committed has local jurisdiction. On the basis of the previously quoted definition of the place where the offence was committed, formulated in Article 6 § 2 CC, one can distinguish a number of its determinants referring to:

- where the perpetrator acted or omitted to act, which he or she was obliged to do;
- where the effect constituting the hallmark of the forbidden act occurred;
- where the effect constituting the object of the offence was intended by the offender to occur.

Each of these determinants is of equal value (theory of equivalence, multiple locations of the crime).[21] If their use leads to a finding that a crime was committed in the districts of two or more courts (eg the action took place in Warsaw, the effect took place in Katowice, while according to the perpetrator's intention it was to take place in Krakow), the local jurisdiction of the court is determined by the rule of anticipation, ie the competent court is the one in whose district preparatory proceedings were first instituted (Article 31 § 3 CPC).

In the case of an offence committed on a Polish ship or aircraft, when the criteria relating to the place where the offence was committed cannot be applied, the court of the ship's home port has jurisdiction (Article 31 § 2 CPC).

If it is not possible to determine the locally competent court on the basis of the basic criterion (criterion of the first degree), auxiliary criteria (criteria of the second degree) are applied, which are set out in Article 32 § 1 CPC. According to this provision, if it is not possible to determine the place where the crime was committed, the locally competent court is the court in whose district:

[18] ibid 146.
[19] Grzegorczyk and Tylman (n 3) 219; Waltoś and Hofmański (n 3) 158–59.
[20] Marszał (n 9) 198.
[21] See eg Wróbel and Zoll (n 16) 141–43.

1. the crime was disclosed (*forum manifestationis*);
2. the accused was apprehended (*forum deprehensionis*);
3. prior to the commission of the offence, the accused resided permanently or temporarily (*forum domicili*).

These subsidiary criteria are equivalent. If they coincide, the rule of anticipation described above shall be decisive in determining the locally competent court.[22] This regulation of subsidiary criteria also applies if the offence was committed abroad (Article 32 § 2 CPC).

If according to the first- and second-degree criteria it is not possible to determine the locally competent court, the third-degree criterion provided in Article 32 § 3 CPC is ultimately applicable, according to which the case is heard by the competent court for the Śródmieście district of the capital city of Warsaw.

Special Jurisdiction

Special jurisdiction includes cases where a court is authorised to hear a particular case on the basis of criteria which result from special regulations and introduce an exception from the scope of applying the previously presented criteria of jurisdiction *ratione materiae* and *ratione loci.* Within the framework of special jurisdiction, a distinction can be made between jurisdiction on the basis of the joinder of cases (*forum connexitatis causarum*) and jurisdiction resulting from a transfer of a case (by delegation).[23]

The joinder of criminal cases justifies the overcoming of the general criteria arising from subject matter jurisdiction and local jurisdiction.[24] Joint examination of cases related to each other in a specific way serves to ensure optimal conditions for a comprehensive examination of the case in a single proceeding (jointly), both in respect of criminal activity of several persons (perpetrators, instigators, assistants, etc) and in respect of a larger number of crimes charged against a single accused. Such a solution is also dictated by procedural economy which sets the order to best achieve the objectives of the criminal trial.[25]

Liaison may take the form of subjective, objective and subjective–objective (mixed) liaison.[26]

Subjective connectivity occurs when one person (the accused) is responsible in one criminal trial for several crimes. In such a case, the entire case shall be heard by the court in whose district the pre-trial proceedings were first instituted (the rule of anticipation) if the cases, according to the criteria of jurisdiction *ratione materiae*, belong to courts of the same order (Article 33 § 1 CPC). If individual crimes, linked by the person of the perpetrator, belong to the jurisdiction of courts of different ranks, the court of a higher rank is competent to hear the entire case (Article 33 § 2 CPC).

[22] Zagrodnik (n 1) 196.
[23] Marszał (n 9) 196.
[24] Grzegorczyk and Tylman (n 3) 220.
[25] See Kalinowski (n 10) 181; Decision of Appellate Court in Cracow, 1 September 2003, II AKz 347/03, Lex no 82897; Decision of Appellate Court in Katowice, 4 April 2012, II Akz 206/12, Lex no 1171018.
[26] Grzegorczyk and Tylman (n 3) 220.

Objective connection occurs when several persons are liable in a single proceedings, each for their 'own' criminal act that remains in a material (object) connection with the criminal acts of others, eg co-perpetrators, instigators or assistants. In such a case, the entire case shall be heard by the court having jurisdiction over the principal offender(s) if the proceedings with respect to persons whose offence remains in close connection with the offender's offence are pending simultaneously (Article 34 § 1 CPC). The condition of simultaneity of ongoing proceedings is fulfilled if the trial of individual cases, between which there are subjective links, is in relation to individual persons (eg the perpetrator and the instigator) at the *in personam* stage of pre-trial proceedings or at the jurisdictional stage.

Subjective–objective unity occurs when, in a single trial, one of the defendants is responsible for several crimes, while the other is responsible for a crime that has a substantive connection to one of the crimes charged against the co-defendant. In such a procedural configuration, the determination of the court competent to hear the entire case is based on the criteria outlined above, as set forth in Articles 34 § 1 and 33 CPC (Article 34 § 2 CPC).

It is necessary to emphasise that the special jurisdiction due to the cumulative nature of the cases is prescribed by criminal procedural law.[27] Therefore, the joint cognisance of cases related by subject or object in the manner described above does not require the issuance of a ruling on this issue.[28]

The second type of special jurisdiction, namely jurisdiction from referral (from delegation), is a derogation from the rules of jurisdiction *ratione loci*, but never *ratione materiae*. Unlike jurisdiction from the joinder of cases, it does not derive from a law, but is based on a decision of the relevant higher court in relation to that court, which has jurisdiction on the basis of *ratione loci* criteria.[29] It results from the possibility of transferring the case to another court of equal jurisdiction in relation to the one which has jurisdiction to hear the case. This may, in the current state of the law, occur in the following cases:

- For reasons of procedural economy, if the majority of persons who must be summoned to the trial reside in the neighbourhood of the latter court and far from the court having jurisdiction over the case (Article 36 CPC); in such a case, the competent court may request the superior court to transfer the case to another equivalent court; the decision of the superior court to transfer the case is binding on the court to which the case is delegated.[30]
- For interests of justice – the criterion of 'the interests of justice' is vague and has a wide range of meanings; by way of example, it can be said to be fulfilled if the accused in a given case is a judge of a court with territorial jurisdiction to hear the case,[31] or if a judge of that court is the victim or an auxiliary prosecutor;[32] whether

[27] Zagrodnik (n 1) 198; Decision of Apellate Court in Cracow, 1 September 2003, II AKz 347/03, Lex no 82897; Decision of Apellate Court in Katowice, 4 April 2012, II Akz 206/12, Lex no 1171018.
[28] Kalinowski (n 10) 182.
[29] Grzegorczyk and Tylman (n 3) 221.
[30] Supreme Court Decision, 11 July 2018, III KO 17/18, Lex no 2559402.
[31] Supreme Court Decision, 22 July 2010, IV KO 84/10, Lex no 843850.
[32] Supreme Court Decision, 15 April 2010, IV KO 44/10, Lex no 843814.

the interests of justice require that the case be transferred to another court equivalent to the court competent to hear the case according to the general criteria of jurisdiction *ratione loci* is a matter for the Supreme Court; the decision of this Court to transfer the case takes the form of a decision.

- On account of the exclusion of all the judges of a given court from hearing the case. If, for this reason, it is not possible to hear the case in a given court, the higher court that decides to exclude the last judge of the court in question shall transfer the case to another equivalent court (Article 43 CPC).[33]
- For utilitarian reasons. If it is not possible to hear the case in a court established on the basis of *ratione loci* criteria within the time limit securing the avoidance of the statute of limitations for the punishability of the offence, as defined in Article 101 CC, at the request of this court the court of appeal may transfer the case for hearing to another equivalent court (Article 11a of the Act of 6.06.1997 – Introductory Provisions to the CPC; Journal of Laws No 89, item 556 as amended).

Examination of Jurisdiction with Consequences of Violating its Rules

The court is obliged to examine its jurisdiction ex officio, and this in every setting of the case, regardless of the initiative of the parties in this regard (Article 35 § 1 in principio CPC). This obligation concerns both jurisdiction *ratione materiae* and *ratione loci*.[34] It arises in any proceedings conducted before a court, so not only in proceedings on the issue of criminal responsibility of a particular person prosecuted for the act charged, but also in proceedings on incidental issues, eg when a motion for pre-trial provisional detention is filed or a complaint is filed.[35]

If the court finds that the case does not fall within its jurisdiction, the rule is to refer the case to the competent court or other authority (Article 35 § 1 in fine CPC). This rule applies whenever it is determined that a court lacks jurisdiction to hear a case before the main hearing. It also applies in further proceedings, but only if such lack results from the application of criteria *ratione materiae*.[36] These criteria must be taken into account throughout the proceedings before the district court, because their violation by this court and the issuance of a decision in a case that falls under the jurisdiction of a regional court is an absolute ground for reversing the ruling (Article 439 § 1, point 4 CPC).

The situation is different in the case of a finding that the court has no local jurisdiction or a finding by the regional court that the case does not fall within its jurisdiction according to the criteria *ratione materiae*.[37] If this occurs only at the main hearing, the

[33] Supreme Court Resolution, 30 June 2004, I KZP 9/04, Lex no 108174.
[34] Supreme Court Judgment, 1 December 2010, III KK 224/10, Lex no 653509.
[35] Zagrodnik (n 1) 200.
[36] Waltoś and Hofmański (n 3) 163.
[37] Marszał (n 9) 196.

court may declare itself lacking jurisdiction and transfer the case to the court of competent jurisdiction only if it becomes necessary to adjourn the trial for another reason (Article 35 § 2 CPC). It can be said that in this procedural configuration, when the main hearing begins, the jurisdiction of the court before which the case is pending is petrified,[38] as if it were a court with no jurisdiction or a court of a higher rank than the court to which the case belongs according to the criteria *ratione materiae*. Referral to the court of competent jurisdiction in such a case is exceptional and optional.[39] The mere fact of adjourning the trial is not sufficient for this. The adjournment must be based on real existing circumstances, which indicate that there are no reasons to consider it sufficient to order a break in the trial.[40] However, even the necessity to adjourn the trial in a specific case should not lead to transferring the case to the competent court, if this is opposed by considerations of procedural economy in the broad sense, in particular if it would be unjustified in view of the progress of the examination of the case at the main hearing.[41]

A finding by the court that the case does not belong to its jurisdiction requires the issuance of a decision on jurisdiction of the court, which may be complained against (Article 35 § 3 CPC).

When a court decides that a case is not within its jurisdiction and transfers the case to a court of competent jurisdiction, it ends the criminal trial in that court, but it does not end it permanently because it continues before another court of competent jurisdiction.[42]

Conflicts of Jurisdiction

A conflict of jurisdiction (dispute of competence) occurs when two or more courts consider themselves competent to hear a case (positive dispute) or when no court wants to hear a case because it considers that the case does not fall within its jurisdiction *ratione materiae* or *ratione loci* (negative dispute).[43] A positive dispute has little practical significance.[44]

A negative dispute can only arise when there is a final transfer of a case to one court by another court which has determined that the case does not belong to its jurisdiction. The court to which the case has been transferred can no longer make the same finding and transfer the case to another court, because there would be a danger that at least some cases, instead of being heard, would be transferred between courts. The court to which the case has been transferred may either hear the case or initiate a dispute if it disagrees with the transfer decision. The initiation of a dispute shall be effected by a decision to transfer the case to a higher court having jurisdiction over the

[38] Zagrodnik (n 1) 200.
[39] Decision of Appelatte Court in Katowice, 14 February 2001, II AKz 122/01, Lex no 48333.
[40] Hofmański et al (n 11) vol I, 224.
[41] Decision of Appelatte Court in Katowice, 14 February 2001, II AKz 122/01, Lex no 48333.
[42] Zagrodnik (n 1) 200.
[43] Grzegorczyk and Tylman (n 3) 226.
[44] Marszał (n 9) 203.

seat of the court that initiated the dispute. This leads to to settle the dispute between the courts.[45] A jurisdictional dispute between a district court and a regional court shall be resolved by a court of appeal, and a jurisdictional dispute between a court of appeal and another common court by the Supreme Court (Article 38 § 1 CPC). The court resolving the dispute is not limited by the possibility to refer the case only to one of the courts in dispute. It may also assert the jurisdiction of another court.[46] The decision of a higher court over the court that initiated the dispute is binding on the court to which the case is referred.[47]

During the course of a dispute, each court that remains in the dispute should undertake actions that are urgent (Article 38 § 2 CPC), ie actions that are necessary because of the danger of losing the possibility of their later performance or because of an obligation to perform them within a statutorily specified time.[48]

As an aside to the above findings, it should be stressed that a competence dispute between common courts and military courts is not possible.[49] This is clear from the content of Article 39 CPC, which states:

> If a military court refers a case to a common court or refuses to accept a case referred to it by a common court, the case shall be heard by the latter.

Hence, the cited provision establishes an irrebuttable legal presumption of the jurisdiction of the common court in cases where the military court refers a case to a common court or refuses to accept a case referred to it by a common court. It follows that the common court is bound by the decision of the military court as to jurisdiction. At the same time, this presumption precludes the possibility of successfully raising in an appeal against a judgment a plea that the common court lacks jurisdiction to hear a particular case.[50]

Staffing of the Courts: Professional and Lay Judges

A Polish criminal court shall in any event be composed of at least one professional judge. No provision is currently made for a court to hear criminal cases composed solely of a lay judge or judges. Such a solution harmonises with the content of Article 182 PC, which provides that citizens, to the extent specified by statute, may participate in the administration of justice. It follows that the administration of justice cannot be wholly placed in the hands of the representative of the community.[51] The conditions for obtaining the status of professional judge and lay judge in the common courts are set out in the LSCC.

[45] ibid 203; see also D Świecki, in D Świecki, *Kodeks postępowania karnego. Komentarz* (Warsaw, Wolters Kluwer, 2022) vol I, 252–53.
[46] Decision of the Appellate Court in Katowice, 15 October 2008, II AKo 216/08, Lex no 477920; Zagrodnik (n 1) 201.
[47] Supreme Court Decision, 19 September 2006, III KO 53/06, Lex no 2531561.
[48] See Świecki (n 45) vol I, 254–55.
[49] Supreme Court Decision, 21 October 2010, III KO 92/10, Lex no 843506.
[50] Supreme Court Judgment, 9 July 1982, V KR 100/82, OSNKW 1982, no 12, poz 98.
[51] Zagrodnik (n 1) 77–78.

Article 55 § 1 LSCC provides that a judge of a common court is a person appointed to that position by the President of the Republic of Poland who has taken an oath before the President of the Republic of Poland. This appointment is not to the position of a judge *in genere*, but to the position of a judge of a specific court, ie a district court, regional court or appellate court. This means that promotion of, for example, a judge of a district court to the position of a judge of a regional court requires a separate appointment by the President of the Republic (Article 55 § 2 LSCC). This is further confirmed by the first sentence of Article 55 § 3 LSCC, under which the appointment to perform the duties of a judge is followed by the designation of the judge's official seat by the President of the Republic.[52] Candidates for the positions of judges of common courts are considered by the National Council of the Judiciary before they are presented to the President. In this regard, it is necessary to emphasise the defectiveness of the appointment procedure and the politicisation of the current composition of this Council, created by amendments introduced by the Act of 8 December 2017 amending the Act on the National Council of the Judiciary and certain other acts (Journal of Laws of 2018, item 3).[53] These factors cause issues with the procedure for vetting and presenting candidates for judicial positions to the President of the Republic of Poland, and, in turn, with the possibility of objectively perceiving the composition of the court in which the judge appointed as a result of such procedure sits as an impartial and independent court. In the case of judges of common (and military) courts, mainly due to the differentiation of the scale of defects in the procedures for appointment to the office of a judge as used by the National Council of the Judiciary – formed according to the procedure set out in the provisions of the Act of 8 December 2017 amending the Act on the National Council of the Judiciary and certain other acts (Journal of Laws of 2018, item 3) – and the differentiation of the status of the participants, it cannot be excluded, despite the violations of the procedure for appointment to the position of a judge, that the resulting doubts about his or her impartiality in the realities of specific cases will not find confirmation, and consequently, the court in which such a judge participates will meet the minimum requirements for maintaining independence and impartiality.[54] This, however, requires verification and a determination as to whether, from the perspective

[52] A judge's place of duty may be changed without a change of position in the following cases: 1. The abolition of a position caused by a change in the organisation of the judiciary or the abolition of a given court or a local division or the transfer of the seat of the court; 2. Admissibility of occupying the position of a judge in a given court due to a relationship of kinship in a straight line or affinity in a straight line, a relationship of adoption, marriage or sibling with a judge, court assessor or court referendary in the same division of the court; 3. As required by the solemnity of the position, on the basis of a ruling of a disciplinary court issued at the request of the collegium of the competent court or the National Council of the Judiciary; 4. As a result of a disciplinary penalty (§ 2 of the cited provision).

In the cases presented, the Minister of Justice decides on the transfer of a judge (Article 73 *in principio* of thef Common Courts). In cases referred to in subparagraphs 1 and 2 above, the decision of the Minister of Justice may be appealed against to the Supreme Court (Article 73 of thef Common Courts).

[53] J Zagrodnik, *Obrońca i pełnomocnik w procesie karnym i karnym skarbowym* (Warsaw, Wolters Kluwer, 2020) 522–23.

[54] Supreme Court Resolution, 15 January 2020, BSA I-4110-1/20, www.sn.pl. See also ECHR Judgment, 7 August 2021, *Xero Flor w Polsce sp. z o.o. v Poland*, Application no 4907/18; ECHR Judgment, 22 November 2021, *Case of Reczkowicz v Poland*, Application no 43447/19. Powołaną uchwałę w sposób bezprawny zakwestionował politycznie motywowany Trybunał Konstytucyjny in Decision, 28 January 2020, Kpt 1/20, Lex no 2770026.

of an objective observer with sufficient insight into the circumstances relevant to forming certain conclusions based on them, the conditions are met for a particular judge to be perceived as impartial and independent and the court as independent, despite the defects in the competition procedure. In a sense, this means weighing the impact of a defects in the procedure for appointing a judge against compliance with the standards of impartiality and independence. According to the position of the Supreme Court as presented in the resolution of the combined Chambers of 23 January 2020, the following criteria and circumstances should be taken into account in doing so:

1. The criterion of the level of the court whose staffing is the result of a defective procedure. Put simply, the higher the level of the court, the higher should be the level of requirements for minimum conditions of impartiality and independence.
2. The importance for the executive of the issues to be decided by the court on which the judge appointed following the flawed competition procedure sits. The greater the importance, for example in the case of the financial interests of the Treasury or in criminal matters, where the executive has certain public expectations of the courts, the more justified are doubts about the impartiality and independence of the appointment of a judge following a flawed, politically motivated procedure.
3. Special circumstances relating to the judge himself, namely: (i) involvement immediately prior to appointment to the office of judge in units subordinate to the Minister of Justice or other bodies of the executive power or the National Council of the Judiciary at a time when the leadership of the supreme bodies of these units was shaped by the parliamentary majority enacting the Act of 8 December 2017 amending the Act on the National Council of the Judiciary; (ii) the judge's attitude to the legislative changes made, publicly expressed in the competition procedure or later, especially in terms of acceptance of unconstitutional actions of the executive authorities against the courts, including the Supreme Court, or acceptance of the loss of the attribute of independence by the National Council of the Judiciary.
4. Failure to exclude individual members of the National Council of the Judiciary in proceedings for appointment to the office of judge conducted in relation to persons associated with them.
5. Positive decisions regarding competitions for the office of judge in favour of persons obtaining administrative promotions within the judiciary by arbitrary decisions of the Minister of Justice.
6. A particular lack of transparency in the competition procedures due to part of the proceedings of the National Council of the Judiciary or its panels being secret, the lack of possibility to learn about the proceedings of a given competition, voting by members of the proceedings of a given competition, and voting by members of the Council *in pleno* without specific justification contrary to the opinions of the Council's panels.
7. Nomination of the Council for the office of a judge in the absence of the opinion of the judicial self-government authorities or after obtaining an opinion that clearly shows a lack of support for the candidature, in particular by not obtaining a majority of votes in favour or obtaining a clearly lower support than another candidate running in the same competition, and without reasonable justification for such a decision or after the candidate had already obtained a delegation to a higher court

on the basis of an arbitrary decision of the Minister of Justice that had no rational justification regarding the quality of the work of the given judge.

8. Appointment to the position of a judge despite the fact that other persons participating in the competition had greater competence.
9. In the case of the promotion procedure, the nature of the promotion, in particular the speed with which it was achieved and the level of promotion; in this respect, the promotion of a judge of a district court to, for example, a judge of a court of appeal may raise significant doubts as to his independence, given the suspicion that he/she owes his/her position primarily to political support.[55]

As a consequence of recognising, on the basis of the above criteria and circumstances, that objective conditions for perceiving a given judge as impartial are not met, hearing the case and issuing a ruling with the participation of such a judge should be qualified as a defect requiring reversal of the ruling irrespective of the boundaries of the appeal on the grounds the panel was improperly constituted (Article 439 § 1 point 1 *in principio* CPC).[56]

Leaving aside the very procedure of appointment of a professional judge in the current legal and political reality, which raises significant reservations from the point of view of the standards of a democratic state of law, attention may be directed to the requirements for candidates for the position of a judge of a public court in the Polish legal system. The basic requirement, from which there is no exception, is to have completed higher legal studies in the Republic of Poland and to have obtained a professional master's degree or undertaken foreign legal studies recognised in the Republic of Poland. In typical cases of appointment as a judge, the educational path leading to this includes, in addition to academic training, vocational training as part of the judicial training programme organised and held at the National School of Judiciary and Public Prosecution in Krakow. In addition to legal education, candidates for the position of judge are required:

1. to be exclusively a citizen of Poland and have full civil and public rights, and not have been validly convicted of an intentional crime prosecuted by public indictment or an intentional fiscal crime;
2. to be of impeccable character;
3. to be able, in terms of health, to perform the duties of a judge;
4. to be at least 29 years of age;
5. to have passed the exam for judge or prosecutor;
6. to have performed the duties of a judge for at least three years while holding the position of assistant judge (Article 61 § 1 LSCC).

The last two requirements do not apply to persons who, prior to their appointment as a judge of a district court, held the position of a judge of an administrative court or military court, the position of a prosecutor, who worked at a Polish higher-education

[55] Supreme Court Resolution, 15 January 2020, BSA I-4110-1/20, www.sn.pl. See also ECHR Judgment, 7 August 2021, *Xero Flor w Polsce sp. z o.o. v Poland*, Application no 4907/18; ECHR Judgment, 22 November 2021, *Case of Reczkowicz v Poland*, Application no 43447/19.

[56] See Świecki (n 45) vol I, 227; Zagrodnik (n 53) 522–23.

institution, the Polish Academy of Sciences in a research institute or other scientific institution and have the academic title of professor or be a doctor habilitated (*doktor habilitowany*) in legal sciences, as well as persons who have practised the profession of a barrister, legal adviser or notary for at least three years or have held the position of president, vice-president or adviser of the Solicitors' Office of the Republic of Poland for at least three years (Article 61 § 2 LSCC).

Further requirements are imposed on candidates for judges of higher courts (Articles 63 and 64 LSCC). Taking into account the classic path of judicial career development, promotion to the position of judge of a higher court is based on specific practical experience connected with working as a judge in a lower court for a statutorily determined minimum period of time. Thus, a judge of a district court or military garrison court may be appointed to the position of judge of a regional court if he/she has at least four years of work experience as a judge of a district court or military garrison court or in the position of a prosecutor (Article 63 § 1 LSCC). On the other hand, a judge of a common court or military court who has had at least ten years of service as a judge or prosecutor may in principle be appointed to the position of judge of an appellate court (Article 64 § 1 LSCC). A specific period of holding the position of judge of a lower court or practising another legal profession is not required for appointment to the position of judge of a regional court or appellate court in the case of employees of a Polish higher-education institution, the Polish Academy of Sciences, a research institute or other research institution who have the academic title of professor or are a doctor habilitated in legal sciences (Article 63 § 2 pkt 2 and Article 64 § 2 pkt LSCC). It is also not required for appointment to the position of regional court judge in the case of administrative court judges and military regional court judges (Article 63 §2 pkt 3 LSCC of Common Courts) and for appointment to the position of appellate court judges in the case of administrative court judges (Article 64 §2 pkt 3 LSCC).

Lay judges in the Polish legal system are both judges of fact and judges of law.[57] In deciding individual cases, they have rights equal to those of judges and court assessors (Article 4 § 2 LSCC), which means that their vote when voting on a decision is equivalent to that of a professional judge or court assessor. Therefore, given that the majority rule applies when voting on the verdict, the possibility of a professional judge (assessor) being outvoted by a lay judge cannot be completely ruled out. In practice, however, such cases are quite isolated. Like professional judges, lay judges enjoy the attribute of independence in their adjudication, which means that they are subject only to the constitution and statutes (Article 169 § 1 LSCC).[58]

The restriction that lay judges are equal to professional judges in the sphere of adjudication is matched by a provision stating that a lay judge may not preside over a trial or deliberation or perform the duties of a judge outside the trial unless a specific provision to the contrary directs otherwise (Article 169 § 2 LSCC). It can therefore be said that activities outside the sphere of adjudication, often of an administrative nature, eg related to the organisation of the main hearing or activities of the so-called material or formal management of the hearing, are entrusted exclusively to

[57] Marszał (n 9) 70–71.
[58] See Waltoś and Hofmański (n 3) 245–46.

professional judges, as presiding judges. It should be emphasised in this connection that Polish law does not provide for any limitation on the information that lay judges may obtain in the course of a trial. This means that they also have access to such information whose evidentiary use is inadmissible. In the case of such information, it is the role of the professional judge as presiding judge to instruct the lay judges in connection with the evaluation of the evidence gathered in the case that it may not be taken into account as the basis for the verdict due to its illegality, eg the prohibition on proving by specific evidence (eg prohibition on proving by witness testimony as to circumstances covered by legal privilege).

District and regional court lay judges are elected for a four-year term (Article 165 § 1 in principio LSCC). After the expiration of that term, a lay judge may only participate in the examination of cases that have been commenced with his or her participation, until their conclusion (Article 165 § 2 LSCC). Lay judges are selected by the councils of municipalities within the jurisdiction of those courts by secret ballot (Article 160 § 1 LSCC). Candidates may be nominated by presidents of competent courts, associations, other social and professional organisations registered under the provisions of law, excluding political parties, or at least fifty citizens who have the right to vote permanently residing in the area of the commune making the election (Article 162 § 1 LSCC). For our purposes, we can confine our discussion to pointing out who can be elected a lay judge and who is excluded from election. In accordance with Article 158 § 1 LSCC, a lay judge must be a person who is a Polish citizen and enjoys full civil and civic rights; is of unimpeachable character; is at least thirty years of age; is employed, runs a business or has resided in the place of candidacy for at least one year; is under seventy years of age; is fit to perform the duties of a lay judge in view of his or her state of health; and has at least a high school or intermediate professional education. Every lay judge must meet all of these conditions. At the same time, even if these conditions are fulfilled, election as a lay judge is excluded in the case of persons employed in courts of general jurisdiction and other courts, as well as in the public prosecutor's office, persons who are members of bodies whose decisions may be required to institute court proceedings, police officers and other persons who hold positions related to the prosecution of crimes and offences (eg Border Guard officers), attorneys and trainee attorneys, legal advisors and trainee legal advisors, clergymen, soldiers in active military service, prison officers and municipal, district and provincial councilors (Article 159 § 2 LSCC).

Composition of the Court's Panel

In the regulation of the composition of the court panel there is always an expression of the degree to which the principle of collegiality and the principle of participation of a social factor in administering justice have been implemented in a given criminal procedural system.[59] In the Polish legal order an imbalance is currently apparent in the proportions between what follows from the aforementioned principles and what constitutes a deviation from them. This is particularly pronounced and difficult to accept with

[59] Zagrodnik (n 1) 202; see also Grzegorczyk and Tylman (n 3) 228.

regard to the composition of the panel of judges at the main trial. Given that this is the forum in which the legal dispute between the prosecution and the defence is revealed in its full form, requiring a formalised evidentiary hearing, the existing solution, which provides in principle for the case to be heard at the main hearing by a single judge, seems impossible to reconcile with the desire to ensure the highest substantive value of sentencing and thus the proper administration of justice.[60]

It would not be appropriate to present in this study the entire complex legal regulation concerning the composition of courts adjudicating in criminal cases. Therefore, the following remarks will be focused on the composition of the trial court. Thus, following this assumption, it can be stated that at the main trial, ie in the proceedings before the court of first instance, both district and regional, the rule is, as already noted above, that the case be heard by a single professional judge.[61] Such a judge has the rights and duties of the presiding judge (Article 28 § 1 CPC). Two groups of exceptions to one-person adjudication at the main trial can be distinguished. The first group consists of cases of felonies. It should be borne in mind that these comprise only a few percent of all criminal cases.[62] In this category of cases, the regional court panel generally comprises one professional judge and two lay judges (Article 28 § 2 CPC). This composition must by law be expanded to two professional judges and three lay judges in cases involving felonies for which the law provides for deprivation of liberty for life (Article 28 § 4 CPC). The second group of exceptions includes situations, rare in practice, in which a single-judge court decides that a case should be heard by three judges or one judge and two lay judges because of its particular importance or complexity. For the reasons given above, one judge and two lay judges may decide a case should be heard by three judges in felony cases (Article 28 § 3 CPC).

For appeal and cassation trial, the rule is that the court decides as a panel of three professional judges (Article 29 § 1 CPC). There are several exceptions to this rule, namely:

1. it is for a court sitting in a panel of five judges to hear an appeal or cassation appeal against a judgment that adjudicates life imprisonment or requests this penalty (Article 29 § 2 CPC);
2. in cases in which the pre-trial proceedings have been completed in the form of a simplified investigation and in private prosecution cases, the appellate court shall adjudicate at the trial in a panel composed of one judge, unless the challenged ruling was issued by the court of the first instance in a panel other than a panel composed of one judge (Article 449 § 2 CPC);
3. a panel of seven judges of the Supreme Court (Article 534 § 2 CPC) shall hear the cassation appeal against a decision of the Supreme Court issued by a panel other than a single judge.

[60] See A Murzynowski, 'Składy wyrokujące w sądach I instancji, (w:) Rozprawa główna. Problemy podstawowe' (1985) *Studia Iuridica* no 13, 37; J Zagrodnik, 'Garść refleksji w sprawie kolegialności składu sądu wyrokującego w pierwszej instancji', in M Rogacka-Rzewnicka and H Gajewska-Kraczkowska (eds), *Istota i zasady procesu karnego 25 lat później. Księga poświęcona pamięci Profesora Andrzeja Murzynowskiego* (Warsaw, Wolters Kluwer, 2020) 537–38.

[61] Grzegorczyk and Tylman (n 3) 229.

[62] See further: https://stat.gov.pl/download/gfx/portalinformacyjny/pl/defaultaktualnosci/5515/2/20/1/rocznik_statystyczny_rzeczypospolitej_polskiej_2020_korekta_30.09.2021.pdf.

In the case of sessions, the rule is that the court is composed of one person (Article 30 § 1 in principio CPC). This also applies to sessions of an appellate court (Article 30 § 2 in principio CPC).[63]

Exclusion of Judges

The ability to exclude a judge is a guarantee of the impartiality of the judiciary.[64] It should be seen as the concretisation of the requirement provided in Article 45 paragraph 1 of the Constitution of the Republic of Poland that the court hearing the case should be competent, impartial and independent. This requirement clearly refers to the treaty standard of a fair and public hearing within a reasonable time by an independent and impartial tribunal established by law (Article 6(1) ECHR, Article 14(1) ICCPR). Adopting a slightly different optic, it can be said that at the heart of the institution of the exclusion of a judge lies the assumption that there is no guarantee of justice without ensuring that a judge in respect of whom circumstances are revealed that call into question his or her impartiality and independence will not take part in the examination of the case and in the substantive adjudication.[65]

The mechanism for excluding a judge allows only for exclusion of a named judge. It is not possible to exclude the entire court through a single procedural act (a single motion for exclusion of the court).[66] Although the regulation of the exclusion mechanism is directly related to professional judges, it is appropriately applied to lay judges (Article 44 CPC).[67] This seems fully understandable, even necessary, if one takes into account what has already been established earlier, namely that lay judges are equal to professional judges in terms of adjudication. The mechanism for the exclusion of a judge also applies *mutatis mutandis* to court clerks under the cited provision. Without losing sight of the application of this mechanism to lay judges and court clerks, in connection

[63] There are many exceptions to this rule. For example, it may be indicated that one group of such exceptions, common for the court of first instance and the appellate court, consists of cases where the court examines the case at a session of three professional judges based on an order of the court president issued due to the particular complexity of the case or its importance (Art 30 § 1 and 2 CPC). Another group of exceptions to the rule of a one-person composition of the court adjudicating at a session are cases where the law provides for a different regulation as to the composition of the court adjudicating a specific issue (Art 30 §§ 1 and 2 CPC). This applies, inter alia, to:

1. situations in which it is necessary to make a ruling during a break in the trial; in such cases, the court should rule on the composition of the court hearing the case, or, if it is impossible to form one, on the same composition, i. a composition of a kind (Article 403 CPC);
2. power of the court of first instance to consider the complaint in its entirety in the same roll call in which the court made the appealed decision (Article 63 CPC);
3. a request for pardon is heard by a district or regional court in the same formation in which it heard the case (Article 562 § 1 CPC)

[64] E Kruk and E Skrętowicz. [w:] *System Prawa Karnego Procesowego*, P. Hofmański (ed.), t. 5, *Sądy i inne organy postępowania karnego*, Z. Kwiatkowski (ed.), (Warsaw, Wolters Kluwer, 2015) s 522.

[65] See eg Supreme Court Resolution, 15 January 2020, BSA I-4110-1/20, www.sn.pl; ECHR Judgment, 15 January 2008, *Micaleff v Malta*, Application no 17056/06, Lex no 336953; ECHR Judgment, 7 August 2021, *Xero Flor w Polsce sp. z o.o. v Poland*, Application no 4907/18; ECHR Judgment, 22 November 2021, *Case of Reczkowicz v Poland*, Application no 43447/19.

[66] Marszał (n 9) 206.

[67] Supreme Court Judgment, 2 December 2004, III KK 107/04, Lex no 146302.

with its detailed discussion, for the sake of clarity of consideration, it is necessary to focus attention on judges.

Considering the type of reasons for the exclusion of a judge, it is necessary to distinguish:

1. exclusion by law (*ex lege*) due to unfitness to judge a case (*iudex inhabilis*);
2. exclusion upon request due to the suspicion that the judge may be biased in the case (*iudex suspectus*).[68]

The first of these points concerns the circumstances resulting in the exclusion of a judge from participation in a case, which are listed taxatively (enumeratively) in Article 40 § 1 CPC. This provision states that a judge shall be disqualified from a case by virtue of law if:

1. the case concerns them directly;[69]
2. they are the spouse of a party, the injured person or the defence counsel, attorney or statutory representative of the foregoing, or are cohabiting with one of these persons;[70]
3. they are a direct relative by blood or affinity, and in the case of sibship, down to the level of the children of the sibling of the persons listed under subparagraph (2), or are related to any such person by adoption, custody or guardianship;[71]
4. they were a witness to the act from which the pending case arises[72] or have appeared as a witness or an expert witness in the same;
5. they have participated in the case as a public prosecutor, defence counsel, attorney, statutory representative of a party to the proceedings, or have conducted investigation in the case;[73]
6. they have participated in the issuance of a contested ruling or have themselves issued a contested order;[74]
7. they have participated in the issuance of a ruling which has been set aside;[75]
8. they have participated in the issuance of a ruling subsequently objected against;[76]
9. they have conducted mediation.

According to Article 40 § 2 CPC:

> The grounds for disqualification shall continue to be valid even if the ties of marriage, cohabitation, adoption, guardianship or custody cease to exist.

Furthermore:

> A judge who has participated in the issuance of a ruling covered by a motion for reopening, appealed against under a cassation procedure or covered by an extraordinary complaint shall not decide on such a motion, cassation appeal or complaint. (Article 40 § 3 CCP)[77]

[68] Marszał (n 9) 207; Grzegorczyk and Tylman (n 3) 233.
[69] See eg Supreme Court Decision, 10 January 2002, IV KZ 83/01, Lex no 559991.
[70] Supreme Court Judgment, 21 April 2005, IV KK 92/05.
[71] Supreme Court Decision, 12 January 2011, III KK 203/10, Lex no 736751.
[72] Supreme Court Decision, 18 October 2001, II KKN 124/99, Lex no 51579.
[73] See eg Supreme Court Decision, 9 January 2019, IV KK 723/18, Lex no 2604050.
[74] Supreme Court Decision, 12 February 2014, V KO 4/14, Lex no 1427480.
[75] Supreme Court Judgment, 31 March 1988, II KR 36/88, Lex no 20303.
[76] Supreme Court Judgment, 15 November 2013, III KK 227/13, Lex no 1403880.
[77] See eg Supreme Court Judgment, 31 March 1988, II KR 36/88, Lex no 20303.

Since the presented catalogue of reasons for excluding a judge *ex lege* is closed, it cannot be expanded through interpretation.[78] The exclusion of a judge for these reasons from participation in the case means that he or she may neither participate in the main trial nor make any decisions on issues concerning the case.[79]

The second type of reasons for the exclusion of a judge is set out in Article 41 § 1 CPC:

> A judge shall be disqualified if there are circumstances that can give rise to reasonable doubts as to the judge's impartiality in a given case

This provision is a *sui generis* supplement to the catalogue of grounds for exclusion provided in Article 40 CPC, which aims to remove a judge from a case whenever there are circumstances that can give rise to reasonable doubts as to his/her impartiality. Establishing the existence of such circumstances does not require a firm determination of the judge's actual bias or that he or she would be biased in the case. The analysed reason for the exclusion of a judge also occurs when the judge is objectively and subjectively impartial, but there is a justified conviction that his or her impartiality in the external perception (external impartiality) is in doubt.[80] The exclusion of a judge on the basis of Article 41 § 1 CPC should therefore be linked to the disclosure of circumstances of such a nature that it is not possible for any reasonable person who had doubts about the judge's impartiality to be convinced that these circumstances would not affect the objectivity of the examination of the case and the content of the judgment being the final outcome of the criminal trial.[81] As a rule, political or religious beliefs of a judge do not constitute such circumstances, unless they are the background of a 'dispute' between the judge and a party, following a polemic in the press or even a scientific debate, and thus when such beliefs affect or may affect his attitude towards the parties.[82] Views publicly expressed by a judge on political or religious matters will constitute grounds for his or her exclusion under Article 41 § 1 CPC if they give rise to a presumption that he or she will be biased in his or her rulings, and these views are adverse to the interests of either party.

The case law and doctrine provide numerous examples of situations and behaviours that should be qualified as a reason for excluding a judge under Article 41 § 1 CPC. These may include:

1. statements made by the judge before the end of the trial that indicate an attitude towards the accused that casts doubt on his or her impartiality, such as a statement that 'the accused's truthfulness may not be as good as his or her own' or that the defendant is a 'fraudster';[83]
2. ironic or polemical language used by the judge at the trial that demonstrates that judge has taken a predetermined view on a factual issue to the exclusion of opposing reasons and inferences;[84]

[78] Hofmański et al (n 11) 247 (2004); Świecki (n 45) vol I, 259.

[79] Decision of the Appellate Court in Katowice, 21 March 2005, II AKz 644/05, KZS 2006, no 2, pos 65.

[80] Supreme Court Judgment, 31 May 2010, II Aka 103/10, KZS 2011, no 1, pos 80.

[81] Supreme Court Judgment, 1 August 2001, II Ako 312/01, KZS 2001, no 12, pos 39.

[82] E Skrętowicz, *Iudex inhabilis i iudex suspectus* w polskim procesie karnym, Lublin 1994, 51; K Papke-Olszauskas, *Wyłączenie uczestników procesu*, Gdańsk 2007, 164–65.

[83] eg Court Judgment 19 July 1962, no 2, pos 51.

[84] See eg Supreme Court Decision, 24 September 2008, III KK 73/08, Lex no 465883.

3. the judge's disclosure of his or her view of the case before or during the hearing, clearly indicating judge's orientation intended to confirm his or her initial assessment of the case,[85] or articulating his or her attitude toward a party;[86]
4. disclosure by the judge of his or her own and emotional attitude toward a particular category of persons to which a party belongs, such as in the statement 'I would lock up all the drivers';[87]
5. the judge's bias against a particular class of persons, eg physicians, related to having been injured by a physician's actions in similar circumstances to those included in the charge against the accused physician;
6. a judge's consideration of a case in which members of the judge's family or the judge's supervisor appear as witnesses, or in which the judge's spouse is an expert witness;[88]
7. the judge's biases based on nationality, race, religion, politics, etc;[89]
8. the judge's previous participation in a panel of judges in a (professional) disciplinary responsibility proceedings in which the same facts were considered and the same evidence was available as in the criminal case under consideration,
9. taking a position by a judge in another case previously heard, which is in close and indissoluble connection with the case currently heard by him/her,[90] even if this position was expressed only in the justification of an earlier decision made with the participation of a particular judge;[91]
10. the judge's assessment of the evidence and conviction as to the criminal liability of one of the perpetrators of the act, if the same evidence were to form the basis for an assessment as to the criminal liability of another perpetrator of the same act.[92]

Taking a different point of view, it may be stated that the following circumstances do not constitute sufficient grounds for excluding a judge from participating in the examination of a case:

1. incidental contacts of the judge with the victim's family and these contacts, the nature of which should be considered as purely neutral or even official;[93]
2. the performance of the function of judge in a lower court by a person who acts as a victim in the case;[94]

[85] Supreme Court Judgment, 31 May 1985, V KRN 333/85, OSNPG 1985/10, pos 129; Supreme Court Judgment, 27 January 1971, III KR 213/70, Lex no 479162; M Jankowski, 'Instytucja wyłączenia sędziego w polskim procesie karnym' (1986) *NP* no 9, 68–70.

[86] Supreme Court Judgment, 1 June 2021, II DIZ 27/21, Lex no 3190963.

[87] Papke-Olszauskas (n 82) 165.

[88] Skrętowicz (n 82) 54; Supreme Court Judgment, 6 July 1967, VI KZP 18/67, OSNKW 1967, no 11, pos 14.

[89] Decision of the Appellate Court in Cracow, 13 November 1997, II Aka 210/97, KZS 1997, no 11–12, pos 55.

[90] Supreme Court Judgment, 8 November 2001, IV CCN 169/97, Lex no 51606; Supreme Court Judgment, 29 August 2006, V CC 107/05, OSNKW 2006, no 10, pos 96; Supreme Court Judgment, 2 June 2011, III CC 328/10, Lex no 860618.

[91] Supreme Court Judgment, 18 March 2009, IV CC 380/08, Lex no 491543.

[92] Supreme Court Judgment, 26 April 2007, I KZP 9/07, OSNKW 2007, no 5, pos 39.

[93] Court of Appeal Judgment 6 November 2019, II Aka 188/19, OSAS 2019, no 4, 39–41.

[94] L Paprzycki, Iudex inhabilis, 396–97.

3. the formulation of judicial assessments that are within the bounds of the arguments judging the case, and beyond this not exceeding and devoid of personal or group bias;[95]
4. examining a witness and critically evaluating his or her testimony in an earlier case when he or she subsequently appears as an accused;[96]
5. rejection of an evidentiary motion of either party;[97]
6. the previous hearing of another case of the same accused by the judge concerned;
7. the fact that the participating judge once served as a prosecutor and prosecuted the accused in another case, as well as the mere fact that another case of the accused was tried by the same judge.[98]

So far, the circumstances that cause or may cause the exclusion of a judge have been presented. The modes in which this may occur are set forth in Article 42 CPC: 'The disqualification shall take place at the judge's request, ex officio or upon a motion of a party of the proceedings.'

The exclusion of a judge on the judge's request takes place on the basis of a declaration by the judge of his/her will to exclude himself/herself from participation in the case, which is linked to a declaration of knowledge of the existence of circumstances justifying his/her exclusion *ex lege* (*argumentum ex* Article 40 § 1 in conjunction with Article 42 § 2 CPC).[99] In the event of the occurrence of such circumstances, judge shall disqualify herself or himself by making a written statement recorded in the case files and shall be substituted by another judge.[100]

Exclusion of a judge ex officio consists in the court commencing, on its own initiative, proceedings for this exclusion. This mode of exclusion is primarily applicable to the reasons for the exclusion of a judge *ex lege* (set out in Article 40 CPC), but cannot be completely excluded for the reasons for the exclusion of the *iudex suspectus* (set out in Article 41 CPC).[101] As regards the grounds for exclusion of a judge *ex lege*, the rule should be that the judge should make a written statement in the file that there is, however, one of the circumstances causing his exclusion *ex lege*. If a judge makes such a declaration of knowledge, another judge takes his/her place (Article 42 § 2 CPC), so a court decision to exclude the judge is not necessary.[102] Only if the described 'self-exclusion' of a judge has not taken place, and the court comes into possession of information about the existence with respect to a judge of circumstances that constitute grounds for exclusion *ex lege* is it obliged to initiate ex officio proceedings for the exclusion of such a judge.[103]

[95] Court of Appeal Judgment in Cracow 12 November 1998, II Aka 199/98, KZS 1998, no 12, pos 34.
[96] Supreme Court Judgment, 16 November 1970, I KR 109/70, OSNPG 1971, no 2, pos 39.
[97] Court of Appeal in Łódź, Judgment 7 February 2001, II Aka 269/00, KZ 2002, no 11, pos 41.
[98] Supreme Court Judgment, 10 July 2001, II CCN 538/98, OSP 2003, pos 25.
[99] See Świecki (n 45) vol I, 284.
[100] R Kmiecik, 'Tryb wyłączenia sędziego i prokuratora w kodeksie postępowania karnego' (1999) 11–12 *Prok i Pr* 23; Hofmański et al (n 11) 253 (2004); differently Świecki (n 45) vol I, 284.
[101] Kmiecik (n 100) 25–26.
[102] Kmiecik (n 100) 23; Hofmański et al (n 11) 253.
[103] Hofmański et al (n 11) 253; differently E Kruk in Z Kwiatkowski (ed), *System Prawa Karnego Procesowego* (Wolters Kluwer) vol 5, 577.

The third mode of exclusion of a judge is exclusion upon motion of a party to the proceedings. A logical and linguistic analysis and application of systemic rules of interpretation to Article 42 § 1 CPC supports the conclusion that this procedure is applicable not only in the case of the exclusion of a judge for the reason stipulated in Article 41 CPC (*iudex suspectus*), but also in relation to circumstances prejudging the exclusion of a judge *ex lege* (*iudex inhabilis*), when they have not been taken into account by the judge concerned or other members of the judging panel.[104] The motion for the exclusion of a judge is a declaration of intent of a postulatory nature, aimed at removing from participation in the case a judge in respect of whom there are circumstances that constitute grounds for his/her exclusion (as specified in Articles 40 or 41 CPC). The parties and their procedural representatives have the right to file such a motion. In terms of its content, the motion must be specific both as to the grounds for exclusion and as to the person of the judge.[105] The right to file a motion to exclude a judge on the grounds set forth in Article 41 CPC is subject to a time limit. Its exercise may in principle take place up until the commencement of the judicial examination. A motion commenced after this deadline is left without examination (Article 41 § 2 CPC). This time limit on the right to file a motion to exclude a judge on the grounds specified in Article 41 § 1 CPC does not apply, however, if this reason had arise or had become known to the party after the commencement of the judicial examination (Article 41 § 2 CPC).

If in a motion for the exclusion of a judge a party raises the existence of a reason for the exclusion of the judge *ex lege*, the judge who is the subject of the motion may make a statement as described above confirming the existence of such a circumstance. Since the filing of such a declaration in fact means that the judge himself/herself has been excluded from participation in the case (Article 42 § 2 CPC), it becomes pointless in the situation described above for the court to consider the party's motion and issue a decision on the issue of exclusion. If a party submits a motion to exclude a judge for a reason specified in Article 41 CPC, the judge to whom the motion pertains may file an appropriate statement in which he or she responds to the motion (Article 42 § 3, first sentence CPC).

With the exception of the situation described above, in which a judge, as a result of a motion filed, makes a statement causing his or her self-exclusion from the case (Article 42 § 2 CPC), a motion to exclude a judge is subject to examination by the court and requires the issuance of an exclusion decision.[106] As a rule, the court with jurisdiction to hear the motion to exclude a judge is the court before which the proceedings are pending (Article 42 § 4, first sentence CPC). The judge concerned shall not participate in the panel adjudicating on the disqualification. If no such panel can be formed, the ruling on disqualification shall be made by a higher court (Article 42 § 4 CPC). If disqualification of judges makes it impossible for a given court to examine a case, a higher court shall refer the case to another court of the level of the former court for examination (Article 43 CPC).

[104] Kmiecik (n 100) 23–24; Zagrodnik (n 1) 206; differently Kruk (n 103) 578–80.
[105] Kruk (n 103) 581.
[106] Hofmański et al (n 11) 254.

The decision of the court to exclude a judge is not subject to complaint. However, if the motion to exclude a judge has not been granted, the issue of the judge's non-exclusion may be raised in an appeal against the judgment as a plea of violation of criminal procedural law that may have affected the content of the judgment (Article 447 § 4 CPC).[107]

Counteracting procedural obstruction based on the abuse of the right to file a motion for exclusion of a judge is provided by Article 41a CPC, according to which a motion for exclusion of a judge based on the same factual grounds as a previously examined motion is left without examination.[108]

The procedural consequences of a judge ruling with regard to whom there were circumstances justifying his or her exclusion vary depending on the reasons for the judge's exclusion. Participation in the judgment by a judge who was excluded *ex lege* constitutes an absolute ground for overturning the judgment (Article 439 § 1.1 CPC). Participation in the decision by a judge with respect to whom there was a reason for excluding him/her from participating in the case as specified in Article 41 § 1 CPC may be classified as a violation of procedural law that could have affected the content of the ruling (Article 438, point 2 CPC).[109]

Criminal Prosecution

Public Prosecution Service

In Polish criminal procedure, the prosecutor plays the main role in criminal prosecution in the pre-trial phase and in accusation in court proceedings.[110] The prosecutor, not the public prosecutor's office, is the procedural authority and participant with respect to criminal prosecution and accusation.[111] A prosecutor is vested with powers of authority, in the exercise of which he or she uses the material and personal resources of the prosecution service. The prosecution office and its particular organisational units constitute the technical and organisational base for the prosecution authority. At the same time it can be said that the prosecutor's office is an organisation that includes individual prosecutors.[112] The prosecutor's office, as an organisational whole, is responsible for carrying out its tasks in the prosecution of offences and upholding the rule of law (Article 2 LPO).

The prosecution system in Poland is currently regulated by the Act – Law on the Prosecutor's Office of 28 January 2016. It provides for basing the system of the prosecutor's office on the classical model, according to which the functions of the Minister of Justice and the Prosecutor General are fulfilled by the same person. Such a solution raises many objections in practice, primarily concerns about the political

[107] Świecki (n 45) vol I, 288.
[108] See Supreme Court Decision, 31 May 2019, III KO 74/18, Lex no 2690396.
[109] Grzegorczyk and Tylman (n 3) 233.
[110] Marszał (n 9) 226.
[111] Waltoś and Hofmański (n 3) 245–46; Zagrodnik (n 1) 213.
[112] P Hofmański and S Waltoś, *Proces karny. Zarys systemu* (Warsaw, 2016) 169.

motives of prosecutors in individual cases.[113] Even if one were to theoretically assume that the holder of the office of Minister of Justice would exercise restraint in shaping criminal policy by influencing the prosecution of particular cases, as a consequence of this personal union, it is impossible to avoid the suspicion that the actions of the Prosecutor General and the prosecutors under his/her control are politically motivated.[114] This undermines confidence in the activities of the prosecution service and its bodies as a whole and, consequently, in the proper administration of justice. Therefore, *in posterum* we should expect a departure from the systemic solution based on a personal union of the Minister of Justice and the Prosecutor General. At the same time, the independence of the prosecution system and prosecutors could be founded on entrusting the election of the Prosecutor General to the General Assembly of Judges of the Supreme Court from among candidates presented by the National Council of the Prosecution Service.[115]

In the current legal state, the public prosecution service is composed of the Prosecutor General, the National Prosecutor, other Deputy Prosecutors General and prosecutors of common organisational units of the public prosecution service and prosecutors of the Institute of National Remembrance – Commission for the Prosecution of Crimes against the Polish Nation (Article 1 §1 LPO). The Prosecutor General, who is, as already indicated, the Minister of Justice, is the chief organ of public prosecution (Article 1 § 2 LPO).

Prosecutors of common organisational units are appointed to the position of prosecutor by the Prosecutor General by a motion of the National Public Prosecutor (Article 74 § 1 LPO). The requirements to be met by prosecutors are similar to those presented earlier for persons appointed as judges. The differences are:

- the age limit, which in the case of prosecutors is set at 26 years;
- the period of employment on the position of prosecutorial or judicial assessor, which is shorter than in the case of judges and must be at least one year; and
- the introduction of a requirement equivalent to the assessorship in the form of serving a period of service in military organisational units of the prosecutor's office as provided for in the regulations on military service.

In addition, it is also envisaged that a person may be appointed to the position of a prosecutor only if he or she has not served in a professional capacity, worked or collaborated with organs of state security listed in Article 5 of the Act of 18 December 1998 on the Institute of National Remembrance – Commission for the Prosecution of Crimes against the Polish Nation (Journal of Laws of 2019, item 1882 and of 2020, item 1273), or was a judge who, when ruling, offended the dignity of the office by betraying judicial independence, which was established by a final ruling (Article 75 § 1 LPO).

[113] Marszał (n 9) 178; Zagrodnik (n 1) 212.

[114] S. Waltoś, *Prokuratura – jej miejsce wsród organów władzy; struktura i funkcje*, Państwo i Prawo (PiP) 2002, nr 4, 7.

[115] Zagrodnik (n 1) 212; see also Waltoś (n 114) 7 et seq; T Grzegorczyk, 'Niezależność prokuratury i prokuratorów w świetle znowelizowanej ustawą z dnia 9 października 2009 r. ustawy o prokuraturze' (2010) *Prok i Pr* nos 1–2; P Kardas, 'Rola i miejsce prokuratury w systemie organów demokratycznego państwa prawnego' (2012) *Prok i Pr* no 9.

In typical situations, the training of prosecutors, like that of judges, takes the form of a prosecutor's apprenticeship, which takes place within the National School of Judiciary and Public Prosecution in Krakow. Upon its completion, a prosecutor's examination is held. As with judges, appointment to the position of prosecutor does not require the prosecutor's or judge's exam be taken by persons who have other professional legal training clearly outlined in the Act, such as attorneys or legal advisors who have practised law for at least three years, as well as professors and persons with a postdoctoral degree of legal sciences from Polish schools of higher education, the Polish Academy of Sciences and research institutes and other scientific institutions. For example, the aforementioned categories of persons are also exempt from the condition of employment for a specified period of time in the position of a prosecutor assessor or court assessor (see Article 75 § 1a and § 2 LPO). It is worth mentioning that with regards to the appointment to the position of a prosecutor in a regional prosecutor's office, provincial prosecutor's office or National Prosecutor's Office, there are additional requirements provided for in the Act, concerning the length of service in the position of a prosecutor or judge and the period of practice of a specific legal profession, such as a solicitor or legal advisor (see Article 76 §§ 1–3 LPO).

The intention of more fully illustrating the structural and functional realities of the prosecutor's office and the specificity of the legal situation of particular prosecutors as procedural organs leads us to briefly present the organisational and operational principles of the prosecutor's office in the Polish legal order.

The first group of principles identified includes: the principle of unity, the principle of centralism, the principle of hierarchical subordination, the principle of 'one-man' management and the principle of independence.[116]

According to the first of these principles, all the organisational units of the public prosecution service constitute one organisational whole.[117] Thus, the organisational units appear to the public not on their own behalf but on behalf of the entire prosecutor's office. A specific manifestation of the principle of unity is the absence of a statutorily defined competence *ratione materiae* and *ratione loci* of the organisational units of the public prosecution service in criminal matters.[118] The principle of centralism means that all organisational units of the prosecution service and all prosecutors are subject to one supreme authority – the Prosecutor General, who is also the Minister of Justice. It follows from the principle of hierarchical subordination that this subordination is not direct, but occurs through higher-level organisational units.[119] It can be said that the orders of the Prosecutor General reach the lower-level units through these levels of the organisational structure of the prosecution service. Under the principle of 'one-man' management, both the entire organs of the prosecution service and each of its organisational units are always headed by a 'one-man' (monocratic) organ.[120]

[116] See Marszał (n 9) 179–80; Waltoś and Hofmański (n 3) 169; Grzegorczyk and Tylman (n 3) 248–50; RA Stefański, in Z Kwiatkowski (ed), *System Prawa Karnego Procesowego* (Warsaw, Wolters Kluwer, 2015) vol 5, 805 et seq.

[117] Marszał (n 9) 179; Stefański (n 116) vol 5, 805.

[118] See Stefański (n 116) vol 5, 806.

[119] Marszał (n 9) 179; Stefański (n 116) vol 5, 814.

[120] Marszał (n 9) 179; Stefański (n 116) vol 5, 814–15.

The principle of independence requires slightly more attention, primarily because of its impact on shaping the actual position of individual prosecutors. Externally, this principle means that prosecutors, in the exercise of their functions, are not subject to influence from other organs of the state. Internally, this principle must be linked to the independence of prosecutors in the performance of their duties.[121] The independence of a prosecutor, unlike independence which is an attribute vested in judges, does not have an absolute dimension. It suffers limitations within the scope arising from Articles 7 §§ 2–6, 8 and 9 LPO. For our purposes,[122] it must suffice to note the following in this regard:

1. The prosecutor is obliged to carry out orders, guidelines and instructions of the superior prosecutor (Article 7 § 2 LPO); bearing in mind the hierarchical organisational structure of the prosecutor's office, it is impossible to escape the fear that through successive levels of the organisational structure of the prosecutor's office, instructions of the Minister of Justice concerning particular cases, dictated mainly by reasons of a political nature, will be sent to the prosecutors.[123]
2. Instructions of a superior prosecutor may concern the content of a procedural act (*argumentum ex* Article 7 § 3 sentence 1 LPO), eg ordering a discontinuance of proceedings or withdrawal of an indictment; this power of a superior prosecutor raises important doubts as to the independence of the prosecutor running the case;[124] it is not abolished by the requirement to preserve the written form or to justify the instruction at the request of the public prosecutor to whom it is addressed (Article 7 § 3 LPO). Prima facie, it could seem that a certain security of the prosecutor's independence is the possibility to demand a change of the order concerning the content of the procedural action or to exclude him/her from performing the action or from participating in the case (Article 7, paragraph 4, sentence 1 LPO); however, if the previously presented organisational principles of the prosecutor's office are taken into account, first of all the principle of centralism and hierarchical subordination, it is very difficult to suppose that prosecutors would risk making such a request and exposing themselves to negative consequences from prosecutors at a higher level, not excluding the Prosecutor General;[125]
3. A superior prosecutor shall have the right to reverse or amend the decision of a subordinate prosecutor; the amendment or reversal of the decision shall be in writing and shall be included in the case file; the amendment or reversal of the decision served on the parties, their attorneys or defence counsel and other entitled entities may take place only in accordance with the procedure and rules set out in the law (Article 8 LPO). The presented solution, primarily because of the lack of clearly defined grounds and thus the ease of reversal or amending the decision by a superior prosecutor if it was not served to entitled entities, limits the prosecutor's independence, because it puts him/her in a situation, where at the moment

[121] Stefański (n 116) vol 5, 818.
[122] See further Stefański (n 116) vol 5, 814; Hofmański et al (n 3) 173–74.
[123] See Marszał (n 9) 178.
[124] Zagrodnik (n 1) 214.
[125] ibid 214–15.

> of making the decision he/she has to take into account a possibility of its negative verification by a superior; this, at the same time, results in the fact that the content of the decision may be influenced by the pursuit of approval from a superior, and this – in the present realities of politicisation of the public prosecution service – does not necessarily go hand in hand with the interest of criminal prosecution, and above all with the protection of citizens from being involved in the course of the criminal process without sufficient justification, and thus creating a state of risk of criminal responsibility.[126]

The second group of principles distinguished, concerning the activity of the prosecutor's office, consists of: the principle of legalism, the principle of impartiality, the principle of ex officio activity, the principle of cooperation with other public and self-government bodies, cooperative and social organisations, the principle of 'one-man' operation, and the principle of substitution, devolution and indifference.[127] Since some of these principles have already been presented within the framework of the discussion of the constitutional and organisational principles or the procedural principles, we describe briefly here the last three mentioned principles. Thus, as far as the principle of substitution is concerned, first of all attention should be drawn to its regulation in Article 9 § 1 CPC, according to which a public prosecutor in a superior position may entrust subordinate public prosecutors with the performance of activities which belong to his/her range of activity, unless the act of law reserves a given activity exclusively to his/her competence. Delegation of the activity does not depend on whether the subordinate prosecutor is directly subordinate to the superior prosecutor. This means that, for example, the Prosecutor General may delegate the activity to a district prosecutor with no intermediate links. The principle of substitution is subject to exception in cases in which the binding regulations reserve the activity to the competence of a prosecutor of a given rank (see Article 263 § 4 CPC) and also should the regulations exclude the possibility of assessor prosecutors carrying out certain activities (see Article 173 § 1 LPO).[128] The principle of devolution is normalised in Article 9 § 2 LPO. This provision states that a superior prosecutor has the right to take over cases conducted by subordinate prosecutors and perform their duties, unless the provisions of the act exclude that, eg when taking over certain duties for execution by the Prosecutor General would result in depriving the litigant of his/her right to complain. The principle of indifference means that for a procedural action to be effective, it does not matter which prosecutor performs it. Each prosecutor may perform any procedural act reserved for prosecutors.[129] The division of tasks between prosecutors shall be purely internal unless otherwise provided by law in specific cases. The exceptions to the principle of indifference are closely related to the exceptions to the principle of substitution or the principle of devolution as indicated by the examples.[130]

[126] ibid 215–16.
[127] Marszał (n 9) 179. Differently, Stefański (n 116) vol 5, 814; Zagrodnik (n 1) 216.
[128] Marszał (n 9) 181; Stefański (n 116) vol 5, 828; Waltoś and Hofmański (n 3) 174–75; Zagrodnik (n 1) 216.
[129] Marszał (n 9) 181; Stefański (n 116) vol 5, 828; Waltoś and Hofmański (n 3) 173–74; Zagrodnik (n 1) 217.
[130] Marszał (n 9) 181; Zagrodnik (n 1) 217.

Against the background of the above systemic issues, the role of the prosecutor at various stages of the criminal trial can be presented.

In the first procedural stage, ie in the pre-trial proceedings, the prosecutor is the organ in charge of the criminal trial.[131] Hence, he or she is referred to as the *dominus litis* in pre-trial proceedings. He or she is thus the main body responsible for the implementation of the function of criminal prosecution in the criminal process. To his/her exclusive competence is reserved the conduct of preparatory proceedings in the form of the principal investigation in cases concerning criminal offences prosecuted by public indictment.[132] The prosecutor may also conduct investigations in this category of cases (Article 311 § 1 and Article 325a § 1 CPC). In the course of pre-trial proceedings, it is the prosecutor's responsibility to carry out procedural actions, including, of course, evidentiary actions, ie the questioning of the accused or witnesses, and to issue binding procedural decisions, including as to the course of the criminal trial, eg decisions to discontinue proceedings. To the extent that the public prosecutor does not him/herself conduct the pre-trial proceedings, he/she exercises supervision over them (Article 298 § 1 CPC).[133] Within the scope of his/her supervision, the prosecutor should undertake actions aimed at guaranteeing the efficient implementation of the objectives of the pre-trial proceedings[134] with respect for the provisions of law, especially with regard to respecting the rights vested in the parties and other procedural participants. The prosecutor's supervision includes not only verifying the correctness of procedural actions and identifying shortcomings, but also drawing consequences from their disclosure, by removing irregularities and preventing them in the future.[135] If in the course of pre-trial proceedings the court performs certain actions, eg examines a witness pursuant to Article 316 § 3 CPC,[136] the public prosecutor has the rights of a party to the proceedings in connection with the actions of the court (Article 299 § 3 CPC).[137]

In court proceedings, the prosecutor acts as a procedural party. He/she is a public prosecutor (Article 45 § 1 CPC). He/she is a party of a special character. Unlike other litigants, he/she is not limited in his/her activity to the realisation of his/her own (private) legal interest in the narrow sense.[138] The absolute determinant of

[131] Marszał (n 9) 175; Grzegorczyk and Tylman (n 3) 243; Stefański (n 116) vol 5, 835.

[132] As a side note, it should be noted that in cases of fiscal offences, the power to investigate is vested, in addition to the prosecutor, in the financial organs of pre-trial investigation (Art 151a § 1, second sentence CPC).

[133] Stefański (n 116) vol 5, 836–37.

[134] According to the Art 297 of CPC, the objectives of investigation are as follows:

1. establishing whether a prohibited act has been committed and whether it constitutes a criminal offence;
2. detecting the perpetrator and, if necessary, apprehending them;
3. collecting data, in conformity with Articl13 and 214;
4. elucidating the circumstances of the case, including the identification of injured persons and the extent of the damage;
5. collecting, securing, and – to the extent necessary – preserving evidence for the court.

[135] F Prusak, *Nadzór prokuratora nad postępowaniem przygotowawczym* (Warsaw, Wydawnictwo Prawnicze, 1984) 99.

[136] According to this regulation, if there is a danger that it may not be possible to hear a witness at the trial, a party or the public prosecutor or another body conducting proceedings may submit a motion to the court demanding that the witness be heard by the court.

[137] See further Stefański (n 116) vol 5, 836.

[138] Grzegorczyk and Tylman (n 3) 278; Zagrodnik (n 1) 222.

the prosecutor's procedural activity is the public interest in prosecution.[139] This *sui generis* motor of the public prosecutor's procedural activity directly imposes an obligation on the prosecutor to maintain impartiality in the exercise of the prosecution function. This obligation is, moreover, directly expressed in Article 6 LPO. In close connection with this obligation, there remains the regulation of cases, in which the prosecutor (public prosecutor) is subject to exclusion from the case (Article 47 CPC).[140]

The prosecutor is the main accuser in cases of crimes prosecuted by public indictment.[141] This follows unambiguously from Article 45 CPC, which states that the prosecutor is a public prosecutor before all courts (§ 1), while another state authority may be such a prosecutor only by virtue of a specific provision of the law, defining the scope of its activities (§ 2). In relation to his or her role in judicial proceedings, the public prosecutor either brings and supports an indictment before the court or supports an indictment brought before the court by another body. In the latter situation, in cases of common crimes, his or her involvement in the judicial process usually results in the exclusion of the other body that acted as a public prosecutor in connection with the filing of the indictment before the court.[142]

The public prosecutor also has the power to bring and support an indictment in cases of offences prosecuted by private prosecution, eg in cases of defamation or infringement of bodily inviolability, if, in his opinion, the public interest so requires (Article 60 § 1 CPC).[143]

Sometimes the public prosecutor acts in court proceedings not as a party-public prosecutor (spokesman for the prosecution), but as a spokesman for the public interest, eg when he/she applies for an obligation to pay restitution to the injured party (Article 49a CPC) or makes an appeal in favour of the accused (Article 425 § 4 CPC).[144]

[139] P Wiliński, 'Materialny ciężar dowodu winy oskarżonego – przyczynek do rozważań', in Ciężar dowodu i obowiązek dowodzenia w koncepcji Mariana Cieślaka in W.Jasiński (ed.), J.Skorupka (ed.), Ciężar dowodu i obowiązek dowodzenia w procesie karnym, Warsaw 2017

P Kardas, T Sroka and W Wróbel (eds), *Państwo prawa i prawo karne. Księga jubileuszowa Profesora Andrzeja Zolla* (Warsaw, Wolters Kluwer, 2012) 1851; J. Zagrodnik, *Ciężar*, 151–52.

[140] Prosecutors are excluded from the case, if:

1. the case concerns them directly;
2. they are the spouse of a party, the injured person, or the defence counsel, attorney, o statutory representative of the foregoing, ofr emain in cohabitation with one of such a persons;
3. they are a direct relative by blood or affinity, and in the case of sibship, – dn to the degree between the children of the sibling of the persons listed under subparagraph (2), or are related to any such person by adoption, custody or guardianship;
4. they were a witness to the act from which the pending case arises or have appeared as a witness or an expert witness in the same (Article § 1–4 WWZ, Article 1 CPC);
5. there are circumstances that can give rise to reasonable doubts as to the prosecutor's impartiality in a given case (Article 4 ZWZ, Article 41 CPC);
6. they have participated in the case as a defence counsel, an attorney, a social representative or a statutory representative of a party (Article 47 CPC).

[141] Marszał (n 9) 225.

[142] Zagrodnik (n 1) 236–37.

[143] Marszał (n 9) 246–47; K Marszał, *Ingerencja prokuratora w ściganie przestępstw prywatnoskargowych w polskim procesie karnym* (Warsaw, Wydawnictwo Prawnicze, 1980) passim.

[144] See further Stefański (n 116) vol 5, 837–40.

Police and Other Law Enforcement Authorities

The police are a uniformed and armed formation which serves the public and are intended to protect the safety of the people and to maintain public security and order (Article 1.1 Police Act (PA)). The police are headed by the Chief Constable. He/she is a central organ of government administration, subordinate to the minister in charge of internal affairs (Article 5 section 1 PA). At the lower levels, the police organs are regional (voivodeship) police chiefs, poviat chiefs, district (city) chiefs and chiefs of police stations (Article 6 PA). Voivodeship police chiefs and district (city) police chiefs are the superiors of police officers within their area (Article 6f PA).

The police undertake six types of service: criminal, investigative, internal affairs, preventive, counterterrorist and those supporting police activities in organisational, logistic and technical areas (Article 4 paragraph 1 PA).[145]

Within the framework of police tasks, three basic groups of activities can be distinguished: investigative, operational-exploratory[146] and administrative-order activities (Article 14, paragraph 1 PA).[147] Furthermore, the police also carry out activities upon the order of, inter alia, a court or prosecutor to the extent in which such an obligation is provided for in separate acts (Article 14(2) PA), eg in the provisions of the CPC.

The first of these groups of activities, investigative activities, includes the police investigation of crimes and carrying out investigations within the scope entrusted to the police by a public prosecutor or performing the entrusted activities. The police are the main body carrying out the aforementioned tasks (argument ex Article 311 § 2 and Article 325a § 1 CPC). This corresponds to the tendency, present throughout the criminal procedural law systems of European countries, to transfer the burden of explaining the case and taking evidence at the first procedural stage to the police.[148] This should not

[145] In addition, the police include: the judicial police, as well as the Higher Police School, training centres and police schools, separate prevention units and research centres (Art 4 paras 2 and 3 of the Police Act). It should be noted that the task of the aforementioned judicial police is to ensure security and public order in courts and in prosecutor's offices and to carry out auxiliary tasks, consisting, among others, in carrying out orders of the court, eg those concerning expulsion of a given person from the courtroom, or transporting and escorting people by order of the court, prosecutor or relevant police chief (see the regulation of the Minister of Internal Affairs and Administration of 16.08.2007 on the detailed scope of tasks and rules of organisation of the judicial police, Journal of Laws No 155, item 1093). Its tasks do not, unlike those of the police *judiciaire* in the French legal system, include conducting preparatory proceedings and taking evidence. See eg J. Hodgson, *French Criminal Justice. A Comparative Account of the Investigation and Prosecution of Crime in France* (Oxford, Hart Publishing, 2005) 93 and n; Grzegorczyk and Tylman (n 3) 252.

[146] Police operational and exploratory activities are covert actions undertaken for exploratory, preventive, detection and evidential purposes. This category includes both simple forms of operational work, eg operational intelligence, and complex forms of these activities, eg operational control (Art 19 APS), controlled purchase (Art 19a APS) or secretly supervised dispatch (Art 19b APS).

[147] These actions are taken for the following reasons:

1. identification, preventioning, and detection of crimes, and fiscal offences;
2. identification, prevention and detection of crimes, fiscal offences and misdemeanours;
3. search for persons who, due to the occurrence of an event that makes it impossible to determine their whereabouts, need to be found in order to ensure the protection of their life, health or freedom (Art 14 para 1 AP).

[148] J Zagrodnik, *Model interakcji postępowania przygotowawczego oraz postępowania głównego w procesie karnym* (Warsaw, Wolters Kluwer, 2013) 219 et seq.

be surprising if we take into account the ever-growing scale of crime, assisted by rapid scientific and technological developments that open the door to new forms and ways of committing crimes and evading justice, as well as human mobility and anonymity guaranteed by prevailing social relations. In such realities, the staffing and technical resources of prosecutors in each country are clearly insufficient to enable prosecutors alone to meet the challenges of modern criminal prosecution and to take on the full range of pre-trial investigations, especially since, as already established above, they are also tasked with supporting the prosecution in court proceedings. In the context of the broadly defined, real role of the police in the sphere of criminal prosecution at the first procedural stage, the appropriate system of educating the corps of police officers authorised to conduct preparatory proceedings should be of significant importance. The current system of educating police officers or qualifying them to carry out investigative activities in Poland does not provide sufficient guarantees of maintaining appropriate standards in this area, taking into account not only the interests of criminal prosecution, but also the rights and freedoms of accused and injured persons. Therefore, it is difficult to accept the current possibility in the Polish criminal procedure of an essentially unlimited flow of protocols of evidentiary activities carried out in the first stage of the trial by police officers to the main hearing and, consequently, their inclusion in the evidentiary basis of the court's judgment.[149] The detailed powers of the police related to conducting pre-trial proceedings or performing therein the investigative activities entrusted by the prosecutor will be presented as part of the discussion of the course of pre-trial proceedings.

The powers of the police with respect to conducting pre-trial investigations outlined above are also vested in the following bodies:

1. the Border Guard, the Internal Security Agency, the National Treasury Administration, the Central Anti-Corruption Bureau and the Military Police, within their respective fields of competence;
2. other bodies set forth in special regulations, eg the Trade Inspectorate and the State Sanitary Inspectorate (see Regulation of the Minister of Justice of 22 September 2015 on the bodies authorised, in addition to the police, to conduct simplified investigations, and the bodies authorised to file and support charges before first-instance court in cases in which simplified investigation has been conducted, as well as the scope of cases entrusted to these bodies, having regard to the statutory scope of their competences, Dz U of 2018, item 522), or forest guards, who have the right to conduct investigations and to bring and support indictments if the object of the offence is a tree or timber from forests owned by the State Treasury (Article 47.2.7 of the Act of 28.09.1991 on forests, ie Dz U of 2020, item 1463).

Some of the bodies mentioned above, such as the Border Guard, the State Sanitary Inspectorate or forest guards, also have the right, to the extent that they are authorised to investigate, to bring an accusation and act as a public prosecutor before a court. They act in this role instead of the prosecutor, which means that the prosecutor's takeover of the accusation excludes these bodies from further acting as an accusing party in court proceedings.[150]

[149] ibid; Zagrodnik (n 60) 133.
[150] Marszał (n 9) 229; Grzegorczyk and Tylman (n 3) 281.

Defence

Concept of Suspect and Accused

Suspect and accused are terms for the person against whom criminal proceedings have been formally initiated. They are defined in the CPC. Their distinction is linked to the division of the criminal process into stages. The term 'suspect' refers to pre-trial proceedings. According to Article 71 § 2 CPC a person shall be considered a suspect if an order has been made about charging them or if they have been charged without such an order in relation to questioning them as a suspect. The term 'accused', in the strict sense, refers to the judicial stage of a criminal trial. Such status is held by a person against whom an accusation has been brought before a court, as well as by a person with respect to whom the prosecutor has filed a motion indicated in Article 335 § 1 CPC or a motion for conditional discontinuance of proceedings (Article 71 § 2 CPC). In a broad sense, the term 'accused' also encompasses a suspect (Article 71 § 3 CPC). The term is used in this sense (accused *sensu largo*) in the present study.

In addition to the accused and the suspect, the CPC refers to a suspected person. This is a person in respect of whom there is a good reason to suppose that he or she has committed a criminal offence, but no formal criminal prosecution has been directed against him or her.[151]

The accused (*sensu largo*) is the central figure of the criminal trial as a person threatened with criminal punishment in connection with the crime formally charged. By virtue of this he/she is entitled to the status of a litigant. In pre-trial proceedings he/she acts in this role as a suspect (Article 299 § 1 CPC).

The provisions of the CPC link the right to defence, including the right to the assistance of a defence counsel, with the status of an accused *sensu largo* (Article 6 CPC). This right is not granted to a suspected person. This person has narrowly defined rights connected with procedural actions taken against him, eg a search (Article 236 § 1 in conjunction with Articles 219 et seq CPC) or detention (Article 244 § 1 CPC). Leaving a suspected person outside the subjective scope of the right to defence raises significant reservations, not only from the point of view of constitutional standards, but also from the point of view of the compatibility of the provisions of the CPC with Article 6(3) ECHR and the provisions of Directive 2013/48/EU of the European Parliament and of the Council of 22 October 2013 on the right of access to a lawyer in criminal proceedings and European Arrest Warrant proceedings and on the right to communicate with third parties and consular authorities during the deprivation of liberty.[152] On the basis of these legal acts, Polish and European jurisprudence uniformly accepts that the right to defence does not depend on the formal bringing of charges against a specific person, but is vested from the moment of the actual criminal prosecution against a specific person. In other words, the very first action of the procedural authorities aimed at

[151] Grzegorczyk and Tylman (n 3) 319–20; E Kowalewska-Borys, in C Kulesza (ed), *System Prawa Karnego Procesowego* (Warsaw, Wolters Kluwer, 2016) vol 6, 711–22; Zagrodnik (n 1) 261.

[152] Zagrodnik (n 60) 124–25; J Zagrodnik, 'The Right to the Assistance of the Defense Counsel in the Light of the European Court of Human Rights Case Law' (2022) *Radca Prawny* no 2.

prosecuting a specific person, which has a serious impact on his or her procedural situation as a potential suspect, makes that person a beneficiary of the right of defence.[153] Perhaps the clearest manifestation of such a concept of defence rights is the right, provided for in Articles 3(2)(a) and 3(3) of Directive 2013/48/EU, to have contact with a defence counsel even before the first interrogation as a suspect by the police or other law-enforcement authority or a judicial authority. Although Polish legislation implements the provisions of Directive 2013/48/EU in the CPC, it is not fully reflected in detailed solutions of the Criminal Procedure Act.[154] In order for the realisation of the right of defence in the case of a suspected person not to remain only in the declarative sphere, changes in the existing legal order are necessary, although it is highly doubtful whether they can be expected in the current political reality, in which the rights and freedoms of citizens lose out to penal populism.

The right of defence of the accused consists of many partial rights, which may serve either to repel the accusation or to mitigate the responsibility of the accused accordingly. In this chapter, we must limit ourselves to presenting the most important of them. Thus, in addition to the aforementioned right to the assistance of a defence counsel, we may distinguish between rights that the accused has by virtue of his/her status as a litigant and such rights that are strictly connected with acting as an accused person and result from the fact that a criminal trial is directed against him/her.[155] The first group includes, for example:

- the right to participate in procedural activities – the accused has the right to participate in the court session if the law so provides or requires (Article 96 § 1, first sentence CPC); he/she also has the right to participate in the main trial (Article 374 § 1 CPC); his/her participation in the trial is mandatory if the presiding judge or the court deems his/her presence mandatory (Article 374 § 1, second sentence CPC), as well as in the initial phase of the trial in cases related to felonies (Article 374 § 1a CPC);
- the right to be informed of his or her procedural rights – the scope of this information is specified in detail in the provisions with respect to the individual stages of the criminal trial (Articles 300 § 1, 338 § 1a, 353 § 4, 386 § 1 CPC);
- the right to file motions for evidence (Article 168 CPC);
- the right to use appeal measures against a ruling rendered in the first instance (Article 425 § 1 CPC).

Among the rights vested exclusively in the accused due to the criminal prosecution against him/her is the submition of explanations. The explanations of the accused, in

[153] On the ground of European jurisprudence, see judgment of 10 December 1982 in *Corigliano v Italy*, A 57; judgment of 10 December 1982 in *Foti and others v Italy*, A 56; judgment of 21 February 1984 in *Öztürk v Germany*, A 73. On the ground of Polish jurisprudence analogously: Judgment of the Constitutional Tribunal of 3 June 2008, ref K 42/07, OTK-A 2008, no 5; Judgment of the Constitutional Tribunal of 11 December 2012, K 37/11, OTK-A 2012, no 1; Judgment of the Supreme Court of 9 February 2004, V CC 194/03, OSNKW 2004, no 4, item 42. See also Zagrodnik, 'The Right to the Assistance of the Defense Counsel' (n 152).

[154] J Zagrodnik (ed), *Kodeks postępowania karnego. Komentarz praktyczny do nowelizacji 2019* (Warsaw, 2020) 21–25.

[155] Marszał (n 9) 138.

addition to being his/her tool of defence, also constitute evidence on which the factual findings of the judgment may be based. Unlike witnesses who testify, the accused is not obliged to tell the truth in his/her explanations, ie he or she is not criminally liable for telling an untruth or concealing the truth in them (*argumentum ex* Article 233 CC).[156] The right to provide explanations is accompanied by the right to refuse to provide them, as well as to refuse to answer questions without having to justify one's position (Article 175 § 1 CPC). Thus, it can be said that he/she has the right to remain silent.[157] Closely related to the right to remain silent and the presumption of innocence of the accused is the lack of obligation to provide evidence against him/her, which is an expression of the principle *nemo se ipsum accusare tenetur*.[158] The absence of such a duty should be referred to the sphere of activity of the accused. It does not imply the absence of an obligation on the part of the accused to put up with certain actions taken against him/her and providing evidence against him/her, if they are within the limits of interference with his/her rights and freedoms provided for by law.[159] Such acts to which the accused is required to submit include:

1. an external examination of their body and other examinations not involving any infringement of bodily integrity[160] – in particular, the fingerprints of the accused may be taken; they may be photographed and presented to other persons in order to establish the identity of the accused;
2. psychological and psychiatric examinations and examinations involving certain tests conducted upon their body, except surgical procedures, provided that the examinations are carried out by an authorised healthcare specialist according to the principles of medical knowledge and do not constitute any threat to the health of the accused – provided that such examinations are indispensable; in particular, the accused shall be obliged, in conformity with the aforementioned conditions, to submit to blood,[161] hair and excretory sampling, subject to the provisions of subparagraph (3);
3. a buccal swab test carried out by a police official, provided that this is indispensable and if there is no fear that it could threaten the health of the accused or of other persons (Article 74 § 1 CPC).

[156] KT Boratyńska, in C Kulesza (ed), *System Prawa Karnego Procesowego* (Warsaw, Wolters Kluwer, 2016) vol 6, 734–36;Zagrodnik (n 1) 266.

[157] Boratyńska (n 156) vol 6, 732–34; Zagrodnik (n 1) 266; see further A Sakowicz, *Prawo do milczenia w polskim procesie karnym* (Białystok, Wydawnictwo Temida 2020) 2.

[158] See eg Supreme Court Decision, 4 February 2008, III KK 363/07, Lex no 357459; Supreme Court Judgment, 15 October 2015, III KK 206/15, Lex no 1948886; Decision of the Appelate Court in Cracow, 25 April 2001, II AKa 674/01, Lex no 49587. See further Z Sobolewski, *Samooskarżenie w świetle prawa karnego (zasada nemo se ipsum accusare tenetur)* (Warsaw, Wydawnictwo Prawnicze, 1982) Cz Kłak, '"Osoba podejrzana" oraz "potencjalnie podejrzana" w polskim procesie karnym a zasada nemoseipsumaccusareten-etur' (2012) *Ius Novum* no 4.

[159] See eg Supreme Court Judgment, 12 January 2000, IV KKN 269/99, Lex no 51139; Supreme Court Judgment, 21 July 2000, II KKN 108/00, Lex no 50904; Decision of the Appelate Court in Katowice, 29 November 2018, II Aka 171/18, Lex no 2690783.

[160] See Supreme Court Judgment, 12 January 2000, IV KKN 269/99, Lex no 51139.

[161] See Supreme Court Decision, 17 March 2008, V KK 73/08, Lex no 549321.

Defence Counsel

A defence counsel is a professional who provides legal assistance to an accused in a criminal trial. His or her basic duty is to undertake all legally permissible (legal) actions aimed at ensuring that an innocent person does not bear criminal liability, and that a guilty person does not bear liability greater than that deserved by the specific factual and legal situation.[162] The activity of a defence counsel, which constitutes a sui generis correction of criminal prosecution, contributes significantly to preventing miscarriages of justice.[163]

The Polish legal system does not provide for a system of non-means-tested legal assistance by a public defender, which could be used by any accused if he/she so requested. The exercise of the right to legal assistance by an accused person is in principle carried out privately, through his/her own choice,[164] and only in the cases strictly specified by the law, can he/she demand the appointment of a public defender. It may therefore be said that the form of exercise of this right is defence by choice or defence ex officio. In addition to this division, a distinction may be made between mandatory and optional defence, depending on whether or not the provisions stipulate that the accused must have a defence counsel regardless of whether he or she wants one.[165] These two divisions are cross-referenced, as will be discussed later.

It is a specific feature of the Polish legal system that the competence to act as defence counsel is vested in professional lawyers belonging to two separate professional corporations, namely solicitors and legal advisers (Article 82 CPC in conjunction with Articles 1(1) and 4(1) of the pr. adw, Article 6 ust. 1 of the u.r.p.).[166] Both solicitors and legal advisers must have similar legal qualifications as judges or prosecutors, so in addition to completing higher law studies and obtaining a master's degree, they must complete a corresponding professional traineeship and pass the relevant examination. Among others, professors and persons with a postdoctoral degree in legal sciences are exempted from the latter requirements.[167] It is sometimes stereotypically assumed that judicial training provides better preparation for the profession than attorney-at-law adviser training, mainly due to a more rigorous selection process for candidates for judges and a smaller number of places on judicial training. This is a rather one-sided view, disregarding the fact that a trainee attorney-at-law can perform the activities of a solicitor or legal adviser after six months of training, while whereas judicial training is only considered as preparation for the profession of judge for its entire duration.

[162] See further Zagrodnik, 'The Right to the Assistance of the Defense Counsel' (n 152).

[163] See M Cieślak, 'Sytuacja prawna obrońcy w świetle nowego ustawodawstwa polskiego' (1969) *Palestra* no 8, 39; Grzegorczyk and Tylman (n 3) 353.

[164] Grzegorczyk and Tylman (n 3) 360.

[165] Z Kulesza, in C Kulesza (ed), *System Prawa Karnego Procesowego* (Warsaw, Wolters Kluwer, 2016) vol 6, 902.

[166] The only difference between the rights of solicitors and legal advisors to provide legal assistance as defence counsel stems from a wider range of forms of professional activity of legal advisors. Apart from, for example, acting within their own law firm, they may also work within an employment relationship, in which case acting as defence counsel is excluded.

[167] However, in order for them to act as defence counsel, they must be entered on the list of active solicitors or legal advisers. See more Zagrodnik (n 53) 24–30.

A defence counsel is a procedural representative of the accused.[168] This stems from the fact that the defence counsel is entitled to perform actions in the name and on behalf of the accused and to represent their interests in the criminal trial. It logically follows from the representative nature of the defensive relationship that the scope of the defender's authority is essentially determined by the scope of the authority vested in the accused as a litigant. Two features distinguish the representative nature of the defence case.[169] First, the independence of the defence counsel vis-à-vis the accused. It means that the defence counsel is not bound by the instruction of the accused and has the ability to act even against his/her will in the scope of his powers. It can be said that the defence counsel and the accused, acting side by side, maintain autonomy within the framework of their trial activity. Second, the duty of the defence counsel to act exclusively for the benefit of the accused (Article 86 § 1 CPC).[170] From this obligation may be derived a prohibition on the defence counsel undertaking actions that are unfavourable to the accused. Actions taken in breach of this prohibition should be deemed ineffective. The accused may not be burdened with negative legal consequences of negligence or improper performance of duties by the defence counsel.[171] Strictly connected with the prohibition of the defence counsel acting to the detriment of the accused is the prohibition of the defence of several accuseds if their interests conflict (Article 85 § 1 CPC). Such a contradiction occurs, for example, when the accuseds accuse each other.[172] It is for the court to determine whether there is a conflict of interests between the accuseds and to issue a decision to that effect.[173] This decision may be challenged by both the accused and the defence counsel (Article 85 § 2 CPC).

As mentioned above, in the Polish legal order, a distinction can be made between discretionary and mandatory defence by counsel. As a rule, the accused decides on his/her own whether he/she wishes to have the assistance of a defence counsel. However, in certain cases, the law provides for an obligation on the part of the accused to have a defence counsel, regardless of whether they themselves wish to do so. This obligation may relate to the entire criminal proceedings or to a specific stage thereof.[174]

The obligation extends to the entire proceedings in the situations specified in Article 79 § 1 and § 2 CPC. According to these provisions the accused must have a defence counsel if:

1. they are below the age of eighteen;[175]

[168] W Daszkiewicz, *Prawo karne procesowe. Zagadnienia ogólne* (Bydgoszcz, 1999) vol 1, 276; Cieślak (n 1) 44; T Grzegorczyk, *Obrońca w postępowaniu przygotowawczym* (Łódź, 1988); Zagrodnik (n 53) 29–31. Different view: S. Śliwiński, *Proces karny. Zasady ogólne* (Warsaw, 1948) 395 et seq; C Kulesza, in C Kulesza (ed), *System Prawa Karnego Procesowego*, vol VI: *Strony i inni uczestnicy postępowania karnego* (Warsaw, 2016) 920.

[169] Grzegorczyk and Tylman (n 3) 354–55; Zagrodnik (n 53) 33–43.

[170] See further P Kruszyński, *Obrońca w postępowaniu sądowym* (Warsaw, 1994) 5.

[171] For example, violation of the time limit for filing a complaint due to the fault of the defence counsel constitutes grounds for restoring the time limit for filing such a complaint pursuant to Art 126 CPC.

[172] See eg Supreme Court Decision, 13 October 2011, III KK 98/11, Lex no 1144036; Supreme Court Judgment, 26 October 1971, V KRN 375/71, OSNKW 1972, no 2, pos 36; Supreme Court Decision, 28 January 2015; V KO 50/14, Lex no 1628968.

[173] See Decision of the Appellate Court in Katowice, 19 April 2005, II Akz 215/05, Lex no 1642059.

[174] Grzegorczyk and Tylman (n 3) 365–66; Zagrodnik (n 53) 33–43.

[175] Supreme Court Decision, 2 February 2016 r, IV KK 337/15, OSNKW 2016, no 3, pos 21.

2. they are deaf, mute or blind;[176]
3. there is a justified doubt whether their ability to recognise the meaning of a given act or direct their behaviour was not excluded or significantly limited when committing the act;[177]
4. there is a justified doubt whether their mental health allows for their participation in proceedings or for running a defence in an independent and reasonable manner;[178]
5. when the court deems that necessary because of other circumstances impeding the defence.[179]

If one of the circumstances listed in subparagraphs 1–4 occurs or the court takes the decision indicated in subparagraph 5, the participation of the defence counsel is mandatory in the main hearing (Article 79 § 3 CPC), the appeal hearing (Article 450 § 1 in conjunction with Article 79 CPC), the cassation hearing (Article 450 § 1 in conjunction with Articles 79 and 518 CPC), as well as in those court sessions in which the participation of the accused is mandatory (Article 79 § 3 in fine CPC).[180] Mandatory defence related to the presented cases ceases when the circumstances that determine it become obsolete, eg the accused turns eighteen years old. In the cases set forth in points 3 and 4 above, in order for the obligatory defence to cease, it is necessary for the court to issue a decision stating that the participation of the defence counsel in the trial is not mandatory. The basis for such a decision is that the court valid as reasonable the opinion of experts in which they expressed the opinion that the act of the accused was not committed under conditions of exclusion or significant limitation of the ability to recognise the meaning of the act or to direct the accused person's behaviour and that the state of mental health of the accused allows for participation in the proceedings and for running a defence in an independent and reasonable manner (Article 79 § 4, first sentence CPC). This decision only means the transformation of compulsory defence into optional defence. If the accused was assisted by a defence counsel ex officio, a separate decision of the court or the president of the court is necessary to release him/her from his/her defence obligations (Article 79 § 4, second sentence CPC).[181]

A basic example of mandatory defence relating to a specific stage of the proceedings is the obligation, regulated in Article 80 CPC, for the accused to have a defence counsel in proceedings before a regional court if he/she has been charged with a felony. In such a case, the defence counsel must take part in the main hearing, and pursuant to Article 450 § 1 in conjunction with Article 80 CPC, his/her participation is also

[176] Supreme Court Decision, 27 January 2010 r, II KK 299/09, Lex no 1746671; Supreme Court Decision, 9 January 2013, III KK 330/12, Lex no 1277747; Supreme Court Decision, 29 June 2017, III KK 225/17, Lex no 2342144.

[177] Supreme Court Resolution, 21 January 1970, VI KZP 23/69, OSNKW 1970, nos 2–3, pos 15; Supreme Court Decision, 24 January 2007, II KK 251/06, OSNwSK 2007, no 1, pos 267; Supreme Court Judgment, 26 May 2015, SNO 29/15, Lex no 1711701.

[178] RA Stefański, 'Obrona obligatoryjna po 1 lipca 2015 r', in P Wiliński (ed), *Obrońca i pełnomocnik w procesie karnym po 1 lipca 2015 r. Przewodnik po zmianach* (Warsaw, 2015) 38.

[179] Supreme Court Decision, 17 February 2004, II KK 277/02, OSNKW 2004, no 4, pos 43; Decision of the Appellate Court in Cracow, 28 October 2002, II AKz 456/02, KZS 2002, no 10, pos 59.

[180] See Grzegorczyk and Tylman (n 3) 364; Zagrodnik (n 53) 33–43.

[181] Supreme Court Decision, 27 October 2005, I KZP 30/05, OSNKW 2005, no 11, pos 107.

mandatory at the appeal hearing and also, in conjunction with Article 518 CPC, at the cassation hearing.[182]

Violation of provisions on mandatory defence in the course of court proceedings is an absolute reason for repealing a ruling (Article 439 § 1, point 10 CPC).[183]

Mandatory defence is closely related to one of the two groups of cases in which a public defender is appointed for the accused. If the defence is mandatory and the accused does not have a defence counsel of his/her own choice, the competent court authority (the court president or a clerk of the court) or the court is obliged to appoint a defence counsel ex officio (Articles 81 and 81a § 2 CPC). The second group of cases includes, first of all, the appointment of a public defender at the request of the accused if he/she can duly prove that they are unable to bear the costs of defence without it affecting their ability to support themselves and their family (Article 78 § 1 CPC).[184] Such proof must be supported by relevant documents, eg income certificates, medical bills or bills of payments for accommodation.[185] This group also includes, among other things, the appointment of a public defender to participate in a court session on the extension of temporary custody and the examination of a complaint against the use or extension of this preventive measure, if the accused who does not have a defence counsel of his/her choice so requests (Article 249 § 5 CPC).

The order of a court authority or decision of the court to appoint a public defender should indicate a particular solicitor or legal adviser who is to act in that procedural role. The appointment is made from the list of defence counsel (Article 81a § 1 in connection with Article 88 CPC), and thus from among the attorneys-at-law who have expressed their readiness to provide legal assistance ex officio. The refusal to appoint a public defender may be contested. The complaint against the order of the court president or court clerk is examined by the court having jurisdiction to hear the case, and against the court's decision by another equivalent composition of that court (Article 81 § 1a CPC). In the event of a repeated motion for the appointment of a public defender based on the same grounds, it is not subjected to a substantive assessment, but is left without examination (Article 81 § 1b CPC).

[182] Grzegorczyk and Tylman (n 3) 364; Zagrodnik (n 53) 116; differently D Świecki, in D Świecki (ed), *Kodeks postępowania karnego. Komentarz* (Warsaw, Wolters Kluwer, 2018) vol II, 587.

[183] See eg Supreme Court Judgment, 10 October 2001, II KKN 581/98, OSNKW 2002, no 3–4, pos 22; Grzegorczyk and Tylman (n 3) 366.

[184] Making such a demand in court proceedings has been subjected to temporal rigours by the amendment of the CPC of 19 July 2019. As a consequence of this change, it should be made in full effect within seven days from the date of service of the copy of the indictment. This guarantees its recognition before the date of any trial or session; it's about a session, where motions aimed at the substantive resolution of the case are considered without the need to refer it to the main trial. In other cases, if the consideration of the motion required a change of the date of the trial or the indicated session, also due to, for example, the need to supplement the motion, it would be subject to postponement until the end of a given trial or session (Art 338b § 2 CPC). A similar solution is envisaged with respect to filing a request for the appointment of a defence counsel after the first trial or session date (Art 338b § 3 CPC). The outlined norms raise reservations from the standpoint of guaranteeing the right to the assistance of counsel, particularly with respect to the main trials described above, as the appointment of counsel after they have already been conducted and a judgment has already been passed in the court of first instance means depriving the accused of the right to counsel in those main trials – see for more detail J Zagrodnik, *Obrońca i pełnomocnik w procesie karnym i karnym skarbowym* (Warsaw, Wolters Kluwer, 2020) 135–36.

[185] See Supreme Court Judgment, 1 July 2009, III KK 3/09, OSNwSK 2009, no 1, pos 1447; Supreme Court Decision, 17 July 2014, V KZ 26/14, KZS 2014, no 12, pos 21.

In justified cases, appointment of another public defender may take place. The justification of the motion in this regard must indicate specific, important circumstances, which prove that in order to ensure the right of defence it is necessary to entrust the role of defence to another solicitor or legal adviser.[186] A groundless statement of lack of confidence in the assigned public defender is not sufficient in this respect. This fact must be supported by factual argumentation, which of course does not mean that the accused is to betray the defence strategy adopted in the case.[187] The solicitor or legal adviser may themselves request to be released from their duties as defence counsel only for important reasons (Article 28 paragraph 1 of the pr.adw, and Article 22 paragraph 1 of the u.r.p.), eg due to illness or retirement.[188]

Against the background of the above findings in the matter of appointing a public defender, it should be stressed that this form of exercising the right to exercise the assistance of a defence counsel is of an accessory nature, which means that it may take place only when the accused does not have a defence counsel of choice. It follows from the accessory nature of ex officio defence that it persists as long as the accused fails to appoint a defence counsel of choice.[189]

Designation of a defence counsel, as already stated above, is an essential manifestation of the right to the assistance of a defence counsel (establishment of the defence relationship).[190] Such designation may either fulfil the obligation of the accused to have a defence counsel, or it may be a manifestation of discretionary representation. Empowerment of the defence counsel is in such a case based on a unilateral declaration of will of the entity that is to be represented.[191] It may be made in writing or orally into the record (Article 83 § 2 CPC). If the accused is deprived of liberty, eg due to pre-trial provisional detention in another case, a so-called temporary authorisation to represent him may be granted by another person (Article 83 § 1 CPC).[192] If the accused accepts the temporary counsel, the defence relationship is transformed into its ordinary form; otherwise the temporary authorisation expires (*argumentum ex* Article 83 § 1 PCC).[193]

The accused may use a maximum of three counsels of choice (Article 77 CPC). This limitation prevents the demonstration of defenders in the criminal trial, which could impede its smooth course.[194] If the accused is assisted by more than one defence counsel, the appearance of one of them is sufficient for the activity to take place (Article 117a § 1 in principio CPC). With the consent of the accused, if the defence is not compulsory, it is also possible to carry out the activity despite the non-appearance of all the defence counsels whom the accused has appointed (Article 117a § 1 in fine CPC).

[186] Supreme Court Decision, 27 November 2014, IV KK 351/14, Lex no 1545168; Zagrodnik (n 53) 139.

[187] Supreme Court Judgment, 12 October 2006, IV CC 199/06, OSNKW 2007, pos 34; Supreme Court Judgment, 18 July 2013, III CC 51/13, Lex no 1353227.

[188] See Zagrodnik (n 53) 139.

[189] Marszał (n 9). See also C Kulesza, in C Kulesza (ed), *System Prawa Karnego Procesowego* (Warsaw, Wolters Kluwer, 2016) vol 6, 909–17.

[190] Grzegorczyk and Tylman (n 3) 361.

[191] If the accused is either totally or partially incapacitated, then the defence counsel shall be appointed by his/her legal representative or a person under whose custody the accused remains (Art 76 CPC).

[192] Supreme Court Decision, 11 May 2017, WZ 6/17, Lex no 2309633.

[193] Grzegorczyk and Tylman (n 3) 360.

[194] Marszał (n 9) 254.

Due to the contractual nature of the defence relationship by choice, both the accused and the defence counsel may terminate it. This termination is binding on the trial authorities. The law shall only regulate the consequences of termination of the defence relationship in cases of mandatory defence.[195] In these cases, depending on the stage of the proceedings, the president of the court or a court clerk (outside the trial) or the court (during the trial) shall appoint a defence counsel for the accused ex officio if he/she has not appointed another defence counsel of his/her own choice (Article 81 § 1 and Article 378 § 1, first sentence CPC). When this occurs during the trial, the court may decide to interrupt or adjourn the trial (Article 378 § 1, second sentence CPC). In addition, it shall concurrently decide whether the existing defence counsel may, without detriment to the accused person's right of defence, carry out their duties until the defence is taken up by a new defence counsel (Article 378 § 3 CPC). This solution serves to provide the new defence counsel with time for a thorough familiarisation with the case.[196]

Designation of a defence counsel or appointment of an ex officio defence counsel shall apply to the entire course of proceedings, including all actions taken after the ruling has become final, unless such a designation or appointment is restricted (Article 84 § 1 CPC).[197] The duty of a defence counsel to act ex officio is delimited somewhat more narrowly, as it extends to actions preceding the final conclusion of the proceedings (Article 84 § 2, first sentence CPC),[198] which does not exclude the possibility of the defence counsel undertaking actions after that time, on his or her own initiative. The defence counsel has the right of substitution, ie transferring his/her right to represent the accused to another solicitor or legal adviser.[199] If an accused has chosen his/her defence counsel based on trust in a particular solicitor or legal adviser, the right to substitution may be subject to exclusion or limitation in the act of appointing the defence counsel (power of attorney).[200]

An important guarantee of proper exercise of the function of a defenders is the duty of professional discretion imposed on solicitors and legal advisers. It is the foundation of the accused's trust in his/her defence counsel, which is the condition for free and open sharing of defence-relevant information with him/her.[201] In the case of relations between the accused and the defence counsel, the obligation to maintain professional discretion is the content of defence secrecy, which under Article 178 (1) CPC remains protected in the form of a prohibition to question the defence counsel as a witness about facts of which he/she became aware of while providing legal assistance or conducting the case as the defender. This absolute prohibition of questioning by means of specific evidence also extends to information that a solicitor or legal adviser obtains when contacting a detainee and providing him/her with legal advice when he/she does not yet have the formal status of a defence counsel in a criminal trial.[202]

[195] Zagrodnik (n 53) 125–27.
[196] See Supreme Court Decision, 26 August 2010, V KK 335/09, Lex no 612952.
[197] Supreme Court Decision, 25 September 2014, III KZ 50/14, Lex no 1551522.
[198] Supreme Court Decision, 26 June 2007, II KZ 14/07, Lex no 460037.
[199] Grzegorczyk and Tylman (n 3) 363; Zagrodnik (n 53) 144–48.
[200] See Grzegorczyk and Tylman (n 3) 363; A Bojańczyk, 'Jakie konsekwencje procesowe wywołuje niezaakceptowanie przez mandanta osoby obrońcy substytucyjnego' (2013) *Palestra* nos 3–4, 228.
[201] F Payen, *O powołaniu adwokatury i sztuce obrończej* (Sopot, 2007) 128.
[202] See further eg Z. Krzemiński, 'Problem tajemnicy zawodowej adwokata w świetle przepisów prawnych' (1959) *Palestra* no 10; Z Kwiatkowski, *Zakazy dowodowe w procesie karnym* (Warsaw, Wolters Kluwer, 2005)

Victim, Injured Person

The CPC does not use the concept of a victim. It uses a related but at the same time slightly narrower term 'injured person'. This is defined in Article 49 §§ 1 and 2 CPC.

> Article 49
>
> §1. The injured person is a natural or legal person whose legal interest has been directly violated or threatened by a criminal offence.
>
> § 2. The injured may also be a following person without legal personality:
>
> 1) state or local government institution;
> 2) other organisational unit having legal capacity based on separate regulations.

The connection of harm on the grounds of the above definition with the state of direct violation or threat to a legal good caused by a criminal offence clearly proves its material and legal character. This should not be surprising in fact, because harm is a passive correlative of perpetration – an objective state remaining in an inseparable relationship with human conduct, which under the binding provisions of substantive criminal law constitutes a prohibited act that exhausts the elements of a given type of crime.[203] It follows from the material-legal anchoring of harm, that in order to determine whose legal good could have been directly violated or threatened by a crime *in concreto*, it is necessary to refer to the provisions of substantive criminal law.[204] In the provisions of substantive criminal law, the injured party may be defined in a certain way, eg a minor (Article 208 CC), a person under fifteen years of age (Articles 200, 200a, 210 CC) or a public official (Articles 222–23, 226 CC). Most often, however, the criminal law does not provide for such a tightening of the circle of injured parties, which means that it can be any person.[205] At the same time, it follows from the substantive law that harm within the meaning of Article 49 § 1 CPC can be said only when the (individual) legal good directly violated or threatened by a crime is also a direct object of criminal law protection.[206] The requirement of directness of violation or threat of a legal good by means of a crime means that there must be no intermediate links between the act, which exhausts the attributes of a crime, and violation or threat of a legal good

78–79; P Kardas, 'Konstytucyjne i ustawowe aspekty ochrony tajemnicy zawodowej powierzanej przedstawicielom zawodów zaufania publicznego' (2014) *CPKiNP* no 4; J Warylewski, 'Tajemnica adwokacka i odpowiedzialność karna za jej naruszenie (ujawnienie)' (2015) *Palestra* nos 5–6; J Giezek, 'O granicach tajemnicy adwokackiej oraz zgodzie "dysponenta" na jej ujawnienie' (2014) *Palestra* no 9; M Rusinek, *Tajemnica zawodowa i jej ochrona w polskim procesie karnym* (Warsaw, 2007); J Zagrodnik, 'Aspekty karnoprocesowe tajemnicy zawodowej radcy prawnego', in R Stankiewicz (ed), *Tajemnica zawodowa radcy prawnego* (Warsaw, Wydawnictwo OBSIL KRRP, 2018).

[203] R Kmiecik, 'Ustawowa definicja pokrzywdzonego (uwagi na tle Article 40 CPC)' (1977) 24 *AUMCS* 164–65.

[204] Daszkiewicz (n 168) 212–13; Zagrodnik (n 1) 243.

[205] Marszał (n 9) 235.

[206] In order to properly determine what good constitutes, in the case of a specific type of a prohibited act, the object of direct criminal law protection, it is necessary to carefully examine the circumstances of the specific conduct in connection with which the criminal trial is conducted, and to determine the scope of protection and whether there is a connection between the statutory elements of the offence and the individual interest of the specific subject. See: Resolution of the Supreme Court of 25 March 2003, I KZP 50/02, OSNKW 2003/3–4, item 28.

of a specific subject.[207] In other words, directness occurs (exists) if a criminal act or omission directly strikes a legal good subject to criminal law protection.[208]

For the injured person to have standing to be a party, it is not necessary to firmly establish that the crime directly threatens or violates his or her legal good. It is sufficient that the violation or threat is hypothetical, in the sense that it is plausible in the light of the evidence.[209] What should be decisive in this respect is the legal classification adopted by the trial authorities at the individual stages of the proceedings (in the decision to initiate the investigation, the decision to present charges, the indictment). Verification of the aggrieved party hypothesis usually takes place only in the form of a final ruling on the subject of the trial.[210] Only exceptionally does it occur earlier, when the procedural body can establish with certainty with respect to a specific entity the lack of the right to act as a injured. This may be expressed by refusal to accept an appeal measure from such a subject (Article 429 § 1 CPC).[211]

It follows from the definition contained in Article 49 § 1 CPC that the injured parties are not entities that have repaired the damage caused by a crime and on this account have a recourse claim against the perpetrator of the crime. This is specifically confirmed in Article 49 § 3 CPC, from which it follows that an insurance company is not an injured party, but should be considered an injured party to the extent that it has covered the damage caused to the injured party by the crime or is obliged to cover it.

The procedural status of the injured person in a certain sense depends on the procedural stage in which the injured person appears.[212] In the pre-trial stage the injured person is a party to the trial by virtue of the very fact of a direct threat or infringement of his/her legal interests by a crime (Article 299 § 1 CPC). In court proceedings he/she is a party to the proceedings if he/she acts as a private prosecutor or an auxiliary prosecutor, which will be discussed later. If injured does not make use of such a possibility, he/she does not have the status of a party and enjoys only such rights as are granted to him/her by the provisions of the Criminal Procedure Act due to the fact that he/she has been injured by a crime, eg the right to participate in a trial (Article 384 § 2 CPC), to file a motion for a justification of a verdict conditionally discontinuing proceedings issued during a sentencing session (Article 422 § 1 CPC) and to appeal against such a verdict (Article 444 CPC). As a rule, the injured person is also a personal source of information about the crime. On this account he/she gives testimony in a criminal trial as a witness.

A private prosecutor is an injured person who has filed and supports the accusation of an offence prosecuted by private indictment.[213] Offences prosecuted by private indictment are those for which such a mode of prosecution is provided in the provisions of the Criminal Code or in special laws, eg the offence of defamation (Article 212 §§ 1 and 2 CC) or violation of physical integrity (Article 217 § 1 CC). The prosecution

[207] See eg Supreme Court Resolution, 12 May 1993, I KZP 6/93, OSNKW 1993, nos 5–6, pos 28; Supreme Court Resolution, 28 April 1980, VI KZP 1/80, OSNKW 1980, nos 5–6, pos 42.

[208] Daszkiewicz (n 168) 212.

[209] Supreme Court Resolution, 14 February 1931, II Pr. 28/31, OSP 1931, no 6, pos 294.

[210] Daszkiewicz (n 168) 214.

[211] ibid 214. See also Zagrodnik (n 1) 245.

[212] Daszkiewicz (n 168) 216–20; Zagrodnik (n 1) 245–46.

[213] See further Daszkiewicz (n 168) 231; Marszał (n 9) 245.

of these offences is, as a rule, subject to the demand of the injured party because this strikes directly at the private interest of a designated person or persons, and only indirectly at the public interest.[214]

An auxiliary prosecutor appears in court proceedings in cases of offences prosecuted by public indictment.[215] In this role, the injured person may act as a secondary accuser alongside or instead of the public prosecutor. Two basic variants of the injured person's activity as an auxiliary prosecutor can be distinguished, namely as an accessory auxiliary prosecutor and as a subsidiary auxiliary prosecutor.[216]

An accessory auxiliary prosecutor is, in principle, an injured person who in the course of judicial proceedings in cases of crimes prosecuted by public indictment supports the accusation in addition to the public prosecutor (Articles 54 § 1, 55 § 4, 60 § 2 CPC) or the subsidiary auxiliary prosecutor (Article 55 § 3 CPC).[217] He or she may also exceptionally support the accusation in place of the mentioned prosecutors in procedural situations in which they themselves withdraw from further support of the accusation (Articles 54 § 2 and 56 § 2 in connection with Article 55 § 3 CPC). The basic procedure for becoming an accessory auxiliary prosecutor is regulated in Article 54 § 1 CPC. Pursuant to this provision, if an indictment is brought by the public prosecutor, the injured person is entitled, until the commencement of the judicial examination at the main hearing, to make a declaration that he/she will act as an accessory auxiliary prosecutor (Article 54 § 1 CPC). A similar procedure for acquiring the status of an accessory auxiliary prosecutor is envisaged in the case of court proceedings inaugurated by a subsidiary auxiliary prosecutor. In such a procedural system, other persons injured by the same act may, until the commencement of the judicial examination at the main hearing, join the proceedings and act alongside the auxiliary prosecutor instead of the public prosecutor (Article 55 § 3 CPC).[218]

The construction of the subsidiary auxiliary prosecution (subsidiary complaint) is based on the assumption that in certain cases, upon the fulfilment of conditions strictly defined by law, which are part of the scheme of control of decisions not to prosecute (decisions on refusal to initiate or to discontinue preparatory proceedings), the injured person may exceptionally obtain the right to file and support an indictment before the court in the case of an offence prosecuted by public indictment instead of by the public prosecutor.[219] At the moment of filing such an indictment, referred to as a subsidiary indictment, he/she acquires the status of a subsidiary auxiliary prosecutor. This option is aimed, on the one hand, at guaranteeing the principle of legalism by ensuring judicial control of the abandonment of criminal prosecution, and on the other hand, at safeguarding the interests of the injured person in the criminal process and injured's right to being heard in court.[220] The path leading to the right of the injured person to initiate court proceedings in a public-complaint case is complicated

[214] Marszał (n 9) 235; Zagrodnik (n 1) 258.
[215] Daszkiewicz (n 168) 224; Marszał (n 9) 245.
[216] Grzegorczyk and Tylman (n 3) 295–96; Zagrodnik (n 1) 249.
[217] Daszkiewicz (n 168) 225–26; Grzegorczyk and Tylman (n 3) 295–96; Zagrodnik (n 1) 249–51.
[218] Zagrodnik (n 1) 251.
[219] See further J Zagrodnik, *Instytucja skargi subsydiarnej w procesie karnym* (Warsaw, CH Beck, 2005).
[220] ibid ix.

and requires a significant commitment from them. It consists of the implementation of the following conditions:

1. issuance of a decision on refusal to initiate, or to discontinue an investigation;
2. filing of a complaint by the injured party against the decision on refusal to initiate, or to discontinue, an investigation,
3. revoking the decision on discontinuing an investigation or on refusing to institute it by the court and referring the case to the authority conducting preparatory proceedings,[221] indicating the reasons thereof, and, when necessary, also the circumstances which shall be clarified or actions which shall be conducted;
4. again issuance by the authority conducting preparatory proceedings of a decision on refusal to initiate, or to discontinue, an investigation;
5. filing of a complaint by the injured party against the repeated decision[222] on refusal to initiate, or to discontinue, preparatory proceedings and upholding of the challenged decision by a superior public prosecutor (*argumentum ex* Article 55 § 1, Article 306 § 1 and 1a, Article 325e, 330 and 465 § 2 CPC).[223]

In order for the injured person to acquire the right to lodge a subsidiary indictment when the decision not to prosecute is upheld again, he or she must – *verba legis* – 'exercise the rights provided for in Article 306 § 1 and § 1a' (Article 330 § 2, third sentence CPC), and thus complain twice against the decision to refuse to initiate, or to discontinue, an investigation.[224] The right to file a subsidiary indictment is time limited. The injured party may exercise it only within one month of the date of being served the notification of the decision of the superior public prosecutor upholding the repeated challenged decision refusing to initiate, or to discontinue, the investigation (Article 55 § 1 CPC). The established time limit is of a preclusionary nature, which means that after its expiration, the filing of a subsidiary indictment is ineffective in the sense that it does not lead to the initiation of judicial proceedings. The time limit cannot be restored.[225] This regulation of the time limit raises objections from the point of view of the guarantee of the rights of the injured person, since it makes him/her bear the negative consequences of the lapse of the time limit in question even if it is caused by circumstances beyond his/her control.[226] With respect to preparing and signing the subsidiary indictment, the law provides for so-called compulsory representation by a lawyer, ie the requirement that these actions be carried out by a solicitor or a legal adviser (Article 55 § 2 CPC). The indictment is accompanied by one duplicate for each of the accused and for the public prosecutor (Article 55 § 1 CPC). The bringing of an indictment shall be notified to other injured parties known to the court (Article 55 § 2a CPC).

[221] See Supreme Court Judgment, 5 December 2012, III KK 122/12, OSNKW 2013, no 1, pos 9.

[222] Supreme Court Resolution, 17 May 2000, I KZP 9/00, OSNKW 2000, nos 5–6, pos 42; Supreme Court Judgment, 9 November 2011, III KK 134/11, OSNKW 2011, no 12, pos 111.

[223] See further ibid 115–270.

[224] J Zagrodnik and P Trzeja, 'Instytucja skargi subsydiarnej oraz oskarżenie posiłkowe w świetle ustawy nowelizującej kodeks postępowania karnego z 19 lipca 2019 r' (2020) 2(23) *Radca Prawny* 160.

[225] Constitutional Court Judgment, 4 October 2012, SK 28/10, OTK-A 2012, no 8, pos 96.

[226] J Zagrodnik, 'Termin do wniesienia aktu oskarżenia według art. 55 § 1 k.p.k. a data wejścia w życie ustawy z 23.091997 o zmianie k.p.k. Glosa do uchwały SN z 20.03.2008 r., I KZP 39/07' (2009) *PiP* no 1, 127 et seq.

The auxiliary prosecutor, both accessory and subsidiary, shall enjoy full rights arising from the status of a party unless they are restricted by an express provision. For example, he/she has the right to participate in the trial (Article 384 § 1 CPC), as well as in court hearings (eg Articles 343 § 1 or 5 CPC), the right to ask questions, submit motions and statements (eg Articles 167 and 368 CPC), the right to be assisted by a solicitor or legal counsel (Article 87 § 1 CPC) and the right to appeal against rulings and orders issued in court proceedings (Article 425 § 1 CPC). The auxiliary prosecutor has an independent position in court proceedings, even if he/she acts alongside the public prosecutor.[227] He exercises his/her rights independently and his/her motions for evidence or formulated claims do not have to correspond with motions or claims of the public prosecutor or other auxiliary prosecutors. The *spiritus movens* of the procedural activity of an auxiliary prosecutor is his/her own private interest resulting from a direct infringement or threat to his/her legal interest from a crime. It should be noted, however, that activities undertaken in this interest usually serve at the same time to secure the public interest in the conditions of a criminal proceeding.[228] This is an obvious consequence of the fact that the activity of an auxiliary prosecutor consists in supporting prosecution in cases of offences directly threatening a public interest.

At the end of this part of the book it should be pointed out that in certain cases the act grants certain entities the right to exercise the rights of an injured person, including the right to act as a prosecutor (private or auxiliary). This applies primarily to persons closest to the injured person and dependent on him or her, who may exercise his or her rights in the event of the death of the injured party (Article 52 § 1 CPC). Pursuant to Article 49 § 3a CPC in cases related to criminal offences against rights of persons engaged in gainful employment, referred to in Articles 218–21 and Article 225 § 2 CC, the bodies comprising the National Labour Inspectorate may exercise the rights of the injured person if they have discovered the criminal offence or requested the commencement of proceedings within their capacity. In turn, according to Article 49 § 4 CC in cases arising out of criminal offences which have inflicted damage upon property of an institution or organisational unit referred to in § 2, if the injured institution's or organisational unit's body is not operating, the rights of the injured may be exercised by state inspection bodies which, within their capacity, have discovered the criminal offence or requested the commencement of proceedings.

[227] Marszał (n 9) 243.
[228] Zagrodnik (n 219) 361–64.

4

Coercive Measures

Coercive measures are strictly connected with the essence of a criminal trial as a dynamic social phenomenon subordinated to the realisation of the aim of justice in the form of a proper settlement of the issue of criminal liability of a given person for the deed of which he or she is accused.[1] The procedural activities undertaken in the course of the trial, which are aimed at achieving this goal, by their very nature are not indifferent from the point of view of the rights and freedoms of the person against whom the criminal prosecution is directed, as well as other participants of the criminal trial or third parties.[2] Criminal procedural law must, on the one hand, guard these rights and freedoms and, on the other hand, safeguard the interests of justice. Thus, it must define the permissible framework of interference in the sphere of rights and freedoms of the accused and other participants of the trial for the purpose of creating conditions for achieving the objectives of justice.[3] If this interference is based on state coercion, or the possibility of its use, its criminal procedural form is coercive measures. It can be said that coercive measures constitute a category of legal measures (legal instruments), which aim to secure the proper course of the criminal trial and the goals of the justice, and which consist in interference, by means of state coercion, in the sphere of rights and freedoms of the persons to whom they are applied.[4] In this chapter, the most important coercive measures used in Polish criminal proceedings will be analysed.

The Principle of Proportionality and the Rule of Moderation in the Context of Using Coercive Measures

The use of coercive measures may infringe human rights and freedoms, which are guaranteed on the constitutional and convention level, in the following spheres:

- personal freedom (Article 41 sections 1–5 of the Constitution of the Republic of Poland, Article 5 ECHR), in particular in the case of detention and pre-trial detention;
- personal inviolability (Article 41 section 1 of the Polish Constitution), eg with respect to forced examination of the accused or a witness;
- privacy, eg regarding the secrecy of communications and inviolability of dwellings (Articles 47, 49 and 50 of the Constitution of the Republic of Poland, Article 8 ECHR);

[1] T Grzegorczyk and J Tylman, *Polskie postępowanie karne* (Warsaw, LexisNexis, 2014) 554.
[2] K Marszał, *Proces karny. Zagadnienia ogólne* (Katowice, Volumen, 2013) 429–30.
[3] See more Grzegorczyk and Tylman (n 1) 554–55.
[4] Marszał (n 2) 429.

- property and other property rights (Article 64 of the Constitution of the Republic of Poland, Article 1 of Additional Protocol No 1 to the ECHR), eg as a result of a property surety, decision on its forfeiture or application of security on property;
- freedom of movement within the country, choice of place of residence (whether permanent or temporary), and freedom to leave the country (Article 52 sections 1–3 of the Constitution of the Republic of Poland, Article 2 of Additional Protocol No 4 to the ECHR).[5]

The regulation of interference in the sphere of the aforementioned constitutional rights and freedoms within the framework of the application of measures of penal-procedural coercion must meet the conditions set out in Article 31 section 3 of the Constitution of the Republic of Poland.[6] This provision states that any limitation upon the exercise of constitutional freedoms and rights may be imposed only by statute, and only when necessary in a democratic state for the protection of its security or public order, or to protect the natural environment, health or public morals, or the freedoms and rights of other persons. Such limitations shall not violate the essence of freedoms and rights. It follows from this provision, first and foremost, that encroachment into the sphere of civil liberties and rights, including by means of coercive measures, must be based on a legislative act with the rank of a statute. The implementation of this condition requires precision in the wording of the provisions regulating the use of coercive measures, in order to exclude the possibility of broadening the scope of restrictions on the rights and freedoms of the individual on an interpretative level by interpreting provisions that are too broadly worded.[7] Consideration of the exclusive statutory regulation of limitations on civil rights and freedoms leads to the conclusion that, with regard to the grounds for the use of coercive measures, there is no room for inference *per analogiam* or recourse to custom or sub-statutory provisions. From the 'necessity' referred to in the aforementioned provision follows the second condition for the restriction of constitutional rights and freedoms, which is formulated as a principle (test) of proportionality.[8] The content of this principle is formed by the following three directives:

1. The utility directive, according to which a restriction of rights and freedoms is justified only when it is connected with the use of effective legal means, ie actually serves the purpose intended by the lawmaker.
2. The directive of indispensability, which implies that interference in the scope of constitutional rights and freedoms must be dictated by a real need connected functionally with the protection of the values indicated in Article 31 paragraph 3 of the Constitution (security of the state, public order, protection of the environment, health and public morals, freedoms and rights of others). In accordance

[5] ibid 429–30. See also W Daszkiewicz, *Prawo karne procesowe. Zagadnienia ogólne* (Poznań, Branta, 2000) 159–60; K Dudka, in K Dudka and H Paluszkiewicz (eds), *Postępowanie karne* (Warsaw, Wolters Kluwer, 2021) 350–51.

[6] Constitutional Court Judgment, 23 April 2008, SK 16/07.

[7] Marszał (n 2) 429; Daszkiewicz (n 5) 160; S Waltoś and P Hofmański, *Proces karny. Zarys systemu* (Warsaw, Wolters Kluwer, 2016) 425.

[8] Judgment, 22 September 2005, Kp 1/05, OTK ZU nr 8/A/2005, pos 93; Constitutional Court Judgment, 13 March 2007, K 8/07, OTK ZU no 3/A/2007, pos 26.

with this directive, legal measures restricting the rights and freedoms of individuals must meet the subsidiarity test, ie ensure the protection of the indicated values in such a manner or to such an extent that could not be achieved by the use of other means. This test also requires recourse to legal measures that are as least onerous as possible for the entities whose rights or freedoms are to be restricted.

3. The proportionality directive (principle of proportionality *sensu stricto*), according to which the effects of a legal regulation and the legal measures it provides for, which involve a limitation of constitutional rights and freedoms, must be proportionate to the burden imposed on the subject to which they apply. In other words, the potential negative effects of certain limitations (legal measures) should never outweigh and must always remain in reasonable proportion to the intended purpose and the content of the freedoms and rights guaranteed by constitutional norms.[9]

The principle of proportionality has a limiting function. The principle of proportionality fulfils a limiting function when it comes to the freedom of the legislator within the scope of statutory regulation of the principles and procedure of rationing constitutional rights and freedoms. It thus serves to secure citizens against the legislator's discretion in the specified scope. Its significance is not limited to the sphere of lawmaking. It should be assumed that this principle must be taken into account at the level of interpretation of the provisions providing for interference in constitutional rights and freedoms of the individual, including obviously the provisions regulating the use of coercive measures.[10] In the field of law enforcement, it is reflected in the form of the rule of moderation, which requires:

1. the application of an appropriate coercive measure, ie one by means of which it is possible to achieve a certain goal – thus, a measure will not be properly applied if by means of it the procedural goal cannot be achieved.
2. to use, from among the appropriate penal procedural measures, the one which *in abstracto* and *in concreto* encroaches less on the sphere of citizens' freedoms and rights. It can be said that the measure to be used is the one which is least onerous for the subject whose rights and freedoms are subject to limitation.
3. the use of a coercive measure which does not cause an intrusion into the sphere of individual rights and freedoms that is obviously disproportionate to the intended objective, ie the use provisional detention instead of arrest and enforced appearance when there is a justified fear that a given person will not turn up for certain tests with his/her participation.[11]

As an aside to the comments made so far, it is worth noting that from the perspective of protecting individuals against unjustified interference in the sphere of their rights and freedoms, an optimal solution would be to reserve the competence to apply coercive measures for the court as a body endowed with the attribute of independence,

[9] Constitutional Court Judgment, 5 February 2008, K 34/06, OTK-A 2008, no 1, pos 2.
[10] Marszał (n 2) 431–32. See also Dudka (n 5) 351–52.
[11] K Marszał, *Proces karny* (Katowice, Volumen, 1998) 278.

essentially free from executive influence, which can be seen in the case of prosecutorial bodies. A deviation from the implementation of this guarantee could be accepted in cases requiring the immediate application of certain measures, such as the arrest of a person, seizure of property or the conduct of a search. In such cases, however, it should be up to the court to approve the use of a particular coercive measure.[12] The presented optimal guarantee standard, as far as the authority authorised to apply coercive measures is concerned, is not currently implemented in the Polish legal system. Apart from narrowly defined cases in which the decision to apply such measures is reserved for the court, eg in relation to provisional detention, the rule is that the court applies the measures in question in court proceedings, whereas in pre-trial proceedings it is for other authorities, primarily the prosecutor. In the cases mentioned above, the minimum guarantee is to ensure judicial review of the decision of another authority to apply the coercive measure.

System of Coercive Measures

In terms of the system of coercive measures in the Polish legal order, there is no unanimity in the doctrine of criminal procedure. However, it seems that for the purpose of this study it is enough to refer to the most convincing classification of these measures, taking into account their essence and function.[13] Based on these criteria, the following categories of coercive measures can be distinguished:

1. arrest;
2. precautionary measures (the group of these measures is presented in more detail below);
3. penalties for breach of order, which include:
   - penalties for breach of order *stricto sensu*, taking primarily the form of financial penalty that is imposed, inter alia, on a witness, expert, translator or specialist in the event of failure to appear when summoned by the body conducting the proceedings or leaving the place of the activity before its completion without the consent of that authority (Article 285 § 1 CPC);
   - coercive sanctions, aimed at – mainly by means of a pecuniary penalty – inducing a specific procedural participant to fulfil his/her procedural obligation (Article 287 § 1 CPC); where a witness persists in evading to give testimony or where an expert witness, an interpreter or a specialist persists in evading their respective duties, or if a person involved persists in refusing to surrender an object, irrespective of a financial penalty, a detention may be applied for a period not exceeding thirty days (Article 287 § 2, first sentence CPC);

[12] Marszał (n 2) 432–33.

[13] ibid 434–36; Dudka (n 5) 352–53. Differently eg Waltoś and Hofmański (n 7) 423–24; Grzegorczyk and Tylman (n 1) 555. See also K Amelung and K Maszał, *Stosowanie środków przymusu w procesie karnym* (Katowice, Wydawnictwo Uniwersytetu Śląskiego, 1990).

4. forced execution of an action, which is the broadest category of coercive measures, within which one can distinguish:
   - enforced appearance;
   - forced search for, extraction and retention of evidence for the purpose of a pending criminal trial – this sub-group of coercive measures may also be included in the category of coercive evidence-seeking activities based on the use of state coercion;
   - forced medical or psychological examinations – this sub-group consists primarily of examinations of the accused, including tests to determine his or her mental condition, combined with placement in a medical facility, and the collection of blood, mucosal swabs or other bodily secretions from the accused;
   - forcibly carrying out activities for evidentiary purposes, eg taking fingerprints;
   - enforcing order in the courtroom, eg removing the accused from the courtroom in the event that, despite being warned by the presiding judge, he conducts himself in a manner which disturbs the order of the trial, or is incompatible with the dignity of the court (Article 375 § 1 CPC);
   - security on property, the essence of which is to secure the enforceability of a ruling on penalties, punitive measures or other measures of a property nature on the property of the accused or the person obliged to return the property gain resulting from the offence (Article 291 CPC).

Arrest

Arrest consists in the brief deprivation of liberty of a specified person. This measure is applied in order to apply a precautionary measure or to forcibly bring a specified person before a procedural authority.[14] Based on the provisions of the CPC and within the framework of the criminal process, the following three forms of procedural detention can be distinguished:

1. apprehension in the act of committing a crime;
2. proper arrest;
3. arrest and enforced appearance.[15]

The first of the distinguished forms of procedural arrest consists in apprehension in the act of committing a crime (*in flagranti*) or in a pursuit undertaken directly following a criminal offence (Article 243 § 1 CPC). Apprehension *in flagranti* means the capture of the perpetrator of a crime during its commission, or after its commission but still at the scene of the crime. Capture in pursuit may occur when the pursuit is undertaken directly after the commission of the offence and is conducted in an uninterrupted manner.[16] *Verba legis*, apprehension in the act of committing a criminal offence can be made by

[14] Waltoś and Hofmański (n 7) 425.
[15] Marszał (n 2) 434–36. See also Grzegorczyk and Tylman (n 1) 558–66.
[16] See further Judgment of the Appellate Court in Szczecin, 3 July 2008, II AKa 78/08, OSA 2010, no 6, ss 3 et seq.

anyone.[17] Therefore, it should be assumed that in addition to citizens themselves, this right is also enjoyed in principle by officers of state bodies, local government bodies, or institutions or social organisations.[18] However, the police do not have this right because in the case of this procedural body, the legal basis and conditions for apprehending a person, including in the act of committing a crime or in the pursuit of such a crime, are regulated separately in Article 244 CPC. An additional condition for apprehension in the commission of a crime is a risk that such a person may go into hiding or that their identity could not be established. These circumstances form a joint alternative. Thus, it can be concluded that for red-handed apprehension to be legal the occurrence of one of these conditions is sufficient.[19] A necessary consequence of such apprehension is that the apprehended person is immediately handed over to the police (Article 243 § 1 CPC). Failure to comply with this obligation or failure to comply with the described conditions for apprehension red-handed in the commission of an offence shall be classified as a crime of unlawful deprivation of liberty as defined in Article 189 CC.[20]

Proper arrest is regulated in Article 244 CPC. It is done by the police. A suspected person is subject to arrest. The status of this person is closely linked to the factual basis for the proper arrest, which in any case is a good reason to suppose that the person has committed a criminal offence. This basis means the state of procedural knowledge necessary for the arrest be legally admissible. The state must be supported by the evidence gathered.[21] In addition, proper (real) arrest is generally possible if there is a risk that the suspected person may go into hiding, destroy the evidence of the criminal offence, or if their identity could not be established, or there are grounds to carry out an expedited procedure with regard to such a person (Article 244 § 1 CPC). Article 244 §§ 1a and 1b CPC specifically regulate the conditions for the arrest of a person suspected of committing a criminal offence with the use of violence to the detriment of a person remaining in a common household with them. According to the first-mentioned provision, it is sufficient to arrest if there is a risk that a suspect may commit a criminal offence involving violence again against such an injured person, especially when the perpetrator threatens to do so (Article 244 § 1a CPC). The second provision establishes an obligatory form of arrest. Pursuant to Article 244 § 1b CPC, arrest must take place if there is a good reason to suppose that an offence involving violence to the detriment of a person remaining in a common household with the suspect has been committed in a qualified form, namely, with the use of a firearm, knife or other dangerous object, especially when the perpetrator threatens to do so. Immediately after arresting a suspect, the police must proceed to collect necessary data and inform the public prosecutor about the arrest. If there are grounds referred to in Article 258 §§ 1–3 CPC, a motion shall be filed with the public prosecutor for applying to the court for provisional detention (Article 244 § 4 CPC).

[17] Judgment of the Appellate Court in Poznań, 20 September 2012, XVI k 62/12, Lex no 1237538.

[18] RA Stefański, 'Zatrzymanie według nowego kodeksu postępowania karnego' (1997) *Prok i Pr* no 10, 32; J Zagrodnik, in L Wilk and J Zagrodnik (eds), *Prawo i proces karny skarbowy* (Warsaw, C.H.Beck, 2016) 506–07.

[19] K Dudka and H Paluszkiewicz, *Postępowanie karne* (Warsaw, Wolters Kluwer, 2021) 357.

[20] Grzegorczyk and Tylman (n 1) 558.

[21] Supreme Court Resolution, 23 May 2006, I KZP 5/06, OSNKW 2006, no 6, pos 55; Judgment of the Appellate Court in Wrocław, 3 March 2016, II AKa 35/16, Lex no 2023602.

The third form of detention distinguished is regulated in Article 247 CPC. It is applied in pre-trial proceedings and concerns a suspect and a suspected person.[22] The premises for the arrest of these persons under the indicated provision are as follows:

1. a justified risk that they will not appear when summoned in order to carry out, with their participation, activities connected with presenting charges or extending or modifying the charges;[23]
2. a justified risk that they will not appear when summoned in order to conduct, with their participation, examinations or activities specified in Article 74 §§ 2 and 3 CPC,[24] to which the suspect and the suspected person are obliged to submit (Article 247 § 1 point 1 CPC);
3. a justified risk that they could impede the proceedings in another illegal way (Article 247 § 1 2 CPC);
4. there is a need of immediate application of a precautionary measure (Article 247 § 2 CPC).

The public prosecutor has the authority to issue a decision for detention and enforced appearance. It shall be executed by the police or another authority within its jurisdiction if it is authorised by law to carry out arrest activities.[25] In connection with the arrest in question, a search may be carried out if the suspect or suspected person is in hiding and there is a reasonable suspicion that he/she is in a particular place (Article 247 § 3 CPC). To minimize the inconveniences that naturally arise from arrest and enforced appearance, the time of this arrest is limited, based on the assumption that arresting a suspect or suspected person is carried out immediately and that they are released afterwards (Article 247 § 4 CPC). The same idea guides the norm contained in Article 247 § 5 CPC, according to which, taking the decision whether to apply a precautionary measure, the public prosecutor shall either immediately release the arrested person or file a motion with the court for provisional detention.

Whatever form of arrest is finally arrived at, it is necessary to distinguish between arrest carried out for the purpose of enforcing the appearance of an accused or another

[22] Waltoś and Hofmański (n 7) 431.

[23] See eg Judgment of the Appellate Court in Białystok, 9 October 2014, II AKa 192/14, Lex no 1532567.

[24] As was mentioned, the provision of Art 74 § 2 CPC provides that the accused shall be under the obligation to submit themselves to:

1. an external examination of their body and other examinations not involving any infringement of bodily integrity; in particular, the fingerprints of the accused may be taken; they may be photographed and presented to other persons in order to establish the identity of the accused;
2. psychological and psychiatric examinations and to examinations involving certain tests conducted upon their body, except surgical procedures, provided that the examinations are carried out by an authorised health care spcialist according to the principles of medical knowledge and do not constitute any threat to the health of the accused, – provided that such examinations are indispensable; in particular, the accused shall be obliged, in conformity with the above mentioned conditions, to submit to blood, hair and excretory sampling, subject to the provisions of subparagraph (3);
3. a buccal swab test carried out by a police official, provided that this is indispensable and if there is no fear that it could threaten the health of the accused or of other persons.

According to Art 74 § 3 the examinations and actions referred to in § 2 (1) may also be performed with respect to a suspected person, and in conformity with the conditions referred to in § 2 (2) or (3) – their blood, hair samples, buccal swabs, or excretory samples may also be taken.

[25] Marszał (n 2) 438.

procedural participant specified in the law, eg an expert, which takes place on the basis of Articles 75 § 2 and 285 § 2 CPC. The premise of the arrest provided for in these provisions is unjustified failure to appear when summoned by the trial authority. Thus, it constitutes a reaction to failure to comply with a procedural obligation to appear.[26] Such arrest involves depriving a person of the freedom to choose his or her place of residence for a period of time that is absolutely necessary for the purpose of bringing the person to the place of the procedural act.

The duration of arrest is regulated in Article 41, paragraph 3 of the Polish Constitution and Article 248 CPC. It follows from these provisions that it may amount to a maximum of 72 hours. Within this time frame, two periods should be distinguished.[27] The basic provision is 48 hours of arrest. This is the time for which the arrested person must be placed at the disposal of the court with a request for temporary arrest or immediate release. The second period includes an additional 24 hours of arrest. It is provided for the court's consideration of the application for provisional detention. The arrested person must be released immediately if, during this additional time, he/she has not been served with the court's decision on provisional detention together with the charges (Article 41(3) of the Constitution of the Republic of Poland, Article 248 §§ 1 and 2 CPC) or if the decision has not been announced to the arrested person at a session conducted online (Article 250 § 3b CPC).[28] It cannot escape notice that the first of these periods raises objections in the context of international standards for the protection of human freedom, which require the arrested person be brought promptly before a court (Article 5(3) ECHR, Article 9(3) ICCPR).

The duration of arrest is counted according to the rules of *computatio naturalis*, that is, *ad momentum a momentum*.[29] Apart from cases related to the expiry of this time, the arrested person must also be released immediately after the reasons for their arrest cease to exist and upon instruction of the court or public prosecutor (Article 248 § 1 CPC). A particular person may be arrested only once on the same grounds. A rearrest of the suspected person on the grounds based on the same facts and evidence shall be inadmissible (Article 248 § 3 CPC).

In connection with an arrest under Article 244 § 1 CPC or a surrender to the police under Article 243 CPC, an arrested person has a number of rights. First of all, he or she has the right to obtain information about the reasons for the arrest. Immediate provision of this information in a manner understandable to the arrested person is a constitutional obligation (Article 41, section 3 of the Polish Constitution). Moreover, arrested person should be informed of their rights and the time limits of their arrest. The catalogue of rights of the arrested person is quite broad. At their head is the right to the assistance of a solicitor or legal counsel. The arrested person, upon their demand, shall be given an opportunity to contact a solicitor or a legal counsel and also to talk directly with them (Article 245 § 1, first sentence CPC).[30] In exceptional cases justified

[26] Grzegorczyk and Tylman (n 1) 566.
[27] Marszał (n 2) 436.
[28] See Consitutional Court Judgment, 6 December 2004, SK 29/2004, OTK-A 2004, no 11, pos 114.
[29] Waltoś and Hofmański (n 7) 429.
[30] See Supreme Court Decision, 13 October 2011, III KK 64/11, OSNKW 2012, no 1, pos 9.

by particular circumstances, the person who made the arrest may reserve the right to be present when such a conversation takes place (Article 245 § 1, second sentence CPC). This restriction on the confidentiality of the arrested person's contact with a solicitor or legal adviser must be based on specific circumstances indicating the need to safeguard the proper course of the proceedings in this way, eg by eliminating any 'leakage' of information that could result in illegal tampering with evidence.[31] The form of direct contact between an arrested person and a solicitor or legal adviser is not strictly defined in the Act. In practice, it is accepted that direct contact with a solicitor or a legal adviser may be ensured through a telephone conversation. In any case, such contact must give the arrested person the possibility to consult about his/her legal situation with a person professionally trained to provide legal assistance.[32]

An arrested person also has the right to request that a closest relative by blood or affinity of the arrested or another person indicated by him/her be notified of the arrest (Article 261 §§ 1 and 2 in conjunction with Article 245 § 3 CPC). He/she has the right to be heard immediately after arrest (*argumentum ex* Article 244 § 2 *in fine* CPC). In the exercise of this right, he/she may present information in the light of which the arrest proves to be unjustified. In connection with the right to a hearing remains the right to submit a statement and to refuse to submit a statement. The second of these rights is a manifestation of the broader right to silence.[33]

Among the key rights of an arrested person is undoubtedly the right to initiate judicial review of arrest, which is an emanation of the guarantees provided for under the Constitution (Article 41, paragraph 2 of the Constitution of the Republic of Poland) and the Convention (Article 5(4) ECHR, Article 9(4) ICCPR). Pursuant to Article 246 § 1 CPC, an arrested person has the right to lodge a complaint with a court in which he/she may request an examination of the grounds and legality of their arrest, and the correctness thereof. The criteria of control in the form of legality and grounds of arrest refer to the decision-making stage of applying this coercive measure. The assessment of the legality of arrest is focused on its compliance with the applicable law.[34] Assessment of the justifiability arrest consists of verification of the conditions for its use, as set out above in Article 244, §§ 1, 1a and 1b CPC. It also includes a check of the proportionality of the use of this coercive measure.[35] The criterion of the correctness of arrest concerns the enforcement stage. It refers both to the assessment of the manner in which the procedural act itself was carried out, as well as to the assessment of the conditions prevailing at the place of arrest. For example, the review for correctness is subject, on the one hand, to the promptness and completeness of the instruction of the detainee about his/her rights, and, on the other hand, to whether or not the conditions in the place of

[31] J Zagrodnik, *Obrońca i pełnomocnik w procesie karnym i karnym skarbowym* (Warsaw, Wolters Kluwer, 2020) 185.

[32] ibid 184–85.

[33] See Judgment of the Appellate Court in Wrocław, 29 May 2018, II AKa 85/18, Lex no 2522786.

[34] See further A Ludwiczek, 'Problematyka kontroli zatrzymania w nowym kodeksie postępowania karnego' (1998) *Prok i Pr*, nos 11–12, passim; 'Zatrzymanie według nowego kodeksu postępowania karnego' (1997) *Prok i Pr* no 10, 41.

[35] Judgment of the Appellate Court in Warsaw, 12 September 2019, II AKa 129/19, Lex no 2726842.

their arrest offended their dignity or the means of direct coercion applied led to their humiliation.[36]

Any such complaint should be lodged with the authority that carried out the arrest. It should be immediately referred to the district court having jurisdiction for the place of arrest or proceedings, which shall examine the matter immediately (Article 246 § 2 CPC). In the event that the arrest is found to have been unjustified or illegal, the court shall order immediate release of the arrested person (Article 246 § 3 CPC).[37] If the arrested person is released before the complaint is heard, the court shall *post factum* declare the arrest to be unjustified, illegal or inadequate. In the case of ascertaining the lack of justification or illegality or incorrectness of the arrest, the court shall notify the public prosecutor and the superior body of the body which has made the arrest (Article 246 § 4 CPC). In the case of undoubtedly unjustified arrest an arrested person is entitled to compensation from the State Treasury for the damage suffered and for the harm suffered (Article 552 § 4 CPC).[38]

The period of arrest in criminal proceedings, rounded up to a full day, is credited towards the imposed penalty (Article 63 § 1 CC).

Here, it is worth noting that in addition to the forms of procedural arrest analysed above, Polish law provides for arrest outside the criminal process and not for its purpose, so-called extra-procedural arrest. There are different types of such arrest: preventive arrest, administrative arrest (in a 'drying-out' facility) and penal arrest (in connection with the execution of a precautionary measure or a custodial sentence). The most important of these varieties is preventive arrest, carried out by the police against persons who clearly pose a direct threat to human life and health, as well as to property (Article 15, section 1, item 3 of the Public Security Act).[39]

The Main Precautionary Measures

Introduction

Precautionary measures are the most important category of coercive measures. Their primary purpose is to secure the proper course of proceedings by preventing the accused from evading justice or obstructing proceedings in some other unlawful manner. Extraordinarily, they may have the additional purpose of preventing the accused from committing a new serious crime. Sometimes the established objectives of precautionary measures are accompanied by other extra-procedural objectives, eg protection against

[36] eg further: European Court of Human Rights Judgment 12 May 2005, 46221/99, *Öcalan against Turkey*, Lex no 151118; European Court of Human Rights Judgment 16 May 2002, 39474/98, *DG against Ireland*, Lex no 75634. See further: K Marszał and J Zagrodnik, 'Zatrzymanie właściwe z perspektywy sądowej kontroli postępowania przygotowawczego', in S Lelental, J Kudrelek and I Nowicka (eds), *Czynnoci dochodzeniowo-śledcze i działania operacyjne Policji a rola sądu w postępowaniu przygotowawczym* (Szczytno, 2008) 101 et seq.

[37] Supreme Court Judgment, 4 July 1991, WZP 1/91, OSNKW 1992, nos 1–2, pos 10.

[38] See Judgment of the Appellate Court in Katowice, 18 Junauary 2018, II AKa 576/17, Lex no 2490943.

[39] See further Grzegorczyk and Tylman (n 1) 557–58; Marszał (n 2) 436–37; Waltoś and Hofmański (n 7) 425–26.

negative consequences of continuing a certain professional activity (Article 276 CPC).[40] Considerable inconvenience and significant interference in the sphere of fundamental human rights and freedoms which is connected with the application of precautionary measures, especially provisional detention, leads to the conclusion that non-trial goals, eg general preventive or educational ones, may by no means constitute an absolute determinant of their application.[41] For the reasons given above, precautionary measures may only be applied to the person against whom criminal proceedings have been formally instituted (the accused *sensu largo*).[42]

In principle, precautionary measures are divided into isolating and non-isolating measures. The former involve the actual deprivation of liberty of the accused. This group of measures essentially consists of provisional detention. The second of these groups is more extensive. It consists of all other (apart from provisional detention) precautionary measures, consisting in restriction of the defendant's freedom or interference with his/her other rights and freedoms. This group includes:

1. bail (Articles 266, 271 and 272 CPC);
2. police supervision (Article 275 CPC);
3. prohibition from leaving the dwelling premises occupied jointly with the wronged party (Article 275a CPC);
4. suspension from official functions or the performance of profession, or an order to refrain from a specific type of activity or from driving a specific type of vehicle, or forbidden from participating in public procurement procedures for the period of the proceedings (Article 276 CPC);
5. prohibitions related to the protection of medical personnel (Article 276a CPC);
6. prohibition preventing the accused from leaving the country (Article 277 CPC).

The 'relation' between provisional detention (isolation measure) and other precautionary measures is based on which of the discussed measures is the *ultima ratio* in terms of achieving their goals.[43] Or to put it another way, we can say that this relationship is characterised by subsidiarity. It manifests itself in two ways. First, provisional detention shall not be used if another preventive measure is sufficient (Article 257 § 1 CPC). Second, if a non-isolating precautionary measure proves to be insufficient, provisional detention is applied.[44] It additionally follows from the presented characteristics that provisional detention is characterised by the independence of its application. This means that while it is possible to apply two or more non-custodial precautionary measures jointly, eg bail and police supervision, the combination of provisional detention with any other precautionary measure is excluded.[45]

[40] Marszał (n 11) 284.
[41] See more Grzegorczyk and Tylman (n 1) 568–69; Dudka (n 5) 376–79.
[42] Marszał (n 2) 436–37; Waltoś and Hofmański (n 7) 432; Dudka (n 5) 370.
[43] Dudka (n 5) 368.
[44] Marszał (n 2) 440.
[45] Supreme Court Resolution, 22 January 2003, I KZP 36/02, OSNKW 2003, nos 1–2, pos 2; Decision of the Appellate Court in Warsaw, 14 May 1996, II AKz 387/96, OSA 1998, no 3, pos 18.

Conditions for Applying Precautionary Measures

The admissibility of the application of precautionary measures is determined by the fulfilment of a number of statutorily defined conditions. They may be divided into substantive conditions and formal conditions.[46] The first group includes:

1. the existence of an adequate evidentiary basis;
2. the existence of a special basis for the precautionary measure.[47]

The evidentiary (factual) basis for the application of precautionary measures is defined in Article 249 § 1 CPC, according to which it is constituted by evidence collected in the case indicating a high probability that the accused has committed a crime. The requirement of a high probability that the accused has committed a crime means that its degree must be higher than that which is required for the presentation of charges,[48] and at the same time it does not have to be so high that the probability borders on certainty.[49] What is important is that the high probability of the accused committing the crime is supported by the evidence gathered in the pre-trial proceedings.[50] It is subject to assessment in terms of verification of the established degree of probability at the time of taking a decision on the precautionary measure. In this assessment, in the case of examining a motion for applying or extending provisional detention, the court is not bound by the legal classification of the act charged against the suspect, adopted in the motion. It is incumbent upon it to verify the legal classification of the offence charged against the suspect as established by the prosecutor.[51]

The special basis of a precautionary measure is a state of threat to the proper course of a criminal trial or specific goods and values subject to protection, concretised in the law, the occurrence of which justifies the application of the measures in question.[52] The special grounds for a precautionary measure are defined primarily in Article 258 §§ 1–3 CPC. According to these provisions, precautionary measures may be applied if:

1. there is a justified risk that the accused may take flight or go into hiding, particularly if their identity cannot be established or the accused has no permanent residence in the country;[53]

[46] Marszał (n 2) 441.

[47] See also eg Grzegorczyk and Tylman (n 1) 573–74; Dudka (n 5) 443.

[48] At this point, it is really important to note that the presentation of the allegations follows, if the data existing at the time of the institution of or collected in the course of a principal investigation provide grounds sufficient to suspect that an act has been committed by a specified person (Art 313 § 1 CPC).

[49] See eg Supreme Court Decision, 26 July 2000, V KZ 95/00, Lex no 1212036; Supreme Court Decision, 22 November 2018, VII KZ 17/18, Lex no 2591571.

[50] Supreme Court Decision, 10 June 2008, WZ 43/08, Lex no 609907; Supreme Court Decision, 3 September 2008, WZ 57/08, Lex no 609916.

[51] Supreme Court Judgment, 10 March 2007, WZ 8/07, OSNwSK 2007/1, poz 654; Supreme Court Judgment 27 January 2011, KZP 23/10, OSNKW 2011/1, poz 1.

[52] Supreme Court Judgment, 17 April 2007, WZ 12/07, OSNwSK 2007, no 1, pos 843.

[53] See eg Supreme Court Decision, 17 April 2008, WZ 27/08, OSNwSK 2008, no 1, pos 926; Decision of the Appellate Court in Cracow, 9 March 2018, II AKz 105/18, Lex no 2574275.

2. there is a justified risk that the accused would induce other persons to give false testimony or attempt to obstruct the criminal proceedings in some other illegal manner (Article 258 § 1 CPC);[54]
3. where the accused has been charged with a felony or a delinquency punishable by imprisonment of a maximum of at least eight years or where the court of the first instance has sentenced the accused to a penalty of imprisonment of not less than three years; in that case the need to apply provisional detention for the purpose of securing the correct conduct of proceedings may be justified by the severe character of the penalty that may be imposed on the accused (Article 258 § 2 CPC);[55]
4. when there is a justified risk that the accused charged with a felony or an intentional delinquency would commit a criminal offence against life, health or public safety, particularly if they threatened to commit such a criminal offence; on this basis a precautionary measure may be applied in exceptional cases (Article 258 § 3 CPC).[56]

The first two grounds are strictly procedural in nature and dictate the use of precautionary measures to secure the proper course of the criminal trial.[57] The risk that the accused may evade justice or otherwise obstruct the criminal proceedings, which constitutes their content, must be justified, ie it must have a real dimension supported by the circumstances of the case and the evidence collected. The third of these grounds is connected with securing the proper administration of justice, but it also has a strong extra-procedural (material and legal) tinge, as it is in fact a severe penalty threatening the accused. This ground relates only to the use of provisional detention and is based on the presumption that those accused of crimes threatened with severe punishment may attempt unlawful actions aimed at disrupting or preventing the proper course of the criminal trial. Because this presumption is legal in nature, it is not necessary to prove that the accused took specific actions in the indicated direction.[58] Thus, it is not really necessary to concretise the threats to the proper course of the criminal trial that would justify resorting to pre-trial detention. Against this background, there is a fear of automatism in the decision to apply this measure due to the threat of a severe punishment for the accused. This concern is deepened by the controversial standpoint of the Supreme Court expressed in the resolution of 19 January 2012,[59] according to which the grounds specified in Article 258 § 2 CPC is an independent special ground allowing the use of provisional detention if it is accompanied by a high probability that the accused will commit a crime. We cannot agree with this view to the extent to which it creates a possibility of applying an isolative precautionary measure despite the absence of a real threat, supported by specific facts, on the part of the accused to the proper course of

[54] Supreme Court Decision, 27 November 2003, WZ 60/03, OSNwSK 2003, no 1, pos 2562; Supreme Court Resolution, 7 May 2008, SNO 43/08, Lex no 1288900.

[55] Supreme Court Decision, 26 July 2000, V KZ 95/00, Lex no 1212036; Supreme Court Decision, 15 July 2003, WZ 30/03, OSNwSK 2003, no 1, pos 1557.

[56] Supreme Court Decision, 26 March 2013, V KK 365/12, Lex no 1312375.

[57] Marszał (n 2) 447.

[58] Court of Appeal Judgment in Wrocław, 5 January 2012, II AKz 12/12, Lex no 1108801; Court of Appeal Judgment in Katowice, 3 November 2011, II AKz 708/11, Lex no 1102946.

[59] I KZP 18/11, OSNKW 2012, pos 1.

the criminal trial.[60] This possibility is unacceptable from the perspective of the principle of proportionality of interference in the sphere of human rights and freedoms (Article 31 paragraph 3 of the Polish Constitution) and the standard of statutory specification of conditions for restriction or deprivation of personal freedom (Article 41 paragaph 1 of the Polish Constitution).[61] The last of the special grounds for a precautionary measure mentioned so far has a clearly extra-procedural character.[62] It allows the use of a precautionary measure for preventive reasons, in order to prevent the accused from committing a new serious crime (the predelictive (anticipatory) aspect of the use of precautionary measures). The statutory uniqueness of the ground in question dictates restraint in the use of precautionary measures for preventive purposes. Deciding upon the application of a specific precautionary measure, the type and nature of risk indicated in Article 258 §§ 1–3, adopted as the grounds to apply a given measure, shall be taken into account, as well as their significance in the context of the correct course of proceedings at its individual stage (Article 258 § 4 CPC).

Although it follows from the above considerations, it is nevertheless worth clearly emphasising that concerning the material conditions for the application of precautionary measures, for such a measure to be applied it is sufficient, assuming the existence of an established evidentiary basis, that one of the following occurs.[63]

The second distinguished group of conditions for the application of precautionary measures, i.e. formal conditions, includes:

1. legitimacy of the procedural authority;
2. issuance of a decision on the presentation of charges;
3. a hearing before the application of a precautionary measure;
4. issuance of a decision in the form of an order.[64]

In the aspect of the legitimacy of the procedural body to apply precautionary measures there is a differentiation of competence based on two criteria, the type of precautionary measure and the state of advancement (development) of the criminal process. Provisional detention is applied exclusively by the court (Article 250 § 1 CPC).[65] Reservation of the competence to apply provisional detention to this authority is the implementation of the constitutional standard (Article 41 of the Constitution of the Republic of Poland) and the Convention standard (Article 5(3) ECHR). During an investigation, provisional detention shall be applied, upon a motion of the public prosecutor,[66] by the district court in whose region the proceedings are conducted, and in cases of utmost urgency, also by another district court. After an indictment has been filed, provisional detention shall be applied by the court before which the proceedings are pending

[60] See Waltoś and Hofmański (n 7) 436; K Eichstaedt, in D Świecki (ed), *Kodeks postępowania karnego. Komentarz* (Warsaw, Wolters Kluwer, 2021) vol I, 993–94.

[61] See also R Renkun-Werner, 'Glosa do uchwały SN z 19.1.2012 r., I KZP 18/11' (2013) *Palestra* nos 11–12; M Drewicz, Glosa do uchwały SN z 19.1.2012 r., I KZP 18/11, OSP 2013, pos 6.

[62] Dudka (n 5) 384.

[63] See further Marszał (n 2) 287.

[64] Marszał (n 2) 442.

[65] See further Eichstaedt (n 60) vol I, 956–57.

[66] See Decision of the Appellate Court in Gdańsk, 28 June 2017, I AKz 388/17, Lex no 2566609.

(Article 250 § 2 CPC).[67] As for the other precautionary measures, in terms of their application, there is a division of competence between the prosecutor and the court related to the development phase of the criminal process. In pre-trial proceedings, these measures are applied by the prosecutor. In court proceedings, the legitimacy to apply them lies with the court (Article 250 § 4 CPC). It must be emphasised that precautionary measures may under no circumstances be applied by another authority, such as the police.

The second of the formal conditions concerns preparatory proceedings. A precautionary measure may be applied in court proceedings also when the presentation of charges in the first procedural stage took place without issuing a decision in this respect (pursuant to Article 325g § 2 CPC). This is excluded in the case of pre-trial proceedings. This means that in simplified investigations where the presentation of charges may take place by proceeding to the interrogation of the suspect, which begins with informing him/her of the content of the charge entered in the minutes, for the application of a precautionary measure it is necessary to direct criminal prosecution against a specific person in a more formalised manner, ie by issuing a decision on the presentation of charges, pursuant to Article 313 § 1 CPC.[68]

The third condition, namely the hearing of the accused before the application of the precautionary measure, is of significant guarantee importance.[69] It promotes the correct verification of the legitimacy and grounds for the application of precautionary measures and the circumstances excluding their application, as well as the determination of which preventive measure would *in concreto* be sufficient to secure the proper course of the proceedings or prevent the defendant from committing another serious crime. The obligation to question the accused by the court or prosecutor applying the precautionary measure is not absolute.[70] It falls away if questioning the accused is not possible due to the latter being in hiding or abroad (Article 249 § 3, first sentence in fine CPC). The defence counsel appointed shall be admitted to be present if they appear. Notifying the defence counsel of the date of questioning is not obligatory, unless requested by the accused, provided that it does not render the action difficult (Article 249 § 3 second sentence CPC).[71] In all cases of questioning by the court, the public prosecutor must be notified of the date of this action (Article 249 § 3, third sentence CPC).

The last of the formal conditions distinguished means that precautionary measures are applied by decision (Article 251 §§ 1 and 2 CPC). This decision shall contain the name of the person, the act imputed to them, its legal qualification and the legal basis for the application of such a measure (Article 251 § 1 CPC). The decision on provisional detention shall additionally set forth the duration of the detention and designate the time limit for the detention. The determination of the duration of the provisional detention requires the determination of the period (in days, weeks or months) for which the measure is to be applied, while the determination of the time limit requires the indication of a specific date up to which the detention is to be applied.[72] The obligation to

[67] See Decision of the Appellate Court in Katowice, 28 November 2007, II AKz 808/07, Lex no 446685.
[68] Eichstaedt (n 60) vol I, 946.
[69] See Decision of the Appellate Court in Cracow, 10 June 2016, III AKz 199/16, Lex no 2057796.
[70] Eichstaedt (n 60) vol I, 947.
[71] ibid 947–48.
[72] Decision of the Appellate Court in Katowice, 9 October 1996, II AKo 379/96, OSA 1997, no 7–8, pos 31.

each time designate the time limit for the detention shall apply until the ruling closing the proceedings becomes final (Article 251 § 2 CPC). An integral part of the decision on the application of a precautionary measure is its justification, which shall present evidence demonstrating that the accused committed a criminal offence and refer to the facts indicating the existence of threats as to the correct course of the proceedings or a possibility of committing another serious criminal offence by the accused should the precautionary measure not be applied, as well as a specific basis for the application and the necessity of application of a given measure. In the case of provisional detention, it shall also explain why another precautionary measure has not been deemed sufficient (Article 251 § 3 CPC). It is undisputed that a statement of reasons, in which the procedural authority merely quotes the content of regulations specifying the grounds for the application of precautionary measures, does not meet the requirements for such a statement.[73] A statement of reasons does not meet the requirements of a statement of reasons either, if it simply refers 'to the evidence gathered'.[74] The court should clearly indicate in the statement of reasons on which evidence it bases its assessment as to the existence of a specific type of threat to the proper conduct of the criminal proceedings.[75] The statement of reasons must demonstrate beyond any doubt that the court has considered whether it is feasible to secure the proper course of the proceedings through the application of non-insulation measures of restraint.[76]

Additionally, it must be noted that the decision to apply provisional detention shall be served on the defendant. The decision to apply a different precautionary measure shall be served on the defendant if they were not present at the delivery of that decision (Article 251 § 4 CPC).[77]

System of Control of Precautionary Measures

The profound interference in the sphere of human rights and freedoms that is associated with the use of precautionary measures, especially provisional detention, makes it important that the legitimacy and legality of their use be extensively controlled. This is guaranteed by an extensive system of control over the use of precautionary measures, including the following three modes:

1. complaint mode;
2. ex officio control mode;
3. the request mode.[78]

The first of these modes is based on the filing of a complaint against a decision on a precautionary measure. This applies both to the decision on the application of such a

[73] Supreme Court Judgment, 15 October 1996, II KZ 78/96, OSNKW 1996, nos 11–12, pos 84.
[74] Appeal Court Judgment in Katowice, 20 January 2010, II AKz 17/10, Lex no 574487.
[75] European Court of Human Rights Judgment, 13 September 2005, 44165/98, *Skrobol against Poland*.
[76] Appeal Court Judgment in Wrocław, 29 October 2008, II AKz 565/08, OSA 2009/6, poz 23; European Court of Human Rights Judgment, 13 September 2005, 44165/98, *Skrobol against Poland*; European Court of Human Rights Judgment, 4 October 2005, 17732/03, *Krawczyk against Poland*; European Court of Human Rights Judgment, 28 July 2005, 751112/01, *Czarnecki against Poland*.
[77] See Eichstaedt (n 60) vol I, 967.
[78] Marszał (n 2) 443.

measure, as well as, for example, to the decision on its refusal, extension or revocation.[79] The complaint against a decision on a precautionary measure is available pursuant to general provisions, unless the Act stipulates otherwise (Article 252 § 1 CPC). A decision of the public prosecutor on a precautionary measure may be challenged in the district court before which the proceedings are pending (Article 252 § 2 CPC). Referring to the general principles mentioned above, it may be stated that the parties are entitled to lodge a complaint within the scope of their legal interest (Article 459 § 3 CPC). This means that in the case of, for example, a court decision on provisional detention, a complaint may be filed by the prosecutor, the suspect affected by the decision and the victim if the decision violates his or her interests.[80] The complaint against a decision on a precautionary measure shall be immediately examined by the court. However, a complaint against a decision on provisional detention shall be examined no later than before seven days have elapsed as of submitting the complaint to the court along with the necessary files (Article 252 § 3 CPC).

The second mode, the control mode, is closely related to the obligation of the trial authority to carry out ongoing, 'permanent' verification of the collected evidence and the resulting findings in terms of the need for further application of the precautionary measure (the directive to adapt the precautionary measure to the procedural situation of the accused).[81] If the reasons for the application of the precautionary measure cease to exist, or reasons justifying its revocation or amendment arise or come to light, it shall immediately be revoked or amended (Article 253 § 1 CPC). The rule is that the decision to revoke or amend a precautionary measure ex officio shall be taken by the authority before which the proceedings are pending. Therefore, in accordance with Article 253 § 2 CPC a precautionary measure applied by the court may, in an investigation, be revoked or amended to a milder measure also by the public prosecutor (Article 253 § 2 CPC).[82] In the aspect of compensation, it is worth noting that failure to promptly revoke the provisional detention or to change this precautionary measure to another in the event of the occurrence of grounds justifying such revocation or change may lead to the assessment that from that moment the provisional detention is undoubtedly unjust within the meaning of Article 552 § 4 CPC.[83]

A special variety of ex officio control of the applied precautionary measure was introduced in Article 258a CPC by means of the Act of 31 March 2020 amending the Act on special solutions related to prevention, counteracting and fighting COVID-19, other infectious diseases and crisis situations caused by them and some other acts (Journal of Laws of 2020, item 568 as amended). According to this provision, if the accused prevents or hinders the performance of a preventive measure applied against the accused or has intentionally violated the obligation or prohibition related to the use of such measure, the court or the public prosecutor shall apply a precautionary measure guaranteeing the effective performance of the purposes of its application. In essence,

[79] See Decision of the Appellate Court in Warsaw, 18 January 2011, II AKz 16/11, Lex no 1094410.

[80] See Supreme Court Resolution, 23 May 1974, VI KZP 3/74, OSNKW 1974, nos 7–8, pos 131.

[81] Supreme Court Decision, 3 June 1976, I KZ 59/76, OSNKW 1976, nos 7–8, pos 98; Supreme Court Decision, 25 October 2004, WZ 62/04, OSNwSK 2004, no 1, pos 1910.

[82] Judgment of the Appellate Court in Warsaw, 23 February 2006, II AKa 471/05, Lex no 1642480.

[83] Supreme Court Judgment, 24 January 2007, II KK 152/06, Lex no 249199.

this provision provides for an obligation to change the precautionary measure in use to a more effective one for a particular accused. It may be thought that this change will, as a rule, consist in the application of a more severe preventive measure, or at any rate one that is more onerous for the accused. The need for the introduction of the presented legal regulation is questionable to the extent that the possibility of an appropriate change of the precautionary measure, including a more severe one, is clearly provided for in the provision of Article 253 § 1 CPC discussed above.

The third mode of control may be initiated only by a suspect (accused) or his/her defence counsel on the basis of a motion for revoking or amending the applied precautionary measure. The right to submit such a motion is available at any time, so there are no temporal limits within which its use would have to be contained.[84] The review on request is complementary to the review of the complaint, so it should not essentially consist in duplicating it using the same reasoning. The filing of a motion may be justified on the grounds that, for example, in connection with the taking and recording of evidence in the pre-trial proceedings, fears of unlawful alteration of evidence by the accused should cease. The motion for modification of the precautionary measure may also aim to change the conditions of its application, eg the scope of obligations imposed on the accused in connection with the application of police supervision.[85] The analysed motion shall be resolved by the public prosecutor not later than three days after filing or, if the indictment has already been filed, by the court before which the case is pending (Article 254 § 1 in fine CPC). The decision on the motion requires the issuance of a decision by the prosecutor or the court. In order to guarantee the smooth course of the trial and to avoid the danger of its inhibition in connection with the control of precautionary measures carried out upon request, the Act provides for a limitation of the appealability of the decision issued following the examination of the application for revocation or modification of this precautionary measure.[86] Pursuant to Article 254 § 2 CPC, a suspect may file a complaint against this decision, provided that the application was filed after at least three months have elapsed from the date of the decision on the precautionary measure. Under this provision, 'a decision on a precautionary measure' means both a decision issued as a result of the examination of a previously filed motion for the repeal or modification of a precautionary measure in a given case, as well as a decision on the application of a precautionary measure and on the extension of its application, and also a decision maintaining the application of this measure in connection with the transition of a trial from the pre-trial stage to the court stage.[87] The presented time limitation on the complaint against the decision on the motion for abrogation or change in provisional detention means that in practice, especially in pre-trial proceedings, the possibility of its filing will come into play only occasionally. The examination of the complaint against the prosecutor's decision on the motion to repeal or change the temporary arrest is the responsibility of the district court in whose district the

[84] Marszał (n 2) 444; Grzegorczyk and Tylman (n 1) 595.

[85] Supreme Court Decision, 30 September 1998, I KZP 12/98, OSNKW 1998, nos 9–10, pos 46.

[86] See Marszał (n 2) 444.

[87] P Hofmański, E Sadzik and K Zgryzek, *Kodeks postępowania karnego. Komentarz* (Warsaw, CH Beck, 2004) vol I, 1046; Appeal Court Judgment in Katowice, 15 September 2004, II AKz 672/04, (2005) *Prok i Pr* no 10, pos 27.

proceedings are conducted (Article 252 § 2 CPC). A complaint against a court's decision shall be examined by the same court by a panel of three judges (Article 254 § 2 CPC).[88]

Provisional Detention

Provisional detention consists of actual deprivation of liberty of the accused, which takes place in the course of a criminal trial before a final decision on its subject and a possible determination of the accused's guilt.[89] It is a coercive measure causing the deepest interference in the sphere of individual rights and freedoms.

Detention, which may be applied on the basis of Article 287 CPC for a period not exceeding thirty days, should be distinguished from provisional detention, especially where a witness persists in evading giving testimony or where an expert witness, an interpreter or a specialist persists in evading their respective duties, or if a person involved persists in refusing to surrender an object, irrespective of a financial penalty. This detention is not a precautionary measure, but is a sanction aimed at enforcing the performance of a specific procedural duty. Arrest should also be distinguished from provisional detention, which is a punishment provided for in Article 18(1) of the Code of Petty Offences, imposed by the court for committing a minor offence which is a petty offence.[90]

The main function of provisional detention is to prevent the defendant from evading justice and illegally obstructing the criminal trial. The protective (predelictive) function of provisional detention, which boils down to protection against the defendant committing a new serious crime, has an accessory character.[91] Only in the category of derivative functions mentioned above, can extra-procedural functions of provisional detention be considered, eg the general-preventive (educational) function, connected with the effect of discouraging (deterring) the commission of crimes, or the repressive function, resulting from the fact that provisional detention entails a real inconvenience for the accused, which is particularly reflected in the normative obligation to count it against sentences imposed against the accused (Article 63 §§ 1 and 2 CC).[92]

The use of provisional detention by the court is a power and not an obligation of this authority.[93] This power exists when, as already indicated earlier in the context of precautionary measures in general, one of the special grounds for these measure occurs in addition to one material condition in the form of an adequate evidentiary basis. The experience of the practice of provisional detention still provides examples of excessively hasty acceptance by courts of prosecutors' motions to apply this measure and thus unjustified recourse to it, often under the influence of public expectations, in particular those of the mass media and strongly populist statements of representatives of authorities, including the Ministry of Justice. Unfortunately, the elimination of such cases

[88] Decision of the Appellate Court in Lublin, 23 March 2010, II AKz 133/10, Lex no 658513.
[89] Marszał (n 2) 445; Waltoś and Hofmański (n 7) 441.
[90] Dudka (n 5) 385.
[91] See ibid 376–77. See also Marszał (n 2) 445–46.
[92] See further Waltoś and Hofmański (n 7) 434.
[93] Marszał (n 2) 446.

from practice is not supported by the specific grounds for provisional detention, which was subjected to a critical assessment earlier, and which refers to the threat of a severe punishment for the accused, and is based on the presumption that due to this threat he/she will make attempts to destabilise the course of the criminal trial.[94]

The exceptional annoyance of provisional detention, immanently connected with the actual deprivation of freedom, which constitutes its essence, justifies a number of restrictions on the use of this precautionary measure.[95] These restrictions are relative in the sense that they provide for the exclusion or waiver of the use of provisional detention, unless there are special circumstances that 'neutralize' this exclusion or waiver. These limitations can be divided into subjective and objective limitations.

Subjective limitations include, first of all, humanitarian injunctions against provisional detention, particularly if depriving the accused of their liberty might seriously jeopardise the life or health of the accused or would entail an excessive burden on the accused or their next of kin.[96] These orders apply if special considerations do not stand in the way of waiving pre-trial detention (Article 259 § 1 CPC). These considerations must be identified with circumstances, eg the intensity of the risk of escape or concealment of the accused, in the face of which provisional detention remains the only effective means of securing the proper course of the criminal trial.[97] In connection with the assessment of the impact of deprivation of liberty on the defendant's health, the court must take into account the possibility of imposing provisional detention in the form of placing the accused in a suitable medical establishment, including a psychiatric establishment (Article 260 § 1 CPC).[98] In principle, it is only when it is not possible to provide adequate healthcare in such a facility, eg due to the need for specialised cancer treatment, that it is justified to waive provisional detention on the basis of Article 259 § 1 CPC.[99]

Subjective limitations on the use of provisional detention also result from privileges granted to certain persons in the form of immunities, eg diplomatic immunity, unless the sending state expressly waives immunity in relation to them (Article 578 in conjunction with Article 580 CPC) or immunity connected with the exercise of the profession of prosecutor or judge.[100] In addition, they are also bound by the protection afforded to defendants or witnesses, taking the form of a safe conduct (Article 281 CPC)[101] or a so-called quasi-safe conduct (Article 589 CPC).[102]

[94] See further J. Skorupka, 'Tymczasowe aresztowanie w praktyce stosowania prawa' (2021) *Palestra* nos 1–2.
[95] Grzegorczyk and Tylman (n 1) 580.
[96] ibid 580.
[97] T Grzegorczyk, *Kodeks postępowania karnego. Komentarz* (Warsaw, Publisher, 2003) 680.
[98] Decision of the Appellate Court in Cracow, 18 March 1992, II AKz 54/92, Lex no 27806.
[99] Supreme Court Decision, 21 February 1995, WZ 35/95, OSNKW 1995, nos 7–8, poz 52.
[100] Dudka (n 5) 387.
[101] In accordance with Art 282 § 1 CPC a safe conduct shall grant the accused the right to remain at liberty until the moment in which the proceedings are validly concluded, provided that the accused:

1. appears at the time designated by the court, and in the investigation -, so at the time designated by the public prosecutor;
2. does not leave their chosen place of stay in the country unless permitted to do so by the court;
3. does not induce witnesses to give false testimony or explanations, or attempt in any other manner to obstruct the criminal proceedings.

[102] Pursuant to Art 589 § 1(1) CPC, a witness or expert witness who is not a Polish citizen and who, when summoned from abroad, appears voluntarily before the court, may not be prosecuted or arrested, or put

The subject-matter (objective) limitations consist in excluding the possibility of provisional detention in the following situations:[103]

1. when the facts of the case make it possible to presume that the court would sentence the accused to the penalty of imprisonment with conditional suspension of execution, or to a milder penalty, or that the term of provisional detention would exceed the expected sentence of imprisonment without a conditional suspension (Article 259 § 2 CPC);[104]
2. where the criminal offence is punishable by imprisonment for a term not exceeding one year (Article 259 § 3 CPC).[105]

Their relative nature is determined by the fact that they shall not apply if the accused has remained in hiding, persistently failed to appear when summoned, impeded the proceedings in another illegal manner or when their identity cannot be established.[106] The restriction provided in the first point shall not apply also when there is a high probability of adjudicating a preventive measure consisting in placing the perpetrator in a closed establishment (Article 259 § 4 CPC).

A separate category of restrictions on the use of provisional detention are temporal restrictions related to the time limits for the use of this precautionary measure. Their introduction is in line with the statutory assumption of temporariness of this measure.[107] They also have a disciplinary function, as they should stimulate the efficiency of procedural authorities.

Finally, they play an important role as guarantor, because due to them the accused has an orientation as to the period after which he/she can realistically expect to be released from provisional detention, unless there are special circumstances justifying the prolongation of pre-trial detention.[108] The temporal limits of provisional detention need to be presented separately in relation to pre-trial proceedings and court proceedings.

In an investigation, according to Article 263 § 1 CPC, the court applying provisional detention shall designate a period of detention not exceeding three months. This is the basic period of provisional detention. The period shall include the time of detention (Article 265 CPC). The decision on provisional detention should clearly indicate the duration of this measure.[109] The court may apply provisional detention within this three-month period for a shorter period. It is also possible for the same court to extend the provisional detention, as long as it remains within the basic three-month period.[110] If due to the particular circumstances of the case it was impossible to complete the investigation within the basic time frame (three months), then – upon request of the

under provisional detention by reason of the criminal offence to which the criminal proceedings refer or of any other criminal offence committed before they crossed the Polish border.

[103] Dudka (n 5) 388.

[104] See eg Supreme Court Decision, 15 April 2004, WZ 28/04, OSNwSK 2004, no 1, pos 716; Supreme Court Resolution, 27 January 2011, I KZP 23/10, OSNKW 2011, no 1, pos 1.

[105] Supreme Court Decision, 16 February 2001, V KKN 456/98, Lex no 1632407.

[106] See further Supreme Court Decision, 12 April 2010, V KK 308/09, Lex no 583934.

[107] Dudka (n 5) 389.

[108] See Grzegorczyk and Tylman (n 1) 582–83.

[109] Decision of the Appellate Court in Katowice, 28 May 2008, II AKz 401/08, Lex no 465063.

[110] Marszał (n 2) 449.

public prosecutor – the first-instance court competent to examine the case may extend the provisional detention, if needed, for a period which shall not exceed twelve months in total (Article 263 § 2 CPC). The concept of 'particular circumstances of the case' should be associated with objectively existing obstacles of a factual, evidentiary or procedural nature, which obstructed the course and prevented the completion of pre-trial proceedings.[111] In practice, such obstacles usually arise from the complexity of the subject or object of the case, the need to carry out actions by way of legal assistance, the need to obtain expert evidence or the need to conduct forensic psychiatric observation of the accused. In the category of special circumstances of the case, the inability to complete the preliminary investigation due to organisational inefficiency or even slowness of the criminal prosecution authorities cannot be considered.[112] To avoid ambiguity, it should be noted that in addition to the described special circumstances that prevented the completion of the pre-trial proceedings, in order to extend the provisional detention it is necessary that the grounds (evidentiary and special) for the application of this preventive measure continue to exist.[113] If the pre-trial investigation could not be completed within twelve months, a so-called extraordinary prolongation of the provisional detention[114] on a motion of the competent public prosecutor who is a direct superior of the public prosecutor conducting or supervising the principal investigation may take place. It is reserved for the appellate court and can take place if deemed necessary in connection with a suspension of criminal proceedings, actions aimed at determination of the accused person's identity, conducting evidentiary actions in a particularly intricate case or abroad, as well as intentional protraction of proceedings by the accused (Article 263 § 4 CPC). The catalogue of circumstances justifying extraordinary prolongation of provisional detention is limited in scope.[115]

In court proceedings there is in principle one relatively maximum term of provisional detention.[116] It applies to the proceedings before the court of first instance and includes the period of provisional detention in the investigation, if at this stage this measure has already been applied.[117] According to Article 263 § 3 CPC, the combined period of provisional detention applied before the first judgment issued by the court of the first instance may not exceed two years. If provisional detention has already been used in pre-trial proceedings and the period until which it was supposed to last expires, after the indictment is filed the court before which the proceedings are pending is obliged to decide on the further use of this precautionary measure, including its extension, provided of course that it does not exceed the indicated period of two years. The time limit is relatively maximum, because the so-called extraordinary prolongation of the provisional detention in court proceedings is also possible in the same cases, listed above, in which the extraordinary prolongation of the provisional detention in pre-trial

[111] Appeal Court Judgment in Lublin, 6 October 1999, II AKz 240/99, (2000) *Prok i Pr* no 5, pos 24.

[112] See eg Supreme Court Decision, 12 March 2009, WZ 15/09, OSNKW 2009, no 7, pos 52; Decision of the Appellate Court in Katowice, 14 December 2005, II AKp 352/05, Lex no 174780.

[113] Supreme Court Decision, 18 March 2008, WZ 20/08, OSNwSK 2008, no 1, pos 684; Decision of the Appellate Court in Cracow, 5 May 2016, II AKz 151/16, Lex no 2031143.

[114] Decision of the Appellate Court in Katowice, 14 December 2005, II AKp 352/05, Lex no 174780.

[115] Eichstaedt (n 60) vol I, 1019. See also Waltoś and Hofmański (n 7) 447.

[116] Waltoś and Hofmański (n 7) 436.

[117] Dudka (n 5) 390.

proceedings may take place. Likewise, the decision in this matter is also reserved to the competence of the appellate court, which takes it at the request of the court before which the case is pending (Article 263 § 4 CPC).

The appellate court may exceptionally extend the pre-trial detention several times.[118] The decision of that court may be contested before an appellate court adjudicating in a panel of three judges (Article 263 § 5 CPC). In view of the possibility of an extraordinary prolongation of the provisional detention it seems quite obvious that the Polish law does not provide an absolute maximum term of provisional detention, which would be impossible to exceed. This state of law is difficult to accept, especially if one takes into account the practice, of which isolated cases still occur, of several years of provisional detention simply because the defendant is threatened with a severe punishment.[119] A certain substitute for definite time limits for the use of provisional detention may be found in the regulation contained in Article 263 § 4a CPC.[120] According to this provision, an extraordinary extension of provisional detention is not possible in pre-trial proceedings, where the penalty to which the accused may be subjected for the criminal offence with which they are charged does not exceed three years of imprisonment, and in court proceedings, when it does not exceed five years of imprisonment, unless the necessity of such an extension results from intentional protraction of proceedings by the accused. It should be noted, however, that even these limitations on the possibility of extraordinary extension of provisional detention are not absolute, since they do not apply in the case of intentional protraction of proceedings by the accused (Article 263 § 4a in fine CPC).

In the aforementioned situations, when the provisional detention is prolonged upon the request of either the public prosecutor or the court before which the case is pending, such a request should be submitted, together with the case file sent to the competent court, no later than fourteen days before the expiry of the temporary arrest measure (Article 263 § 6 CPC). The purpose of the deadline is to give the competent court the time necessary to schedule a hearing on the extension of the provisional detention and, above all, a real opportunity acquaint itself with the often voluminous evidence in the case.[121]

These terms of provisional detention and the conditions of their prolongation do not apply after the first judgment of the court of first instance. When that happens (the issuance of such a judgment), the provisional detention is decided by the court before which the case is pending. Once a ruling closing proceedings has been issued, it will be the court that issued that ruling, and if the case has been referred to the second instance, it will be the appellate court (Article 251 § 2, third sentence CPC). If there is a need to use provisional detention after the first judgment of the first-instance court, each time the provisional detention may be prolonged for a period not longer than six months (Article 263 § 7 CPC). The extension of the provisional detention for the indicated period may take place several times,[122] but it may not exceed this period at

[118] Marszał (n 2) 450; Grzegorczyk and Tylman (n 1) 585.
[119] See Marszał (n 2) 450; Grzegorczyk and Tylman (n 1) 582–86.
[120] Waltoś and Hofmański (n 7) 448.
[121] Eichstaedt (n 60) vol I, 1023.
[122] ibid 263.

any one time. To the extent the cited provision does not clearly define the grounds for extending provisional detention after the first judgment of the court of first instance, it violates the constitutional standard of defining clear and precise rules of deprivation of liberty in the law, resulting from Article 41 section 1 of the Polish Constitution.[123]

The findings so far focused on the presentation of the limitations on the use of provisional detention require some supplementary remarks concerning the procedure and the evidentiary basis for ruling on provisional detention.

In pre-trial proceedings, the incidental court proceedings on provisional detention are initiated on the basis of a written motion of the prosecutor to apply this precautionary measure.[124] The prosecutor's motion, in addition to meeting the general conditions of a pleading (Article 119 § 1 CPC), shall include evidence indicating a high probability that the accused has committed a criminal offence, circumstances supporting the existence of threats to the correct course of proceedings or a possibility of committing another serious criminal offence by the accused, as well as the specific basis for application of this precautionary measure and the necessity of its application (Article 250 § 2a CPC). Where there is a well-founded fear of a threat to the life, health or freedom of a witness or a person close to the witness, the public prosecutor may enclose with the indicated motion, in the form of a separate group of documents, evidence from the testimony of the witness that shall not be made available to the accused and their defence counsel (Article 250 § 2b CPC).[125] This solution undoubtedly serves to strengthen the protection of witnesses who are subject to any such fear.[126] However, it raises important objections from the perspective of the defence, because keeping the evidence justifying the motion for detention secret from the accused and their defence counsel means that they do not have access to some of the evidence (Article 156 § 5a CPC[127]) on which the examination of the motion for the application or extension of the provisional detention is based (Article 249a § 1.2 CPC). This clearly puts into question the reality of the right to effectively challenge the grounds for the application or extension of provisional detention. The effectiveness of the fight against organised crime is not a sufficient justification for the presented limitation of the right to defence.[128] It should be recognised that it violates European standards of access of the defence to information on the grounds for provisional detention.[129] Against the background of the formulated assessment of the legal regulation contained in Article 250 § 2b CPC, the

[123] The same opinion can be found in a Constitutional Court Judgment. See further: Constitutional Court Judgment, 20 November 2012, SK 3/12 (Dz U poz 1237), where judges declared Art 263 § 7 unconstitutional.

[124] See Eichstaedt (n 60) vol I, 957–58.

[125] Before requesting pre-trial detention, the public prosecutor shall determine by order, to be annexed to the file in the handwritten file, which evidence from the testimony of witnesses which is to form the basis for pre-trial detention shall not be made available to the accused and the defence counsel (§ 148(1) of the Public Prosecutor's Regulations).

[126] Zagrodnik (n 31) 250.

[127] The cited provision provides that should a motion be filed in the course of an investigation to apply or extend provisional detention, the suspect and their defence counsel shall immediately be granted access to the case files in the part containing the contents of the evidence enclosed with the motion, excluding the evidence from witness testimonies referred to in Article 250 § 2b.

[128] Zagrodnik (n 31) 250.

[129] Constitutional Court Judgment, 15 January 2008, 28481/03, *Łaszkiewicz against Poland*; see also: Directive of the European Parliament and of the Council 2012/13/UE, 22 May 2012, the right to an information in criminal proceedings, Dz Urz UE L142, 1.

obligation of a strict interpretation of this provision deserves emphasis. This gives rise to the assertion that the 'danger to life, health or freedom of a witness or a person close to the witness', which constitutes a premise for withholding a part of the detention case file from the defence, must have a real dimension, and not merely a hypothetical one, dictated by the subjective feelings of the witness. This rationale cannot be established solely on the basis of the type, number and nature of the charges against the accused.[130] The indicated danger must be objective, ie it must be confirmed by the circumstances of the case resulting from the evidence conducted during the pre-trial proceedings.[131] The issue of judicial review of the legitimacy of the prosecutor's withholding of part of the evidence justifying the detention request is discussed below in the context of the basis for the arrest decision.

When sending the motion for provisional detention to the court together with the case file, the public prosecutor instructs the suspect on his/her rights in the event that this precautionary measure is applied and orders that he/she be brought to court (Article 250 § 3 CPC). This also entails placing the suspect at the disposal of the court until the motion for provisional detention is considered (§ 181 Regulations of the Prosecutor). The prosecutor's motion for provisional detention is subject to examination by the court at a session to be scheduled immediately after the motion is received (§ 317 Regulations of the Court). By way of the Act of 19 June 2020 on interest rate subsidies for bank loans granted to entrepreneurs affected by COVID-19 and on simplified proceedings for approval of an arrangement in connection with the occurrence of COVID-19 (Journal of Laws of 2021, item 1072, as amended), the possibility of holding an online session on provisional detention was introduced. According to Article 250 § 3b CPC, the compulsory appearance of the suspect in court may be waived if their attendance at a session is ensured, especially if they testify, with the use of technical devices enabling this procedural action to be conducted remotely with a simultaneous direct transmission of image and sound. This possibility does not apply to cases where the accused is a deaf, mute or blind person (Article 250 § 3f CPC). A court clerk or assistant judge, employed by the court in whose district the suspect or prison service officer, if the suspect is in prison or custody, shall attend the remote court session at the place where the defendant is staying (Article 250 § 3c CPC). The defence counsel shall be present at a remote court hearing at the place of stay of the defendant, unless the defence counsel appears in court for this purpose or the court obliges them to appear at the session held in the court building due to the need to mitigate the risk of not making a decision regarding the motion to apply provisional detention before the period for which the defendant may be detained expires (Article 250 § 3d CPC). If the defence counsel is present at a session while being in a different location than the defendant, the court may order an adjournment for a definite period of time at the motion filed by the defendant or the defence counsel and permit the defence counsel to contact the defendant by telephone, unless granting the motion may disrupt the proper course of the proceedings or create risk that the motion to apply provisional detention will not be decided prior to the expiry of the period for which the defendant may be detained

[130] Eichstaedt (n 60) vol I, 926.
[131] Zagrodnik (n 31) 250.

(Article 250 § 3e CPC). The construction of a remote court session certainly offers an improvement in the mode of detention proceedings. However, it raises significant objections from a guarantee perspective, and not only because direct contact between the court and the suspect, to whom provisional detention may be applied, seems to be the optimal form of verifying the legitimacy and grounds for applying this measure and an accurate assessment whether in a specific situation and with regard to a specific person it would not be sufficient to secure the proper course of proceedings to apply another precautionary measure. Also, and in fact above all, because the remote session procedure may result in a serious limitation of the right to a defence in terms of ensuring that the accused has adequate contact with his/her defence counsel. A threat to the exercise of this right becomes evident in situations where the defence counsel is not in the same location as the accused due to the possibility of the court refusing to grant a request for permission for the defence counsel to contact the accused by telephone, eg on the grounds that this might interfere with the proper conduct of the remote session. It should be concluded that refusal to allow the accused (defence counsel) to contact the defence counsel (accused), for the reason given as an example, violates the standard of the right to defence, shaped on constitutional and convention levels (Article 42(2) of the Constitution of the Republic of Poland, Article 6(3)(b), (c) ECHR). Looking ahead, one should opt for a reduction of the possibility to hold a remote session on a motion for provisional detention to situations in which this would be absolutely necessary due to an epidemic or a threat of an epidemic or other similar threats to life or health of session participants.[132]

The issue of the participation of the defence counsel and the notification of the defence counsel and the public prosecutor about the session on the application of the provisional detention has already been discussed above in connection with the discussion of the formal conditions for the application of precautionary measures. Thus, it remains here to draw attention to the regulation of the participation of the prosecutor and the defence counsel in the session of the court concerning the prolongation of the application of provisional detention, as well as the examination of the complaint against the decision to apply or prolong the application of this precautionary measure. It is subordinated to the assumption that the said subjects are entitled to participate in the said sessions, which means that they should be notified of the time and place of the session (*argumentum ex* Article 249 § 5 sentence 1 in conjunction with Article 117 § 1 CPC).[133] Upon request of an accused person who does not have a defence counsel, an ex officio defence counsel shall be appointed for the purposes of that action. A failure to appear by the defence counsel or public prosecutor, if they were duly informed about the date, shall not impede case examination (Article 249 § 5, second and fourth sentences CPC).

In the course of the arrest session, the defence counsel, by means of questions, statements and motions, should first seek to challenge the grounds for the application of pre-trial detention, pointing out the absence in the case of evidence that would justify the high probability of the commission of an offence, ie the evidentiary basis for the

[132] Similarly Eichstaedt (n 60) vol I, 962–63.
[133] ibid 950.

application of provisional detention (Article 249 § 1 CPC) or the lack of evidence or at least circumstantial evidence (eg mutual connections to an organised criminal group), which would make it probable that the suspect will undertake actions aimed at obstructing the ongoing proceedings in an unlawful manner or another special reason for the use of precautionary measures (Article 258 §§ 1 and 2 CPC).[134] The defence counsel may also argue the existence in the case of the limitations on the use of provisional detention described above (Article 259 §§ 1–3 CPC). Finally, the defence of a suspect may focus on demonstrating that the use of non-insulating precautionary measures is sufficient to secure the proper course of proceedings. In this connection, the defence counsel may propose to stipulate in the decision on the application of provisional detention the transformation of this measure into a bail as soon as a specific object or sum of money is deposited, which will be discussed separately hereinafter.[135]

In the light of the considerations presented so far, the thesis that the court is not bound by the prosecutor's motion for provisional detention may be regarded as obvious.[136] The examination of the motion should consist of a thorough analysis of the grounds for the use of provisional detention, examination of whether there are any circumstances excluding the use of temporary arrest and verification of the necessity of the use of the discussed precautionary measure to secure the objectives of the trial.[137] The point of reference for the court is the description of the act charged against the suspect, and not its legal qualification, specified in the motion.[138] The provision of Article 249a CPC provides for raising the requirements concerning the evidentiary basis for provisional detention.[139] According to its content, the basis for a ruling on the application or extension of provisional detention may be constituted by findings made on the basis of evidence open to the accused and their defence counsel, and evidence from witness testimonies that have been withheld by the prosecutor from the accused and their defence counsel due to a well-founded fear of danger to the life, health or freedom of the witness or a person close to them (Article 249a § 1 CPC). The restriction presented at the end on the access of the accused and defence counsel to evidence supporting the motion for application or extension of provisional detention is subject to review by the court examining the motion. If the court finds that the prosecutor's excluding access to the witness's testimony was unjustified, it is obliged to disregard it as part of its ruling on the issue of provisional detention.[140] This should not be surprising if one only takes into account that apart from exceptional cases, objectively justified by the fear of danger for the life, health or freedom of a witness or a person close to the witness, only evidence that is open to the defendant and his or her defence counsel may constitute the basis for deciding on the merits of a motion for the application or extension of provisional detention. In the analysed situation, the court is obliged to disclose,

[134] Zagrodnik (n 31) 262–64.
[135] ibid 254–55, 264.
[136] ibid 255.
[137] See further Supreme Court Judgment, 17 April 2007, WZ 12/07, OSNwSK 2007/1, pos 843; Court of Appeal Judgment in Lublin, 3 October 2007, II AKz 321/07, Lex no 357179.
[138] See Supreme Court Judgment, 20 March 2007, WZ 8/07, OSNwSK 2007/1, pos 654; Supreme Court Judgment (7), 27 January 2011, I KZP 23/10, OSNKW 2011/1, pos 1.
[139] Decision of the Appellate Court in Cracow, 10 October 2017, II AKz 396/17.
[140] Zagrodnik (n 31) 254.

after notifying the prosecutor, the classified testimony of the witness and take it into consideration within the framework of the session in connection with the motion under consideration, if the circumstances favourable for the accused arise from it (Article 249a § 2 CPC).[141]

If the court issues a decision on the application of provisional detention, there is an obligation to serve it on the accused as well as on his defence counsel (Article 250 § 4 in conjunction with Article 140 CPC).[142] If provisional detention is applied in court proceedings, the court shall advise the accused of their rights in the case of provisional detention immediately after announcing or serving on the accused the decision on the application of the precautionary measure (Article 250 § 3a CPC). The decision on the extension of the provisional detention shall be served on the accused and his/her defence counsel if they were not present when the court's decision was announced (Article 100 § 4 in conjunction with Article 140 CPC).

The decision on the application of provisional detention may take a conditional form (the so-called conditional provisional detention),[143] which has already been mentioned above. It consists in the fact that the court may stipulate that this measure shall be changed on condition that a specified bail is deposited not later than within the set time limit (Article 257 § 2 in principio CPC). Upon a justified request of the accused or their defence counsel, filed not later than on the last day of the set time limit, the court may extend the time limit for depositing the bail (Article 257 § 2 in fine CPC). Such a motion should indicate that the extension of the time limit for depositing the bail is necessary due to the need to apply for a loan, for example, and the time needed to obtain one, or the time needed to gather the bail amount by selling certain items.[144]

If the bail is lodged within the time limit (original or extended), the provisional detention basically ceases to be valid *ex lege*, and the detainee should be released immediately if there is no basis for his/her detention in another case.[145] 'Basically', because the enforceability of the decision of provisional detention to the extent that it provides for its change to a bail in the event of its filing is suspended until it becomes final, if the change is objected to by the prosecutor at the latest at the detention's session (Article 257 § 3 CPC). The prosecutor's objection results in the fact that, despite the timely filing of the bail by the suspect, the provisional detention continues until the indicated court decision becomes final. It serves as a *sui generis* notice of complaint against the court's decision on provisional detention to the extent of changing this precautionary measure to a bail. It may be assumed that the intention is to prevent situations in which a challenge by the appellate court, as a result of complaint review, to the change of provisional detention to a bail would occur at a time when the suspect would have already been released from custody due to the submission of a bail. From the

[141] Eischstaedt (n 60) vol I, 923.

[142] See further ibid.

[143] Zagrodnik (n 31) 256–58; Eichstaedt (n 60) vol I, 981–82.

[144] In the event of failure to comply with the original or extended time limit for posting a bail, the temporary arrest shall be maintained. If the bail is lodged after the expiration of the time limit, a separate decision on the matter is required in order to have the effect of changing the temporary arrest to a bail. Such a motion may be filed under Art 254 § 1 of the CPC by the defendant themselves or by their defence counsel.

[145] Supreme Court Decision, 25 Februrary 2016, I KZP 18/15, OSNKW 2016, no 4, pos 24; Zagrodnik (n 31) 257.

perspective of the suspect and defence counsel, this solution in fact means continuation of detention, ie continuation of actual deprivation of liberty without a court sentence, despite the fact that due to the submission of a bail it is not – according to the decision of the court of first instance – necessary to secure the proper course of proceedings, but occurs in a sense 'just in case', if the appellate court would agree with the prosecutor's assessment of the need to apply an isolation measure against the suspect. This cannot be accepted.[146] First of all, because the consequences of the prosecutor's objection seem impossible to reconcile with the constitutional principle of proportionality (Article 31 paragraph 3 of the Constitution of the Republic of Poland) and the directive resulting from Article 257 § 1 CPC and Article 5(3) ECHR to minimise precautionary measures, according to which provisional detention as an *ultima ratio* may be applied or continued only as a last resort, when the application of any of the non-insulating (liberty) precautionary measures is not sufficient to secure the proper course of proceedings.[147] To the extent that the provision in question provides for the continuation of provisional detention until the court decision issued under Article 257 § 2 CPC becomes final, in essence based on the prosecutor's objection, it undermines the principle of a judicial decision as to the application of this precautionary measure.[148]

Humanitarian considerations dictate the informational obligations incumbent upon a court applying provisional detention.[149] Among the most important of these is the obligation to notify the person closest relative by blood or affinity of the accused of the application of this precautionary measure. This may be a person indicated by the accused (Article 261 § 1 CPC). Upon motion of the accused, another person may also be notified instead of or in addition to the person indicated above (Article 261 § 2 CPC). The court shall be obliged to promptly notify the employer, school or university, or in the case of a soldier, their commander-in-chief, and in the case of an entrepreneur or a member of management body or an entrepreneur who is not an employee, upon motion of that member, the person managing the enterprise, of the imposition of provisional detention (Article 261 § 3 CPC).

The use of provisional detention, meaning the actual deprivation of liberty during its use in the conditions of a provisional detention facility or a relevant treatment facility (Article 260 CPC), naturally has a negative impact on the suspect's ability to freely contact his defence counsel.[150] The contact of a provisionally arrested person with his defence counsel is to some extent regulated. A defence counsel intending to communicate with his or her client must obtain the consent of the authority at whose disposal the provisionally arrested person remains (Article 215 § 1 CPC), which in pre-trial proceedings is the prosecutor at whose request this measure was first applied (§ 187(1) of the procuratorial regulations). Article 73 §§ 2 and 3 CPC provide for a significant limitation of the freedom of communication between a provisionally detained person and his/her defence counsel. It follows that the prosecutor may reserve his/her own presence or a

[146] See further ibid 257–58.

[147] See Supreme Court Judgment, 4 October 2005, 17732/03, *Krawczak against Poland*; Constitutional Court Judgment, 28 July 2005, 751112/01, *Czarnecki against Poland*.

[148] See also Ł Chmielniak, M Klonowski, A Rychlewska-Hotel and J Zagrodnik (eds), *Kodeks postępowania karnego. Komentarz praktyczny do nowelizacji 2019* (Warsaw, Wolters Kluwer, 2020) 95–97.

[149] See Marszał (n 2) 451–52; Grzegorczyk and Tylman (n 1) 581–82.

[150] Zagrodnik (n 31) 259–60.

person designated by him/her during the suspect's contact with counsel and reserve control of the suspect's correspondence with counsel. The prosecutor's decision in this respect is not subject to appeal. These reservations may take place in particularly justified cases, when the good of the pre-trial proceedings requires it. The cases in question are those where the suspect would take steps to provide the defence counsel with, or through him, information, which could lead to taking actions aimed at obstruction of the proceedings, eg covering up traces of a crime.[151] To make the right to defence of a suspect more realistic,[152] and in a way to discipline the criminal prosecution authorities, a temporal limitation of the objections presented serves the purpose, according to which they may neither be maintained nor made after fourteen days have elapsed from the day of provisional detention (Article 73 § 4 CPC). This makes it possible to conclude that it is only when this time limit expires that the detained suspect and defence counsel can count on full confidentiality, unencumbered by any reservations, enabling them to communicate unhindered, which determines a viable and effective defence.[153]

Since provisional detention is a nuisance consisting of the actual deprivation of liberty of the accused, it shall be counted towards the sentence imposed, on the assumption that one day of the actual deprivation of liberty is equal to one day of the penalty of deprivation of liberty, two days of the penalty of limitation of liberty or two daily rates of fine (Article 63 § 1 CC). The sentence of deprivation of liberty shall also include any period of provisional detention served by the accused in another case in which the proceedings were simultaneously pending, and in which a final ruling of acquittal was rendered or the proceedings were discontinued or there was a renouncement of punishment (Article 417 CPC).[154]

Bail

Along with a guaranty given by an employer and a guaranty from a trustworthy person (non-material guarantyship),[155] bail is one of the types of measures that give a warranty that the accused will not evade justice or unlawfully obstruct the proceedings. Bail in its current form in Polish criminal proceedings differs from bail in its classic form, in which it exists primarily in the common law system. It is a precautionary measure independent of provisional detention,[156] one of several to choose from, while in its classical

[151] Similarly, Eischstaedt (n 60) vol I, 380.

[152] See more about suspect's right to freely contact with his defence counsel: J Zagrodnik, 'The Right to the Assistance of the Defense Counsel in the Light of the European Court of Human Rights Case Law' (2022) *Radca Prawny* no 2.

[153] It is worth noting that the contact between the provisionally arrested person and his/her defence counsel may be facilitated, especially in the case of the use of detention in the jurisdictional stage of the criminal trial, by the right of the provisionally arrested person to use a telephone apparatus under the rules set out in the organisational and order regulations for the execution of pre-trial detention, with the consent of the authority at whose disposal he/she remains (Art 217c § 1(1) Code of Petty Offences). It should be noted that a temporarily arrested person does not have the possibility of using other means of wire or wireless communication (Art 217c § 1(2) Code of Petty Offences).

[154] Judgment of the Appellate Court in Łódź, 9 April 2013, II AKa 47/13, Lex no 1323129.

[155] See further eg Dudka (n 5) 398–400; Marszał (n 2) 455–56.

[156] Dudka (n 5) 393.

form it is used in principle as a substitute for provisional detention. Comparing bail with provisional detention, it is assumed that it constitutes a *sui generis* contract between the trial authority and the bail provider, by virtue of which the trial authority assures the accused that he will remain at liberty in exchange for a guarantee of appropriate behaviour, which will not impede the proper course of the criminal proceedings.[157] In the case of bail, this guarantee is based on certain property rights. According to Article 266 § 1 CPC, the subject of the bail may be money (in domestic or foreign currency), securities (domestic and foreign), as well as pledges and mortgages. It can be submitted by the accused or another person. It is permissible to accept a bail from several people.[158] The source of bail cannot be a donation to the accused or any other person posting bail, made for that purpose. The acceptance of bail may be conditioned by the court or public prosecutor on the person posting bail proving its source (Article 266 § 1a CPC).[159] The property deposited with the court or secured by it does not cease to be the property of the entity granting the bail. The bail only restricts the guarantor's authority over these assets.[160]

In accordance with the previously discussed general rules for the application of non-insulating precautionary measures, bail shall be applied by a decision of the prosecutor in pre-trial proceedings, and by the court in court proceedings. This decision should be specified the amount, type and conditions of the bail, and particularly the time limit for depositing it. The determination of these components of the decision must take into account the financial condition of the accused and the person depositing the bail, the gravity of the damage inflicted and the character of the act committed (Article 266 § 2 CPC). If the person depositing the bail is not the accused, there is an obligation to notify him/her of each summons of the accused to appear (Article 267 in principio CPC). This aims to ensure that the person standing surety can influence the accused and ensure that he or she appears when summoned by the trial authority. Failure to comply with this information obligation, which prevents the person depositing a bail from knowing what he or she is obliged to do, precludes the possibility of ruling on the forfeiture of the property constituting the bail or the collection of the sum pledged.[161]

In a sense, the effectiveness of a specified bail is based on the threat of forfeiture of certain property rights, which are the subject of the bail, by imposing their forfeiture or collection of the bail sum, in cases of defendant's evasion of justice or in cases of otherwise obstructing the course of the criminal proceedings.[162] Depending on what the defendant's bail of justice consists of, we may distinguish mandatory and optional forfeiture of the bail object or recovery of the bail sum.[163] A decision to this effect shall be mandatory in the case of the taking flight or hiding of the accused. Taking flight is when the accused leaves his/her place of residence without providing a new address and without intending to return soon. It is not taking flight if the accused leaves for a short

[157] Decision of the Appellate Court in Cracow, 22 November, II AKa 385/16, Lex no 2287990. See Waltoś and Hofmański (n 7) 451; Hofmański et al (n 87) vol I, 1099.

[158] Hofmański et al (n 87) vol I, 1103–04.

[159] See further Eichstaedt (n 60) vol I, 1040–43.

[160] Marszał (n 2) 454.

[161] Appeal Court Judgment in Cracow, 5 September 2011, II AKz 353/11, KZS 2011, no 10, poz 31.

[162] Waltoś and Hofmański (n 7) 452.

[163] Marszał (n 2) 454; Grzegorczyk and Tylman (n 1) 602–03; Dudka (n 5) 396.

period of time without providing a new address if it can be established that he/she will soon return to his place of residence.[164] Hiding of an accused person consists of failure to appear as required at the body conducting the proceedings and avoiding contact with that authority combined with the accused's knowingly preventing that authority from contacting him/her.[165] Forfeiture of the bail object or collection of the bail sum is optional if the accused hinders the course of the criminal proceedings in any other way than taking flight or hiding. The hindering must obviously be unlawful. It can consist, for example, of inducing witnesses to give false testimony, encouraging fellow suspects to give false explanations, using violence or unlawful threats to influence a witness, expert or interpreter, or influencing judges or prosecutors by means of bribery.[166] A prerequisite for a decision on forfeiture of the surety object or recovery of the surety sum is that the person posting the surety is properly warned about the prerequisites for such a decision (Article 268 § 1 CPC), as well as its consequences (Article 269 CPC).[167] *Lege non distinguente*, it should be assumed that such a warning must also be given to whoever has deposited the bail (Article 268 § 3 CPC).

The forfeiture of the property constituting the bail or the collection of the sum pledged shall be ordered by the court before which the proceedings are pending, while in the investigation by the court having jurisdiction over the case, upon motion of the public prosecutor (Article 270 § 1 CPC). Reservation of the decision on forfeiture of the subject of the bail or collection of its amount to the competence of the court implements the standard set out in Article 46 of the Polish Constitution, according to which property may be forfeited only in cases specified by statute, and only by virtue of a final judgment of a court.[168] There should be absolutely nothing surprising in this if we consider that the decision in question is the most far-reaching interference in the sphere of the right to property, consisting in depriving a specific entity of this right in relation to designated property values. The importance of the decision determines the adversarial nature of the session set to consider the issue of forfeiture of the surety's object or collection of the surety sum.[169] According to the first sentence of Article 270 § 2 CPC, the accused, the person depositing the bail and the public prosecutor shall have the right to participate in the court session or to file written statements. The right to participate in the session shall be restricted in the case of a defendant deprived of liberty, who shall be brought to the session if the president of the court or the court itself consider it necessary (Article 270 § 2, second sentence CPC).[170] The court's decision to forfeit the property constituting the bail or to the collection of the sum pledged may be contested by way of complaint (Article 270 § 3 CPC). However, no complaint may be lodged against a decision refusing to impose a forfeiture of the property constituting the

[164] See further Eichstaedt (n 60) vol I, 1045–46.
[165] Hofmański et al (n 87) vol I, 1106.
[166] Eichstaedt (n 60) vol I, 1047–48.
[167] Supreme Court Resolution, 20 May 1992, I KZP 17/92, OSNKW 1992, nos 7–8, pos 53.
[168] Waltoś and Hofmański (n 7) 452.
[169] Similarly Waltoś and Hofmański (n 7) 452.
[170] It cannot be ruled out that the issue of forfeiture of the surety's assets or collection of the surety's amount will be considered at the trial (*argumentum ex* Article 95 § 1, sentence 2 CPC). However, it is then necessary to notify the surety of the date of the trial, if it is not the defendant, indicating that the indicated issue will be subject to consideration in this forum.

bail or to impose a collection of the sum pledged.[171] A complaint may be filed not only by the parties, but also by a person depositing a bail who is not a party, whose rights are directly affected by the court's decision (*argumentum ex* Article 459 § 3 CPC).

In adjudicating the forfeiture or collection of property constituting the subject of the bail, the court may decide on a partial forfeiture or collection of the said property, applying concurrently with regard to the accused also another precautionary measure, taking account of the requirements of Article 258 § 4 CPC, except for provisional detention (Article 268 § 1a of the CPC). Again drawing on the *lege non distinguente nec nostrum est distinguere* rule, it should be noted that partial forfeiture or collection of property constituting the subject of the bail may take place both in cases where forfeiture or recovery of the bail is optional and where it is mandatory. The use of this option should act as a spur to the person depositing a bail, who is not an accused, to ensure that the accused person for whom he/she has provided surety duly fulfils his/her obligations in the subsequent proceedings on pain of forfeiture of the remaining bailed assets. In the case of the accused him/herself, as the provider of the bail, the primary motivation for fulfilling his/her procedural obligations in the event that the bail remains in place, in part, should be that the alternative to this is actual imprisonment under provisional detention.[172] It is very likely that this measure would be applied if an accused continued to obstruct the proceedings. The obligation to apply at the same time another non-insulating precautionary measure is mainly intended to counterbalance the weakening of the guaranty arising from the bail as a result of the ruling in part of the forfeiture or the collection of the sum of property constituting the subject of the bail.

The property or sum of money constituting a bail which has been forfeited or collected shall be transferred or paid to the State Treasury; the injured shall then have priority in satisfying with them the injured person's claims resulting from the crime if damages cannot be redressed by other means (Article 269 § 1 CPC).

The bail ceases, and the property constituting the same and the sum of money pledged shall be released, upon the issuance of a decision to waiver the application of this precautionary measure or to change it to another measure, or upon the entry into force of a judgment ending the proceedings in the case. The withdrawal of the bail or its change to another precautionary measure shall entail the return of the property constituting a bail or the release of the sum of bail, unless the change is a consequence of a ruling on the forfeiture of that object or the collection of that sum. In the event that provisional detention is used in lieu of bail, bail shall not cease until the defendant is remanded in custody.[173] In the case of a judgment ending the proceedings in a case, if it is a judgment issuing a sentence of deprivation of liberty without conditional suspension of its execution, the return of the property constituting a bail or the release of the sum of bail occurs only at the time when the accused begins to serve his/her sentence, ie when he/she appears in prison for this purpose.[174] In the case of other decisions ending proceedings, this occurs at the time when they acquire the attribute of validity.

[171] Eichstaedt (n 60) vol I, 1059.
[172] ibid 1048–49.
[173] Supreme Court Judgment, 22 January 2003, I KZP 36/02, OSNKW 2003, nos 1–2, poz 2.
[174] Decision of the Appellate Court in Katowice, 1 June 2016, II AKz 241/16, Lex no 2139312.

A property surety may be withdrawn before its termination. The withdrawal of bail is an autonomous decision of the person depositing the bail and the underlying cause is irrelevant. However, it takes effect only with the receipt of another bail, the imposition of another precautionary measure, or the waiver of the relevant precautionary measure (Article 269 § 3 PCC),[175] unless a decision on forfeiture of the bail or on the collection of the sum pledged has been issued.

Search and Seizure

Search and seizure – the terms are also used in evidentiary law – are coercive procedural measures that serve to search for, extract and collect evidence for a pending criminal trial.[176]

Search

Search is a coercive measure that involves interference of procedural authorities in several aspects of the sphere of human constitutional rights and freedoms, first of all personal inviolability, inviolability of the home and the right to protection of personal and family life.[177] The annoyance and invasiveness of a search in with respect to legal freedom makes it important to define by law the purpose, conditions and scope of this procedural activity. These issues are regulated in Articles 219 and 200 CPC.[178] The first of these provisions states that the search may be conducted for the following purposes:

- to detect or arrest a suspected person or to enforce their compulsory appearance;
- to locate objects which might serve as evidence in a case or be subject to seizure in criminal proceedings.[179]

The material premise (material condition) of a search is the existence of reasonable grounds to suppose that the wanted suspected person is in the place to be searched, or that the things sought are in that place or with a certain person, including among the objects belonging to that person.[180] The subjective element of this condition

[175] Decision of the Appellate Court in Cracow, 23 August 2001, II AKz 266/01, Lex no 49496.

[176] See further Marszał (n 2) 462–65.

[177] See eg Zagrodnik (n 31) 99–100.

[178] In addition to the CPC, they are regulated by the Law of 10.6.2016 on anti-terrorist activities (Journal of Laws of 2021, item 2234). Pursuant to Art 25 of this Act, in the case of suspicion or attempted commission or preparation of an offence of a terrorist nature, in order to detect or detain or forcibly bring in a suspected person, as well as in order to find items that may constitute evidence in the case or that are subject to seizure in criminal proceedings, the prosecutor may decide to conduct a search of premises and other places located in the area indicated in the decision, if there are reasonable grounds to believe that the suspected person or the listed items are located in that area. A search may also be conducted of persons, their clothing and nearby objects in the area specified in the order in order to find the specified items. A search may be conducted at any time of day.

[179] Grzegorczyk and Tylman (n 1) 99–100.

[180] See further J Grochowski, 'Definicja i elementy składowe instytucji przeszukania w procesie karnym' (1990) *Problemy Prawa Karnego* no 16, 80–91; idem, 'Podstawy dowodowe przeszukania w kodeksie postępowania karnego' (1992) *Problemy Prawa Karnego*, no 18, 41–48.

(supposition) must be supported by objective information arising from the evidence obtained in the course of the criminal trial and recorded in accordance with the rules of evidence or, in cases of urgency, subject to procedural verification and recording in evidentiary form following a search.[181] This does not entirely remove doubts raised by the overly general formulation of the material premise from the perspective of the protection of constitutional rights and freedoms that are restricted by a search.[182] From the perspective of these rights and freedoms, it would be appropriate *de lege ferenda* to assume a higher degree of probability that the wanted person or thing is in a specific place or remains at the disposal of a specific person. A search may cover premises and other places (Article 219 § 1 CPC), persons, as well as objects and information systems (Article 219 § 2 in connection with Article 236a CPC).

The formal condition for a search is, in principle, the issuance of a decision on this matter by the court or prosecutor (*argumentum ex* Article 220 § 2 CPC). The prosecutor may conduct the search personally. Upon his/her order or the order of the court, which is supported by a decision to search, this act is performed by the police, and in cases indicated by law, also by another authority, such as the Internal Security Agency or Border Guard (*argumentum ex* Article 220 § 1 in conjunction with Article 312). Exceptionally, in cases of utmost urgency, if the decision of a court or public prosecutor could not be issued, the person carrying out the search shall present an order of the manager of their unit or an official identity card, and then without delay request the court or the public prosecutor to approve the search (Article 220 § 3, first sentence CPC). The phrase 'case of utmost urgency' is vague and has a considerable range of meaning. A narrower interpretation is required to avoid abuse of this exception.[183] A case of utmost urgency may be considered, for example, a case in which delaying the search to await a court or prosecutor's decision would realistically threaten the loss of evidence.[184] The court or prosecutor shall, within seven days of the search being carried out, issue a decision approving the search. A positive decision must be preceded by a finding that at the moment of commencing the search the material grounds for this activity and the situation of urgency existed, and the search was conducted and documented in accordance with the provisions in force.[185] Otherwise, the competent authority is obliged to issue a decision refusing to approve the search. Such a decision means that the search is ineffective and determines the immediate return of the items seized as a result of this action. The decision of a court or public prosecutor as regards the approval shall be served on the person at the premises of whom the search was carried out, within seven days as of the date of the procedural action, upon request of that person included in the record.

[181] Grochowski (n 180, 1992) 47.

[182] See A Sakowicz, 'Poszanowanie życia prywatnego w postępowaniu karnym' (2000) *Jurysta* no 6, 21.

[183] A Sakowicz, 'Przeszukanie mieszkania a prawa do poszanowania prywatności jednostki. Uwagi na marginesie przepisów Konstytucji RP oraz umów międzynarodowych', in A Michalska-Warias, I Nowikowski and J Piórkowska-Flieger (eds), *Teoretyczne i praktyczne problemy współczesnego prawa karnego. Księga jubileuszowa dedykowana Profesorowi Tadeuszowi Bojarskiemu* (Lublin, 2011) 923.

[184] K Zgryzek, 'Przeszukanie jako czynność procesowa i kryminalistyczna' (1977) *Palestra* no 2, 44; K Łojewski, 'Problematyka rewizji domowej i osobistej w kodeksie postępowania karnego' (1967) *Palestra* no 4, 78.

[185] K Kremens, in P Hofmański, and J Skorupka (eds), *System Prawa Karnego Procesowego*, vol VIII, *Dowody* (Warsaw, 2019) part 3, 3859.

Such a person shall be advised of the right of including such a request in the record (Article 220 § 3 second sentence and third sentence CPC).

A person on whose premises the search is to be conducted shall be notified before the commencement of the search of its objective and summoned to surrender the objects sought (Article 224 § 1 CPC).[186] If as a result of a summons to surrender the objects sought all of them are surrendered, the search shall be abandoned.[187] In such a case, its performance would constitute an unacceptable interference in the sphere of constitutional rights and freedoms of the person to whom the action would be directed, violating the principle of proportionality and the rule of moderation in the use of coercive measures. Adopting a different approach, it may be stated that a summons to surrender the objects sought is an expression – corresponding to the rule of moderation – of recourse to possibilities less invasive for the person with respect to whom the activities aimed at finding the object or suspected person are undertaken. A person on whose premises the search is undertaken has the right to be present at the search, in addition to the person designated for that purpose by the person conducting the search. Furthermore, the search may be attended by a person designated by the occupant of the premises searched, provided that this does not seriously obstruct the search or render it impossible (Article 224 § 2 CPC).[188] The presence of such a person is intended to ensure the validity of the search, also in terms of its conduct in accordance with the standards arising from the constitutional principle of proportionality.[189] In the event that the search is performed in the absence of the owner of the premises, at least one adult member of the household or a neighbour shall be called on to attend the search (Article 224 § 3 CPC). The summoning of a person other than those listed in the cited provision does not invalidate its guarantee purposes if a person not connected with the law-enforcement agency carrying out this activity is selected to attend the search, eg an employee of the company administering the building in which the search was carried out.[190] The procedure for searches of premises and other places is further subject to the following rules:

1. Searches of occupied premises shall be conducted at night only in cases of utmost urgency; night shall be understood as the period from 10 p.m. to 6 a.m. (Article 221 § 1 CPC); a search commenced by day may be continued into the night (Article 221 § 2 CPC). An occupied premises is not only an apartment in a house, but also a hotel room, as well as a caravan or motor home in which someone resides, even temporarily.

[186] Although this solution explicitly refers to a search the purpose of which is to find specific items, by analogy it should be assumed that also in the case of a search with the aim of discovering a suspected person, the person with whom the search is to be conducted should be summoned in order to induce the suspected person to come forward. See Hofmański et al (n 87) vol I, 936.

[187] Hofmański et al (n 87) vol I, 936; Eichstaedt (n 60) vol I, 857.

[188] Incidentally, it is worth noting that in the case of a search that could result in the disclosure of professional secrecy, solicitors and legal advisers are under an obligation to request the participation of a representative of their professional body (§ 20 KEA and Art 18 KERP). This deontological obligation arises not only in the case of a search of a solicitor's or legal adviser's office, but also in the case of a search of a solicitor's or legal adviser's home or other place of employment.

[189] Zagrodnik (n 31) 101.

[190] Appeal Court Judgment in Białystok, 4 May 2015, II Aka 50/15, Lex no 1730145.

2. Premises that are open at night (from 10 p.m. to 6 a.m.) to the public (an unspecified number of people) or that are used to store objects may be searched at the indicated time (Article 221 § 3 CPC).
3. A closed premises or place belonging to a state or local government institution may be searched provided that the manager of such an institution or their deputy, or a relevant body of control is notified of the intended search when it begins and they are admitted to the activity (Article 222 § 1 CPC).
4. A search of military premises shall be conducted only in the presence of the commander-in-chief or a person designated by them (Article 222 § 2 CPC).

Article 225 CPC regulates a special procedure for dealing with writings or other documents found during a search that contain classified information or news covered by professional or other legally protected secrets or of a personal nature. This procedure serves to protect such information and knowledge from disclosure and violation of the related duties of discretion.[191] According to Article 225 § 1 CPC, if the manager of a state or local government institution subject to search or the person from whom objects have been seized, or whose premises are searched, declares that a letter or other document surrendered or discovered during the search contains classified information or information protected by professional secrecy or other legally protected secrecy,[192] or is of a personal nature, the body conducting the search shall immediately transmit such a letter or document in a sealed container without prior reading to the public prosecutor or the court. The obligation to transmit to the said bodies the documents found without reading them also applies to psychiatric records found in the course of a search (Article 225 § 4 in conjunction with Article 225 § 1 CPC). In the light of the cited provision, it seems obvious that the authority executing the search has no right either to examine the content of specific letters or documents or to verify the statement made by the person with whom the search is conducted.[193] An exception in this respect concerns procedural situations in which the public prosecutor is the body executing the search. This results from the power vested in the prosecutor to acquaint him/herself with the content of documents containing information covered by certain types of secrecy, and, for example, to release from the obligation to maintain them, or – as in the case of the general secrecy of solicitor's or legal adviser's secrecy or medical secrecy – to decide to apply to the court for release from secrecy, which would open the way for evidentiary use of certain documents (see Article 180 § 2 CPC).[194] The above procedure for dealing

[191] See further eg M. Całkiewicz, 'Materialne i formalne podstawy prawne przeszukania w kancelarii radcy prawnego', in R. Stankiewicz (ed), *Tajemnica zawodowa radcy prawnego* (Warsaw, Wydawnictwo OBSIL KIRP, 2018) 43–72.

[192] It is worth noting that if a search is conducted at the premises of a solicitor or legal adviser and documents covered by the solicitor's or legal adviser's professional secrecy are found, they are required to make the statement referred to in the cited Art 225 § 1 CPC. This obligation, being a manifestation of the statutory obligation to maintain professional secrecy, finds its normative anchoring in corporate laws (Art 6(1) of the Polish Bar Council Act and Art 3(3) ARP). It also stems from the deontological norms, ordering to take all the measures provided by law for securing solicitor or legal adviser secrecy from disclosure (§ 19(1) KEA and Art 19 KERP). Failure to do so by a solicitor or legal adviser should be considered in terms of disciplinary liability.

[193] See RA Stefański, 'Wykorzystanie dokumentów zawierających tajemnicę państwową, służbową lub zawodową w nowym kodeksie postępowania karnego' (1998) *Prok i Pr* no 5, 114.

[194] See eg Całkiewicz (n 191) 58–60.

with letters and documents in respect of which a statement has been made pursuant to Article 225 § 1 CPC is subject to exception in the cases set out in Article 225 § 2 CPC, where the holder of such documents, and in the case of documents of a personal nature also their author or addressee, is a person suspected of committing an offence. It should be noted in this context that the inclusion of letters or other documents containing classified information or covered by professional secrecy, eg in the collection of documents found in the course of a search or their transmission in a sealed package to the court or prosecutor, does not prejudge their use as evidence in a criminal trial. For this, it is necessary for the competent authority to secure the release of the documents from secrecy, eg the court from the secrecy of solicitor or legal advisor (*argumentum ex* Article 226 CPC).[195] Compared to Article 225 § 1 CPC, a higher standard of protection of secrecy is provided for in Article 225 § 3 CPC with respect to defence counsel secrecy. Under this provision, if a defence counsel or another person of whom it is demanded to surrender objects, or whose premises are searched, declares that letters or other documents discovered in the course of a search relate to circumstances connected with the performance of the function of defence counsel, the body conducting the actions shall leave these documents with such a person without getting acquainted with their contents or appearance. The said declaration is absolutely binding if it comes from the solicitor or legal adviser who is the defence counsel.[196] Verification of the declaration is not possible.[197] The situation is different if the declaration is made by a person other than the defence counsel who is requested to surrender the objects sought or is searched. Such a person may be an employee of a solicitor's or legal adviser's office or a legal trainee who is in possession of certain documents in connection with the preparation of a draft of a pleading.[198] If the declaration of such a person gives rise to doubts, the body conducting the actions shall transmit the documents, in a sealed container, to the court. Having acquainted itself with the documents, the court shall return them in their entirety or in part, in a sealed container, to the person from whom they were taken, or issue a decision on their seizure for the purposes of the proceedings (Article 225 § 3 second sentence CPC). The court decides to return documents primarily when they contain information covered by defence secrecy. Exemption from such secrecy and thus the evidential use of such documents is inadmissible (*argumentum ex* Article 178 § 1 in conjunction with Article 226, first sentence CPC). Documents should also be returned in cases where the court finds that, although they do not contain information covered by defensive secrecy, they are not useful in resolving the case.[199]

In terms of the mode of searching a person and clothes on him/her, Article 223 CPC provides that a search should be conducted, as far as possible, by a person of the same sex as the person searched. This solution serves to protect the person searched

[195] This provision provides that, as regards the use of documents containing classified information or professional secrets as evidence in criminal proceedings, the prohibitions and limitations set forth in Articles 178–181 shall apply accordingly. In an investigation, however, the use of documents covered with medical secrecy as evidence pursuant is decided upon by the public prosecutor.

[196] See further Zagrodnik (n 31) 105.

[197] The only thing that can be checked is whether the declaration comes from a person who is a defence counsel.

[198] Całkiewicz (n 191) 64.

[199] ibid 66.

from excessive embarrassment associated with, for example, having to undress in front of a person of the opposite sex.[200] However, it is not absolute. Performing a search of a person by a person of the other sex may take place in urgent cases, when there is a threat of, for example, distortion of evidence. This guarantee standard does not apply to a search of a person's belongings, such as a purse or bag.

In any case, any search of objects shall be conducted in accordance with the objective of the action, with moderation and within the limits necessary to achieve the objective of those actions, with due diligence and respect for the privacy and dignity of the persons to whom the action relates, and without unnecessary damage or hardship (Article 237 CPC). The search standards established in the cited provision reflect constitutional standards concerning the conditions and limits of interference in the sphere of individual rights and freedoms. Their violation does not entail direct consequences in terms of the effectiveness of the search. However, it may be the subject of a complaint concerning the manner in which this procedural act was carried out.[201]

A record of the search must be drawn up (Article 143 § 1(6) CPC). Specific requirements of the protocol recording the course of this activity include a designation of the case to which the seizure of objects or the search is related, an indication of the precise time of the commencement and completion of the action, a detailed list of the objects seized, and, as necessary, a description of those objects, as well as an indication of the warrant of a court or a public prosecutor. Where no warrant was issued prior to the action, the record shall contain a note stating that the person on whose premises the action was carried out has been advised that a decision concerning the approval of the action shall be served on them upon their request (Article 229 CPC).[202]

A decision concerning a search, that is, a decision to search or a subsequent decision to approve the search, and the manner in which this procedural action was carried out, may be complained against by persons whose rights have been violated. A complaint against a decision issued or an action performed as part of an investigation shall be examined by the district court within whose territorial jurisdiction the investigation is conducted (Article 236 § 1 CPC).[203]

Seizure

The basic regulation for seizure is Article 217 CPC. The seizure is a coercive measure aimed at obtaining for the purposes of a criminal trial objects which may serve as evidence, or be subject to seizure in order to secure financial penalties, criminal measures involving property, forfeiture, compensation measures and claims to redress damage. This measure infringes first of all the right to property, because it leads to depriving the holder of the property of their power over it, also against their will by using coercive elements to overcome their possible resistance (*argumentum ex* Article 217 § 5 CPC). Its core part is the requirement of the person who is in possession

[200] Hofmański et al (n 87) vol I, 935.
[201] ibid 944.
[202] See Judgment of the Appellate Court in Cracow, 31 August 2005, II AKa 16/05, KZS 2005, no 10, pos 28.
[203] Further Eichstaedt (n 60) vol I, 884–86.

of the aforementioned things to surrender them. This allows us to conclude that the material premise of the request is credible information indicating that a certain thing or things are at the disposal of a specific person. This request shall be made by a court or a public prosecutor, and in urgent cases by the police or another authorised body, eg Internal Security Agency or Border Guard (Article 217 § 1 in fine in connection with Article 312 CPC).[204] A formal condition for submitting such a request is, in principle, a decision of a court or prosecutor in this matter.[205] In such a decision, it is necessary to specify the exact purpose of the seizure, the item to which it relates and to identify the person with respect to whom it is to be carried out.[206] If a body other than the court or the public prosecutor requests surrender, it is obliged to present the decision to the person against whom the request is directed. Exceptionally, in urgent cases, e.g. when there is a risk of loss or deformation of evidence, the Police or other authorised body may request surrender of an item without a prior decision of the court or prosecutor on this issue (Article 217 § 1 in fine of the CPC). The authority requiring surrender in such cases is obliged to produce an order of the manager of their unit or an official ID card. The person who surrenders the object has the right to immediately submit an application for a decision of the court or of the public prosecutor relating to the approval of seizure to be drawn up and served on them, and such a person shall be advised of that right. The said application shall be served within fourteen days of the seizure (Article 217 § 4 CPC). In connection with the presented regulation, it is worth emphasising that, unlike a search, the seizure of objects does not require in every case the approval of a subsequent court or a prosecutor's decision. Based on the findings to date, it may be concluded that such an obligation arises when requested by the person who surrenders the object. A decision approving the seizure should be issued within seven days of the seizure of the object. If this does not occur, the object must be returned immediately to the authorised person (Article 230 § 1 CPC).

According to Article 227 CPC, seizing objects shall be conducted in accordance with the objective of the action, with moderation and within the limits necessary to achieve the objective of those actions, with due diligence and respect for the privacy and dignity of the persons to whom the action relates, and without unnecessary damage or hardship.[207] With regard to the procedure for the seizure of property, the rule is that in advance of the possible use of coercive elements, the person holding the property subject to surrender is called upon to release this voluntarily (Article 217 § 2 CPC). Only if the person refuses to surrender the object voluntarily may its seizure be enforced (Article 217 § 5 CPC).[208] In this case, if the request to surrender was not based on a prior decision of the court or the prosecutor, the seizure also requires a subsequent decision of one of these authorities, approving this action. If it is not issued within seven days of the forcible seizure, the surrended objects must be returned immediately to the authorised person (Article 230 § 1 CPC). The decision approving the seizure of an item

[204] ibid 841.
[205] Marszał (n 2) 300.
[206] See J Skorupka, in J Skorupka (ed), *Kodeks postępowania karnego. Komentarz* (Warsaw, CH Beck, 2021) 551–52.
[207] ibid 551.
[208] Hofmański et al (n 87) vol I, 920.

following its forcible seizure shall be delivered to the person from whom the item was seized upon his/her request in the record of seizure (Article 220 § 3 in conjunction with Article 217 § 5, second sentence CPC). It does not seem superfluous to point out that the action of approving the seizure, especially when it is related to its forced execution, cannot be treated mechanically.

The authority approving the seizure is obliged to examine whether this action was justified, whether there was an urgent case justifying the seizure without a prior decision of the court or prosecutor, and whether the seizure was carried out and documented in accordance with the requirements set out in the CPC.[209] As far as the documentation of the seizure of property is concerned, it should be noted that a record is drawn up on the seizure of property (Article 143 § 1(6) CPC), both when the seizure has been effected by way of the voluntary handing over of property and when it has been effected by forcible collection of objects subject to seizure.[210] As in the case of a search, in addition to the general requirements of a record of procedural actions set forth in Article 148 CPC, such a record should include a designation of the case to which the seizure of objects is related, an indication of the precise time of the commencement and completion of the action, a detailed list of the objects seized, and, as necessary, a description of those objects, as well as an indication of the warrant of a court or a public prosecutor. Where no warrant was issued prior to the action, the record shall contain a note stating that the person on whose premises the action was carried out has been advised that a decision concerning the approval of the action shall be served on them upon their request.

A decision concerning a seizure of objects may be complained against by persons whose rights have been violated (Article 236 § 1, first sentence CPC). Such a decision is both a decision on the seizure and on its subsequent approval. A complaint against a decision issued as part of an investigation shall be examined by the district court within whose territorial jurisdiction the investigation is conducted (Article 236 § 1, second sentence CPC).

The conditions and procedures for seizure set out above apply accordingly to the administrator and user of a device containing IT data or of an IT system, in the scope of data stored on that device or in that system, or on a carrier administered or used by such a person, including e-mail correspondence. The administrator is the one who has control of the system. The user is the one who has the right to use the system and derive certain benefits.[211] Bearing in mind the content of the above-cited Article 227 CPC, which requires seizure to be carried out in the least disruptive manner possible, it should be assumed (in conjunction with Article 236a CPC) that if for the purposes of the proceedings it is sufficient and at the same time possible to obtain only computer data, detention should not extend to the carrier of such data.[212]

[209] The presented elements of the assessment of the detention of things before its approval are directly mentioned in a sub-statutory act, namely in § 160 of the Regulation of the Minister of Justice of 7.4.2016 – Rules of internal office of the organisational units of the prosecutor's office (Journal of Laws, item 177, as amended).

[210] Hofmański et al (n 87) vol I, 922.

[211] See further A Lach, 'Gromadzenie dowodów elektronicznych po nowelizacji kodeksu postępowania karnego' (2003) *Prok i Pr* no 10, 20.

[212] See further A Lach, 'Karnoprocesowe instrumenty zwalczania pedofilii i pornografii dziecięcej w Internecie' (2005) *Prok i Pr* no 10, 52–62.

Pursuant to Article 218 CPC, the scope of admissible seizure in criminal proceedings is extended to correspondence and mail as well as data specified in the Telecommunications Law, namely in Article 180c and Article 180d of the Act of 16 July 2004 – Telecommunications Law (Journal of Laws of 2018, item 1954, as amended), where they are of importance for the proceedings under way.[213] The rationale for seizure, indicated at the end, is formulated in an overly general manner, which gives rise to a serious risk of abuse of the coercive measure in question, primarily with regard to data specified in the telecommunication law provisions cited above. A consequence of these provisions is that the seizure may concern retention data, which consist of data necessary to identify the network termination point, the telecommunication terminal equipment, the end-user who initiates the call and the one to whom the call is directed, determination of the date and time of the call and its duration, the type of call (voice call, MMS, audiovisual call, eg Google Meet) and the location of the telecommunication terminal equipment. The discussed regulation of the seizure differs significantly in several points from its basic form, set forth in Article 217 CPC.[214] Firstly, the circle of addressees of a request to surrender correspondence, parcels and certain retention data is limited. These include offices, institutions and entities operating in the field of postal or telecommunications services, customs and tax offices, and transportation institutions and companies. Secondly, in all cases, a request for the surrender of designated items, addressed to the listed entities, must take the form of a court or a prosecutor's decision. This excludes requests such as those made by the police in urgent cases. Thirdly, the surrender takes place to the court or public prosecutor. Only the court or a public prosecutor shall have the right to open them or to order their opening (Article 218 § 1, second sentence CPC). Fourthly, serving of the decision on the addressees and the telephone subscriber or on the sender whose list of calls or other data transmissions was surrendered may be postponed by a specific time, necessary in the context of the interest of the case, but in any case by no longer than until the final conclusion of the proceedings (Article 218 § 2 CPC).

Coercive Medical and Psychological Examination

The issue of admissibility and the conditions for carrying out medical and psychological examinations in the Polish criminal process deserve to be illustrated with regard: (i) to the accused (suspect) and the suspected person, (ii) to the witness, and (iii) to using the examinations for elimination and verification purposes, which will be discussed in more detail below.

The basic provision concerning the issue of compulsory examination in a criminal trial is Article 74 § 2 CPC. This defines the scope and conditions for subjecting the accused to such examinations and taking body samples from him/her, as well as photographing and presenting him/her for identification purposes. This provision also indicates the entities entitled to conduct certain examinations or take certain body

[213] See further Skorupka (n 206) 553–55.
[214] ibid 554–55.

samples from the accused.[215] Under this provision the accused shall be under the obligation to submit themselves to the following examinations:

1. An external examination of their body and other examinations not involving any infringement of bodily integrity. In particular, the fingerprints of the accused may be taken; they may be photographed and presented to other persons in order to establish the identity of the accused.
2. Psychological and psychiatric examinations and to examinations involving certain tests conducted upon their body, except surgical procedures, provided that the examinations are carried out by an authorised healthcare specialist according to the principles of medical knowledge and do not constitute any threat to the health of the accused – provided that such examinations are indispensable. In particular, the accused shall be obliged, in conformity with the aforementioned conditions, to submit to blood, hair and excretory sampling,[216] subject to the provisions of subparagraph (3).
3. A buccal swab test carried out by a police official, provided that this is indispensable and if there is no fear that it could threaten the health of the accused or of other persons.

The presented obligations of the accused, mainly concerning submission to certain tests and collection of body samples, constitute an exception to the *principle nemo se ipsum accusare tenetur*, according to which the accused is under no obligation to submit evidence incriminating them (Article 74 § 1 CPC).[217] In this connection, it should be stressed that their fulfilment does not generally require active action on the part of the accused.[218] Taking a different view, it can be said that the aforementioned obligations of the accused consist mainly of passive submission to the actions of the procedural organ or other competent entity, and thus boil down to not disturbing (*non facere*) and enduring (*pati*) certain discomforts associated with the external examination of the body, other examinations or collection of trace evidence.[219] The most conspicuous examples of deviations from this rule are psychological and psychiatric examinations, the sense of which depends on cooperation on the part of the accused with a psychologist or psychiatrists.[220] In this connection, it should be noted that while it is possible

[215] Grzegorczyk and Tylman (n 1) 330–31.
[216] Such secretions include substances secreted by the human body as a result of metabolism, eg urine, sweat, and substances secreted by glands of the human body, eg bile, sperm. An odour trace does not constitute a secretion of the organism, therefore odour samples are taken from the accused according to the principles set out above in point 1 (Art 74 § 2 (1) CPC). See SN judgment of 12.1.2000, ref no IV CCN 269/99, Lex no 511139.
[217] P Starzyński, in *System Prawa Karnego Procesowego*, P Hofmański (ed), vol 6, *Strony i inni uczestnicy postępowania karnego*, C Kulesza (ed) (Warsaw, Wolters Kluwer, 2016) 796.
[218] Supreme Court Judgment, 21 July 2000, II KKN 108/00, Lex no. 50904.
[219] Starzyński (n 217) 797.
[220] Another example would be phonoscopic examinations and the taking of writing samples. In this connection, it is worth noting that it does not follow from the absence of an obligation on the part of the accused to show activity in obtaining certain evidence that the use in evidence of such material, obtained by the trial authority in the course of the proceedings, can only take place with his/her consent. If the trial authority has in its possession, for example, a voice recording or a handwritten letter made by the accused, there is nothing to prevent its use even if the accused has refused to record a voice sample or to submit a sample letter. It is irrelevant when such comparative evidence was created – before or after the refusal to record the voice or

to force the accused to undergo these examinations, as will be discussed below,[221] it is not possible to compel him/her to be active during them, eg to engage in conversation, answer questions or fill in questionnaires or tests, mainly because of the guarantee *nemo se ipsum accusare tenetur*.[222] The exceptional character of the obligations set out in Article 74 § 2 CPC, which appears against the background of this guarantee, determines that their list should be considered exhaustive.[223] A different view would make this guarantee largely illusory.

Some of the listed obligations are also incumbent on the suspected person. This person has the obligation to submit themselves to an external examination of their body and other examinations not involving any infringement of bodily integrity. The fingerprints of the suspected persons may be taken. They may be photographed and presented to other persons in order to establish the identity of the accused. Moreover, in conformity with the conditions referred to in points 2 and 3, their blood, hair samples, buccal swabs or excretory samples may also be taken (Article 74 § 3 CPC).[224]

The obligations of the accused and the suspected person as provided for in Article 74 §§ 2 and 3, respectively, of the CPC are an integral part of the corresponding evidentiary procedural actions, which usually lead to obtaining evidence in the form of an expert opinion. For example, a cheek swab taken by an officer gives rise to a DNA analysis. However, the result of this analysis does not constitute evidence in itself. Evidence in the present case is the opinion of an expert, who was appointed by the trial authority pursuant to Article 192 § 1 CPC to carry out the test.[225] Coercion is not a necessary ingredient of the fulfilment of the analysed procedural obligations. The accused (*sensu largo* of course) or the suspected person shall be summoned to submit themselves to these obligations (Article 74 § 3a, first sentence CPC).[226] They may be encouraged or verbally persuaded to do so. If the accused or the suspected person refuses to submit themselves to these obligations, they may be taken and brought compulsorily, and physical force or technical measures to overpower them may be used to the extent necessary to carry out a given action (Article 74 § 3a, second sentence CPC). The use of this force or measures should be viewed in terms of *ultima ratio*.[227]

The rule is that if necessary for the purposes related to evidence, a consenting witness may be submitted to an examination of their body and to medical or psychological examination (Article 192 § 4 CPC).[228] This is closely related to the assumption that a witness should not suffer any inconvenience beyond that which is strictly connected

handwriting sample – as well as whether the accused was aware that his/her statement would be recorded. See judgment of the Supreme Court of 21.7.2000, II CCN 108/00, Lex no 50904. See also Judgment of the Appellate Court in Katowice, 29 November 2018, II Aka 171/18, Lex no 2690783.

[221] Supreme Court Judgment, 9 January 2001, V KKN 461/00, Lex no 50912; Supreme Court Judgment, 21 July 2000, II KKN 108/00, Lex no 50904.

[222] A Gaberle, *Dowody w sądowym procesie karnym. Teoria i praktyka* (Warsaw, Publisher, 2010) 157. See also Supreme Court Judgment, 9 January 2001, 4, V CCN 461/00, Lex no 50912.

[223] Starzyński (n 217) 796.

[224] See further E Kowalewska-Borys, in *System Prawa Karnego Procesowego* (n 217) 717–18.

[225] See eg W Achrem, P Wolańska-Nowak and I Sołtyszewski, 'Opinia biegłego z zakresu badań genetycznych' (2015) *Prok i Pr* no 10, 142 et seq.

[226] Skorupka (n 206) 234.

[227] See ibid; Eichstaedt (n 60) vol I, 403.

[228] See Judgment of the Appellate Court in Łódź, 14 June 2016, II AKa 97/16, Lex no 2080323.

with giving testimony in a criminal procedure.[229] There are two exceptions to this rule. The first relates to cases in which the witness is also the victim of a crime. In that case, if criminal liability for an act depends on his/her health condition, the latter shall not refuse an examination of their body or a medical examination, provided that no surgical procedure or observation at a healthcare institution is involved (Article 192 § 1 CPC). This applies, for example, to acts that include bodily harm as one of their constituent elements. It also applies to acts in the case of which an examination may make it possible to establish whether a specific event has taken place at all, eg rape.[230] The second exception is provided for in Article 192 § 2 CPC, according to which, if there is any doubt as to the witness's mental condition, their cognitive skills, or ability to perceive or recollect perceived things, the court or the public prosecutor may order that such a witness be examined with the participation of a medical expert or an expert psychologist, and the witness may not refuse this. The doubt indicated must be real and supported by facts arising from specific procedure or factual situations.[231] For example, it may be necessary to question a witness with the participation of an expert psychologist if there are doubts about his or her ability to perceive or reproduce events, such as when a witness states that due to a head injury he or she suffers from memory lapses and is unable to fully recount the course of events he or she participated in or observed.[232] The above exceptions do not apply to persons who refuse to testify due to being very close relatives, by blood or affinity, of the accused (Article 182 §§ 1 and 2 CPC) or are exempted from the obligation to testify due to their particularly close relationship with the accused (Article 185 CPC). Obviously, pursuant to the wording of Article 192 § 4 CPC, there are no obstacles to a person who refuses to testify agreeing to undergo an examination and a medical or psychological examination.

A broad – in terms of subjects and objects – possibility of conducting examinations, or strictly speaking, taking certain body samples, is provided for in Article 192a CPC. This provision provides the legal basis for so-called screening (elimination) examinations,[233] sometimes referred to as 'trawling',[234] and so-called verification examinations. The former serve the purpose of narrowing down the circle of suspected persons in cases where it is very broadly, because out-of-process information and evidence obtained in the case give rise to very general conclusions, eg that the perpetrator of the crime may be a person between eighteen and forty-five years of age, living or residing in a certain area, exhibiting certain features, eg a handsome face, stocky build and average height. Sometimes it is a matter of 'fishing out' the perpetrator by means of these tests from among several or several thousand potential suspected persons.[235] Verification examinations aim at eliminating those from among the revealed and secured traces, which have no connection with the crime that is the subject of the ongoing criminal proceedings.

[229] Marszał (n 2) 400.
[230] Supreme Court Decision, 10 December 2010, II KK 238/11, Lex no 1084719.
[231] Appeal Court Judgment in Cracow, 27 May 1999, II Aka 80/99, *Prok i Pr*, no 11–12, poz 24.
[232] See eg Supreme Court Judgment, 23 November 1984, Rw 445/84, OSNKW 1985, nos 5–6, pos 43; Supreme Court Decision, 28 April 2015, II KK 89/15, Lex no 1682543.
[233] Supreme Court Decision, 18 October 2017, II KK 280/17, Lex no 2407824.
[234] I Sołtyszewski, K Krassowski and E. Gruza, 'Możliwości wykorzystania badań przesiewowych w praktyce śledczej' (2012) *Prok i Pr* no 12, 136.
[235] ibid 136–37.

According to the content of the cited provision, in order to limit a group of suspected persons in number or to determine the evidentiary value of discovered traces, fingerprint data, buccal swabs, hair, saliva, handwriting samples and smell samples may be collected, or a photograph of a person may be taken, or their voice recorded. After being used in the case for the purposes of which the material was collected or recorded, the collected or recorded material that is no longer needed in the proceedings shall be immediately removed from the files and destroyed. Material redundant to the proceedings shall include, in particular, material that has no relation to the subject matter of the case, those parts of the collected material which originate from persons who, according to the research, were mistakenly included in the circle of suspected persons or persons with regard to whom there were no precise suspicions, but subjecting them to the screening procedure was justified by the need to narrow the circle of such persons, as well as material obtained, for example, through the use of hypnosis or chemical agents.[236] However, even if the material used for screening tests was not considered redundant to the case, it cannot be transformed, along with the initiation of proceedings against a specific person, into evidence and used as a basis for the factual findings of the judgment. In order to obtain such evidence, connected with the taking of traces of the offence specified in Article 192a CPC, it is necessary to conduct examinations in respect of the accused on the basis and under the conditions specified in Article 74 § 2 CPC, cited above.[237]

For the purposes specified above, ie an order to limit a group of suspected person's in number or determine the evidentiary value of discovered traces, upon consent of the person subject to examination, an expert witness may also use technical measures aimed at checking unconscious responses of that person (Article 192a § 2 CPC). A polygraph (lie detector) is such a measure. It can only be used as part of a general questioning of persons belonging to, for example, a wide range of suspected persons selected on the basis of certain general characteristics.[238] Therefore, it cannot be used during a formal questioning of a person having a procedural status of a witness or suspect.[239] The required consent for polygraphic examination must be given explicitly to the expert conducting this activity.[240] Such an expert, however, does not constitute an evidentiary source within the meaning of the rules of evidence, but acts as an expert qualified in the use of the polygraph.[241] He does not produce an opinion from this activity which could be used as evidence in the course of further criminal proceedings against a particular person.[242] Looking from a different perspective, it can be said that the importance of the polygraph examination and the role of the expert who conducts it are limited to the screening or verification tasks that these examinations serve.

[236] Supreme Court Judgment, 20 January 2010, IV CC 364/09, Lex no 560612; Supreme Court Judgment, 9 February 2010, II CC 198/09, OSNKW 2010, no 5, pos 47.

[237] See Supreme Court Decision, 9 February 2010, II KK 198/09, OSNKW 2010, no 5, pos 47.

[238] Supreme Court Decision, 12 June 2014, WO 2/14, Lex no 1476977; Supreme Court Decision, 18 October 2017, II KK 280/17, Lex no 2407824.

[239] Judgment of the Appellate Court in Białystok, 25 Febrauary 2014, II AKa 28/14, Lex no 1438984.

[240] Judgment of the Appellate Court in Lublin, 9 September 2014, II AKa 154/14, Lex no 1515269. See also Hofmański et al (n 87) vol I, 823.

[241] Hofmański et al (n 87) vol I, 823.

[242] Judgment of the Appellate Court in Wrocław, 19 October 2015, II AKa 204/16, Lex no 2484973; see also Supreme Court Decision, 18 October 2017, II KK 280/17, Lex no 2407824.

Surveillance and Recording of Conversations

Modern criminal procedure faces the challenge of combating crimes that take increasingly sophisticated and complex forms, often involving the use of technological advances. Criminal procedural law must therefore provide for measures to meet these challenges that are appropriate to the modern technology used to commit the crime.[243] Such measures include the surveillance and recording of conversations, which are intergral components of wiretapping (*podsłuchu*), which is an important tool for collecting and detecting evidence. Wiretapping is also an important tool for preventing and combating crime, especially that which takes organised form or involves the commission of serious crimes.[244] Thus, its use certainly serves to ensure public security and order. At the same time, wiretapping is one of the most controversial methods of obtaining evidence[245] because it is a drastic infringement of civil liberties and a profound interference in the constitutionally protected freedom of communication and related secrecy (Article 47 of the Constitution of the Republic of Poland) and the right to privacy (Article 47 of the Constitution of the Republic of Poland).[246] For this reason, the subjective and above all objective limits of wiretapping, apart from the fact that they should be defined particularly precisely by law, should also be formulated in a restrictive way,[247] limiting the use of this measure to cases where it is justified by the need to obtain evidence significant from the point of view of ongoing proceedings for a serious crime or from the perspective of preventing the commission of such a crime. In the CPC, these limits are defined in relation to the so-called procedural wiretapping (procedural surveillance and recording of conversations), which can only be applied within the framework of ongoing criminal proceedings.[248] Further detailed comments are devoted to this subject. It should be noted, however, that the Polish law also provides for so-called out-of-process (operational) wiretapping (out-of-process surveillance and recording of conversations), which is one of the forms of operational control and is regulated in police acts.[249] This control takes place within the framework of operational and exploratory activities.[250]

[243] Eichstaedt (n 60) vol I, 890.

[244] Hofmański et al (n 87) vol I, 961.

[245] K Dudka, 'Kontrola i utrwalanie rozmów telefonicznych w projekcie kodeksu postępowania karnego z 1991 r' (1994) *Przegląd Sądowy* nos 7–8, 127.

[246] See further I Dyś, 'Dopuszczalność dowodu z podsłuchu w postępowaniu karnym w świetle konstytucyjnej wolności i ochrony tajemnicy komunikowania się; (2016) *Przegląd Prawa Konstytucyjnego* no 1, 81 et seq; Eichstaedt (n 60) vol I, 891.

[247] Noteworthy is the accurate statement of the Supreme Court that even a great public interest cannot justify violation of regulations governing the search for and obtaining of evidence from (telephone) wiretapping; see Judgment of the Supreme Court of 24.10.2000, WA 37/00, Lex no 332949.

[248] M Rogalski, 'Kontrola i utrwalanie rozmów w procesie karnym' (2017) *Prok i Pr* no 6, 5–6.

[249] These are laws regulating the activities of the Police Service, the Internal Security Agency, the Central Anti-Corruption Bureau, the National Fiscal Administration, the Border Guard, the Military Police, the Military Intelligence Service, the Military Counterintelligence Service and the State Protection Service.

[250] They can be conducted before proceedings are instituted as well as during them, as they are subordinated both to such goals that are connected with the pre-frontline of a criminal procedure (prevention and detection of crimes), and to those that also concern pending proceedings (identification of perpetrators, obtaining and recording of evidence). On the example of the police, it can be noted that operational control, including out-of-process wiretapping, can be a tool for achieving the indicated goals in cases of the most serious crimes, enumerated in the law, if other measures have proved to be ineffective or will be useless for achieving these goals. The ordering of an operational control is decided by a regional court in the form of a

The core of the regulation of procedural wiretapping in Chapter 26 CPC are the provisions on control and recording of telephone conversations (telephone eavesdropping) conducted with the use of telecommunication networks.[251] Under Article 241 CPC these provisions shall apply respectively to the surveillance and recording, by technical means, of the content of other conversation or information transmissions, including e-mail correspondence. This means that the admissibility of the surveillance and recording of conversations shall be extended to all conversations other than telephone conversations conducted over a telecommunications network, regardless of where and how they are conducted (at work, at home, in the open air, in a shopping centre or on means of transport).[252] In addition, the provisions on procedural wiretapping apply to the control and recording of communications other than by telephone (eg via the internet or radio).[253]

Surveillance and recording of conversations are ordered by the court in the form of a decision (Article 237 § 1 CPC). In this decision the court makes the wiretapping more specific by specifying its object and subject boundaries.[254] In pre-trial proceedings, the court grants prior permission for the application of procedural surveillance and recording of conversations upon a motion of the public prosecutor.[255] Such a motion should specify the purpose of the use of this coercive measure, the crime in connection with which it is to be used and the subject who is to be wiretapped.[256] It must contain a justification. As an exception, in cases of utmost urgency,[257] the surveillance and recording of conversations may be ordered by the public prosecutor who shall be obliged, however, to file with the court a motion for approval of the decision within three days (Article 237 § 2, second sentence CPC). The court's permission in this case is subsequent to the wiretapping activity. Its granting, in the form of a decision, in fact means the legalisation of the wiretapping ordered by the prosecutor. In order to issue such a decision, it is necessary for the court to determine, first, that there was an urgent case justifying the prosecutor's wiretapping order, and, second, that the conditions for the application of this coercive measure were fulfilled, which will be discussed further

decision on a written motion of the Chief Commander of the Police, Commander of the Central Bureau of Investigation, Commander of the Police Internal Affairs Bureau or Commander of the Central Bureau for Combating Cybercrime, submitted after obtaining a written consent of the regional prosecutor competent for the seat of the requesting police authority (Art 19(1) of the Police Act). If it is necessary to order operational control against a suspected or accused person, the application for ordering operational control shall include information on the proceedings pending against that person (Art 19(5) of the Police Act). In urgent cases, where this could result in the loss of information or the obliteration or destruction of evidence of an offence, one of the above-mentioned Chief Constables or the relevant regional Police Chief may order, after obtaining the written consent of the competent regional prosecutor, an operational control, at the same time applying to the locally competent regional court for a decision in this matter. If the court does not give its consent within five days from the date of ordering the operational control, the authority in charge suspends the operational control and destroys, by means of a protocol, the materials collected during its use (Art 19 (3) of the Police Act).

[251] Sz Stypuła, 'Podsłuch procesowy na gruncie znowelizowanego kodeksu postępowania karnego' (2012) *Palestra* nos. 7–8, 91 et seq.

[252] Waltoś and Hofmański (n 7) 383.

[253] Hofmański et al (n 87) vol I, 976.

[254] Supreme Court Judgment, 3 December 2008, V KK 195/08, Lex no 482213.

[255] See Supreme Court Decision, 25 March 2010, I KZP 2/10, Lex no 564518.

[256] Hofmański et al (n 87) vol I, 967.

[257] See Decision of the Appellate Court in Cracow, 5 February 2009, II AKz 6/09, Lex no 500219.

below.[258] The verification of a 'case of utmost urgency' requires reference to the purpose of the wiretapping and consequently examining whether achieving this would realistically be jeopardised by postponing the application of this measure until a prior decision on the matter has been issued by the court.[259] In the analysed, exceptional, procedural configuration the court shall issue a decision on the motion for approval of the public prosecutor's decision within five days in a session without participation of the parties (Article 237 § 2, second sentence CPC). The failure of the court to meet this time limit and to grant subsequent approval after the deadline has passed does not delegitimise the surveillance and recording of the conversations themselves.[260] However, should a decision of the public prosecutor not be approved, the court, in its decision on the motion, shall order that all recorded contents be destroyed. A contestation of the decision suspends its execution (Article 237 § 2, third and fourth sentences CPC).[261]

By placing emphasis on the definition in Article 237 § 1 CPC it may be stated that the ordering of the wiretapping is based on the conviction of the authority applying this measure that it will lead to the detection and obtaining of evidence for the ongoing proceedings in a case for an offence falling within the material scope of permissible wiretapping (evidential purpose) or to prevent the commission of a new offence (preventive purpose), belonging to this material scope, about which there is a reasonable fear of its commission (*argumentum ex* Article 237 § 3 in principio CPC). Additionally, taking into account the content of Article 237 § 3a CPC, it should be recognised that the rationale for procedural surveillance and recording of conversations is also the belief that this will make it possible to disclose property threatened with forfeiture as provided in Article 45 § 2 of the Penal Code and Article 33 § 2 of the Fiscal Penal Code.[262] The object (material) scope of procedural wiretapping includes crimes belonging to the catalogue specified in Article 237 § 3 CPC.[263] It is essentially composed of crimes of

[258] Hofmański et al (n 87) vol I, 969.
[259] See eg Decision of the Appellate Court in Cracow, 5 February 2009, II AKz 6/09, Lex no 500219.
[260] Supreme Court Judgment, 3 December 2008, V CC 195/08, OSNKW 2009, no 2, pos 17.
[261] Further Stypuła (n 251) 93.
[262] Similarly Eichstaedt (n 60) vol I, 892.
[263] This catalogue consists of the following types of offences

1) homicide;
2) causing a danger to the public or causing a catastrophe;
3) human trafficking;
4) abduction of a person;
5) ransom extortion
6) hijacking of an aircraft or ship;
7) robbery, robbery with violence, or extortion by force;
8) attempt against the sovereignty or independence of the State;
9) attempt against the consitutionl order of the State or against its supreme bodies, or against a unit of the armed forces of the Republic of Poland;
10) espionage or disclosure of classified information with the clause 'secret' or 'top secret';
11) amassing weapons, explosives or radioactive materials;
12) counterfeiting and circulating counterfeit monies, payment means or instruments, or tradable documents entitling to receive a cash amount, commodity, cargo, or in-kind prize, or tradable documents providing for an obligation of capital contribution, contribution of interest, share in profits or statement of interest in a company;
12a) the forgery or modification of invoices or the use of invoices forged or modified within the scope of factual circumstances that might influence the determination of the amount of the public-law liabilities or their refund, or the refund of other tax liabilities, and the issuance and use of invoices

high gravity,[264] which are often committed in the realm of organised crime. Although this catalogue is quite extensive, perhaps too extensive insofar as it extends to crimes against the administration of justice (Article 237 § 3 16a–16g CPC), it has the advantage of being a *numerus clausus*.[265] This provides citizens with a guarantee[266] (see, however, further comments on Article 237a CPC) that the use of wiretapping against them may take place only in cases of clearly defined crimes; as a rule, those that are marked by considerable gravity and social harmfulness.[267]

The personal scope of procedural wiretapping is defined in Article 237 § 4 CPC. According to this provision, this measure shall be permitted with regard to a suspected person, the accused, and with regard to the injured or another person whom the accused may contact or who might be connected with the perpetrator or with an imminent criminal offence. The person with respect to whom a procedural surveillance and recording of conversations is applied should be clearly identified in the decision to order the wiretapping.[268] This does not mean that only the telephone or other device belonging to that person may be wiretapped. The wiretap applied to him/her may concern an official telephone or a telephone of a third party not connected with the proceedings, if

certifying false information concerning factual circumstances that might influence the determination of the amount of the public liabilities or their refund, or the refund of other tax liabilities;
13) manufacturing, processing, trading, and smuggling dugs, precursors, substitutes, and psychotropic substances;
14) organised crime group;
15) property of significant value
16) use of violence or unlawful threats in connection with criminal proceedings;
16a) giving false testimony and the presentation of a false opinion, expert opinion or translation by an expert witness, qualified expert, or translator;
16b) a false accusation of a criminal offence, fiscal offence, or fiscal delinquency against another person;
16c) producing false evidence or taking other deceptive actions directing prosecution for a crime, fiscal offence, or fiscal delinquency against another person, or taking such actions in the course of the proceedings;
16d) concealing evidence demonstrating the innocence of a person suspected of committing a criminal offence, fiscal offence, or fiscal delinquency;
16e) notifying a prosecution body of a criminal offence or fiscal offence that has not been committed;
16f) acting as an accessory after the fact;
16g) failure to report a criminal offence;
17) bribery and influence peddling;
18) procurement or facilitation of prostitution;
19) criminal offences defined in Chapter XVI of the Actof 6 June 1997 –- the Criminal Code (Journal of Law of 2020, items 1444 and 1517), as well as in Articles 5– to 8 of the Roe Statute of the International Criminal Court, drawn up in Rome on 17 July 1998 (Jou of of 2003, item 708 and of 2018, item 1753), hereinafter referred to as "'Rome Statute'".

[264] Hofmański et al (n 87) vol I, 969.

[265] Grzegorczyk and Tylman (n 1) 550.

[266] Decision of the Appellate Court in Katowice, 24 November 2014, II AKa 363/17, Lex no 2461354.

[267] In determining whether an offence in connection with which criminal proceedings are pending belongs to the catalogue specified in Art 237 § 3 CPC, the court deciding on the application of procedural wiretapping is guided primarily by the legal qualification adopted – depending on the stage of proceedings – in the decision to initiate criminal proceedings, the decision to present charges, or possibly in the indictment. This qualification is not binding on the court. The court is not only entitled but also obliged to independently verify whether a specific act, as it results from the evidence gathered, meets the criteria of one of the 'catalogue offences' specified in the cited provision. In cases in which a procedural wiretap is dictated by the fear of committing a new crime, belonging to the 'catalogue offences', the key is the evidence on the basis of which this fear finds factual justification.

[268] Supreme Court Judgment, 3 December 2008, V KK 195/08, Lex no 482213.

there are reasons to believe that it will be used by the person against whom the wiretap was ordered.[269]

A serious and dangerous breach in the scope of permissible procedural surveillance and recording of conversations is provided for in Article 237a CPC. According to this provision where, as a result of an inspection, evidence has been obtained that a person against whom the inspection has been applied has committed a criminal offence prosecuted ex officio or a fiscal offence other than the criminal offence covered by the inspection order or that a person not covered by the inspection order has committed a criminal offence prosecuted ex officio or a fiscal offence, the public prosecutor shall take a decision as to the use of such evidence in the criminal proceedings. This provision raises significant concerns,[270] not only because it allows the possibility of evidentiary use of evidence obtained as a result of a procedural surveillance and recording of conversations within a broader scope (in terms of subject or object) than that resulting from the court's decision to apply this coercive measure, but also because the use of this possibility is decided by the prosecutor, which means that on the basis of the decision of a non-judicial body there is an actual expansion of the evidentiary use of the material resulting from the procedural wiretapping compared to that established in the court decision ordering the procedural surveillance and recording of conversations.[271] The fundamental interpretative doubt under the cited provision is whether it authorises the prosecutor to use material obtained by means of procedural wiretapping in cases of offences not found in the catalogue of offences set out in Article 237 § 3 CPC. The linguistic interpretation of this provision in principle leads unambiguously to an affirmative answer to this question.[272] However, it would be difficult to accept such a result of interpretation from the perspective of the protection of the constitutional right to secrecy of communication (Article 49 of the Constitution of the Republic of Poland) and the right to privacy (Article 47 of the Constitution of the Republic of Poland), whose essential guarantee is – as noted earlier – the *numerus clausus* of offences to which procedural surveillance and recording of conversations may relate.[273] Therefore, one should opt for a pro-constitutional and pro-guarantee interpretation of Article 237a CPC and thus exclude the possibility of the prosecutor deciding on the evidentiary use of the material obtained as a result of procedural wiretapping with respect to offences other than the 'catalogue offences' defined in Article 237 § 3 CPC.[274] This does not dispel all doubts that arise against the background of Article 237a CPC. It requires the intervention of the legislator and restoration of the previous provision in the Act giving the court permission for evidential use of the material obtained as a result of procedural wiretapping concerning a catalogue offence, but other than

[269] See K Eichstaedt, in D Świecki (eds), *Kodeks postępowania karnego. Komentarz* (Warsaw, Publisher, 2018) vol I, s 864.

[270] J Machlańska, 'Procesowe wykorzystanie podsłuchu w nowelizacji Kodeksu postępowania karnego oraz niektórych innych ustaw z dnia 11 marca 2016 r. w świetle prawa do obrony' (2016) XXV(4) *Studia Iuridica Lublinensia* 134 et seq; Eichstaedt (n 60) vol I, 901.

[271] Machlańska (n 270) 134.

[272] Similarly ibid 134.

[273] Decision of the Appellate Court in Katowice, 24 November 2014, II AKa 363/17, Lex no 2461354.

[274] M Błoński, in D Świecki (ed), *Meritum. Postępowanie karne* (Warsaw, Wolters Kluwer, 2019) 635; Decision of the Appellate Court in Katowice, 24 November 2014, II AKa 363/17, Lex no 2461354.

the one specified in the decision on the application of wiretapping or committed by a person other than the one specified in this decision.

The use of procedural wiretapping is temporally limited. The surveillance and recording of telephone conversations may be carried out for a period not exceeding three months, with a possibility of extension, in particularly justified cases, for a period no longer than a further three months (Article 238 § 1 CPC). 'Particularly justified case' is a vague phrase, which may lead in the practice of applying the law, on the one hand, to unjustified differentiation of the situation of the subjects subject to wiretapping, and, on the other hand, to abuse of the possibility of extending the application of this measure. It is sometimes assumed that the condition for prolonging the use of procedural surveillance and recording of conversations is fulfilled when the case concerns a crime of high gravity.[275] This position is not fully convincing if we consider that the application of procedural surveillance and recording of conversations generally concern serious crimes. Thus, the proposed criterion does not allow for a clear distinction between those cases in which the procedural wiretap is applied within the basic term and those in which its application may exceptionally be extended for another three months.

The general indication that the phrase 'particularly justified case' cannot be freely extended,[276] although useful in the practice of law enforcement, does not lead to its clarification. Above all, it does not allow citizens to see the circumstances in which the procedural authorities are entitled to use such a measure as wiretapping, which deeply interferes with their fundamental rights and freedoms.[277] Therefore, it seems necessary *de lege ferenda* to concretise the grounds for prolongation of the procedural surveillance and recording of conversations, eg by assuming that it is the disclosure of new, significant circumstances in the case that justify the advisability of further application of the coercive measure in question. In addition to the temporal limitation, procedural wiretapping is limited by the circumstances determining its purposefulness and the permissible scope of its application (Article 238 § 2 in conjunction with Article 237 §§ 1–3 CPC). Thus, if, for example, the need to prevent the commission of a specific 'catalogue offence' ceases to exist or it is revealed that the act subject to investigation should be qualified on the basis of a different provision typifying an offence which does not belong to the 'catalogue offences', the procedural surveillance and recording of conversations should be terminated immediately.

The decision on ordering the surveillance and recording of conversations (procedural wiretapping) must be delivered to the person against whom this measure is applied, because he/she has the right to lodge a complaint against this decision (*argumentum ex* Article 100 § 4 in conjunction with Article 240 CPC). It is also obvious that an immediate announcement (delivery) of this decision to the indicated person could frustrate the achievement of the objectives that the procedural interception is intended to achieve.[278] Therefore, it is possible to adjourn the announcement of the decision to control and record conversations for the time necessary in the interest of the

[275] Hofmański et al (n 87) vol I, 972.
[276] Supreme Court Judgment, 19 January 2011, WZ 53/10, OSN 2011, no 3, pos 28.
[277] Constitutional Court Judgment, 30 July 1998, *Valenzuela Contreras against Spain*, 27671/95, Lex no 78163.
[278] Hofmański et al (n 87) vol I, 973.

case (Article 239 § 1 CPC). In the case of procedural wiretapping applied in pre-trial proceedings, the announcement of the decision to order the surveillance and recording of conversations may be adjourned no further than until the investigation is completed (Article 239 § 2 CPC). As already indicated, a decision regarding the surveillance and recording of telephone conversations may be contested. In their complaint, a person to whom such a decision relates may demand that the validity and legality of the surveillance and recording of telephone conversations be controlled (Article 240, first and second sentences CPC). Decisions to apply to prolong the application or approve the prosecutor's decision to apply a procedural wiretap, and decisions to refuse to apply to prolong or approve the prosecutor's decision are both subject to appeal.[279] Review of these decisions from the perspective of legitimacy requires verification of the necessity and advisability of the application of a procedural wiretap. The review by the prism of legality focuses on the assessment of the compliance of the decision on procedural wiretapping with the applicable law.[280] The complaint against a decision of a public prosecutor is considered by the court (Article 240, third sentence CPC).

Offices, institutions and entities carrying out telecommunications activities or a telecommunications operator within the meaning of the Act of 16 July 2004 – the Telecommunications Law – shall be obliged to facilitate the execution of a decision of the court or public prosecutor regarding the surveillance of telephone conversations, and to ensure that the conduct of such a surveillance is registered (Article 237 § 5 CPC). The legal-organisational form in which the listed entities conduct their communications activities is irrelevant. It is also irrelevant whether they are state or private entities.[281] According to Article 237 § 6 CPC only the court and a public prosecutor shall be entitled to play the recordings, and in cases of utmost urgency, the police with the approval of the court or public prosecutor. This subjective restriction is intended to protect the persons against whom the wiretap is applied. The recording of their conversations, in addition to information of evidentiary value for the ongoing proceedings, will generally contain a large amount of information related to the private life of the wiretapped person, which remains irrelevant in the criminal procedural aspect. The purpose of the presented statutory solution is to provide access to such information, and thus an insight into the privacy of the wiretapped person, to a maximally narrow circle of subjects.[282] It is obligatory to draw up a record of the playback of recorded conversations (Article 143 § 1, point 7 CPC). The right to acquaint oneself with the register of telephone conversation surveillance is also reserved for the court and prosecutor in preparatory proceedings (Article 237 § 7 CPC).

According to Article 238 § 3 CPC, if the entire recordings recorded as a result of wiretapping are not relevant to the proceedings, the prosecutor shall, upon completion of the inspection, apply to the court to order the destruction of all such recordings. The court shall issue a decision on the motion without delay, in a session without

[279] M Rogalski, (in:) System Prawa Karnego Procesowego, red. P. Hofmański, t. 8, cz. 3, Dowody, J.Skorupka (ed.), Warsaw 2019, Wolters Kluwer, p. 4051.

[280] Hofmański et al (n 87) vol I, postępowania karnego. Komentarz, Warsaw 2004, t. I, p. 975.

[281] M Rogalski, in *System Prawa Karnego Procesowego*, P Hofmański (ed), vol 8, cz 3, *Dowody*, red J Skorupka (Warsaw, Wolters Kluwer, 2019) 4008.

[282] ibid 4013–14.

participation of the parties. After the investigation is completed, the public prosecutor shall file a motion ordering the destruction of the recordings in whole or in the part of no relevance to the criminal proceedings in which the surveillance and recording of telephone conversations have been ordered; they shall not constitute the evidence referred to in Article 237a. The court shall issue a decision on the motion in a session that may be attended by the parties (Article 238 § 4 CPC). In addition to the situations outlined above in which the prosecutor is obliged to request the destruction of records of recorded conversations (in whole or in part), a right is provided for the person against whom the wiretapping is applied to file such a request (Article 238 § 5, first sentence CPC). This right is an important guarantee as it gives the entitled person the opportunity to take an initiative aimed at destroying recorded recordings that violate his/her privacy and may expose him/her to disgrace or humiliation in public opinion, or even rejection in a particular professional or social environment. It may be used no earlier than after the investigation is completed. The court shall issue a decision on the motion in a session that may be attended by the person who filed the motion (Article 238 § 5, second sentence CPC).[283]

[283] See further Skorupka (n 206) 588–89.

5

Pre-trial Investigation

Pre-trial Investigation Model

Based on the findings made in chapter two, it may be stated that the importance and model shape of pre-trial proceedings is determined by the system of relations (interaction) occurring between the proceedings at this stage and the court proceedings.[1] While a judicial trial is undoubtedly the culmination of a criminal proceedings in terms of resolving the case due to the fact that it is there that the substantive decision on the subject of the trial is made, in terms of explanation of the circumstances of the case the model of the criminal proceedings is subordinated to the concept assuming the supremacy of preparatory proceedings (investigation) over the judicial trial.[2] The supremacy of the pre-trial proceedings over the trial in terms of clarifying the case is fully understandable in the case of the consensual model of trial, in which the judgment is delivered at a session, in a sense replacing the main hearing, without examining evidence, and thus based on the evidence gathered in the pre-trial proceedings. In cases that come up for examination at the main trial, it should be assessed critically, as has already been mentioned. One of the basic manifestations of this supremacy with respect to the main trial is the enormous influence of the evidence taken at the first trial stage on the determination of the case in this forum, resulting from the wide-ranging possibility of using this evidence as the basis for the judgment issued at trial.[3] These few observations, reiterated in a slightly different context, allow us to note that, in the current legal state, the clarification of the case in the pre-trial proceedings largely determines the judicial trial in the Polish criminal trial, either by providing, in principle in its entirety, the evidentiary basis for the judgment in the consensual model of trial (at the sentencing session) or by significantly influencing the shaping of this basis and delineating the direction of the evidentiary proceedings in cases heard at the main trial. Adopting a different point of view, we can say that preparatory proceedings go far beyond mere preparation of a case so that it can be examined (explained) by the court, as it comes to gathering

[1] J Zagrodnik, *Model interakcji postępowania przygotowawczego oraz postępowania głównego w procesie karnym* (Warsaw, Wolters Kluwer, 2013) 108–19.

[2] See L Schaff, *Zakres i formy postępowania przygotowawczego* (Warsaw, Państwowe Wydawnictwo Naukowe, 1961) 128 et seq. See also T Grzegorczyk and J Tylman, *Polskie postępowanie karne* (Warsaw, LexisNexis, 2014) 619–21; S Waltoś and P Hofmański, *Proces karny. Zarys systemu* (Warsaw, Wolters Kluwer, 2016) 489–90, S Waltoś, *Model postępowania przygotowawczego na tle prawnoporównawczym* (Warsaw, Państwowe Wydawnictwo Naukowe, 1968) passim.

[3] Schaff (n 2) 86 et seq.

evidence that serves the court's authority to decide the case.[4] In these procedural realities, it is important to ensure the right of defence of the person against whom the criminal prosecution is directed, including the possibility to effectively act and participate in the activities of taking evidence and to influence their scope. In this chapter we will look at the most important structural components of pre-trial proceedings, which determine its model shape, in particular, the authorities conducting these proceedings, its objectives (tasks) and forms, the participation of parties in these proceedings and the main activities that determine its course.[5] The final section deals with the issue of the principal criminal complaint, which is indeed subject to preparation within the investigation, but serves to launch the next procedural stage, namely the judicial proceedings.

Before proceeding to the discussion of the specified issues, it is necessary to emphasise that the investigation is an obligatory stage of criminal proceedings in cases concerning criminal offences prosecuted by public indictment. In these cases, the completion of the tasks of the preparatory proceedings conditions the passage of the trial to the second stage, ie the judicial proceedings (*argumentum ex* Articles 10 and 303 CPC).[6] As a rule, it does not occur in cases of offences prosecuted by private prosecution (eg insult (Article 216 CC) or violation of personal inviolability (Article 217 CC)), in which the criminal trial begins with the filing of a private indictment by the injured party with the court.

Pre-trial proceeding is the non-judicial stage of criminal proceedings.[7] The master of these proceedings (*dominus litis*) is the prosecutor.[8] He or she conducts preparatory proceedings or exercises supervision over preparatory proceedings conducted by the police or other bodies that have police powers. The prosecutor bears responsibility for the implementation at this stage of the procedural activity that makes up the function of criminal prosecution (Articles 311 and 326 CPC). Without in any way undermining the expressed view, it should be noted that in practical terms the basic organ conducting preparatory proceedings, but under the supervision of the prosecutor, is the police.[9]

This role of the police as the body conducting pre-trial proceedings, which in fact corresponds to a pragmatic trend that can also be observed in the organisation of criminal prosecution in other European countries, should in the future find clear support at the normative level. This would be conducive to realising the proposed need to raise the level of qualifications of police officers who are responsible for conducting pre-trial proceedings, so that their procedural activities would meet the highest standards of fairness and guarantee standards related to the rights of parties or other participants in procedural activities (eg the person being searched, or witnesses being questioned).[10]

[4] Zagrodnik (n 1) 31–34. See also Grzegorczyk and Tylman (n 2) 632.

[5] K Marszał, *Proces karny. Zagadnienia ogólne* (Katowice, Volumen, 2013) 329.

[6] RA Stefański, in *System Prawa Karnego Procesowego*, red P Hofmański, vol 10, *Postępowanie przygotowawcze*, RA Stefański (ed) (Warsaw, Wolters Kluwer, 2016) 37.

[7] Marszał (n 5) 330.

[8] Grzegorczyk and Tylman (n 2) 640.

[9] At the same time, the most recent accurate data in this regard, from 2019, indicate that investigations conducted by the prosecutor alone accounted for only 7% of the total number of principal investigations, and in only less than 9% of simplified investigations did the prosecutor conduct the preliminary investigation.

[10] See further Zagrodnik (n 1) 230, 286.

Polish criminal procedural law does not provide for either the institution of an investigating judge, known, for example, in the French and Belgian systems of criminal procedural law,[11] or the institution of a judge for an investigation, as exists, for example, in German and Italian criminal procedure (*Ermittlungsrichter*, *guidice per la indagni preliminari*).[12] This does not mean that the judicial factor is absent in Polish pre-trial proceedings: taking into account the constitutional and convention-related conditions – connected, for example, with guarantees of the right to personal freedom – its complete elimination from the pre-trial proceedings is simply impossible.[13] In the Polish legal system the presence of the judicial factor in the pre-trial proceedings manifests itself in certain activities of the court at this stage of the process. Generally speaking, they are a guarantee of the legality of the activities of the investigation authorities and the observance of the limits of interference in the sphere of human rights and freedoms in the pre-trial proceedings.[14] They are not of a uniform nature.[15] Their main group consists of control activities related to examination of complaints against the prosecutor's decisions, eg on refusal to initiate or discontinue preparatory proceedings (Article 306 in connection with Article 465 § 2 CPC), on refusal to provide access to files in preparatory proceedings (Article 159 in fine CPC), on securing property (Article 293 § 3 of the CPC) and – as already noted in the previous chapter – on decisions on precautionary measures other than provisional detention (Article 252 §§ 2 and 3 CPC). In addition, the court makes decisions in an investigation which are the result of a legal and factual review of actions taken in this proceedings and which are subject to further instance review, eg in the matter of the application of provisional detention (Article 250 § 1 CPC), on the forfeiture of the property constituting the bail or the collection of the sum pledged (Article 270 § 1 CPC) and on referring the accused for a psychiatric examination combined with an observation in a healthcare establishment (Article 203 §§ 2 and 3 CPC). Finally, the court exceptionally performs certain procedural acts in investigation that do not involve issuing a decision or reviewing the prosecutor's decision, eg questioning a witness if there is a danger that it may not be possible to hear a witness at the trial (Article 316 § 3 CPC).

In the model aspect – in the context of differences between investigation in Polish criminal proceedings and criminal proceedings in England and Wales – it should be emphasised that in the Polish legal system, a full and thorough explanation of the case in investigation, providing evidence indicating that a specific person has committed an offence and allowing proof of his or her guilt, leads to a formal accusation to the court,

[11] See eg J Fermon, F Verbruggen and S. De Decker, 'The Investigative Stage of the Criminal Process in Belgium', in E Cape, J Hodgson, T Prakken and T Spronken (eds), *Suspects in Europe: Procedural Rights at the Investigative Stage of the Criminal Process in the European Union* (Antwerp and Oxford, Intersentia, 2007) 30; J Hodgson, *French Criminal Justice: A Comparative Account of the Investigation and Prosecution of Crime in France* (Oxford and Portland, OR, Hart Publishing) 66 et seq.

[12] C Roxin, *Strafverfahrensrecht* (München, CH Beck, 1998) 70 et seq.

[13] See further Zagrodnik (n 1) 239; D Salas, 'The Role of the Judge', in M Delmas-Marty and JR Spencer (eds), *European Criminal Procedure* (Cambridge, 2002) 488 et seq. Historically see R Gneist, *Vier Fragen zur Deutschen Strafprozeßordnung mit einem Schlußwort über die Schöffengerichte* (Berlin, 1874) 77–78.

[14] Salas (n 13) 533 et seq; Hodgson (n 11) 66; Zagrodnik (n 1) 247–50.

[15] Further K.Marszał (n 5) 330–31; Grzegorczyk and Tylman (n 2) 714–20; K Eichstaedt, *Czynności sądu w postępowaniu przygotowawczym w polskim procesie karnym* (Warsaw, CH Beck, 2008).

initiating proceedings before this body.[16] As a rule, this accusation takes the form of an indictment, or less formally, a motion for conviction without trial (Article 335 § 1 CPC) or a motion for conditional discontinuance of proceedings (Article 336 CPC). There is no alternative to bringing one of these actions and initiating court proceedings in the form of the possibilities, known to the Anglo-Welsh system, of terminating a criminal trial at the pre-trial stage by applying certain measures of penal response to the offender (eg informal warning, formal police cautions, conditional cautions).[17] There is also no other way to initiate court proceedings in a criminal case except by filing the above-mentioned criminal complaints with the court. Along with their filing, an investigation file with annexes is sent to the court (Article 334 § 1 in conjunction with Article 335 § 3 and Article 336 § 4 CPC).[18]

In the initial phase of the judicial proceeding, the investigation files, or more precisely, the evidence contained in them, are the basis for the decision on the merits of the case at the 'sentencing session', without referring the case to the main trial, if the prosecutor has filed a motion for a judgment on conviction without a trial (autonomous (Article 335 § 1 CPC) or non-autonomous (Article 335 § 2 CPC)) or a motion for conditional discontinuance of the proceedings (Article 336 § 1 CPC), or if the defendant filed a motion for the issuance of a judgment of conviction and the imposition of a specific penalty or a criminal measure upon them or for ordering forfeiture or a redress measure without an evidentiary hearing being conducted (Article 338a CPC).[19]

On the basis of the investigation files, the court also conducts a preliminary examination of the case in the indicated procedural phase with a view to, for example, checking whether there are circumstances due to which the proceedings are inadmissible and must be discontinued (Article 339 § 3 points 1 and 2 CPC) or should be suspended (Article 339 § 3 point 6 CPC). If the accused is under provisional detention, the court, as part of its preliminary examination of the case, shall decide on maintaining, amending or revoking that measure ex officio. When necessary, the court may also decide upon other precautionary measures (Article 344 CPC). The court's obligation in this respect has a guarantee function. Its purpose is to ensure that in connection with a significant change in the procedural arrangement, resulting from the initiation of court proceedings and thus the completion of evidentiary activities in the pre-trial proceedings, the premises for the continued use of pre-trial detention will be reviewed.[20]

In the course of pre-trial proceedings, two main phases may be distinguished, namely proceedings *in rem* (anonymous prosecution) and proceedings *in personam* (named personal prosecution, proper criminal prosecution). They are separated by a

[16] Marszał (n 5) 493; K Zgryzek, in J Zagrodnik (ed), *Proces karny* (Warsaw, Wolters Kluwer, 2021) 486.

[17] A Ashworth and M Redmayne, *The Criminal Process* (Oxford, Oxford University Press, 2005) 148–49.

[18] Critical about this solution Waltoś (n 2) 153–54; Zagrodnik (n 1) 183–86. See also eg Ch Ernst, *Das Gerichtliche Zwischenverfahren nach Anklageerhebung* (Frankfurt am Main, Bern and New York, Peter Lang, 1986) 92 et seq; B Schünemann, 'Die Zukunft des Trafverfahrens – Abchied vom Rechtsstaat?' (2007) *ZStW* no 4, 951; G Illuminati, 'The Frustrated Turn to Adversarial Procedure in Italy' (2005) 4 *Washington University Global Studies Review* 572.

[19] See further S Steinborn, *Porozumienia w procesie karnym, Kantor Zakamycze* (Kraków, Zakamycze, 2005) 27 et seq.

[20] K Zgryzek, 'Obligatoryjne posiedzenie przygotowawcze przed rozprawą w polskim procesie karnym', in *Współczesne problemy procesu karnego i wymiaru sprawiedliwości. Księga ku czci Profesora Kazimierza Marszała* (Katowice, Wydawnictwo Uniwersytetu Śląskiego, 2003) 517.

set of actions comprising the presentation of charges, as a result of which a suspect (accused *sensu largo*) appears in the criminal process.[21] In the first of these phases, a search takes place with the aim of collecting and preserving evidence of a crime and verifying hypotheses constructed on their basis concerning the course of the event in connection with which the criminal trial is conducted, allowing for the eventual identification of the alleged perpetrator and his/her possible apprehension. In the second phase, the activities of the procedural body focus on collecting evidence that make it possible to prove the guilt of a certain person in court proceedings. The charge that begins the personal prosecution phase does not have to be identical to the charge that is the essential substantive component of the indictment. Sometimes, however, the changes in the description or legal qualification of the act charged against the suspect in the presentation of charges are so far-reaching that it is necessary to repeat the activities connected with the presentation of charges; this will be discussed in more detail in the section devoted to the Presentation of Charges.

Irrespective of the above distinction of the two phases of pre-trial proceedings, certain fundamental points can be delineated in its course on which the presentation of the process of the first procedural stage will further focus, namely the initiation of pre-trial proceedings, the presentation of charges, the closing of the investigation or simplified investigation, and the drafting of the principal criminal complaint.

Tasks (Objectives) of Pre-trial Proceedings

The tasks (objectives) of pre-trial proceedings are specified in Article 297 CPC. They should be seen as a concretisation, from the point of view of the first procedural stage, of the general objectives of the criminal trial set out in Article 2 § 1 CPC.[22] They determine the scope of clarification of the case and evidentiary activities in investigation.

The basic task of investigation is to establish the basis for bringing an indictment (the emergence of a judicial proceeding). This is achieved by the accomplishment of sub-tasks, which include.

1. establishing whether a prohibited act has been committed and whether it constitutes a criminal offence;
2. detecting the perpetrator and, if necessary, apprehending them;
3. collecting data, in conformity with Articles 213 and 214 CPC;[23]
4. elucidating the circumstances of the case, including the identification of injured persons and the extent of the damage (Article 297 § 1, subparagraphs 1-4 CPC).

[21] Waltoś and Hofmański (n 2) 501–02.

[22] J Tylman, in 'System Prawa Karnego Procesowego', red P Hofmański, vol 10: *Postępowanie przygotowawcze*, RA Stefański (ed) (Warsaw, Wolters Kluwer, 2016) 135–38.

[23] According to Art 213 CPC:

- following shall be determined in an investigation: the identity of the accused, their number in the Universal Electronic System for Registration of the Population [Powszechny Elektroniczny System Ewidencji Ludności [tPESEL), and in the case of a person having no PESEL number assigned; the number and name of the identity document and the name of the body by which that document was issued, as well as the age of the accused, their family and property relationships, level of education,

Establishing whether a crime has actually been committed requires an examination of whether specific conduct has occurred, whether it constitutes a prohibited act and whether it meets the conditions set out in criminal law that determine its criminality. A positive result of this examination is the driving force behind criminal prosecution – the initiation and conduct of pre-trial proceedings in order to carry out the other tasks of this procedural stage.[24] The determination of the perpetrator of the crime is a further consequence. Personal identification tests of the accused, consisting of the collection of data specified in Articles 213 and 214 CPC, is aimed at ensuring the implementation of the directive of individual prevention when deciding on the subject of the trial.[25] The task of clarifying the case is primarily to enable the procedural authority to decide whether there are grounds for bringing an indictment, or whether criminal proceedings should be discontinued or another appropriate decision taken (eg on supplementing the investigation). This task consists, apart from determining the time, place, manner of committing the crime and its consequences, of clarifying the circumstances concerning the culpability of the perpetrator, the subjective and objective elements affecting the assessment of the act, as well as other circumstances relevant under criminal law due to their significance for the final decision on the subject of the trial (eg circumstances excluding or limiting criminal liability).[26] Although in the current state of the law there is no obligation to explain the case in an exhaustive manner in pre-trial proceedings,

profession, sources of income, criminal record, and – whenever possible – the telephone number, telefacsimile number and electronic mail address enabling contact with the accused, and the Taxpayer Identification Number (NIP), if such has been assigned; in the case of the accused person being a public officer at the time of committing the act or during the proceedings, data concerning the performance of public service by the accused and any disciplinary distinctions and sanctions shall also be collected (§ 1);

- where necessary, the public prosecutor, another body conducting the investigation, or the court shall obtain from the ICT system of the minister responsible for finance information concerning the property relationships and sources of income of the accused, including pending and completed fiscal proceedings, on the basis of up-to-date data available in the system. Such information shall be obtained by electronic means (§ 1a);
- in proceedings in cases concerning offences related to land transport specified in Chapter XXI of the Criminal Code, information concerning the accused shall also be obtained from the central driver register and from the register of drivers breaching road traffic regulations kept by the Police; if 6 months have passed from the preparation of such information, the information shall be obtained again (§ 1b).

Article 214CPC provides the community inquiry. According to § 1 of this provision. should a need arise, and in particular when it is necessary to determine data related to the personal characteristics and conditions, as well as the way of life of the accused until present, the court, and in an investigation, – the public prosecutor, shall order a community simplified investigation to be carried out with regard to the accused by a probation officer or another entity authorised on the basis of separate regulations, and in particularly justified cases, by the police (§ 1) A community simplified investigation is compulsory in cases related to felonies and with regard to the accused who, at the time of committing the act, was under twenty-one years of age if charged with an offence against life (§ 2).

[24] J Zagrodnik, in J Zagrodnik (ed), *Proces karny* (Warsaw, Wolters Kluwer, 2021) 509. Similarly M Kurowski, in D Świecki (ed), *Kodeks postępowania karnego. Komentarz* (Warsaw, Wolters Kluwer, 2021) vol I, 1155.

[25] Zagrodnik (n 24) 509.

[26] See J Tylman, 'Cele i zadania postępowania przygotowawczego w procesie karnym', in *Współczesne problemy procesu karnego i wymiaru sprawiedliwości. Księga ku czci Profesora Kazimierza Marszała* (Katowice, Wydawnictwo Uniwersytetu Śląskiego, 2003) 423; Zagrodnik (n 24) 509–10.

in practice, this usually takes place, which, in connection with numerous exceptions to the directive of direct examination of evidence before the court adjudicating at the main trial, translates into an increased impact of investigation on the examination of the case by the court and the factual findings of this body, on which the judgment is based.[27]

The basic task of preparatory proceedings is inextricably linked with another one, which consists of the collection of evidence. The clarification of the case in the course of pre-trial proceedings, in order for it to be the basis for a decision on bringing an indictment, or a decision on discontinuance of a criminal trial, must be supported by the evidence carried out at this stage of the trial in accordance with the formal rigours set out in the applicable regulations (eg for the testimony of a witness or the explanation of the accused).[28] Criminal procedural law provides in several cases for the possibility of limiting the scope of evidentiary actions taken during the investigation. According to Article 325 h § 1, first sentence CPC, a simplified investigation may be limited to determining whether there are sufficient grounds for filing an indictment or for another closure of the proceedings (so-called summary investigation). The use of this possibility depends on the decision of the authority conducting the proceedings. This should be expected in less complex cases. The provision of Article 325h § 1, second sentence CPC delineates the limits of simplification of a summary investigation. It lists the activities that must necessarily be carried out in this investigation.[29] Under this provision activities related to the final acquaintance with the investigation materials shall be carried out, the suspect and the injured shall be questioned, and any actions which cannot be repeated shall be carried out and documented in records. Other evidentiary actions shall be documented in the form of a record limited to the most important statements of persons participating in the action (Article 325h § 1, third sentence CPC).[30] Limitation of evidentiary actions in pre-trial proceedings may furthermore take place if the accused pleads guilty, and in the light of their explanations the circumstances in which the criminal offence was committed and the responsibility of the accused are beyond doubt, and the attitude of the accused indicates that the objectives of investigation would be achieved (Article 335 § 1, first sentence CPC).[31] In that case further action may be abandoned if the prosecutor decides to file a motion to convict the accused at the sentencing hearing instead of an indictment. However, the necessary steps should be taken to secure traces and evidence of a criminal offence against loss, distortion or destruction (Article 335 § 1, third sentence). If there is a need to evaluate the reliability of the explanations submitted, evidentiary actions shall be carried out only in the scope necessary thereto (Article 335 § 1, second sentence CPC). Another type of limitation of investigation is provided for in Article 315a CPC. Under this provision an injured party may not be questioned in the capacity of a witness where this is not essential for making

[27] Zagrodnik (n 24) 509. Similarly Kurowski (n 24) vol I, 1156.

[28] Tylman (n 26) 425; J Tylman, in *System Prawa Karnego Procesowego*, red P Hofmański, vol 10, *Postępowanie przygotowawcze*, red RA Stefański (Warsaw, Wolters Kluwer, 2016) 145; Zagrodnik (n 24) 510–11.

[29] Kurowski (n 24) vol I, 1273.

[30] See further Grzegorczyk and Tylman (n 2) 697–700.

[31] Further Kurowski (n 24) vol I, 1332; Zagrodnik (n 24) 583.

findings of fact. This solution is justified on pragmatic grounds.[32] It gives the investigating authority the possibility to refrain from questioning all the injured parties, which in some cases may number hundreds or even thousands, without being exposed to the risk of returning the case in order to supplement the investigation (pursuant to Article 344a § 1 CPC).[33]

The last basic task of pre-trial proceedings is to secure and, to the extent necessary,[34] preserve evidence for the court. This includes material evidence, as well as the explanations of the accused, witness statements and observations or impressions resulting from visual inspection. The preservation of evidence takes place in the form of record (Article 143 CPC).[35] These records are part of the investigation file, which, as already stated above, is sent to the court following the filing of the principle complaint triggering the court proceedings. The preservation of evidence for the court and the full access of this body to the investigation file raise questions in cases referred to the main hearing.[36] This access essentially means that the adjudicating court proceeds to hear the case and evaluate the evidence at the main hearing, acting essentially under the suggestion of the investigation file, which contains mainly evidence that is obviously tainted with an accusatory bias. There is no mechanism that would ensure sui generis neutralisation of the indicated suggestion and attitude, and this significantly weakens the guarantees of independent evaluation of evidence and impartial assessment of the case by the court. Access to the investigation file also provides an opportunity for the adjudicating court to get an idea of what questions to ask personal sources of evidence or what other evidence to take in order to prove the validity of the prosecution's thesis. Consequently, it is a breeding ground for 'hyperactivity' on the part of the presiding judge and the court during the examination of the evidence, usually manifests in the field of taking evidence in favour of the prosecution.[37] It leads to an unacceptable distortion of the fundamental division of procedural roles between prosecution, defence and adjudication anchored in the accusatory principle, which should be fully reflected in relation to the legal dispute at the main trial.

[32] Kurowski (n 24) vol I, 1228–29; Zagrodnik (n 24) 511; Ł Chmielniak, M Klonowski, A Rychlewska-Hotel and J Zagrodnik (eds), *Kodeks postępowania karnego. Komentarz praktyczny do nowelizacji 2019* (Warsaw, Wolters Kluwer, 2020) 104–05.

[33] For example, the described limitation may concern cases of misappropriation offences or fraud offences, where harming a large number of people is very often a consequence of multistep, but at the same time, identical, homogeneous behaviour of the perpetrator, who acts according to a predefined pattern, using the same, or similar in important respects, opportunities to take over someone else's property, or to bring about its disposal. From the legal point of view, such behaviours are subject to qualification under Art 12 of the Penal Code, which regulates the so-called continuous offence, or under Art 91 § 1 of the Penal Code, which regulates the construction of the so called sequence of crimes.

[34] See Decision of the Appellate Court in Warsaw, 6 June 2010, II AKz 474/10, Lex no 832782.

[35] Tylman (n 26) 426.

[36] See further Waltoś (n 2) 153–54; Zagrodnik (n 1) 183–86.

[37] See further Zagrodnik (n 1) 181–94, 423–81. See also J Zagrodnik, 'Model procesu karnego status quo i status futurus – kilka refleksji na temat dwóch rzeczywistości, nie tylko normatywnych' in *W pogoni za rzetelnym procesem karnym. Księga dedykowana Profesorowi Stanisławowi Waltosiowi* (Wolters Kluwer, Warszaw, 2022) 125–26.

Scope and Forms of Activity of Parties and their Representatives in an Investigation

The tasks of investigation as defined in the previous section in practice determine the subordination of its course to the investigative principle and the dominant influence of the investigative factor. The prosecutor, who conducts or supervises the criminal trial at this stage, has a superior position to the accused and defence counsel, as well as the injured person and his/her attorney. The prosecutor concentrates in his/her hands the tasks that are a manifestation of the realisation of the function of criminal prosecution, he/she makes procedural decisions that are binding for the parties, thus realising the function of ruling, and to the extent that he/she is obliged to maintain impartiality takes into account the circumstances in favour of the accused (Article 4 CPC), and he/she performs the activities comprising the realisation of the function of defence.[38] At the same time, he/she is *de facto* a party to a legal dispute, the binding resolution of which is a matter for the court at the next procedural stage (judicial trial).[39]

Due to the presented procedural position of the prosecuting authority, it is quite obvious that in the case of investigation there can be no question of shaping the process on the adversarial pattern in the form of a dispute of equal parties before an impartial arbiter. This does not mean that inquisitorial pattern reigns in this procedural stage in an absolute way.[40] In the realities of the modern criminal trial, in which guarantees provided, inter alia, in Article 6 ECHR are in force, this is basically impossible. The imbalance of power between the parties to the criminal law dispute in the pre-trial proceedings, resulting from the dominant position of the prosecutor, cannot constitute a basis either for negating the manifestations of adversarialism (manifestations of the dispute) at the first procedural stage, or even more so for crossing out, in relation to this procedural stage, the dispute itself. This dispute is fully developed with the referral of criminal proceedings against a specific person (suspect) as a result of the hypothesis of a collision between a specific behaviour of this person and the legal interest, subject to protection under the norms of substantive criminal law.[41]

The manifestations of adversarialism in investigation are directly related to the rights to active action at this stage, which are vested in the procedural parties and their representatives.[42] It should be recalled, referring to the findings of chapter three,

[38] See A Murzynowski, 'Model postępowania przygotowawczego w europejskich państwach socjalistycznych' (1983) *ZN ASW* no 3, 97. See also M Cieślak, 'Przygotowawcze stadium procesu karnego (pojęcie-zakres-funkcje-struktura)', in M Cieślak and WE Czogunow (eds), *Postępowanie przygotowawcze (Węzłowe problemy na tle radzieckiego i polskiego prawa karnego procesowego)*, ZN UJ, no 61, 22 et seq; Z Doda, '"Kontradyktoryjność" postępowania przygotowawczego na tle polskiego prawa karnego procesowego, in *Postępowanie przygotowawcze*, ibid, ZN UJ, no 61, 93.

[39] Another proof of this can be the regulation contained in Art 299 § 3 CPC, according to which in court actions within an investigation, the public prosecutor shall have the rights of a party.

[40] Doda (n 38) 93; Zagrodnik (n 1) 321.

[41] Doda (n 38) 88–89.

[42] In cases provided for by law, certain rights are also vested in non-parties (Art 299 § 2 CPC), eg concerning complaints against the decision not to open an investigation (Art 306 § 1 CPC) or complaints about inaction of a law enforcement agency (Art 306 § 3 CPC).

that the parties in the first procedural stage are the suspect and the injured person (Article 299 § 1 CPC). Their procedural status, but above all, equipping them with the right to actively act in the investigation, is a testimony to their procedural empowerment. This is particularly important in the case of a suspect, who is thus no longer a subject (object) of investigative activities, as was the case in the extremely inquisitorial criminal trial, but a subject of the trial in the investigation. An important guarantee of the rights of the parties at this stage, making their use realistic, is the obligation of the criminal prosecution authority to instruct them about their rights (Article 300 §§ 1 and § 2 CPC).[43] The same can be said of the right of access, in principle with the consent of the pre-trial investigation authority, to the investigation file (Article 156 § 5 CPC).[44] In principle, the right of the parties to be assisted by a professional legal representative – a defence counsel in the case of a suspect and an attorney in the case of an injured person – should be assessed in an analogous manner.[45]

The current legislation gives the parties and their representatives significant possibilities to influence the scope and course of the investigation and to control its correctness. These include the right to submit a motion for evidence (Article 167 CPC), including, for example, the right to submit a motion to the court demanding that the witness be heard by the court if there is a danger that it may not be possible to hear a witness at the trial (Article 316 § 3 CPC), the right to participate in the activities of pre-trial proceedings, to appeal against procedural decisions and to communicate with the opposing party (Article 23a § 1 CPC), also within the framework of mediation proceedings, which may provide grounds for, for example, a motion for sentencing without main trial.[46]

The most important manifestations of adversarialism in the first procedural stage include the aforementioned participation of parties in evidentiary actions carried out at this stage. It opens the way for the use of instruments of procedural activity in the form of motions and statements which are subject to recording (Articles 143 and 148 § 2 CPC). It also plays an important role from the point of view of controlling the correctness of evidence-gathering activities.[47] The regulation of the participation of parties and their representatives in evidentiary activities in preparatory proceedings is not uniform. It depends on the type of actions, as well as on the initiative of the parties to carry them out.[48] In order to present them in more detail, we should distinguish between the following:

1. So-called non-repeatable activities, ie activities with regard to which there is a justified fear that it will not be possible at all or will become pointless to carry them out in the evidentiary proceedings before the court,[49] eg the suspect, the injured

[43] Kurowski (n 24) vol I, 1167–76.

[44] ibid 633–36; P Kardas, 'Standard rzetelnego procesu a prawo wglądu do akt sprawy w postępowaniu w przedmiocie tymczasowego aresztowania, czyli historia jednej nowelizacji' (2010) *Prok i Pr*, nos 1–2, 99 et seq.

[45] See eg W Posnow, 'Udział obrońcy w przygotowawczym stadium procesu karnego – aspekty realizacji niektórych uprawnień', in J Skorupka (ed), *Rzetelny proces karny. Księga jubileuszowa Profesor Zofii Świdy* (Warsaw, Wolter Kluwers, 2009) 416–37.

[46] See further K Dudka, in *System Prawa Karnego Procesowego*, red P Hofmański, vol 10, *Postępowanie przygotowawcze*, RA Stefański (ed) (Warsaw, Wolters Kluwer, 2016) 895–924.

[47] Zagrodnik (n 24) 514.

[48] Dudka (n 46) et seq.

[49] T Grzegorczyk, *Obrońca w postępowaniu przygotowawczym* (Łódź, Wydawnictwo Uniwersytetu Łódzkiego, 1988) 190; Dudka (n 46) 911–18; J Zagrodnik, *Obrońca i pełnomocnik w procesie karnym i karnym skarbowym* (Warsaw, Wolters Kluwer, 2020) 211–15.

person and their legal representatives, as well as the defence counsel and attorney, if they have already been appointed in the case, shall be admitted to participate in the action, unless there is a danger of loss or distortion of evidence in the event of delay (Article 316 § 1 in fine CPC). The appearance of a suspect deprived of liberty shall not be procured if a delay could lead to a danger of loss or distortion of evidence (Article 316 § 2 CPC).

2. The examination of witnesses by the court in the cases specified in Article 185a–c CPC.[50] The regulations contained in these provisions are based on the assumption that certain categories of witnesses can be examined only once; these are, for example, witnesses under the age of fifteen at the time of examination who are injured in cases involving crimes against liberty (Chapter XXIII of the Penal Code), against sexual freedom and decency (Chapter XXV of the Penal Code), against the family and guardianship (Chapter XXVI of the Penal Code), and also in cases involving crimes committed with the use of violence or unlawful threats (Article 185a § 1 CPC) or witnesses injured by the crime of rape (Article 197 of the Penal Code), taking advantage of another person's helplessness or lack of capability of recognising the significance of the act or controlling one's conduct due to a mental impairment or a mental illness (Article 198 of the Penal Code) or the crime of abusing a relation of dependence (Article 199 CPC), who is fifteen years of age or older at the time of questioning (Article 185c § 1a in conjunction with § 1 CPC). The one-off nature of the examination is intended to prevent secondary victimisation.[51] The act of examining witnesses from the categories listed as examples is reserved for the court. The right to participate in the court session is generally vested in the public prosecutor, who in this case enjoys the rights of a party, defence counsel and attorney for the injured party. The suspect him/herself does not have such a right; in most of the indicated cases, if the accused notified of the procedural action in consideration remains without a defence counsel of their choice, the court shall appoint an ex officio defence counsel for them (Article 185a § 2, fourth sentence, in connection with Article 185a § 4 and Article 185b § 1 CPC).
3. Actions requested by a party or his/her procedural representative. The party who submitted a motion to cause certain actions to be performed, as well as their defence counsel and attorney, may not be refused the possibility to participate in the action if they so demand (Article 315 § 2, first sentence CPC);[52] an exception applies to a suspect deprived of liberty, who shall not be brought in if this would involve serious difficulties (Article 318, second sentence, in conjunction with Article 315 § 2, second sentence CPC).
4. Activities related to the appointment of an expert witness. If evidence based on an opinion issued by an expert witness, a scientific or specialised institution is admitted, the suspect and their defence counsel, as well as the injured and their attorney, shall be served the decision on admission of the evidence and permitted

[50] See more Kurowski (n 24) vol I, 758–67; Zagrodnik (n 49) 215–19.

[51] Supreme Court Decision, 15 March 2012, III KK 244/11, OSNKW 2012, no 6, pos 68; Supreme Court Decision, 27 September 2016 r, V KK 246/16, Lex no 2148670. See also Judgment of the Apellate Court in Wrocław, 21 May 2008, II Aka 104/08, (2009) *Prok i Pr* nos 7–8, pos 46.

[52] See more Dudka (n 46) 902–07.

to participate in the questioning of expert witnesses, and to acquaint themselves with the opinion, if one has been prepared in writing. The appearance of a suspect deprived of liberty shall not be procured if it were to involve serious difficulties (Article 318 CPC).[53]

5. Other actions of evidence in the investigation. According to Article 317 § 1 CPC, the parties, and a defence counsel and an attorney if already appointed in the case, shall also be admitted upon request to participate in other actions of the investigation.[54] The request of a party or its procedural representative may be refused only by the prosecutor in the form of a decision. The refusal may take place only in particularly justified cases, if the important interest of the investigation so require (Article 317 § 2 in conjunction with Article 325a § 2 CPC). The prosecutor may also refuse to bring in a suspect who is deprived of liberty if this would cause serious difficulties (Article 317 § 2 in fine CPC).

Against the background of the presented normative solutions, a few additional words of attention are required on the issue of activity at the first stage of the trial of the parties' procedural representatives, in particular the defence counsel of the accused.[55] There is no doubt, given the representative character of activities of defence counsel and attorney in criminal proceedings, which has already been established in chapter **3**, that apart from situations in which certain rights are directly provided by law with respect to these professional entities (see above, Article 317 § 1 CPC), they generally exercise the rights vested in the parties they represent, eg they are entitled to file motions for evidence or complain against procedural decisions.[56] Of no small importance in terms of the scope of their actual activity in the pre-trial proceedings is the significant impact of the evidence gathered at this stage on the examination and resolution of the case by the court, either at the 'sentencing session' (*posiedzeniu wyrokowym*, the session at which judgment is handed down), or – as mentioned earlier – at the main trial. With some simplification, it can be said that their activity should be directly proportional to this influence, especially when it comes to the participation of the defence counsel in questioning suspects and witnesses during the first trial stage. This participation should serve to ensure that the course of the interrogation is fairly reflected in the record, in particular that those evidentiary statements which are important for an effective defence in the subsequent proceedings are included therein with maximum precision.[57] The defence counsel cannot count on the fact that the procedural body, focused in its activities on criminal prosecution and accusation, will be equally sensitive to the circumstances in favour of the accused. Thus, by not participating in the activity of interrogation, the defence counsel risks that information that could be useful to the defence case will not be exposed, will be obliterated or will be trivialised. The participation of the defence counsel in the evidentiary activities in the investigation and the possibility of influencing through it the scope of the evidence gathered at this stage acquires full significance if

[53] ibid 923. See also Zagrodnik (n 49) 220–23.
[54] Dudka (n 46) 921; Zagrodnik (n 49) 223–25.
[55] See further C Kulesza, in *System Prawa Karnego Procesowego*, red P Hofmański, vol 10, *Postępowanie przygotowawcze*, RA Stefański (ed) (Warsaw, Wolters Kluwer, 2016) 946–1011.
[56] Grzegorczyk and Tylman (n 2) 353; Zagrodnik (n 49) 31.
[57] Zagrodnik (n 49) 31, 154–55.

we take into account not only the fact that this evidence usually constitutes the basis for the factual findings of the verdict, but also what has already been indicated, namely that if evidence resulting from the reading of the investigation file is sufficiently strong, in the current inquisitorial model the court holding the judicial trial forms its own picture of the case and proceeds to examine it. These few observations lead to the conclusion that the participation of the defence counsel in the examination of the suspect and witnesses in the pre-trial proceedings, contrary to traditional deontology, which was characterised by the passivity of the defence counsel at the first stage of the trial, should be perceived in terms of the deontologically conditioned duty of this procedural representative. A different approach is required to assess the activity of the defence counsel in respect of posing questions to witnesses and in terms of taking the initiative for evidence in preparatory proceedings. In this respect the cardinal maxim determining the battle strategy will often come into play, according to which all available forces serving the purpose of defence should be used as simultaneously as possible, and in any case at the place of a decisive clash,[58] which in criminal procedural terms should be equated with evidentiary proceedings and final votes at the main trial. This may dictate the abandonment of asking witnesses questions, eg questioning their credibility, or making requests for the admission of certain defence evidence in investigation for the sake of its more effective use in court proceedings.[59]

Forms of Pre-trial Proceedings

The forms of preparatory proceedings are its generic varieties.[60] Polish law provides for two such forms, namely principal investigation and simplified investigation. Within each of these forms preparatory proceedings include the previously distinguished *in rem* and *in personam* phases, which makes it possible to note that their distinction, although it would be reasonable, does not provide a basis for differentiating the forms of preparatory proceedings.[61] In each of these forms, preparatory proceedings are subject – directly or under supervision – to the prosecutor. In the current state of the law, both principal investigation and simplified investigation are the principal forms of preparatory proceedings,[62] representing the typical course of the criminal process in its first stage in the corresponding categories of cases. If it is possible to speak of a certain superiority of a principal investigation over a simplified investigation, it is given that in every case in which pre-trial proceedings may be conducted in the form of an simplified investigation, it is at the same time permissible to conduct them in the form

[58] Carl von Clausewitz, O wojnie, bez daty i miejsca wydania, wyd. Mireki, Warszawa 2006, ss 153–59.

[59] Zagrodnik (n 49) 31, 154–55.

[60] Cieślak (n 38) 33; Marszał (n 5) 336. See also Waltoś (n 2) p. 15; S Waltoś, 'Dochodzenie uproszczone w polskim procesie karnym', in M Cieślak and W E Czogunow (eds), *Postępowanie przygotowawcze (Węzłowe problemy na tle radzieckiego i polskiego prawa karnego procesowego)*, ZN UJ, no 61, 157.

[61] L Schaff, *Zakres i formy postępowania przygotowawczego* (Warsaw, Wydawnictwo PWN, 1961) 159.

[62] See S Waltoś, 'Postępowanie przygotowawcze we współczesnym polskim procesie karnym', in *Współczesne problemy procesu karnego i wymiaru sprawiedliwości. Księga ku czci Profesora Kazimierza Marszała* (Katowice, Wydawnictwo Uniwersytetu Śląskiego, 2003) 461.

of a principal investigation. This does not work in reverse, at least to the full extent.[63] In cases where an principal investigation must be conducted (mandatory principal investigation), a simplified investigation is inadmissible and therefore illegal.[64]

The fundamental differences between principal investigation and simplified investigation concern the following:

1. The gravity of the act for which the investigation is conducted. A principal investigation is mandatory in the following cases:
   (a) in which the examination in the first instance belongs to the competence of a regional court;
   (b) related to misdemeanours – where the suspect is a judge, a public prosecutor or an officer of the police, Internal Security Agency, Foreign Intelligence Agency, Military Counterintelligence Service, Military Intelligence Service, State Protection Service, Speaker's Guard, Customs and Tax Service or Central Anti-Corruption Bureau;
   (c) related to misdemeanours – when the suspect is an official of the Border Guard, the Military Police (Żandarmeria Wojskowa), of a financial investigative body, or of a superior body of a financial investigative body, as far as cases belonging to the capacity of these bodies or related to misdemeanours committed by these officials in connection with the performance of official duties are concerned;
   (d) related to misdemeanours in which simplified investigation is not conducted.

   apart from the cases mentioned, a principal investigation may be conducted in the form of an investigation if the public prosecutor decides so due to the significance or complexity of the case; in other cases, the appropriate form, which in practice is the predominant one,[65] is simplified investigation.
2. The bodies conducting the investigation. The body exclusively entitled to conduct a principal investigation is the public prosecutor (Article 311 § 1 CPC). A simplified investigation shall be conducted by the police or bodies that exercise police powers, unless it is conducted by the public prosecutor (Article 325a § 1 in conjunction with Article 312 CPC).
3. The duration of the pre-trial investigation. The basic principal investigation period is three months (Article 310 § 1 CPC); in justified cases, the period of principal investigation may be extended for a further period designated by the public prosecutor supervising the principal investigation or by the public prosecutor directly superior to the public prosecutor who conducts the principal investigation, but for no longer than one year. In particularly justified cases, the competent superior public prosecutor of the public prosecutor supervising or conducting the principal investigation may extend its period for a further specific time (Article 310 § 2 CPC).

[63] A Kiełtyka, in *System Prawa Karnego Procesowego*, red P Hofmański, vol 10, *Postępowanie przygotowawcze*, RA Stefański (ed) (Warsaw, Wolters Kluwer, 2016) 412; Zagrodnik (n 24) 520.

[64] Supreme Court Decision, 17 November 2005, I KZP 39/05, OSNKW 2005, no 12, pos 116. See also Judgment of the Appellate Court in Katowice, 14 September 2006, II AKa 196/06, OSA 2006, no 4, pos 15.

[65] Referring to recent years' data, it can be noted that in 2020, investigations accounted for 85.4%, and in 2019 88.2% of all pre-trial investigations. Data source: Statistical reports for 2020 and 2019: pk.gov.pl.

A simplified investigation should be completed within two months; the public prosecutor may extend this period to three months, and in particularly justified cases to a longer specified period (Article 325i § 1 CPC).[66]

The differences presented are fluid: they do not draw a rigid line between a principal investigation and simplified investigation.[67] This is perhaps most evident in the case of the duration of the pre-trial proceedings, which in practice may be identical for principal investigations and simplified investigation. As regards the legitimacy to conduct pre-trial proceedings, the broadly defined possibility to entrust a principal investigation, in a specific scope or in whole, or the performance of individual actions of the principal investigation, to the police (Article 311 § 2 CPC) supports the formulated assessment. The use of this possibility in practice is so wide that, in principle, the actual performance of evidentiary activities in preparatory proceedings conducted in the form of principal investigation may be associated with the police.[68] In the discussed context, it is additionally necessary to emphasise that the regulation of the course of preparatory proceedings in each of its forms is essentially based on the provisions concerning principal investigations, and only exceptionally, with regard to simplified investigations, are special provisions applied, which provide certain differences in the course of the first procedural stage in this form (Article 325a § 2 CPC).

The *sui generis* liability of criteria differentiating principal and simplified investigations that emerges against the background of the above observations, which also concerns the formalism of procedural actions, combined with the fact that in the case of each of these forms, evidence conducted in preparatory proceedings may flow, and in practical terms does flow, in a wide stream to the main trial, gives grounds to state that further maintenance of separateness of the forms in which the first stage of a criminal trial may take place has no rational justification.

Initiation of Investigation

The initiation of pre-trial proceedings is a duty of the criminal prosecution authorities[69] if there is a good reason to suspect that a criminal offence has been committed (Article 303 CPC). This obligation is the essence of the principle of legalism, to which the mechanism of criminal prosecution in Poland is subordinated. This principle is subject to a few deviations in favour of opportunism, by which it is possible to consider the advisability of criminal prosecution despite the fact that there are factual grounds

[66] See Marszał (n 5) 337; P Hofmański and S Waltoś, *Proces karny. Zarys systemu* (Warsaw, Wolters Kluwer, 2016) 494. Further: D Tarnowska, *Różnice między dochodzeniem a śledztwem w polskim procesie karnym* (Szczecin, Wydawnictwo Uniwersytetu Szczecińskiego, 2009); Kiełtyka (n 63) 411.

[67] Marszał (n 5) 337; Hofmański and Waltoś (n 66) 494.

[68] Hofmański and Waltoś (n 66) 495. For the sake of accuracy, it should be noted that entrusting a principal investigation shall not cover actions related to the presentation of the charges, the amendment or supplementation of a decision on the presentation of the charges, and the completion of the principal investigation (Art 311 § 3 CPC).

[69] S Cora, in *System Prawa Karnego Procesowego*, red P Hofmański, vol 10, *Postępowanie przygotowawcze*, RA Stefański (ed) (Warsaw, Wolters Kluwer, 2016) 586; Kurowski (n 24) vol I, 1181.

for it and it is legally permissible. These, however, only materialise following the initiation of investigation and are connected, for example, with the possibility of the so-called absorption discontinuance of criminal proceedings (Article 11 § 1 CPC)[70] or discontinuance of proceedings against a suspect who has been granted the status of a crown witness (Article 9 CC).

The factual basis for the initiation of preparatory proceedings is the reasonable suspicion that an offence has been committed. It is related to the degree to which the authority entitled to initiate investigation or prosecution is informed about the factual event in connection with which the investigation or prosecution would be conducted.[71] Such a basis occurs if the authority obtains objectively convincing information justifying the hypothesis that a crime has been committed, which leads it to believe that a crime may have occurred.[72] A conjecture or assumption that an unspecified crime has been committed, which is not supported by objective information making such a fact probable, is not sufficient to initiate a pre-trial investigation.[73] If the information obtained by the prosecuting authority is uncertain or insufficient to raise a reasonable suspicion of a crime, it may be verified in the course of checking (verification) proceedings (Article 307 CPC).[74] These proceedings are situated in the foreground of a possible criminal proceeding, so they are not a component of it.[75] Consequently, if it does not provide information justifying the initiation of a investigation, the institution of the investigation should be refused.

The principal form of the institution of an investigation is the issuance of a formal decision to initiate it.[76] In the event of submission a notification of a criminal offence, such a decision, or a decision to refuse to institute an investigation, should be issued without undue delay.[77] The delay may be justified by the necessity to carry out the

[70] Pursuant to the mentioned provision, the proceedings in a case of misdemeanour subject to imprisonment for up to five years may be discontinued if the imposition of the penalty on the perpetrator would be manifestly inexpedient in the light of the type and extent of a penalty finally adjudicated for another criminal offence, and as long as the interest of the injured is not prejudiced.

[71] See more J Izydorczyk, '"Prawdopodobieństwo popełnienia przestępstwa" oraz jego stopnie w polskim procesie karnym na podstawie k.p.k. z 1997 r.', in T Grzegorczyk (ed), *Funkcje procesu karnego. Księga jubileuszowa Profesora Janusza Tylmana* (Warsaw, Wolters Kluwer, 2011) 175–82.

[72] Marszał (n 5) 342; Cora (n 69) 592–94. See also Supreme Court Decision, 7 December 2005, III SW 67/05, OSNAPiUS 2006, nos. 7–8, pos 139.

[73] L Schaff, *Zakres i formy postępowania przygotowawczego* (Warsaw, Wydawnictwo PWN, 1961) 30.

[74] Verification may follow the filing of a notification of criminal offence or serve to verify the criminal prosecution authorities' own information, leading them to suppose that a criminal offence has been committed. There are two basic forms of checking activities, namely demanding that the data contained in the criminal offence notification be supplemented within a specified period of time, or verifying the facts indicated in the notification or arising from the law enforcement authorities' own information (Art 307 § 1 CPC). Under the first of these forms, actions may also be completed by a questioning of the notifying person in the capacity of a witness (Art 307 § 3 CPC). In the case of checking the facts contained in the notification of a crime, the checking procedure should be completed within an instructional period of thirty days from the receipt of this notification. Within this period, the authority is obliged to issue a decision on the initiation or refusal to initiate preparatory proceedings.

[75] This is the way in the verification procedure: no evidence of an expert opinion or actions requiring records are undertaken, except for receiving an oral notification of a criminal offence or a motion for prosecution, and the questioning of the notifying person in the capacity of a witness (Art 307 § 2 CPC).

[76] P Hofmański, E Sadzik and K Zgryzek, *Kodeks postępowania karnego. Komentarz* (Warsaw, CH Beck, 2004) vol I, 27.

[77] Judgment of the Appellate Court in Łódź, 27 November 2012, I ACa 856/12, Lex no 1267346.

aforementioned verification procedure. The decision on the institution of a principal investigation must contain two components: the determination of the act which is the subject of the proceedings and its legal qualification (Article 303 in fine CPC). In the case of a principal investigation, this decision is made exclusively by the prosecutor (Article 305 § 2 CPC).[78] According to Article 325e § 1 CPC, the decision to institution a simplified investigation shall be issued by the police or another authority conducting the proceedings (prosecutor or criminal procedure authority vested with police powers). It may be included in the protocol referred to in Article 304a CPC (protocol of oral notification of a crime and examination as a witness of the notifying person) and does not require justification.[79] This simplification may or may not be used. The person who, or the state, local government or soc (ial institution which, submitted a notice of a criminal offence, and the injured disclosed shall be notified of the institution of an investigation (Articles 305 § 4 and 325a § 2 CPC).[80]

In addition to the described, formal institution of pre-trial proceedings, this may indeed take place by undertaking urgent actions, the so-called 'proceedings (investigation) in the necessary scope' or 'case of utmost urgency'.[81] This is regulated in Article 308 § 1 CPC, according to which within the limits necessary to secure traces and evidence of a criminal offence against loss, distortion or destruction, the public prosecutor or the police may, in each case, in the event of utmost urgency, still before issuing a decision on the institution of a principal or simplified investigation, carry out necessary procedural actions. Having regard to this provision, two conditions for proceedings in the necessary scope can be distinguished:

- the existence of a basis for the institution of investigation, ie a good reason to suspect that a criminal offence has been committed;
- the occurrence of an urgent situation in which a threat of immediate loss, distortion or destruction of traces or evidence of a criminal offence is revealed.[82]

In such situations, the institution of an investigation takes place at the time of the first action provided for by the provisions of the CPC to secure traces or evidence of a criminal offence.[83] Article 308 § 1 CPC specifies exemplarily such actions, including an inspection, if a need arises with the participation of an expert witness, a search, and the taking of blood, hair and excretory samples. A person suspected of committing a criminal offence may be questioned as a suspect prior to the issuance of a decision on the presentation of charges, if there are grounds for the issuance of such a decision.

[78] If the police or other law enforcement authority receives a report of an offence that requires investigative investigation, or the police or other authority has data indicating that such an offence has been committed, it shall immediately forward it to the public prosecutor for the purpose of issuing a decision to initiate an investigation.

[79] Kurowski (n 24) vol I, 1183.

[80] The CPC does not provide for an obligation to notify the prosecutor about the opening of investigations by other criminal law enforcement bodies. The absence of such an obligation is difficult to reconcile with the prosecutor's duty to exercise supervision over investigations to the extent that he/she does not conduct them him/herself (Art 326 § 1 CPC). After all, it is difficult to expect its actual performance from the moment they are initiated, if he/she has no knowledge that a particular investigation is being conducted.

[81] Marszał (n 5) 348.

[82] Supreme Court Decision, 11 April 2012, II KK 313/11, OSNKW 2012, no 9, pos 96.

[83] Supreme Court Judgment, 8 March 2017, IV CSK 254/16, OSNC 2017, no 10, pos 119.

The questioning shall begin with informing the suspect of the contents of the charge (Article 308 § 2 CPC). The investigation, in cases of utmost urgency, shall be completed within five days of conducting the first evidentiary act (Article 308 § 3 CPC). Once it is completed, the rule will be to issue a decision to initiate a simplified investigation or to transfer the case file to the prosecutor in order to issue a decision to initiate an principal investigation, if it is required to conduct preparatory proceedings in this form (Article 308 § 1, second sentence CPC). Issuance of one of these decisions means transformation of the investigation in the necessary scope into a proper principal investigation or simplified investigation.[84] If a particular person has been questioned as a suspect and the proceedings should be conducted in the form of a principal investigation, within five days of questioning a decision on presentation of charges shall be issued, or in the case there are no grounds to draw up such a decision, the investigation shall be discontinued with respect to the person questioned (Article 308 § 3 CPC). If, as a result of urgent actions, it turns out that there are no factual grounds or exist legal obstacles to continue the criminal proceeding, then the instituted proceedings shall be discontinued.

To conclude this section, a few words should be devoted to the refusal to institute an investigation. As a rule, this takes a formal shape in cases of notification of the commission of a criminal offence.[85] Then, in accordance with Article 305 § 1 CPC, the criminal prosecuting authority is obliged to issue a decision on refusal to institute preparatory proceedings if it does not issue a decision to the contrary. Confronting these two decisions leads inevitably to the conclusion that one refuses to institute of an investigation when there are no grounds for doing so (instituting of investigation), ie when there is no good reason to suspect that a criminal offence has been committed.[86] This is the basic premise of a refusal decision. If the information about a crime does not come from a notice of its commission, its statement is usually made in an official note.[87] This does not preclude a formal decision to refuse to initiate an investigation. It should be issued in particular when a potential injured person is identified. This is supported by guarantee considerations, related to ensuring the possibility of initiating judicial review of a refusal to institute investigation on the basis of Article 306 § 1 CPC.[88] Apart from the indicated reason of factual nature (factual premise), refusal to institute investigation may be a consequence of stating one of the procedural obstacles of a legal nature, specified in Article 17 § 1, points 2–11 CPC.[89] Their occurrence results in a refusal to initiate preparatory proceedings, even when there is a justified suspicion that an offence has been committed (the factual basis for the criminal trial).

The authorities entitled to issue a decision on refusal to institute an investigation are: the public prosecutor, the police and other authorities vested with police powers (Article 305 § 3 in conjunction with Articles 311–12 and Articles 325a § 2 and 325f CPC), with the proviso that a decision not issued by a prosecutor requires his/her written approval (Article 305 § 3 and Article 325e § 2 CPC). Without approval, the decision

[84] Marszał (n 5) 349.

[85] Zagrodnik (n 24) 542.

[86] Judgment of the Appellate Court in Lublin, 13 November 2013, I ACa 327/12, Lex no 1444780; Stefański (n 6) 676.

[87] Grzegorczyk and Tylman (n 2) 656–57; Zagrodnik (n 24) 542.

[88] Grzegorczyk and Tylman (n 2) 657.

[89] These obstacles are detailed in ch 2 above. See Stefański (n 6) 675.

of the 'non-prosecutor' criminal prosecuting authority has no procedural effect; it is something like a draft decision.[90] The person who, or the state, local government or social institution which, submitted a notice of a criminal offence, and the injured disclosed shall be notified of the refusal to institute a principal or simplified investigation (Article 305 § 4, first sentence CPC).[91]

Presentation of Charges

The presentation of charges comprises a set of actions that demarcate the investigation in the *in rem* phase and the *in personam* phase, as a result of which criminal proceedings are directed against a specific person.[92] These actions are carried out by the criminal prosecution body that directs the pre-trial proceedings. In those cases where the prosecutor entrusts the conduct of the investigation to the police or to another body exercising police powers, the performance of these activities is reserved for the prosecutor (Article 311 § 3 in principio CPC).[93]

If there are grounds for presentation of charges against a particular person, questioning this person as a witness should be regarded as inadmissible as it would lead to violation of the principle *nemo se ipsum accusare tenetur* (Article 74 § 1 CPC) and of the suspect's right to refuse to give explanations and to refuse to answer questions (Article 175 § 1 CPC).[94] Such grounds consist of evidence of the commission of an offence to the extent allowing for subjective concretisation of a criminal prosecution. Article 313 § 1 CPC provides in this respect that if the data existing at the time of the institution of or collected in the course of a principal investigation provide grounds sufficient to suspect that an act has been committed by a specified person, a decision on the presentation of charges shall be drawn up and announced without delay to the suspect, who shall then be subjected to questioning, The data referred to in the cited provision denote the necessary minimum evidence so that the presentation of a charge against a specified person may be considered sufficiently justified. A hypothesis that a specific person has committed a crime must be supported by evidence that allows the trial authority to gain 'subjective certainty' about its accuracy.[95]

[90] A Gaberle, *Umorzenie postępowania przygotowawczego w polskim procesie karnym* (Warsaw, Wydawnictwo Prawnicze, 1972) 53; Stefański (n 6) 686.

[91] The injured, the state, local government or social institution which submitted a notice of criminal offence (Art 306 § 1 items 1 and 2 and Art 325a § 2 CPC) have the right to lodge a complaint against the decision to refuse to initiate an investigation. A person who submitted a notice of criminal offence is also entitled to challenge this decision if, as a result of the crime, his or her rights have been breached (Art 306 § 1 point 3 in connection with Art 325a § 2 CPC).

[92] Marszał (n 5) 349–50; J Kosonoga, in *System Prawa Karnego Procesowego*, red P Hofmański, vol 10, *Postępowanie przygotowawcze*, RA Stefański (ed) (Warsaw, Wolters Kluwer, 2016) 733–34.

[93] An exception to this proviso is made in cases in which the presentation of charges is made as part of urgent actions (see Art 308 § 2 in conjunction with Art 311 § 3 *in fine* CPC).

[94] Supreme Court Judgment, 21 January 1982, II KR 338/81, OSNKW 1982, no 3, pos 14; Supreme Court resolution, 26 April 2007, I KZP 4/07, OSNKW 2007, no 6, pos 45.

[95] Supreme Court Resolution, 23 February 2006, SNO 3/06, OSNSD 2006, no 1, pos 25.

The cited provision provides a basis for distinguishing the fundamental activities that make up the sequence forming the presentation of charges. These actions include:

1. drawing up a decision on the presentation of charges, which should contain the identity of the suspect, detailed data on the charged act and the legal classification thereof (Article 313 § 2 CPC);[96]
2. announcing its contents to the suspect without delay;
3. questioning of the suspect.[97]

As a rule, in order to effectively direct criminal proceedings against a certain person (to issue a decision to present charges) it is necessary to carry out all the listed actions. It is not sufficient to draw up the decision on the presentation of charges, which is a technical act conditioning the possibility of considering this decision as issued.[98] An exception relates to situations in which the suspect is in hiding or staying abroad and it is not practically possible to carry out the entire sequence of activities comprising the issuance of the decision to present charges, because the criminal prosecution authority has no contact with the person concerned (Article 313 § 1 in fine CPC).[99] In such cases, effective referral of proceedings against a specific person is based on the preparation of the indicated procedural decision.[100] The basic activities described above are supplemented by instructing the suspect about his/her right to demand that he/she be informed orally about the grounds for the charge without delay, as well as to demand that a statement of reason for the charge be prepared in writing, and without delay the charges announced orally to the suspect or a statement of reasons be prepared in writing and served on the suspect and the defence counsel (Article 313 §§ 1 and 3 CPC). The content of the substantiation of the decision to present charges is defined in the law in a very sparse manner. According to Article 313 § 4 CPC, the statement of reasons shall indicate, in particular, the facts and evidence assumed as the basis for the charges. By its very nature, the statement of reasons must convince that there are grounds to bring criminal proceedings against a specific person.[101]

The first questioning of the suspect in connection with the presentation of charges against him/her must be preceded[102] by instructions on his/her rights and obligations,

[96] See RA Stefański, 'Czynności przedstawienia zarzutów' (2013) *Prok i Pr* nos 7–8, 21 et seq.

[97] Supreme Court Decision, 16 January 2009, IV KK 256/08, Lex no 486201; Supreme Court Judgment, 2 June 2010, V KK 376/09, OSNwSK 2010, no 1, pos 1151. See more Kosonoga (n 92) 733 et seq; Zagrodnik (n 49) 191.

[98] Supreme Court Judgment, 2 June 2010, V KK 376/09, OSNwSK 2010, no 1, pos 1151. See further RA Stefański, 'Skuteczność przedstawienia zarzutów' (2013) *Prok i Pr* no 6, 8 et seq.

[99] Supreme Court Judgment, 5 March 2014, IV KK 341/13, Lex no 1444341; Supreme Court Judgment, 5 March 2015, III KK 414/14, OSP 2017, no 5, pos 47.

[100] Its promulgation and interrogation as a suspect shall be postponed, but shall take place immediately after the cessation of one of the specified reasons preventing this action immediately after the drafting of the charging order.

[101] See further Kosonoga (n 92) 790–98; Zagrodnik (n 49) 200–02.

[102] Judgment of the Appellate Court in Gdańsk, 22 January 2014, II AKa 447/13, Lex no 1430707.

which are set out in detail in Article 300 § 1, first sentence CPC. According to this provision, a person who is to be questioned as a suspect is instructed in particular:

1. of their rights:
   - to submit explanations, to refuse to provide explanations or to refuse to answer questions (Article 175 § 1 CPC);[103]
   - to information on the contents of the charges and amendments thereto (Article 313 § 1 and Article 314 CPC);
   - to submit motions for actions in the principal or simplified investigation (Article 315 § 1 CPC);
   - to receive assistance from a defence counsel, including the right to apply for a public defence counsel in the case defined in Article 78 and of the contents of Article 338b;
   - to the final acquaintance with the investigation materials (Article 321 § 1 CPC);
   - to submit a request for the case to be referred to mediation proceedings (Article 23a §1 CPC);
   - to a free-of-charge aid of an interpreter if he or she does not speak Polish sufficiently well (Article 72 § 1 CPC);
   - to access to the investigation files, and make copies or extracts and obtain certified copies or extracts against payment (Article 156 § 5 CPC);
   - to request to be questioned in the presence of the appointed defence counsel (Article 301 CPC);
   - to agree to the motion for a conviction to be issued in a session as well as for adjudicating penalties (Article 335 CPC);
   - to file, before a notification of the date of the trial is served on them, a motion for the issuance of a judgment of conviction and the imposition of a specific penalty or a criminal measure upon them or for ordering forfeiture or a redress measure without an evidentiary hearing being conducted (Article 338a CPC);
   - to submit, until the completion of the first questioning of all accused persons at the main trial, a motion for a judgment of conviction and for the imposition of a specific penalty or criminal measure upon them or for ordering forfeiture or a redress measure without an evidentiary hearing being conducted (Article 387a CPC);
2. of the obligations:
   - to undergo external examination of their body and other examinations specified in Article 74 § 2 CPC (described in chapter **4**);
   - to notify the authority conducting the proceedings of each change in their place of residence or of stay lasting longer than seven days, including also as a result of imprisonment in connection with another case, as well as of each change in their details enabling contact with them, indicated in Article 213 § 1 CPC, of which the accused knows that they are known to the authority conducting the

[103] Supreme Court Decision, 25 June 2014, II KK 124/14, Lex no 1480317.

proceedings; the accused shall also be obliged to appear upon each call in criminal proceedings (Article75 CPC);
- to indicate an addressee for service in the country or in another Member State of the European Union if they do not reside there; if they fail to do so, a letter sent to their last known address in the country or in another Member State of the European Union or, if there is no such address, enclosed with the case file, shall be deemed to have been served (Article 138 CPC).[104]

The suspect is advised in writing about indicated above – duties and rights; the suspect shall confirm the receipt of the advice with their signature (Article 300 § 1, second sentence CPC).[105]

Against the background of the presented rights of the suspect, it is worth recalling what has already been pointed out in chapter **3**, namely that the CPC does not guarantee a person who is to be questioned as a suspect that he/she may in any case have contact with a defence counsel before the first interrogation. At the same time, there is no guarantee of the participation of the defence counsel in the activities that make up the presentation of charges.[106] There is no doubt that the contact of the person to be questioned as a suspect with the defence counsel before his/her first questioning is of fundamental importance from the point of view of the defence, determining its strategy and tactics. In the current state of the law, the right of a suspect to request that he be questioned in the presence of the appointed defence counsel (Article 301 CPC) may be used to obtain such contact.[107] At the same time, two circumstances should be noted. First, that the condition in the form of appointment of a defence counsel is to be regarded as fulfilled if the suspect appeared at the summons of the trial authority to present charges together with a solicitor or a legal adviser, or gave to a solicitor or a legal adviser authorisation to represent him/her in the criminal trial in connection with the summons to appear for questioning as a suspect, and then, as soon as the questioning in this capacity commenced, demanded that the solicitor or legal adviser be allowed to participate in the proceedings as a defence counsel.[108] Second, that a failure to appear by the defence counsel shall not prevent the questioning from being conducted (Article 301, second sentence CPC).[109] The right of a suspect to request to be questioned with the participation of an appointed defence counsel is of a one-time nature.[110]

The order of activities comprising the presentation of charges presented so far may be subject to certain reductions in formalism in the case of simplified investigation (Article 325g § 2 CPC) and investigation in cases of utmost urgency, within the limits necessary to secure traces and evidence of a criminal offence against loss, distortion or

[104] See further Kosonoga (n 92) 770–76.

[105] Judgment of the Appellate Court in Wrocław, 23 October 2007, II AKa 290/07, OSA 2008, no 5, pos 24.

[106] Critical of this lack of guarantee to the right to defence, Zagrodnik (n 37) 124–25. See also J Zagrodnik, 'The Right to the Assistance of the Defense Counsel in the Light of the European Court of Human Rights Case Law' (2022) *Radca Prawny* no 2.

[107] J. Kosonoga, 'Przedstawienie i modyfikacja zarzutów a rola obrońcy', in P. Wiliński (ed), *Obrońca i pełnomocnik w procesie karnym po 1 lipca 2015 r. Przewodnik po zmianach* (Warsaw, Wolters Kluwer, 2015) s 111.

[108] Kulesza (n 55) 952.

[109] Kurowski (n 24) 1177; Kulesza (n 55) 952; Zagrodnik (n 49) 195.

[110] Kulesza (n 55) 952; Zagrodnik (n 49) 31, 195. Differently Kosonoga (n 107) 110.

destruction (Article 308 § 2 CPC). They basically consist in the possibility to refrain from drawing up a decision on the presentation of charges (simplified presentation of charges).[111] Such a presentation of charges takes place by informing a specified person of the contents of the charge, which is simultaneously entered into the record, and then proceeding to interrogate that person as a suspect. Entering the charge into the record is equivalent to the preparation of a decision to present charges, which is drawn up in the formalised form of the presentation of charges, while the notification of the contents of the charge is equivalent to the announcement of this decision. In the case of a simplified presentation of charges, a specific person is deemed to be a suspect as soon as his/her questioning begins, which, as already noted, takes place by announcing the contents of the charge (Article 308 § 2, second sentence and Article 325g § 2, second sentence CPC).[112] The described possibility to refrain from drawing up a decision on the presentation of charges in an investigation does not apply to investigations in which the suspect is subject to provisional detention (Article 325g § 1 in fine CPC) or there is a need to apply another precautionary measure against him (*argumentum ex* Article 249 § 2 CPC), as well as when the suspect does not have sufficient command of the Polish language, because in such a case there is an obligation to serve him/her with a translation of the decisions on presenting, supplementing or amending the charges (Article 72 § 3 in connection with Article 72 § 1 CPC).

The detailed data on the alleged act of the suspect by way of presenting charges is of significant guarantee importance, as it outlines the programme of the investigation against a specific person.[113] It has already been said earlier that the charge made in the investigation and the resulting programme of proceedings need not be identical with the charge resulting from the indictment, setting out the programme for the determination of the case in court proceedings. Sometimes the natural changes in the programme of the investigation, dictated by the dynamics of the cognitive process at this stage of the proceedings and the enrichment by the trial authority of its knowledge of the criminal offence under investigation, are so significant that even before the charge in the indictment, it is necessary to repeat the steps comprising the presentation of the charge in order to allow the suspect to adjust his/her defence accordingly.[114] This must occur in three procedural situations, namely if during principal investigation it turns out that:

1. the accused shall be charged with an act not included in a previous decision on the presentation of charges;
2. an act essentially different in nature or form from the one attributed to them therein;[115] or
3. the alleged act shall be classified under a more strict provision (Article 314 CPC).[116]

The first two situations are related to factual findings, whereas the third situation is related to the legal assessment of the act charged against the suspect.

[111] Kosonoga (n 92) 741–43.
[112] Stefański (n 98) 23.
[113] Grzegorczyk and Tylman (n 2) 669.
[114] Kosonoga (n 92) 820; Zagrodnik (n 24) 550–51.
[115] See Decision of the Appellate Court in Katowice, 19 August 2009, II AKz 553/09, OSA 2009, no 3, pos 18.
[116] Supreme Court Judgment, 30 September 2009, I KZP 1/09, OSNwSK 2009, no 1, pos 1904.

Closure of a Principal Investigation or a Simplified Investigation

At the outset, it should be emphasised that the closure of an investigation does not mean the end of the proceedings at the first procedural stage (the end of pre-trial proceedings), because this stage still includes – in accordance with the Code's systematics (Section VII CPC) – the drafting of an indictment or other substantive criminal complaint.[117]

Closing an investigation should be viewed institutionally, assuming that it does not constitute a single action, but a certain sequence of actions preceding the decision to close. These actions are taken if the evidence gathered in the investigation allows the procedural authority to come to a subjective conviction that the suspect is the perpetrator of a criminal offence (the perpetrator of a specific type of criminal act in the case of insanity of the suspect) and that the case should be heard and decided by a court.[118] Adopting a different optics, it can be stated that the closure of the principal investigation or simplified investigation takes place in situations where the preparatory proceeding has provided grounds for drawing up and filing an indictment (Articles 331 and 335 § 2 CPC) or a motion for a judgment of conviction to be issued in a session and to order the penalties of other measures provided for the misdemeanour (Article 335 § 1 CPC) or a motion for conditional discontinuance of proceedings by the court at the hearing (Article 336 CPC) or a motion on discontinuance of the proceedings due to insanity of the perpetrator and on the application of preventive measures (Article 324 CPC).[119] In the established sequence of activities, the following two links may be distinguished:

1. activities related to the final acquaintance of the suspect and his/her counsel with the materials of the investigation;
2. formal closure of the principal investigation or closure of the simplified investigation.[120]

The basic activities related to the final aquaintance with the pre-trial materials include the following:[121]

1. Notifying the suspect and defence counsel of the date of final acquaintance with the materials of the proceedings, at the same time instructing them on the right to review the files in advance within a time frame appropriate to the importance or complexity of the case, determined by the procedural authority;[122] these actions are of optional nature – they take place upon a request of a suspect or his/her

[117] Marszał (n 5) 353; Stefański (n 6) 1263–66.
[118] Stefański (n 6) 1014.
[119] Zagrodnik (n 24) 553.
[120] Stefański (n 6) 1031.
[121] ibid 1031–32.
[122] The time frame for the suspect to become acquainted with the investigation materials should be set so that at least seven days will have passed from the date of service of the notification of that time frame on the suspect and their defence counsel (Art 321 § 2 CPC). The seven-day time limit is the minimum time limit that must be respected by the trial authority in every case. When setting a deadline for the final familiarisation with the materials of the proceedings, the criminal enforcement authority should be guided by the desire to guarantee the accused a real opportunity to familiarise him/herself with the case file within limits not exceeding a reasonable need. It should take into account, inter alia, the breadth and complexity of the evidence, as well as

defence counsel for the final aquaintance with the materials of the proceedings (Article 321 § 1 CPC). Such a request is *spiritus movens* for the actions comprising this acquaintance; when it is not submitted, the closure of the investigation boils down to issuing a decision in this respect.

2. Making the investigation file available to the suspect and his/her defence counsel for personal viewing. The procedural authority may not deny them access to the investigation file in this phase of the process.[123] The procedural authority is obliged to provide appropriate technical and organisational conditions for this purpose.[124] The prosecutor may also make the files available in electronic form (Article 156 § 5, sixth sentence and Article 321 § 1, second sentence CPC).
3. The acquaintance the suspect and his/her defence counsel with all the materials of the investigation. Participation in this activity is the right of the said subjects; a failure of the suspect or his/her defence counsel to appear for which no justification has been provided shall not obstruct the further course of the investigation (Article 321 § 4 CPC). Acquaintance should take the form of an oral presentation by the procedural authority of the evidence collected in the case;[125] this would certainly serve the purpose of self-control of procedural authorities as regards the legality and legitimacy of procedural actions, as well as putting in order the evidence collected in the investigation. In practice, however, it is not infrequently limited to expressing the trial authority's conviction as to the realisation of the elements of the criminal offence charged against the suspect on the basis of a general reference to the files of the investigation, with which the suspect and his or her counsel have or could have become acquainted; this leaves little room for the suspect and defence counsel to comment on individual pieces of evidence. Although the law does not provide for an obligation to finally question the suspect in this procedural phase, there is no obstacle to the suspect giving explanations; if he/she is willing to do so, the procedural authority should, in principle, give him/her an opportunity to do so.
4. Taking record of the final acquaintance of the suspect with the materials of the investigation (Article 143 § 1 (8) CPC); this is obligatory.
5. Submission by the parties of motions to supplement the principal investigation or simplified investigation within three days from the final acquaintance with the materials of the proceedings (Article 321 § 5 CPC);[126] this time limit is not a manifestation of evidence preclusion,[127] so there is no obstacle, for example, to

the suspect's individual perception abilities related, for example, to his/her education or health condition. See Decision of the Appellate Court in Katowice, 26 August 2009, II AKz 566/09, OSA 2009, no 4, pos 25.

[123] Refusal to grant access to files due to the need to secure the proper course of proceedings or protect an important interest of the state, as provided for in Art 156 § 5 CPC (the provision of Art 321 § 1 CPC constitutes a *lex specialis* with respect to the indicated regulation), is out of the question.

[124] Stefański (n 6) 1036.

[125] ibid 1038–40.

[126] It follows from the cited provision that not only the defendant (and his/her defence counsel), but also the victim (and his/her attorney) have the right to file a motion. The exercise of this right by the victim may encounter significant difficulties, because he/she is not familiarised with the materials of the pre-trial proceedings, nor is he/she notified of the date of this procedural action, which is connected to the beginning of the three-day period for submitting a request for evidence.

[127] See R Olszewski, 'Zasadnicze zmiany dotyczące procesowych uprawnień oskarżonego i pokrzywdzonego w nowelizacji z 27 września 2013 r', in T. Grzegorczyk (ed), *Funkcje procesu karnego. Księga jubileuszowa Profesora Janusza Tylmana* (Warsaw, Wolters Kluwer, 2011) 263.

the accused requesting the examination of evidence, which is already known to him at the time of closing the investigation, only at a subsequent stage of criminal proceedings.[128]

If, as a result of the activities related to the final acquaintance of the suspect or his/her counsel with the materials of the preparatory proceedings, the need to supplement the principal investigation or simplified investigation does not become apparent as a result of the motions of the parties or their procedural representatives or on the procedural authority's own initiative, the investigations are formally closed. In the case of a principal investigation, it is necessary for the prosecutor to issue a decision on its closure. It shall be announced or its contents shall be communicated to the suspect and their defence counsel (Article 321 § 6 CPC). Although in a simplified investigation it is not required to issue a decision to close it, unless the suspect is not subject to provisional detention (Article 325g § 1 CPC), there are no obstacles to the authority conducting the investigation issuing such a decision.[129]

Following the closure of the principal investigation, the prosecutor proceeds to draw up and file the indictment. In the framework of a simplified investigation conducted by the police or another body exercising police powers, it is for these bodies to draw up the indictment. However, it generally requires the approval of the prosecutor, who also files it to the court (Article 331 § 1 CPC). An exception applies to the authorities listed in the regulation of the Minister of Justice, issued on the basis of the statutory delegation contained in Article 325d CPC (e.g. the Trade Inspectorate, the State Sanitary Inspectorate), which may file the indictment to court independently, ie without approval, unless the prosecutor decides otherwise (Article 331 § 2 CPC).

An alternative to the described closing of a principal or a simplified investigation is the unconditional discontinuance of criminal proceedings, which interrupts the course of the trial and causes its cessation. It also ends the preparatory proceedings.[130] At the stage of criminal proceedings under discussion, it may be the result of determining that the evidence gathered in the case does not provide grounds for bringing an indictment or other principal criminal complaint, or that one of the procedural obstacles specified in Article 17 § 1 CPC occurs.[131] A decision on discontinuance of a principal or simplified investigation may be contested by the parties, by the state or local government institution which has provided the notice of the criminal offence, and by a person who has submitted the notice of a criminal offence defined in Articles 228–31, 233, 235, 236, 245, 270–77, 278–94 or 296–306 CC, provided that criminal proceedings have been instituted as a result of the notice and the rights of that person have been breached as a result of the criminal offence (Article 306 § 1a CPC). The persons authorised to file the complaint shall have the right to view the files (Article 306 § 1b CPC). It shall be for the court to examine the complaint (Article 465 § 2 in conjunction with Article 55 § 3 and Article 330 § 2 CPC).

[128] Zagrodnik (n 24) 555–56.
[129] Stefański (n 6) 1047–48.
[130] Marszał (n 5) 353.
[131] Grzegorczyk and Tylman (n 2) 677.

Principal Criminal Complaint

A principal criminal complaint, hereinafter abbreviated as a principal complaint, is a complaint that initiates integral proceedings before the court as to the main object of the trial, ie court proceedings as to the criminal liability of a specific person prosecuted for the offence charged.[132] In the Polish criminal trial, which is based on the accusatory principle, the fundamental criminal complaint is the foundation of court proceedings as to the merits of the trial and constitutes the condition of its admissibility (a procedural ground – Article 17 § 1 point 9 CPC). In order for this condition to be fulfilled, the complaint must meet two necessary requirements, which are *essentialia negotii* of the complaint, namely it must identify the person accused and contain a description of the criminal offence charged.[133] The essence of the principal criminal complaint is a demand that the court examine the case for the offence charged against the accused and draw the criminal law consequences resulting from its commission.[134] The basic form of such a demand is an indictment.

On the example of an indictment, the essential functions of a criminal complaint can be presented, which include the following:

- The balancing function, consisting in the fact that the indictment is the expression of a summary and analysis of the results of the preparatory proceedings (investigation), which, as a rule, precedes the judicial stage of the criminal trial.[135]
- The initiating function,[136] also called the function of the procedural impulse;[137] its sense is expressed in the fact that the filing of an indictment sets in motion legal proceedings and causes a state of *lis pendens* before the court (*litis pendentio*) without the need for the judicial authority to take any action in this regard. The court does not decide whether or not to institute legal proceedings, since this follows from the filing of the complaint. The complaint is *sui generis* the motor of the criminal proceedings before the court of first instance, setting in motion the mechanism for the examination and determination of the case by said authority.
- As indicated above, the indictment sets out a programme for the court to examine and determine the case (programmatic funkction). The court is bound by this programme, which means that it cannot go beyond the subjective and objective (subject-matter) boundaries of the programme as set out in the principal complaint;[138] the former apply to the accused himself. Court proceedings may

[132] Zagrodnik (n 24) 570. See also S Waltoś, *Akt oskarżenia w procesie karnym* (Warsaw, Państwowe Wydawnictwo Naukowe, 1963) 7 et seq; M Cieślak, *Polska procedura karna. Podstawowe założenia teoretyczne, Dzieła wybrane* (Wydawnictwo Uniwersytetu Jagiellońskiego, Kraków 2011) vol II, 260.

[133] Marszał (n 5) 361.

[134] See further S Stachowiak, *Funkcje zasady skargowości w polskim procesie karnym* (Poznań, Wydawnictwo Uniwersytetu im. Adama Mickiewicza w Poznaniu, 1975) 26 et seq.

[135] Marszał (n 5) 363; differently also Waltoś (n 132) 14. See also Supreme Court Judgment, 4 December 2007, II KK 88/05, OSNwSK 2007, no 1, pos 2752.

[136] Cieślak (n 132) 260; Marszał (n 5) 363; Stefański (n 6) 1561.

[137] Waltoś (n 132) 11 et seq; Stachowiak (n 134) 26.

[138] S Kalinowski, *Polski proces karny* (Warsaw, Wydawnictwo PWN, 1970) 416; Cieślak (n 132) 260; Marszał (n 5) 363–64.

proceed only against the person who has been named as the accused in the indictment. The subject-matter boundaries are connected with the offence charged against the accused in the indictment. The court may not extend the proceedings to other acts not specified therein;[139] an exception in this respect is the so-called 'incidental process' (*proces wpadkowy*)[140] – if, by reason of circumstances newly disclosed at the trial, the prosecution counsel has charged the accused with committing an act in addition to those contained in the indictment, the court may, if the accused consents thereto, hear the new charges at the same trial, unless it becomes necessary to institute investigation with respect to the newly disclosed act (Article 398 CPC).

- The function of procedural information. This is closely related to the principle of a fair trial and to the principle of publicity. The indictment is a source of information about the matter of the proceedings, both for the accused and his/her defence counsel and for other parties and participants involved in the trial.[141]

The principal (main) complaint comes in different generic varieties. The basic one, as already stated, is the indictment, in its ordinary form and its other variants. In addition to it, one can distinguish principal complaints that replace the indictment in a criminal trial and principal complaints that do not belong to any of the categories distinguished earlier (other principal criminal complaints).[142] All these variants of the principal complaint will be briefly introduced below, with particular emphasis on the ordinary form of the indictment.

The ordinary indictment is the typical principal complaint. It must be in writing, which serves to preserve the precision of its wording and ensures its permanence. Being in writing also guarantees the accused that an act (in the real sense) other than that set forth in the indictment will not be imputed to him in the judgment.[143] The order of the content structure of the indictment as envisaged in the Polish criminal trial is based on the Germanic model, which is characterised by the inclusion of a statement of reasons at the end of this pleading.[144] According to Article 332 §§ 1 and 2 in connection with Article 119 § 1 CPC, the content components of the indictment, constituting its formal requirements, are the following:

1. The first and last name of the accused and their other personal data, including their telephone number, fax number and e-mail address, or confirmation that the accused does not have these or that they cannot be determined, and data on the application of a precautionary measure and security on property (Article 332 § 1 pkt 1 CPC). These particulars define the subjective boundaries of the case being examined in court proceedings.[145]
2. A detailed determination of the alleged act of the accused with an indication of the time, place, manner and circumstances related to its commission as well as of the consequences, and particularly of the value of the resulting damage (Article 332

[139] Marszał (n 5) 364.
[140] ibid 364.
[141] Marszał (n 5) 364; Waltoś (n 132) 13.
[142] Zagrodnik (n 24) 570–74.
[143] Waltoś (n 132) 9. See also Zagrodnik (n 1) 348.
[144] Zagrodnik (n 24) 575.
[145] Waltoś (n 132) 54; Stefański (n 6) 1586.

§ 1 pkt 2 CPC).[146] This is the so-called conclusion of the indictment,[147] which must correspond to the disposition of the provision of substantive criminal law in the sense that it should indicate specific facts fulfilling the disposition of the provision defining the offence in connection with which the proceedings are conducted.[148] The act described in the conclusion sets the subject-matter boundaries of the court proceedings.[149]

3. An indication that the act has been committed under the conditions specified in Articles 64 or 65 CC, or Article 37 § 1 of the Penal Fiscal Code (Article 332 § 1 pkt 3 CPC). The first of these provisions regulates criminal liability for a crime committed under conditions of recidivism; the second concerns the criminal liability of the perpetrator who has adopted commission of crimes as a regular source of income or has committed a crime acting in an organised criminal group or organised criminal association aiming at perpetrating crimes, and to the perpetrator of a crime of a terrorist character; the third one concerns committing a fiscal offence in conditions justifying an extraordinary aggravation of punishment, specified in Article 37 § 1 of the Penal Fiscal Code.
4. An indication of the criminal statute under which the alleged act is classifiable (Article 332 § 1 pkt 4 CPC).[150]
5. An indication of the court competent to examine the case (Article 332 § 1 pkt 5 CPC).
6. The date and signature of the person filing such a pleading (Article 119 § 1 pkt 4 CPC).

In the current state of the law, the statement of reasons is an obligatory component of the content of the indictment only in cases in which the preparatory proceedings ended in the form of a principal investigation. Where an investigation has ended in the form of a simplified investigation, the indictment may not contain a statement of reasons (Article 332 § 3 CPC). This, of course, does not preclude its provision and, it may be said, as a rule, the indictment also contains an announcement of a judgment in cases where a simplified investigation has been carried out.[151] A statement of reasons should indicate the facts and evidence on which the charge is founded and, insofar as it is necessary, explain the legal basis for the charge and describe the circumstances cited by the accused in their defence (Article 332 § 2 CPC).

According to Article 333 § 1 CPC, an indictment should also contain:

1. a list of persons that the prosecution counsel requires to be summoned;
2. a list of other evidence that the prosecution counsel requires to be examined in the main trial.

[146] Supreme Court Judgment, 24 March 1983, II KR 49/83, OSPIKA 1984, no 6, pos 126. See also Waltoś (n 132) 59.

[147] Similarly Stefański (n 6) 1591.

[148] Supreme Court Judgment, 22 March 2012, IV KK 375/11, OSNKW 2012, no 7, pos 78; Decision of the Appellate Court in Katowice, 16 January 2014, II AKa 397/13, Lex no 1428051; Judgment of the Appellate Court in Szczecin, 28 September 2017, II AKa 192/16, Lex no 2391897.

[149] Supreme Court Decision, 13 November 2003, WK 19/03, OSNwSK 2003, pos 2413. About language, Decision of the Appellate Court in Białystok, 10 April 1991, II AKz 13/91, OSA 1992, no 1, pos 10.

[150] Further Waltoś (132) 82; Stefański (n 6) 1610–15.

[151] Similarly Kurowski (n 24) 1315.

The list of evidence that indicates the evidentiary basis for the indictment is at the same time a motion for evidence that is addressed to the court, aiming to examine the evidence listed therein.[152] The public prosecutor may put forward a motion for the abandonment of summoning of the witnesses who have been questioned, who are staying abroad or who state circumstances that are not so important that it is necessary to question the witnesses directly at the trial, in particular circumstances not denied by the accused in their explanations (Articles 332 § 2 and 350a CPC). This shall not apply to the persons listed in Article 182, who have the right to refuse to testify.

A list of injured parties disclosed, with their addresses, as well as addresses of persons who the prosecution counsel requires to be summoned, shall be attached to the indictment, for the court's information. The telephone numbers, fax numbers and e-mail addresses of the persons indicated in the first sentence shall also be provided, unless this information cannot be determined (Article 333 § 3 CPC). An indictment shall be accompanied by a list of the injured who have submitted requests to be informed about the manner of concluding the case with an ordinary letter sent to the address indicated by the injured, by fax or by e-mail, along with a copy of the final ruling concluding the investigation or an excerpt therefrom, which may be sent in electronic form (Articles 333 § 3a and Article 299a § 2 CPC). A public prosecutor may also enclose with an indictment a motion calling for adjudication with regard to the obliged entity specified in Article 91a of the return of a material benefit or its equivalent to the entitled entity or adjudication of forfeiture of a benefit or its equivalent to the State Treasury. Such a motion shall contain a justification (Article 333 § 5 CPC).

An indictment sent to the court shall be accompanied by the investigation files, including annexes thereto. The following shall also be enclosed with an indictment address annex to the case files and one duplicate of that indictment for each of the accused, and in the case defined in Article 335 § 2 CPC (see below), also for each of the injured (Article 334 §§ 1–2 CPC). The court shall be provided with all the material gathered at the pre-trial proceedings. It is not allowed to make any selection of the collected material.[153]

Under Article 335 § 2 CPC the public prosecutor may enclose with an indictment a motion for a judgment of conviction to be issued in a session and to order the penalties of other measures provided for the misdemeanour, determined in consultation with the accused and also taking into account the legally protected interests of the injured, where the circumstances in which the criminal offence was committed and the guilt of the accused are beyond doubt, the evidentiary testimony given by the accused is not inconsistent with the findings made, and the attitude of the accused indicates that the objectives of the proceedings will be achieved. The agreement may also cover the issuance of a specific resolution as to the incurrence of costs of proceedings (Article 335 § 1 fifth sentence and Article 335 § 2 second sentence CPC). A submitted motion for conviction without trial, because it is subject to being attached to the indictment, is referred to as non-self-contained. If attached to the indictment, the complaint need not

[152] Zagrodnik (n 24) 577. See further Zagrodnik (n 1) 353–56; Stachowiak (n 134) 174; Waltoś (n 132) 105.

[153] S Stachowiak, in K Marszał, S Stachowiak and K Zgryzek (eds), *Proces karny* (Katowice, Volumen, 2005) 68; similarly Zagrodnik (n 24) 578–79.

contain a list of persons that the prosecution counsel requires to be summoned and a list of other evidence that the prosecution counsel requires to be examined in the main trial. The statement of reasons for the indictment shall be limited to an indication of the evidence showing that the circumstances in which the criminal offence was committed and the guilt of the accused are beyond doubt and that the objectives of the proceedings will be achieved without a trial being conducted (Article 335 § 3, second sentence in conjunction with Article 335 § 2, second sentence CPC). The motion in question serves to create an opportunity for the court to resolve the case under the consensual model of trial, without the need for evidence to be taken at the main trial.[154] In this model, the defendant avoids the stigma associated with sitting on the defendant's bench at a public main hearing, can expect a quick explanation of his legal situation and often also a lighter sentence. From the injured person's perspective, a resolution of the case under the consensual model of trial makes it possible, above all, to obtain compensation for damage or harm suffered relatively quickly.

In addition to the ordinary indictment, which has been discussed above, three special forms of it can be distinguished:

1. The summary indictment – this differs from the ordinary indictment only in that it does not contain a statement of reasons, and this, as already established above, is possible in cases where the preparatory proceedings have ended in the form of an simplified investigation (Article 332 § 3 CPC).[155]
2. A simplified indictment, brought to court by the injured person in cases under private indictment (Chapter 52 CPC), eg in cases involving offences of personal violation or offences of defamation.[156] Such an indictment may be limited to the designation of the accused, of the act imputed to them, and to the indication of the evidence on which the indictment is founded (Article 487 CPC). A further facilitation for the injured of an offence prosecuted by private prosecution arises from the wording of Article 488 § 1 CPC, which requires the police to accept an oral or written complaint at the request of a designated entity, if necessary, secure the evidence, and to transmit the complaint to the competent court.[157]
3. An oral indictment, which initiates the so called 'incidental process',[158] mentioned above (Article 398 CPC). Such an indictment requires a precise statement of the facts. It seems obvious that such an indictment must contain the elements of the content structure of an ordinary indictment, which can be regarded as necessary from the point of view of the essence of the principal criminal complaint, ie it should name the accused, precisely define the offence charged (the conclusion of

[154] See more S Steinborn, *Porozumienia w polskim procesie karnym* (Kraków, Kantor Zakamycze, 2005) passim; H Paluszkiewicz, *Pierwszoinstancyjne wyrokowanie poza rozprawą w polskim procesie karnym* (Warsaw, Wolters Kluwer, 2008) 240 et seq; Zagrodnik (n 1) 370 et seq; Zagrodnik (n 37) 125, 133.

[155] Marszał (n 5) 363.

[156] ibid 363.

[157] See further K Eichstaedt, in D Świecki (ed), *Kodeks postępowania karnego. Komentarz* (Warsaw, Wolters Kluwer, 2021) vol II, 506–16; D Gil, *Postępowanie w sprawach z oskarżenia prywatnego w polskim procesie karnym* (Warsaw, Wolters Kluwer, 2011).

[158] Marszał (n 5) 363; Grzegorczyk and Tylman (n 2) 785; Eichstaedt (n 157) vol I, 506–16.

the indictment) and indicate its legal qualification;[159] it should also contain information about committing the act under the conditions specified in Articles 64 or 65 CC or Article 37 § 1 of the Penal Fiscal Code.

Moving on to outline the other varieties of principal complaints in Polish criminal proceedings, we should begin with complaints that replace the indictment, which perform all of its functions, as illustrated earlier. The following two principal complaints belong to this group:

- A motion for conditional discontinuance of criminal proceedings. This is drawn up by a prosecutor or a non-prosecutorial procedural body authorised to file and support a charge in cases of offences prosecuted by public indictment (Articles 336 and 325i § 3 CPC). The drawing up and filing of such a motion takes place if the grounds for the application of a probationary measure in the form of conditional discontinuance of criminal proceedings are met; these conditions are set out in Articles 66 § 1 and 2 CPC. It follows from these provisions that the court may conditionally discontinue the criminal proceedings if the perpetrator's fault and social harmfulness of the act are not substantial, the circumstances of the committed crime subject to the penalty of deprivation of liberty exceeding five years are indubitable, and due to the demeanour of the perpetrator, who has not been previously sentenced for an intentional crime, his/her characteristics, personal conditions and previous way of life, it is reasonable to expect that, in spite of the discontinuance of the proceedings, he will respect the legal order, especially by not committing a crime. In general, a motion for conditional discontinuance of criminal proceedings must contain most of the components that constitute the formal requirements of an ordinary indictment.[160] Its statement of reasons may be limited to an indication of the evidence showing that the guilt of the accused is beyond any doubt, as well as an indication of the circumstances supporting a conditional discontinuance (Article 336 § 2 CPC). The motion may indicate a suggested probation period, obligations to be imposed on the accused and, depending on circumstances, a motion regarding the supervision (Article 336 § 3 CPC).
- A motion for the case to be tried in expedited proceedure. This motion shall be drawn up and forwarded to the court by the police together with the gathered evidence if the conditions for the case to be tried in expedited proceedings exist (Article 517d § 1 CPC).

Unlike the principal complaints listed at the end, the others do not fulfil the essential functions that are inherent in an indictment. This is clearly revealed against the background of the regulation of the manner of their negative disposal, which results in transferring the case to the prosecutor in order to continue the preparatory proceedings or to take another decision in the case (Articles 324 § 2 and 343 § 7, first sentence CPC). This excludes the continuation of the examination of the case by the court until it is resolved on the merits, as is generally the case in the cases of principal complaints

[159] Judgment of the Appellate Court in Warsaw, 23 October 2013, II AKa 85/13, Lex no 13112111.

[160] K Zgryzek, 'Skargi zastępują ce akt oskarżenia w polskim procesie karnym', in Gerecka-Żołyńska et al, *Skargowy model procesu karnego*.

presented earlier which replace the indictment. The characterised group of criminal complaints includes the following:

- The prosecutor's motion on discontinuance of the proceedings and on application of preventive measures. This may be filed if it is established that the suspect committed the act in a state of insanity and that there are grounds for applying to him/her the preventive measures specified in Article 93a § 1 CC (electronic monitoring of a person's location, therapy, addiction therapy, placement in a psychiatric facility) or to impose, as a preventive measure, orders or bans defined in Article 39 §§ 2–3 CC (eg prohibition from occupying a specific position, practising a specific profession or operating a specific business activity, prohibition from entering a mass event, prohibition from entering gambling facilities and engaging in gambling games, order to leave, for a determined period of time, the premises occupied together with a harmed party, prohibition from operating vehicles).
- An independent motion for a judgment of conviction to be issued in a session (without a main trial) and to order the penalties of other measures provided for the misdemeanour, which is regulated in Article 335 § 1 CPC. This motion differs from a non-self-contained motion on the same subject in that it requires that the defendant plead guilty. The plea of guilty is an expression of his or her desire to expiate; the plea of guilty must be complete (*confesio plena*), which means that it should relate to all the relevant circumstances of the case relating to the issue of perpetration, guilt and legal classification. The accompanying explanations of the defendant are in fact the foundation of the factual findings on which the judgment on criminal responsibility is based. If there is a need to evaluate the reliability of the explanations submitted, evidentiary actions shall be carried out only in the scope necessary thereto (Article 335 § 1, second sentence CPC); in the other case, if the accused pleads guilty, and in the light of their explanations the circumstances in which the criminal offence was committed and the responsibility of the accused are beyond doubt, and the attitude of the accused indicates that the objectives of investigation would be achieved, further actions may be abandoned (Article 335 § 1, first sentence CPC). However, procedural actions necessary to secure traces and evidence of the criminal offence against their loss, distortion or destruction must be carried out, including, inter alia, external examination of the body, searches, and blood, hair and excretory sampling (Article 335 § 1, third sentence CPC).

6

Proceedings before the Court of First Instance

Preparation for the First-Instance Trial

Submission to Court

In the doctrine, two different meanings are used to designate the institution of trial submission indicated here. The first of them – submission to court *sensu largo* – is a procedural act of a specific authority or person, based on which a person is indicted for the act he or she is accused of and is answerable to the court, which is to decide on the subject of the proceedings, ie on the guilt or innocence of that person and on the other consequences of the act, as provided for in substantive criminal law.

Submission to court *sensu stricto* means a judicial act of review by the court of the merits of the accusation before the commencement of the main trial. This institution is also sometimes referred to as 'submission of the case to the court by the court', which emphasises the role of the court at this stage of the trial. It is for the court to determine whether the substantive conditions for consideration of the case brought by the prosecution exist. In this way, the court determines whether the conditions for scheduling a main trial have been met.

In fact, this preliminary review of the accusation may take place before or after the charge is brought before the court. In the first case, the court allows the indictment to be brought or decides that the evidence gathered in the case is not sufficient to bring the designated person to trial. In this way, by exercising this preliminary review, the court protects the person suspected of a crime from being unjustifiably charged. It is for this reason that the court, when deciding that the accusation is unfounded, does not allow the accusation to be made in public, ie during the trial. As a result of the post-indictment review, it is only at this stage that the court, depending on the outcome of the review, either schedules a trial or takes any other appropriate decision.

Submission of the case to the court by the court may occur in two forms: mandatory or facultative. The first of these may take place in all cases or only in cases of more serious offences, eg in cases of crimes. Facultative submission the case by the court, on the other hand, means that the question of whether a preliminary examination is necessary is left to the discretion of a particular judicial authority. Such optional submission occurs only if specific conditions expressly set by law are met.[1]

The Polish CPC has adopted a mixed solution with respect to the institutions indicated here. In some situations it provides for mandatory submission of the case to the court by the court, while in other cases it leaves this matter to the discretion of the presiding judge. The president of the court may commit the case to session where the accused who has been charged with a criminal offence punishable by imprisonment for a term not exceeding fifteen years, before the service upon them of the notification of the date of the trial having been set, has submitted the motion referred to in Article 338a and the president of the court decides that the objectives of the proceedings do not preclude the examination of the case in a session (Article 339 § 3a CPC).

The submission of the case to the court by the court has a number of advantages. It is a guarantee of protection of the interests of the accused in the criminal trial. It ensures that no one becomes a victim of unfounded and unjustified accusations, especially those without sufficient factual basis, and is protected from the reputational damage of wrongfully sitting on the prosecution bench at a public hearing. Moreover, it saves costs to the authorities and litigants and protects the court and the parties from unnecessary actions. It also strengthens the authority and dignity of the state power by favouring the elimination of wrongful accusations, for nothing can be more detrimental to a democratic state of law, a status that the Republic of Poland enshrines in Article 2 of its constitution, than the presence on the bench of an accused person against whom the accusation in court turns out to be completely unfounded. Finally, judicial review is supported by the fact that the legitimacy of the accusation is reviewed by a judicial authority, and thus objectively and impartially, without succumbing to accusatory tendencies that sometimes characterise the entity bringing the charge before the court.[2]

The institution of submission of the case to the court by the court includes the control of the formal conditions of the indictment and the control of the case.[3]

[1] H Paluszkiewicz, *Pierwszoinstancyjne wyrokowanie merytoryczne poza rozprawą w polskim procesie karnym* (Warsaw, Wolter Kluwer, 2008); K Zgryzek, 'Obligatoryjne posiedzenie przygotowawcze przed rozprawą w polskim procesie karnym', in pod red P Hofmański (ed) and K Zgryzek, *Współczesne problemy procesu karnego i wymiaru sprawiedliwości. Księga ku czci Profesora Kazimierza Marszała* (Katowice, Wydawnictwo Uniwersytetu Śląskiego, 2003).

[2] D Drajewicz, 'Ingerencja sądu w postępowanie przygotowawcze' (2013) *PS* no 3; E. Łuszczyk, 'Kontrola czy nadzór sądu nad postępowaniem przygotowawczym', in T Kalisz (ed), *Nowa kodyfikacja prawa karnego* (Wrocław, Wydawnictwo Uniwersytetu Wrocławskiego, 2012) vol XXVIII; D Stachurski, 'Sądowa kontrola zaniechania ścigania karnego – rzeczywiste czy pozorne wzmocnienie zasady legalizmu w procesi karnym?' (2012) *PS* no 3.

[3] Ł Supera and D Wyszkowski, 'Subsydiarny akt oskarżenia w ujęciu konstytucyjnym' (2016) *Pal* nos 7–8; R Zawłocki, 'Akt oskarżenia jako przedmiot procesowego sporu przed kontradyktoryjną rozprawą', in P Wiliński (ed), *Obrońca i pełnomocnik w procesie karnym po 1 lipca 2015 r Przewodnik po zmianach* (Warsaw, Wolters Kluwer, 2015) R Kaczor, 'Akt oskarżenia jako pisemna forma skargi oskarżyciela publicznego. Uwagi polemiczne' (2012) *Prok i Pr* no 4; A Narowska, M. Pańczyk and M Szybowska, 'Skarga subsydiarna oraz rola oskarżyciela posiłkowego subsydiarnego w polskim procesie karnym' (2012) *WPWS*; R Kmiecik, 'Akt oskarżenia jako pisemna forma skargi oskarżyciela publicznego' (2010) *Prok i Pr*, nos 1–2; P Hofmański and S Zabłocki, 'Granice skargi oskarżycielskiej w świetle najnowszego orzecznictwa', in A Gerecka-Żołyńska, P Górecki, H Paluszkiewicz and P Wiliński (eds), *Skargowy model procesu karnego. Księga ofiarowana Profesorowi Stanisławowi Stachowiakowi* (Warsaw, 2008); E Skrętowicz and E Kruk, 'Granice skargi oskarżycielskiej w świetle najnowszego orzecznictwa', in Gerecka-Żołyńska et al, *Skargowy model procesu karnego*; K Zgryzek, 'Skargi zastępujące akt oskarżenia w polskim procesie karnym', in Gerecka-Żołyńska et al, *Skargowy model procesu karnego.*

The control of the formal conditions of the indictment[4] is subject not only to the fulfilment of the specific formal conditions provided for in the provisions on the indictment, but also to the fulfilment of the general formal conditions to which pleadings should conform. Thus, two provisions coexist – one that deals fully with the specific pleading that is the indictment (Article 332 CPC), and another that deals with the formal conditions for pleadings (Article 119 § 2 CPC).

The control of the formal conditions of the indictment is exercised by the president of the court (Article 337 § 1 CPC); his/her powers – depending on the internal division of activities in the court – may be exercised by the president of the division or an authorised judge (*argumentum ex* Article 93 § 2 CPC). This control may also be exercised by a court clerk (Article 93a § 2 CPC), who in the proceedings before the court may issue orders to call for rectification of formal deficiencies in the indictment within seven days, as well as declaring a deficient and uncompleted letter ineffective. Such a definition of the scope of authority of the entities mentioned herein should help streamline criminal proceedings at their initial stage.

The president of the court (president of the division, an authorised judge or a court clerk) is obliged to examine each indictment filed with the court for compliance with the formal requirements. The presiding judge shall examine the indictment filed for formal requirements pertaining only to the indictment, but also those peculiar to any pleading. If the president finds formal defects, ie if he/she finds that the indictment does not meet the conditions, he/she returns it to the prosecution counsel, calling for its supplementation within seven days (Article 337 § 1 CPC). The Code thus implements the principle that all formal defects in the indictment should be treated equally. This proves that the indictment is a special pleading, the procedural significance of which is completely different from that of other pleadings. Thus, while in the case of pleadings that are not indictments the need to remedy the deficiency arises only if the pleading cannot proceed because of a formal deficiency, such effect is produced by any formal deficiency in the indictment.[5]

A special procedure for examination of formal conditions of an indictment concerns both the indictment brought by the public prosecutor and the indictment brought by a subsidiary or private prosecutor (injury person).

Moreover, the provisions relating to the indictment shall apply mutatis mutandis to the motion for conditional discontinuance of proceedings in lieu of the indictment, so the motion must meet the same formal requirements as the indictment (Article 336 § 2 CPC). A motion for a penalty under the expedited procedure drawn up by the police also serves as a substitute for the indictment. The motion should, therefore, also be examined for compliance with the formal conditions governing an indictment, since it should contain all the information that should characterize an indictment (Article 517d CPC).

[4] P Brzeziński, 'Kontrola formalna aktu oskarżenia' (2006) *Prok i Pr* no 10; RA Stefański, 'Formalna kontrola aktu oskarżenia w nowym kodeksie postępowania karnego' (1998) *Prok i Pr* no 9; S Stachowiak, 'Sądowa kontrola wymagań formalnych skargi w polskim procesie karnym' (1973) NP no 12.

[5] H Kuczyńska, 'Kompetencja sądu do zmiany kwalifikacji prawnej czynu przedstawionej w akcie oskarżenia (zagadnienie kompatybilności instytucji procesowych)' (2017) *Prok i Pr* no 2.

As regards returning the indictment to the prosecutor, the president of the court (presiding judge, authorised judge, court clerk) shall issue an order[6] in which he/she shall specify all formal defects of the indictment and set a time limit by which these defects should be removed. However, it is not always necessary for the president of the court to return the indictment itself, as in some cases it may be sufficient to motion the prosecutor to attach to the indictment a missing document, such as a list of persons whom the prosecutor demands be summoned to the trial. In some cases, therefore, the author of the indictment may be summoned to the court premises in order to rectify the formal deficiency of the indictment (as it seems that the lack of the signature of the indictment could be rectified in this way, the return of the indictment for this purpose seems to be too great a formalisation of the control of the indictment). However, it is not permissible to return the case to the prosecutor to extend the indictment to other acts of the accused, even if they are within the group of acts already charged. The court examines the case within the limits of the indictment set forth by the description of the facts in the complaint initiating the case, and a violation of this principle would be a violation of the principle of complaint.

The accuser may complain against the order issued by the president of the court to the court competent to examine the case (Article 337 § 2 CPC), ie to the court that would hear the case if the indictment met the relevant conditions. It should be noted that the complaint may be filed by any prosecutor who has filed the indictment with the court, so not only by the prosecutor. Contrary to the general rule, according to which the complaint against the order of the president of the court is examined by the appellate court (Article 466 § 2 CPC), the complaint against the order of returning the indictment for the purpose of correcting the definciencies s is not examined by the superior instance court, but by the court that has jurisdiction over the case. If the prosecutor does not file a complaint or if the complaint is not granted, the prosecutor is obliged to file a corrected or supplemented indictment within the prescribed time limit, in accordance with the position of the president of the court expressed in the order to return the indictment. If, on the other hand, the complaint filed by the prosecutor is accepted, the president of the court is obliged to take further actions related to the filed indictment and related to the preparation of the main trial.

It is undoubtedly true that, although the president of the court is obliged to return the indictment to the prosecutor if he/she finds that it has (any) deficiencies, the prosecutor cannot be compelled in any way to file a corrected or supplemented indictment, as this would be in conflict with the aforementioned principle of complaint.[7] Therefore, if the formal deficiency in the indictment is not removed within the time limit, the indictment is deemed ineffective. Therefore, if the public prosecutor fails to file a corrected indictment with the court within the time limit, the *litis pendens* before the court will cease and the case will return to the pre-trial phase (the body in charge of this phase of the proceedings will be the prosecutor to whom the indictment was returned). If we treat

[6] A Kiełtyka, 'Zwrot sprawy w trybie art 345 k.p.k., po uchyleniu wyroku' (2007) *Prok i Pr* no 3; T Retyk, 'Zwrot sprawy prokuratorowi w trybie art 345 § 1 k.p.k. na tle orzecznictwa i praktyki' (2011) *Prok i Pr* no 3; S Cora, 'Zwrot sprawy do uzupełnienia postępowania przygotowawczego a art 397 k.p.k. (2005) *Prok i Pr* no 10.

[7] T Grzegorczyk, 'Przekazanie przez sąd sprawy prokuratorowi do przeprowadzenia postępowania przygotowawczego na zasadach ogólnych' (2008) *PS* no 2; Cora (n 6).

the ineffective lapse of the time limit set for the elimination of the formal deficiency as the same as a procedural obstacle (lack of a complaint by the authorised prosecutor), then the proceedings would have to be discontinued for the sole reason that the prosecutor did not manage to remove the deficiency found by the president of the court. Such a solution, creating a state of *rei iudicatae*, would be highly socially unjust. It should therefore be concluded that the seven-day time limit for the purpose of correcting the definciencies in the indictment is a decisive time limit, as this group of time limits also includes those the violation of which (in other words, failure to perform an act within the prescribed time limit) renders the act ineffective.[8]

The defective indictment shall be returned to the prosecutor. It is obvious that this refers not only to the public prosecutor, but also to the private prosecutor and the auxiliary prosecutor. However, in the case of an indictment brought by the public prosecutor, it will be about any formal deficiency, while in the case of the other two types of prosecutors, it will only be about such deficiencies that make it impossible to proceed. Thus, if a private or subsidiary prosecutor fails to remedy the deficiency within the time limit, then such an indictment cannot be regarded as a complaint initiating proceedings, and the proceedings must be dismissed for lack of a complaint from a legitimate prosecutor. If not prevented by other procedural reasons (eg statute of limitations), such indictment corrected and filed after the time limit set by the presiding judge in the order will have the procedural effect of setting up the procedure before the court as of the date of filing the amended indictment with the court.

If the president of the court determines that the filed indictment complies with the formal conditions or if the deficiencies found by him/her have been removed within the prescribed time limit, he/she shall order that a copy of the indictment be served on the accused and on his/her counsel (Article 338 § 1 CPC), if he/she has been appointed in the case. Such an indictment will create a state of *lis pendens* before the court as of the date of its filing; thus, in the case of an indictment with deficiencies, if the deficiencies were corrected within the time limit, there is a certain legal fiction of treating such an indictment as if it had no deficiencies from the moment of its filing with the court. Where the indictment contains a motion to convict the accused without main trial (Article 335 §§ 1 or 2 CPC), a copy of the indictment shall also be served on each disclosed injured person (Article 338 § 1b CPC). The president of the court shall also summon the accused to submit evidentiary motions, setting a seven-day time limit for this purpose (Article 338 § 1 CPC). The firmness of the wording of the provision constituting the basis for dismissing the evidentiary motion suggests that we are dealing here with evidentiary preclusion, the existence of which would be contrary to the defendant's right of defence. It is clear that the legislature, through this time limit, aims to concentrate the evidence, but at the same time it does not deprive the accused of the possibility of submitting evidence motions after this time limit. The relevant provision does not allow dismissal of a motion to take evidence if such a motion, submitted after the time limit, for a circumstance which is to be proved, is significant for determining whether a criminal act was committed, whether it constitutes a crime and what kind of crime it is, whether the act was committed under the conditions referred to in Article 64 or 65 CC,

[8] H.Kuczyńska, *Kompetencja sądu do zmiany kwalifikacji prawnej czynu przedstawionej w akcie oskarżenia (zagadnienie kompatybilności instytucji procesowych)*, PiP 2017, no 2, *passim*.

or whether the conditions for imposing a stay in a psychiatric facility pursuant to Article 93g CC exist. It should be remembered, however, that the submission of motions for evidence is the right of the accused and falls within the scope of certain defence tactics – his or her defence counsel.[9]

In the present legal state, with respect to the initiative of taking evidence, which the accused is called upon to take after being served with a copy of the indictment, there is a clear imbalance in the procedural balance between the parties, ie a violation of the adversarial principle. Here, the defendant is emphatically called upon to make evidentiary submissions within seven days of service of the copy of the indictment (Article 338 § 1 CPC), while the other party (in this case, the injured person) is not called upon to do the same.

An important element of the indictment is the statement of reasons, which is a basis for the court, the parties to the proceedings and other participants in the proceedings to know what evidence has been collected in the case for the act charged. The indictment shall be served on the defendant and his/her counsel, always with a statement of reasons, unless there is a fear of disclosure of 'secret' or 'top secret' classified information, in which case the indictment shall be served on the accused without a statement of reasons (Article 338 § 3 CPC) but it shall be made available subject to the rigours specified by the president of the court or the court. As regards service of a copy of the indictment, the president of the court or a court clerk shall issue an order, instructing the accused on the contents of the provisions referred to in Article 338 § 1a CPC, as well as instructing him/her on the possibility of filing a motion for appointment of a defence counsel ex officio, but no later than within seven days from the date of the delivery of a copy of the indictment. The motion shall be accompanied by proof demonstrating that the accused is unable to bear the costs of defence without it affecting their ability to support themselves and their family (Article 338b § 1 CPC). If the submission of such a motion after the expiry of the time limit would necessitate a change to the date of a trial or the session referred to in Article 341, Article 343 or Article 343a, the demand shall be examined immediately after the date of the trial or session. This provision shall apply accordingly if the demand is submitted within the time limit but does not meet the formal requirements referred to in Article 120 § 1 or the proof referred to in the second sentence of § 1 has not been enclosed (Article 338b § 2 CPC).

An important element of the accused's right of defence is the right to file a written response to the indictment within seven days from the date of service of this letter (Article 338 § 2 CPC);[10] the accused should be instructed about this right of defence, even if he/she has a defence counsel. It is worth noting that the previously applicable CPC

[9] J Kosonoga, 'Oddalenie obstrukcyjnego wniosku dowodowego' (2019) *Ius Novum* no 1; M Kościelniak-Marszał, 'Oddalenie wniosku dowodowego zmierzającego w sposób oczywisty do przedłużenia postępowania', in S Steinborn and K Woźniewski (eds), *Proces karny w dobie przemian. Zagadnienia ogólne* (Gdańsk, Wydawnictwo Uniwersytetu Gdańskiego, 2018) vol I; K Zgryzek, 'Oddalenie wniosku dowodowego w nowelizacji kodeksu postępowania karnego z 2003 roku', in M Płachta (ed), *Aktualne problemy prawa i procesu karnego. Księga ofiarowana Profesorowi Janowi Grajewskiemu* (Gdańsk, GSP, 2003) no 1.

[10] PK Sowiński, Odpowiedź oskarżonego na akt oskarżenia (art 388 § 2 KPK), (2007) *ZN UR* no 41; RA Stefański, Odpowiedź na akt oskarżenia (2005) *Prok i Pr* no 5; K Woźniewski, Odpowiedź na akt oskarżenia jako nowa instytucja prawa dowodowego oraz gwarancja rzetelnego procesu (w świetle wybranych standardów procesowych Europejskiej Konwencji Praw Człowieka) (Gdańsk, GSP, 1999) no 4.

did not provide for this right of the accused, which strengthens the adversarial system and the right of defence. This written response to the indictment does not have the character of an objection, but usually constitutes a form of a first written polemic against the theses included in the indictment. We can say, that the essence of the defendant's (or his/her counsel's) response to the indictment, therefore, boils down to presenting to the court the defendant's position on the indictment so that, if the need arises, the case can be referred by the presiding judge for a pre-trial session. The filing of a written response does not necessarily require that the case be referred to a pre-trial session, but the president of the court may determine that there is a need to do so – for example, when it appears necessary to consider the possibility of discontinuing the proceedings because of a manifest absence of any factual basis for the charge, or when there is a need to to issue a decision on provisional detention or other coercive measures. In practice, the response to the indictment often includes a motion by the accused or his/her defence counsel for the case to be referred to a pre-trial session. Like the time limit for submitting evidence after receiving a copy of the indictment, the seven-day time limit for filing a response to the indictment is not decisive, which means that the accused does not lose his/her right to file a response setting out his/her views on the case at a later date.

If the indictment was erroneously not returned for the purpose of correcting the formal deficiencies and a hearing has been scheduled, the court may order the return of the indictment after the case has been called at main trial, but before the commencement of the judicial examination, ie before the concise presentation of the charges. If, on the other hand, the deficiencies are discovered after the presentation of the charge, ie after the commencement of the judicial examination, the return of such an indictment for the purposes of correcting the formal deficiencies is not admissible; in that case, it must be assumed that the proceedings before the court were instituted by the defective indictment, and the court will be under an obligation to do what the prosecutor should have done if the indictment had been returned to it.[11] It should be noted, that if, for example, the lack of an indictment consists in the failure to attach to the indictment evidence showing the circumstances of the alleged act, the prosecutor may, at any time, present such evidence by formulating an appropriate motion for evidence.[12]

It should be emphasised that the control exercised by the president of the court may only relate to the formal conditions of the indictment,[13] and may not be connected to the substantive examination of the case. In the current state of the law, there is no provision that would oblige the president of the court (or other entities authorised to carry out such control) to carry out a formal review of the indictment within a certain time limit.

[11] E Kruk, Skarga oskarżycielska jako przejaw realizacji prawa do oskarżania uprawnionego oskarżyciela w polskim procesie karnym (Lublin, AUL, 2016).

[12] M Kurowski, 'Wpływ zmian w zakresie prawa dysponowania skargą przez oskarżyciela publicznego na wybrane zasady procesowe', in pod red M Rogackiej-Rzewnickiej and H. Gajewskiej-Kraczkowskiej (eds), *Istota i zasady procesu karnego 25 lat później. Księga poświęcona pamięci Profesora Andrzeja Murzynowskiego* (Warsaw, Wolters Kluwer, 2019).

[13] M Poliwka-Pacana, 'Sądowa kontrola wymagań„ formalnych oskarżenia prywatnego w polskim procesie karnym', in I Nowikowski (ed), *Problemy stosowania prawa sądowego. Księga ofiarowana Profesorowi Edwardowi Skrętowiczowi* (Lublin, Wydawnictwo Uniwersytetu Marii Curie-Skłodowskiej, 2007; D Osowska, *Sądowa kontrola oskarżenia w polskim procesie karnym* (Warsaw, Poznań„ Toruń„ Państwowe Wydawnictwo Naukowe, 1977); A Kaftal, *Kontrola sądowa postępowania przygotowawczego* (Warsaw, Wydawnictwo Prawnicze, 1974).

Preliminary Examination of the Case

Proceeding to the next stage of the procedure before court of the first instance is possible only when the indictment complies with all the formal conditions stipulated by the provisions of the CPC, although in practice it may happen that a defective indictment can seep into main trial by oversight. Thus, if the indictment has been returned to the prosecution counsel for the purpose of correcting the deficiencies, until it is corrected, the case may not be referred to the pre-trial session, and if this is not necessary or needed, to the trial.

The activities performed in the so-called preliminary examination of the case are carried out in two stages. One of them was mentioned above; at this stage, the examination is conducted by the president of the court (the president of a division, the president of the adjudicative panel or a duly authorised judge) and it concerns only the formal conditions of the indictment filed with the court. The second stage of preliminary review is of a substantive nature and is carried out exclusively by the court at the session preceding the main trial. The case is commited to the session by the president of the court on his/her own initiative; although the present CPC, unlike the previous one, does not mention the right of the parties to file a motion to commit the case to the session, it does not mean that the parties (or their representatives) cannot file such a motion. The right of the parties (as well as other persons directly concerned) to make an appropriate motion clearly indicates that the fact that a procedural authority takes a certain action ex officio (on its own initiative) does not mean that other parties cannot make a motion for such an action; such a motion by a party or a person directly concerned may be an impulse for the president of the court (see Article 9 § 2 CPC) to consider the need to commit the case to a session and undoubtedly strengthens the adversarial nature of the trial.

Preliminary examination of the case by the court before the main trial has been significantly extended in the current CPC and expanded by new procedural steps.

In the previous legal state, in none of the procedural situations was the president of the court obliged to commit the case to a pre trial session; therefore, in each situ ation he/she examined whether there was such a need. In the current legal state, the necessity of commiting a case to a session before trial has been settled legally in certain situations.[14] Such referral should be made no later than thirty days from the date of filing the indictment with the court (Article 339 § 4a CPC); undoubtedly, the purpose of this solution is to streamline the course of the proceedings and prevent unnecessary delay in this regard; however, this time limit is an instructional time limit, since its violation has not been provided with any procedural consequences.

Parties, defence counsel and attorneys may participate in court sessions, which are held on an obligatory basis in the event that the grounds specified in Article 339 § 1 CPC exist. These entities may also participate in sessions at which the court considers the possibility of discontinuance of the proceedings, also due to a manifest absence of factual basis of the charge, and the issuance of a decision on provisional detention

[14] Zgryzek (n 1); W Boczkowski, 'Z problematyki posiedzenia przygotowawczego przed rozprawą', (1975) *NP* no 7–8.

or other coercive measure. However, when the subject of the session is the issue of a ruling on a preventive measure, the participation in the session of the prosecutor and defence counsel is mandatory (Article 339 § 5 first instance CPC). The said parties, defence counsel and attorneys have the right to participate in the other session if they appear; their notification of the date of the session is not compulsory, and the examination of the case in their absence does not affect the admissibility of the actions taken (Article 96 § 2 CPC). The law introduces certain exceptions to this rule ('unless the statute stipulates otherwise'); this applies e.g. to adjudication at a session on conditional discontinuance of proceedings, on indictment containing a motion of the prosecutor to convict the accused without a hearing; to adjudication on the extension of provisional detention; to adjudication on the discontinuance of proceedings due to insanity of the perpetrator of a prohibited act and application of a protective measure against him/her; and to issuance of an injuctive judgment.

In the course of further proceedings, and especially at the main trial, the court shall neither be bound by the factual nor by the legal evaluations which have served as a basis for the decisions and orders issued at the session (Article 347 CPC).[15] Thus, if, for example, the court at the session found that there were no procedural obstacles, this does not mean that in further proceedings the basis for its discontinuance cannot be precisely a procedural obstacle. Similarly, if the court at the session determines that there is no need to discontinue the proceedings due to a manifest absence of factual grounds for the charge, this does not prevent the court from issuing an acquittal after a main trial in the future, if the evidence gathered in the case indicates such. Neither does the fact that the legal classification of the act adopted in the indictment was found to be incorrect at the session prevent the judgment from adopting the same legal classification that was indicated in the indictment. Thus, the aforementioned provision (Article 347 CPC) confirms the principle of jurisdictional independence of the court.

Due to the nature of the reason to commit the case to a session, one may speak of an obligatory and a facultative pre-trial session.

An obligatory session of the court before the main trial takes place when the CPC itself requires in certain situations that the main trial be preceded by such a session; in such cases the president of the court is obliged[16] to commit the case to a session of the court, and the Code does not leave this issue to his/her discretion. This occurs when:

1. the prosecutor has submitted a motion for adjudication of preventive measures;
2. there is a need to consider conditional discontinuance of proceedings, especially when the prosecutor has filed the relevant motion for conditional discontinuance;

[15] Kuczyńska (n 5); J Izydorczyk, 'Obowiązek badania kwalifikacji prawnej czynu przez organy stosujące tymczasowe aresztowanie' (2015) *Studia Prawnoekonomiczne* XCVII; E Klimowicz-Górowska, 'Zmiana kwalifikacji prawnej a niezmienność przedmiotowych granic rozpoznania sprawy', in P Hofmańskiego (pod red), *Węzłowe problemy procesu karnego* (Warsaw, Wolters Kluwer, 2010); S Stachowiak, P Wiliński and B Janusz-Pohl, 'Zmiana kwalifikacji prawnej w toku postępowania karnego (jednolitoÅ›Ä‡ prawa karnego)', in Z Ćwiąkalski and G Artymiak (eds), *Współzależność prawa karnego materialnego i procesowego. W świetle kodyfikacji karnych z 1997 r i propozycji ich zmian* (Warsaw, Wolters Kluwer, 2009).

[16] Zgryzek (n 1).

3. the indictment is accompanied by an motion for a judgment of conviction to be issued in a session and to order the penalties or other measures provided for the misdemeanour, determined in consultation with the accused (motion referred to in Article 335 § 2 CPC);
4. the public prosecutor has filed in place of indictment the independent motion for a judgment of conviction to be issued in a session (without a main trial) and to order the penalties or other measures provided for the misdemeanour, which is regulated in Article 335 § 1 CPC;
5. the defendant is in provisional detention – in order to decide on maintaining, amending or revoking the detention order; if necessary, the court may also decide on other precautionary measures at the session (Article 339 § 1 and Article 344 CPC).

The prosecutor's motion on discontinuance of the proceedings due to insanity of the perpetrator and on the application of preventive measures shall, in principle, be directed to the main trial, unless in the light of the investigation materials there are no doubts about the suspect having committed the prohibited act and about their insanity at the time of the act, and the president of the court finds purpose in hearing the case in a session with the participation of the public prosecutor, defence counsel and suspect. The suspect shall not participate in the session if the opinions of expert witnesses indicate that it would be inadvisable, unless the court finds their participation necessary. The injured shall have the right to participate in the session; the injured shall be informed of this right and notified of the date of the session (Article 354 point 2 CPC).

After the decision on discontinuance of preparatory proceedings becomes final and valid, the public prosecutor, if he/she determines that there are sufficient grounds, shall submit only a motion to the court to rule, as a preventive measure, on forfeiture (Article 324 CPC). The prosecutor may also submit such motion in the case of discontinuance of proceedings due to failure to detect the perpetrator of a criminal offence, fiscal offence or fiscal delinquency, if the provision envisages adjudication of forfeiture (Article 323 § 3 CPC). The court shall decide on the forfeiture during a session. A person claiming right to benefits or objects, the forfeiture of which was ruled as a preventive measure,[17] may assert his/her claims only in civil proceedings.

A conditional discontinuance of proceedings may also take place at a pre-trial session if a motion to that effect has been filed by the prosecutor. If the prosecutor's motion is justified, the court decides on the conditional discontinuance of the proceedings at a session by way of a judgment (Article 341 § 5 CPC), but if it decides that the conditional discontinuance is unjustified or if the defendant objects to the conditional discontinuance, the court commits the case to trial. In such a case, the motion replaces the indictment (Article 341 § 2 CPC).

The public prosecutor, the accused and the injured shall have the right to participate in the session[18] related to conditional discontinuance of the proceedings; however, if the presiding judge or the court so orders, their participation in the session is mandatory

[17] K Bratek, 'Glosa do post. SN z 27.2.2013 r., I KZP 27/12' (2014) *WPP* no 2.

[18] W Jasiński, 'Udział stron, obrońców i pełnomocników w czynnościach postępowania przygotowawczego – uwagi de lege lata i de lege ferenda' (2010) *AUW* LXXXII.

(Article 341 § 1 CPC).[19] The court may condition the application of conditional discontinuance on the defendant's agreement with the injured party on redressing damage or compensation. To this end, it may adjourn the session by setting an appropriate time limit for the parties, and shall order a suitable break or adjourn the session if the defendant and the victim file a motion to that effect on the grounds of the need to reach an agreement (Article 341 § 3 CPC).

Sentencing the defendant without trial (Article 335 §§ 1 and 2 CPC) is an institution introduced to the Polish criminal procedure by the 1997 CPC.[20] In the current legal status, the institution of sentencing the defendant without trial is conditional on the prosecutor filing a motion for such a sentencing (motion for a judgment of conviction to be issued in a session and to order the penalties or other measures provided for the misdemeanour, determined in consultation with the accused),[21] which may take two forms.[22]

The motion is an independent motion, ie one that the prosecutor files with the court instead of an indictment (Article 335 § 1 CPC). It may also take the form of a non-self-contained motion when the prosecutor attaches it to the indictment filed with the court (Article 335 § 2 CPC).[23] The substance of both motions is the prosecutor's demand that a conviction be handed down at a session and that penalties or other measures prescribed for the offence charged be agreed with the accused, also taking into account the legally protected interests of the injured person. The agreement may also cover the issuance of a specific resolution as to the incurrence of costs of proceedings. A motion for sentencing without trial is considered at a session where no evidence is taken (Article 343 § 3 CPC).[24]

The public prosecutor, the accused and the injured have the right to participate in the session, and their participation shall be mandatory if the president of the court or the court orders so. When being notified of a session, the injured shall also be advised of the possibility of closing the proceedings without a trial and of early submission of the statement that he or she will act as an auxiliary prosecutor (Article 343 § 5 CPC). This means that the rule according to which this statement may be made until the commencement

[19] A Baj, 'Udział, stron postępowania przygotowawczego w czynnościach powtarzalnych' (2019) *Prok i Pr* no 2; M Kurowski, 'Udział, osób trzecich w czynnościach procesowych w postępowaniu przygotowawczym i jego wpÅ‚yw na zakres i sposób dokumentowania przebiegu czynności', in S Steinborn and K Woźniewski (ed), *Proces karny w dobie przemian. Przebieg postępowania* (Gdańsk, Wydawnictwo Uniwersytetu Gdańskiego, 2018) vol II.

[20] BJ Stefańska, 'Skazanie na posiedzeniu bez przeprowadzenia postępowania dowodowego', in T Grzegorczyk and R Olszewski (ed), *Verba volant, scripta manent. Proces karny, prawo karne skarbowe i prawo wykroczeń po zmianach z lat 2015–2016* (Warsaw, Wolters Kluwer, 2017); B Myrna, 'Skazanie bez przeprowadzenia postępowania dowodowego w świetle nowelizacji kodeksu postępowania karnego', in L Bogunia (ed), *Nowa kodyfikacja prawa karnego* (Wrocław, Wydawnictwo Uniwersytetu Wrocławskiego, 2004) vol XVI.

[21] RA Stefański, 'Wniosek prokuratora o skazanie oskarżonego bez rozprawy' (1998) *Prok i Pr* no 2; M Żbikowska, 'Wniosek o skazanie bez rozprawy po noweli k.p.k. z dnia 27 września 2013 r. (kilka uwag do artykułu I. Pączek)' (2016) *Prok i Pr* no 7–8.

[22] A Bartha, 'Wniosek oskarżonego w trybie art 338a ustawy Kodeks postępowania karnego a sprawność (szybkość) postępowania jurysdykcyjnego', in S Steinborn and K Woźniewski (ed), *Proces karny w dobie przemian. Przebieg postępowania* (Gdańsk, Wydawnictwo Uniwersytetu Gdańskiego, 2018) vol II.

[23] See more on these motions and conditions for filing them in ch 5.

[24] M Garwol, 'Proceduralne aspekty tzw. skazania bez rozprawy po wejściu w życie nowelizacji z 11 marca 2016 r.' (2016) *CzPKiNP* no 3; M Drewicz, 'Skazanie bez rozprawy (art 335 k.p.k.) i dobrowolne poddanie się odpowiedzialności (art 387 k.p.k.) a przestępstwa o strukturze wielopodmiotowej' (2015) *CzPKiNP* no 3.

of the judicial examination at the main trial does not apply here. If the injured party or other entitled person has not applied for compensation for the damage caused by the offence in whole or in part, then the court may condition the granting of the application for sentencing the accused without a main trial on redressing the damage in part or in whole, or on providing compensation for the harm inflicted. In order to reach an agreement between the defendant and the injured as to redressing damage or compensation, the court may adjourn the session and designate a suitable time limit for the parties. The court may condition the granting of the motion on making a change in it by the public prosecutor, as specified by the court and accepted by the accused (Article 343 § 3 CPC). The court shall instruct the accused that the grounds for an appeal against a judgment granting the motion for sentencing without main trial may not be allegations related to the content of the agreement between the accused and the injured (Article 343 § 5a CPC).[25]

Granting the motion, the court sentences the accused under a judgment (Article 343 § 6 CPC). Granting the motion is the court's prerogative and is possible only when the injured, while being duly informed of the date of the session, does not object (Article 343 § 2 CPC).

The consequences of the court finding that there are no grounds to grant the prosecutor's motion referred to in Article 335 § 1 or Article 335 § 2 CPC vary depending on whether the motion was filed on its own or whether the motion was attached to the indictment (a non-self-initiated motion). In the former case (independent motion), the court refers the case back to the public prosecutor. In the case of a motion that is not self-contained, the case shall be examined in line with general principles, and the public prosecutor, within seven days as of the session, shall supplement the indictment by a list of persons that the prosecution counsel requires to be summoned, and a list of other evidence that the prosecution counsel requires to be examined in the main trial, and in addition, the public prosecutor may motion for the abandonment of summoning of the witnesses who have been questioned, who are staying abroad or who are to give evidence of circumstances that are not so important that it is necessary to question these witnesses directly at the trial, in particular circumstances not denied by the accused in their explanations (Article 343 § 7 in connection with Article 333 §§ 1 and § 2 and with Article 350a CPC).

The accused themselves may also file a motion for the issuance of a judgment of conviction and the imposition of a specific penalty or a criminal measure upon them or for ordering forfeiture or a redress measure without an evidentiary hearing being conducted.[26] This is possible if the offence charged against the accused is punishable

[25] A Lach, 'Obrońca i pełnomocnik wobec instytucji skazania bez rozprawy', in P Wiliński (ed), *Obrońca i pełnomocnik w procesie karnym po 1 lipca 2015 r. Przewodnik po zmianach* (Warsaw, Wolters Kluwer, 2015); J Duży, 'Porozumienia procesowe przewidziane w art 335 i 387 k.p.k. w kontekście zasady legalizmu i prawdy materialnej', in A Przyborowska-Klimczak and A Taracha (ed), *Iudicium et Scentia. Księga jubileuszowa Profesora Romualda Kmiecika* (Warsaw, Wolters Kluwer, 2011); KT 'Boratyńska, "Skazanie bez rozprawy" (art 335 KPK) w ocenie prokuratorów', in C Kulesza (ed), *Porozumienia karnoprocesowe w praktyce wymiaru sprawiedliwości* (Białystok, Temida2, 2010).

[26] Z Kwiatkowski, 'Wniosek oskarżonego o wydanie wyroku skazującego bez postępowania dowodowego na rozprawie w świetle nowelizacji kodeksu postępowania karnego', in T Grzegorczyk and R Olszewski (red), *Verba volant, scripta manent. Proces karny, prawo karne skarbowe i prawo wykroczeń po zmianach z lat 2015–2016. Księga pamiątkowa poświęcona Profesor Monice Zbrojewskiej* (Warsaw, Wolters Kluwer, 2017); Stefański (n 21).

by imprisonment for a term not exceeding fifteen years; a motion filed under this procedure may also concern a specific decision on payment of the trial costs (Article 338a CPC). This motion may be filed by the accused before a notification of the date of the trial is served on them, which in practice may cause significant difficulties in determining whether the time limit for filing this motion by the accused has passed. In order to avoid the related interpretation problems, the accused should file this motion immediately after receiving the copy of the indictment (preferably together with the response to the indictment).

Finally, the last reason for the obligatory referral of the motion to trial is the need to examine the appropriateness of the further use of provisional detention. This issue is obvious at every stage of criminal proceedings, since the court, and in preparatory proceedings, the prosecutor, are obliged to examine whether or not the reasons for which this measure was applied have ceased to exist.[27] Therefore, if the accused is under provisional detention, then in each such case, after the indictment is filed, the appropriateness of the continuation of this measure, the need for its modification or revocation must be examined. If necessary, the court shall also rule on other precautionary measures (Article 344 CPC). The court is obliged to make a decision in this regard ex officio, but this does not mean, however, that the parties and persons directly concerned may not file motions to this effect.

An facultative pre-trial hearing takes place instead of an obligatory one when the presiding judge commits a case to a session if, in his/her opinion, there is a need to make a decision (other than those that make it mandatory to commit the case to a session) that exceeds his/her powers, ie when there are conditions that require the court to make a decision (Article 339 § 3 *in principio* CPC). The CPC leaves the existence of such a need to the president's assessment alone, although it may undoubtedly be influenced by relevant motions of the parties and persons directly involved.

The CPC, as an example of such situations, indicates the need to:

1. Discontinuance of proceedings due to inadmissibility of the process (pursuant to Article 17 § 1 (2) to (11) CPC). The court examines the existence of procedural obstacles ex officio, as the existence of one of them is sufficient for criminal proceedings to be discontinued.[28]
2. Discontinuance of proceedings due to a manifest absence of any factual basis for the charge (Article 339 § 3 point 2 CPC). A condition for the discontinuance of proceedings on this ground is the prior determination of the completeness of the preliminary investigation; this means that the preliminary investigation must not be affected by deficiencies. Discontinuance occurs when the absence of factual basis for the charge is manifest. This means that the aforementioned provision may apply when the absence of evidence justifying the accusation is clear and conspicuous,

[27] J Izydorczyk, 'Wniosek prokuratora o zastosowanie tymczasowego aresztowania', in S Stachowiaka (ed), *Współczesny polski proces karny. Księga ofiarowana Profesorowi Tadeuszowi Nowakowi* (Poznań, 2002); E Kutek, 'Wniosek prokuratora o zastosowanie tymczasowego aresztowania', in L Boguni (ed), *Nowa kodyfikacja prawa karnego* (Wrocław, Wydawnictwo Uniwersytetu Wrocławskiego, 2006) vol XIX.

[28] B Nita-Światłowska and A Światłowski, 'Przeszkoda procesowa z art 17 § 1 pkt 6 k.p.k. wobec zmian terminów przedawnienia (kontekst konstytucyjny)' (2018) *Prok i Pr* no 10.

ie when it can be determined without the need for additional examination. The assessment of the president of the court should therefore be made with particular caution, since a decision to commit a case for this reason for a session expresses the president's conviction that there is (or, more precisely, that there is not) a basis for prosecution. The case law emphasises that a manifest absence of factual basis for the accusation occurs, inter alia, in the absence of any evidence that the accused has committed the act attributed to him/her, but it cannot be the result of their assessment.

3. Issue a decision on the lack of jurisdiction of the court (Article 339 § 3 point 3 CPC). The court examines its jurisdiction ex officio, and if it finds that it lacks jurisdiction, it refers the case to the competent court or other body.
4. Return the case to the public prosecutor for the purpose of rectifying major deficiencies in the investigation (Article 339 § 3 point 3a CPC). This return occurs when the court sees an opportunity to supplement the materials of the proceedings, and the existing evidence is insufficient for the case to go to main trial. A significant deficiency of preparatory proceedings is, first of all, a deficiency of an evidential nature, but it also includes, for example, failure to observe the legally required form of preparatory proceedings (despite the obligatory principal investigation, a simplified investigation was carried out).
5. Issue a decision on suspension of the proceedings; the basis for issuing such a procedural decision is the appearance of an obstacle of a factual nature, the duration of which cannot be estimated, after the indictment has been filed with the court. Article 22 § 1 CPC, listing by way of example these obstacles, indicates the impossibility of apprehending the accused and the impossibility of his/her participation in the proceedings due to mental illness or other serious illness. These obstacles are to be of a long-term nature and the proceedings shall be suspended for their duration.[29]
6. Iissue a decision on provisional detention or other coercive measure (Article 339 § 3 point 6 CPC), when the provisional detention or other coercive measure has not previously been used or when there is a need to adjudicate on such other a coercive measure; thus, the court may issue a decision on maintaining, amending, revoking or – if it has not been used so far – on applying a coercive measure (eg surveillance and recording of conversations pursuant to Article 237 CPC).[30]
7. Issue an injunctive judgment if there are grounds for doing so (Article 339 § 3 point 6 CPC).[31]
8. Consider whether to refer the case to mediation (Article 339 § 4 CPC).

[29] B Szyprowski, 'Umorzenie postępowania z powodu oczywistego braku faktycznych podstaw oskarżenia' (2005) *Prok* no 1.

[30] M Latos, 'Merytoryczne podstawy przekazania sprawy ze względu na dobro wymiaru sprawiedliwości' (2017) *PS* no 2; idem, 'Zażalenie na postanowienie w przedmiocie właściwości (2016) *AUL* no 6; M Błoński, 'Praktyczne aspekty dotyczące właściwości miejscowej sądu' (2013) *PS* nos 7–8.

[31] R Olszewski, 'Ujawnianie przez sąd i usuwanie istotnych braków dochodzenia lub śledztwa w polskim procesie karnym' (2007) Łódź; J Radlińska, 'Usunięcie istotnych braków postępowania przygotowawczego w trybie art 397 k.p.k.' (2004) *Prok i Pr* no 9; idem, 'Glosa, I KZP 68/98' (1998) *OSP* no 10; Z Młynarczyk, 'Glosa do post. SN z 1 VIII 1986' (1987) *NP* no 6; K Zgryzek, 'Glosa do w. z 18 III 1982, I KR 323/81' (1984) *Prok i Pr* no 3.

9. Decide at this stage of the trial on other issues not listed above, the resolution of which is either necessary or expedient in the interest of procedural economy before the main trial is held, as long as it exceeds the authority of the president of the court. These issues are, for example, the need to exclude part of the case for separate examination, to exclude the openness of the main trial, to consider the issuance of an order to search for the accused by wanted notice.

Among the reasons for facultative refering the case to a session before the trial are those that precede the trial (eg issuance of a decision to suspend the proceedings) and those for which the order excludes the need for a future trial (eg when the proceedings are discontinued due to a procedural obstacle or due to a manifest absence of factual grounds for the accusation).

Preliminary Hearing

During the preparation phase for the main trial, it is clearly important for the efficient conduct of the trial to organise many of its activities, as their implementation after the commencement of the judicial examination may significantly slow down the course of the trial, and in some situations even make it impossible. In the literature it has been repeatedly stated that one of the most serious shortcomings of the Polish criminal trial is the lengthiness of the proceedings, and among the causes of this is the poor organisation of procedural activities during the main trial. Undoubtedly, a preparatory session ordered by the president of the court may be considered one way to improve the existing situation.[32]

If the expected scope of an evidentiary hearing provides grounds to suppose that the judicial examination shall not be closed at the first session of the trial, the president of the court shall immediately appoint a judge or members of the adjudicative panel, and the president of the adjudicative panel shall refer the case for a preliminary hearing. The preliminary hearing may be set to be held on the same day as the first session of the main trial (Article 349 § 1 CPC). The parties and other individuals whose participation in the preliminary hearing is mandatory, as well as other parties and the aggrieved party, may present a position as to the process of planning and organisation of the main trial. The position shall be presented in writing and may also be presented verbally at the hearing. The presiding judge may summon parties and other individuals obligated or entitled to participate in the preliminary hearing to present, inter alia, written statements on the proposed trial dates and periods of objective obstacles preventing participation in the trial, motions for evidence to be heard directly or to be presented, motions for evidence to be heard in a specific order, and motions to bring material evidence to the trial or for the court to obtain a specific official document of relevance to the resolution

[32] D Świecki, 'Posiedzenie przygotowawcze do rozprawy głównej w świetle nowelizacji z 27 września 2013 r', in *Złota Księga Jubileuszowa prof. zw. dr hab. dr honoris causa Brunona Hołysta* (Warsaw, Fundacja 'Ubi societas, ibi ius', 2015); Boczkowski (n 14) nos 7–8; H Paluszkiewicz, *Pierwszoinstancyjne wyrokowanie merytoryczne poza rozprawą w polskim procesie karnym* (Warsaw, Wolters Kluwer, 2008).

of the case (Article 349 §§ 3 and 4 CPC).[33] The presiding judge, taking into consideration indicated statements and motions or other positions, makes the decision, by way of an order, regarding circumstances covered by motions and other circumstances relevant to the efficient and due performance of judicial examination, schedules at least five trial dates, provided that the scope of an expected evidentiary hearing does not justify a smaller number of trial dates, and announces them to the parties and other individuals participating in the hearing. The announcement of scheduled trial dates is equivalent to being summoned to appear at the trial or notified of its date (Article 349 § 8 CPC).

The outlined regulation is undoubtedly an expression of the care taken over the implementation of the principle of concentration of evidence. At the same time, it is an expression of the assumed that only a case that is well-prepared in terms of its merits and organisation should be admitted to main trial, and that all those issues that can be resolved before it is commenced, in particular, before the commencement of judicial examination, should be resolved at this preliminary stage of the judicial proceedings.

Actions Related to the Organisation of the Main Trial

In cases in which a preliminary hearing has not been scheduled, the president of the court (the president of a division, a duly authorised judge) shall issue a written order indicating the judge or members of the panel of judges (Article 350 § 1 CPC).

If the indictment filed with the court meets the formal requirements or if the identified deficiencies of the indictment have been corrected in a timely manner, and furthermore if there are no obligatory or optional reasons for commit the case to a pre-trial session or no decision ending the proceedings has been issued after the session (eg proceedings have not been discontinued due to the existence of procedural obstacles or due to the existence of an manifest absence of factual basis for the prosecution) or if a preliminary hearing has already been held, or if a preliminary hearing has not been scheduled, the president of the court (chairman of the department, authorized judge) shall issue a written order on scheduling a main trial. He/she shall indicate in it (Article 350 § 2 CPC):

1. the judge or members of the adjudicative panel, at the same time appointing the president of the adjudicative panel;
2. the day, time and courtroom;
3. the parties and other persons who shall be summed to the trial or notified of its date;
4. other actions necessary for the preparation of the trial.

The president of the adjudicative panel may decide not to summon to the trial witnesses who have been questioned, who are staying abroad or who are to give evidence about circumstances that are not so important that it is necessary to question the witnesses

[33] H Paluszkiewicz, 'Udział obrońcy w posiedzeniu organizacyjnym jako element budujący strategię obrony oskarżonego w stadium jurysdykcyjnym', in P. Wiliński (ed), *Obrońca i pełnomocnik w procesie karnym po 1 lipca 2015 r. Przewodnik po zmianach* (Warsaw, 2015).

directly at the trial, in particular circumstances not denied by the accused in their explanations. This does not apply to persons closest relative, by blood or affinity, of the accused, as well as such witness who is accused of complicity in another pending case with regard to the criminal offence covered with the proceedings (Article 350a and 182 §§ 1 and 3 CPC). Undoubtedly, this provision may have an impact on speeding up the evidentiary proceedings, but it significantly limits the rule of directness in taking evidence at trial. Approval of this solution should be combined with the absence of objection from the accused to such a limitation of the evidentiary proceedings.

The designation of the judge and the members of the adjudicative panel[34] is an extremely important issue from the perspective of implementing the principle of objectivity and judicial independence, as expressed in the institution of the statutory judge. It should be known in advance to which cases a judge will be assigned, so that an administrative factor cannot decide the composition of the court at its own discretion. In the previous legal state, in the absence of a statutory regulation of this issue, the president of the court had too much discretion in this respect.

The rules for assignment cases to individual judges and court assessors have been significantly altered by modifications introduced to the Act on the Common Court System.[35] Under those amendments, cases are assigned to judges and assessors at random, unless the case is assigned to the on-duty judge. The assignment of cases is, as a rule, equal, unless it has been reduced because of the function performed, participation in the allocation of cases of another category, or for other reasons provided by law. These rules shall apply mutatis mutandis to the assignment of cases to court clerks. If a case has been assigned that requires an extraordinary workload, the reporting judge may motion the president of the court to suspend the assignment of further cases for a specified period; the president shall consider the motion without delay and his/her decision shall be delivered to the judge concerned and shall be communicated to the judges of the court concerned. That decision may be questioned. It should be noted that the rules for random assignment of cases to a judge indicated herein seemingly only streamline and reveal the rules for determining the composition of the court. In fact, they may lead to a violation of the principle of impartiality and independence of judges, due to the lack of precision in specifying the reasons for departing from the rules of random assignment of cases to specific judges. It also needs to be emphasised that significant powers in this respect were given to the president of the court, who is directly subordinate to the executive power, and furthermore that under the previous legal status, derogation from the composition of the adjudicative panel according to the impact of the case was only possible due to a judge's omission due to illness or other serious impediment, which had to be indicated in the order setting the trial. The changes in the rules for determining the composition of the court are intended to clearly demonstrate the subordination of

[34] Z Kwiatkowski, 'Wyznaczanie składu orzekającego w sprawach karnych' (2018) *Problemy Prawa Karnego* II; I Nowikowski, 'Skutki niedochowania reguł dotyczących wyznaczania składu orzekającego w procesie karnym', in S Steinborn and K Woźniewski (ed), *Proces karny w dobie przemian. Zagadnienia ogólne* (Gdańsk, Wydawnictwo Uniwersytetu Śląskiego, 2018) vol I.

[35] Law amending the Law on the organisation of the common law courts' (DzU of 2001, no 98, heading 1070).

the judiciary, hitherto protected by the principle of impartiality, to the executive power. These changes cannot be approved under any circumstance.[36]

Failure to comply with the rules of determining the composition of the court constitutes an absolute reason for reversing the ruling, referred to as improperly constituted panel (Article 439 § 1.2 CPC).

When determining the place of main trial, the president of the court shall indicate the courtroom or decides that the trial will be held in an away session.

The duties of the president of the court related to the organisation of the future main trial also include determining the persons who should be summoned or notified of the trial. People who are obliged to attend the trial shall be summoned, while those who are entitled to attend the trial but not obliged to do so shall be notified. Witnesses and experts shall be summoned; if the court deems the presence of the accused obligatory, the accused shall also be summoned. However, other litigants shall be notified, as well as those persons who appear at the trial in the capacity of a litigant's representative (defence counsel, attorney). A public prosecutor shall be notified of trials and sessions by service of a list of cases to be heard on a given day (Article 135 CPC). The CPC allows a letter to be delivered to the addressee also by fax or e-mail; in such a case, the proof of receipt is constituted by a confirmation of data transmission (Article 132 § 3 CPC).[37] If the defendant is deprived of liberty in this or any other case, it is necessary to issue an order to bring him/her to trial (see more Article 350 § 3 CPC). If a party has more than one defence counsel or attorney, the procedural action may be carried out in the case of appearance of at least one of them, unless the party consents that the action be carried out without any defence counsel or attorney, and the participation of the latter is not mandatory (Article 117a § 1 CPC). This provision should be regarded as significantly limiting the scope of the accused's right of defence. Because the law allows the accused to have no more than three defence counsels, it should not be permissible to conduct the proceedings without their participation. Acceptance of this solution would have to involve consent of the accused, but only if at least one of the appointed defence counsel was to participate in the activity. These rules apply mutatis mutandis to the attorney of a person who is not a party.

The president of the court shall also issue an order to admit evidence and bring it to trial. He/she does so ex officio or at the motion of the parties.

When setting the date of the trial, the president of the court must at the same time ensure the defendant's right to defence. Therefore, he or she must ensure that at least seven days elapse between the service of notification and the day on which the main trial is to be held (the start of the trial). If the time limit is not observed with respect to the accused or their defence counsel, then on their motion, filed before the commencement

[36] A Łozińska-Piekarska, 'Nowy sposób wyznaczania składów orzekających w procedurze karnej – większy obiektywizm, czy wydłużenie postępowania sądowego?' (2017) *INov* no 1; D Świecki, 'Zasady wyznaczania składu orzekającego i konsekwencje ich naruszenia' in A Lach (ed), *Postępowanie karne po nowelizacji z dnia 11 marca 2016 roku* (Warsaw, Wolters Kluwer, 2017).

[37] A Baworowski, 'Doręczenia elektroniczne w toku postępowania przygotowawczego' (2007) *Prok i Pr* no 11; M Górtowski, 'Poczta elektroniczna w postępowaniu karnym' (2007) *Prok i Pr* no 11; M Żak, 'Wnoszenie pism drogą elektroniczną oraz elektroniczne doręczenia w procesie karnym [I KZP 39/08]' (2010) *CzPKiNP* no 3; J Kudrelek, 'Rola doręczania pism procesowych a sprawność postępowania karnego, cz. 1, cz. 2' (2004) *Przegl Pol* nos 1–2, 3.

of the judicial examination, the trial shall be adjourned (Article 353 § 2 CPC); in such a case, the court will not examine whether the failure to meet the time limit actually caused a violation of the defendant's right of defence, as the motion itself is sufficient in this regard. If, despite the motion, the trial is continued, this may constitute grounds for reversal of the questioned ruling if the violation could have affected its content. If the accused has a defence counsel, failure to file such a motion does not constitute an obstacle to the continuation of the trial; however, if the accused appears in the trial without a defence counsel, he/she should be instructed on this right so that the lack of the motion is not a result of the accused being unaware of his/her right. A motion for adjourned of the trial is only a right of the accused or his/her defence counsel, as despite the failure to observe the seven-day time limit, the accused and his/her defence counsel may be prepared to defend themselves and have no interest in adjourn of the main trial.

The seven-day time limit applies only to the accused and his counsel; other parties cannot therefore motion for an adjournment of the main trial for this reason. Along with the service of the summons to the trial or notification of its date, the accused shall be instructed on the right to appeal decisions, including those issued outside the trial, on the right to participate in the trial, on the possibility of conducting the trial in spite of the absence of the accused at it, if he or she left the courtroom without permission from the president of the adjudicative panel, on the possibility of announcing the judgment in spite of the failure to appear of the parties and their defenders and attorneys, about the right to motion for a statement of reasons, and about the fact that in the event of an appeal against a judgment rendered following the granting of a motion for conviction to be issued in a session, without main trial (Article 335 §§ 1 and 2 CPC), or a motion for voluntary submission to criminal responsibility (Articles 338a and 387 CPC), the grounds for appeal cannot be allegations of error in factual findings or of strikingly disproportionality of punishment if they relate to the content of the agreement that gave rise to the granting of the said motions (Article 353 § 4 CPC).

General Characteristics of the Main Trial

The main trial is the most important stage of criminal proceedings from the perspective of deciding the subject of the process.[38] Apart from exceptional situations (verdict conditionally discontinuing the proceedings; conviction of the accused by a sentence without a trial), in principle, it is only at this stage of proceedings that a judgment of guilty or not guilty of the accused can be issued. All earlier stages of criminal proceedings are preparatory in nature. Their purpose is to ascertain the existence of grounds for indicting a certain person and to secure evidence for the main trial (trial). When examining the claims of the indictment, the court becomes acquainted with the information gathered as a result of the evidentiary proceedings carried out at the preliminary

[38] D Świecki, 'Rola i znaczenie rozprawy głównej w procesie karnym (rozważania o forach orzekania)' (2018) *Prok i Pr* no 10; M Rzeszutko, *Rozprawa sądowa w świetle lingwistyki tekstu* (Lublin, Wydawnictwo Uniwersytetu Marii Curie-Skłodowskiej, 2003); J Tylman, *Postępowanie przed sądem pierwszej instancji* (Warsaw, Wydawnictwo Prawnicze, 1999).

(preparatory) stage of the criminal trial (in the principal or simplified investigation). On their basis, it makes findings as to the guilt or innocence of the accused. The basis for these findings can be only such circumstances that were disclosed at the main trial (Article 410 CPC). This fact emphasises the role of the main trial in the course of a criminal procedure and proves that the basis for findings cannot be circumstances not disclosed during the main trial (this does not apply to notoriety, which should, however, be notified to the parties). Thus, only those evidentiary facts (disclosed during the trial) about which the parties had an opportunity to comment (pose questions, make statements, or submit evidentiary motions) may form the basis of findings. This statement is of great importance from the perspective of the principles of the right to defence and the principle of an adversarial process.

The stage of the criminal process in the form of the main trial is also distinguished by the fact that procedural principles, eg the principle of objective truth, the principle of directness, the principle of audience, the principle of orality, are most widely applied therein. The main trial also has important educational functions; therefore, it is very important to take care of the appropriate level of culture of the main hearing. This circumstance is clearly emphasised in case law and literature.

As a rule, the trial is directed by the president of the adjudicative panel (presiding judge), but certain actions related to directing the trial are the responsibility of the entire panel. The president of the adjudicative panel (presiding judge) shall direct the main trial, supervising its proper course. These are activities connected with the order of the trial, included in the so-called formal management of the trial. The presiding judge is also responsible for a significant part of the activities of the so-called material management of the trial, ie activities related to clarifying the circumstances of the case.The presiding judge should ensure that all important circumstances of the case are explained and aim at reaching a decision on the case at the first main trial (Article 366 CPC).

The powers of the presiding judge as part of the trial management include:

- deciding on the opening and closing of the trial;
- verifying the attendance of persons summoned to the trial;
- directing the evidence proceeding;
- deciding whether to grant a motion for evidence, unless it has been contested by another party;
- exercising sessional police, ie issuing all orders necessary to maintain order and peace in the courtroom;
- ordering an interruption in the trial;
- giving the floor to the parties and other participants in the proceedings;
- directing the conduct of deliberation and voting;
- announcing the judgment and instructing on the right, time limit and manner of appealing it.

The presiding judge shall also be obliged to ensure that the other members of the panel have an opportunity to acquaintance themselves with the case files and shall be obliged to ensure that the main trial starts on time.

Certain activities of the presiding judge are also performed by the entire panel. The court may also perform acts of formal management, such as ejecting individuals from the room if they violate the solemnity, peace or order of the proceedings or the entire audience due to their improper behaviour, as well as acts of substantive management, such as dismissing a motion for evidence (Article 368 § 1 CPC). This is because these decisions must be made only in the form of a decision.

The court's powers in this regard include, among others, such actions as:

- deciding an immediate contest against an order of the presiding judge made at the trial, unless the rulings are issued by one judge;
- to excluding the public from a trial;
- allowing representatives of mass media to use equipment to record image and sound during the course of a trial;
- adjourning the trial;
- dismissing a motion to take evidence.

In the course of the main trial, the following stages may be distinguished:

1. the preliminary part of the trial;
2. the judicial examination;
3. final statements;
4. adjudication.

Preliminary Part of the Main Trial

The first phase of the main trial is the introductory part. The main trial, and thus its first phase, commences with the calling of the case, which consists of announcing loudly in the waiting room outside the courtroom that the next case on the list of cases (calendar, roll) is to be heard, stating its number (reference number), the name of the accused, and the act charged. The calling of a case is of such importance for criminal proceedings that from that moment the principle of continuity (with invariability of the panel of judges) begins to operate. The trial thus commenced should be completed on a single date, unless, exceptionally, it is necessary to order an interruption or adjourn the trial. Unfortunately, in practice, the requirement to finish the trial at the first main trial has become an exception, whereas interruption or adjournment of the trial has become the rule. The timing of the call of the case may be important for the realisation of the rights of the parties. For this reason, the case should not be called earlier than the time set for the trial to commence.

The preliminary part of the main trial serves primarily to check the presence of the summoned persons and to examine whether there are any obstacles to the hearing of the case. Other issues may also be dealt with at this phase. As part of the preliminary part of the main trial, activities are carried out, which can be divided into four groups:

- checking the presence of summoned and notified persons;
- checking whether there are any obstacles to the examination of the case;

- performing actions that can be performed at the latest before the commencement of the judicial examination;
- the settlement of other issues connected with the course of the trial.

If the parties or their representatives fail to appear, it is necessary, first of all, to establish whether they were properly summoned or notified of the date of the main trial, ie in accordance with the provisions on service, and then whether they excused their absence in accordance with the relevant provisions. In the absence of proof of proper service of the summons or notice, the trial shall be adjourn. The same procedure should be followed if these persons excused their absence or if there is a good reason to suspect that the absence was caused by natural disasters or other extraordinary circumstances (Article 117 § 2 CPC). An excuse for a failure to appear due to illness of the accused, witnesses, defence counsels, attorneys and other participants of the proceedings whose presence was obligatory or who have applied for admission to an action while being persons authorised to participate in it, requires the provision of a statement confirming the inability to appear upon call or a notification of the body conducting the proceedings, issued by a court physician (Article 117 § 2a CPC). However, the failure to appear of a party who has been duly notified of a procedural action, irrespective of the reasons for that failure, poses no obstacle to conducting that procedural action if his/her defence counsel or attorney has appeared (Article 117 § 3a CPC). This does not apply to actions in which the participation of the party is mandatory. It should be pointed out that this provision severely restricts the right of defence of the accused, especially if we consider the admissibility of carrying out the action despite the failure of the accused to appear, regardless of the reason for the failure to appear.

If the summons or notice is properly served and the absence is not sufficiently excused, the consequences of the failure to appear depend on the role in which the designated person appears in the criminal trial.[39] Thus:

- The accused has the right to take part in the trial, but the presiding officer or the court may consider his/her presence mandatory (Article 374 § 1 CPC). In cases related to felonies, the presence of the accused is mandatory during the actions specified in Articles 384 and 385 CPC (Article 374 § 1a CPC). The presiding judge may issue an order to prevent the accused from leaving the court before the termination of the trial (Article 374 § 2 CPC). Exceptionally, only in the absence of the accused is it allowed to conduct the trial if the accused:
  - due to their own fault, works themselves up into a condition making them unfit to participate in a trial where their presence is deemed mandatory (Article 377 § 1 CPC);
  - whose presence at the trial is compulsory, having been notified of the date and time of the trial, declares that they will not participate in the trial, makes it impossible to bring them to the trial or, having been notified of it personally, fails to appear at the trial without excuse; however, the court may order arrest and enforced appearance of the accused. The decision on arrest and enforced

[39] D Drajewicz, 'Zatrzymanie i przymusowe doprowadzenie w przypadku nieusprawiedliwionego niestawiennictwa oskarżonego?' (2008) *Prok* no 1; K Marszał, 'Skutki niestawiennictwa oskarżyciela prywatnego na posiedzenie pojednawcze' (1965) *NP* no 10.

  appearance may be contested before another equivalent panel of the court (Article 377 § 3 CPC);
  - failed to appear at the trial in the proceedings for the rendering of a cumulative judgment; however, the court may decide otherwise and declare the appearance of the accused to be compulsory (Article 573 § 1 CPC).
- Failure of the defence counsel to appear results in adjournment of the trial both when defence is compulsory and when defence is not compulsory, but the defendant declares that he/she wishes to be assisted by a defence counsel (see, however, Article 378a CPC).
- The consequences of the prosecutor's non-appearance should be assessed depending on whether his/her presence at the trial is compulsory or not (Article 46 CPC). The failure of the public prosecution counsel to appear in a trial shall not obstruct the course of the trial, where an investigation has ended in the form of a simplified investigation (Article 46 § 2 CPC). The prosecutor's participation in the trial is not compulsory in private prosecution cases (unless there has been an interference of the prosecutor in such a case) and in cases initiated as a result of filing the so-called subsidiary indictment by the injured person.
- The failure of the private prosecution counsel and their attorney to appear at a conciliation session without justification shall be treated as withdrawal from the charge; in such a case, the person conducting the session shall discontinue the proceedings (Article 491 § 1 CPC).
- In the case of the non-appearance of a witness, irrespective of imposing a financial penalty and ordering the arrest and enforced appearance of a witness (see Article 285 §§ 1 and 2), a decision shall be made to hold a trial or to adjourn it. The decision to conduct a trial shall be made if it will be possible to read the testimony of this witness or if the court has the opportunity to conduct partial evidence, and in order to take evidence from the testimony of an absent witness the presiding judge will order an interruption in the trial or the court will adjourn the trial.
- Failure of the interpreter to appear will make it impossible to conduct the proceedings, unless the defendant himself/herself also fails to appear.
- Failure of an expert or specialist to appear will most often result in the trial being interrupted or adjourned.

The preliminary phase of the main trial also checks the existence of other circumstances that prevent the trial from taking place on the scheduled date. Such circumstances include the need to suspend the proceedings, as well as the failure to observe the seven-day time limit between the notification of the defendant about the trial and the trial date. In the latter case, if the defendant or his/her counsel motion adjournment of the trial, before the commencement of the judicial examination, the court is obliged to issue a decision to that effect (Article 353 § 2 CPC).

The duty to check the existence of procedural obstacles[40] is incumbent on the trial authority at every stage of the proceedings, and therefore at this phase of the proceedings

[40] M Rogalski, 'Glosa do post. SN z 28.10.2009 r., I KZP 21/09' (2011) *OSP* no 1.

also, the finding of a procedural obstacle must result in the issuance of a decision to discontinue the proceedings. However, the inability to assign guilt to the perpetrator of the act does not exclude the proceedings on the application of preventive measures.

An extremely important moment in the trial is the commencement of judicial examination.[41] It begins with a concise presentation of the charges by the public prosecution counsel; however, if the prosecutor does not participate in the trial, a briefly presentation of the charges against the accused is made by the presiding judge (Article 385 § 1 CPC). The presiding judge shall also inform of the contents of the answer to the indictment, if filed (Article 385 § 2 CPC). It seems that the obligation to present the charge of the indictment should rest solely with the prosecutor, as the presiding judge's performance of this act violates the principle of impartiality.

The admissibility of many procedural actions ceases with the commencement of judicial examination. These actions can be performed in the preliminary part of the main trial, and some of them can be performed even earlier, because they can already be done in the preparatory proceedings. If, for some reason, the proceedings return to the phase before the commencement of the judicial examination (eg the time limit for which the judgment was adjourned has been exceeded or the case has been referred back to the main trial after the appellate court reversed the judgment), these actions may be performed again until the judicial examination is 'reopened'. If such an action was made earlier, but the court did not make a decision on it, or if it was made in the preliminary part of the main trial, the court should make an appropriate decision on such an action before the commencement of the judicial examination. The following actions belong to this group:

- Withdrawal of a prosecution motion with the court's consent. A motion may be withdrawn in court proceedings, with the consent of the court, up until the conclusion of the judicial examination within the first main trial. In cases where the indictment was brought by a public prosecution counsel, the withdrawal of a motion after the commencement of the judicial examination shall be effective if the public prosecution counsel present at the trial or hearing does not object to this (Article 12 § 3 CPC).
- Withdrawal of the indictment by the public prosecutor. During the judicial examination before a first-instance court, an indictment may be withdrawn only upon the consent of the accused (Article 14 § 2 CPC).[42]
- Filing of a motion for exclusion of a judge due to the existence of circumstances that can give rise to reasonable doubts as to the judge's impartiality in a given case; such a motion may be filed after the judicial examination has been commenced, if the grounds for disqualification had arisen or had not become known to the party concerned until after the commencement of the examination (Article 41 CPC).

[41] S Stachowiak, 'Rozpoczęcie przewodu sądowego na rozprawie głównej jako czas wygaśnięcia niektórych uprawnień procesowych' (2005) *Prok i Pr* no 11; Z Jankowski, *Postępowanie karne przed sądem pierwszej instancji w aspekcie prakseologicznym* (Warsaw, Wydawnictwo Prawnicze, 1986).

[42] M Kurowski, 'Cofnięcie aktu oskarżenia przez oskarżyciela publicznego a prawo pokrzywdzonego do sądu', in C Kulesza and A Sakowicz (ed), *Ewolucja polskiego wymiaru sprawiedliwości w latach 2013-2018 w świetle standardów rzetelnego procesu* (Białystok, Temida2, 2019).

- Filing a statement by the injured on their intention to act as an auxiliary prosecutor (Article 54 § 1 CPC).
- Other persons injured by the same act may join the proceedings (Article 55 § 3 CPC).
- Filing a motion to adjourn the trial if less than seven days have elapsed between the service of the notice and the trial date (Article 353 § 2 CPC).
- Transferring the case to a competent court if it is found that the act of the defendant constitutes a delinquency.
- Discontinuance of proceedings without the consent of the accused in a case for an act prosecuted by private prosecution if the private prosecutor withdraws from the charge (Article 496 § 2 CPC).
- Filing against the private prosecutor who is an injured party a reciprocal charge for an act subject to prosecution under private indictment being related to the act imputed to the accused (Article 497 § 1 CPC).
- Withdrawal of the objection against the injunctive judgment (Article 506 § 4 CPC).[43]

The preliminary part of the trial should also include actions related to the course and organisation of the future trial. In this group, it would be appropriate to indicate, for example, the following actions:

- the court by a decision shall allow representatives of the mass media to use equipment to record image and sound during the course of a trial (Article 357 § 1 CPC);
- unless there is any concern for the proper conduct of the proceedings, the court, upon motion of a party, shall allow such a party to record the course of the trial using sound recording equipment (Article 358 CPC);[44]
- the court may also issue a decision on the exclusion of all or part of the trial from public view (Article 360 § 1 CPC);
- the presiding judge may issue an order to render it impossible for the accused to leave the courthouse before the termination of the trial (Article 374 § 2 CPC);
- the presiding judge may issue an order for persons who cannot participate in the trial to leave the room (Article 356 § 3 CPC);
- the presiding judge may allow certain persons to attend the trial (Article 356 § 2 CPC).

[43] J Żylińska, 'Cofnięcie sprzeciwu od wyroku nakazowego w procesie karnym' (2019) *Prok i Pr* no 2; S Durczak-Żochowska, 'Glosa do wyr. SN z 21.8.2008 r., III KK 224/08' (2011) *OSP* no 1; A Pawłowska, 'Sprzeciw od wyroku nakazowego – uwagi dotyczące jego charakteru i skutków' in I Nowikowskiego (pod red), *Problemy stosowania prawa sądowego. Księga ofiarowana Profesorowi Edwardowi Skrętowiczowi* (Lublin, 2007; S Stachowiak, 'Sprzeciw przeciwko postanowieniu o warunkowym umorzeniu postępowania karnego' (1971) *NP* no 10; K Zgryzek, 'Glosa do u. SN z 15 IV 1986, VI KZP 8/8' (1987) *Pal* no 12.

[44] A Taracha, 'Rejestracja czynności dowodowych w postępowaniu karnym przy użyciu urządzeń utrwalających obraz i dźwięk (zagadnienia wybrane)' (2012) *WSS* no 3; H Gajewska-Kraczkowska, 'O audiowizualnych rejestracjach rozprawy głównej – de lege ferenda', in S Waltoś przy współpracy Z Dody, A Światłowskiego, J Rybaka and Z Wrony (eds), *Problemy kodyfikacji prawa karnego. Księga pamiątkowa ku czci Profesora Mariana Cieślaka* (Kraków, Wydawnictwo Uniwersytetu Jagiellońskiego, 1993).

Decisions on these issues may be made by the court or the presiding judge, respectively, also in the course of the trial, if the need for such a decision becomes apparent only after the commencement of the trial.

If all the steps in the preliminary part of the main trial have been taken, the presiding judge shall determine, on the basis of personal data or other data, whether any of the witnesses has the right to refuse to testify, either as a person closest relatives by blood or affinity to the accused (Article 182 CPC) or because of a particularly close personal relationship with the accused (Article 185 CPC). As emphasised in the literature, a 'particularly close personal relationship' is one that is not based on blood or affinity, but is socially accepted, or at least tolerated, such as engagement, cohabitation of persons of the same sex, kinship or affinity with the defendant's spouse, friendship or other such personal relationship. The judicature, on the other hand, indicates that if such a relationship is based on the existence of only a loose relationship between the interrogated person and the accused person, eg typical of youth culture, this requires particular insight and reasonableness from the interrogating authority assessing this fact. Such a witness must be warned of his/her right to refuse to testify on these grounds. If it is determined that the witness is not entitled to refuse to testify, the presiding judge shall instruct the witness of his/her obligation to tell the truth and warn him/her of his criminal liability for giving false testimony.

Witnesses summoned to the trial shall wait outside the courtroom until they are summoned to give their testimony, remaining at the disposal of the court, but if the witness is an injured party, he or she shall be examined first in order to participate in all the activities of the evidentiary proceedings, and at the same time to comply with the rule that a witness who has not yet given his or her testimony should not take part in the examination of another witness (Article 384 § 2 CPC). Assessing which witness's testimony is 'more important', and thus which witness should be examined first, can be subjective and difficult to make before the testimony is taken. As seems appropriate, the court should hear the parties' positions on this issue before making a decision. If the court finds it purposeful, it may obligate the injured to be present throughout the trial or a part thereof (Article 384 § 3 CPC).

Similar principles to those outlined above apply to expert witnesses, except that they may remain in the courtroom, unless otherwise ordered by the presiding judge (Article 384 § 1 CPC).

After all the actions discussed above have been completed, the presiding officer shall order the commencement of the judicial examination, unless there are no obstacles to the continuation of the trial.

Judicial Examination

The judicial examination is a sub-phase of the trial in which all the evidence providing information allowing the court to make factual findings is conducted. Under the conditions of the adversarial principle, it is possible to clarify all relevant circumstances of the case, which are necessary to decide on the subject of the trial.

The judicial examination shall commence with a concise presentation of the charges by the public prosecution counsel (or the presiding judge), and ends with the presiding judge's order to close the judicial examination. The judicial examination can be divided into four distinct phases as follows.

The first of these is a concise statement by the prosecutor of the charges against the accused. In an adversarial trial, in which the court acts as an impartial arbiter, the reading of the indictment should be done by the prosecutor him/herself, as doing so by the court violates the balance of parties and puts the court in the role of an accuser. This solution should be rejected *a limine*, as it is a manifestation of the inquisitorial nature of the trial. In the present state of the law, in principle, the first way of familiarising the court, the parties and other persons participating in the trial with the charges of the prosecution has been adopted. In cases concerning criminal offences prosecuted by public indictment, the public prosecutor presents the charges, in criminal offences prosecuted by private indictment, the private prosecutor performs this task, and in proceedings initiated as a result of filing a subsidiary indictment, the subsidiary prosecutor does this. However, where no prosecution counsel is participating in a trial, the presiding judge shall briefly present the charges of the prosecution. It does not have to be explained that this solution should be regarded as violating the principle of an adversarial and impartial court. Therefore, in the cases discussed the reading out the charges (without any limitation to briefly presentation of the charges) should be entrusted to a recording clerk, even if this would significantly prolong this part of the trial. In practice, such an action, ie a reading of the charges of the indictment by the recording clerk, does not violate any of the provisions of the CPC and is certainly a better solution than the presentation of the charges by the presiding judge. The restriction to a brief presentation of the charges in the indictment thus means that the sometimes very extensive statement of reasons for the indictment will not be read out either.

If a response to the indictment has been filed, the presiding judge shall inform only of its contents (Article 385 § 2 CPC), and thus shall not quote it *in extenso*.[45]

A concise presentation of the charges of the indictment will have to be repeated when the main trial is conducted again, from the beginning. This type of situation occurs eg as a result of an adjournment of the trial, or exceeding the time limit of the adjournment rendering of a judgment, after the judgment has been set aside and the case has been referred for re-examination.

After the charge of the indictment is presented, the proceedings proceed to the phase of the defendant's explanations. If the accused participates in the main trial, the presiding judge, after presenting the charges, shall advise the accused of the right to provide explanations, refuse to provide explanations, answer questions, and file motions for evidence, as well as of the consequences of not exercising this right, and then the presiding judge shall ask the accused whether they plead guilty to the alleged act and whether and what explanations they wish to provide (Article 386 § 1 CCP). The accused

[45] PK Sowiński, 'Odpowiedź oskarżonego na akt oskarżenia (art 388 § 2 KPK)' (2007) *ZN UR* no 41; RA Stefański, 'Odpowiedź na akt oskarżenia' (2005) *Prok i Pr* no 5.

shall be instructed about the indicated rights if he/she appears for the first time at the subsequent main trial (Article 386 § 3 CCP).

If the accused decides to give explanations, he/she must be allowed to do so under conditions of free speech; questions may be put to him/her only after he/she has given his/her account.[46]

Until the completion of the first questioning of all accused persons at the main trial, an accused who has been charged with a criminal offence punishable by imprisonment for a term not exceeding fifteen years may submit a motion for a judgment of conviction and for the imposition of a specific penalty or criminal measure upon them or for ordering forfeiture or a redress measure without an evidentiary hearing being conducted.[47] This is known as sentencing the defendant without a hearing.[48] Such a motion may also concern the issuance of a specific decision as to the payment of the costs of the proceedings. Where the accused has no defence counsel of their choice, the court may, at the request of the accused, appoint a public defence counsel for them ex officio (Article 387 § 1 CPC). Before granting the defendant's motion, the court shall instruct the defendant that the appeal, if any, may not be based on charges of error in the findings of fact constituting the basis of the judgment and strikingly disproportionality of the penalty or penalty measure, forfeiture or compensation measure (Article 387 § 1a CCP).

The court may grant the motion of the accused to issue a judgment convicting the latter only if the circumstances related to the criminal offence and the responsibility of the accused do not give rise to doubt, and if the objectives of the proceedings are to be achieved in spite of the trial not being conducted in full.[49] Granting of the motion is possible only when the public prosecutor, as well as the injured duly informed about the date of the trial and advised of the possibility of submission of such a motion by the accused, do not object to that (Article 387 § 2 CPC). The court may make the granting of the motion of the accused conditional on introducing into it an amendment indicated by the court (Article 387 § 3 CPC). On the motion of the accused or the injured party, the court may adjourn the hearing, setting an appropriate time limit for the parties to make arrangements.

[46] E Gruza, 'Przyznanie sie do winy oskarżonego jako element dowodu poszlakowego', in M Rogacka-Rzewnicka and H. Gajewska-Kraczkowska (eds.), *Istota i zasady procesu karnego 25 lat później. Księga poświęcona pamięci Profesora Andrzeja Murzynowskiego* (Warsaw, Wolters Kluwer, 2019); A. Sakowicz, 'Zakres przedmiotowy prawa do milczenia w polskim procesie karnym', in Istota i zasady procesu karnego 25 lat później, ibid; M Kucharczyk, *Wyjaśnienia oskarżonego jako dowód w polskim procesie karnym* (Katowice, PhD thesis, 2017).

[47] M Tokarska and J Pawlikowska, 'Skazanie bez dowodów? Czyli wokół procesów poszlakowych – o "lepszych" i "gorszych" dowodach w procesie karnym', in D Gila (pod red), *Dowód w procesie karnym w perspektywie porównawczej* (2016) *WPWS* no 6; M Żbikowska, 'Wybrane aspekty instytucji skazania w trybie art 335 k.p.k.' (2016) *PS* n 9; M Błaszczyk, 'Skazanie bez rozprawy i dobrowolne poddanie się odpowiedzialności karnej w nowym modelu procesu karnego', in T Gardocka and M Jakubik (eds.), *Szkice o nowym modelu procesu karnego* (Warsaw, Dom Wydawniczy Elipsa, 2014).

[48] S Cora, 'Kontrola sądowa wymogów wniosku o skazanie bez rozprawy określonych w art 335 k.p.k.' (2005) *Prok i Pr* no 6.

[49] S Steinborn, *Porozumienia w polskim procesie karnym. Skazanie bez rozprawy i dobrowolne poddanie się odpowiedzialności karnej* (Kraków, Zakamycze, 2005); W Marcinkowski, Nowelizacja trybu dotyczącego wniosku prokuratora o skazanie oskarżonego bez przeprowadzenia rozprawy' (2003) *Prok* no 2; E Kruk, 'Istota instytucji skazania bez rozprawy', in S Stachowiaka (ed), *Współczesny polski proces karny. Księga ofiarowana Profesorowi Tadeuszowi Nowakowi* (Poznań, 2002).

If the motion is not granted and there are no grounds to convict the accused without an evidentiary hearing, the court shall continue the judicial examination under the general rules.

If the explanations of a defendant who has pleaded guilty do not give rise to doubt, the court – upon obtaining the consent of the parties present – may conduct evidentiary proceedings only partially, if the evidence carried out allows verification of their credibility (Article 388 CPC).

The accused may give explanations, but may refuse to do so.[50]

Where the accused has failed to appear at the trial, refuses to give explanations, gives explanations inconsistent with those given previously or claims that they are unable to recall certain particulars, at the trial, the records of their explanations given previously when the accused was the accused in the given case or another case, in the investigation or before court, or in other proceedings provided for in the statute, eg in disciplinary proceedings, may be read out only in the appropriate scope (Article 389 § 1 CPC). After reading the record, the presiding judge shall request the accused to state their opinion as to the contents of the record and to explain any existing inconsistencies (Article 389 § 2 CPC). The reading of the record of the defendant's explanations is not only the court's right, but also its duty, as failure to do so may lead to factual findings that are not true. It is irrelevant for the reading of the record of the defendant's explanations whether their content is favourable or unfavourable to the defendant. The reading of the record of the accused's statements is an exceptional solution, as it constitutes a derogation from the principle of directness, which means that it cannot be interpreted broadly. The record of explanations made by the accused before foreign law enforcement authorities, in the course of legal assistance or in proceedings before taking over the prosecution, is also subject to reading.

The reading of the record of the testimony that the accused gave as a witness in the preparatory proceedings in the case in question shall not be admissible even if the accused motions it, since the evidentiary prohibition prevents the granting of such a motion. This is fully understandable: since the accused does not have to give explanations and does not have to tell the truth, so his/her testimony given as a witness, who is obliged to give truthful testimony, cannot be read out. The reading of the record of the explanations of an accused who has died is permitted (Article 389 § 3 CPC). In the current state of the law, it is also possible to read those records which were made in other proceedings, but only such as are provided by law. On this basis, it is permissible to read out records from any disciplinary proceedings, as long as their course is regulated by statute, although this undoubtedly expands the scope of derogations from the principle of directness.

After questioning the accused, the presiding judge shall instruct them of their right to address questions to the persons subject to questioning and to give explanations concerning each item of evidence (Article 386 § 2 CPC).[51]

[50] A Sakowicz, *Prawo do milczenia w polskim procesie karnym* (Białystok, Temida2, 2019).

[51] J Kosowski, 'Pouczenie świadka w procesie karnym a kwestia odpowiedzialności karnej (zagadnienia wybrane)', in I Nowikowski (ed), *Problemy stosowania prawa sądowego. Księga ofiarowana Profesorowi Edwardowi Skrętowiczowi* (Lublin, 2007); idem, 'Pouczenie oskarżonego (podejrzanego) w procesie karnym a kwestia odpowiedzialności karnej i wymiaru kary – zagadnienia wybrane', in Z Ćwiąkalski and G Artymiak (eds.),

All parties and their representatives may be present during the taking of evidence. The accused may be present at all evidentiary proceedings, regardless of whether his or her appearance at the trial is mandatory or not. In exceptional circumstances, if there is a justified risk that the presence of the accused may have an inhibiting effect on the explanations given by their co-accused or the testimony of a witness or an expert witness, the presiding judge may order that the accused leave the courtroom for so long as such other person is being questioned (Article 390 § 2 CPC); the case law emphasises that this should be done only exceptionally. If the accused, whose presence is compulsory, after making explanations, leaves the courtroom without permission of the chairman, the court may complete the trial in the absence of the accused. However, the court shall order arrest and enforced appearance of the accused if it deems their presence necessary (Article 376 § 2 CPC). Evidentiary proceedings may proceed without the participation of the accused (even if he/she has not yet given explanations) when he/she has become incapable of participating in the trial due to his/her fault (see Article 377 § 1 CPC).

Of course, the right to participate in the activities of the evidentiary proceedings is also vested in the accused's defence counsel. In the case of mandatory defence, the participation of the defence counsel in the procedural actions is mandatory, which means that without the participation of such counsel, the procedural actions cannot be carried out.[52] If, in a case in which the accused must have a defence counsel and they use a defence counsel of their choice, and the defence counsel or the accused terminate the defence relationship, the court, the president of the court, or a court clerk shall appoint an ex officio defence counsel, provided that the accused has not appointed a defence counsel of their choice. If there is such a need, the trial shall be interrupted or adjourned (Article 378 § 1 CPC), which means that a defence counsel may be appointed immediately, unless the accused submits an empowerment for a new defence counsel or at least indicates his willingness to designate a new defence counsel. In a case in which the accused benefits from the services of an ex officio defence counsel, the court, upon a justified motion of the defence counsel or of the accused, shall release the defence counsel from their duties and appoint another ex officio defence counsel for the accused (Article 378 § 2 CPC). When appointing a new defence counsel, the court shall concurrently decide whether the existing defence counsel may, without detriment to the accused person's right of defence, carry out their duties until the defence is taken up by a new defence counsel (Article 378 § 3 CPC).

The parties and their representatives present at the hearing during the taking of evidence are entitled to make statements in relation to any evidence taken. The presiding judge should permit the aforementioned subjects to express themselves on any matter which is to be resolved. If one of the parties expresses themselves on a matter, every other party shall also be entitled to do the same. However, the defence counsel of the accused and the accused shall have the right to the last word (Article 367 § 2 CPC);

Współzależność prawa karnego materialnego i procesowego w świetle kodyfikacji karnych z 1997 r. i propozycji ich zmian (Warsaw, 2009).

[52] D Jagiełło, 'Udział radcy prawnego w procesie karnym po nowelizacji K.p.k. Z 27 września 2013 r' (2015) *Ius Novum* no 1; C Kulesza, 'Udział obrońcy i pełnomocnika w rozprawie – obowiązek czy uprawnienie po dniu 1 lipca 2015 r', in P Wiliński (ed), *Obrońca i pełnomocnik w procesie karnym po 1 lipca 2015 r. Przewodnik po zmianach* (Warsaw, Wolters Kluwer, 2015).

this is understandable if one considers that the accused is the subject of punishment in a criminal trial.

In the course of further evidentiary proceedings, evidence in support of the accusation should be taken as far as possible before evidence for the defence (Article 369 CPC). This regulation is related to the person of the (public) accuser, on whom the burden of proof rests. An exception to the specified order of evidence taking applies, for example, to situations when some of the witnesses who are to support the prosecution fail to appear at the trial and the court decides to hold a trial. Evidence will be taken in a similar order when a motion for evidence in favour of the accused is made and favourably decided earlier than the one supporting the prosecution case. Considering the order in which the evidence is to be taken, the Code provides for a slight preponderance of evidence in favour of the defence over that in support of the prosecution's case. This advantage is confirmed by the provisions granting the accused the right to the last word (*favor defensionis*). This advantage, by virtue of the accused's right of defence, is fully justified.

Next to the accused, the most common personal source of evidence is the witness.[53] The witness shall be given an opportunity to express themselves freely, and then may be questioned by trial participants in the following order: the public prosecutor, the auxiliary prosecutor, the attorney of the auxiliary prosecutor, the private prosecutor, the attorney for the private prosecutor, expert witnesses, defence counsel, the accused, and members of the adjudicative panel (Article 370 § 1 CPC). In practice, this order is often violated; the principle of adversarial proceedings and the principle of the right to defence suffers. The party based on whose motion the witness was admitted shall ask questions before the other parties (Article 370 § 2 CPC). The members of the adjudicative panel may ask additional questions at any time (Article 370 § 2a CPC); the CPC permits members of the panel to ask questions out of turn, which may in some cases upset the balance of the parties and thus compromise the adversarial principle. The presiding judge shall dismiss any questions that suggest an answer or that he/she finds improper for other reasons (Article 370 § 4 CPC).

A witness shall be examined in the absence of other witnesses who have not yet testified; an exception to this is the right of the injured party who is to testify as a witness to remain in the courtroom even if other witnesses have not yet testified; the court should examine such an injured party first (Article 384 § 2 CPC). The Code imposes an obligation on the presiding judge to take steps necessary to prevent communication between persons already questioned and those awaiting the questioning (Article 371 § 2 CPC).[54]

[53] J Gurgul, 'Jeszcze o dowodzie z zeznań i wyjaśnień nietrzeźwego' (2018) *Prok i Pr* no 1; M Kierska, 'Prawo do przesłuchania świadków oskarżenia w świetle orzecznictwa Europejskiego Trybunału Praw Człowieka' (2017) *Pal* no 6; KJ Pawelec, 'Wyjaśnienia i zeznania obciążające w znowelizowanej procedurze karnej. Zagadnienia wybrane' (2016) *PS* no 6; L Lapawa, 'Problem pouczenia świadka o prawie do uchylenia się od odpowiedzi na pytanie' (2013) *WPP* no 1; M Kornak, *Dziecko jako świadek w polskim procesie karnym* (Warsaw, Wolters Kluwer, 2009).

[54] Ł Cora, 'Wyjątkowość dopuszczalności ponownego przesłuchania pokrzywdzonego w trybie art 185a i 185c k.p.k.', in L Mazowiecka, W Klaus and A Tarwacka (eds.), *Z problematyki wiktymologii. Księga dedykowana Profesor Ewie Bieńkowskiej* (Warsaw, Wolters Kluwer, 2017); M Kierski, 'Jednokrotne przesłuchanie pokrzywdzonego w trybie art 185a k.p.k. – reguła czy wyjątek?' (2018) *Prok i Pr* no 11.

The testimony of a witness or an expert witness shall be recorded by means of image and sound recording equipment when there is a risk that taking the testimony from that person might not be possible later in the proceedings or if the examination is carried out by means of the procedure of taking evidence by requisition; the person examined shall be informed about the recording before the device is activated (Article 147 § 2 CPC). The provisions of the CPC set forth the rules for recording the course of a trial and the extent to which its openness is excluded due to the fear of disclosure of classified information categorized as 'secret' or 'top secret' (see Article 147 § 2c CPC).

A derogation from the principle of directness is the reading of the records of the testimony of a witness. If a witness refuses without any justification to give testimony, gives testimony inconsistent with the testimony given previously or claims that they are unable to recall certain circumstances, or if they are staying abroad or it has been impossible to serve a summons on them, or if they have failed to appear due to obstacles that could not be removed, or the presiding judge has refrained from summoning the witness pursuant to Article 350a, as well as where the witness has died, the records of the testimonies given previously by the witness in the investigation or before court in the given case or in another case, or in other proceedings provided for in the statute, may be read out to the appropriate extent (Article 391 § 1 CPC).[55]

The reading of the record of a witness's testimony is possible only in the situations listed in the provisions of the Code. These provisions are of an exceptional nature, which means that their broadening interpretation is inadmissible. The reading of the record of the testimony of a witness is not subject to the consent of the parties. The record of the testimony of a witness may be read ex officio or at the motion of the parties. The reading of the record of the testimony of a witness given in the preparatory proceedings or before the court in this or another case, or even in other proceedings provided for by law, shall be allowed only in the situations specified in this provision. The court may also read the record of the testimony of a witness when the witness in another pending case is accused of complicity in the crime under investigation. The court may also read the record of the explanations that the witness gave earlier when acting in a different procedural role, ie as an accused.

The CPC provides for broad possibilities of reading out at the trial any records of questioning of witnesses and accused persons, drawn up in investigation or before court, or in other proceedings provided for in the Act, when direct taking of evidence is not necessary and none of the parties present objects to that, but any objection from a party to whom testimonies or explanations do not relate shall not prevent the reading of the record (Article 392 of the CPC). The assessment of the necessity to take evidence in a direct way is the responsibility of the court; the inclusion of this condition in practice allows for fairly free use of this form of taking evidence, as long as none of the parties present at the trial objects to it.

Obligatory reading of the record of testimony of a witness who is under fifteen years of age and is an injured party is also obligatory in cases of crimes against sexual freedom

[55] A Gaberle, 'Glosa do wyr. SN z 6.12.2006 r., III KK 181/06' (2007) *OSP* no 10; RA Stefański, 'Glosa do wyr. SN z 6.12.2006 r., III KK 181/06' (2007) OSP no 10.

and morality.[56] This obligation arises from the fact that, as a rule, the CPC provides for the admissibility of only a single hearing of such a witness, unless significant circumstances are disclosed and there is a need for repeated questioning to clarify these, or the accused who remained without a defence counsel during the first questioning of the injured party demands so (Article 185a CPC).[57] The Code does not normalise the question of the procedural moment at which such a one-time examination of a minor injured is possible, so it must be assumed that it is admissible both in preparatory and judicial proceedings. The image and sound recorded with the use of appropriate equipment shall be played at the main trial and the record of the interrogation shall be read out.

During the trial, reports from visual inspections, searches and seizures of objects, as well as opinions of expert witnesses, institutes, establishments or institutions, criminal records, results of community inquiries, and any official documents submitted in the course of the investigation or the court proceedings, or in other proceedings provided for in the statute, may be read. However, it is not allowed to read out the notes on the actions for which a protocol is required to be drawn up (Article 393 § 1 CPC). In other respects, the official notes shall be read out. In addition, the following may be read at the trial: the notification of criminal offence, unless it was filed to the record; any private documents prepared outside the criminal proceedings, in particular statements, publications, letters and notes,; records of the most significant statements of the persons participating in the procedural action, if these were recorded by means of a transcript or a sound recording device; records of the testimony of an anonymous witness, but then the publicity of the trial shall be excluded, and persons of the parties' confidence may not participate in the trial (Article 393 §§ 2–4 CPC). Personal data of the accused and the results of a community inquiry shall be read out upon request of the accused or the defence counsel (Article 394 § 1 CPC).

Upon the conclusion of the judicial examination, all records and documents subject to reading out at the trial that were not read out shall be revealed without being read out (Article 405 § 2 CPC). The records and documents subject to reading at the trial shall be read out upon motion of a party that has had no opportunity to become familiar with their contents or if the court deems it necessary. The motion of the party who is not affected by the content of the document does not create an obligation to read out the records (Article 394 § 2 CPC).

The regulations indicated above, which provide for admissibility of reading out the records and documents, and revealing them without being read out, are intended to streamline and expedite evidence proceedings.

Questioning of a witness in the course of court proceedings may also take place in the form of the so-called requisitioning examination of evidence. If a witness has failed to appear due to some insurmountable obstacles, the court may order that a witness be questioned by a judge designated from the panel or by another court appointed for that

[56] J Żylińska, Obecność osoby wymienionej w art 51 § 2 k.p.k. przy przesłuchaniu małoletniego pokrzywdzonego przestępstwem przeciwko wolności seksualnej i obyczajności a swoboda wypowiedzi' (2019) *Prok i Pr* no 12; T Lenartowicz, 'Dopuszczalność ponownego przesłuchania małoletniego pokrzywdzonego przestępstwem seksualnym' (2018) *CzPKiNP* no 4.

[57] See further ch 5.

purpose in the region in which the witness stays (Article 396 § 2 CPC). The parties, the defence counsels and attorneys have the right to participate in this action; therefore, they should be notified of the date of the action. An accused deprived of liberty shall be brought to court only if the court finds it necessary (Article 396 § 3 CPC). This solution is to be considered as a significant infringement of the accused's right to defence, as the participation of the accused's defence counsel (if he/she has one, of course) is not sufficient in such a case.

If a party has filed a motion for bringing physical evidence or the court has deemed it necessary and the viewing of the physical evidence by the entire panel involves serious difficulties or if the parties consent to this, the court shall designate a judge from the panel to perform this action or shall appoint another court for that purpose (Article 396 § 1 CPC).

Requisitioning carrying out evidence by the summoned court is also possible through the use of technical equipment that makes it possible to perform this action remotely, which may contribute to a significant improvement of the evidentiary proceedings before the court, as well as to the safety of the persons participating in these actions, but this may take place only exceptionally.[58]

If necessary, evidence of an expert witnesses, procedural experiment or inspection shall be carried out. It should be recalled that any evidence may be taken at the analyzed stage of the proceedings, as long as it is not inadmissible or illegal.

Interruption and Adjournment of the Trial

Interruption and adjournment of a trial are procedures that constitute an exception to the principle of concentration of evidence, and, in particular, to the principle of continuity of the trial expressed in the directive that the criminal process, and especially the main trial, should constitute a compact course of procedural facts, carried out without unnecessary interruptions and inhibitions.[59]

The interruption of the trial is ordered by the presiding judge, while the adjournment of the trial is decided by the court. A party may appeal against the order for interruption immediately to the panel of judges. In that case, the issue shall be decided by the court as a whole, ie without excluding the chair, ie the person who issued the appealed order. If, however, the court rules by a single judge, then, obviously, the orders of the presiding judge cannot be challenged in the absence of a body empowered to hear the complaint. The decision of adjournment is not subject to complaint, as it does not belong to the category of appealable decisions, nor does it close the way to the judgment, nor is the

[58] P Korbal, 'Podstawy prawne "wideokonferencyjnego" przesłuchania na odległość w polskiej procedurze karnej', in L Paprzycki and Z Rau (eds), *Praktyczne elementy zwalczania przestępczości zorganizowanej i terroryzmu* (Warsaw, Wolters Kluwer 2009); A Lach, *Przesłuchanie na odległość w postępowaniu karnym* (Warsaw, 2009); G Kopczyński, 'Przesłuchanie świadka na odległość w polskim procesie karnym' (2005) *AUW* LXXII.

[59] A Bojańczyk and T Razowski, 'W kwestii optymalnego czasu przerwy i odroczenia w postępowaniu karnym' (2009) *CzPKiNP* no 3; A Kordik, 'Przerwa i odroczenie rozprawy głównej w procesie karnym' (1995) *AUW* no 32; C Kwiecień, 'Problem przerwy i odroczenia rozprawy w procesie karnym' (1976) Probl Praw nos 1–2.

admissibility of the complaint directly provided for in the provisions on the interruption and adjournment of the trial.

The reasons for the interruption and adjournment of a trial are similar.[60] The interruption is ordered so that the parties could prepare motions for evidence or to have a piece of evidence brought to court, or to take a rest, and finally for any other substantial reason. Such an substantial reason may be, for example, the non-appearance of a defence counsel or the leaving the courtroom by the defence counsel before the end of the trial, when the participation of the defence counsel in the trial is mandatory. Other reasons may cause an interruption only if they are important reasons, ie if they are significant. It is accepted in the case law that the necessity to order a interruption in the trial on the grounds of rest is not only dictated by humanitarian reasons, for the removal of fatigue, but also in order for the parties to be able to actively, genuinely control the course of procedural actions; thus, it is not only about the fatigue of the judges, but also of the parties and other persons participating in the trial.

The court may adjourn the trial only if ordering an interruption would not be sufficient. Reasons may include, for example, the failure of a defence counsel to appear if his or her presence is mandatory, or the failure of the defendant to appear at the trial if his or her presence is mandatory; or, for example, if the defendant or his/her counsel motions that the trial be postponed due to failure to observe the seven-day period between the delivery of the notice of the trial date and the date of the main trial.

In contrast to adjournment, a maximum period of forty-two days has been provided for the interruption. The legislator assumed that this is the period during which the facts revealed at the trial do not fade in the judges' memory. The judicature and the literature aptly emphasise that multiple and multi-day interruptions in the trial for which there are no important reasons are obviously contrary to the principle of continuity of the trial.[61] The period of forty-two days mentioned here is a term belonging to the group of other decisive terms. The procedural effect of exceeding this time limit is that the trial is deemed to be adjourned. When announcing an interruption, the presiding judge shall at the same time indicate the time and place where the further continuation of the trial will take place.

If an interruption in the trial has been ordered, the trial shall be continued after its resumption. However, if the panel of the court has been altered or if the court finds it necessary, the trial shall be held from the beginning again (re-commenced). If during such an interruption it is necessary to make a decision on a certain issue, eg on a precautionary measure or a motion for evidence, the decision shall be made by the panel hearing the case (the same personal composition), and if it is impossible to reconstruct the panel – by a panel of the same type of composition, ie in a changed personal composition (Article 403 CPC).

[60] Bojańczyk and Razowski (n 58); J Kudrelek, 'Zasada ciągłości a sprawność postępowania karnego' (2006) *Przegl Pol* no 3; Kordik (n 58); Kwiecień (n 58).

[61] J Kudrelek (n 59); A Murzynowski, 'Zasada ciągłości rozprawy w polskim procesie karnym', in P Hofmańskiego and K Zgryzka (pod red), *Współczesne problemy procesu karnego i wymiaru sprawiedliwości. Księga ku czci Profesora Kazimierza Marszała*, (Katowice, Publisher, 2003); A Kabat, 'Zasada bezpośredniości i ciągłości na tle przepisów kodeksu postępowania karnego – próba oceny i propozycje zmian' (1981) *Prob Praw* nos 8–9.

The adjourned trial shall be conducted on the new date from the beginning. However, this is a rule, because an adjourned trial may exceptionally be conducted with continuity; it should be assumed that it is possible only if the evidence carried out at the previous trial is not significant for the determination of the degree and scope of guilt of the accused, otherwise the court should conduct the postponed trial from the beginning.

A change in the composition of the court (even a change of only one judge) will always result in the necessity to conduct the case from the beginning again even if the parties agreed to continue the trial despite the change in composition.

The current regulations do not specify the duration of the adjournment. The case law rightly assumes that if a trial is to be continued after an adjournment, then due to the exceptional nature of this provision, which is a departure from the principle of continuity of the trial, as well as due to its similar nature of the interruption and the adjournment of the trial, the duration of the adjournment of the trial cannot be significantly longer than the period provided for the interruption in the trial.

If the presiding judge, when ordering an interruption, at the same time designates the date and place for the resumption of the trial, the persons present at the interrupted trial, whose presence was obligatory, shall be obliged to appear on the new date without special summons. Persons authorised to appear need not be notified of the new date, even if they did not participate in the interrupted trial (Article 402 § 1 CPC).

Interruption and Adjournment for the Presentation of Evidence

The institution of an interruption and adjournment of a trial to present evidence is completely new in Polish criminal procedure, with no equivalent previously existing in the provisions of the CPC. Its introduction is supposed to be connected with a strengthening of the accusatory principle, binding in the modern criminal trial, which imposes on the prosecutor the obligation to provide the court with evidence confirming the thesis of the accusation. Its purpose is also to confirm the constitutional principle of impartiality, obliging the court to consider all the evidence gathered in the case impartially and objectively, without considering only the role played by the prosecutor in a criminal trial.[62]

However, if the court, on its initiative, sets a deadline for the public prosecutor to present evidence that will enable a proper decision to be made within a reasonable time, the court loses its impartiality, since it thereby forces the public prosecutor to present evidence to support the indictment.[63]

[62] K Zgryzek in J Zagrodnik (ed), Proces karny (Warsaw, Wolters Kluwer, 2021) 637.

[63] See more J Skorupka, 'Ciężar dowodu i ciężar dowodzenia w procesie karnym' in T Grzegorczyk (ed), *Funkcje procesu karnego. Księga jubileuszowa Profesora Janusza Tylmana* (Warszaw, Wolters Kluwer, 2011) 133–34; J Zagrodnik, *Model interakcji …*, 418–19 and 439 et seq; P Hofmański and S Waltoś, *Proces karny. Zarys systemu* (Warsaw, Wolters Kluwer, 2016) 535.

The court does not return the case to the public prosecutor to complete the preliminary investigation, but interrupts or postpones the trial, which means that the pendency of the case before the court does not cease.

It is undoubtedly true that the deficiencies of the preparatory proceedings should be eliminated before the main trial, so that they interfere minimally with the trial itself.[64] However, it may happen that in the course of the trial significant deficiencies of the pre-trial proceedings are found, the elimination of which by the court would prevent the issuance of a correct decision within a reasonable time. If these obstacles cannot be removed by carrying out the so-called requisition of evidence the court does not return the case to the prosecutor for the elimination of these deficiencies, but interrupts or postpones the trial for this purpose, setting a reasonable time limit for the public prosecutor to present evidence, the carrying out of which would allow the elimination of the perceived deficiencies. The court continues to act as the governing body and takes all procedural decisions regarding the case, except, of course, for decisions related to the collection of evidence to fill the identified deficiencies. This is undoubtedly intended to force greater procedural activity on the bodies of pre-trial proceedings, as well as to encourage that cases brought to court are complete in terms of evidence. From this point of view, the discussed institution should be assessed positively. On the other hand, however, the evidentiary activity of the court violates the constitutionally guaranteed principle of impartiality, because if the court expects evidentiary support from the public prosecutor, it must necessarily support the prosecution, not the defence.

The public prosecutor given a deadline to gather evidence that would fill in the essential gaps in the pre-trial proceedings may first of all undertake the relevant activities himself, while the prosecutor may also commission the police to undertake the relevant activities.[65] These actions should be taken within a time limit set by the court, which may be extended if necessary. The time limit set by the court should be realistic, ie make it possible to gather relevant evidence. If the deadline set by the court cannot be met, the public prosecutor may motion an extension of the deadline set by the court. It should be assumed that the public prosecutor, when filing the motion, should indicate the reasons for failure to meet the deadline set by the court.[66]

The court, finding significant deficiencies in the preliminary investigation and ordering their elimination, assumes that it is likely to collect such evidence that will fill these deficiencies.[67] If, however, the prosecutor fails to produce the relevant evidence within the prescribed time limit, the court shall resolve doubts arising from the failure to produce such evidence in favour of the accused. It is therefore the court's duty in such a case to apply the *in dubio pro reo* rule, as the doubts arising from the failure to take evidence that the prosecutor expected to be taken have not been removed.[68]

[64] See more R Olszewski, *Ujawnianie przez sąd i usuwanie istotnych braków dochodzenia lub śledztwa w polskim procesie karnym* (Łódź, Wydawnictwo Uniwersytetu Łódzkiego, 2007).

[65] R Ponikowski and J Zagrodnik in J Skorupka (ed), *Kodeks postępowania karnego. Komentarz* (Warsaw, CH Beck, 2021) 1149.

[66] D Świecki in D Świecki (ed), *Kodeks postępowania karnego. Komentarz* (Warsaw, Wolters Kluwer, 2021) vol I, 1662.

[67] See P Hofmański, E Sadzik and K Zgryzek, *Kodeks postępowania karnego. Komentarz* (Warsaw, CH Beck, 2004) vol II, 448–49.

[68] ibid 448–49.

The decision to interrupt or to adjourn the trial to present evidence may be made ex officio or at the motion of a party.[69] In justifying its decision, the court should indicate the evidence (or the type of evidence) it expects to be presented. However, the procedural position of the court in the proceedings does not allow it to indicate, for example, the evidence in the form of testimony of a witness against the defendant. At most, it would be a matter of indicating that the evidence that the court expects to be presented could be used to prove a proof thesis set forth in indictment. However, the court should refrain from indicating in its reasons that the evidence in question is evidence unfavourable to the defendant.[70]

The institution discussed herein may be used only in cases involving crimes prosecuted ex officio, and, moreover, only when the public prosecutor is the entity bringing the indictment. This is because only this entity can be obliged by the court to perform actions that may result in supplementing evidence gathered in the case. Therefore, if a private prosecutor has filed an indictment or an subsidiary auxiliary prosecutor has filed it in a case for an act prosecuted by public indictment, this institution cannot be used in such a case.

Transfer of the Case to the Prosecutor to Complete the Principal Investigation or Simplified Investigation

In January 2017, the June 2016 amendment to the CPC came into force, which differs significantly from the one discussed above. The difference basically comes down to the entity initiating the need to supplement the evidence collected in the case. In the case of the first institution, we are dealing with the initiative of the court, in the opinion of which, without additional evidence, it will not be possible to resolve the case and will lead to the application of the rule *in dubio pro reo*, while in the case of the institution in question, the entity that will take the initiative to supplement the evidence is the prosecutor, making an appropriate motion to the court.[71]

The motion of the prosecutor may be submitted before the judgment is issued. This means that it may take place, for example, immediately after the case is called for the so-called publication date, at which the judgment is to be announced, and thus even after speeches of the parties, in which the assessment of the evidence gathered in the case should be presented to the court. It is difficult to establish unequivocally what had to happen in the case, so that immediately before the judgment the prosecutor could submit the abovementioned motion. Such a reason can probably only be the 'escape' from a possible acquittal of the accused, when the evidence gathered in the case does not support the prosecution case. This solution should be regarded as puzzling.

The amendment excludes the possibility of reviewing the court's decision following a complaint, and it does not indicate the authority that should determine the existence of these important circumstances or the need to search for evidence or conduct

[69] Ponikowski and Zagrodnik (n 65) 1149.
[70] Zgryzek (n 62) 639.
[71] ibid 640.

other activities to clarify the circumstances of the case. However, the court may refer the case for supplementation of the investigation only if the prosecutor submits the relevant motion. So, only the prosecutor can be the entity that may consider the need to supplement evidence as justified. It also clearly follows from the provision (verba legis: 'the court shall, upon motion, transfer') that the court is bound by the prosecutor's motion, which is all the more surprising as it is the court that conducts proceedings at this stage. The return of the case for supplementation of preparatory proceedings shall not apply in cases where the indictment was brought by an auxiliary prosecutor (Article 5 §3 of the Act of 5 December 1996 on the Medical Profession). This allows us to conclude that it may apply in cases where an indictment was brought by an entity other than the auxiliary prosecutor, for example, police. Nota bene, it should be noted that the public prosecutor may join the case initiated by an auxiliary prosecutor (Article 5 §3, sentence 2 CPC of the above mentioned act) and, as a result, 'take up' the case in which he previously saw no basis either for initiating preparatory proceedings or for bringing an indictment. Although the body conducting preparatory proceedings is an entity other than the public prosecutor, the prosecutor is the addressee in returning the case for supplementation.

After completing the relevant actions aimed at supplementing the investigation, the public prosecutor may file a new indictment, motion for conviction, motion for conditional discontinuance of proceedings and motion for discontinuance of preparatory proceedings and application of precautionary measures; he/she may also sustain the previously filed indictment, but he/she should do it not later than six months from the date of transferring the case.

The prosecutor, by using the institution discussed herein, may effectively block the efficient conduct of judicial proceedings.

It is to be hoped that in practice this institution will not be used to block the possibility of acquittal of the accused or discontinuance of the proceedings against him when the evidence collected before the supplementation does not allow for his conviction, but the return will be done de facto in order to search for evidence leading to a conviction.[72]

Substantive Extension of the Charges

Extension of the indictment at trial against the same accused for an act other than that charged in the indictment is exceptionally possible and does not constitute a departure from the accusatory principle, since such an extension requires the filing of a complaint charging the commission of a specific offence, but the complaint is oral. The present extension of the indictment is admissible when circumstances which are newly disclosed at the trial, occurring cumulatively, indicate that the accused has committed another act in addition to those contained in the indictment; the accuser accuses the accused of having committed this act at the trial and demands that the proceedings be extended immediately to include this act (in this case, the accusation is made orally); the accused agrees to examine the act under the new indictment at

[72] ibid 642.

the same trial; and there is no need to conduct preliminary proceedings with respect to the new act.

Circumstances that show that the accused committed an act other than the one contained in the indictment filed with the court must be disclosed only at trial, ie after it has been called; the act disclosed at trial is not the act charged against the accused in a substantially changed form, but a new act that the law enforcement authorities and the judiciary had no knowledge of having been committed by the accused before.[73] The prosecutor must express his will to charge the disclosed act; this will is manifested in the formulation of the so-called oral indictment (this is one of the special forms of the indictment), the contents of which are recorded in the minutes of the trial.[74] The defendant himself must expressly and unambiguously agree to the verbal accusation;[75] his counsel cannot make a statement to this effect for him and it must be recorded in the minutes of the trial. This extension of the indictment is not permissible if there is a need to conduct a principal or simplified investigation into the new act. This follows from the directive of truth, according to which it is necessary to collect adequate and sufficient evidence to judge the act. The court may take cognisance of the charge formulated in the oral indictment, but it is not obliged to do so. In other words, the indictment itself does not have an initiating function, which means that the court is not obliged to take cognisance of the new charges.[76] This is therefore a different situation from that which arises from the filing of an ordinary indictment in court.

The court may also postpone the trial if the accused agrees to be tried on a new indictment but does not agree to do so immediately, believing that he should have time to prepare his defence. In this case, the pendency of the case before the court for the acts included in the ordinary and oral indictment shall not cease, but the prosecutor shall file a new or additional indictment, which shall allow the accused to prepare his defence.[77] In this case, the written indictment should be served on the accused prior to trial, and the accused may submit a response to the indictment.

This extension of the indictment may take place not only in cases of crimes prosecuted by public indictment, but also in cases of crimes prosecuted by private indictment.

Change of Legal Classification of an Act at Trial

It follows from the programmatic function of the indictment that the court shall examine the case within the limits of the indictment, ie as to the accused who is identified in the indictment and as to the act formulated therein, with exceptions allowing for the subjective extension of the indictment. The act charged against the accused determines the subjective limits of examination of the case. During the trial, the court is not bound by the description of the act or the legal classification applied to it.

[73] Judgment of the Appellate Court in Warsaw, 12 September 2012, II AKa 244/12, Lex no 1238639.
[74] See Judgment of the Appellate Court in Warsaw, 3 April 2013, II AKa 85/13, Lex no 1312111.
[75] Judgment of the Appellate Court in Szczecin, 9 November 2016, II AKa 170/16, Lex no 2231155.
[76] Ponikowski and Zagrodnik (n 65) 1153.
[77] See Judgment of the Appellate Court in Szczecin, 9 November 2016, II AKa 170/16, Lex no 2231155.

During the trial it may turn out that the form of the act described in the indictment was modified due to revealed circumstances. The description of the act must therefore be adjusted to the evidence presented at the trial under one condition: it must relate to the same event (act) as the one charged in the indictment.

Legal qualification is the application of a substantive law standard to the established facts, which constitute a criminal act. The change of legal qualification may be either primary or secondary. The primary change of legal qualification of an act does not involve a change in the factual findings, as they were made correctly, and only an incorrect legal qualification was applied. A secondary change of legal qualification occurs when a change in the description of the charged act (in terms of factual findings) entails a change in its legal qualification.[78]

The court is not bound by the legal classification of the act. It may be changed, depending on the findings or assessments of the court.[79] It is admissible only within the scope of the indictment, ie only with respect to the subject of the procedure delimited by the indictment, and it cannot result in a modification of the subject of the trial. The act of the accused may be qualified under another provision of substantive law, but only within the limits of the indictment.[80] The court should warn the parties present at the trial about the intended change. This notification should take the form of a decision signalling the possibility of qualifying the act under a different substantive law provision indicated in the decision.

At the motion of the defendant, a trial may be interrupted to allow him/her to prepare for his/her defence (Article 399 § 2 CPC). An interruption of the trial in such a case is not mandatory, but in practice, especially when a change may result in the application of a more severe provision, an interruption should be treated as the rule.[81]

Conclusion of Judicial Examination

The conclusion of the judicial examination is an action that falls within the competence of the presiding judge. It is tantamount to the closing of evidence process; therefore, after the conclusion of the judicial examination, no change in the evidentiary basis for the decision on the merits of the case is possible. In order to make such a change, it is necessary first to reopen the judicial examination.[82] Conclusion of the judicial examination plays a role in proceedings before a court similar to the one played by the institution of closing preparatory proceedings.

Before the conclusion of the judicial examination, the presiding judge should ask the parties whether they wish to supplement the evidence, and if they do not answer in the affirmative, the presiding judge will announce the judicial examination to be concluded

[78] K Marszał, *Proces karny* (Katowice, Vademecum, 1998) 395.
[79] Supreme Court Judgment, 30 September 2014, II KK 234/14, OSNKW 2015, no 2, pos 14.
[80] Supreme Court Judgment, 5 September 2006, IV KK 194/06, OSNwSK 2006, no 1, pos 1663; Supreme Court Judgment, 27 January 2006 r, WK 27/05, OSNwSK 2006, no 1, pos 234.
[81] See Judgment of the Appellate Court in Warsaw, 16 July 2019 r, II AKa 23/19, Lex no 2712649.
[82] T Grzegorczyk and J Tylman, *Polskie postępowanie karne* (Warsaw, Wolters Kluwer, 2014) 791.

(Article 405 § 1 CPC). Upon the conclusion of the judicial examination, all records and documents subject to being read out at the trial that were not read out shall be revealed without being read out (Article 405 § 2 CPC).

Re-opening the Judicial Examination

Re-opening the judicial examination means withdrawal of the process to the judicial examination. The re-opening of the judicial examination trial may take place from the adjudication phase (but only until the judgment is pronounced) or from the final statements of the parties. Re-opening the judicial examination requires a decision of the court. The law does not exhaustively enumerate the reasons for re-opening the judicial examination. Reasons for re-opening may include, for example, the need to warn the parties about the possibility of changing the legal classification of the act under another legal provision if this was not done in the course of the judicial examination.

The need to reopen the judicial examination also exists when the court, in anticipation of the possibility of conditional discontinuance of the proceedings or the possibility of imposing a sentence with conditional suspension of execution, deems it appropriate to set a reasonable time limit for the parties in view of the possibility of an agreement between the defendant and the injured party on reparation on redress damage inflicted by a crime or to compensate for the suffered harm. Judicial examination may also be re-opened if the court comes to the conclusion that it is necessary to conduct additional evidence or retry evidence in order to make a correct judgment.[83]

In the resumed judicial examination, the action for which the re-opening was made shall be performed.

Having done so, the presiding judge shall ask whether the parties motion that the trial be supplemented, and if they reply in the negative and all evidentiary possibilities have been exhausted, he shall announce the judicial examination to be concluded.

The presiding judge shall then give the floor to the parties during the final statement even if they have already had the opportunity to speak previously.

Final Statements

Final statements of the parties are a separate phase of the main trial. This phase takes place after the Judicial examination, ie after all the evidence has been exhausted. This does not mean, however, that information (circumstances) revealed at this stage of the trial, eg arising from the last word of the accused, cannot be taken into account in establishing the facts.[84] The final statements are a phase closely related to the adversarial construction of the main trial. Notwithstanding the general right of the parties to speak during the trial as to any issue to be decided and as to any evidence taken, the parties are entitled to a final speech after the close of the evidence.

[83] Marszał (n 78) 396; Świecki (n 66) 1722–23.
[84] Grzegorczyk and Tylman (n 82) 791.

The final statements serve to express their own views on the results of the evidence.[85] They are a stage containing an evaluation of the evidence from the point of view of the individual litigants and their representatives.[86] They may also include evidence which has come to the attention of the parties at this stage, or which has not gained the approval of the court earlier. If the court grants them, the concluded judicial examination requires re-opening.

They shall speak in the following order: the public prosecutor, the subsidiary prosecutor or the private prosecutor (depending on whether the criminal proceedings are conducted in public or private prosecution mode), the social representative, the defendant's counsel and the defendant (Article 406 § 1 CPC). The aforementioned subjects are entitled by law to speak. The opportunity to speak is not subject to the permission of the presiding judge. Those entitled should be given the floor by the presiding judge in the order provided for in the CPC. Otherwise, he exposes himself to the charge of violating a rule of criminal procedure. Trial representatives of the parties speak before those parties they represent in the trial.

It is noteworthy that the accused is always entitled to speak last. This normalisation is understandable if one considers that he is at risk of being punished for committing a crime. By speaking last, he can respond to the statements and conclusions of those who have spoken before. This is a defence privilege referred to as *favor defensionis*.[87]

If the accuser speaks again (reply), the accused's defence counsel also has the right to speak. The accused is also entitled to speak last in this situation.

The speeches of the parties may effect the final form of the ruling on the subject of the criminal trial. Therefore, an important role is played by the following elements: the structure, content and form of the speech of the parties, and the persuasiveness of the arguments presented in them.

If the defendant does not speak Polish, the full content of the speeches should be given to the accused through an interpreter.

Adjudication

Adjudication is the phase of the trial in which a decision is made on the subject of the trial.[88] This decision takes the form of a judgment (Articles 413 and 414 CPC).

As a rule, the court shall proceed to judgment immediately after final statements of the parties; however, in a complex case, or for other important reasons, it may adjourn its judgment for a period not exceeding fourteen days. The court should proceed to judgment immediately on the basis of the evidence fresh in its memory from the trial

[85] See Supreme Court Judgment, 13 January 2017, SNO 57/16, Legalis.

[86] A Murzynowski, 'Formułowanie wniosków prokuratora co do wymiaru kary' (1980) *Palestra*, no 5; JR Kubiak, 'W sprawie wniosków prokuratora co do wymiaru kary' (1982) Palestra, nos 1–3, 103 et seq; Grzegorczyk and Tylman (n 82) 791; Ponikowski and Zagrodnik (n 65) 1178.

[87] Ponikowski and Zagrodnik (n 65) 1181.

[88] Supreme Court Judgment, 21 January 2004, II KK 168/03, OSNKW 2004, no 3, pos 28.

and discussed by the parties in their final statements.[89] It is rightly assumed that the court should proceed to deliberate on the verdict when it is directly impressed by the parties' statements, so that the store of information about the case is not impoverished by the passage of time, which may undoubtedly have a negative effect on the content of the judgment. It is also about eliminating the possibility of influencing the position of the judge by means of, for example, mass media.

The following stages may be distinguished in the course of sentencing: deliberation of the judgment, voting on the judgment, drawing up of the judgment in writing, pronouncement of the judgment, oral presentation of the most important reasons underlying the judgment, and instruction as to the right, time limit and manner of appealing the judgment.[90]

Deliberation and Voting on the Judgment

In the course of deliberation, the court may come to the conclusion that there is a need to re-opening judicial examination in order to carry out certain actions or to give additional voice to the parties.

If the case is ripe for resolution, ie if the evidence gathered in the case allows it, the court proceeds to deliberate and vote.

Adjournment Rendering of a Judgment

Adjournment rendering of a judgment is an institution that is an exception to the principle of continuity of the trial and means, in fact, an interruption in the trial, ordered in the course of adjudication before the pronouncement of the judgment.

The reasons for the adjournment rendering of a judgment are not listed exhaustively. Adjournment rendering of a judgment is possible in a complex case or for other substantial reasons.

The complexity of the case may concern both factual and legal aspects. Other important reasons may include, for example, late time or fatigue, which significantly limits proper judgment.

The court shall adjourn the judgment by a decision, in which the time (date of publication) and place of announcement of the judgment shall be indicated. Adjournment rendering of a judgment is possible for a period not exceeding fourteen days. In the original wording of the current Code, the time limit was seven days, whereas in the previous CPC of 1969 it was only three days, which probably disciplined the court most strongly to render a judgment when it was still impressed by the arguments presented in the final statements.

[89] Ponikowski and Zagrodnik (n 65) 1183.
[90] Świecki (n 66) 1719.

The term of adjournment is decisive (it belongs to the group of other firm terms). The total time of this adjournment may not exceed the indicated term.[91] If it is exceeded, the trial shall be conducted from the beginning, and the Code does not provide for any exceptions in this respect. Conducting the trial from the beginning means conducting it from the very beginning.

Adjourned rendering of the judgment should be of an exceptional nature.[92] In practice, the judgment is increasingly announced on the so-called publication date, after adjournment rendering of a judgment.

Making a Judgment in Writing

The judgment should be drawn up in writing immediately after the vote has been completed.[93] Writing and announcement is a ground for the validity of the judgment.[94] The judgment shall be signed by all members of the adjudicative panel, thus including the member of the panel which voted otherwise. The absence of one of the signatures results in the judgment not being announced. As long as it is an internal act of the court it may be debated by the court.[95]

The judgment is pronounced on behalf of the Republic of Poland, which means that it has a ceremonial form.

The CPC specifies the components that every judgment should contain. In addition, the conviction should contain a detailed description of the act ascribed to the accused and its legal qualification, as well as decisions as to the penalty and the criminal measures, and forfeiture, and – where necessary – as to offsetting them against the periods of actual deprivation of liberty.

The term 'act ascribed' refers to the description of the act as established by the court. This description does not have to coincide in detail with the description of the act described in the indictment (the act charged).[96] However, it is necessary to preserve the identity of the act, because otherwise the rule of invariability of the subject of the criminal trial will be violated.

This means that the description should accurately indicate the time, place and acts of execution, as well as the legal goods attacked by the act, and the effects of the act, especially the damage done. The description of the act in the conviction should include all the elements of the perpetrator's action that are of significance for the legal classification of the act.[97]

The court's findings should be based on persuasiveness. The court must not be in doubt as to those facts on which it makes its findings. If doubts have arisen and cannot

[91] See Supreme Court Judgment, 16 December 1982, Rw 1107/82, OSNKW 1983, no 6, pos 47.
[92] Supreme Court Judgment, 3 December 2002, III KKN 351/00, KZS 2003, no 5, pos 30.
[93] See more E Skrętowicz, *Wyrok sądu karnego pierwszej instancji* (Lublin, Wydawnictwo UMCS, 1989).
[94] Supreme Court Decision, 19 January 2012, I KZP 19/11, OSNKW 2012, no 1, pos 3.
[95] Marszał (n 78) 400; Ponikowski and Zagrodnik (n 65) 1191.
[96] Supreme Court Decision, 2 February 2007, V KK 126/06, OSNwSK 2007, no 1, pos 353.
[97] Supreme Court Decision, 18 February 2008, V KK 245/07, OSNwSK 2008, no 1, pos 299; Supreme Court Judgment, 29 May 2012, III KK 87/12, (2012) Prok i Pr no 12, pos 15.

be dispelled by the evidence gathered in the case, they should be interpreted in favour of the accused in accordance with the rule in *dubio pro reo*.

By changing its description, while maintaining the identity of the act, the court may not acquit the accused of the fragments of the charged act not confirmed in the trial.[98] The adjudication rules do not provide for acquittal of individual elements contained in the description of the charged act or the legal qualification established in the indictment. For the description of the act attributed to the perpetrator and all its elements, it is not necessary to use the words of the statute, but the point is that this description corresponds to the meaning of all the statutory elements of the specific crime.[99]

The judgment shall also rule on the unconditional or conditional discontinuance of criminal proceedings, on the payment of punitive damages to the injured party, on the obligation to redress the full damage inflicted by a crime, or to redress part of it, or to compensate for the suffered harm, provided that the claim resulting from the commission of the criminal offence is not the subject of other proceedings or a final ruling has not been issued with regard to the claim; the subject of the judgment shall also be the costs of proceedings.[100]

If one of the procedural obstacles occurs, the court shall discontinue the proceedings by judgment. However, if it is found that the act was not committed or that there are no sufficient grounds to suspect that it was committed, or if the act does not have the features of a prohibited act, or when it is acknowledged by the law that the perpetrator has not committed a criminal offence, the court shall render a judgment of acquittal, unless the perpetrator was insane at the time of the act.[101]

Pronouncement of the Judgment

The pronouncement of the judgment is a legal act, causing it to become binding from that moment on; it can no longer be changed by the authority that issued it. The pronouncement of the judgment thus constitutes the moment that creates the judgment.[102] A document that is called a judgment but is not signed and pronounced is not a judgment, but only a draft of this procedural act.

A judgment is always pronounced publicly, even if the trial was held in camera (Article 418 § 1 CPC).[103] The judgment shall be announced by reading it out, which shall be done by the presiding judge.[104] When the judgment is pronounced, all those present, with the exception of the panel of the court, shall stand.

[98] Supreme Court Judgment, 7 February 1979, IV KR 5/79, OSNKW 1979, no 6, pos 75.
[99] Supreme Court Decision, 2 April 2003, V KK 281/02, OSNKW 2003, nos 5–6, po. 59.
[100] See more Ponikowski and Zagrodnik (n 65) 1197–1201; Świecki (n 66) 1735–42.
[101] See eg Supreme Court Decision, 15 June 2016, V KK 104/16, Legalis; Supreme Court Judgment, 13 May 1977, IV KR 81/77, OSNKW 1977, nos 7–8, pos 88.
[102] Decision of the Appellate Court in Gdańsk, 9 June 1999, II AKo 113/99, OSAG 2000, no 1, pos 1; Supreme Court Decision, 19 January 2012, I KZP 19/11, OSNKW 2012, no 1, pos 3.
[103] K Eichstaedt in Świecki (n 66) 1753.
[104] Ponikowski and Zagrodnik (n 65) 1215.

The non-appearance of the parties, their defence counsels and attorneys shall not preclude the pronouncement of the judgment (Article 419 § 1 CPC).[105]

The time limit for filing a motion for its statement of reason shall be calculated from the time of pronouncement of the judgment (Article 422 § 1 CPC). For an accused deprived of liberty who has no defence counsel and – despite the fact that a motion was submitted to bring them to the trial on the date on which the judgment was pronounced – was not present during the pronouncement of the judgment, the time limit specified in Article 422 § 1 shall run from the date of service of the judgment on the accused (Article 422 § 2a CPC).

Should a judgment be issued in a session held in camera, for example, an injunctive judgment, the contents of the judgment shall be made public by depositing its duplicate in the court secretariat for a period of seven days, which shall be mentioned in the record or in the official note from the session (Article 418a CPC). Essential critical remarks against this provision have been made in the doctrine of criminal process.[106]

Oral Presentation of the Most Important Reasons Underlying the Judgment

The statement of reasons for a judgment is not, as a rule, prepared at the same time as the judgment. An oral presentation of the most important reasons underlying the judgement serves as a substitute for the statement of reasons.[107] The oral reasons for the judgment must set out the factual and legal grounds for each decision in the judgment and must correspond in substance to the future written statement of reason for judgment.[108] The reasons underlying the judgment may be stated orally by the presiding judge or a member of the adjudicative panel. As a rule, oral presentation of the most important reasons underlying the judgment is done in public. Exceptionally, if the hearing has been fully or partially closed to the public, the most important reasons underlying the judgment may also be given orally in full or partially closed to the public.

Information on the Right, Time and Method of Appeal

It follows unquestionably from the principle of a fair trial that the parties and their representatives should be informed of their rights, including in particular the right to appeal a procedural decision infringing (in their view) their procedural interest. It needs to be emphasised that the procedural body should instruct the participants in

[105] See eg Supreme Court Decision, 6 November 2003, IV KK 456/02, OSNKW 2004, no 3, pos 23; Supreme Court Decision, 11 May 2004, II KZ 26/04, Lex no 109492.

[106] See more, for example, S Durczak-Żochowska, 'Udostępnienie treści wyroku nakazowego' (2009) *Prok i Pr*, no 2, 47–51; S Zabłocki, 'Publiczne ogłoszenie wyroku wydanego na posiedzeniu – realna gwarancja czy fikcja' (2003) *Gdańskie Studia Prawnicze*, no 2, 311–22; Glosa do uchwały Sądu Najwyższego z dnia 25 marca 2004 r, I KZP 46/03, OSP 2005, no 6, 188–190.

[107] Eichstaedt (n 103) 1756.

[108] Supreme Court Decision, 6 July 2006, IV KK 174/06, OSNwSK 2006, no 1, pos 1361.

the proceedings about their right to implement an appeal and of the time limit and the procedure for the implementation of such a measure, or of the fact that the judgment may not be appealed against (Article 100 § 8 CPC). Lack of instruction or erroneous instruction may not cause negative procedural effects for the entitled person (Article 16 § 1 CPC).[109] It shall be given in such a way as to enable the party concerned to understand it and consequently to exercise their rights.

Closing of the Main Trial

The main trial ends with its closing. This decision takes the form of an order of the presiding judge.[110]

Sometimes, between the instructions on the right, time and manner of appealing the judgment and the closing of the trial, the court announces decisions on, for example, the immediate release of the accused under provisional detention. The court may also decide on provisional detention.

Final Actions in the Court of First Instance

General Considerations

Within the framework of this phase of criminal proceedings, many different activities are carried out, which are related to the completion of the proceedings before the court of first instance.[111] It should be borne in mind that just as the end of proceedings before the court of first instance is not, as a rule, the same as the end of criminal proceedings in general, the end of the trial does not mean the end of activities before the court of first instance.

The statutory time limit for filing a motion for a statement of reasons in writing runs from the service of the judgment, or sometimes from the service of a copy thereof to the accused. When an entitled person files such a motion, it triggers the obligation to prepare a statement of reasons and to serve it along with a copy of the judgment on the person who filed the motion.[112] The date of service of a copy of the judgment with a statement of reasons, in turn, opens the time limit for filing an appeal.[113] Filing appeal results in moving the proceedings to the next stage of the trial: the appeal proceedings.

If no motion for statement of reasons for the judgment is filed, or if it is filed by an unauthorised person or after the time limit set forth by law for that purpose, or if the time limit for filing a motion for statement of reasons the judgment is not restored, or if no appeal is filed, the judgment becomes final.

[109] Supreme Court Resolution, 19 March 1970, VI KZP 1/70, Lex no 18058.
[110] Marszał (n 78) 403.
[111] ibid 403; Hofmański and Waltoś (n 63) 544.
[112] Supreme Court Resolution, 15 November 1973, VI KZP 36/73, OSNKW 1974, no 1, pos 2.
[113] Grzegorczyk and Tylman (n 82) 808.

Final actions include actions performed between the closing of the main trial and the filing of an appeal, and, if the judgment of the court of first instance becomes final, between the closing of the main trial and the sending of the judgment for execution.[114]

Among the activities carried out at this phase there may be some that are connected both with ascertaining that the judgment is legally valid and with conducting incidental proceedings, eg concerning a precautionary measure, when a party, for example, files a motion for revoking provisional detention.

The most important groups of final actions include: serving a copy of the judgment on the accused, if required by law; filling a motion for a written statement of reasons for the judgment of the court of first instance; preparing a statement of reasons for the judgment; actions related to making the judgment final; and supplementing the judgment.

Notification of a Copy of the Judgment to the Defendant

As a rule, the judgment will not be served on the defendant, but will usually be announced to them. The time limit for filing a motion for a written statement of reasons for the judgment starts when the judgment is announced. The judgment will only be served on the defendant in exceptional circumstances, ie if the defendant, who was deprived of liberty and had no defence counsel, was not brought to the trial to hear the judgment (Article 422 § 2a CPC).[115]

If the defendant does not have a sufficient command of Polish, the judgment shall be served upon him together along with translation (Article 72 §§1 and 2 CPC).

A copy of the judgment shall be served to the accused without delay. Serving the judgment on the accused, he shall be informed in writing of his right, time limit and manner of filing an appeal. In such a case, the time limit for filing a motion to prepare a statement of reasons for the judgment shall run from the date of serving it on the accused.

Motion for a Statement of Reasons

As mentioned above, the statutory time limit for filing a motion for a statement of reasons to be drawn up in writing and served on it runs from the service of the judgment, or sometimes from the service of a copy thereof. Such a motion may be filed by a party, and in the case of a verdict conditionally discontinuing proceedings, also by the injured party, regardless of whether or not they appeared as a litigant in the proceedings before the court.[116] The motion must be made in writing; therefore, it cannot be submitted on the record or before the judgment is pronounced.[117]

The seven-day time limit for submitting the motion for a written statement of reasons for the judgment is a final time limit, which means that any act done after the

[114] Marszał (n 78) 404.
[115] See more Ponikowski and Zagrodnik (n 65) 1231–32.
[116] See more Eichstaedt (n 103) 1766–67.
[117] Ponikowski and Zagrodnik (n 65) 1229.

time limit expires is ineffective. However, it is possible to restore the time limit.[118] If the persons entitled to file the motion intend to file an appeal against the judgment, they should first file a motion for drafting a written statement of reasons for the judgment. The party filing a motion for a statement of reasons is not obliged to file an appeal against the judgment, nor does it have to explain the reasons why it files a motion for a written statement of reasons.[119]

If the motion for a statement of reasons in writing is filed out of time or by an unauthorised person, the president of the court will refuse to accept it; the same procedural effect will arise if the motion for the restoration of the time limit for filing a motion for a statement of reasons is not granted.[120]

The fact that a statement of reasons for a judgment is drawn up ex officio does not exempt a party from making the motion in question.[121] The application must be made in writing. The motion should indicate whether it relates to the judgment as a whole, or to some of the acts that the prosecution has charged the accused with having committed, or only to the decision on the penalty and other legal consequences of the act. If the motion does not come from the accused, it should also indicate the accused to whom it refers.[122]

Persons entitled to submit a motion may, within the time limit for submitting a motion to prepare a statement of reasons, file an appeal. In other words, the filing of an appeal is not absolutely conditional on the prior receipt of a statement of reasons for the judgment and the prior submission of a motion to that effect. In such a case, it should be assumed that the appeal complaint also includes the motion to prepare a written judgment.[123] After receiving a copy of the judgment with a statement of reasons, an entity that has filed an appeal before the lapse of time limit for filing a motion for the preparation of a statement of reasons may supplement its earlier appeal within the time limit for filing it.[124]

The filing of a motion for a statement of reasons for a judgment triggers the obligation to prepare it in writing and to serve a copy of the judgment with a statement of reasons on the person who filed such a motion. Thus, the statement of reasons for the judgment is not served on the person who has not filed the relevant motion. On the other hand, the time limit for filing an appeal extends from the date of service of the copy of the judgment with a statement of reasons for the judgment to the person who filed a motion for a statement of reasons to be drawn up and to be served on them.

In certain situations, the justification for the judgment is prepared ex officio. This occurs when the court of first instance is a military court with the exception, however, of situations in which the court grants the motion of public prosecutor for a judgment

[118] Supreme Court Decision, 26 April 2018, IV KZ 17/18, Lex no 2499860.

[119] Ponikowski and Zagrodnik (n 65) 1227.

[120] ibid 1233–34.

[121] Marszał (n 78) 404.

[122] See more Supreme Court Decision, 13 June 2017, V KK 480/16, Lex no 2357440; Decision of the Appellate Court in Katowice, 13 January 2016, II AKz 725/15, Lex no 2023133; Ponikowski and Zagrodnik (n 65) 1229–31.

[123] See J Zagrodnik, *Obrońca i pełnomocnik w procesie karnym i karnym skarbowym* (Warsaw, Wolters Kluwer, 2020) 467.

[124] Marszał (n 78) 405–06.

of conviction to be issued in a session and to order the penalties of other measures provided for the misdemeanour or grants motion of accused for a judgment of conviction and for imposition of a specific penalty or criminal measure upon them. However, this does not exempt the aforementioned subjects from filing a motion for serving a justification.[125]

Statement of Reasons for the Judgment

Filing an effective motion for justification of the judgment triggers the obligation to prepare a statement of reasons for the judgment. A statement of reasons for a judgment shall be prepared within fourteen days from the date on which the motion for the preparation of the statement is received by the court, or, where a statement of reasons is prepared ex officio, from the date on which the judgment is pronounced (Article 423 § 1 CPC). The time limit is of an ordinal nature, which means that drafting the grounds after the deadline does not render the action ineffective.[126] Exceeding this time limit may only cause extraprocedural (disciplinary) consequences for the judge who caused the failure to meet the time limit.[127] Therefore, in a complex case or for another important reason, where it is impossible to prepare a statement of reasons within the time limit, the president of the court may extend the time limit for a specified period (Article 423 § 1 CPC). However, excessive extension of the time limit violates the principle of speedy proceedings and principle of fair trial.

Statement of reasons for a judgment plays an important role, as it has an educative function.[128] Due to well-chosen arguments, precision of wording and logic of reasoning, the justification should convince the participants of the proceedings of the correctness of the decisions contained in the judgment.[129] Defective, legally unsuccessful and socially erroneous statement of reasons for the judgment are harmful from the perspective of the court's educational functions. The written justification plays an important role for the parties and for the appellate court. The justification of the judgment allows the parties to get an idea of the reasons that guided the court in reaching its verdict. A convincing statement of reasons for the judgment may influence a party to abandon its intention to appeal the judgment. For the appellate court, the statement of reasons is a document that allows to review the correctness of the decisions made in the judgment.

The statement of reasons is a reporting document; it should indicate facts which the court found to be proven or not proven and what evidence it relied on in this respect,

[125] Judgment of the Appellate Court in Cracow, 7 November 2002, II AKa 226/02, KZS 2002, no 12, pos 46.
[126] Judgment of the Appellate Court in Cracow, 7 November 2002, II AKa 226/02, KZS 2002, no 12, pos 46.
[127] Supreme Court Decision, 1 July 2010, IV KK 163/10, OSNwSK 2010, no 1, pos 1364.
[128] See more K Zgryzek, 'Zwięzłe uzasadnienie – czy to jeszcze uzasadnienie?' in P Hofmański (ed), *Fiat iustitia pereat mundus. Księga jubileuszowa poświęcona Sędziemu Sądu Najwyższego Stanisławowi Zabłockiemu z okazji 40-lecia pracy zawodowej* (Warsaw, LexisNexis, 2014) 663 et seq; E Skrętowicz, 'Istota i znaczenie uzasadnienia wyroku sądu karnego po nowelizacji z 2003 r' in L Leszczyński, E Skrętowicz and Z Hołda (eds), *W kręgu teorii i praktyki prawa karnego. Księga poświęcona pamięci Profesora Andrzeja Wąska* (Lublin, Wydawnictwo UMCS, 2005) 679 et seq; C Kulesza and R Starzyńska, 'Obowiązek uzasadniania orzeczeń sądowych a prawo do obrony' (2010) *Prok i Pr*, no 5, 12 et seq.
[129] Judgment of the Appellate Court in Cracow, 16 December 2013, II AKa 153/13, Lex no 1466276.

as well as why it did not accept evidence to the contrary. It should also explain the legal basis of the judgment.[130]

Under the current legal status, a justification should be a concise document. The CPC does not leave, in this respect, any room for discretion for the authority drawing up the written statement of reasons, as it provides that 'The statement of reasons should contain concise ... ' (Article 424 §1 CPC). The aforementioned provision does not explain what a 'concise' statement of reasons is.

The regulation allowing for concise presentation of the statement of reasons largely furthers the interests of the administration of justice, but does not take into account the procedural interests of the parties, who should have the right to question the arguments presented in the statement of reasons – a concise statement of reasons is not conducive to such a task.[131] These are not, however, all the changes introduced to the criminal procedure, as a rule was introduced under which a justification shall be drawn up on a form.[132] In this way, the activity of preparing the statement of reasons becomes automatic, which certainly does not help protect the interests of litigants, especially the defendant.

The statement of reasons is usually prepared by the presiding judge or the reporting judge, unless it is prepared by another judge, court assessor or lay judge. If a written statement of reasons is not possible, the presiding judge shall make a note to that effect in the case file. If the written statement of reasons is drawn up by a lay judge, the presiding judge, if necessary, can designate a judge or court assessor to assist the lay judge in drawing up the statement of reasons.[133]

If the motion for a written statement of reasons is made only in respect of a part of the judgment, for example, a certain act whose commission was charged to the accused by the prosecution counsel (subject limitation), or a certain accused person (personal limitation), the court may limit the scope of the statement of reasons only to those parts of the judgment to which the motion relates (Article 423 §2 CPC). This power may, in practice, make it possible to relieve judges of a great deal of unnecessary work.

The statement of reasons for the judgment is signed by the persons issuing the judgment, including each person who voted otherwise (Article 115 §1 CPC). If the case was heard by a judge and two lay judges, only the presiding judge signs the statement of reasons, unless a dissenting opinion has been filed. In cases heard by two judges and three lay judges, the statement of reasons shall be signed by both judges, unless a dissenting opinion has been expressed (Article 115 § 2 CPC). If a dissenting opinion is expressed by any of the judges (and thus also by a lay judge), the statement of reasons are always signed by the entire panel of adjudication, even if the judgment was issued by the panel with lay judges. If the signature of the presiding judge or any other member of

[130] Judgment of the Appellate Court in Cracow, 20 February 2019, II AKa 285/18, Lex no 2718716.

[131] Zgryzek (n 128) 671–74.

[132] Critically about this resolution, H Paluszkiewicz, 'Glosa do wyroku Sądu Najwyższego z dnia 11 sierpnia 2020 r' (2020) I KA 1/20 *Dyskurs Prawniczy i Administracyjny*, no 1, 221 and n; A Kotowski, 'O formularzach uzasadnień w sprawach karnych' (2020) *Prok i Pr* nos 7–8, 144–74; Ponikowski and Zagrodnik (n 65) 1239–40.

[133] See more Ponikowski and Zagrodnik (n 65) 1236.

the adjudicative panel cannot be obtained, one of the signatories shall note that fact in the statement of reasons for judgment, indicating its cause.[134]

The fourteen-day time limit for filing an appeal runs from the date of delivery of the copy of the judgment with the statement of reasons. The filing of the appeal triggers the appeal proceedings. If the appeal is not filed or if the president of the first instance court refuses to accept the appeal on the grounds that it was filed out of time or by an unauthorised person, or is inadmissable under law (Article 429 §1 CPC), the judgment of the first instance court becomes final.

Actions Related to Making a Judgment Final

Finality entails the enforceability of the judgment, and thus the institution of enforcement proceedings if the judgment contains enforceable decisions.[135]

As part of the final action, a supplementary decision may be issued if the judgment contains no decision on forfeiture, or on including in the sentence to be served the period of the actual deprivation of liberty, the period of the seizure of the driving licence or another relevant document or the period of the application of the precautionary measures listed in Article 276, or on the imposition of the obligation to return a document authorising driving of a vehicle, or on physical evidence (Article 420 § 1 CPC). The court shall rule on this by decision at a session. Pursuant to Article 420 § 3 CPC, the parties shall have the right to participate in a session if its object is to decide on forfeiture or on physical evidence. An accused deprived of liberty shall be brought to a session only if the president of the court or the court deems it necessary.[136]

[134] Grzegorczyk and J Tylman (n 82) 811–12; Marszał (n 78) 406.
[135] Marszał (n 78) 407.
[136] Grzegorczyk and J Tylman (n 82) 807.

7

Evidence

Introduction

Evidence has a fundamental importance to the purpose of a criminal trial. Information obtained by means of them constitutes the basis for factual findings, which determine the content of decisions made in a criminal trial, especially decisions about the subject of the trial.[1]

Every crime, to a greater or lesser degree, leaves certain 'traces'. These may be physical 'traces' of a given act in the place where it was committed (eg tools of the crime, footprints, fingerprints, other biological traces), or traces left in the psyche of people who were victims of or witnessed the criminal behaviour. These persons, by perceiving, remembering (eg by fixing an image in memory), are the 'bearers of traces' of the committed crime. 'Traces' play a decisive role in reconstructing the specific conduct that is the subject of the criminal trial, or establishing its absence. This reconstruction is done in the course of the process to determine whether the act occurred, whether it constitutes a crime, and who is criminally responsible for the act. This reconstruction is similar to the work of a historian. This is because in a criminal trial, certain behaviours that occurred in the past are reconstructed. In both cases the material for such reconstruction is information obtained from various sources ('traces').

Reaching these sources and obtaining necessary information in a criminal trial is possible in the way determined by the law, namely through searching for, preserving, introducing to the process and conducting evidence. Evidence with preserved 'traces' of a crime are sources that allow us to obtain the information needed to reconstruct the event that is the subject of the criminal trial. Depending on whether the 'traces' of a crime are left on things or in the psyche of individuals, we speak of material or personal sources of evidence. At the time of initiation of preparatory proceeding, the trial authority is most often in a situation where the initial information about the criminal act is incomplete and, moreover, usually of a circumstantial nature (unless the perpetrator has been apprehended red-handed when committing a criminal offence). Often the perpetrators themselves do not provide the trial authority with complete and truthful information about their act. This authority enriches its knowledge about a particular act by collecting further information by means of taking evidence. Although extra-procedural activities, eg operational activities, may also be a source of this knowledge,

[1] M Cieślak, 'Zagadnienia dowodowe w procesie karnym' in S Waltoś (ed), *Dzieła wybrane* (Kraków, Wydawnictwo Uniwersytetu Jagiellońskiego, 2017) vol I, 5.

for the purposes of factual findings concerning the subject matter of the trial only such information may be recorded and used which results from the evidence gathered (including evidence obtained in the course of operational activities). Evidence gathered in preparatory proceedings (principal or simplified investigation) authorises an authority (usually the prosecutor) to file an indictment or obliges it to refrain from further prosecution. After an indictment is filed, the court, at a main trial, with the participation of the litigants, decides on the subject matter of the trial on the basis of the evidence gathered. This is provided for in Article 410 CPC, which expressly states that the court shall base its judgment solely on the basis of all circumstances disclosed at the main trial. The regulations in force provide also for the possibility to pass substantive judgments at a session (Articles 341, 343 and 500 § 4 CPC). With regard to these situations, there are no separate regulations specifying the grounds for passing a sentence thereunder. In this respect, a general provision is applicable, according to which a ruling may be based only on all the circumstances disclosed in an investigation and relevant to the determination of the case. (Article 92 CPC). It seems that the basis of a judgment rendered at a session (no main trial) should be clearly defined at the normative level, taking into account the fact that in the course of a session no evidentiary proceedings are conducted, so the court in fact bases its findings on the evidence gathered in the preparatory (pre-trial) proceedings.

All the provisions relating to evidence contained in the CPC are referred to by the name 'law of evidence'.[2] It regulates not only what is to be considered as a source or means of evidence, but also a whole range of activities relating to evidence, which is referred to as 'evidence proceedings'.

The Concept of Evidence

The term 'evidence' is used in many provisions of the CPC. In fact, in each of the sections of this Code this term is used – in provisions on parties, and in the provisions regulating pre-trial (simiplified and princpila investigation), main trial and appeal proceedings. However, it is significant that in none of these provisions we will find the an actual definition of the term 'evidence'. Reaching for the dictionary meaning of the term, it should be noted that the term 'evidence' has many conceptual scopes.[3] In a criminal trial the scope of this term is also not unambiguous. This ambiguity of the term "evidence" comes down to the assumption that evidence is a source of information, a form of information, an evidentiary fact, but also all procedural activities related to obtaining information, its introduction and externalisation in a criminal trial. The analyzed term is also used to define the final result of the course of thought.[4] Presented ambiguity is accepted in the doctrine as well as in the judicature. Here we assume that the term will be used later in this book in the context of evidentiary source, evidentiary means and evidentiary fact.

[2] ibid 7; T Grzegorczyk and J Tylman, *Polskie postępowanie karne* (Warsaw, LexisNexis, 2014) 1027; P Hofmański and S Waltoś, *Proces karny. Zarys systemu* (Warsaw, Wolters Kluwer, 2016) 352.

[3] K Marszał, *Proces karny. Zagadnienia ogólne* (Katowice, Volumen, 2013) 337. See also Cieślak (n 1) 37–38; Hofmański and Waltoś (n 2) 353.

[4] See eg Marszał (n 3) 337–40; Hofmański and Waltoś (n 2) 353–54.

There is essentially no dispute in the doctrine that a source of evidence may be the person or thing that provides the means of proof. As a result, evidentiary sources may be personal (eg witness, defendant, expert witnesses) or material (eg objects relevant to the case – material evidence, crime scene traces, etc). This division raises some doubts about the classification of a designated evidentiary source into one or the other of these groups. An example is a document. Its intellectual layer may lead to treating it as a personal source of evidence, while on the other hand it may be considered as a material source of evidence when analysed as an object. In this situation it should be assumed that a document as a source of evidence should be qualified to separate groups of sources of evidence – personal and material at the same time.

An evidentiary means is a form of conveying information (observations) that is obtained from a source of evidence with which the procedural authority is in direct contact when it takes evidence, such as eg the testimony of a witness. Evidence is a kind of link between the source of evidence and the procedural authority. In this sense, we can say that the accused is a source of evidence and his/her explanations are a means of evidence. A witness is a source of evidence and his/her testimony is a means of evidence. Similarly, in the case of an expert witness, who as a source of evidence provides the procedural authority with a means of evidence in the form of an opinion or testimony. A document whose contents or the material from which it was prepared or by means of which information was recorded shall also be a source of evidence. Material evidence is a source of evidence, and its characteristics are a means of evidence; a trial experiment may also be a source of evidence, and its results are a means of proof.

Evidentiary facts are the individual pieces of information (links in the information carrier) contained in an item of evidence, eg in an explanation or testimony, concerning the circumstances of a specific conduct on which a given criminal proceeding is pending. Since, for example, the testimony of a witness is a means of evidence, the information given in that testimony about specific conduct or about a specific state of affairs will be evidentiary facts that make it possible to reconstruct the specific conduct in accordance with the actual state of affairs. These facts may directly indicate that the accused committed the crime charged, or indirectly (circumstantial evidence) prove that the accused committed the crime.

The literature distinguishes between several types of evidence. Here we limit ourselves only to the most important ones.

The division of evidence into personal, material and personal–material (documents) has already been presented above. Additionally it can only be emphasised that the criterion for this division is the type of evidence source, ie whether it is a person or thing.

Based on the content of the evidence, we can distinguish conceptual evidence and sensory evidence. The category of conceptual evidence includes, for example, witness testimony, explanations by the defendant, expert opinions and the contents of documents. The category of sensory evidence, on the other hand, includes physical evidence obtained on the basis of the sensory perception of the persons collecting the evidence, including the properties of the scene, items (including documents) or human body.

Taking into account the number of links that occur between the procedural body and the known reality, in connection with which the criminal trial is conducted, evidence can be divided into primary and derivative. If there is only one link, we talk about primary evidence; if there are more links, we talk about derivative evidence.[5]

In addition to these, doctrine sometimes distinguishes between direct evidence, which points to the main fact, and indirect evidence, which together with other evidence give rise to a conclusion about the guilt or innocence of the accused.[6] A distinction can be made between strict (formal) and free (informal) evidence.[7] The division of evidence into incriminating and exculpatory evidence is of practical value.

However, not everything in a criminal trial can be evidence in a case. It is important to determine whether what is proposed in an evidentiary motion or what is intended to be introduced into the trial ex officio to obtain information can be evidence at all. The CPC distinguishes between the explanation of the accused, witness testimony, expert witnesses' opinion, documents, inspection (examination), inquiry with community and procedural experiment.

Against this background, however, the question arises as to whether only the aforementioned named evidence is admissible in a criminal trial or also other evidence not mentioned in the provisions of the criminal procedural law, ie unnamed evidence.[8] This issue is not easy to resolve. Certainly, there may be a tendency to use any existing evidence in a criminal trial, whether it belongs to the categories enumerated in the criminal procedural law or not, if it serves to clarify a circumstance relevant to the determination of the subject matter of the trial. Underlying this approach is the directive of truth. However, on the other hand, it should be noted that the fundamental purpose of the formalised taking of evidence is precisely the implementation of the directive arising from the principle of truth. It follows from this directive, that only those pieces of evidence that are provided for (named) in the criminal procedural law are admissible, and thus, that those that are not named in the provisions of the CPC are not admissible. This approach cannot be fully accepted.[9]

The literature is dominated by an accurate position that in a criminal trial admissible evidence is that which is not prohibited. This is a position in favour of non-formalised criminal proceedings, and the provisions of the CPC are aimed at creating the most favourable conditions for the discovery of the so-called material truth, which also relates to the problem of admissibility of evidence.

One should advocate the admissibility in a criminal process of both named evidence and unnamed evidence. However, in order for unnamed evidence to be admissible, it is necessary for it to meet two conditions: if the new evidence is based on new research methods, these should be sufficiently tested and the findings resulting from the use of these methods should be certain; and furthermore, the research methods or evidence used must not violate the procedural guarantees of the process subjects, especially the accused.

[5] Cieślak (n 1) 73.

[6] See further W Daszkiewicz, *Prawo karne procesowe. Zagadnienia ogólne* (Poznań, Branta, 2001) 70–71.

[7] See further S Śliwiński, *Polski proces karny przed sądem powszechnym. Zasady ogólne* (Warsaw, Wydawnictwo Gebethner i Wolff, 1961) 19 et seq.

[8] Marszał (n 3) 340–42.

[9] See ibid 340–42. Differently Daszkiewicz (n 6) 96–97.

Evidentiary Prohibitions

The essence of evidentiary prohibitions boils down to the proposition that making factual findings in a criminal trial cannot be done at any cost. In certain situations, it is necessary to protect a certain interest, even at the expense of making true findings of fact. It is obvious that the ruling should be based on truthful findings of fact, but in some situations reaching the truth may be impossible or at least hindered, when the legislator assumes that the implementation of the principle of truth in a criminal trial must give way to the need to protect a specific interest – public or private. This is when we talk about evidentiary prohibitions.[10]

The term 'evidentiary prohibitions' may be used in both a narrow and a broad sense. In a narrow sense, it refers to restrictions on the taking of specific evidence, provided in Article 178 and subsequent provision of the CPC, while in a broad sense it should be understood as all kinds of restrictions on the possibility of proving, introducing and conducting evidence, as well as using this in a criminal process.[11]

The term 'evidentiary prohibitions' should therefore refer to (i) prohibitions on proving a specific thesis or proving by means of specific evidence, (ii) prohibitions on using inadmissible methods of proving and (iii) prohibitions on using evidence.[12] The term 'prohibitions on proving' covers those situations in which, by virtue of express provisions, the proving of a specific thesis or the proving it by means of a specific piece of evidence that is generally admissible is excluded.

It follows from the prohibition of proving a specific thesis that a certain circumstance may not be proved by any means of evidence.[13] We are dealing here with the most far-reaching restriction, and the need for such a prohibition arises for important social reasons. It is possible only if an express provision provides for such a prohibition. Such a prohibition applies:

- to deliberations and voting on a ruling, which are secret, and a waiver of secrecy in this regard is not permissible (Article 108 § 1 CPC),
- to proving contrary to the findings of a final judgment another court's establishing legal rights or legal relationship (argumentum ex Article 8 § 2 CPC), unless the factual basis for these findings has changed, and
- to statements by the accused, regarding the alleged act, made to an expert or doctor providing medical assistance (Article 199 CPC).

The latter case is covered by the subject matter and means that the accused's statements – regarding the alleged act, made to the expert or doctor providing medical assistance – are

[10] See further B Janusz-Pohl, 'Rozdział VIII. Zakazy dowodowe w ujęciu dyrektywalnym – zarys problematyki', in J Skorupka and A Drozd (eds), *Nowe spojrzenie na model zakazów dowodowych w procesie karnym* (Warsaw, CH Beck, 2015); A Baj, 'Zakazy dowodowe dotyczące świadka koronnego' (2007) *Prok i Pr* no 1; Z Kwiatkowski, *Zakazy dowodowe w procesie karnym* (Katowice, Wydawnictwo Uniwersytetu Śląskiego, 2005); RA Stefański, 'Rozdział VII. Zakazy dowodowe – czy potrzebne są zmiany?', in J Skorupka and A Drozd (eds), *Nowe spojrzenie na model zakazów dowodowych w procesie karnym* (Warsaw, CH Beck, 2015); J Skorupka, 'Rozdział II. Zakazy dowodowe a prawo konstytucyjne', in *Nowe spojrzenie*, ibid.

[11] Marszał (n 3) 343.

[12] ibid 343. Similarly K Zgryzek, in J Zagrodnik (ed), *Proces karny* (Warsaw, Wolters Kluwer, 2021) 352.

[13] See further Kwiatkowski (n 10) 116–19.

not subject to proving. The content of these statements cannot be proved either by the testimony or opinion of an expert, or by the testimony of a witness of the doctor who provided medical assistance to the accused. It appears that these statements also cannot be proved by other evidence, such as the testimony of a witness who was present when the accused made such statements (eg a nurse); the case law takes a similar position.[14] This prohibition extends to any statement by the accused relating to the alleged act.

The prohibition of proving by means of specific evidence covers with its scope the possibility of both introducing and conducting specific evidence in a criminal trial due to a designated social interest.

Taking specific evidence may serve the interest of justice, but at the same time it may undermine the equally important social good. Then a conflict of interest arises. This applies in situations when, for example, the taking of evidence would violate a specific type of secrecy. In such a situation the legislator must make a choice between interests (goods), guided by their respective values. When the taking of evidence could bring greater social harm in comparison with the benefits for the interest of justice, prohibitions on proving by a particular means of evidence are established. These prohibitions also protect the witness from internal conflict when he/she would have to testify about, perhaps against, a person close to him/her. The witness would be trapped between his/her duty to testify to the truth and the need to protect the interest of a person close to him/her during the interview.

These prohibitions apply only to the extent that they are expressly established by the applicable law.

Within these prohibitions, a distinction may be made between absolute prohibitions on proving by means of specific evidence and relative prohibitions on proving by means of specific evidence.[15] The criterion for division between these groups boils down to the nature of the prohibition, ie whether it is definitive, not providing for any exception, or whether it allows the taking of evidence upon the fulfilment of a condition specified by law.

Absolute prohibitions on proving by certain evidence are absolute in nature, and evidence covered by such a prohibition is inadmissible within its limits. Such prohibitions include: prohibition on questioning an defence counsel or solicitor, or legal counsel acting pursuant to Article 245 § 1 CPC, with regard to the facts communicated to them while giving legal advice or conducting a case; prohibition on questioning a priest on facts communicated to him in confession; prohibition on reading or reproducing previously given testimony if the witness has exercised his or her right to refuse to testify or has been exempted from the obligation to give testimony; prohibition to read the record of an examination of a witness if that person is subsequently examined as an accused; prohibition on recording statements made by the examined person including a confession to a criminal offence, which also applies to documentation concerning examinations carried out at the motion of an authorised body; prohibition on questioning persons obliged to maintain secrecy under the provisions of the Act on the Protection of Mental Health as witnesses to the statements made by a person with regard to whom

[14] Marszał (n 3) 343–44.
[15] Kwiatkowski (n 10) 116–19.

actions under the said Act have been taken (this prohibition applies mutatis mutandis to a doctor acting as an expert witness).[16]

Relative prohibitions by means of specific evidence admittedly exclude the use of specific evidence in a criminal trial, but if the conditions provided for by the law are met, this evidence may be used in a criminal trial. Such a condition may be, for example, obtaining the consent of the relevant authority. The relative prohibitions of evidence include prohibition due to the obligation to keep in secrecy classified information categorized as 'secret' and 'top secret', prohibition due to the obligation to keep in secrecy classified information categorized as 'reserved' or 'confidential' or due to obligation to keep a secret connected with profession or office, or prohibition due to the right to refuse to testify, and the exemption from testifying of a person who is in a particularly close personal relationship with the accused.[17]

The first of the prohibitions listed here concerns a defence counsel or a solicitor or legal counsel acting pursuant to Article 245 § 1 CPC (Article 278 point 1 CPC), and stems from the need to fully guarantee the accused's confidence in his or her defence counsel, thus enabling the accused to exercise his or her right of defence unhindered.[18] This prohibition is addressed to all procedural authorities, as it applies not only in judicial proceedings, but also in pre-trial proceedings. The prohibition on questioning a defence counsel as a witness applies to a defence counsel who has acted as such in a criminal case, as well as to a lawyer who has provided legal advice to the accused, and to a lawyer when a suspected person has been arrested. This prohibition occurs regardless of who appointed the defence counsel – the accused him/herself, the president of the court ex officio, the court or another person or statutory representative. However, this prohibition does not extend to a solicitor or legal counsel acting as a party's attorney in a criminal process. The prohibition here covers only those facts of which defence counsel became aware while giving legal advice to the accused or while conducting his/her case, or in the course of contact with an arrested person. The prohibition thus covers any information of which a defence counsel has become aware while giving legal advice or while conducting a case, regardless of the source of such information, ie regardless of whether they come from the accused or from any other source. The prohibition on questioning the defence counsel or the solicitor, or legal counsel acting pursuant to Article 245 § 1 CPC is absolute, as it cannot be lifted even at the motion of the defence counsel or the solicitor or legal counsel him/herself or with the consent of the accused. However, it does not cover informations that reached the defence counsel before he/she appeared in the case in that capacity, eg as a witness to a specific event. In any event, in

[16] Zgryzek (n 12) 354–55.

[17] See further P Kardas, 'Tajemnica adwokacka a procesowe zakazy dowodowe', in J Giezek and P Kardas (eds), *Etyka adwokacka a kontradyktoryjny proces karny* (Warsaw, Wolters Kluwer, 2015); J Sobczak, 'Tajemnica dziennikarska. Zakres, rola gwarancyjna, zakazy dowodowe – aspekty procesowe i skutki w zakresie prawa karnego materialnego', in Z Ćwiąkalski and G Artymiak (eds), *Współzależność prawa karnego materialnego i procesowego. W świetle kodyfikacji karnych z 1997 r. i propozycji ich zmian* (Warsaw, Wolters Kluwer, 2009) 387–412; Baj (n 10) 111–22.

[18] See further P Kardas, 'Konstytucyjne i ustawowe aspekty ochrony tajemnicy zawodowej powierzanej przedstawicielom zawodów zaufania publicznego' (2014) *CzPKiNP* no 4, 41 et seq; J Zagrodnik, 'Aspekty karnoprocesowe tajemnicy zawodowej radcy prawnego', in R Stankiewicz (ed), *Tajemnica zawodowa radcy prawnego* (Warsaw, Wydawnictwo OBSIL KRRP, 2018) 200–10; J Zagrodnik, *Obrońca i pełnomocnik w procesie karnym i karnym skarbowym* (Warsaw, Wolters Kluwer, 2020) 77–83.

this situation, the solicitor or legal counsel should consider the question of admissibility of undertaking the duty of defence counsel in this case.

The prohibition against questioning a priest in the capacity of witness does not include a prohibition against examining him/her in evidence as a witness in general, but only against questioning him/her with respect to facts communicated to him in confession (Article 178 point 2 CPC). This prohibition is anchored in the constitutionally guaranteed freedom of conscience and religion (Article 53 (1) PC). According to the view of the Supreme Court, the prohibition in question applies to clergy of all churches in which individual confession is practised. The prohibition on questioning a priest is absolute and means that it is inadmissible even if the confessor has abandoned the priestly state. It should also be assumed that it applies only to those confessions in which the sacrament of confession is in force.[19]

The prohibition of disclosure of previously given testimony is closely related to the right to refuse to testify and the right to exempt from the obligation to give testimony. In the event of using the right to refuse to testify or exempting from the obligation to give testimony, a testimony previously given, cannot be read out or reconstructed. There is no derogation from this prohibition. By this prohibition, reconstructions of previously given testimony – by means a official note or questioning of a person who has conducted the hearing of a witness, who has refused to testify or who has been released from the obligation of a waiver – is not covered. However, body inspection records prepared in criminal proceedings are subject to disclosure at the trial, even if the person subjected to the inspection exercised the right to reject to testify.

Persons obliged to keep in secrecy classified information categorised as 'secret' or 'top secret' may be questioned as to the circumstances to which this obligation extends only if released from the obligation to preserve such a secret by an authorised superior body. The definition of classified information is contained in the Classified Information Protection Act 2010. If the examination is to cover circumstances covered by secrecy, the examination should be waived, even if the person to be interrogated is ready to give evidence. In such a case, the court or public prosecutor should apply to an authorised superior body requesting a release from the obligation to maintain secrecy (Article 179 § 1 CPC). Such a release may be refused only if giving testimony might result in serious damage to the interest of the state (Article 179 § 2 CPC). If release from secrecy of classified information is refused, the court or public prosecutor may apply to an appropriate supreme body of central administration requesting that a witness be released from the obligation to observe secrecy, provided that specific Acts do not provide otherwise (Article 179 § 3 CPC). The decision of this supreme body shall be final.[20] With the broad scope of the secrecy of classified information categorised as 'secret' or 'top secret', the Supreme Court, sitting with a single judge, should ultimately decide *de lege ferenda* on the releasing from this secrecy, as *de lege lata* the lack of releasing from the obligation to observe secrecy may be dictated by the unjustified protection of a particular official.[21]

[19] A Gurbiel, 'Tajemnica spowiedzi – zbieg instytucji prawa kanonicznego i państwowego czy efekt oddziaływania systemów prawnych? (2018) *Jurysta* no 6.

[20] Kwiatkowski (n 10) 185–96.

[21] Marszał (n 3) 349.

When a witness is released from secrecy of classified information, he or she is questioned at the hearing in camera. However, when an exemption from secrecy has been granted under the provisions of the Physician and Dentist Professions Act, the patient or his or her representative may give consent to the disclosure of the secret, but only after having informed the patient about the adverse consequences of its disclosure; and in addition, when the release from confidentiality occurred on the basis of the Act on Patient's Rights and the Commissioner for Patient' Rights ie when the patient or the patient's legal representative consents to the disclosure of the secret, or when a person close to the deceased patient consents to the disclosure of the secret by a medical practitioner, unless another close person objects. If the exemption from secrecy has been granted on the basis and under the principles set forth in the above-mentioned Acts, the circumstances covered by secrecy that were revealed at a trial held in camera may be disclosed to the public by the person whose consent was required for the exemption from secrecy.[22]

In addition to the issue of the obligation to waive preservation of a secret that includes 'secret' or 'top secret' circumstances, persons obliged to keep secret classified information described as 'restricted' or 'confidential' or secrets connected with their profession or office may refuse to testify as to the circumstances to which this obligation extends, unless they have been released by the court or the public prosecutor. Professional secrecy may be related to the exercise of a profession or function. Secrecy connected with a profession may be understood in two ways. Namely, it may include information concerning the private life of certain persons, which the person obliged to keep in secrecy obtained by virtue of his/her profession or function. This may include medical secrecy, solicitor or legal counsel secrecy, etc. It may also refer to the obligation to maintain secrecy of information concerning a given profession or its organisation. The scope of professional secrecy understood in this way will include, for example, details concerning the production of certain items, issues related to patents, etc.

The obligation to keep secrect classified information categorised as 'restricted' or 'confidential' and the obligation of professional secrecy are not absolute.[23] The court or prosecutor may release persons testifying as witnesses from the obligation to keep a secret, determining whether the release is indispensable for the judgment of the case and is in the interests of the judiciary. The release should take the form of a decision, in which specific circumstances justifying the lifting of secrecy should be indicated. Other authorities authorised to conduct pre-trial proceedings, such as police authorities, do not have this power. If it is necessary to question a person in a simplified investigation or principal investigation about facts covered by professional or official secrecy, a prosecutor's decision is necessary.[24] After release, the person in possession of information protected by secrecy is obliged to testify.

[22] M Prusek, 'Utajnienie zezna świadka w procesie karnym a realizacja konstytucyjnej zasady proporcjonalności' (2017) *Pal* nos 7–8, 30 et seq; R Teluk, 'Nieodtajnienie materiałów niejawnych jako przyczyny zwrotu sprawy do uzupełnienia' (2010) *Prok i Pr* no 11, 113–22; R Netczuk, 'Tajny agent policji w świetle nowego kodeksu postępowania karnego i ustawy o Policji' (2001) *PPK* 24.

[23] See more Kwiatkowski (n 10) 196–228.

[24] Marszał (n 3) 351.

The hearing of a witness released from the obligation to maintain secrecy of classified information categorised as 'restricted' or 'confidential' or from the obligation of professional secrecy shall be held at a hearing in camera. The examination records of such witnesses shall be stored in the same way as the examination records of a witness released from the obligation to maintain secrecy of classified information categorized as 'secret' or 'top secret'.

A separate regulation concerns the obligation of professional secrecy: notaries, solicitors, legal counsels, tax advisers, physicians, journalists, or statisticians, and persons obliged to protect the secrets of the Solicitors' Office of the Republic of Poland. Persons obligated to maintain such professional secrecy may be questioned as witnesses about facts covered by such secrecy only when this is necessary for the sake of justice and the circumstances cannot be determined on the basis of other evidence.[25] The questioning or permission for questioning shall be decided exclusively by the court, including in pre-trial proceedings (in investigation). In investigation the court shall render its decision at a session without the participation of the parties, within a period not longer than seven as of the date of service of the prosecutor's motion. The decision of the court may be contested (Article 180 § 2 CPC). It should be assumed that both the decision to questioning or permitting questioning as to the facts covered by professional secrecy and the decision to refuse the motion in this regard are subject to appeal.

With respect to journalistic secrecy, there is a more complete legal regulation. The release of a journalist from the obligation to keep a secret may not relate to data enabling the identification of the author of a press material, letter to the editor or another material of the same nature, as well as identification of persons providing information published or passed to be published, if these persons reserved the right to keep the data secret (Article 180 § 3 CPC). There are specific exceptions to this rule. In practice, against the background of the above regulation, difficulties may arise in identifying the perpetrator of the crime, and without identifying the perpetrator no indictment may be filed.

The person closest relatives, by blood or affinity, of the accused[26] is free to choose between testifying and refusing to testify as a witness (Article 182 § 1 CPC). The question of who is the closest person is regulated by the provisions of the Criminal Code, according to which the closest relatives, by blood or affinity, of the accused person are: a spouse, an ascendant, a descendant, a siblings, a relative by marriage in the same line or degree, a person in an adoption relationship or this person's spouse, and also a domestic partner (Article 115 § 11 CC). It should be added that this status is not lost in the case of termination of marriage or adoptive relationship (Article 182 § 2 CPC). A relative by marriage in a descendant line is, for example, a stepson. The essential and necessary elements of being domestic partner are mental and physical cohabitation, economic community and permanence of the relationship. The list of the closest

[25] See further M Rusinek, in *System Prawa Karnego Procesowego*, (ed) P Hofmański, vol 8, cz 2, *Dowody*, J Skorupka (ed) (Warsaw, Wolters Kluwer, 2016) 2059–92.

[26] R Krajewski, 'Osoba najbliższa w prawie karnym' (2009) *PS* no 3, 103–13; K Wróblewski, 'Osoba najbliższa i osoba w szczególnie bliskim stosunku osobistym jako osobowe źródło dowodowe w postępowaniu karnym' (2009) *AUW* no LXXXI, 107–15; M Jachimowicz, 'Osoba najbliższa w prawie karnym' (2008) *Jurysta* nos 11–12; M Płachta, 'O prawie odmowy zeznań osoby najbliższej' (1988) *Prok i Pr* no 10, 168 et seq.

persons is exhaustive, so their circle cannot be expanded by interpretation. Such a status is not held, for example, by a person under the actual custody of the accused.

The right to refuse to testify shall be vested also in a witness who is accused of complicity in another pending case with regard to the criminal offence covered with the proceedings (Article 182 § 3 CPC). If this right is exercised, the record of the witness's previous explanations as an accused person may be read out.[27]

When examining a witness, his/her relation to the accused shall be checked in order to determine whether he/she has the right to refuse to testify, and it shall be checked whether the witness is accused of complicity in another pending case with regard to the criminal offence covered with the proceedings. The witness shall also be advised of his/her right to refuse to testify, taking into account his/her age and stage of development. It does not matter for what reason the witness exercised his/her right to refuse to testify or did not exercise his/her right, as the decision in this regard is the sole prerogative of the witness, and the trial authority cannot assess the validity of the choice made by the witness.

If a witness has exercised his/her right to refuse to testify at an earlier stage of the process, he/she may change his/her mind at the main trial and express his/her willingness to testify. If the right to refuse to testify is exercised no later than before the commencement of the first testimony in court proceedings, the previously given testimony of that person may not serve as evidence nor be reproduced. As soon as the witness gives his first testimony in the court proceeding, he/she loses the right to refuse to testify. This right shall not be renewed when the case is referred by the appellate court to the first instance court for re-examination, or reffered to the public prosecutor in order to complete a principal or simplified investigation and then referred to the court of first instance, or when the trial is held again from the beginning. The right to refuse to testify is vested in a witness regardless of age; a minor need not act through his or her statutory representative for this purpose.

Doubts arise when there are more defendants in the case and the witness is in a closest relatives, by blood or affinity, of the only one (some) of them. If it can be established that despite the closest relation his/her testimony concerns only another co-defendant, it can be assumed that the witness cannot exercise the right to refuse to testify.[28] The issue becomes more complicated when the witness's testimony concerns both a defendant who is closest to the witness and a co-defendant who is a stranger to the witness. Two solutions can be considered in this case: first, assume that the witness may exercise the right to refuse to testify; and second, assume that the witness should testify but that this testimony cannot be taken into account in the determination of the defendant closest to the witness. It seems that the first of presented solutions should be favoured, as it is supported by the *ratio legis* of the institution of refusal to testify.[29]

A separate issue is whether the testimony of a witness closest to the accused given in the pre-trial proceeding may be read out if the witness died before the main trial. In

[27] See more Rusinek (n 26) 2095–2108.
[28] Supreme Court Decision, 22 January 2014, IV KK 313/13, OSNKW 2014, no 6, pos 49.
[29] ibid 2095–96.

the case law of the Supreme Court under the previous legal status such a possibility was not excluded. A more convincing view seems to be the one accepting the possibility of reading the testimony of a deceased witness when he or she was warned about the right to refuse to testify.

The right to refuse to testify applies to the entirety of the witness's testimony, so it is not possible to refuse to testify in part and to testify in part.[30] A witness may exercise the right to refuse to testify only with respect to the accused for whom he is the closest person.

A witness may decline to answer a question if such an answer might expose the witness themselves or their closest relatives by blood or affinity to liability for a criminal or fiscal offence (Article 183 § 1 CPC). As the law currently stands, the term 'criminal liability' includes liability for both a crime and a fiscal crime, but does not include liability for delinquency.[31] Refusal to answer a question is not equivalent to refusal to testify. The witness in such a case is obliged to testify, and is exempted only from answering the question.[32] The presiding judge of the panel of the court should determine on the basis of a preliminary examination of the case whether this is the case. If so, he/she should instruct the witness on the right to decline to answer the question put to him/her. This instruction should not be construed as an invitation to decline to answer the question.[33] The witness is not obliged to explain the reasons for his/her refusal to answer the question put to him/her, but he/she should ask to be excused.[34]

A person having a particularly close relationship with the accused may be exempted from the obligation to give testimony or provide answers to questions if this person applies[35] for such an exemption (Article 185 CPC). The Code does not specify what is meant by a particularly close relationship between a witness and the accused. It certainly does not refer to the relationship of closeness by blood or affinity to the accused or to the fact that persons of the opposite sex are domestic partner, as these cirmustancies are grounds for refusal to testify. In practice, it is assumed that what is at stake here may be, for example, further kinship than that defined in Article 115 of the Criminal Code, including having children together,[36] engagement, actual care of person with diabilities, etc. Whether such a relationship exists must be decided by the trial authority in the pre-trial or judicial proceedings against the background of the specific circumstances.[37] Thus, it is not sufficient to merely cite the existence of such a relationship.

It is up to the decision of the trial authority to exempt an expert from testifying or answering a question. As follows from the provisions of the CPC, persons to whom the reasons indicating the admissibility of refusal to testify or answer questions apply, or

[30] Rusinek (n 26) 2105–2106.

[31] D Lapawa, 'Osoba najbliższa w prawie karnym, Problem pouczenia świadka o prawie do uchylenia się od odpowiedzi na pytanie' (2013) *WPP* no 1; see also M Jeż-Ludwichowska, 'Glosa do wyr. SN z 6.4.1977 r., II KR 38/77' (1978) *Prok i Pr* nos 8–9.

[32] Rusinek (n 26) 2123.

[33] Supreme Court Decision, 17 September 2014, V KK 204/14, Lex no 1537573.

[34] Supreme Court Decision, 8 February 2006, IV KK 394/05, OSNwSK 2006, no 1, pos 306.

[35] Judgment of the Appellate Court in Cracow, 13 November 2014, II AKa 203/14, Lex no 1711349.

[36] Supreme Court Decision, 22 February 2006, III KK 222/05, OSNKW 2006, no 5, pos 46.

[37] Supreme Court Decision, 27 May 2003, IV KK 63/03, Lex no 80281.

who may be exempted from testifying, may also not be experts, and the opinion submitted by such a person may not constitute evidence in the case (Article 196 § 1 CPC).[38]

Prohibition on Substitution of Testimony or Explanation

The evidence from explanations of the accused or testimony of a witness cannot be substituted with contents of documents, notes and official notes (Article 174 CPC). This evidentiary prohibition applies only to the accused or a witness,[39] but not to an expert.[40] It is addressed to the trial authorities, who may not substitute the explanations of the accused or the testimony of a witness for the contents of letters, notes or official papers. This does not mean a prohibition on the use of any kind of writings, notes or official notes in criminal proceedings, but rather a prohibition on their substitution for the explanations of the accused or the testimony of a witness. An official note is not a prohibited form of documenting actions; on the contrary, this form is expressly provided for in the Code (see Article 143 § 2 CPC). The official note may be evidence in a criminal trial as long as it does not replace the defendant's explanation or the testimony of a witness. However, it is not permissible to read the official note of an activity for which a record is required (Article 393 §1 CPC). Substitution of witness's testimony and substitution of explanations of the accused is also not possible by questioning of a person who took testimonies or explanations.

The analysed prohibition does not cover written materials, such as private notes, secret messages, diaries etc, and documents created outside criminal proceedings, in particular statements, publications, letters and memos. Such materials may be read at the trial (Article 393 § 3 CPC).

It should be noted that an accused may make his/her explanations in writing in the pre-trial proceedings (Article 176 § 1 CPC).[41] The written explanations of the accused, signed by him/her, indicating the date of their submission, shall be annexed to the record.

Prohibition on the Use of Inadmissible Methods of Proof

The prohibition indicated here is a safeguard of the rules of a democratic criminal trial, which ensures the freedom of expression of the person being questioned. The CPC not

[38] See more J Konecka-Misztala and J Konecki, 'Wyłączenie biegłego w postępowaniu karnym' (2010) *Prok i Pr* nos 7–8, 149–64; K Papke-Olszauskas, *Wyłączenie uczestników procesu karnego* (Gdańsk, Wydawnictwo Uniwersytetu Gdańskiego, 2007); K Papkę-Olszauskas, 'Instytucja wyłączenia uczestnika procesu karnego po noweli styczniowej' in Z Sobolewski, G Artymiak and CP Kłak (eds), *Problemy znowelizowanej procedury karnej* (Kraków, Zakamycze, 2004) 447–54.

[39] F Prusak, 'Zakaz substytuowania dowodu z wyjaśnień oskarżonego w procesie karnym' (1973) *Nowe Prawo* no 10.

[40] See Supreme Court Decision, 3 March 2003, II KK 175/02, Lex no 184723.

[41] Supreme Court Decision, 30 June 2016, Wa 6/16, Lex no 2139265.

only provides for relevant prohibitions in this regard, but also establishes serious consequences for their non-compliance.[42]

According to applicable provisions, it is inadmissible to influence the statement of the questioned person by means of coercion or unlawful threats, and to use hypnosis or chemical or technical measures influencing the psychological processes of the person subject to questioning or are aimed at checking their unconscious responses in connection with the questioning (Article 171 § 5 CPC). Against violation of these prohibitions is secured by the provision according to which explanations, testimonies or statements made in conditions precluding freedom of expression or obtained in breach of the indicated prohibitions listed may not constitute evidence (Article 171 § 7 CPC).[43] In this way, all forms of coercion (physical or mental) that preclude the ability to behave according to one's own will have been eliminated.

Physical coercion is also understood as torture in the broad sense, applied by the interrogator or by another person with his consent. Unlawful threat includes both:

- the threat of committing a crime against particular person or against this person's immediate family member, if the threat induces a reasonable fear in the threatened person that it will be carried out; and
- a threat of bringing about criminal proceedings or other proceedings in which a pecuniary administrative penalty may be imposed or broadcasting information that is damaging to the threatened person's honour or this person's immediate family member; a declaration of bringing about criminal proceedings or other proceedings in which a pecuniary administrative penalty may be imposed with the sole purpose of protecting legal interest infringed by the crime or the behaviour subject to a pecuniary administrative penalty does not constitute a threat Article 115 § 12 CC).[44]

Narcoanalysis is fairly universally recognised as an unacceptable method of truth-seeking in the criminal process, and involves subjecting the accused to narcotic drugs, the use of which removes or substantially reduces the psychological resistance to the accused's confession. It is a method that cannot be reconciled with the defendant's right to remain silent or the witness's right to refuse to testify or answer questions. Hypnosis constitutes a method of 'unlocking memory' and the use of this method in a criminal trial as part of an examination is expressly prohibited.[45]

[42] See further W Jasiński, *Nielegalnie uzyskane dowody w procesie karnym. W poszukiwaniu optymalnego rozwiązania* (Warsaw, Wolters Kluwer, 2019); H Kuczyńska, 'Model reguł dopuszczalności dowodów w państwach anglosaskich na przykładzie Wielkiej Brytanii' in R Olszewski (ed), *Artes serviunt vitae. Sapientia imperat. Proces karny sensu largo. Rzeczywistość i wyzwania. Księga jubileuszowa Profesora Tomasza Grzegorczyka z okazji 70. urodzin* (Łódź, Wolters Kluwer, 2019) 622–40; M Rusinek, *Z problematyki zakazów dowodowych w postępowaniu karnym* (Warszaw, Wolters Kluwer, 2019); Ł. Cora, 'Aksjologia procesowa a dopuszczalność dowodu z art 168a k.p.k.' (2018) *Prok i Pr* no 10; T Grzegorczyk, 'Kodeksowe legalizowanie w procesie karnym, przez nowelizację z 11 marca 2016 r. dowodów uzyskanych za pomocą przestępstwa albo poza granicami zgody udzielonej przez sąd na wkroczenie w sferę konstytucyjnie chronionych wolności jednostki', in S Steinborn and K Woźniewski (eds), *Proces karny w dobie przemian. Zagadnienia ogólne* (Gdańsk, Wydawnictwo Uniwersytetu Gdańskiego, 2018) vol I, 323–38.

[43] See eg Judgment of the Appellate Court in Cracow, 3 July 2002, II AKa 134/02, Lex no 55888.

[44] See M Kurowski, in D Świecki (ed), *Kodeks postępowania karnego. Komentarz* (Warsaw, Wolters Kluwer, 2021) vol I, 704.

[45] See Judgment of the Appellate Court in Cracow, 3 July 2002, II AKa 134/02, Lex no 55888.

Polygraph tests and their results are a separate issue. The Code provides for the prohibition of the use of technical means aimed at checking unconscious responses of the body in connection with questioning. A polygraph (lie detector) is such a measure. It must be assumed that the term 'in connection with questioning' must mean not only 'during questioning' but also 'before or after' questioning. Explanations, testimony and statements obtained in contravention of discussed prohibition cannot constitute evidence (Article 171 §§ 5 point 2 in conjunction with § 7 CPC).[46] It is widely undisputed that the legislature, by the provision invoked, originally intended to eliminate polygraphic examination from the criminal trial.

An amendment was introduced to the Code, according to which the use of technical measures in an examination by an expert witness with an aim of checking unconscious responses of the person subject to examination is possible only with the consent of that person (Article 199a CPC). A second provision, among others, states that in order to limit a group of suspected persons in number or determine the evidentiary valuc of discovered traces, upon consent of the person subject to examination, an expert witness may use technical measures aimed at checking unconscious responses of that person (Article 192a § 2 CPC).[47]

Prohibitions on the Use of Evidence in a Criminal Trial

The essence of title prohibitions boils down to the mere use of evidence; then this prohibition can be described as an independent prohibition on the use of evidence. It may also be a consequence of another regulation in the form of a prohibition of evidence.[48] One or the other form of prohibition of the use of evidence is dealt with when it is expressly provided for in the sphere of criminal procedural law.

Among the independent prohibitions on the use of evidence we should distinguish:

1. a prohibition on the use of the contents of a statement of the the accused, regarding the alleged act, made to an expert witness or to a physician providing medical aid, which, however, does not apply to a polygraph examination (Article 199 CPC);
2. a prohibition on the use at trial of the record of testimonies as a witness of a person who is questioned as an accused (*argumentum a contrario* from Article 391 § 1 CPC and Article 389 § 1 CPC);
3. the suspect's explanations, which may not be used as evidence if the prosecutor has not applied to the court to grant the suspect the status of a crown witness or if the court by decision has rejected to allow evidence from the testimony of a crown witness (Article 6 Crown Witness Act).

The *non*-independent prohibitions on the use of evidence are:

1. procedural situations when, despite the prohibition on proving a specific evidentiary thesis or the prohibition on proving with the help of specific evidence, the

[46] See further Supreme Court Judgment, 29 January 2015, I KZP 25/14, Lex no 1621318.
[47] See more on Art 192a CPC in ch 4.
[48] Marszał (n 3) 361–62.

evidence will be taken; such evidence, as illegal, must be disregarded in the scope of factual findings;
2. a prohibition on the use of explanations, testimony or statements made in conditions of using inadmissible methods of evidence (Article 171 § 7 CPC);
3. a prohibition on the use of testimony, explanations or statements made in conditions precluding freedom of expression, when they were obtained by abusing the natural conditions of examination, such as by prolonged questioning, including at night or by an intoxicated person;
4. a prohibition on using an opinion submitted by an expert who, after being appointed an expert, was found to have grounds for being excluded (Article 196 § 2 CPC).

The above prohibitions are only examples of prohibitions on the use of evidence in a criminal trial, although they are sufficient to show the essence of the indicated prohibitions.[49]

The 2013 amendment to the CPC provided for the inadmissibility of conducting and using evidence that was obtained for the purposes of criminal proceedings by means of a prohibited act. Unfortunately, the 2016 counter-reform not only abolished the prohibition introduced by the 2013 amendment, but introduced the opposite solution. As a result, a piece of evidence shall not be deemed inadmissible exclusively on the grounds that it has been obtained as a result of an infringement of the procedure or a forbidden act referred to in Article 1 § 1 CC, unless the piece of evidence has been obtained in connection with the fulfilment of the official duties by a public officer, as a result of: homicide, causing deliberate damage to health or deprivation of liberty (Article 168a CPC). This solution is aptly regarded as contrary to the foundations of the functioning of the rule of law, including the Constitution of the Republic of Poland.

Proving

Preliminary Remarks

Proving process is a cognitive process aimed at gathering all the 'traces' of a crime committed and reconstructing the act in connection with which the criminal trial is pending. Proving process is a particular process, involving both the 'taking of evidence' and the corresponding type of reasoning, which involves proving something. It is a particular chain of evidentiary actions. This chain of evidence is legally regulated in terms of the 'taking of evidence'.[50]

[49] See further Kwiatkowski (n 10) 326–431.
[50] M Klejnowska, 'Dowodzenie co do meritum w sprawie karnej w postępowaniu apelacyjnym' (2007) *RPEiS* no 1, 101–18; K Juszka and E Żywucka-Kozłowska, 'Wykrywanie i dowodzenie za pomocą niekonwencjonalnych metod śledczych' (2005) *AUW* LXXII; M Wantoła, 'Dowodzenie okoliczności negatywnych w polskim procesie karnym na tle rozwiązań przyjmowanych w krajach systemu common law' in D Gil (ed), *Dowód w procesie karnym w perspektywie porównawczej* (2006) *WPWS* no VI.

The proving process, which is a set of activities, begins in principle from the initiation of the proceedings, continues until its final conclusion, and occurs even after the final conclusion of the trial. In the proving process (this term should not be confused with the course of a trial), stages can be distinguished according to the functions performed, namely the search for and initial securing of evidence, the introduction of evidence into the criminal trial, the taking of evidence, and the evaluation of the evidence taken and the making of findings of fact.[51]

The process of reasoning, especially deductive reasoning, occurs from the very first procedural step, and is based on the suspicion of a crime, which must arise from specific information. When this information creates a probability that a crime has been committed, a decision is issued to initiate an principal investigation or simplified investigation. The description of the prohibited act contained in the opening decision is a hypothesis that needs to be tested. The description of this act, as the knowledge about it enriches, may be corrected. Such a description of the act with an increased probability of its commission is included in the decision to present charges. Finally, the description of the act charged in the indictment is formulated on the basis of all the material collected during the pre-trial proceedings. In cases where the court considers the case at main trial, after the judicial examination has been held and all available evidence has been exhausted, it proceeds to judgment. All collected evidence disclosed at the main trial constitutes the evidentiary basis of the case. The court makes its findings of facts based on the positively verified evidence (the basis of the judgment).[52]

Object of Proof

What Is the Object of Proof?

The object of proof is that which is to be proven, demonstrated in a criminal trial. These objects include circumstances of a factual nature and circumstances of a normative nature.[53]

Any factual circumstance is subject to proof if it is relevant to the case. The term 'circumstance' is used in a broad sense, including both specific human conduct, which constitutes a specific act, as well as its individual components, ie single facts. Circumstances may also be certain states, features, phenomena or relations that are significant for the settlement of the subject matter of the case or for the issuance of another ruling, eg to discontinuace of the proceeding or significant for the assessment of the penalty. When proving the existence or non-existence of certain facts, one proves at the same time the truth or falsity of statements about these facts.[54]

[51] See further M Klejnowska, 'Dowód, ślad, informacja – wyjaśnienie znaczenia pojęć w procesie dowodzenia w sprawie karnej', in P Hofmański (ed), *Węzłowe problemy procesu karnego* (Warsaw, Wolters Kluwer, 2010) 288–312.

[52] Marszał (n 3) 366–67.

[53] M Cieślak, *Zagadnienia dowodowe w procesie karnym* (Warsaw, Wydawnictwo Prawnicze, 1955) 44.

[54] See further KJ Pawelec, *Proces dowodzenia w postępowaniu karnym* (Warsaw, LexisNexis, 2010) passim; H Paluszkiewicz, 'Z problematyki dowodzenia na posiedzeniu wyrokowym', in J Skorupka (ed), *Rzetelny proces karny. Księga jubileuszowa Profesor Zofii Świdy* (Warsaw, Wolters Kluwer, 2009) 403–15.

Therefore, the subject of proof is each circumstance significant to the case, unless it concerns facts of common knowledge or such facts that have been found in a final determinations of a court establishing legal rights or legal relationship.[55]

The subject of proof is also 'uncontroverted' circumstances, admitted by the accused.[56] A confession by the accused does not constitute the highest evidence and is subject to examination as to its truthfulness. Only if the explanations of the accused who admits guilt are beyond doubt may the court, with the consent of the parties present, take evidence in part (Article 388 CPC). It is a matter of dispute whether normative circumstances, ie first of all the provisions of the applicable law, can be the subject of evidence. A judge with a legal and professional background should be able to interpret even the most detailed provisions of the applicable law.[57] Admitting expert evidence in this respect in one case would create a temptation to use this evidence more and more in the main proceedings. Therefore, one must opt for the inadmissibility of evidence as to normative circumstances of national law. However, there is no obstacle to foreign law being the subject of proof.[58]

Notoriousness

Notoriousness may be common or official.[59] The former includes facts that are commonly known and is relative in nature, which means that in one place a given circumstance may be commonly known, while in another it may not. Its boundaries cannot be determined in a strict manner. Facts of common knowledge are facts known to a wide range of people. Facts of common knowledge do not require proof (*notoria non egent probatione*).[60] Official notoriousness includes facts known to the trial authority, especially the court, ex officio, which is referred to as 'judicial notoriousness'. The knowledge of these facts arises from the office of the procedural authority. The circumstances covered by official notoriousness must be notified to the parties. The court should draw the attention of the parties and their representatives to the fact that the designated facts are known to it ex officio (Article 168 CPC), as they may be unknown to the parties.[61] A lack of notification could surprise the parties and their representatives. Drawing their attention to it will enable them, for example, to make statements or submit relevant motions for evidence, should such a need arise in their opinion.

Presumptions

As far as the subject of proof is concerned, presumptions are not without significance. We distinguish between legal presumptions (*praesumptiones iuris*) and factual

[55] Marszał (n 3) 367. Similarly J Skorupka, in *System Prawa Karnego Procesowego* (n 26) 635.

[56] Marszał (n 3) 367.

[57] S Śliwiński, *Polski proces karny przed sądem powszechnym. Zasady ogólne* (Warsaw, Wydawnictwo Gebethner i Wolff, 1961) 307. Differently Cieślak (n 1) 255 et seq.

[58] Marszał (n 3) 368.

[59] See KJ Pawelec, in *System Prawa Karnego Procesowego* (n 26) 656–57.

[60] Marszał (n 3) 368.

[61] Supreme Court Decision, 29 March 2018, V KK 353/17, Lex no 2536286.

presumptions (*praesumptiones facti*).[62] The legal presumption is applied when a legal regulation connects one fact (the basis of presumption, the predecessor of presumption) with the existence of another fact (the successor of presumption). If the existence of the fact constituting the basis of the presumption is demonstrated, the existence of the successor is presumed by virtue of the legal provision, and this regardless of whether or not it corresponds to the objective state of affairs.

The legal presumption is divided into those that abolish counter-evidence (*praesumptio iuris tantum*) and those that do not abolish counter-evidence (*praesumptio iuris ac de iure*).[63] In the first case it is possible and in the second it is inadmissible to give evidence against the successor of the presumption. In criminal trials, presumptions play a lesser role. An example can be private prosecution proceedings, which in the case of the non-appearance of the private prosecutor and his/her representative at the main trial are subject to discontinuance regardless of whether or not the non-appearance of these subjects is justified Article 496 § 3 CPC).

Factual presumptions are more common in criminal trials than in legal ones. They consist in that on the basis of one established fact, conclusions are drawn about the existence of another fact, due to the presence of a causal link between these facts, which justifies an inference based on probability.[64]

Probability

In a criminal trial, as a rule, the subject matter of the trial should be decided on the basis of findings based on proven facts. However, in some cases, probability may suffice.[65]

Probability should not constitute a derogation from the principle of truth and justify the abandonment of its examination. Probability should not be understood as a manifestation of the principle of informalism introducing the possibility for the court to reach an internal conviction about a proven fact without a formal procedure of proof and therefore by means of free evidence.[66]

In fact, the probability is applied in all those cases where the applicable provisions of the criminal procedural law make the relevant consequences, eg taking a procedural decision, dependent on 'reasonable doubt', 'high probability', 'justify risk', 'sufficient suspicion', etc.

Circumstantial Evidence

The term 'circumstantial evidence' means a fact that does not directly prove that a certain person committed a crime, but taken together with other facts and evidence allows an

[62] Pawelec (n 61) 656–57.

[63] See eg Marszał (n 3) 369–70.

[64] See, first of all, ibid 370; Pawelec (n 61) 678–81. See also M Gutowski and P Kardas, 'Domniemanie konstytucyjności a kompetencje sądów' (2016) *Pal* 5, 44 et seq.

[65] Pawelec (n 61) 666–67.

[66] See further J Nelken, 'Uprawdopodobnienie w procesie karnym' (1980) *Nowe Prawo* no 4; R Kmiecik, 'Uprawdopodobnienie w procesie karnym' (1983) *Nowe Prawo* no 5.

indirect conclusion as to the crime and the perpetrator.[67] It is a fact indirectly indicating the commission or non-perpetration of a crime. Circumstantial evidence makes it possible to infer the truth or falsity of the main evidentiary fact. The more circumstantial evidence, the greater the probability of confirming the evidentiary thesis.[68]

The Legal Duty of Proof and the Burden of Proof

The legal duty of proof is sometimes referred to as the formal burden of proof. It is a consequence of the presumption of innocence of the accused.

The duty of proof (*onus probandi*) is the obligation to take all relevant evidence, whether favourable or unfavourable to the accused, and is imposed on the trial authorities alone. In particular, it is imposed on the court regardless of the activity of the parties.[69] The issue of imposing this obligation on the public prosecutor and law enforcement authorities is no longer so obvious, since by filing an indictment they become a litigant. The amendment to the CPC dating back to 2013 significantly modified duty of proof by exempting the court from the burden of proof. In 2016, however, there was a return to the previous legal status and, as a result, this duty was again imposed on the court.

The legal duty of proof does not apply to the private prosecutor and the auxiliary (subsidiary) prosecutor. Nor is this duty placed on the accused – he or she is not obliged, but has the power to prove his/her innocence. The accused is under no obligation to prove his innocence, the guilt should be proved to him. The accused is entitled to submit explanations and motions for evidence, but he/she does not have to do so. It follows that even if an attempt to prove an alibi fails, it does not follow that he/she is guilty.

It should be assumed that the legal obligation to prove circumstances favourable to the accused is placed on the defendant's counsel. It is not only their power, but their duty. The defence counsel, even if convinced of the guilt of the accused, should prove circumstances favourable to the accused.[70]

The essence of the burden of proof boils down to the question of who bears the consequences of the lack of evidence or the failure to prove a circumstance relevant to the case being decided.[71] In other words, on whose shoulders falls the disadvantage (burden) of the fact that there is no evidence or that the existence of a certain circumstance relevant to the case was not proved. Undoubtedly, it does not apply to the court, because it is not guided by its own interest when deciding the subject matter of the trial, ie it is impartial. The disadvantage is borne by the active party, ie the prosecutor. It is true that the public prosecutor is not personally affected by such disadvantages

[67] Marszał (n 3) 371.
[68] See further C. Kulesza, in *System Prawa Karnego Procesowego* (n 26) 428–45.
[69] Marszał (n 3) 372.
[70] ibid 372.
[71] Marszał (n 3) 372–73. Similarly Zgryzek (n 12) 378. See also J Skorupka and W Jasiński (eds), *Ciężar dowodu i obowiązek dowodzenia w procesie karnym* (Warsaw, Wolters Kluwer, 2017) passim.

(burden), because he/she is not directly interested in a particular outcome, but acquittal of the accused or adoption of certain decisions in his/her favour is a procedural negative consequence rejecting his/her prosecution theses. As far as other prosecutors are concerned, the consequences of failing to prove the existence of a central fact are even more far-reaching, because in addition to the acquittal, it is the prosecutor who is obliged to bear the costs of the trial.

The burden of proof does not, as a rule, fall on either the accused or his/her counsel. An irresistible defence of the accused, even if it is not proved, leads to a ruling in favour of the accused. The failure to prove a defence thesis does not necessarily cause it to be rejected. For this purpose, its falsity must be shown, otherwise the defence thesis must be accepted. Only in defamation cases can the burden of proof be on the accused. If the prosecutor shows the existence of the elements of the offence of defamation, as to which the accused may carry out the proof of truth, a conviction of the accused may follow if the proof of truth is not carried out under the conditions of the existence of the features of the offence. This constitutes a harsh consequence for the accused of failing to make proof of truth.

Stages of Proving

Preliminary Remarks

Evidence process is a chain of actions. It may be divided into the following stages: the search for and preservation of evidence, the introduction of evidence to the trial, the taking of evidence, and the evaluation of evidence and making findings of fact.[72] As a rule, if the evidence was introduced to the trial at the motion of a party, the first stage is unnecessary; this stage is optional and takes place depending on the situation.

The Search for and Initial Preservation of Evidence

The search for and disclosure of evidence is the responsibility of the trial authorities, especially those who conduct pre-trial proceedings; they may also demand the surrender of objects that may be evidence in the case and in order to find such objects they may search premises, other places and persons or things. The evidence found that is relevant to the case shall be introduced in the trial, and it is also possible to preliminarily secure evidence.[73]

[72] Marszał (n 3) 374–75.

[73] Ł Chojniak, 'Granice poszukiwania prawdy w procesie karnym – uwagi na tle skargi nadzwyczajnej', in C Kulesza and A Sakowicz (eds), *Ewolucja polskiego wymiaru sprawiedliwości w latach 2013–2018 w świetle standardów rzetelnego procesu* (Białystok, Temida2, 2019) 447–62; S Stachowiak, 'Droga poznania prawdy w polskim procesie karnym', in A Choduń and S Czepita (eds), *W poszukiwaniu dobra wspólnego. Księga jubileuszowa Profesora Macieja Zielińskiego* (Lublin, AUL, 2010); S Cora, 'Poszukiwanie dowodów przez sąd w świetle przepisów KPK' (2006) *Pal* nos 3–4, 147–54.

Introduction of Evidence to a Criminal Trial

The introduction of evidence to a trial consists in its inclusion within the scope of a criminal process in progress. In pre-trial proceedings, the evidence introduced and conducted is preserved for the purposes of further criminal proceedings, including the main proceedings.[74]

We can talk about two ways of introducing evidence to a criminal trial, namely ex officio and upon motion.[75]

Introduction of Evidence to a Trial Ex Officio

The ex officio introduction of evidence into a criminal trial plays a greater role in preparatory (pre-trial) proceedings.[76] It is connected with the directive of instructiveness. Law enforcement authorities in pre-trial proceedings, when introducing ex officio evidence, are not obliged to issue a separate decision on the introduction of evidence into the criminal trial. In the main proceedings, the introduction of evidence into the criminal trial ex officio may take place before the trial or at the trial. The president of the adjudicative panel, having examined the motions of the parties, or the court, ex officio, shall admit evidence, and the president shall order that the evidence be submitted to the trial. The provision of Article 368 § 1 CPC shall apply accordingly (Article 352 CPC). The court at main trial, whenever it is necessary to clarify the essential circumstances of the case, may by way of a decision admit evidence not motioned by the parties.[77]

Introduction of Evidence to the Trial Upon Motion

This procedure of introducing evidence to the trial plays a more important role in the judicial proceedings, but it may also take place in the preparatory proceedings. Evidentiary motions may be submitted by the parties and their statutory representatives, defenders and attorneys;[78] a motion submitted by an unauthorised person shall be left unheard. Such a motion, if it contains a circumstance significant for the proceeding, may lead to introduction of evidence in the process ex officio.[79]

In the judicial proceedings, two groups of evidence can be distinguished. The first of these groups includes evidence which has already been introduced to the process at the

[74] See more K Woźniewski, in *System Prawa Karnego Procesowego* (n 26) 3467 et seq.
[75] Grzegorczyk and Tylman (n 2) 475.
[76] Marszał (n 3) 376; Grzegorczyk and Tylman (n 2) 475.
[77] See further Woźniewski (n 76) 3478–3504.
[78] ibid 3520–21.
[79] B Lewandowski, 'Czy na pewno żądanie oskarżonego złożone w trybie art 185a § 1 k.p.k. należy rozpoznawać jak zwykły wniosek dowodowy?' (2016) *Pal* 2016, nos 7–8, 85 et seq; J Skorupka, 'Wprowadzanie i przeprowadzanie dowodów na rozprawie głównej', in P Wiliński (ed), *Obrońca i pełnomocnik w procesie karnym po 1 lipca 2015 r. Przewodnik po zmianach* (Warsaw, 2015); J Jodłowski, 'Wpływ ograniczenia inicjatywy dowodowej sądu na realizację zasady prawdy materialnej w postępowaniu karnym' (2012) *CzPKiNP* no 2, 159–72.

stage of preparatory proceedings, and the second one includes evidence which has been motioned by the parties to the proceedings to be taken by the court.[80]

A motion for evidence may be made orally or in writing. Such a motion shall identify the evidence and indicate the circumstances to be proven; moreover, it may also specify the manner of evidence-taking (Article 169 § 1 CPC). The purpose of the motion to take evidence may also be to reveal or evaluate the relevant evidence (Article 168 § 2 CPC).[81]

A motion for evidence shall be dismissed if the taking of evidence is inadmissible; if the circumstance to be proven is either irrelevant to the resolution of the case;[82] if the circumstance to be proven has already been proven consistently with the statement of the party who has submitted the motion; if the evidence would be irrelevant to establish factuality of a given circumstance;[83] if the evidence cannot be taken;[84] or when the motion for evidence is manifestly aimed at prolonging the proceedings[85] (Article 170 § 1, points 1–5 CPC).

The amendment of 2019 introduced into the criminal trial another ground for dimissing a motion for evidence when this was submitted after the expiry of the time limit set by the procedural body, of which the party submitting the motion had been notified (Article 170 § 1, point 6 CPC). Such a reason for dismissing a motion to take evidence introduces to the Polish criminal trial the institution of evidence preclusion, which doctrine and judicature clearly opposed. It is contrary to the rights of the accused to defend him/herself against the charge and significantly limits the rights of the trial parties to shape the evidentiary basis for the decision.

A motion for evidence shall be dismissed by a decision, regardless of the stage of proceedings.[86] Such a decision may not be contested; however, the objection that the dismiss of motion was unjustified may be raised in an appeal against a judgment, since it could not be the subject of a complaint (Article 447 § 4 CPC).[87] The decision to dismiss the motion for evidence is a typical revocable decision of the body conducting the trial. Dismissal of a motion for evidence does not prevent the later admission of evidence, even if no new circumstances have emerged.

[80] Supreme Court Decision, 11 January 2008, IV KK 419/07, Lex no 534886.
[81] See further Woźniewski (n 76) 3507–13.
[82] Supreme Court Judgment, 8 September 2005, III KK 319/04, Lex no 200247.
[83] Supreme Court Judgment, 11 October 2017, III KK 102/17, Lex no 2390664.
[84] Supreme Court Decision, 29 December 2015, II KK 371/15, Lex no 1959481.
[85] Supreme Court Judgment, 7 July 2009, V KK 1/09, Lex no 518146.
[86] J Kosonoga, 'Oddalenie obstrukcyjnego wniosku dowodowego' (2019) *Ius Novum* no 1, 7–22; M Kościelniak-Marszał, 'Oddalenie wniosku dowodowego zmierzającego w sposób oczywisty do przedłużenia postępowania', in S Steinborn and K Woźniewski (eds), *Proces karny w dobie przemian. Zagadnienia ogólne* (Gdańsk, Wydawnictwo uniwersytetu Gdańskiego, 2018) vol I, 460–69; J Jodłowski, 'Wpływ ograniczenia inicjatywy dowodowej sądu na realizację zasady prawdy materialnej w postępowaniu karnym' (2012) *CzPKiNP*, no 2, 159–72; M Jeż-Ludwichowska, 'Krytycznie o koncepcji prekluzji dowodowej', in A Przyborowska-Klimczak and A Taracha (eds), *Iudicium et Scientia. Księga jubileuszowa Profesora Romualda Kmiecika* (Warsaw, Wolters Kluwer, 2011) 539–52; M Wąsek-Wiaderek, 'Oddalenie wniosku dowodowego zmierzającego w sposób oczywisty do przedłużenia postępowania w polskiej procedurze karnej' in L Leszczyński, E Skrętowicz and Z Hołda (eds), *W kręgu teorii i praktyki prawa karnego. Księga poświęcona pamięci Profesora Andrzeja Wąska* (Lublin, Wydawnictwo Uniwersytetu Marii Curie-Skłodowskiej, 2005) 709–18; K Zgryzek, 'Oddalenie wniosku dowodowego w nowelizacji kodeksu postępowania karnego z 2003 roku', in M Płachta (ed), *Aktualne problemy prawa i procesu karnego. Księga ofiarowana Profesorowi Janowi Grajewskiemu* (Gdańsk, GSP, 2003) vol XI, 169–75.
[87] Marszał (n 3) 380.

The court may not dismiss a motion for evidence by making a negative *a priori* assessment of the value of the evidence (prohibition of anticipation of evidence).[88] If anyone of the reasons for dismissal of the motion for evidence does not apply, the motion should be granted. In pre-trial proceedings the decision on admitting the evidence motioned may take the form of an order. In the main proceedings, the decision on the motion for evidence may take the form of an order issued by the president of the court in preparation for the main hearing or by the presiding judge unless it has been contested by another party. In other cases, the court decides on admitting the motioned evidence by means of an decision.

Taking of Evidence

The manner in which evidence is taken is by examination (interrogation), reading, inspection and, as a rule, procedural experiment.[89]

Examination (Interrogation)

Examination is a method of conducting evidence from personal sources of evidence. This is the way of conducting evidence from the explanations of the accused, the testimony of a witness and the testimony of an expert (expert witness). The vast majority of evidence comes in the form of personal sources of evidence, and it is clear that examination is at the forefront of ways to conduct evidence.[90]

Examination takes place within the framework of general rules that apply to every examination. These include the freedom of the person making the explanations or testimony to speak, the order of questioning, the prohibition on substituting the explanations or testimony with the content of writings, notes or official notes, and the prohibition on asking the person being questioned questions suggesting the content of the answer.[91]

The person questioned must be granted an opportunity to express themselves freely within the limits defined by the purpose of a given action. The first phase within the order of examination is the phase of spontaneous statement,[92] after which questions may be asked in order to complete, explain or verify the explanations or testimony (Article 171 § 1 CPC). This order is prescribed by law and should be followed.

[88] Supreme Court Judgment, 11 December 2002, II KKN 186/01, Lex no 74387.

[89] Marszał (n 3) 379.

[90] R. Koper, 'Przesłuchanie pokrzywdzonego w trybie art 185c k.p.k.' (2019) *PS* no 5, 73–88; E Kruk, 'Znaczenie przyznania się do winy w procesie karnym – zarys problematyki', in R Olszewski (ed), *Artes serviunt vitae, sapientia imperat. Proces karny sensu largo. Rzeczywistość i wyzwania. Księga jubileuszowa Profesora Tomasza Grzegorczyka z okazji 70, urodzin* (Łódź Wolters Kluwer, 2019) 168–77; J Gurgul, 'Jeszcze o dowodzie z zeznań i wyjaśnień nietrzeźwego' (2018) *Prok i Pr* no 11, 94–122; A Malarewicz-Jakubów and Z. Sawicka-Kroczek, 'Wybrane prawne aspekty przesłuchania małoletniego w charakterze świadka w postępowaniu karnym' (2018) *Studia prawnoustrojowe* no 39, 83–93; A Baj, 'Przesłuchanie pełnoletniego pokrzywdzonego w trybie art 185c k.p.k.' (2016) *Prok i Pr* no 1, 100–06; R Teluk, 'Przesłuchanie świadka anonimowego w postępowaniu przygotowawczym i przed sądem' (2013) *Kwart KSSiP* no 4, 55–69; Kucharczyk, *Wyjaśnienia oskarżonego w polskim procesie karnym* (Katowice, PhD thesis, 2015).

[91] Marszał (n 3) 380. Differently Hofmański and Waltoś (n 2) 390 et seq.

[92] Supreme Court Decision, 17 January 2017, V KK 257/16, Lex no 2203534.

The interrogation creates a special situation for the person questioned. It affects his or her psyche to a greater or lesser extent (depending on his or her mental sensitivity). Exclusion of the freedom of expression may take place both under normal interrogation and due to the application of additional pressure on the questioned person.[93] Within the framework of normal interrogation, freedom of expression can be excluded, for example, by applying physical coercion, long hours or repeated examination leading to complete exhaustion of the questioned person, or examination of a person who feels intense thirst, hunger or acute pain, or is in an advanced state of pregnancy and in fear of provisional detention. Such methods are incompatible with a fair trial against a subject who is protected by the right to defence.

The CPC explicitly prohibits the use of means to influence a questioned person, including: influencing the statements of an questioned person by means of coercion or unlawful threats, eg by beating, torture or intimidation and the use of hypnosis or chemical or technical measures influencing psychological processes of an questioned person or aimed at checking the unconscious responses of his/her body in connection to the questioning (Article 171 § 5 CPC). It is debatable whether deception excludes or restricts freedom of expression.[94] While deception cannot be used to elicit statements and cannot be reconciled with the directive on the loyalty of trial authorities, so much is also stated that deception used for an unworthy purpose and not in the fight against crime is reprehensible. It seems that the first of the positions indicated here should be regarded as binding.

The Code not only sets freedom of the person making the explanations or testimony to speak as a rule, but also provides for sanctions for its violation. Evidence statements obtained in conditions that exclude freedom of expression cannot constitute evidence and must be disregarded.[95] In this respect, the trial authority should issue a decision. Such evidence may be used to establish the existence of other evidence, even though the information about it comes from a 'tainted' source.

During interrogation it is not allowed to ask questions that suggest the answer (Article 171 § 4 CPC).[96] It should be stressed that this prohibition is addressed to all the entities participating in the act of interrogation, and therefore also – although then the decision to set aside from such a question may raise certain difficulties – to the body conducting this activity, ie the pre-trial proceedings authority or the court. The questions suggesting an answer shall be set aside by the body conducting a questioning (Article 171 § 6 CPC). If an answer is given to a suggestive question, such a statement is subject to a thorough evaluation by the court at the main trial.

[93] Marszał (n 3) 380–81.

[94] R Koper, 'Problem dopuszczalności stosowania podstępu wobec świadka w procesie karnym' (2018) *Prok i Pr* nos 7–8, 24–47; P Rogoziński, 'Kwestia dopuszczalności stosowania podstępu wobec uczestników procesu a względna postać zasady informacji prawnej (art 16 § 2 k.p.k.)', in W Cieślak and S Steinborn (eds), *Profesor Marian Cieślak – osoba., dzieło, kontynuacje* (Warsaw, Wolters Kluwer, 2013) 1015; M Kornak, 'Swoboda wypowiedzi osoby przesłuchiwanej a możliwość stosowania podstępu w trakcie przesłuchania' (2005) *AUW* no 72; E Niemczyk, 'Problematyka swobody wypowiedzi osoby przesłuchiwanej w polskim procesie karnym' (2004) *WPP* 4; 60; B. Kurzępa, 'Stosowanie podstępu w toku czynności karno-procesowych. Podstęp w trakcie przesłuchania' (2002) *Prok* nos 3–4, 17 et seq; B Kurzępa, *Podstęp w toku czynności karnoprocesowych i operacyjnych* (Toruń, TNOiK, 2003) 15 et seq.

[95] See Supreme Court Judgment, 9 January 2003, III KKN 315/01, Lex no 75375.

[96] See Judgment of the Appellate Court in warsaw, 9 October 2017, II AKa 310/17, Lex no 2404622.

Persons questioned may be subjected to a confrontation, ie brought face to face with witnesses – for example, to clarify contradictions in their testimony, unless the law precludes confrontation (Article 172 CPC).[97] More often than not, expert witnesses are confronted in order to arrive at a uniform result of their opinions.

Another rule of interrogation is the prohibition on substitution of explanations or testimony with the contents of letters, notes or official memos (Article 174 CPC).

Another form of interrogation is presentation, the purpose of which is to identify a person or a material object (Article 173 § 1 CPC).[98] A person, their image or an object shall be shown to the person interrogated. Presentation may concern anyone who is being interrogated, ie a witness, a defendant or an expert, as well as other subjects. The injured person or a third party may also be subject to presentation and identification. When necessary, the presentation of another person may be conducted also in a manner precluding identification of the person subject to questioning by the person to be identified (Article 173 § 2 CPC). The presentation of the object should be accompanied by similar conditions.[99] The presentation of material object is very important for the identification of instruments of the committed crime, as well as objects from the crime. In the doctrine, the question of admissibility of presenting voice or scent traces is disputable. It should be assumed that the presentation of voice or scent traces is admissible.[100] A record shall be drawn up from the presentation.

Reading

Reading is a form of taking evidence from a document at a main trial that concerns its contents.[101] A document shall be read as a whole or in part, if only that part is relevant to the case. The most commonly read documents are records of evidentiary actions, drawn up in preparatory proceedings. This reading is generally done by the presiding judge, but it should be done by the prosecutor. Data on the accused and the results of the community inquiry are considered to be disclosed without being read out. However, if the accused or defence counsel so motions, these documents shall be read out (Article 394 § 1 CPC).

In pre-trial proceedings, documents shall be added to the case file for subsequent presentation to the court.

Upon the conclusion of the judicial examination, all records and documents subject to reading out at the trial that were not read out shall be revealed without being read out (Article 405 § 2 CPC).[102] However, they shall be read out upon motion of a party that

[97] See further Supreme Court Decision, 19 August 2013, WK 15/03, Lex no 152013; Supreme Court Decision, 9 August 2017, II KK 182/17, Lex no 2376889.

[98] P Herbowski and D Słapczyńska, 'Okazanie mowy w polskiej praktyce śledczej' (2016), *Palestra* nos 78, p. 49 et seq; MJ Lisiecki, 'Okazanie cech i właściwości – problemy wykładni obowiązującego stanu prawnego', in P Hofmański (ed), *Węzłowe problemy procesu karnego* (Warsaw, Wolters Kluwer, 2010) 313–17.

[99] See also Judgment of the Appellate Court in Wrocław, 23 October 2013, II Aka 319/13, Lex no 1400517.

[100] See eg Supreme Court Decision, 26 May 2004, V KK 22/04, Lex no 121992.

[101] Marszał (n 3) 384; Hofmański and Waltoś (n 2) 404.

[102] Critically about this solution, see J Zagrodnik, in J Skorupka (eds), *Kodeks postepowania karnego. Komentarz* (Warsaw, CH Beck, 2021) 1173–77.

has had no opportunity to become familiar with their contents or when the court deems it necessary (Article 394 § 2 CPC).

Inspection

The Code distinguishes between inspection of a place, person or material object (Article 207 § 1 CPC). The task of visual inspection is to ascertain the characteristics of the place, body or material object. This activity is carried out not only with the help of the sense of sight (*oględziny*), but it can also include observations made with the help of other senses, such as smell, taste, touch, etc.[103]

If the material object might be damaged or destroyed during the examination, all efforts shall be made to preserve at least part of such an object intact and, if this is not possible, the condition of the object shall be preserved in some other manner (Article 207 § 2 CPC).

Of all the scene inspections, the crime scene inspection is the most important. Its aim is to establish traces of the crime and secure them for evidentiary purposes. A report shall be drawn up on such inspection (Article 143 § 1, item 3 CPC). Appropriate situational sketches are made and photographs are also taken, or a picture of the crime scene is recorded on relevant apparatus.[104]

Inspection of persons is carried out to find traces of the crime; first of all, injuries caused by the perpetrator of the crime or other traces left on the body of the person subjected to inspection are searched for.[105] A witness, if they are injured and criminal liability for an act depends on their health status, shall not refuse an examination of their body or a medical examination, provided that no surgical procedure or observation at a healthcare institution is involved (Article 192 § 1 CPC).

It should be assumed that an inspection is performed by the authority in charge of the trial. In order to determine the type, nature or extent of bodily injuries, it is necessary to call an expert medical doctor. If it is suspected that the death has been caused by criminal means, an inspection of the corpse and a post mortem (autopsy) must always be ordered (Article 209 § 1 CPC). The court or the public prosecutor may order an exhumation to conduct an inspection of a corpse or to perform a post mortem (Article 210 § 1 CPC). Physical evidence is subject to inspection already during the preparatory proceedings. The material evidence shall be attached to the case file.

If the properties of physical evidence do not prevent it, because of its size, weight, permanent connection with the ground, etc, upon motion of a party or if the court deems this necessary, physical evidence shall be brought to the courtroom and made available to the parties, and, where necessary, to witnesses and expert witnesses (Article 395 CPC). If the examination of the physical evidence or the examination by the full courtroom encounters serious difficulties, or if the parties consent to this, the court shall designate a judge from the panel to perform this action or shall appoint another court for that purpose (examination by requisition Article 396 § 1 CPC).

Evaluation should not be confused with a procedural experiment.

[103] Marszał (n 3) 385; Hofmański and Waltoś (n 2) 402.
[104] J Kasprzak in *System Prawa Karnego Procesowego* (n 26) 5141–53.
[105] Marszał (n 3) 385; Kasprzak (n 106) 5154.

Evaluation of Evidence and Making Findings of Fact

Evidence that is illegal should be eliminated from the evidentiary basis of the decision. Such illegality may be caused by the taking of evidence obtained from an illegal source, obtaining evidence in an illegal manner, or conducting evidence illegally.[106]

Evidence is subject to evaluation by the trial authority[107] in accordance with the directives of the presumption of innocence of the accused.

Findings of fact are a descriptive reconstruction of the course of a specific act or specific state of affair. In sentencing, it is a descriptive reconstruction of a specific act that occurred in the past. This reconstruction is made on the evidentiary basis of the judgment in question. As a rule, the factual basis for procedural decisions are proven facts, which we are dealing with when there is objective convincingness of evidence, ie when the confirming facts are objectively convincing and when the trial authority is subjectively convinced of these facts. In the case of ruling on the subject matter of the trial, plausibility is not sufficient, proof is necessary.

Individual Sources and Means of Evidence

The Accused as a Source of Evidence and Their Explanations

The accused,[108] being a party to the trial, may at the same time be a source of evidence.[109] He/she is both entitled to give explanations and obliged to submit to the examinations prescribed by law, although he/she is not obliged to prove his/her innocence or provide evidence to his/her disadvantage.[110] An explanation is any statement of the accused's knowledge providing information about the facts of the case being decided, whether it occurs in the pre-trial proceedings (investigation) or in the later stages of the criminal process.[111] The accused may not be interested in clarifying the truth about the course of the act and its circumstances.[112] He/she may exercise his/her right to defence by giving explanations or by means of the right to remain silent.[113]

The accused has the right to remain silent, and therefore he/she may not give explanations or answer questions put to him/her (Article 175 § 1 CPC). Refusal to answer questions or provide explanations may not result in any adverse procedural

[106] Marszał (n 3) 387–88; D Czerniak, in *System Prawa Karnego Procesowego* (n 26) 3015.
[107] Czerniak (n 108) 3006–11.
[108] A Sakowicz, *Prawo do milczenia w polskim procesie karnym* (Białystok, Temida2, 2019); W Friedrich, 'Oskarżony jako podmiot badań psychologicznych w procesie karnym – aspekty prawne i psychologiczne' (2018) *PS* no 4, 76–86; J Gurgul, 'Jeszcze o dowodzie z zeznań i wyjaśnień nietrzeźwego' (2018) *Prok i Pr* no 4, 94–123; D Margiel, 'Status oskarżonego w polskim kpk, a jego pozycja w świetle wybranych norm prawa UE' (2017) *Jurysta* no 6; M Błoński, 'Wyjaśnienia oskarżonego na tle prawnoporównawczym', in D Gil (ed), *Dowód w procesie karnym w perspektywie porównawczej* (2016) *WPWS* no 3; P Nowak, 'Definicja podejrzanego i oskarżonego a konstytucyjne prawo do obrony' (2016) *CzPKiNP* no 4, 64–85.
[109] Grzegorczyk and Tylman (n 2) 481.
[110] See M Błoński, in *System Prawa Karnego Procesowego* (n 26) 4161–65.
[111] Marszał (n 3) 390.
[112] Supreme Court Decision, 4 February 2008, III KK 363./07, Lex no 357459.
[113] Daszkiewicz (n 6) 97.

consequences for the accused.[114] In case of refusal to give explanations at the main trial, the record of his/her explanations given earlier in this or another case should be read; refusal to give explanations does not eliminate from the trial the explanations previously given by this accused (Article 389 § 1 CPC).

Explanations of the accused, especially a confession, cannot be obtained through expert evidence. An expert cannot be instructed to overcome the mistrust of the accused and induce him/her to give explanations on the facts about which he/she has decided to keep silent before the procedural authority. Statements made by the accused to an expert or to a medical practitioner concerning the alleged act cannot constitute evidence (Article 199 CPC). When giving explanations, the accused – unlike a witness – is not obliged to tell the truth. This does not mean that the accused exercises the right to lie.[115] However, from the right to remain silent flows the right to conceal the truth.

The problem of the limits of the defence of the accused in the framework of explanations is very complex.[116] The question is whether the accused, in his/her explanations, may with impunity accuse another person of committing a crime or of such characteristics or conduct as may degrade him/her in public opinion or expose him/her to the loss of confidence. In the literature, opinions on this issue are divided. On the one hand, it is a matter of providing the accused with maximum freedom to defend themselves against the charges they face, and on the other hand, it is a matter of public interest and the interest of individual persons who are exposed to the activities of the accused, generally contrary to the existing legal order. As it seems, the accused may defend themselves by any means they think will enable them to repel the charge they face. The only limit is that by their conduct they do not violate the criminal law, threatening them with criminal liability. A defendant who falsely accuses another person of committing a criminal act exceeds the limits of his/her defence and may thereby incur criminal liability (false accusation of committing prohibited act or disciplinary delinquency – Article 234 CC). A co-defendant's defamation is sufficient to establish the guilt of the other co-defendant, provided, however, that the defamation is convincing and supported by the circumstances of the entire case.[117]

An admission of guilt shall not constitute prima facie evidence (is not "queen of evidence") – *confessio non est regina probationum*. Only if the confession is beyond reasonable doubt may the court, with the consent of the parties present, take partial evidence or no evidence when an accused submits a motion for the issuance of a judgment of conviction and the imposition of a specific penalty or a criminal measure upon them or for ordering forfeiture or a redress measure without an evidentiary hearing being conducted.[118]

[114] Supreme Court Decision, 4 February 2008, III KK 363/07, Lex no 357459; Supreme Court Decision, 14 March 2008, IV KK 438/07, Lex no 531243.

[115] Judgment of the Appellate Court in Gdańsk, 16 April 1998, II AKa 88/98, Lex no 1681209.

[116] E Gruza, 'Przyznanie się do winy oskarżonego jako element dowodu poszlakowego', in M Rogacka-Rzewnicka and H Gajewska-Kraczkowska (eds), *Istota i zasady procesu karnego 25 lat później. Księga poświęcona pamięci Profesora Andrzeja Murzynowskiego* (Warsaw, Wolters Kluwer, 2019) 81–94; M Kucharczyk, *Wyjaśnienia oskarżonego w polskim procesie karnym* (Katowice, PhD thesis, 2015).

[117] Supreme Court Decision, 8 January 2003, III KK 261/02, Lex no 75374; Supreme Court Decision, 7 May 2014, II KK 81/14, Lex no 1460786.

[118] See Supreme Court Judgment, 6 January 2004, IV KK 276/03, Lex no 162362.

Explanations may be confessing, not confessing, or partially confessing, but this division is irrelevant to the evidentiary value of the explanations, since each explanation is the basis for the decision. If the claims contained in the explanations that point to the innocence of the accused (eg showing his/her alibi) cannot be refuted by other credible and convincing evidence, then they will constitute grounds for a verdict of acquittal.

The Witness and His/Her Testimony

The term 'witness' is not understood unambiguously, nor is it defined in the Code. In the Code, it is used to denote a person present at the commission of an act, who saw its course at least in some part. The literature also uses the term 'foster witness' to denote a person who participated in the act of search.

The term 'witness' is also used in the procedural and in the material sense.[119] In the procedural sense, it is any person who has been summoned as such by the trial authority to give evidence in the course of a criminal trial. The decisive moment for a witness to be called in a trial is when the trial authority summons him or her in this capacity.[120] Such a summons occurs when, according to the data in the possession of the trial authority, the person has information that may be relevant to the pending criminal process. In the procedural sense, it is also a witness who reported to the procedural authority without a summons. Most often it will also be a witness in the substantive (material) sense.[121] A witness is a personal source of evidence and his/her testimony is a means of proof.

The following obligations are imposed on a witness: the obligation to appear when summoned by the procedural authority, the obligation to remain at the disposal of the procedural authority, the obligation to testify, the obligation to take the pledge, and the obligation to testify to the truth.[122]

A person may be obliged to appear as a witness as a result of his/her summons, which is generally made by the authority in charge of the criminal process (Article 177 § 1 CPC). In cases of utmost urgency, a person may be summoned or notified by telephone, or in any other manner appropriate to the circumstances, recording in the case files a copy of any communications sent, signed by the person who sent it (Article 137 CPC). The action shall not be undertaken if the authorised person fails to appear and there is no evidence that they have been notified, and if there is good reason to suspect that such a failure to appear was due to a natural disaster or other extraordinary circumstances (Article 117 § 2 CPC). If a person summoned as a witness is prevented from appearing due to illness, disability or other irremovable obstacle, he or she shall provide an excuse for his or her absence. Excusing the absence of a witness due to illness requires the presentation of a statement confirming the inability to appear upon call or a notification of the body conducting the proceedings, issued by a court physician (Article 117 § 2a CPC).

[119] Marszał (n 3) 394; similarly, Daszkiewicz (n 6) 100.

[120] See Judgment of the Appellate Court in Warsaw, 13 April 2017, I ACa 112/17, Lex no 2455077.

[121] Marszał (n 3) 394.

[122] M Kornak, *Małoletni jako świadek w procesie karnym* (Warszawa, Wolters Kluwer, 2009); P Szustakiewicz, 'Prawa i obowiązki świadka' (1996) *Gaz Praw* no 20; M Dobrowolska and A Oklejak, 'Prawa i obowiązki świadków w procesie sądowym – rozwiązanie prawne i wnioski de lege ferenda' (1978) *ZN IBPS* no 10; Zgryzek (n 12) 396–400.

In the cases presented, a witness may be questioned where he or she is staying. In the course of court proceedings, the institution of a designated judge or a summoned court is used for this purpose (Article 396 § 2 CPC). Failure of a witness to appear at the main trial may cause an interruption or adjournment of the main trial. In the case of unjustified non-appearance of a witness who has been served with a summons, order penalties (financial penalty) may be applied, as well as their arrest and enforced appearance (Article 285 CPC).

A person summoned to appear as a witness shall not only appear at the time and place specified in the summons, but shall also remain at the disposal of the trial authority until he/she is released.[123] As long as the action has not been completed and the authority in charge of the criminal process does not release the witness, the obligation continues.[124]

The legal obligation to testify is, on the one hand, the right of the witness to testify, and, on the other hand, an obligation – social as well as legal – sanctioned by the possibility of the application of procedural coercive measures. The obligation to testify applies both to the evidentiary information in the possession of the witness that is relevant to the pending case and to the data concerning his/her identity.[125] If a witness unjustifiably refuses to testify, he/she must be instructed on his/her obligation to do so, and only then, if he/she continues to reject, may coercive measures be applied.

The obligation to take the pledge is limited to the examination of the witness by the court or the designated judge (Article 187 § 1 CPC).[126] The pledge is not taken from the witness before questioning by criminal prosecution authorities. No religious oath is taken in the Polish criminal trial. The pledge is an additional element intended to strengthen the credibility of the witness's testimony.[127] The obligation to have a pledge given by the witness may be waived if the parties present do not object (Article 187 § 3 CPC). The witness him/herself may not be exempted from this obligation unless the law expressly provides that the pledge shall not be taken from him/her, which shall be the case when the witness is a minor or when he/she has been convicted of giving false testimony (see Article 189 CPC).

The pledge shall be solemn, and during its taking all persons present in the courtroom, not excluding judges, shall stand (Article 188 § 2 CPC). If the witness is deaf or mute, he or she shall take the pledge by signing the text of the pledge (Article 188 § 3 CPC). If a witness has already taken a pledge in a given case, he/she shall be reminded of the pledge upon any new questioning by the court (Article 188 § 4 CPC). However, the court may take another pledge from the witness if it considers this necessary. The obligation to take a pledge may be enforced by Penalties for Breach of Order (Article 287 § 1 CPC).

[123] Decision of the Appellate Court in Katowice, 27 March 2013, II AKz 183/13, Lex no 1341992.

[124] R. Kmiecik, 'Orzekanie kar porządkowych z powodu niestawiennictwa świadka lub bezpodstawnej odmowy zeznań' (2010) *Przegląd Sądowy* no 2, 15 et seq.

[125] Marszał (n 3) 396.

[126] Z. Mitręga, 'Przysięga zamiast przyrzeczenia. Trudna droga do prawdy obiektywnej' (1996) *Rzeczpospolita* no 70; M Płachta, 'Znaczenie przyrzeczenia dla oceny wiarygodności świadka' (1983) *Nowe Prawo* nos. 9–10, 157–68; J Stańda, 'Problematyka przyrzeczenia prawdomówności na tle obowiązującego prawa procesowego' (1973) *Prob Praw* nos 1–2.

[127] Marszał (n 3) 396–97.

The witness is obliged to tell the truth. The obligation to give truthful testimony arises first and foremost directly from substantive law. A ground for criminal responsibility is that the person receiving of the testimony has warned the witness of the criminal liability for giving false testimony or has received a pledge from the witness (Article 233 § 2 CC). The witness should therefore be cautioned about the liability for false testimony before being questioned. The crime of giving false testimony can only be committed intentionally.

The witness also has certain rights.[128] As mentioned above, he or she has the right to refuse to testify or decline to answer questions. In addition, if questions are put that are offensive to the witness, these questions are subject to set aside; the same applies to inappropriate behaviour towards the witness. A witness may demand to be questioned at a trial in camera if the contents of their testimony may expose them or their closest relatives by blood or affinity to disgrace (Article 183 § 2 CPC). The witness is also entitled to reimbursement of expenses incurred for appearing.

A witness may be questioned with the use of technical devices enabling this procedural action to be conducted remotely on the basis of a simultaneous direct transmission of image and sound. In proceedings before court, in a procedural action in the place of stay of the witness, a court clerk, judge assistant, or an official employed at the court in whose region the witness stays, shall participate (Article 177a § 1 CPC).[129] The role of these entities listed at the end is to ensure the technical and organisational conditions for carrying out this activity and to guarantee its correctness. Parties, defenders and attorneys have the right to participate in the remote hearing.

The witness is to testify about facts known to him/her. Unlike an expert witness, a witness is not entitled to express his or her opinions or draw conclusions, but to state facts that he or she has seen or heard or otherwise come into contact with through his or her senses. However, it is not precluded to ask the witness about his/her conclusions.[130] While conclusions and evaluations come to the fore in the opinion of an expert, in the case of the testimony of a witness they indeed recede into the background, but this does

[128] M Kowalewska-Łukuć and Ł Buczek, 'Złożenie przez świadka fałszywych zeznań w sytuacji jego niewiedzy o prawie do odmowy składania zeznań lub uchylenia się od odpowiedzi na pytanie a możliwość pociągnięcia go do odpowiedzialności' (2019) *Prok i Pr* no 12, 99–111; M Derlatka, 'Wspólne pożycie a prawo do odmowy zeznań' (2016) *Pal* nos 1–2, 159 et seq; D Lapawa, 'Problem pouczenia świadka o prawie do uchylenia się od odpowiedzi na pytanie' (2013) *WPP* no 1, https://www.gov.pl/attachment/70ed2bda-1fc4-43ed-8fd5-030aa77827a1; K Zgryzek, 'Zwolnienie świadka z obowiązku zeznawania w trybie art 185 k.p.k.', in A Przyborowska-Klimczak and A Taracha (eds), *Iudicium et Scientia. Księga jubileuszowa Profesora Romualda Kmiecika* (Warsaw, Wolters Kluwer, 2011) 683–96; Paszek and Pawelec (n 20) 119–26; A Bojańczyk and T Razowski, 'Konsekwencje procesowe uzyskania i utraty przez świadka uprawnienia do odmowy składania zeznań' (2007) *Palestra* nos. 3–4, 11–22; PK Sowiński, 'Instytucja odmowy składania zeznań przez świadka, oskarżonego w innej toczącej się sprawie o współudział w przestępstwie objętym postępowaniem (art 182 § 3 k.p.k.)' (2003) *Prok* no 2, 52–61; PK Sowiński, 'Zwolnienie z obowiązku zeznawania w procesie karnym świadka pozostającego z oskarżonym w "szczególnie bliskim stosunku" (art 185 KPK)', in *Jednostka, państwo i prawo dawniej i dziś. Prace ofiarowane Profesorowi Zbigniewowi Sobolewskiemu w siedemdziesięciolecie urodzin* (2003) *ZN UR* no 7, 369–75; Z Gostyński, *Tajemnica dziennikarska a obowiązek składania zeznań w procesie karnym* (Warsaw, Wydawnictwo ABC, 1997) passim.

[129] M Dutkiewicz, 'Przesłuchanie świadka na odległość w świetle art 177 § 1A kodeksu postępowania karnego' (2008) *Palestra* nos 3–4, 74–82; G Kopczyński, 'Przesłuchanie świadka na odległość w polskim procesie karnym' (2005) *AUW* LXXII; A Lach, 'Przesłuchanie na odległość w postępowaniu karnym' (2006) *Prok i Pr* no 12, 81 et seq.

[130] Marszał (n 3) 399.

not mean that a witness cannot express an opinion or draw conclusions at all, especially if he/she has the relevant life experience and knowledge to do so.

In the current state of the law, the restrictions on multiple questioning of an injured person who is under fifteen years of age have been significantly expanded. For example, in cases related to criminal offences committed with the use of violence or unlawful threat, or defined in Chapters XXIII (Crimes against Liberty), XXV (Crimies against Sexual Freedom and Decency) and XXVI (Crimes against Family and Guardiansip) of the Criminal Code, an injured person who is under fifteen years of age at the time of examination shall shall be questioned in the capacity of a witness only when their testimony could be of particular importance for the resolution of the case, and questioned only once, unless significant circumstances are disclosed and there is a need of a repeated questioning to clarify them, or the accused who remained without a defence counsel during the first questioning of the injured demands so (Article 185a § 1 CPC).[131] The questioning shall be carried out by the court in a session, with the participation of an expert psychologist, immediately, not later than within fourteen days from the date of the receipt of the request. The public prosecutor, defence counsel and attorney of the injured have the right to participate in the questioning. If the accused notified of the procedural action in consideration remains without a defence counsel of their choice, the court shall appoint an ex officio defence counsel for them (Article 185a § 2 CPC). The recording of image and sound of the questioning shall be replayed, and the record of the questioning read, at the main trial (Article 185 § 3 CPC).

An 'obligated entity' (a 'quasi-party'[132]) may also be questioned as a witness. Such an entity is a natural or legal person, or an organisational unit without legal personality, which is granted legal personality by separate regulations, who has obtained, in connection with committing a prohibited act, a material benefit or a benefit specified in Articles 405–07, 410 and 412 of the Civil Code from the State Treasury, a local government unit, a state or local government organisational unit, an entity for which a local government authority is the founding entity, or a commercial law company in which the majority of shares are held by the State Treasury or a local government unit. On a motion of the prosecutor, the court, applying the provisions of civil law, obliges the indicated persons or organisational units to return the benefit or its equivalent to the entitled entity or orders the forfeiture of the benefit or its equivalent to the State Treasury (Article 91a § 1 CPC). In the case of an entity other than a natural person, a person or persons authorised to act on its behalf shall be heard (Article 91a § 2 CPC). The person may refuse to testify, and the provisions concerning the right to the assistance of an interpreter, the obligation to appear when summoned, and in the case of unjustified non-appearance, the provisions concerning detention and enforced appearance, the right to have a representative, the right to access to the records of proceeding and the provisions concerning the initiative to take evidence shall apply accordingly (Article 91a § 3 CPC).

A main problem is the issue of examining the witness and causing them further inconvenience. As these burdensome measures are extended, there may be a fear that citizens will be reluctant to act as witnesses, and as a result, the justice system could

[131] See Supreme Court Decision, 24 November 2010, I KZP 21/10, OSNKW 2010, no 11, pos 95.
[132] See Zagrodnik (n 12) 225–29.

be cut off from sources of evidence that are important to it.[133] Such an example of an intractable nuisance could be the examination of a witness's sanity, especially if it were combined with placement in a treatment facility. The authority in charge of the trial should be able to check the possible mental disorders of the witness, but this must not unduly restrict the freedom of the witness and expose him/her to the risk of public verification of his/her mental state. If criminal liability for an act depends on the health condition of the injured, the latter shall not reject an examination of their body or a medical examination, provided that no surgical procedure or observation at a healthcare institution is involved (Article 192 § 1 CPC).[134] However, if the examinations concern persons who have refused to give evidence or have been exempted from this, then the examinations may not be carried out without their consent. The court or the public prosecutor may order the examination of a witness with the participation of a medical expert or expert psychologists, and the witness may not object to this, if there is any doubts as to the witness's mental condition (Article 192 § 2 CPC). In all other cases, the witness's consent shall be required for the medical or psychological examination of the witness.[135] If necessary for the purposes related to evidence, a consenting witness may be submitted to an examination of their body and to medical or psychological examination (Article 192 § 4 CPC).These examinations may not be combined with surgical treatment or observation in a medical institution.

The question remains whether it is possible to combine the role of a witness with other roles in a criminal trial. A witness can act in this role while at the same time being an auxiliary prosecutor or a party's attorney, but combining the role of a witness with a social representative raises objections due to the fact that the social representative has an independent role in the trial, without the need to take sides. Combining the role of a witness with the position of a defence counsel also raises numerous doubts. It seems that in such a situation, for the sake of justice, the advocate or legal adviser should terminate the defence relationship. A witness cannot be both an accused and an expert.[136]

The CPC provides that in situations where there is justified concern for the safety of life, health, freedom or property of considerable size regarding the witness or their closest relative by blood or affinity, the court, and in pre-trial proceedings (investigation) the prosecutor, may issue a decision on keeping secret circumstances making it possible to disclose the identity of the witness,[137] including personal data, if irrelevant for the resolution in the case.[138] The proceedings in this scope shall be carried out without the participation of the parties and covered by secrecy as information classified as 'secret' or 'top secret'. The circumstances referred to in the first sentence shall not be included in the decision (Article 184 § 1 CPC). The justified concern for safety should be based

[133] Marszał (n 3) 400–01.

[134] Supreme Court Decision, 10 December 2010, II KK 238/11, Lex no 1084719.

[135] See Supreme Court Judgment, 27 March 2014, V KK 331/13, Lex no 1463433.

[136] See further Z Martyniak, 'Kumulacja ról procesowych w postępowaniu karnym' (1985) *NP* no 1, ss 47 et seq; M Płachta, 'Kumulacja roli świadka z rolą innego uczestnika procesu (Na tle badań empirycznych)' (1983) *Prok i Pr* no 8; W Jasiński, 'Kumulacja ról oskarżonego i pokrzywdzonego w polskim procesie karnym' (2008) *Prok i Pr* no 1, 85–95; Dopuszczalność kumulacji roli procesowej pokrzywdzonego z innymi rolami procesowymi postępowaniu karnym. (2001) *Problemy Prawa Karnego*, vol 24, ss 144–69.

[137] Judgment of the Appellate Court in Gdańsk, 18 November 1999, II AKa 243/99, OSA 2002, no 4, pos 33.

[138] See P Hofmański, *Świadek anonimowy w procesie karnym* (Kraków, Wydawnictwo Zakamycze, 1998).

on marked, concrete, proven or at least plausible circumstances. Only those circumstances that would allow disclosure of a witness's identity, including personal data, shall be anonymised unless they are 'relevant to the resolution in the case'.[139] As a result of indicated decision by a court or prosecutor, information that would allow the disclosure of a witness's identity or personal data shall be known exclusively to the court, the public prosecutor and, when necessary, to the police official conducting the investigation. The record of the testimony of such a witness may be made available to the accused or their defence counsel in a manner that prevents the disclosure of the identity of the witness or their personal data (Article 184 § 2 CPC). Such a witness shall be examined by the public prosecutor, as well as by the court,[140] which may appoint a judge from its composition to do so, at a place and in a manner making it impossible to disclose circumstances mentioned in Article 184 § 1 CPC. This means that an anonymous witness may not be examined by another criminal prosecution body than prosecutor. When this witness is examined by the court or judge, the public prosecutor, the accused and the defence counsel may be present, but the accused shall be brought in only if the court deems it necessary (Article 184 § 3 third sentence in conjunction with Article 396 § 3 CPC). The questioning of an anonymous witness may be carried out[141] with the use of technical equipment, enabling this activity to be conducted remotely.

The decision on keeping in secrecy the circumstances making it possible to disclose identity may be contested by a witness or the accused, and in proceedings before court also by the public prosecutor, within a period of three days, A complaint against the decision of a public prosecutor shall be examined by the court having jurisdiction over the case (Article 184 § 5 CPC). If the complaint is taken into account, the record of the questioning of the witness shall be destroyed and a note of this shall made in the files of the case (Article 184 § 6 CPC).

Upon closure of the judicial examination before the first-instance court, a witness may file a motion to set aside the decision on the secrecy of the circumstances allowing for the disclosure of the identity of the witness or his/her personal data. A decision related to the motion may be contested. Should the motion be granted, the record of the questioning of the witness shall be disclosed in its entirety (Article 184 § 7 CPC). If it turns out that when the decision of the anonymisation was issued there was no justified concern for the safety of life, health, freedom or property of considerable size of the witness or their closest relatives by blood or affinity, or that the witness has intentionally given false testimony or the testimony has been disclosed, the public prosecutor in the investigation, and the court in the court proceedings, upon request of the public prosecutor, may set the decision aside (Article 184 § 8 CPC).

There is no doubt that the institution of anonymity for witnesses limits the right of defence of the accused. This imposes on the practitioner the obligation to apply this institution prudently in the criminal process in specific cases.[142]

[139] Supreme Court Resolution, 20 January 1999, I KZP 21/98, OSNKW 1999, nos. 1–2, pos 3.
[140] Supreme Court Judgment, 10 July 2007, II KK 387/06, OSNwSK 2007, no 1, pos 1587.
[141] Supreme Court Judgment, 17 December 2003, V KK 131/03, OSNwSK 2003, no 1, pos 2728.
[142] See Supreme Court Decision, 7 January 2003, II KK 320/02, OSNwSK 2003, no 1, pos 5.

The second special form is the crown witness.[143] It is assumed that we deal with a crown witness when the state makes promises to the perpetrator in terms of prosecution or punishment for the act committed by him/her in return for revealing what he/she knows about the crimes of others. This institution creates an opportunity to break collusion (conspiracy) between offenders. It also gives the prosecutor the opportunity to abandon all or part of the prosecution of such a person and call him/her as a witness. Undoubtedly, these are some important advantages of the institution of a crown witness. However, in addition to the advantages, this institution also has a number of drawbacks. First of all, it cannot be reconciled with the principle of legalism. It creates too much freedom for the prosecutor in the choice between prosecuting and not prosecuting a particular person. In addition, the value of testimony obtained in this way may raise significant questions, because the person has a personal interest in 'defaming' other perpetrators and 'whitewashing' themselves.[144]

Only a suspect who has been admitted by decision to testify as a witness may be a crown witness (Article 2 WPA). A suspect may be admitted as a crown witness if all of the following conditions are met (positive conditions): if, by the time the indictment is brought in court as a suspect, he/she has provided the authority conducting the proceeding with information in his/her explanations that may contribute to the disclosure of the circumstances of the crime, the detection of other perpetrators, the disclosure of further offences or the prevention of further offences, and has disclosed his or her and the known assets of the other accomplices to the offence or fiscal offence, and has undertaken to give comprehensive testimony to the court regarding the persons involved in the offence or fiscal offence and the other circumstances of the offence (Article 3 WPA).[145] The provisions on a crown witness shall not apply to a suspect if he/she has attempted to commit or has committed the crime of murder or has participated in the commission of such a crime, if he/she has induced another person to commit a prohibited act to which the institution of a crown witness may be applied in order to bring criminal proceeding against that person, and if he/she has led an organised criminal group or association having as its the purpose of commission a crimes or a fiscal crimes (Article 4 WPA).

In the matter of admitting evidence from the testimony of a crown witness, a decision shall be issued by the regional court having jurisdiction over the place where the pre-trial proceedings are conducted on the motion of the public prosecutor conducting or supervising the proceedings, submitted after obtaining the consent of the Public Prosecutor General or the Deputy Public Prosecutor General authorised by him/her

[143] S Waltoś, 'Świadek koronny – obrzeża odpowiedzialności karnej' (1993) *Prok i Pr* no 2, 13 et seq; E Kowalewska-Borys, *Świadek koronny w ujęciu dogmatycznym* (Kraków, Wydawnictwo Zakamycze, 2004); J Grajewski, 'Instytucja świadka koronnego w procesie karnym' (2012) *WPP* no 4, www.gov.pl/attachment/28f11e86-66a6-4abf-abdd-f1a0f27a013a; EW Pływaczewski, 'Świadek koronny jako instrument zwalczania przestępczości zorganizowanej' (2010) *Prok i Pr* nos 7–8, 93–115; K Bajda, 'Przesłuchania świadka koronnego' (2009) *AUW* no LXXXI, 118–30; LK Paprzycki, 'Instytucja świadka koronnego i świadka *incognito* w świetle Konstytucji RP i Europejskiej konwencji praw człowieka' (2008) *Palestra* nos 5–6, ss 23 et seq; LK Paprzycki, 'Zeznania świadka anonimowego i świadka koronnego w rzetelnym procesie karnym', in EW Pływaczewski (ed), *Przestępczość zorganizowana. Świadek koronny. Terroryzm. W ujęciu praktycznym* (Kraków, Wydawnictwo Zakamycze, 2005).

[144] See further Daszkiewicz (n 6) 122–25; A Lach, in *System Prawa Karnego Procesowego* (n 26) 4862–70.

[145] See Lach (n 147) 4886–88.

(Article 5 section 1 WPA). The court shall issue a decision within fourteen days from the date of receipt of the motion (Article 5 section 5 WPA), specifying therein the time limit and manner of execution of the obligation to return the financial benefit derived from the crime and to redress the damage caused thereby. The public prosecutor is entitled to appeal against this decision (Article 5 section 6 WPA). If a decision is made to admit evidence from the testimony of a crown witness, the proceedings with respect to the person covered by the decision shall be excluded for separate proceedings and then suspended until the proceedings against the other perpetrators are legally concluded (Article 7 section1 WPA).

The perpetrator shall not be punished for the offence in which he/she participated and which he/she, as a crown witness, disclosed. The public prosecutor shall issue an order discontinuing the proceedings within fourteen days of the date on which the decision ending the proceeding against the other perpetrators becomes final. This decision is not subject to appeal (Article 9 UŚK).[146] If there is a threat to the life or health of a crown witness or a person close to him or her, a protection programme providing for personal protection or appropriate assistance may be initiated. This shall be decided by the prosecutor.[147]

The Expert and Their Opinion

An expert is a source of evidence, and his or her opinion is a means of evidence. An expert or experts shall be appointed if specialist knowledge is required to determine the circumstances of significant importance for the resolution of the case (Article 193 § 1 CPC).[148] Specialist knowledge is not known to the layperson, but is obtained through education in a specific field or by practising a specific profession, which allows experience to be gained in a specific field above the usual level in a given profession.[149] The possession of specialist knowledge by the pre-trial investigation authority or a member of the court panel does not relieve the obligation to seek an expert opinion. This view has long been established in case law and literature.[150]

If circumstances arise in the proceeding, the explanation of which requires specialist knowledge, the body directing the trial is obliged to consult an expert opinion. This is an obligation and not a right of the trial authority.[151]

[146] ibid 4890–92.

[147] Daszkiewicz (n 6) 131–32; Lach (n 147) 4909–10.

[148] Marszał (n 3) 410.

[149] Judgment of the Appellate Court in Wrocław, 28 January 2014, II AKa 430/13, Lex no 1467019; Judgment of the Appellate Court in Wrocław, 27 January 2017, II AKa 243/13, Lex no 2388075.

[150] J Berent, 'Biegły lekarz w postępowaniu sądowym', in R Olszewski (ed), *Artes serviunt vitae, sapientia imperat. Proces karny sensu largo. Rzeczywistość i wyzwania. Księga jubileuszowa Profesora Tomasza Grzegorczyka z okazji 70, urodzin* (Łódź, Wolters Kluwer, 2019) 125–31; R Kmiecik, 'Kwestia poczytalności oskarżonego w postępowaniu przyspieszonym' (2017) *Prok i Pr*, no 5, 5–12; B Kmieciak, *Biegły psychiatra jako strażnik praw pacjenta (in:) Biegły w polskim systemie prawnych", B. Lewandowski (ed)*, (Warsaw, Instytut na Rzecz Kultury Prawnej Ordo Iuris, 2016); M Pomper, 'Rola biegłych przy ustalaniu niepoczytalności – analiza porównawcza na tle regulacji innych państw', in D Gil (ed), *Dowód w procesie karnym w perspektywie porównawczej*, (2016) *WPWS* VI.

[151] See eg Supreme Court Judgment, 24 April 2017, SNO 10/17, Lex no 2311193.

The procedural authority addresses an expert or experts to give an opinion. Such an opinion may also be sought from a scientific or specialised institution (Article 193 § 2 CPC). It should be emphasized that evidence provided by a scientific or specialised institution has the same evidentiary value as evidence provided by an individual expert. If expert witnesses of various fields of specialisation are appointed, the procedural body appointing the expert witnesses shall decide whether they shall carry out their research jointly and submit one opinion or separate opinions (Article 193 § 3 CPC). Each person appointed as an expert shall be required to give an opinion to the best of his/her knowledge. Coercive measures may be taken against the expert witness in the event of unjustified evasion of discharging their duties (Article 287 § 1 CPC).

An expert witness shall take the pledge, with the proviso that a court expert witness (listed expert witness) shall make reference to their prior pledge given when they were appointed in such a capaciiy (Article 197 §§ 1 and 2 CPC).[152]

The prohibitions on evidence arising from the secrecy of classified information (with the clause top secret, secret, confidential, restricted) and professional secrecy shall apply accordingly to the expert. The decision on admitting evidence based on an expert opinion shall be made by the authority conducting the proceeding – in pre-trial proceedings by the prosecuting authority, and in the main proceedings by the court (Article 194 CPC). This issue is regulated differently with respect to the appointment of expert psychiatrists; namely, in pre-trial proceedings, the decision in this regard may be issued only by the public prosecutor, so if the proceedings are conducted by another law enforcement body, this body shall submit a motion to the public prosecutor in this regard. In jurisdictional proceedings, the decision to admit evidence from expert psychiatrists shall be issued by the court (Article 202 § 1 CPC). The decision on admitting expert evidence shall be issued upon motion of a party or ex officio. This decision is not subject to appeal, and the parties should be notified of its contents.

The time limit for filing the expert opinion is a time limit set by the procedural authority and may be extended by it.[153] The trial authority is obliged to see to it that the expert's opinion is delivered on time.

The appointed expert witness shall give his/her opinion on the basis of his/her knowledge. Depending on the instruction from the procedural body, an expert witness shall state their opinion orally or in writing (Article 200 § 1 CPC). The opinion of the expert may be subject to control. It may be verified by the parties and their representatives, by asking questions to the expert witness, by making their own submissions challenging the opinion and by pointing out contradictions, ambiguities and implausibility of the opinion.[154] This verification is also carried out by the trial body, and especially by the court in the course of the main trial. If an opinion issued is incomplete or unclear, contains a contradiction in itself, or opinions on the same matter are contradictory, attempts may be made to clarify any points of doubt by asking the expert questions or by calling the expert again for this purpose (Article 201 CPC).[155] If the ambiguities are not clarified,

[152] See Judgment of the Appellate Court in Katowice, 6 August 2003, II Akz 655/03, Lex no 84155.
[153] Kurowski (n 45) 788.
[154] But see Supreme Court Decision, 20 April 2017, II KK 79/17, Lex no 2281249; Supreme Court Decision, 14 January 2021, IV KK 515/00, Lex no 3177739.
[155] T Widła, in *System Prawa Karnego Procesowego* (n 26) 4965–68.

the trial authority may call another expert witness.[156] Another expert witness or expert witnesses may then be called until the circumstances requiring specialist knowledge have been fully clarified. In cases in which a particular circumstance requires clarification by means of expertise, this may be made only on the basis of an expert opinion that the trial body considers satisfactory. The body directing the trial may not reject all opinions on subjects that require specialised knowledge and decide on the basis of its own knowledge.[157]

Sometimes the applicable rules require that more than one expert be examined at the same time. For example, in order to deliver an opinion on the mental condition of the accused, at least two expert psychiatrists must be appointed (Article 202 § 1 CPC). The Code requires the absolute participation of at least two expert psychiatrists, and that they are to be persons who are not married to each other or in any other relationship capable of raising justified doubts as to their independence (Article 202 § 4 CPC). The general provisions on the exclusion of expert witnesses also apply to expert psychiatrists. The defendant is obliged to submit to a psychiatric examination (Article 74 § 2 point 2 CPC).

The basis for admitting evidence of a mental condition examination is the existence of doubts about the mental health of the accused. Such a situation arises when there are facts in the case that create the doubts indicated above in the authority in charge of the trial.[158] These facts may be facts obtained ex officio by the trial authority or presented by a party or their representative. Existing facts cannot be preliminarily reviewed by a single psychiatric expert witness to determine the basis for calling two expert witnesses, as this would circumvent the Code requirement. The need for a mental health examination is decided by the prosecutor or the court on its own, on the basis of its own observation; a defendant's description of his/her illness cannot therefore form the basis for an examination.[159] In doctrine and jurisprudence, however, it is accepted that the assessment of the mental processes of the accused (intent, motives, emotions accompanying the commission of a criminal act) is a matter for the court.

Upon a motion of psychiatrists, an expert witness or expert witnesses of other specialties are also appointed to participate in the preparation of an opinion (Article 202 § 2 CPC). To participate in the preparation an opinion on the state of mental condition of the accused, in the scope of sexual preference disorders, the court, and in the preparatory proceedings (investigation) the prosecutor, appoints an expert sexologist ex officio, ie without waiting for a possible motion from psychiatrists (Article 202 § 3 CPC). In the cases presented, the experts appointed to participate in the preparation of the opinion shall prepare it jointly with the psychiatric expert witnesses. The opinion of expert witnesses shall include statements on both the sanity of the accused at the time of committing the alleged act (*in tempore criminis*) as well as on the current mental condition of the accused, and in particular it shall contain an indication whether that

[156] ibid 4966.

[157] Supreme Court Judgment, 28 June 1932, II K 448/32, OSP 1932, vol 11, pos 491; Supreme Court Judgment, 12 October 1933, 3 K 902/33, OSP 1934, vol 13, pos 78.

[158] Supreme Court Judgment, 12 June 1997, IV KKN 82/97, Lex no 518152; Supreme Court Judgment, 17 June 1997, IV KKN 279/96, Lex no 518150.

[159] See eg Supreme Court Judgment, 11 February 2016, SDI 68/15, Lex no 2004211.

mental condition allows for the participation of the accused in the proceedings and for conducting defence in an independent and reasonable manner (Article 202 § 5 CPC).

The psychiatric examination of the accused may be combined with an observation in a health care establishment, if expert witnesses report such a necessity (Article 203 § 1 CPC). A decision in this regard may be made only by the court. In pre-trial proceedings, the court shall rule on the motion of the public prosecutor (Article 203 § 2 CPC). In principle, the observation in a health care establishment should not last longer than four weeks. However, upon motion of the authorities of the establishment, the court may extend this time limit for a limited period necessary for the completion of the observation. The total duration of the observation in a given case may not exceed eight weeks (Article 203 § 3 CPC). The decision ordering the examination of the defendant in a health care establishment and extending its duration may be appealed against and the court should examine it promptly (Article 203 § 4 CPC).[160]

The CPC does not regulate the admissibility of private, non-procedural opinions. Such opinions may be ordered by litigants and their representatives, who may use them, for example, when asking questions of an admitted expert witness.[161] For such an opinion, the procedural route is not closed, and its verification may take place by questioning its issuer at the trial. Admissibility of the use of such an opinion in a criminal trial results from Article 393 § 3 CPC, in which we read that any private documents prepared outside the criminal proceedings, in particular statements, publications, letters and notes, may be read aloud at the trial. However, this is not an opinion equivalent to an opinion was issued by an expert witness appointed by a procedural body.[162] The latter is evidence in the strict sense, while private opinion has no such value. A private opinion is usually used to verify the opinions of experts appointed by a procedural authority. Like any other evidence in proceedings, after its inclusion in case file, it is subject to free evaluation by the procedural body. As a result, it may constitute the basis for findings of fact in a criminal trial.

Document and its Content

In substantive criminal law, the term 'document' occurs in the context of the legal protection of those objects that take the form of a document. In procedural criminal law, the name is used to refer to a 'carrier' of information that may be relevant in a criminal trial, that is, to a source of evidence in written form.[163] In substantive criminal law, a document is any object or other recorded information carrier to which a specific right is attached, or which constitutes evidence of a right, a legal relationship or a circumstance having legal significance due to its contents (Article 115 § 14 CC).

[160] K Zgryzek, in *System Prawa Karnego Procesowego* (n 26) 5022–32.

[161] See further M Kusak, in *System Prawa Karnego Procesowego* (n 26) 5079–5104.

[162] See also R Ponikowski and J Zagrodnik, in J Skorupka, *Kodeks postępowania karnego. Komentarz* (Warsaw, CH Beck, 2021) 1135–36.

[163] Marszał (n 3) 417; W Daszkieiwcz, *Prawo karne procesowe. Zagadnienia ogólne* (Poznań, Branta, 2001) 143–44.

Unlike substantive criminal law, procedural criminal law does not contain a definition of a document, leaving its specification to the science and practice of criminal procedure. The components of a document in the procedural sense are: a graphic page or an electronic form, the content of the document, its foundation and the author of the document.[164]

An object, in order to be a document, must by its nature be in the form of a record. It should be drawn up by means of appropriate graphic signs or other equivalent record. In a broad sense, graphic symbols (equivalent of graphic signs) can take the form of a sketch, a plan or a recording which preserves sound or image (a tape, CD or DVD, a file which makes it possible to reproduce the content recorded in it, regardless of the electronic format used to create it, including a file stored in the 'cloud'). A document should express a human thought in the form of a declaration of will or knowledge, and thus should be a carrier of a specific intellectual content, for which reason a document becomes a source of evidence in a criminal process.[165]

A document in the procedural sense may be produced outside the trial and then introduced into the trial because of its content. Documents are also 'produced' within the criminal process, especially in the form of evidentiary records. An original document is a primary document and its duplicate is a derivative document. Documents are also divided into those that are issued for a pending trial and those that are issued as part of a particular trial.

The issue relates to the official note, ie whether the official note is a document with evidentiary value. The possibility of its preparation is provided for by the provisions of Article 143 § 2 CPC. Pursuant to these provisions, a record shall be made of other actions if so required by specific provisions, or if the person conducting the action finds it necessary. In other cases an official note shall suffice. A form of documenting official actions outside of a criminal trial is the official note.

Evidence from a document is conducted by reading, reproducing or revelation without reading them. The consent of the parties shall not be required for reading.

Physical Evidence and its Characteristics

Physical evidence deserves special attention in a criminal trial. This is due to the quality of the information it provides. Physical evidence is not subject to deformations in perception, memory and reproduction, as in the case of personal sources of evidence. For example, footprints at the scene and fingerprints on the murder weapon are more reliable material that can be subjected to direct examination.[166] The primary method of gathering physical evidence is inspection. Inspection consists in receiving impressions not only by sight, but also by using other senses, eg smell, touch (temperature, edge sharpness), taste, etc.

[164] Marszał (n 3) 417.
[165] See further Zgryzek (n 12) 416–17.
[166] Marszał (n 3) 422.

The provisions of the CPC make inspection of a place, person or thing the object of visual inspection.[167] Inspection of the place aims, on the one hand, to perceive the existing state of affairs at the crime scene and, on the other hand, to search for traces of the crime committed, including objects with the help of which the crime was committed.[168] The inspection may also be carried out with the participation of an expert or specialist, to whom most of the provisions on experts apply. A bodily inspection of persons is a way of gathering personal evidence when the body of a living person is inspected. The purpose is to find signs of a crime on a person's body. The accused is obliged to submit to bodily examination and other examinations not requiring violation of bodily integrity (Article 74 § 2 point 1 CPC). This obligation may be enforced (Article 74 § 3a CPC). As a rule, it is carried out by a physician. A witness may also be subjected to bodily inspection (Article 192 § 1 CPC).[169] A bodily inspection or examination which may offend the modesty of the person examined shall be conducted by a person of the same sex, unless this involves some special difficulties. A person of the opposite sex may be present during the examination only if necessary (Article 208 CPC). The visual inspection of the body is, like the inspection of the crime scene, more often carried out in the course of pre-trial proceedings than in the course of judicial proceedings, because the traces may be erased after a certain time.

A record is drawn up of the inspection, which is read out at the trial (Article 143 § 1 point 3 CPC).

Inspection of material object is carried out in order to determine their external or internal characteristics.[170] Any properties observed shall be stated in the inspection record.[171] Material objects suitable for this shall be attached to the case file or otherwise secured so that they remain in an unaltered state until the main trial. The procedural authority may demand the surrender of objects of evidentiary importance in the case (Article 217 § 1 CPC). A search may be conducted for this purpose (Article 219 CPC).

A document shall be visually inspected for its material substance (i.e. to verify that it is not forged or counterfeited). If a document is drawn up in electronic form, it may be reproduced.

The Procedural Experiment and its Results

In order to verify circumstances of essential relevance to the case, an experiment during the proceedings may be undertaken, or the course of events under examination may be reconstructed in whole or in part (Article 211 CPC). Such an experiment is an independent source of evidence, and the information obtained by means of it constitutes a means of proof.[172] It cannot be classified as physical evidence, because its essence comes down to the creation by the trial authority of some artificial situation existing at

[167] Further J Kasprzak, in M Kurowski, in *System Prawa Karnego Procesowego* (n 26) 5140–54.
[168] Grzegorczyk and Tylman (n 2) 524.
[169] Examination of the accused's or witness's body is discussed further in ch 4.
[170] Grzegorczyk and Tylman (n 2) 524–25.
[171] Kurowski (n 45) 821.
[172] See further Kurowski (n 170) 5228–30.

the time of the experiment. A trial experiment in the sense of an independent source of evidence is not experiments performed by an expert within the framework of an expert opinion,[173] which are intended to test certain relationships, structure, etc. Independent procedural experiments are more often used in pre-trial proceedings than in the main trial.

The essence of a procedural experiment boils down to the creation of an artificial situation, event or condition that is supposed to correspond to a certain version of reality based on the evidence. Its purpose is to test experimentally the course of certain events to ascertain whether such an event or its course was possible at all, and if so, how it occurred.[174] In this way, a certain version may be accepted as possible or information is obtained to support the belief in the reliability of an explanation or testimony, or that otherwise contradicts such explanation or testimony.[175]

Due to the fact that a reconstruction has a high suggestive power, it is necessary to ensure that the result obtained does not mislead the trial authorities or increase this error. For this reason, the conditions under which the experiment is conducted are important.[176] An expert witness or a specialist, summoned for this purpose by the procedural authority, may participate in performing a reconstruction and obtaining evidence therefrom. Conducting a procedural experiment may be combined with other evidentiary activities, eg with the questioning of the accused. A record shall be drawn up of the course of the reconstruction.

Inquiry within the Community

Inquiry within the community is evidence carried out as part of personal cognitive research. Conducting a community inquiry regarding the accused is ordered by the court, and in pre-trial proceedings (investigation), by the prosecutor. This inquiry is to be carried out with regard to the accused by a probation officer or another entity authorised on the basis of separate regulations, and in particularly justified cases, by the police. Inquiry within the community is ordered (by decision) should a need arise, and in particular when it is necessary to determine data related to the personal characteristics and conditions, as well as the way of life, of the accused, up to the present (Article 214 § 1 CPC).

The order to make an inquiry within the community may be compulsory of optional. A community inquiry is compulsory in cases related to felonies and with regard to an accused who, at the time of committing the act, was under twenty-one years of age if charged with an offence against life (Article 214 § 2 CPC). Optional inquiry within the community is taken when there is such need. A community inquiry may not be carried out in relation to an accused who does not have a permanent place of residence in the country (Article 214 § 3 CPC).

[173] Marszał (n 3) 425; Kurowski (n 170) 5236–37.

[174] Judgment of the Appellate Court in Cracow, 12 April 2006, II AKa 12/06, OSA 2008, no 5, pos 23; Judgment of the Appellate Court in Cracow, 9 May 2018, II AKa 73/18, Lex no 26114576.

[175] Kurowski (n 170) 5228–31.

[176] Judgment of the Appellate Court in Gdańsk, 29 December 2015, II AKa 111/15, Lex no 2034123.

Data of the persons who provide information as part of a community inquiry shall be disclosed by the person carrying out the inquiry only upon the request of the court, and during the investigation, only upon the request of the public prosecutor (Article 214 § 5 CPC). Persons who provide information during a community inquiry may, when necessary, be questioned in the capacity of witnesses (Article 214 § 6 CPC), as may be the persons who conducted the inquiry (Article 216 CPC).

Evidence obtained from an inquiry within the community should be treated like other evidence. It is examined by the right entity authorised by the court or public prosecutor, having jurisdiction over an accused according to his permanent place of residence. Outcomes of a community inquiry shall in particular include information concerning the accused's behaviour, his environmental conditions, including family, school or professional environment, and also information about the material conditions and income sources of the accused. It should also include information concerning the health condition of the accused, as well as concerning the abuse of alcohol, drugs, substitutes or psychotropic substances by him. It should also include the personal observations and conclusions of the person conducting the inquiry. Persons carrying out the inquiry should keep in secret all the circumstances concerning conducting an inquiry within the community.

To a person that carried out an inquiry within community, provisions on judge's disqualification shall be applied.

8

Appeal Measures

System of Appeal Measures

The regulation of the course of criminal proceedings at the pre-trial stage and at the trial stage before the court of first instance should provide optimal conditions for making the correct final decision on the issue of criminal responsibility of a particular person both in terms of facts and applicable legal provisions. However, experience teaches that even with the greatest care in the formulation of the applicable laws and in their application by the trial authorities, there are cases of erroneous procedural decisions.[1] This can be observed also in relation to rulings and orders on incidental issues, which come to light and are subject to resolution within the framework of proceedings on the fundamental issue (the issue of criminal liability of a specific person). Therefore, the modern criminal trial, in the name of guaranteeing the correctness of decisions, must ensure the control of procedural decisions.[2] The system of this control can be more or less developed, eg it can be based on distinguishing two or three control instances. In Polish law the core of this system is the review of rulings based on appeal measures.[3] The scheme of this control is subject to the two-instance rule.[4] It is worth noting that as far as proceedings before the courts are concerned, two instances constitute the minimum guarantee standard, laid down in Article 176(2) of the Constitution of the Republic of Poland, which is fully applicable to rulings on the merits.[5]

According to the two-instance rule, first-instance rulings, whether made by a court or by another authority (eg the prosecutor), may in principle be subject to ordinary appellate review, both in fact and in law, by way of an appeal or a complaint. In principle,

[1] K Marszał and J Zagrodnik, 'Postępowanie odwoławcze' in J Zagrodnik (ed), *Proces karny* (Warsaw, Wolters Kluwer, 2021) 697.

[2] J Wolski, 'Epistemologiczne aspekty środków odwoławczych' in A Gaberle and S Waltoś (eds), *Środki zaskarżenia w procesie karnym. Księga pamiątkowa ku czci Profesora Zbigniewa Dody* (Zakamycze, Wolters Kluwer, 2000) 80; R Kmiecik, 'Nowe skargi "nadzwyczajne" w systemie karnoprocesowych środków zaskarżenia – z problematyki przyzwoitości prawa' in D Szumiło-Kulczycka (ed), *W pogoni za rzetelnym procesem karnym. Księga dedykowana Profesorowi Stanisławowi Waltosiowi* (Warsaw, Wolters Kluwer, 2022) 613–15.

[3] See further A Kaftal, *System środków odwoławczych (rozważania modelowe)* (Warsaw, Państwowe Wydawnictwo Naukowe, 1972); C Kulesza, 'Apelacja po nowelizacji – rozważania modelowe' in A Lach (ed) *Postępowanie karne po nowelizacji z dnia 11 marca 2016 r* (Warsaw, Wolters Kluwer, 2017) 243 et seq.

[4] P Wiliński, *Proces karny w świetle Konstytucji* (Warsaw, Wolters Kluwer, 2011) 154–66.

[5] Supreme Court Judgment, 28 June 2018, I KZP 3/18.

the rule is subject to certain exceptions *in plus* and *in minus*, which will be further illustrated below. Rulings rendered as a result of ordinary appellate control may sometimes be subjected to further review, but this is exceptional in nature and remains, as it were, outside the instance system. The uniqueness of this extraordinary control is expressed in the significant limitation of its material scope to certain categories of rulings, on the one hand, and the type of defects, on the other hand, through the prism of which it is carried out. Such control is triggered by extraordinary appeals measures. Based on this preliminary information, it is possible to distinguish in the Polish system of appeal control:

1. appeal measures that initiate the control of decisions that do not have the characteristics of finality (final and binding);[6] this group includes:
   - appeal, enabling control of judgments (Articles 444 et seq CPC);
   - complaints, which allow the review of decision (under Articles 459 and 302 § 1 CPC), orders (Articles 466 § 1 and 302 § 1 CPC) and other procedural acts (Articles 467 § 1, 246 § 1 and 302 § 2 CPC), as well as the review of inaction on the part of an authority (Article 306 § 3 CPC) and, occasionally, certain settlements contained in a judgment (Article 626 § 3 CPC);
2. extraordinary remedies, which mostly serve to review the final and binding court ruling concluding proceedings; the group of these remedies consists of:
   - cassation (Articles 518 et seq);
   - complaints against appellate court judgments (Article 539a–f CPC);[7]
   - renewal of court proceedings concluded by a final ruling (Articles 540 et seq CPC).[8]

These remedies will be analysed in more detail in the following sections.

Extending the research perspective for a moment, it should be noted that in addition to the appeal measures, the Polish system of decisions and control orders provides for the following remedies:

1. objections and quasi-objections, which are characterised by the fact that their filing causes the ruling challenged by them to lose its legal force *ex lege*, and the case then

[6] Incidentally, it may be recalled that this attribute means that the rulings in question are not open to challenge by ordinary means of appeal, eg because the course of the proceedings has been exhausted, the court of appeal has given judgment or the time limit for appealing against the decision of the authority at first instance has expired for each person entitled to lodge an appeal against it.

[7] See further J Zagrodnik, 'Instytucja skargi na wyrok sądu odwoławczego (rozdział 55a k.p.k.) – zarys problematyki' in T Grzegorczyk and R Olszewski (eds), *Verba volant, scripta manent. Proces karny, prawo karne skarbowe i prawo wykroczeń po zmianach z lat 2015–2016. Księga pamiątkowa poświęcona Profesor Monice Zbrojewskiej* (Warsaw, Wolters Kluwer, 2016) 519–35.

[8] An extraordinary measure, but regulated outside the CPC, is the extraordinary complaint provided for in the Act on the Supreme Court (Art 89–95 SCA). The structure of this complaint is controversial, mainly because it constitutes another means of undermining the stability of final and binding rulings. In the criminal law area, it can be ordered against a final ruling of the court closing the case, if it cannot be annulled or modified by other extraordinary remedies, ie by way of the aforementioned cassation procedure or renewal of the procedure ended by the final decision of the court (Art 89 § 1 SCA). Within the scope not regulated in the Act on the Supreme Court, the provisions of the CPC concerning cassation shall apply to the extraordinary complaint in criminal matters and the proceedings initiated by lodging such complaint (Art 95 § 2 SCA).

proceeds from the beginning, as a rule, before the authority that issued the ruling (cassation and lack of devolution); this group includes, among others:[9]

- objection to an injunctive judgment (Article 506 § 1 CPC);
- objections to orders and instructions of a court clerk (Article 93a § 3 CPC);

2. contest against orders of the presiding judge made during the trial (Article 373 CPC); these orders may be contested before the adjudicative panel, unless the rulings are issued by one judge.

Features of Appeal Measures

The basic feature of all appeal measures is that they require filing a complaint, which means that the review conducted on the basis of them is triggered on demand, ie by filing an appropriate appeal complaint.[10] The only exception in this regard concerns the renewal of court proceedings concluded by a final ruling which may be carried out ex officio in the event of the disclosure of absolute grounds for appeal specifically enumerated in Article 439 § 1 CPC (see below).

The second feature of the analysed measures is the devolutive effect.[11] This consists in the fact that filing an appeal measure causes the case to be transferred for examination to a higher-instance authority. Devolutive effect has an absolute dimension: filing a permissible appeal measure always entails the necessity to move the case to the next tier of court hierarchy for examination. This is the case, for example, in appeals, cassation or complaints against appellate court judgments. It has a relative character when the law allows the appeal measure to be taken into consideration in the instance in which the contested decision was issued. Such a possibility exists in relation to a complaint. In addition, the so-called horizontal devolutive effect can be distinguished, by which the appeal measure is subject to examination at the same level at which the contested decision was made, by another equivalent composition of a specific court – equivalent appellate court panel (Article 426 § 2 CPC).

Another feature is the suspensive effect.[12] This has effects on two planes, namely the finality of the contested decision and its enforceability (its entering into effect). It boils down to the fact that as a result of lodging an appeal measure, the contested decision does not acquire the characteristic of finality and is not subject to execution. Suspension of finality is absolute in the case of lodging an ordinary appeal measure, because in any case it excludes the possibility of the contested decision becoming final. The suspensive effect on this plane does not apply to extraordinary appeal measures, for which the finality of the rulings is a condition for their admissibility. Suspension of enforcement of the contested ruling (the second plane of the suspensive effect) is absolute in the case

[9] K Marszał, *Przebieg procesu karnego. Postępowanie odwoławcze* (Katowice, Uniwersytet Śląski, 1979) 10–11.

[10] A Murzynowski, *Istota i zasady procesu karnego* (Warsaw, Wydawnictwo PWN, 1994) 170; I Nowikowski, *Odwołalność czynności procesowych stron w polskim procesie karnym* (Lublin, Wydawnictwo Uniwersytetu Marii Curie-Skłodowskiej, 2001) 165.

[11] Marszał and Zagrodnik (n 1) 700.

[12] Marszał (n 9) 12.

of appeals. With respect to other appeal measures it is – with certain exceptions[13] – relative, because the suspension of enforcement of the ruling may be effected by a decision of the authority recognising the appeal measure. Such an effect is not produced by the mere filing of those measures.

The last characteristic distinguishing the appeal measures is reformatory, which means that the filing of an appeal triggers substantive control of a ruling, as a result of which the trial authority may not only reverse or sustain contested ruling, but most often also amend it.[14]

Ordinary Appeal Measures

General Rules

The CPC uses the collective term 'appeal measures' to describe appeals and complaints. General provisions in Chapter 48 of the CPC (Articles 425–443a CPC) are devoted to these two means of appeal measures.[15] These provisions normalise the institutions common to both of these types of appeal measures, the most important points of which are illustrated further in this section. The next two chapters of the CPC contain solutions specific to each of these measures separately.

Admissibility of the Appeal Measure

The issue of the admissibility of an appeal measure is closely related to the aforementioned two-instance principle. This principle is reflected in Article 425 § 1 CPC, according to which an ordinary appeal measure is available against rulings rendered in the first instance. There are a number of exceptions to this. Only one exception applies to judgments. It relates to an injunctive judgment and results from the possibility of challenging it only by means of an objection (*argumentum ex* Article 507 CPC).[16] This excludes the possibility of filing an appeal against such a judgment. More exceptions to the two-instance rule are connected with the appeal measure in the form of a complaint. They are not uniform in nature. It can be said that they go in two opposite directions,[17] namely:

1. Extension of the possibility of lodging a complaint by its adoption in relation to certain decisions issued in the second instance. This applies, for example,

[13] For example, the penalties for Breach of Order filing of a complaint shall stay the execution of a decision on detention (Art 290 § 3 CPC).

[14] M Rogacka-Rzewnicka, 'O wyższości apelacji nad rewizją. Rozważania o modelach postępowania odwoławczego w systemie prawa kontynentalnego w aspekcie historyczno-komparatystycznym' (2018) 23(1) *BSP* 139 et seq.

[15] S. Zabłocki, *Postępowanie odwoławcze w nowym kodeksie postępowania karnego* (Warsaw, Ministerstwo Sprawiedliwości, Departament Kadr i Szkolenia, 1997) 16.

[16] Marszał and Zagrodnik (n 1) 705.

[17] Marszał (n 9) 15–17.

to a decision on the application of provisional detention issued as a result of a complaint,[18] as well as to a decision issued during appellate proceedings on the conduct of observation, on the application of a precautionary measure, on the imposition of a disciplinary sanction, on the staying of proceedings, and relating to the costs of proceedings on which an appellate court adjudicated for the first time (Article 426 § 2 CPC). The extension also consists in the admissibility of lodging a complaint against decisions that are not rulings, taking the form of an order, as well as against actions that are not procedural decisions, or even against the absence of actions.

2. Limitation of the possibility to lodge a complaint with respect to decisions by binding it to certain categories of rulings taking this form. According to Article 459 §§ 1 and 2 CPC, complaints may be brought against the decisions which preclude the rendering of a judgment (unless otherwise provided in the CPC), against decisions with respect to a preventive measure, and against other decisions in cases prescribed under the CPC.

The CPC allows for the possibility of challenging the whole or part of a decision (Article 425 § 2, first sentence). Appealing in its entirety means that all settlements of the ruling contained therein are within its scope. An incomplete scope of the appeal measure may result from its subjective, objective or objective–subjective limitation, eg to specific defendants or specific acts.[19] Appeals may be brought against settlement of the ruling on conviction or acquittal of the accused, ie resolution relating to his or her criminal liability, as well as against other settlements of the ruling, eg on the discontinuance of proceedings. It is also permissible to appeal against lack of a specific decision (Article 425 § 2, second sentence CPC).[20] This lack constitutes a normatively created substrate of the appeal measure.[21] It can only be a lack of resolve on an issue that cannot be the subject of proceedings on its own, eg a lack of resolve on the issue of the obligation to repair damages. The party may agree with the decision, while having significant objections to the statement of reasons itself. The answer to this is the possibility of appealing against the grounds of the ruling itself (Article 425 § 2, third sentence CPC), but this can only be done if no settlements of the ruling are contested.[22]

Right to Appeals Measures: Withdrawal of Appeals Measures

The right to appeal lies primarily with the parties (*argumentum ex* Article 425 § 1 CPC). An injured person who does not have the status of a party may appeal against a

[18] See further Constitutional Tribunal Decision, 9 November 2009, S 7/09, OTK-A 2009, no 10, pos 154.
[19] P Hofmański and S Waltoś, *Proces karny. Zarys systemu* (Warsaw, 2016) 553.
[20] See D Świecki in D Świecki (ed), *Kodeks postępowania karnego. Komentarz* (Warsaw, Wolters Kluwer, 2021) vol II, 33.
[21] Supreme Court Resolution, 28 October 2015, I KZP 21/14, OSNKW 2016/1, pos 1.
[22] M Klejnowska, *Ograniczenia sądu odwoławczego orzekającego w sprawie karnej po wniesieniu środka zaskarżenia* (Rzeszów, Wydawnictwo Uniwersytetu Rzeszowskiego, 2008) 553.

judgment conditionally discontinuing proceedings that was issued in a session (Article 444 § 1 CPC). The circle of persons entitled to lodge a complaint is somewhat broader. In addition to the parties, any person directly concerned by the decision may lodge a complaint, unless otherwise provided in the Act (Article 459 § 3 CPC). Such a person is, for example, a person who is not a party at whose place the search was conducted. Pursuant to specific provisions, the right to lodge an appeal measure is also vested in the obliged entity who is affected by the ruling on a motion calling for adjudication with regard to the obligation to return a material benefit or its equivalent to the entitled entity or adjudication of forfeiture of a benefit or its equivalent to the State Treasury (Article 422 § 1a CCP) and the owner of an enterprise at risk of forfeiture (Article 422 § 1 in conjunction with Article 91b CCP). The right to lodge an appeal measure also applies to the procedural representatives of the aforementioned participants in the proceedings, ie their defence counsel and attorneys.[23]

A subject generally entitled to lodge an appeal measure *in concerto* may exercise this right if there is a grievance (*gravamen*) on his/her part resulting from the ruling rendered. This is provided for in the first sentence of Article 425 § 3 CCP, according to which the appealing party may appeal against the resolutions or findings only if these are prejudicial to their rights or interests.[24] The violation of rights or harm to interests that justifies the existence of *gravamen* on the part of the appealing party should not be considered only in the sphere of criminal law. It refers – in the absence of restrictions in this regard in the wording of the cited provision – to the entire functioning of the appealing party in social life, and therefore also to the sphere of civil law, administrative law, and the sphere of economic and social relations.[25] Taking this into account, and taking into account the previously established admissibility of a challenge to the statement of reasons itself, it should be stated that *gravamen* may result from the findings contained in this statement of reasons damaging, for example, to the accused at the level of social relations in relation to his position in society. The requirement of the existence of *gravamen* on the part of the complainant is closely related to the admissibility of the appeal measure, because it causes its limitation.[26] It does not apply to the public

[23] R Ponikowski and J Zagrodnik in J Skorupka (ed), *Kodeks postępowania karnego. Komentarz* (Warsaw, CH Beck, 2019) 1191.

[24] K Marszał, 'Gravamen w postępowaniu odwoławczym w sprawach karnych' in A Przyborowska-Klimczak and A Taracha (eds), *Iudicium et Scientia. Księga jubileuszowa Profesora Romualda Kmiecika* (Warsaw, Wolters Kluwer, 2011) 447–49.

[25] Supreme Court Decision, 19 May 2011, I KZP 2/11, OSNKW 2016, pos 47; Z Doda, *Zażalenie w procesie karnym* (Warsaw, Wydawnictwo Prawnicze, 1985) 141–42; Marszał (n 24) 450–51.

[26] Although the appealing party is not required to demonstrate the existence of gravamen, the hypothesis of the existence of gravamen based on the appealing party's subjective belief must be justified in the light of the circumstances connected with the content of the contested ruling and the content of the appeal measure assessed in the light of the procedural function within the framework of which the complainant takes procedural actions (prosecution, defence). See, for exmple, the judgment of the Supreme Court of 19 March 1997, IV CCN 326/96, OSNKW 1997, nos 7–8, item 64; J Zagrodnik, *Obrońca i pełnomocnik w procesie karnym i karnym skarbowym* (Warsaw, Wolters Kluwer, 2020) 463–64. Negative verification of this hypothesis at the preliminary stage of the appeal proceedings results in refusal to accept the appeal measure (Art 429 § 1 CPC) or leaving it without consideration at the appeal instance (Art 430 § 1 CPC). It may be said that, apart from the situations in which such a review is possible at the initial stage of the appeal proceedings, there is a presumption of gravamen on the part of the appealing party in the subsequent proceedings until the appeal has been examined on the merits.

prosecution counsel (Article 425 § 3, second sentence CPC), who shall also be entitled, contrary to the fundamental direction of his/her procedural activity, to file appeal measures for the benefit of the accused (Article 425 § 4 CPC).

The reverse of the right to file an appeal measure is the possibility to withdraw it. It is provided for in Article 431 § 1 CPC and is a manifestation of the adversarial principle.[27] An effective withdrawal of an appeal measure may take place until an irreversible state arises, ie a ruling is issued by the appellate court following the examination of the measure filed. The principle is that the appeal measure can be withdrawn by the person who filed it. There are exceptions to this rule going in two directions. First, an appeal measure filed for the benefit of the accused shall not be withdrawn without their consent (Article 431 § 3 CPC). This serves to protect the interests of the accused, who, knowing that an appeal measure has been filed in his or her favour, could choose not to file his or her own appeal measure. Thus, by withdrawing such a measure, the accused cannot be surprised. The consent expressed by the accused to withdraw the appeal should be so clear that there can be no doubt that the accused has expressed a wish to that effect.[28] Second, the accused may withdraw an appeal measure for their benefit, unless it has been filed by the public prosecution counsel or an event of compulsory defence, described in Article 79, has occurred (Article 431 § 2 CPC).[29]

A withdrawn appeal does not lose its legal force. In principle, such a measure shall be left unheard (Article 432 *in principio* CPC).[30] This does not happen when one of the grounds of appeal provided for in Articles 439 or 440 is revealed, which are connected with the right of the appellate court to rule ex officio regardless of the limits of the appeal and the charges raised.[31] The aim of this solution is to reverse, or alternatively amend, the decision affected by the most serious defects referred to in the aforementioned provisions without the need to launch extraordinary appeals measures.

Formal Requirements for the Appeal Measure

The appeal measure must be made in writing (Article 428 § 1 CPC). The written form means that it must comply with the general conditions for a pleading set out in Article 119 § 1 CPC (see chapter two).[32] Among the specific requirements of the appeal measure, concerning its content structure, are the indication of the contested decision or finding, ie the determination of the scope of the appeal, and the indication by the appellant of what he or she demand (Article 427 § 1 CPC), ie the formulation of the appeal motions. The law does not impose a general obligation on the appellant to specify the indication of the objections raised against the ruling. This is related to the desire to

[27] B Bieńkowska, 'Dyspozycyjność stron w procesie karnym na tle zasady kontradyktoryjności' (1996) *PS* 6, 34 et seq.

[28] Supreme Court Decision, 26 June 1973, V KRN 163/73, OSNKW 1873, no 12, pos 169; Supreme Court Decision, 04 March 1981, V KRN 32/81, OSPiKA 1981, no 11, pos 205.

[29] Supreme Court Judgment, 19 June 1987, IV KR 197/87, OSNKW 1987, nos 11–12, pos 109.

[30] Supreme Court Decision, 25 April 1975, IV KRN 25/75, OSNPG 1975, no 9, pos 87.

[31] Supreme Court Decision, 16 October 2002, IV KKN 161/99, Lex no 74389.

[32] Marszał (n 9) 18.

formalise the actions, which are often carried out by subjects without adequate legal training. The appeal measure, however, must contain an indication of the objections raised against the decision and a statement of reasons, if it comes from a professional subject, ie a public prosecutor, defence counsel or attorney (Article 427 § 2 CPC).[33]

Objections raised against the decision consist of indications of violations in the contested ruling or in the procedure before court of first instance. The CPC does not specify the categories of violations that may be raised in an appeal measure.[34] Instead, these may be established on the basis of the content of Article 438 CPC, addressed to the appellate court and specifying the types of violations, the establishment of which entails modification or reversal of the ruling in the appellate instance.[35] In order for it to be effective, the appellant who contests a ruling should indicate in the appeal measure such violations that cause the effect specified in Article 438 CPC.[36] There are, however, certain limitations in indication of the objections against a ruling. They are addressed to the appellants and consist in excluding the possibility of raising general or particular types of violations in the appeal measures. Since they basically concern the appeal, they are presented in the section devoted to this measure.

In addition to defining the scope of the appeal measure, formulating appeal motions and raising objections against ruling, the appellant may also, as a rule, indicate new facts or evidence in the appeal measure (Article 427 § 3 CPC). In principle, this power is not available to the appellant if he or she could have invoked a specific fact or evidence in the proceedings before the court of first instance (*argumentum a contrario ex* Article 427 § 3 CCP). Although this exclusion of the right to raise new facts or evidence, being a manifestation of evidentiary preclusion, sounds categorical, this is not the case, due to Article 452 § 2 paragraph 3 CPC, which precludes rejecting a motion for evidence in the appellate instance only on the basis that it concerns evidence or facts that could have been, respectively, referred to or indicated before the court of first instance, if the circumstance that is to be proven, within the limits of the appellate court's examination of the case, is of material importance to the determination whether a prohibited act was committed, whether it constitutes a criminal offence and what criminal offence, whether the prohibited act was committed under the conditions referred to in Articles 64 or 65 CC or whether there are grounds for ordering a stay in a psychiatric hospital pursuant to Article 93g CC (these are facts and evidence concerning the perpetration and guilt of the accused).

In addition to the formal requirements for the appeal measure relating to its content, these requirements include the obligation to attach duplicates to this measure.[37] An appropriate number of duplicates for the opposing parties shall be enclosed with an appeal; one duplicate shall be enclosed additionally with an appeal filed with an appellate court (Article 446 § 2 CPC). In the case of a complaint, the obligation to enclose

[33] K Marszał, 'Problem granic środka odwoławczego w polskim procesie karnym' (1975) *PPK* no 1, 72; Zabłocki (n 15) 28.

[34] Marszał (n 9) 18.

[35] S Kalinowski, *Polski proces karny* (Warsaw, Państwowe Wydawnictwo Naukowe, 1971) 484.

[36] M Cieślak, 'Podstawowe pojęcia dotyczące rewizji według k.p.k.' in S Waltoś (ed), *Dzieła wybrane*, vol IV: *Prawo karne procesowe. Artykuły, studia i inne prace* (Cracow, Wydawnictwo Uniwersytetu Jagiellońskiego, 2011) 148.

[37] D Święcki, *Postępowanie odwoławcze w sprawach karnych* (Warsaw, Wolters Kluwer, 2018) 299–300.

copies with it is provided for in relation to a challenge to a decision concluding proceedings. In such cases, the complaint shall be accompanied by an appropriate number of duplicates for the persons whom the challenged decision directly concerns (Article 461 § 1 CPC).

At this point, it is also worth noting that in the case of an appeal against a judgment of the regional court that is not filed by the public prosecutor the compulsory representation by a lawyer applies (Article 446 § 1 CPC).[38] It must therefore be drawn up and signed by a solicitor, a legal counsel or a counsel of the General Prosecutor to the Republic of Poland.[39]

Inadmissibility of an Appeal Measure and Lack of Entitlement or Violation of a Time Limit for Lodging it; Verification of Formal Requirements for an Appeal

The appeal measure shall be verified in terms of its admissibility, submission by the authorised person and within the applicable time limit. Such verification shall be performed in the first instance by the president of the court of the first instance (Article 429 § 1 CPC). If the result is negative, he/she issues an order refusing to accept the appeal measure. A determination only in the court of appeal that an appeal measure filed after the applicable time limit, filed by an unauthorised person, or one inadmissible under the CPC, results in the court of appeal issuing a decision to leave the appeal measure filed unheard.[40] Such a decision is also made when this court determines that the appeal measure has been admitted as a result of an improper reinstatement of the time limit (Article 430 § 1 CPC).

These decisions may also be a consequence of a finding by the court president or the appellate court that there are defects in the implementation of predefined formal requirements of the appeal measure, concerning its content or the obligation to have it drawn up and signed by a solicitor or legal adviser.[41] However, if such defects are resovable, the competent authority shall first request the appellant to remedy them within seven days on pain of the appeal measure being ineffective (Article 120 § 1 CPC). If the defect is corrected within the prescribed time limit, the appeals measure shall take effect from the day on which it is filed. If the defect is not corrected within the prescribed time limit, the appeals measure shall be considered null and void, and the person filing it shall be advised thereof upon being served the summons.

[38] Supreme Court Decision, 30 September 1996 r, V KZ 47/96, OSNKW 1996, nos 11–12, pos 88.

[39] See further B Nita-Światłowska, 'Przymus adwokacko-radcowski przy wnoszeniu środków zaskarżenia w postępowaniu karnym (cz I)' (2017) *Pal* nos 1–2, 39–51; B Nita-Światłowska, 'Przymus adwokacko-radcowski przy wnoszeniu środków zaskarżenia w postępowaniu karnym (cz II)' (2017) *Pal* no 3, 61–68; P Misztal, *Przymus adwokacko-radcowski w polskim procesie karnym* (Warsaw, Wolters Kluwer, 2020) 203–50.

[40] Supreme Court Decision 18 May 2022, II DIZ 45/21, Lex no 3361578.

[41] If a formal defect in an appeal consists in the failure to attach to it a sufficient number of copies for the opposing parties, it should be remedied by means of an informal request for remedy.

An order to refuse to accept an appeal and a decision to leave it unheard shall be subject to appeal.[42] An exception to this is made in cases where the appeal has been left unheard by the Supreme Court (Articles 429 § 2 and 430 § 2 CPC).

In order to avoid ambiguity, it is worth emphasising that it is not a ground for refusal to accept an appeal measure or leave it unheard if it is filed by an entitled person within the time limit, but to the wrong authority. The competent authority is the authority that issued the appealed ruling, because the appeal is filed through it to the appellate authority (Article 428 § 1 CPC). Despite its erroneous filing to another authority, prior to the lapse of the time limit, it shall be treated as one properly filed (Article 125 CPC).[43] The appeal measure shall then be transferred to the competent authority without delay.

Scope of Appellate Review

The question of scope is one of the fundamental issues of appellate review. It involves determining whether the review is total, ie carried out both legally and factually over the entire ruling because of the appeal measure lodged, or whether it is more narrowly defined because it is carried out essentially through the prism of the objections indicated in the appeal measure. The CPC regulates this issue in Article 433 § 1 CCP, according to which the appellate court shall hear the case within the limits of the complaint, and where objections raised against the decision are indicated in the appellate measure, also within the limits of the objections raised, taking into account the contents of Articles 447 § 1 to 447 § 3 (see further), and, more widely, in the cases indicated in Articles 435, 439 § 1, 440 and 455.[44] Cases of ex officio review of appeals measure beyond the limits of the complaint and objections against the ruling raised, regulated in the four provisions mentioned above, form the group of absolute reasons of appeal. On the basis of the cited provision, one may consequently conclude that the scope of appellate control in the Polish criminal trial is determined by two factors:

1. the limits of the complaints and the limits of the objections raised against the decision (if such objection were raised in the appeal), ie the limits of the appellate control set by the appellant in the appeal measure; and
2. absolute reasons of appeal, which include statutorily defined cases of appellate control beyond its limits indicated in the appeal measure.[45]

Neither the motions for appeal nor the direction of the appeal measure are determinants of the scope of appellate review. Its latter influences the scope of adjudication in the appeal instance.[46]

[42] Supreme Court Decision 15 March 2022, II KZ 3/22, Lex no 3361477.
[43] Supreme Court Decision 27 April 2011, III KZ 16/11, OSNwSK 2011, no 1, pos 882.
[44] Święcki (n 37) 88.
[45] K Marszał and J Zagrodnik in J Zagrodnik (ed) *Proces karny* (Warsaw, Wolters Kluwer, 2021) 721.
[46] Marszał and Zagrodnik (n 1) 723.

Limits of Appellate Control

The limits of appellate control are a fundamental factor determining the scope of examination (control) of a case in the appellate instance. This is best evidenced by the content of Article 433 § 1 CPC, quoted above.[47] It can be said that this provision expresses the principle of the appellate court's examination of the case within the limits of appellate control.[48] For the sake of clarity, it is worth emphasising that these limits are determined by two components of the appeal measure, namely the limits of the complaint and limits of the objections.[49] The limits of the complaint determines the research plane, within which the control of the contested ruling is conducted. In turn, the objection against the decision constitute a *sui generis* prism through which the appellate court controls the contested decision on the plane determined by the limits of the complaint.

The limits of the complaint is a constant determinant of the limits of appellate control, since it must be specified in each appeal. The limits of the complaint is determined by those components of the ruling of the court of first instance against which the appeal measure is directed.[50] As has already been established, the appellant may appeal against the whole or parts of the ruling, ie its individual decisions (settlements of decision or judgment), as well as the lack of a particular decision (settlement of decision or judgment) or the very statement of reasons of the ruling (Article 425 § 2 CPC). In the case of an appeal, the limit of the complaint is extended by law due to the operation of the irrebuttable legal presumptions provided for in Article 447 §§ 1–3 CPC.[51] From these provisions it follows, firstly, that an appeal as to the determination of guilt shall be considered to be directed against the judgment as a whole (Article 447 § 1 CPC); secondly, that an appeal as to the determination of penalty shall be considered to be directed against the imposition of penalty or criminal measures as a whole (Article 447 § 2 CPC);[52] and thirdly, that an appeal concerning a criminal measure, a compensation measure or forfeiture shall be considered as directed against the entire decision on, as appropriate, the criminal measures, compensation measures or forfeiture (Article 447 § 3 CPC).[53] The presumptions presented are aimed at guaranteeing internal coherence in the scope of all decisions composing the content of the ruling (settlements of decision

[47] Supreme Court Decision 21 April 2022, III KK 125/22, Lex no 3431007.

[48] K Marszał, 'Znaczenie granic zaskarżenia i podniesionych zarzutów w postępowaniu odwoławczym w sprawach karnych' (2004) *PPK* no 25, 107.

[49] K Marszał, 'Zasadnicze składniki granic środka odwoławczego' in A Gaberle and S Waltoś (eds), *Środki zaskarżenia w procesie karnym: księga pamiątkowa ku czci prof. Zbigniewa Dody* (Zakamycze, Kantor Wydawniczy Zakamycze, 2000) 52; Supreme Court Decision 12 April 2018, II KK 422/17, OSNKW 2019, no 3, pos 14.

[50] Marszał (n 33) 71.

[51] W Kociubiński, 'Orzekanie przez sąd odwoławczy na niekorzyść oskarżonego w granicach zaskarżenia i zarzutów podniesionych w środku odwoławczym. Glosa do postanowienia Sądu Najwyższego z dnia 12 kwietnia 2018 r., II KK 422/17' (2020) OSP no 4, 104, 105.

[52] Supreme Court Judgment, 20 September 1977, VI KRN 209/77, OSNKW 1978, nos 4–5, pos 54.

[53] M. Klejnowska and M Trybus, 'Zarzut wadliwości orzeczonej kary jako przesłanka odwoławcza – aspekty karno materialne i karnoprocesowe' in Z Ćwiąkalski and G Artymiak (eds), *Współzależność prawa karnego materialnego i procesowego* (Warsaw, Wolters Kluwer, 2009) 631–31.

or judgment), due to the significance of the contested settlement for other settlement contained in the appealed ruling.

The objections against the decision, which are the assertions of violations made in the appeal complaint, are a variable determinant of the limits of appellate control, because they determine the scope of the examination of the case in the appellate instance only if they are raised in the appeal measure. In any case, they determine the limits of appellate control if the appeal measure comes from a professional entity, ie a public prosecutor, defence counsel or attorney, as they are under the obligation to indicate objection against the ruling (Article 427 § 2 CPC). No such obligation is imposed on another appellant, eg the accused, if he or she files the appeal measure independently. However, if the appellant, who is not obliged to raise objections against the decision, does so in the appeal measure, they also set the limits of the appellate control. Adopting a different point of view, it may be said that the objections against the decision do not delimit those boundaries when they are not a component of the appeal measure, and this is legally permissible when this measure comes from an entity other than one of the listed professional entities. In such a case, the only determinant of the limits of appellate control are the limits of complaint. If the limits of complaint covers all the decisions included in the ruling (settlement of ruling), it entails its total control in the appellate instance for all the violations specified in Article 438 CPC (see below).[54]

According to Article 433 § 2 CPC, the appellate court is under an obligation to consider all motions and objections indicated in the appeal measure unless otherwise provided in the CPC.[55] The case in which the CPC provides otherwise is normalised in Article 436 CPC, providing for the possibility of limiting the examination of an appeal measure to individual breaches only, raised by a party or subject to examination ex officio, if the examination in this scope is sufficient to issue a ruling, and the examination of other breaches would be premature or pointless for the further proceedings.[56]

Reasons for Appeal

The reasons for appeal are basically certain types of violations that cause the impugned ruling to be reversed or modified.[57] Some of them, as already noted above, are subject to review and consideration only within the limits of appellate control. They constitute the basic group of reasons for appeal, catalogued in Article 438 CPC and referred to as relative reasons for appeal. A separate group consists of such violations that by virtue of a specific provision should be taken into account irrespective of the limits established for the appeal measure and the objections raised. They form a group of absolute reasons for appeal (Articles 439, 440 and 455 CPC).[58]

[54] Kulesza (n 3) 247; Supreme Court Decision 18 February 2015, II KK 26/15, Lex no 1654740.
[55] Supreme Court Decision, 14 July 2021, II KK 232/21, Lex no 3391084.
[56] Supreme Court Judgment, 4 October 2005, V KK 241/05, Lex no 157212.
[57] Świecki (n 37) 133.
[58] Marszał (n 9) 46.

Relative Reasons for Appeal

The group of relative reasons for appeal includes the following types of violations:

1. a violation of the provisions of substantive law has occurred with regard to the legal classification of the act attributed to the accused;
2. a violation of the provisions of substantive law has occurred in a case other than that indicated in subparagraph 1, unless despite the wrong legal basis, the ruling complies with the law;
3. a violation of procedural provisions has occurred, provided that it may have affected the contents of the ruling issued;
4. an error has occurred in the findings of fact assumed as a basis for rendering the ruling, provided that it may have affected the contents of the ruling;
5. the penalty, criminal measure or exemplary damages imposed are strikingly disproportionate to the offence, or a preventive measure, forfeiture, or another measure has been incorrectly applied or not applied.[59]

Referring holistically to the reasons listed under subparagraphs 1 and 2, it should be emphasised that a substantive law violation may consist in a violation of any area of substantive law, which was or should have been applied in criminal proceedings, ie not only substantive criminal law, but also, inter alia, civil law, eg with respect to ruling on the obligation to redress damage. This type of failure takes the form of an application of an inappropriate norm of substantive law, failure to apply a legal norm the application of which was mandatory in a given case (eg the court failed to apply a ban on practising a profession, even though it was mandatory) or misinterpretation of the provision applied. In each of these forms, the violation of substantive law provisions materialises and at the same time reveals itself through the defective content of the ruling. It is the content of the judgment, which is an act of application of substantive law, that 'offends' this substantive law.[60] If the violation of the substantive law is a consequence of an erroneous factual finding, then the erroneous factual finding must be taken into account first, ie the ground of appeal provided for in Article 438 point 3 CPC.[61]

Violations of procedural law constitute failures of various natures, from those that are, so to speak, insignificant, because in the specific procedural configuration they are irrelevant to the ruling, to those that belong to the category of absolute reasons for appeal and imply, in almost every case, reversal of the appealed ruling without the necessity to examine the impact of the failure on its content. Somewhere in the middle are the violations of procedural law, which constitutes a relative reasons of appeal

[59] In addition to the aforementioned reasons, the decision may be reversed or amended as a result of new facts or evidence discovered after the decision at first instance was issued. These constitute an autonomous ground of appeal if the defect in the judgment becomes apparent only in the light of such facts or evidence. In other cases, which in practice occur far more frequently, new facts or evidence merely provide support for the objections pointing to deficiencies under Arts 438 or 439 § 1 CPC, which constitute proper reasons for appeal.

[60] R Kmiecik, 'Rażące naruszenie prawa materialnego jako „względna" przyczyna kasacyjna' in P Hofmański and K Zgryzek (eds), *Współczesne problemy procesu karnego i wymiaru sprawiedliwości. Księga ku czci Profesora Kazimierza Marszała* (Katowice, Wydawnictwo Uniwersytetu Śląskiego, 2003) 272.

[61] Supreme Court Judgment, 23 July 1974, V KR 212/74, OSNKW 1974, no 12, pos 233; Supreme Court Decision, 29 March 2007, IV KK 32/07, OSNwSK 2007, no 1, pos 751.

(Article 438 point 2 CPC). This category of infringements consists of violations in the field of application of provisions of procedural law, which could have influenced the content of the appealed ruling and do not belong to the category of absolute reasons for appeal regulated in Article 439 CPC. The following violations fall into this category:

1. failure to apply a norm of criminal procedural law that the procedural authority was absolutely obliged to apply (*errores in ommitendo*), eg failure read a witness's previously given testimony when he or she testifies differently at the main hearing;[62] basing the judgment on undisclosed parts of the evidence;[63] failure to warn the parties of a possible change in legal qualification when it was subsequently changed in the judgment;[64] failure to give the accused the last vote;[65]
2. actions contrary to the provisions of procedural law (*errores in faciendo*), eg taking of evidence in violation of the prohibition on substitution of explanations or testimony by the contents of letters, notes or official notes (Article 174 CPC), unjustified dismissal of a motion for evidence,[66] limitation of evidence to a defendant's explanations, despite the fact that the defendant did not admit the fact that he/she committed the crime charged;[67]
3. violation of provisions concerning the construction of the ruling and the ruling itself, in particular the rules of evidence assessment (*errores in iudicando*), eg leading to a contradiction between the content of the ruling and its statement of reasons.

If an objection that there has been a violation of procedural law, which is subject to examination within the limits of appellate control, is to be effective, it is necessary to genuinely prove, based on the circumstances of the specific case, that there is a connection between the objected procedural violation and the content of the ruling, in the light of which the violation is likely to affect the content of the ruling (hypothetical causal link).[68] In this respect, it is not sufficient to make an unfounded statement that the misconduct had or could have had an impact on the content of the ruling.[69]

An error in the findings of fact may result from incompleteness of evidence (so-called error of omission) or from exceeding the limits of free assessment of evidence (so-called error of discretion).[70] Errors of omission occur, for example, when the authority issuing the decision at first instance was not aware of specific evidence that would support

[62] Supreme Court Judgment, 21 May 1984, OSNPG 1984, no 12, pos 114.
[63] Supreme Court Judgment, 30 July 1979, III KR 196/79, OSNPG 1980, no 3, pos 43.
[64] Supreme Court Judgment, 1 June 1994, II KRN 81/94, OSNKW 1994, nos 7–8, pos 48; Supreme Court Judgment, 7 February 2002, VCCN 185/99, OSNKW 2002, nos 5–6, pos 45.
[65] Supreme Court Judgment, 7 January 1972, II KR 163/72, Biul SN 1972, no 4, pos 81.
[66] Supreme Court Judgment, 18 December 1975, Rw 680/75, OSNKW 1976, nos 4–5, pos 69; Supreme Court Judgment, 3 July 1987, IV KR 186/87, OSPiKA 1988, no 3, pos 69.
[67] Supreme Court Judgment, 4 March 1985, V KRN 116/85, OSNPG 1985, no 11, pos 142.
[68] Incidentally, it may be noted that a procedural irregularity which may affect the judgment in one case will not have such an effect in another, eg where the evidence of a witness given in breach of the prohibition on hearing on grounds of medical confidentiality relates to circumstances which are immaterial for the outcome of the case or concerns circumstances which are not relevant to the outcome of the case.– see judgment of the Supreme Court, 17 August 1984, IV KR 180/84, OSNKW 1985, nos 3–4, pos 28.
[69] Z Doda and A Gaberle, *Kontrola odwoławcza w procesie karnym. Orzecznictwo Sądu Najwyższego. Komentarz* (Warsaw, Dom Wydawniczy ABC, 1997) vol II, 116.
[70] ibid 129.

factual findings different from those made. This applies to situations in which after the first-instance court issued its judgment evidence came to light that substantially changes the state of knowledge about the event subject to the court's factual findings.[71] An error of discretion results from an incorrect process of deducing facts on the basis of accumulated evidence. It may be caused by insufficient knowledge of the evidence or violation of the directives governing its assessment. It can be a consequence of basing findings of fact on non-credible evidence or on facts that are not proven, ie facts that do not follow from the evidence held or are a consequence of omitting, within the scope of findings of fact, all facts that follow from the evidence held and that are significant for the outcome of the case.[72] An error of discretion may also manifest itself in contradictory or unjustified conclusions in assessing the causes and consequences of certain facts arising from evidence taken (eg incidental facts in circumstantial procedure). Similarly as in cases of violations of procedural law, the objection of an error in factual findings cannot be reduced to generalities, as it is necessary to prove that it influences the ruling. It is therefore out of the question to merely substantiate the allegation by presenting a different assessment of the evidence. The raising of this objection should be based on a precise definition of what the objection is directed against, eg demonstrating specific irregularities committed by the adjudicating authority with respect to the principles of logical reasoning or in the light of knowledge and life experience.[73]

Striking disproportionality of the penalty, penal measure or exemplary damages imposed, or incorrectly application or non-application of a protective measure, forfeiture or other measure constitutes a violation in the scope of the legal consequences of the act ascribed to the accused. It refers to the sphere of the judge's discretion when assessing the penalty – the judge's discretion when choosing and marking the penalty reaction which is appropriate *in concreto*.[74] Raising it as an independent objection against the judgment is possible if the facts have been properly established and the legal classification of the act ascribed to the accused has been properly applied.[75] In other cases, the failure in question most frequently constitutes a consequence of violation of procedural regulations or error in the findings of fact, and it is these defects that should be the subject of an appeal objection. 'Striking disproportionality' and 'incorrectly' are the quantifiers for the assessment of the judge's choice and the dimension of the measures of penal reaction.[76] In practice, the meaning of 'strikingly disproportionality' raises the most problems. Based on extensive court rulings, it can be stated that such a qualification of a penalty, penal measure or exemplary damages imposed is justified when the sum of disadvantages resulting from the imposition of these measures of penal

[71] M Bielski, 'Zasady konstruowania zarzutów apelacyjnych opartych na względnych przyczynach odwoławczych' in P Hofmański (ed), *Fiat iustiia pereat mundus. Księga jubileuszowa poświęcona Sędziemu Sądu Najwyższego Stanisławowi Zabłockiemu z okazji 40-lecia pracy zawodowej* (Warsaw, Wolters Kluwer, 2014) 38 et seq.

[72] T Grzegorczyk, *Kodeks postępowania karnego. Komentarz* (Warsaw, Wolters Kluwer, 2014) vol I, 1466.

[73] Supreme Court Judgment, 22 January 1975, I KR 197/74, OSNKW 1975, no 5, pos 58; Supreme Court Judgment, 6 February 1992, II AKr 1/92, OSA 1992, no 6, pos 41.

[74] Judgment of the Supreme Administrative Court in Katowice, 28 February 2013, II AKa 550/12, Lex no 1294787.

[75] cf Supreme Court Judgment, 23 October 1974, V KRN 78/74, OSNKW 1974, no 12, pos 234.

[76] Supreme Court Decision, 3 October 2011, V KK 96/11, Lex no 1044083.

response remains in gross disproportion to the disadvantages which the defendant (a similar offender) usually suffers, if the same act is imputed to him/her.[77] Disproportion is striking if it is significant and glaring; it is disproportion of fundamental nature, and unacceptable. Such a disproportion occurs if the sum of imposed penalties, penal measure or exemplary damages imposed does not fully reflect the degree of social harmfulness of the act, the circumstances in which it was committed and its gravity, as well as the personality of the perpetrator and the goals of the punishment.[78]

Absolute Reasons for Appeal

As already indicated above, absolute reasons for appeal concern cases in which the appellate authority is entitled and obliged to rule ex officio regardless of the limits of appellate control (Articles 439 § 1, 440 and 455 CPC), and regardless of the filing of an appeal (Article 435 CPC). Due to its exceptional character, ruling outside the limits of appellate control may take place only in cases expressly specified in the provisions referred to. Based on these, three groups of reasons can be distinguished in which this occurs, namely:

1. absolute reasons for reversing the ruling (Article 439 § 1 CPC);
2. manifestly unjust of the ruling (Article 440 CPC);
3. correction an incorrect legal classification (Article 455 CPC).

The group of absolute reasons for reversing a ruling includes the most serious violations of procedural law, constituting *sui generis* 'procedural cardinal sins'.[79] The rank of these violations determines their impact on the content of the ruling, and therefore it is not necessary to demonstrate this.[80] Due to this rank, they play an important role within the framework of extraordinary appellate control. The consequence of their finding is the obligation to, in principle, reverse the contested ruling and then to refer the case to the first-instance court for re-examination or to discontinue the proceedings. The list of absolute reasons for reversing the ruling in Article 439 § 1 CPC is closed, which excludes the possibility of expanding their number by way of interpretation.[81] According to this provision, irrespective of the limits established for the appeal measure and the objections raised, as well as of the effect of the breach on the contents of the ruling, the appellate court at its session shall reverse the ruling appealed against if:

1. A person unauthorised to adjudicate or incapable of adjudicating, or subject to disqualification pursuant to Article 40,[82] has participated in the rendering of the ruling. In subject terms, these violations refer to both professional judges and lay judges. Unauthorise to adjudicate occurs when a person is not appointed to

[77] Supreme Court Judgment, 14 November 1973, III KR 254/73, OSNPG 1974, nos 3–4, pos 51.
[78] Supreme Court Judgment, 30 June 2009, WA 19/09, OSNwSK 2009, no 1, pos 1255; Supreme Court Judgment, 30 November 1990, WR 363/90, OSNKW 1991, nos 7–9, pos 39.
[79] See Doda and Gaberle (n 69) 523. As a side note, it may be noted that Art 439 § 1 provides for only one failure consisting in violation of substantive law (see para 5 of this provision and further comments).
[80] Supreme Court Judgment, 31 August 2011, II KK 99/11, Lex no 898597.
[81] Supreme Court Decision, 7 July 2010, II KK 95/10, OSNwSK 2010, no 1, pos 1381.
[82] For the grounds for disqualification of the judge set out in Art 40, see ch 4.

adjudicate at all;[83] it is therefore required to establish the absence of an act of appointment as a judge or lay judge in relation to a particular member of the panel.[84] Incapable of adjudication includes cases in which, due to the condition of a particular person at the time of adjudication, he or she should not take part in it; examples of such a condition include intoxication with alcohol, drugs or psychotropic drugs, or insanity.

2. The panel was improperly constituted, or some of its members were not present throughout the trial. An 'improperly constituted panel' is a panel not constituted as it should be;[85] this may result from deviations from the statutory number of members of the court or failure to observe the established proportions between the number of persons of different legal status (judge, lay judge, additional lay judge), as well as situations in which there is a lack of authority to rule in a given court or on a specific case. In terms of determining the conceptual scope of the phrase 'improper manning of the court', the resolution of the Supreme Court of 23 January 2020 is of great importance,[86] which was made against the background of legislative changes inspired by the political environment centred around the current Minister of Justice and constituting a form of attack on the independence of judges and the independence of the courts. This attack, in its basic version, took the form of changes introduced in the Act of 8.12.2017 on amending the Act on the National Council of the Judiciary and some other acts (Dz U of 2018, item 3). In a nutshell, the effect of this change was to shape the composition of the National Council of the Judiciary in a way that violated constitutional norms. This caused the procedure for the Council to present candidates for judge to the President of the Republic of Poland to be affected by defects that put into question the impartiality and independence of judges. According to the cited Supreme Court resolution, about improper composition of the court determines:
   - participation in the composition of the court of a person appointed to the office of a judge of the Supreme Court on the motion of the National Council of the Judiciary formed on the basis of the indicated law;
   - participation in the composition of a court adjudicating criminal cases of a person appointed to the office of a judge of a common court or military court on the motion of the National Council of the Judiciary formed on the basis of the aforementioned procedure, if the defect in the process of appointment leads in specific circumstances to a violation by such person of the standard of independence and impartiality within the meaning of Article 45(1) of the Constitution of the Republic of Poland, Article 47 of the Charter of Fundamental Rights of the European Union (Official Journal of the EU C 202 of 7.06.2016, p 389) and Article 6(1) ECHR.[87]

[83] Supreme Court Decision, 17 January 2012, IV KK 354/11, Lex no 1128203.

[84] Incidentally, it may be noted that the participation in the decision of at least one person who is not entitled to adjudicate is sufficient to constitute an absolute ground for setting aside the decision. If the decision was rendered by a panel in which all the persons were not competent to adjudicate, the 'decision' has only the appearance of a procedural decision (*sententia non existens*).

[85] Supreme Court Resolution, 20 November 1997, I KZP 30/971, OSNKW 1996, nos 9–10, pos 64.

[86] BSA I-4110-1/20.

[87] See more extensive considerations in ch 3 on the staffing of the court.

3. A common court of law has rendered a ruling in a case falling under the jurisdiction of a special court, or a special court has rendered a ruling in a case falling under the jurisdiction of a common court of law.[88] The special courts hearing criminal cases are military courts; the failure presented is directly related to the separation of competences between these courts and common courts.[89]
4. A lower-level court has rendered a ruling in a case falling under the jurisdiction of a higher-level court. A lower-level court is a district court in relation to a regional court and a military garrison court in relation to a military regional court.[90]
5. A penalty, criminal measure, compensation measure or preventive measure has been imposed which is not mentioned in the Act.[91] The violation consists in the imposition of a penalty, criminal measure or preventive measure not at all unknown to the Polish criminal law system, not only therefore to the Criminal Code, eg the punishment of flogging, house arrest, death penalty, confiscation of property in its entirety.[92]
6. The ruling has been issued in breach of the principle of the majority of votes or has not been signed by any of the persons participating in its issuance. A violation of the principle of the majority of votes during voting on the ruling occurs when the ruling was made in a collegial composition not unanimously and its content is inconsistent with the will of the majority of the members of that composition.[93] The signature of the members of the court is a guarantee of the authenticity of the decision, a confirmation that it conforms to the will and knowledge of the signatories, and an indication that the signatories accept responsibility for it;[94] it gives the decision the value of an act of justice, with which the law attaches certain legal consequences. There are no exceptions to the obligation to sign the decision as regards judgments (*argumentum ex* Article 418 § 1 *in principio* CPC). In the case of rulings in form of decisions, an exception applies to those that are in the records of the trial or session (Article 113 *in fine* CPC), to be signed only by the presiding judge or another member of the panel, stating the reason for the lack of the presiding judge's signature (Article 149 §§ 1 and 3 CPC). The lack of a compulsory signature of at least one member of the panel at the moment of pronouncing the ruling is an absolute ground of appeal, regardless of the circumstances that caused the ruling not to be signed. The lack of a signature after the pronouncement of the judgment or decision is ineffective, because this failure cannot be remedied

[88] See Supreme Court Decision, 4 February 1999, WZ 82/94, OSNKW 1999, nos 5–6, pos 32; Supreme Court Judgment, 30 April 1982, I KR 121/82, OSNKW 1982, no 9, pos 64.

[89] See more P Hofmański, E Sadzik and K Zgryzek, *Kodeks postępowania karnego. Komentarz* (Warsaw, CH Beck, 2004) vol I, 628.

[90] See more S Steinborn, 'Stwierdzenie niewłaściwości rzeczowej sądu – art 35 k.p.k.' (2001) *Prok i Pr* no 5, 59; Supreme Court Judgment, 20 October 1994, II KRN 211/94, OSNKW 1994, nos 11–12, pos 75; Supreme Court Judgment, 9 January 2013, V KK 382/12, Lex no 1289073.

[91] Supreme Court Judgment, 8 November 1989, V KRN 267/89, OSNKW 1990, nos 7–12, pos 32.

[92] The imposition of a penalty that is known to the legal system but, for example, is not foreseen for a specific offence qualifies as a relative ground of appeal under Art 438(1a) CPC.

[93] As the deliberation and the vote on the decision are secret, it is in fact possible to establish a violation of the majority vote on the basis of the separate sentence or sentences taken when the decision was signed.

[94] Supreme Court Decision, 28 April 2011, V KK 3/11, Lex no 817556.

after the pronouncement of the ruling, even if it had no effect on the substantive content of the ruling.[95]

7. There is an inconsistency in the content of the ruling making it impossible to enforce it; the inconsistency must genuinely and absolutely make it impossible to the enforcement of the ruling[96] – an apparent inconsistency, resulting from ambiguity or lack of precision in the formulation of individual decisions, which can be explained by way of interpretation, does not meet these criteria.[97] As an example, it can be pointed out that a discrepancy between the amount of the penalty stated in words and in a digital form written in brackets is qualified as a failure under Article 439 § 1 point 7 CPC.[98]
8. The ruling was issued despite the fact that the criminal proceedings concerning the same act committed by the same person had already been validly concluded. This failure consists of a violation of the *ne bis in idem* rule (*res iudicata*) and arises from the existence of a final (validly) ruling concluding the proceedings in a given case; it is irrelevant whether the ruling is a judgment on the merits of the case or, for example, a ruling discontinuing criminal proceedings against a specific person. *Res judicata* is not generated by a decision to discontinue proceedings at the *in rem* stage in the pre-trial investigation.[99]
9. One of the circumstances excluding the proceedings, defined in Article 17 § 1(5), (6) and (8)–(11) CPC, has occurred; this violation consists in issuing a decision despite the occurrence, in the course of the criminal trial, of a procedural obstacle in the form of death of the accused (Article 17 § 1(5) CPC), prescription of criminality (Article 17 § 1(6) CPC), despite not being subject to the jurisdiction of the Polish criminal courts (Article 17 § 1(8) CPC), lack of a complaint by an authorised prosecutor (Article 17 § 1, point 9 CPC), lack of permission for prosecuting or motion to prosecute from an authorised person (Article 17 § 1, point 10 CPC) or other circumstance excluding prosecution (Article 17 § 1, point 11 CPC).[100]
10. The accused had no defence counsel in judicial proceedings in the cases described in Article 79 §§ 1 and 2 and in Article 80 CPC (see above, chapter four),[101] or the defence counsel did not participate in actions in which their participation was mandatory. The second of these violations is a consequence of the separate treatment in the CPC of the obligation to have a defence counsel and of his/her mandatory participation in procedural actions. The former obligation is not necessarily synonymous with an obligation to participate in all actions. As an example, it

[95] Supreme Court Judgment, 2 February 2012, IV CC 18/12, KZS 2012, no 5, pos 27.

[96] Supreme Court Judgment, 15 September 2010, II CC 42/10, OSNKW 2010, no 11, pos 101.

[97] Supreme Court Decision, 17 September 2008, II KK 60/08, Lex no 458853.

[98] Supreme Court Judgment, 8 September 2009, IV CC 223/09, Lex no 608291; Supreme Court Judgment, 22 October 2015, III CC 235/15, Lex no 1820401.

[99] cf Supreme Court Judgment, 15 February 2012, II KK 201/11, OSNKW 2012, no 6, pos 60.

[100] See also S Zabłocki in RA Stefański and S. Zabłocki (eds), *Kodeks postępowania karnego. Komentarz* (Warsaw, Wolters Kluwer, 2003) vol III, 174–75.

[101] Absolute ground for repeal of the decision shall also exist if, in cases provided for in Art 79 §§ 1 and 2 and Art 80 CPC, the accused was formally appointed as a defence counsel, however, it was in fact impossible for this procedural representative to conduct the substantive defence since he/she did not have the opportunity to read the case file, contact the accused and therefore could not prepare the defence concept: Supreme Court judgment of 24 May 1985, IV KR 94/85, OSNPG 1985, no 11, item 143.

may be recalled here, in principle, that in the cases of mandatory defence described in Article 79 §§ 1 and 2 CPC the participation of a defence counsel in the trial is mandatory, also in those sessions in which the presence of the accused is mandatory (Article 79 § 3 CPC); in the cases described in Article 80 participation of the defence counsel in the main trial is mandatory.[102]

11. The case has been heard in the absence of an accused whose presence was mandatory. Absolute reversal of the ruling for this reason is based on the presumption of a violation of the right of defence in the presented procedural situation; this failure is subject to qualification under Article 439 § 1, point 11 CPC, if during the absence of the accused, activities related to the examination of the case were carried out, eg evidence was taken or final statements were made.[103]

Reversing the ruling solely for reasons described above in points 10 and 11 may only be done for the benefit of the accused (Article 439 § 2 CPC). This means that despite the deficiencies listed in these points, ruling to the detriment of the accused is excluded. The *ne peius* principle is regulated in this solution.[104]

The second of the aforementioned absolute reasons for appeal consists in substantive and legal review of the decision outside the limits of appellate control in terms of its manifest unfairness. According to Article 440 CPC, where upholding a ruling would be manifestly unjust, such a ruling shall be subject to amendment in favour of the accused irrespective of the limits of the complaint and the objections raised or – in the case defined in the second sentence of Article 437 § 2 CPC – to revocation.[105] Manifest injustice of the ruling may be a derivative of each of the defects belonging to the category of relative reasons for appeal listed in Article 438 CPC, and thus also of the violation of procedural law provisions. This corresponds to the understanding of 'injustice of a ruling' not only in the material aspect ('material' injustice, eg violation of substantive law), but also in the procedural aspect ('procedural' injustice), ie violation of procedural law, due to which there were manifest violations of the rule of fair trial.[106] For a ruling to be considered manifestly unjust, it is not enough that this injustice is flagrant. It must additionally result from a defect of sufficient gravity, related to its rank (essence) and intensity, such that the ruling cannot in any way be reconciled with the public sense of justice.[107] In the case of violations of procedural law, in order to find manifest unfairness of the ruling it is necessary to establish that due to its nature and intensity it had a real impact on the content of the ruling.[108]

[102] Supreme Court Judgment, 24 May 1985, IV KR 94/85, OSNPG 1985, no 11, pos 143; Supreme Court Decision, 7 December 2004, IV KK 276/04, Lex no 163269.

[103] Świecki (n 20) vol II, 224.

[104] Supreme Court Decision, 11 December 1991, V KRN 304/90, OSNKW 1992, nos 5–6, pos 44.

[105] In view of the presented consequences of the finding of manifest injustice of the ruling in the appellate instance, it should be pointed out that there is an actual legal loophole within the scope of the regulation Article 440 CPC. It consists of remaining outside the scope of this norm the cases where the judgment would have to be amended – in accordance with the direction of the appeal – to the disadvantage of the accused and there are no grounds to set it aside and refer the case for re-examination (Art 437 § 2 CPC).

[106] Supreme Court Judgment, 2 April 2012, III CC 98/12, Lex no 1163194.

[107] Supreme Court Judgment, 30 September 2014, II CC 347/14, Lex no 1541049; Supreme Court Judgment, 22 May 2014, III CC 127/14, Lex no 1467124.

[108] See Hofmański, Sadzik and Zgryzek (n 88) 649.

The last of the identified absolute grounds of appeal concerns the legal qualification of the act ascribed to the accused in the judgment, and thus its assignment to a provision of the criminal statute defining the crime. Based on Article 455 first sentence CPC, without amending the findings of fact, the appellate court shall correct an incorrect legal classification irrespective of the scope of the appeal and objections raised therein. It is clear from this provision that the correction of the legal classification occurs when it is defective, despite the correct findings of fact, reflected in the description of the act and concerning the time, place, manner and circumstances of its commission and the effects of the act.[109] Thus, it can be said that it occurs on the basis of the same findings of fact on which the impugned judgment was based.[110] If, in the application of Article 455 CPC, the appellate court changed the findings of fact and only on this basis changed the legal classification to the detriment of the accused, this would constitute a manifest violation of the cited provision, which could be raised in cassation. A legal classification may be corrected to the disadvantage of the accused only when the appeal measure has been filed to the disadvantage of the accused (Article 455 second sentence CPC).[111]

Direction of the Appeal Measure

The direction of the appeal measure has a significant impact on the scope of the appellate court's ruling following the appellate control, generally within its limits. It constitutes a feature of the appeal measure, which manifests itself, as a rule, in an effort to improve or worsen the situation of the accused. The CPC does not consider an appeal measure that is brought by the parties and is neutral in character, ie is brought in defence of the violated right.[112] The direction of the appeal measure is most often determined by the procedural position of the appellant. This statement is confirmed in all cases in which this measure is brought by an authorised entity that is not a public prosecutor. This follows from the already established obligation of *gravamen* on the part of the appealing person, meaning that he or she may appeal against the resolutions or findings only if they are prejudicial to his or her rights or interests (Article 425 § 3 CPC). The public prosecutor, on the other hand, is entitled to file appeal measure both against and for benefit of the accused (Article 425 § 4 CPC).[113] He/she should make a clear statement in the appeal measure as to whether he/she is appealing in favour or against the defendant. In the absence of such a statement, when the content of the appeal measure does not give an unequivocal answer as to its direction, in the name of *favor rei*, the measure coming from the public prosecutor should be considered as brought for benefit of the accused.[114]

[109] M Kwietniowska, 'Zmiana kwalifikacji prawnej czynu w postępowaniu odwoławczym (art 455 k.p.k.) (2006) *Prok I Pr* no 4, 95.
[110] K Marszał, 'Zmiana kwalifikacji prawnej czynu w postępowaniu rewizyjnym' (1989) *PPK* no 15, 41.
[111] See further Z Doda, 'Uwagi na temat kierunku i granic środka odwoławczego' (1979) *Pal* no 4 72.
[112] Note that the feature of neutrality can be seen in the cassation from the so-called special entities referred to in Art 521 CPC.
[113] See also Supreme Court Judgment, 19 June 1987, IV KR 197/87, OSNKW 1987, nos 11–12, pos 109.
[114] Doda and Gaberle (n 69) 233.

The significant effect of the direction of the appeal measure on the scope of appellate adjudication, identified at the beginning of this section, is based on the principle that the appellate authority shall rule in accordance with the direction of the appeal measure. This principle has an exception only in cases expressly provided by statute. Traditionally, ruling against the direction of the appeal measure ('breaking' the direction of the appeal measure) can be done for benefit of the accused. In the current state of the law, this possibility is significantly limited, because it depends on the finding of manifest violations of the law by the appellate court, causing the state of manifest injustice of the ruling (Article 440 CPC) or the need to correct – in favour of the accused – the incorrect legal qualification of the act pursuant to Article 455 CPC (Article 434 § 2 CPC). This means that the 'breaking' of the direction of the appeal can now take place in conditions allowing rulings outside the limits of appellate control, as set out in Articles 440 and 455 CPC.

Prohibition of *Reformationis in Peius*

Related to the direction of the appeal measure is the prohibition of *reformationis in peius*. Its essence is to provide the accused with a guarantee that the appeal measure filed for his benefit will not worsen their procedural situation in relation to that resulting from the ruling appealed against.[115] If an appeal measure is brought only for the benefit of the accused, 'breaking' its direction is, as a rule, inadmissible. This is because then the analysed prohibition applies. An exception in this respect is connected with exclusion of the operation of this prohibition in cases specified in Article 434 § 4 CPC, which are discussed further below.[116]

The prohibition of *reformationis in peius* fulfils an important function from the point of view of the interests of justice, as it paves the way for the removal within the framework of appeal control of the errors that crept into the ruling when another entitled subject does not file an appeal measure. It should be believed that in the absence of a guarantee in the form of the prohibition in question, the accused would give up filing an appeal measure for fear of worsening his/her procedural situation.[117] As a result, it would not be possible to correct in the appellate instance the errors that crept into the ruling and, despite its defectiveness, it would have to function in legal circulation. The existence of this guarantee, by eliminating any risk that could be associated with the appeal of a ruling made by the accused or by other persons in his/her favour, thus serves to create conditions in which it is possible to correct the decision and at the same time to realise the concept of securing the freedom of complaint by the accused.[118]

The prohibition of *reformationis in peius* exists in the form of a direct prohibition and an indirect prohibition. In each of these forms, the condition for this prohibition to operate is that the ruling must be appealed only for the benefit of the accused.

[115] K Marszał, *Zakaz reformationis in peius w nowym ustawodawstwie karnym procesowym*, (Warsaw, Wydawnictwo Prawnicze, 1970) 77–80.
[116] See also ZDoda (n 110) 62.
[117] K Marszał and J Zagrodnik in J. Zagrodnik (ed), *Proces karny* (Warsaw, Wolters Kluwer, 2019) 709.
[118] See further Marszał (n 114) 77–80.

It is generally excluded if an appeal measure is filed against the accused, regardless of whether or not there is an adjacent appeal measure lodged in favour of the accused. The direct prohibition is addressed to the court hearing the appeal measure (Article 434 § 1 CPC). An indirect prohibition applies in retrial proceedings, after the ruling has been set aside and the case referred to the first-instance court for re-examination (Article 443 CPC). In both forms, the prohibition of *reformationis in peius* has a wide scope of operation and excludes the worsening of the situation of the accused in any point in comparison with the resolution contained in the appealed ruling (eg as to the penalty, findings of fact, obligations imposed or penal measures applied).[119]

In light of what has been said so far, it is clear that the direct prohibition of *reformationis in peius* excludes the possibility of ruling in the appellate instance to the detriment of the accused when an appeal measure is brought solely in his or her favour. Moreover, in situations where the appeal measure has been filed against the defendant, the prohibition analysed precludes the appellate court from ruling in accordance with the direction of the appeal if this would require going beyond the limits of appellate control, unless the law requires ruling outside those limits. It may therefore be stated that, except in situations where the law prescribes that a ruling be given irrespective of these limits, the prohibition of *reformationis in peius* precludes a ruling in accordance with the direction of the appeal measure to the disadvantage of the accused beyond the limits of the appellate control.[120]

The indirect prohibition of *reformationis in peius* means that, if the case is referred for re-examination, the court in such further proceedings may sentence the accused to a penalty more severe than the one imposed in the ruling reversed only if the appeal thereof was an appeal prejudicial to the accused. Thus, if, for example, a ruling has been set aside following an exclusive appeal against the ruling in the defendant's favour, the court to which the case has been referred for re-examination may not in principle pass a more severe sentence in the retrial, irrespective of whether or not new aggravating circumstances have come to light in the retrial. Looking from a different perspective, it may be said that the court to which the case has been referred for re-examination may pass a sentence more severe than one imposed in the ruling reversed as a result of an appeal measure filed against the accused only to the limits of the complaint against the accused and only with respect to those violations that were the subject of the accepted objections raised against the ruling, provided that the objections were raised in the appeal measure[121]

Both the direct and indirect prohibition of *reformationis in peius* may be subject to exclusion in a procedural set-up, in which a conviction takes place with the application of Article 60 §§ 3 and 4 PC and Article 36 § 3 CPC, ie a conviction with the application of an extraordinary mitigation of the penalty due to the fact that the perpetrator

[119] An exception, of great practical importance, is made for the retrial and decision on preventive measures listed in Art 93a § 1 of the Penal Code (eg electronic monitoring of a person's location or placement in a psychiatric facility), which are imposed for reasons of public protection.

[120] Supreme Court Judgment, 13 December 2017, II KK 274/17, Lex no 2434431; Supreme Court Judgment, 16 October 2019, III KK 399/18, Lex no 3147260; Supreme Court Decision, 16 November 2020, IV KK 339/19, Lex no 3080401.

[121] D Świecki, 'Granice orzekania na niekorzyść oskarżonego na podstawie art 434 § 1 i art 443 k.p.k.' (2009) *PS* no 5, 71–72; Supreme Court Judgment, 28 August 2013, V KK 53/13, OSNKW 2014, no 1, pos 7.

who has committed a crime or fiscal offence in complicity with other persons disclosed information concerning the individuals participating in the crime and the substantive circumstances of its commission to a law-enforcement authority responsible for prosecuting crimes.[122] In such a procedural set-up, the prohibition does not operate in the event of revocation or considerable change – after the verdict – of the explanations or testimonies that formed the basis for the accused's obtaining certain benefits provided for in the referred provisions of substantive criminal law and substantive criminal fiscal law.[123] It can be said that the exclusion of the prohibition is determined by the disloyal attitude of the accused who, having taken advantage of the benefit of extraordinary mitigation of the penalty, withdraws the explanation or testimony, 'breaking the word' that constituted its basis.[124] This exclusion becomes obsolete in cases where in an appeal filed solely for benefit of the accused, a objection of violation of substantive law is legitimately raised or where the appellate court finds circumstances justifying the reversion of the ruling, as defined in Article 439 § 1 CPC (Article 434 § 4, second sentence, in conjunction with Article 443 CPC). This stems from the assumption that the violations of substantive law and the failures enumerated in Article 439 § 1 CPC burden the court first and foremost, and consequently the accused should not be exposed to a worsening of his/her legal situation as a result of their raising or their finding by the court ex officio outside the limits of the appeal control caused by the appeal brought exclusively for his/her benefit, despite the fact that he/she revokes or substantially changes the explanations or testimonies that brought him/her to a favourable judgment.[125]

Decisions in the Appellate Instance

Based on Article 437 CPC, it may be stated that the appellate authority shall make one of the following decisions:[126]

1. Sustain the appealed ruling (approbatory ruling) – this is an expression of the controlling nature of the appellate instance and a form of approval of the decision made in the first instance.
2. Amend the appealed ruling (reformatory ruling) – this means adjudicating differently as to its merits as compared in relation to the appealed ruling; for example, the change may consist in acquittal instead of conviction or modification of the judgment with respect to the penalty or legal qualification of the act.

[122] Constitutional Tribunal Judgment 28 April 2009, P 22/07, OTK-A 2009, no 4, pos 55.

[123] See more MJ Szewczyk, 'Ograniczenia zakazu reformationis in peius oraz podstaw apelacyjnych w ujęciu art 434 § 4 k.p.k. i art 447 § 5 k.p.k.' (2017) *Prok i Pr* no 11, 95; K Nowicki, 'Ograniczenia stosowania zakazu reformationis in peius w związku z nielojalnym zachowaniem oskarżonego' (2016) *PS* no 5, 66.

[124] I Fredrich-Michalska and B Stachurska-Marcińczak (eds), *Nowe kodeksy karne – z 1997 r. z uzasadnieniami* (Warsaw, Wydawnictwo Prawnicze, 1997) 155.

[125] See also M Fingas, 'Zakres rozpoznania sprawy przez sąd odwoławczy w przypadku zaskarżenia przez tzw. stronę prywatną orzeczenia wydanego w trybie konsensualnym' in T Grzegorczyk and R Olszewski (eds), *Verba volant, scripta manent. Proces karny, prawo karne skarbowe i prawo wykroczeń po zmianach z lat 2015–2016. Księga pamiątkowa poświęcona Profesor Monice Zbrojewskiej* (Warsaw, Wolters Kluwer, 2016) 604.

[126] Marszał (n 9) 57–59.

3. Reverse the appealed ruling (cassationary ruling) – this is the original decision of the appellate authority, as a result of which the appealed ruling loses its procedural existence, it ceases to be in force. Reversing may concern the whole ruling or its relevant parts (settlements), depending on whether the reason for reversing covers the whole ruling or its individual parts (settlements). In reversing the appealed ruling, the appellate authority has to make a secondary (consequential) decision,[127] ie decide on the fate of further proceedings; secondary decisions take the form of:
   - discontinuance of the proceedings, eg in cases provided for in Article 439 § 1 item 9 CPC; or
   - referring the case to the first-instance court for re-examination in the cases specified in the second sentence of Article 437 § 2 CPC,[128] ie in the event that in the appellate instance:
     (i) violation constituting an absolute reason for reversal (Article 439 § 1 of the CPC), provided that there are no grounds for discontinuance of the proceedings on this ground,[129]
     (ii) a violation that could have had a significant impact on the content of the appealed ruling (Article 438 of the CPC), when at the same time:
       - it is not possible to amend the ruling due to the *ne peius* rule set forth in Article 454 CPC (see next section);[130]
       - it is necessary to carry out the entire judicial examination again (*argumentum ex* Article 437 § 2 sentence 2 *in fine* CPC);[131] this occurs when the entirety of the evidence in the first instance was improperly conducted (formal irregularity) or evaluated (material irregularity), as well as in the case of violations in the course of evidence proceedings affecting the correctness of the entire cognitive process before the first instance-court,[132] eg if a judge was sitting in the court and there were grounds to exclude him/her due to circumstances that can give rise to reasonable doubts as to the judge's impartiality (*iudex suspectus* – Article 41 § 1 CPC). The need to carry out the entire judicial examination again occurs also in cases where a judgment delivered under the consensual model of trial, in which the subject matter of the trial is decided in a session (Articles 343 and 343a CPC) or at a main trial following the direct taking of evidence only of the accused's explanations (Article 387 CPC), is set aside.[133]

[127] Supreme Court Judgment, 21 April 2022, III KS 25/22, Lex no 3430971.
[128] Supreme Court Decision, 9 June 2022, IV KS 16/22, Lex no 3405311.
[129] Supreme Court Judgment, 23 February 2022, III KS 8/22, Lex no 3403026.
[130] Supreme Court Decision, 21 April 2022, III KS 28/22, Lex no 3419090.
[131] Supreme Court Decision, 14 April 2022, I KS 14/22, Lex no 3369238.
[132] Supreme Court Decision, 21 April 2022, V KS 5/22, Lex no 3430989.
[133] M Fingas, 'Prekluzja dowodowa w postępowaniu odwoławczym na tle zmian modelu postępowania jurysdykcyjnego wprowadzonych przez ustawę nowelizującą z dnia 11 marca 2016 r' in S Steinborn and K Woźniewski (eds) *Proces karny w dobie przemian. Przebieg postępowania* (Gdańsk, Wydawnictwo Uniwersytetu Gdańskiego, 2018) 429.

After the appeal against the statement of reasons has been heard, the court decides to sustain or amend the contested statement of reasons in whole or in part by issuing a decision to that effect (Article 443a § 4 in conjunction with Article 93 § 1 and Article 456 CPC). Sometimes the ruling of the appellate authority takes a special form, eg when the appellate court examines a complaint about arrest, it cannot reverse the decision on the subject as it is not made; instead, it can determine that there has been unjustified or illegal arrest and order the immediate release of the arrested person (Article 246 §§ 2 and 3 CPC).[134]

Appeal and Appeal Proceedings

The reflection contained in the previous sections of the chapter was focused on the issues and regulations common to the appeal and complaint. Regulations pertaining exclusively to appeals were only partially discussed, inter alia in connection with the representation of the defence counsel or the attorney-at-law (compulsory representation by a lawyer), extended limits of complaint or absolute reasons for appeal measure in the form of a manifestly unjust ruling and correction of an incorrect legal classification. This section is devoted to the analysis of other regulations, which are of fundamental importance and are specific to the measure in the form of appeal.

We should begin with a reminder that an appeal is a measure that is available against a judgment of the court of first instance, with only one exception, namely an injunctive judgment (Article 444 CPC). Exceptionally, the ruling on the costs of the proceedings in the judgment may be appealed by complaint (Article 626 § 3 CPC).[135] The statement of reasons for the judgment may also be appealed by complaint if no appeal has been lodged (Article 443a § 2 CPC).[136]

In terms of its content, an appeal is subject to two specific limitations on raising objections of appeal.

The first one is provided for in Article 447 § 5 CPC and concerns the appeal against a judgment rendered following the granting of a motion for conviction to be issued in a session, without main trial (Article 335 §§ 1 and 2 CPC), or a motion for voluntary submission to criminal responsibility (Articles 338a and 387 CPC). In the event of an appeal against such judgments, the grounds for appeal cannot be allegations of error in factual findings or strikingly disproportionality of punishment if they relate to the content of the agreement that gave rise to the granting of the said motions. This restriction serves to prevent instrumental use of the institution of sentencing without trial (in a session) and the institution of voluntary submission to criminal responsibility, without a full judicial examination. It is intended above all to prevent disloyalty and abuse of power by an accused who has benefited from the advantages usually accompanying a conviction under Articles 343, 343a or 387 CPC, after which he/she would challenge, on

[134] Marszał and Zagrodnik (n 1) 723.
[135] See also Supreme Court Decision, 10 September 2020, II KZ 17/20, Lex no 3158464.
[136] Supreme Court Judgment, 20 January 2004, WA 64/03, Lex no 3321841.

the basis of the objections indicated above, the agreement that led to it.[137] At the same time, this limitation protects the accused against the possibility that, for example, the public prosecutor, having obtained a conviction at first instance, will break the agreement entered into with him/her, which was the basis for the conviction, and will file an appeal aimed at increasing the penalty imposed on the accused.

The second of the limitations on raising objections in an appeal is dictated by considerations of procedural economy. Pursuant to Article 447 § 6 CPC, an appeal may not be based exclusively on objections that could be taken into account by correcting a judgment (Article 105 CPC), supplementing it pursuant to Article 420 CPC, or as a result of filing and considering a complaint on costs (Article 626 CPC).[138] The purpose of this is to avoid complex appellate proceedings in situations where elimination of specific defects that have crept into the judgment is possible through simpler penal procedural mechanisms, eg by supplementing the judgment with certain resolutions that were omitted therein.[139] Following the example given above, it should be stated that an appeal based solely on objections indicating deficiencies to be corrected by supplementing a judgment should be treated as a motion for such a supplement filed pursuant to Article 9 § 2 CPC (Article 447 § 6, sentence 2 CPC in conjunction with Article 118 §§ 1 and 2 CPC).

A separate group of limitations related to the appeal is constituted by limitations on the scope of adjudication in the appeal instance, resulting from the *ne peius* rule regulated in Article 454 § 1 CPC. They operate despite the fact that an appeal has been filed to the disadvantage of the accused, thus differently from the restrictions arising from the prohibition of *reformationis in peius*.[140] The *ratio legis* of the *ne peius* rules is to guarantee in criminal proceedings the principle of the right to defence and the principle of two-instance proceedings in its material aspect connected with limiting the right of the appellate court to adjudicate on the merits.[141] Regulation of these rules in the invoked provision currently boils down to exclusion of the possibility for the appellate court to convict an accused person who was acquitted in the first instance or in respect of whom the proceedings in the first instance were discontinued. In the situations presented above, the court which, after examining the appeal against the defendant's disadvantage, finds that there are grounds for conviction is left with the possibility of reversing the appealed ruling and referring the case for re-examination to the first-instance court (Article 437 § 2, second sentence CPC).[142] A conviction, in the face of an appeal against the defendant's disadvantage, is therefore possible, but only before the court of first instance. The restriction arising from Article 454 § 1 CPC is absolute. In addition to this provision, the *ne peius* rule is contained in the already discussed Article 439 § 2 CPC, according to which reversing the ruling solely for reasons described in Article 439 § 1 points 9–11 CPC may only be done for the benefit of the accused.

[137] MJ Szewczyk, 'Ograniczenia zakazu reformationis in peius oraz podstaw apelacyjnych w ujęciu art 434 § 4 k.p.k. i art 447 § 5 k.p.k.' (2017) *Prok i Pr* no 11, 95 et seq.
[138] Supreme Court Decision, 28 January 2020, IV KK 768/18, Lex no 3220951.
[139] See also Supreme Court Judgment, 27 October 2011, II KK 125/11, Lex no 1084713.
[140] Zabłocki (n 15) 144–45.
[141] Świecki (n 37) 363–64.
[142] Supreme Court Decision, 8 September 2021, IV KS 31/21, Lex no 3316492.

The appeal must be filed within fourteen days[143] of the delivery to the appellant of the judgment together with the statement of reasons. This is a final time limit, and therefore, it may be reinstated if its failure to do so was due to reasons beyond the control of the appellant (Article 126 § 1 CPC). The ground for lodging an appeal is the submission of the motion for a statement of reasons for the judgment to be made in writing and served within seven days of its announcement, and where the law provides the service of the judgment, a motion of its service (Article 422 §§ 1 and 2a CPC). The preparation of a statement of reasons for the judgment ex officio does not release the appellant from the obligation to file a motion for the statement of reasons to be served on them (Article 422 § 1, second sentence CPC). The procedural effects appropriate to such a motion may be produced by filing an appeal within the seven-day period prescribed for filing the motion (the so-called conversion of procedural actions; Article 445 § 2 *in principio* CPC). In such a case, the appellant has the right to supplement the appeal within fourteen days of being served with the judgment with a statement of reasons, eg to the extent of taking into account the detailed argumentation of the court (Article 445 § 2 *in fine* CPC). It should be emphasised that filing a motion for preparation and delivery of a written statement of reasons of the judgment or filing an appeal is ineffective if it is made before the date of announcement of the judgment.[144] On the other hand, filing an appeal after filing a timely motion for preparation and service of a written statement of reasons for a judgment, but before service of the statement of reasons, and thus *de facto* before the time for filing an appeal commences, should be deemed effective.[145]

As a rule, the time limit for filing an appeal runs separately for each person entitled from the time of service of the judgment with a statement of reasons. A certain deviation from this rule concerns cases in which a motion for a written statement of reasons for the judgment was filed by the accused or by the accused and a defence counsel, and the judgment with a statement of reasons were served to the accused and the defence counsel on different dates. In this procedural situation, the time limit for filing an appeal for both of these entities begins on the date of the later service of the judgment with a statement of reasons.[146] If, on the other hand, the motion for a written statement of reasons for the judgment was submitted on behalf of the defendant exclusively by his/her defence counsel, then, although the defendant acquires the possibility of filing his/her own appeal, the time limit for filing it runs from the date of service of the judgment with the statement of reasons on his/her defence counsel.[147]

In appellate proceedings before the court of first instance (*ad quo* appellate proceedings), the president of the court of first instance, finding that the appeal is admissible, has been lodged in time by an authorised person and meets the formal requirements for an appeal set out in one of the preceding sections, shall issue an order accepting the appeal. A notification of this fact shall be given to the public prosecutor, to defence counsels and attorneys, as well as to the parties; whereupon the files shall be submitted to the appellate court without delay (Article 448 § 1 CPC). A notification shall be

[143] In the accelerated procedure, the time limit for appeal is reduced to seven days (Art 517h § 3 CPC).
[144] Supreme Court Judgment, 11 October 2002, WA 53/02, OSNKW 2003, nos 1–2, pos 15.
[145] Appeal Court Judgment in Lublin, 28 March 2012, II AKz 154/12, Lex no 1210838.
[146] Supreme Court Judgment, 28 April 1980, VI KZP, OSNKW 1980, nos 5–6, pos 43.
[147] Supreme Court Judgment, 14 November 1972, V KRN 437/72, OSNKW 1973, no 4, pos 52.

accompanied by a duplicate of the appeal lodged by the opposing party, unless the trial was held in camera to protect confidential information classified as 'secret' or 'top secret' (Article 448 § 2 CPC).[148] After these steps have been taken, the president of the court of first instance shall immediately send the case file to the court of second instance.

In the appellate proceedings before the court of appeal (appellate proceedings *ad quem*), which begin with the sending of the case file to this court, the following three sub-phases can be distinguished: preparation for the appellate trial, the appellate trial and the final actions. Of paramount importance is the appellate trial, which is the primary forum in which the appellate court's ruling is reached as a result of control of the contested judgment. Its presentation in essential points is the subject of further detailed comments, which make up the content of the current subsection. Before formulating them, however, it should be noted that, by way of exception, the forum for the appellate court's ruling on the merits may be the session. Such an exception is stipulated in Article 439 § 1 CPC and is connected with the possibility to reverse a judgment at a session if one of the violations catalogued in the said provision, constituting absolute reason for reverse the ruling, is raised in the form of a objection in appeal or if the appellate court notices such violations ex officio before an appeal trial is scheduled.[149]

There are few regulations directly concerning the appellate trial. This results from the fact that the regulation of appellate proceedings is based on the reference to the accordingly application of the provisions concerning the proceedings before the court of first instance, at the same time reserving the differences in the scope resulting from the provisions of the chapter on appeals (Article 458 CPC). This chapter autonomously regulates the participation of the parties and their representatives in the appeal trial.[150] According to Article 450 § 1 CPC, this participation is mandatory for the prosecutor, as well as for the defence counsel in cases of obligatory defence regulated in Articles 79 and 80 CPC.[151] The participation in the appeal trial of other parties and their attorneys and defence counsel outside the indicated cases of mandatory defence is mandatory if the president of the court or the court decides so (Article 450 § 2 CPC). A failure of the parties, defence counsels or attorneys, duly notified of the date of a trial, to appear at the trial shall not stay the hearing of the case, unless their participation is mandatory (Article 450 § 3 CPC).[152] If the accused is deprived of liberty, the appellate court shall, upon his or her motion, filed within seven days of service on him or her of the notification of acceptance of the appeal, order that he or she be brought to the appeal hearing. A motion submitted after that time limit shall be examined, unless this would make it necessary to adjourn the trial. The accused shall be advised of the right to file such a motion (Article 451, third sentence CPC in conjunction with Article 113 § 1 CC). The obligation to bring an accused who is deprived of liberty is relative in the sense that the court may consider the presence of defence counsel sufficient and refrain from ordering that the accused be brought,[153] In such a case, the court, the president of the court or the

[148] Świecki (n 37) 313.
[149] Świecki (n 20) vol II, 229.
[150] Supreme Court Judgment, 15 July 2009, III KK 90/09, Lex no 608099.
[151] Supreme Court Decision, 11 December 2013, IV KK 402/13, OSNKW 2014, no 5, pos 39.
[152] Supreme Court Judgment, 21 November 2017 r, III KK 424/17, Lex no 2445786.
[153] Supreme Court Decision, 28 April 2021, IV KK 138/21, Lex no 3252661.

court clerk shall appoint ex officio a public defender for the accused deprived of liberty, unless he/she is already assisted by a defence counsel (Article 451, fourth sentence CPC in conjunction with Article 113 § 1 CPC). However, the principle should be to grant the motion of an accused deprived of liberty to order that he/she be brought to the appeal trial.[154] This is particularly important in view of the wide-ranging possibility of reformatory rulings at the appeal hearing.[155] The presence of a defence counsel should be considered sufficient in cases where appeal objections are limited strictly only to legal issues. On the other hand, such an eventuality (the presence of only a defence counsel) should be eliminated in the case of filing of a appeal to the disadvantage of the accused and objection raised in relation to guilt or penalty.

In the construction of the judicial examination in an appellate court, an important difference can be noticed in comparison with the judicial examination in a first-instance court, closely related to the controlling nature of the appellate proceedings. It concerns the beginning of the judicial examination before an appellate court, which, as a rule, takes the form of a report by the reporting judge, ie a member of the panel of judges who has been entrusted with the case for detailed elaboration.[156] The report is oral and consists of a presentation by the reporting judge of the course and results of previous proceedings, and particularly the contents of the judgment subject to appeal, the objections and motions forming the appeal, and finally the matters that must be resolved ex officio. If necessary, as part of the report, the reporting judge reads out aloud individual excerpts from the case file (Article 453 § 1 CPC). Although the content of the oral report does not need to be recorded, its presentation needs to be noted in the record of the appeal trial. The report is currently not an absolutely necessary part of the proceedings at the appeal trial. The court may dispense with it if nobody appeared at a trial. If only the participants in the proceedings have appeared in this forum, the court may decide, upon motion or with the consent of the present parties, not to deliver an oral report. In presented cases, the judicial examination commences upon announcement of the decision not to deliver an oral report (Article 453 § 1a CPC).

The remainder of the judicial examination at the appeal hearing, following the report of the reporting judge, may be filled with evidentiary proceedings (Article 452 § 2 CPC) or the hearing of the parties, including the submission of explanations, statements and motions by the parties (Article 453 § 2 CPC).[157]

Explanations of each of the parties, their defence counsels and attorneys, submitted at the appeal hearing, do not constitute evidence, but serve the purpose of additional clarification, and provide an explanation of doubts that may arise against the background of the content of the appeal or the arguments used in support thereof, or against the background of the appeal proceedings, eg the report of the reporting judge, when it did not accurately reflect the content of the appeal motions or appeal objections.

Evidentiary proceedings at the appeal hearing are subject to the rule contained in Article 167 CPC, according to which evidence shall be taken at the request of the parties

[154] Supreme Court Judgment, 23 June 2021, V KK 244/21, Lex no 3301574.
[155] Supreme Court Decision, 17 March 2021, IV KK 494/20, Lex no 3159082.
[156] Supreme Court Decision, 13 February 2020, V KK 558/19, Lex no 2784763.
[157] Supreme Court Decision, 3 January 2019, III KK 208/18, Lex no 2602114.

or ex officio. The initiative of the parties to take evidence at the appeal hearing is subject to a number of limitations. In addition to the above-presented limitation, which is a manifestation of evidence preclusion and consists in excluding the possibility of indicating in the appeal new facts or new evidence, if the appellant could have invoked them in the proceedings before the court of first instance (Article 427 § 3 CPC), Article 452 § 2 CPC provides for two grounds to dismiss an evidentiary motion in the appellate instance, complementing the catalogue of grounds for dismissing such a motion contained in Article 170 § 1 CPC. In accordance with Article 452 § 2 point 1 CPC, the appellate court shall dismiss a motion for evidence where the taking of the evidence by that court would not be purposeful for the reasons specified in the second sentence of Article 437 § 2, justifying setting aside the appealed verdict and referring the case for re-examination (passing a cassationary ruling), that is, in the event of the finding of an absolute reason for setting aside the judgment specified in Article 439 § 1 CPC, the actualisation of *the ne peius* rule under Article 454 § 1 CPC or in the event that it is found necessary to carry out the entire judicial examination again.[158] The last-mentioned circumstance justifying the issuance of a cassationary judgment and, at the same time, the dismission of the motion to take evidence gives grounds to conclude that the proceedings to take evidence in the appellate instance may be conducted if it is not necessary to carry out the entire judicial examination again. When such a need arises, it has already been established above when discussing type of decisions of the appellate body. The second of the additional grounds for dismissing a motion to take evidence in the appellate proceedings refers, although not in a fully compatible way, to the regulation of evidence preclusion in Article 427 § 3 CPC.[159] According to Article 452 § 2 point 2 CPC, the appellate court shall dismiss a motion for evidence where the evidence was not invoked before the court of the first instance, despite the fact that the person filing the motion could have invoked it then, or the circumstance that is to be proven concerns a new fact, not being the object of the proceedings before the court of the first instance, and the person filing the motion could have indicated it then. Dismissing the motion for evidence on this ground falls away, however, if the circumstance that is to be proven, within the limits of the appellate court's examination of the case, is of material importance to the determination whether a prohibited act was committed, whether it constitutes a criminal offence and what criminal offence, whether the prohibited act was committed under the conditions referred to in Articles 64 or 65 CC Code or whether there are grounds for ordering a stay in a psychiatric hospital pursuant to Article 93g CC, thus – in short – if is materially important in the matter of perpetration or guilt.[160]

Apart from the presented dissimilarities concerning the regulation of the judicial examination in an appellate court, the evidentiary proceedings before such court follow the same rules as in the court of first instance and are therefore based on the general rules governing the taking of evidence (eg with regard to witnesses, Articles 177 et seq CPC in conjunction with Article 458 CPC). From a model point of view, this means

[158] J Zagrodnik, 'Glosa do uchwały Sądu Najwyższego z dnia 20 września 2018 r, I KZP 10/18' (2019) *OSP* no 8, 67–72.

[159] Supreme Court Decision, 19 October 2017, IV KK 336/17, Lex no 2418090.

[160] Supreme Court Judgment, 5 May 2015, IV KK 428/14, Lex no 1729287.

evidentiary proceedings' subordination to the assumption of the dominant role of the court and the presiding judge, symptomatic of the inquisitorial model of the judicial process in terms of explanation of the case.[161]

Similarly as in the case of the main trial, after the evidence is taken and the judicial examination is closed, the appellate trial moves to the phase of final votes. These are used in appellate proceedings to express, mainly by the parties and their representatives, their own view on the course and results of evidence in the appellate trial. Granting these votes is separately regulated with regard to appeal proceedings in Article 453 § 3 CPC. According to this provision the presiding judge shall grant an opportunity to speak to the parties, their representatives and the social representative (the participants referred to in Article 406 § 1), in the order determined at the discretion of the presiding judge, with the appellant speaking first. If there is more than one appellant, eg the appeal has been brought by the accused and the public prosecutor, the order in which they speak shall be decided by the presiding judge. In such a procedural situation, the appellant who has filed an appeal within a broader scope should generally be given the floor first.[162] The accused and their defence counsel shall not be declined the right to speak after other participants in the proceedings have delivered their statements (Article 453 § 3, second sentence CPC). The right of the participants in the proceedings to speak in closing may in principle only be exercised within the limits of appellate review arising from the appeal(s) filed.

Complaints and Complaint Procedure

A complaint, as previously established, is an appeal measure against a ruling other than a judgment, so having a form of decision, and also serves to review orders, procedural actions that do not involve a decision or even to control a lack of action.[163] The practical significance of this measure is considerable for two main reasons. Firstly, because the right to lodge a complaint is not limited to decisions ending the proceedings, eg decisions to discontinue proceedings or orders to refuse to accept a complaint against a decision to discontinue proceedings, but is provided for in relation to numerous decisions and other procedural actions that are taken as part of a pending criminal trial. Secondly, because not only the decisions and other procedural actions of the court, but also the procedural actions of other procedural organs, first of all, the judicial organs (president of the court, chairman of the adjudicating panel), the prosecutor and the police, are subject to complaint control.

Undoubtedly, the most important group of activities subject to complaint are decisions. This is dictated by the importance of issues that are subject to resolution in this form. Apart from decisions that directly affect the course of a criminal trial (eg decisions

[161] Supreme Court Judgment, 18 March 2015, II KK 317/14, OSNKW 2015, no 8, pos 71.
[162] D Świecki, *Czynności procesowe obrońcy i pełnomocnika w sprawach karnych* (Warsaw, Wolters Kluwer, 2015) 457.
[163] Marszał and Zagrodnik (n 1) 761 et seq.

to discontinue or suspend a trial),[164] this form is also used for decisions that entail a deep interference in the sphere of individual rights and freedoms, especially decisions on the application of coercive measures (see chapter four). The appealability of decisions, as already established earlier, is not provided for in full, but concerns three categories of these, namely decisions which preclude the rendering of a judgment (unless otherwise provided in the CPC), primarily decisions discontinuing proceedings for any reason; decisions with respect to a preventive measure and decisions in cases prescribed under the CPC.[165] The latter category includes, for example, decisions to suspend proceedings (Article 22 § 2 CPC)[166] and decisions on a precautionary measure (Article 252 § 1 CPC). If a decision does not belong to one of these groups (eg a decision to dismiss a request for evidence), an appeal against the judgment may raise objections which have not, or could not, constitute the object of a complaint (Article 447 § 4 CPC).[167] Apart from the decisions, the complaint may be appealed against the orders as well. Moreover, in this case it is not possible to talk about full appealability. A complaint may be lodged against orders which preclude the rendering of a judgment as well as other orders with regard to which the possibility to lodge a complaint is separately provided for by law (Article 465 §1 in conjunction with Article 459 §1 CPC). The latter group includes, for example, the order of the president of the court to return the indictment to the prosecution counsel for the purpose of correcting the deficiencies (Article 337 §§ 1 and § 2 CPC). As an exception, a complaint also serves to challenge the judgment. This applies to its motivational part (statement of reason), if no appeal has been lodged against the judgment (Article 443a § 2, first sentence CPC). The decision on costs contained in the judgment is also subject to appeal if no appeal has been lodged against it (Article 626 § 3, first sentence CPC).[168] If there is a concurrence of a complaint against the statement of reasons of the judgment or the decision on costs, eg brought by the accused, with an appeal, eg brought by the public prosecutor, the complaint is subject to examination by the appellate court together with the appeal (Article 443a § 2, second sentence and Article 626 § 3, second sentence CPC).

In the cases specified in the Code, a complaint may be lodged against actions that do not consist of issuing a decision, as well as against the inaction of the procedural authorities (Article 467 § 1 CPC).[169] Such actions include, for example, arrest (Article 246). A failure to notify a person or institution that has submitted a notification of a criminal offence within six weeks about the instituting or refusal to institute an investigation is a complainable omission (Article 306 § 3 in conjunction with Article 325a § 1 CPC).

Complaints shall be filed basically within seven days as of the date of the announcement of the decision, or if the Act provides for the service of the decision, within seven days from the date of the service.[170] This also covers complaints against resolutions

[164] M Syta, 'Zażalenia na postanowienia zamykające drogę do wydania wyroku podejmowane w toku postępowania przygotowawczego' (2006) *Prok i Pr* no 1, 45; D Drajewicz, 'Zażalenie w postępowaniu karnym' (2013) *MoP*, no 1, 30.

[165] Appeal Court Decision in Katowice, 22 November 2017, II AKz 743/17, Biul SAKa 2017, no 4, pos 23.

[166] See further Supreme Court Decision, 18 July 2017, KSP 6/17, Lex no 2332326.

[167] Appeal Court Decision in Katowice, 22.12.2010, II AKz 842/10, Lex no 785471.

[168] Supreme Court Decision, 10 September 2020, II KZ 17/20, Lex no 3158464.

[169] Supreme Court Decision, 29 November 2016, I KZP 7/16, OSNKW 2016, no 12, pos 83.

[170] Appeal Court Decision in Cracow, 18 March 2010, II AKzw 222/10, KZS 2010, no 3, pos 38.

contained in a judgment and pertaining to costs and charges. However, when an appellant submits a motion for preparation of the statement of reasons for the judgment in writing and for the service thereof, a complaint may be brought within the time limit prescribed for filing an appeal (Article 460 CPC). In some cases, the Criminal Procedure Code provides for shorter time limits for filing a complaint, such as in Article 184 § 5 CPC (three days).

In the complaint procedure *ad quo*, ie before the body of first instance, as in the case of an appeal, the complaint is checked for formal requirements as well as its admissibility, legitimacy to file it and compliance with the time limit in this respect (Article 429 § 1 CPC). A positive result of this control means that the complaint may be considered substantively. The specificity of the complaint procedure lies in the fact that under certain conditions the authority that issued the contested decision is entitled to substantive examination of the complaint.[171] According to the first sentence of Article 463 § 1 CPC a court against whose decision a complaint has been filed may grant such a complaint, provided that it adjudicates in the same panel which issued the decision challenged.[172] Granting the complaint in its entirety ends the complaint proceedings without the need to send the complaint to the second instance.[173] In that event, the court must issue a decision granting the complaint.[174] As it is issued by the court of first instance, it does not benefit from the attribute of non-appealability, so it can be subject of complaint.[175] In other cases, it shall promptly refer the complaint with the case files or necessary copies of the case files to the court competent to examine the complaint (Article 463 § 1, second sentence CPC).[176] As a rule, it will be the court of the second instance, and sometimes another equivalent appellate court panel (Article 426 § 2 CCP) or the court competent to examine the case (eg Article 337 § 2 CCP).[177] A complaint against a decision on provisional detention or on security on property shall be referred for examination within forty-eight hours (Article 463 § 2 CPC). The presented possibility to consider the complaint in its entirety in the *ad quo* instance applies *mutatis mutandis* to the control of orders of judicial authorities and the control of procedural decisions issued by other procedural authorities, such as the prosecutor (Article 463 § 1 in conjunction with Articles 465 § 1 and 466 § 1 CPC).

As already indicated at the beginning of this chapter, unless provided otherwise under the CPC, submission a complaint shall not automatically stay the execution of a decision. However, the court that has issued such a decision or the court designated

[171] K Marszał, 'Względna dewolutywność zażalenia w postępowaniu przygotowawczym' (2003) *Prok i Pr* no 9, 7.

[172] Supreme Court Resolution, 24 August 2001, I KZP 12/01, OSNKW 2001, nos 9–10, pos 73; K Marszał, 'Problematyka względnej dewolutywności zażalenia w procesie karnym' (2003) *Stud Prawn* no 2, 133.

[173] Marszał (n 172) 128–29; D Wysocki, 'Glosa do uchwały SN z dnia 24.08.2001 r., I KZP 12/01' (2002) *OSP* no 3, 42; cf R Kmiecik, 'Glosa do postanowienia SN z dnia 11.12.2002 r., V KK 135/02' (2004) *PS* no 1, 191.

[174] Appeal Court Decision in Wroclaw, 1 April 2009, II AKz 145/09, Lex no 499989.

[175] Supreme Court Judgment, 24 January 2001, I KZP 46/00, Lex no 550515.

[176] Supreme Court Decision, 19 May 2005, WZ 44/05, OSNwSK 2005, no 1, pos 994.

[177] Supreme Court Decision, 24 January 2001, I KZP 46/00, Lex no 550515.

to examine the complaint may stay the execution of such a decision (Article 462 § 1 CPC).[178] This is the relatively suspensive nature of the complaint regarding the enforceability of the decision.[179]

If, in the *ad quem* instance (before the appellate authority), it is up to the court to examine the complaint, this takes place in a session. On the basis of Article 464 § 1 CPC, the parties, defence counsels and attorneys shall have the absolutely right to participate in a session of the appellate court examining a complaint against a decision concluding the proceedings, against a decision on a precautionary measure other than provisional detention, against a decision on property security, and against arrest.[180] They shall have the right to participate in sessions of the appellate court also where they have the right to participate in sessions of the court of the first instance. The parties also have the right to participate in the session of the appellate court examining the complaint against the statement of reasons (Article 443a § 3, first sentence CPC). Apart from the aforementioned cases, the appellate court may allow the parties, or a defence counsel or an attorney, to participate in the session. As regards the participation of a person deprived of his or her liberty in the appellate court session, Article 451 CPC, which has already been set out in the previous section (Article 96 § 1, second sentence and Article 443a § 3, second sentence CPC), applies accordingly.

Evidence in the strict sense shall not be taken in the context of an appellate court session. However, if, before a ruling is issued in a session, a necessity arises to verify the facts, the court can do so on its own or shall appoint a judge from the adjudicative panel for this purpose, or shall request a court of competent territorial jurisdiction to take specified measures (Article 97 CPC).

In addition to the competent court, it is the prosecutor, eg the directly superior public prosecutor (Article 302 § 3 CPC) or the public prosecutor supervising the investigation, who is responsible for investigating the complaint in cases specified by law.[181] The public prosecutor listed last is responsible for examining complaints against a decision issued by the body conducting an investigation other than a public prosecutor (Article 465 § 3 CPC).[182] In the case of the prosecutor's decision, the rule is that the complaint may be lodged with the court competent to examine the case, unless the Act provides otherwise (Article 465 § 2 CPC).

As a result of the control, the competent appellate authority shall take one of the previously discussed decisions provided for in Article 437 § 1 CPC, and a shall adjudicate whether the decision subject to review shall be sustained, amended or reversed, in whole or in part. When granting a complaint against an action or a failure to act, the appellate body states the unlawfulness of an action or a failure to act and orders suitable actions, in particular aimed to remedy the effects of the violation and to prevent similar violations from occurring in the future, and also undertakes other measures provided for in the CPC (Article 467 CPC).

[178] W Daszkiewicz, *Proces karny: część ogólna* (Toruń, Wydawnictwo Naukowe UMK, 1985) vol I, 240.
[179] Z Doda, *Zażalenie w procesie karnym* (Warsaw, Wydawnictwo Prawnicze, 1985) 209.
[180] See also Constitutional Tribunal Judgment, 27 October 2015, K 5/14, OTK-A 2015, no 9, pos 150.
[181] Appeal Court Decision in Cracow, 23 October 2017, II AKz 423/17, Lex no 2566587.
[182] Supreme Court Resolution, 23 February 1999, I KZP 35/98, OSNKW 1999, nos 3–4, pos 13; Appeal Court Decision in Katowice, 5 September 2008, II AKz 661/08, Lex no 477730.

Extraordinary Appeal Measures

Introduction

The model of appellate control in the Polish criminal trial is subordinated to the concept of a two-instance course of proceedings with a simultaneous development of extraordinary appeal measures in the form of a cassation appeal, a complaint against a cassation judgment of an appellate court and renewal of proceedings concluded with a final court judgment. These measures are regulated in Section XI CPC. They mainly serve to eliminate from legal circulation final and binding (valid) judgments of the court ending the proceedings, affected by the most serious defects. The functioning of such judgment in legal circulation is *de facto* in conflict with the sake of justice.[183] This statement applies in its entirety to the cassation appeal and a request for renewal of the proceedings concluded by the final court decision, and therefore they play a fundamental role at the level of extraordinary appellate control. The situation is different in the case of a complaints against appellate court judgment, which is available against a judgment which reverses the appealed judgment and refers the case for re-examination – the nature of this complaint is not to end the proceedings, and the attribute of validity is granted to it in the formal respect.[184]

Having regard to the established fundamental purpose of extraordinary appeal measures, it can be stressed – assuming a certain simplification – that, in the case of a cassation, extraordinary appeal is achieved through the control of the contested judgments from the point of view of their legality. It therefore relates to judgments of courts that contain flagrant infringements of the law (substantive and procedural), while in the case of the renewal of proceedings concluded by a final court judgment, it is about judgments suffering from the most serious errors in the sphere of underlying factual findings. In other words, it can be said that the cassation serves to correct legal errors (errors in the application of legal provisions) that have crept into the judgment, while the renewal of proceedings means sui generis *reasumptio causae* that ended with a final court decision, usually as a result of the discovery of new facts or evidence.[185]

[183] A Murzynowski, 'Prawomocność orzeczeń sądowych jako przesłanka kasacji' in A Gaberle and S Waltoś (eds), *Środki zaskarżenia w procesie karnym. Księga pamiątkowa ku czci Profesora Zbigniewa Dody* (Cracow, Wolters Kluwer, 2000) 193; M Rogacka-Rzewnicka, *Kasacja w polskim procesie karnym* (Warsaw, Wolters Kluwer, 2001) 159; Supreme Court Resolution, 29 November 2016, I KZP 6/16, OSNKW 2017, no 1, pos 1.

[184] Validity *in genere* is the characteristic of a decision which means that it is not subject to challenge by ordinary means of appeal. In formal terms, validity means that the decision may not be challenged by way of ordinary legal remedies to the extent aimed at the continuation of the existing criminal proceedings. See S Steinborn, *Prawomocność części orzeczenia w procesie karnym* (Warsaw, Wolters Kluwer, 2011) 45–69; S Steinborn, 'Skarga na wyroku kasatoryjny sądu odwoławczego na tle systemu środków zaskarżenia w polskim procesu karnym' in T Grzegorczyk and R Olszewski (eds), *Verba volant, scripta manent. Proces karny, prawa karne skarbowe i prawo wykroczeń po zmianach z lat 2015–2016. Księga pamiątkowa poświęcona Profesor Monice Zbrojewskiej* (Warsaw, 2017) 419; similarly Zagrodnik (n 7) 524.

[185] Zagrodnik (n 26) 590; K Dudka and H Paluszkiewicz, *Postępowanie karne* (Warsaw, 2017) 583. It should be noted that the highlighted, essential differences between the cassation and the renewal of the proceedings concluded with a final court ruling have been to some extent blurred as a result of the amendments made to the CPC in 2003 and the introduction of the possibility of renewal of the proceedings *ex officio* due to the determination of one of the infringements listed in Art 439 § 1 CPC, which also constitute grounds for cassation (Art 542(3) CC).

Cassation

The cassation is the principal extraordinary appeal measure. In contrast to the ordinary appeal measures in relation to the cassation appeal, the law defines its grounds addressed to the applicant, which are the categories of violations that may be raised in the cassation appeal. According to Article 523 § 1 CPC a cassation appeal may be filed only due to the violations listed in Article 439 or another flagrant infringement of law where it could have had a significant effect on the contents of the ruling. The violations listed in Article 439 § 1 CPC, which comprise the category of absolute grounds for overturning a ruling, have already been illustrated in detail above in this chapter. They may constitute grounds for cassation, if they occurred in reality, and not, for example, as a result of improper preparation of the record of the main trial.[186] In the light of the wording of Article 523 § 1, there is no doubt that these other infringements may constitute grounds for cassation if they consist in a flagrant violation of law – *lege non distinguente* – both substantive and procedural.[187] *A contrario*, the grounds for a cassation appeal cannot be constituted by violations relating only to the sphere of establishing facts,[188] the legitimacy of the assessment of evidence and the conclusions drawn from it, or the assessment of the credibility of witness testimony, if they remain within the limits of the free assessment of evidence.[189] This does not yet explain what 'another flagrant infringement of law where it could have had a significant effect on the contents of the ruling' consists of. The ground of cassation contained in this normative phrase is based on two vague terms, namely 'flagrant infringement of law' and 'it could have had a significant effect on the contents of the ruling'. In order to concretise it, it is necessary to determine the scope of meaning (set of designations) of these terms. Without this it is basically impossible to show the admissibility of cassation appeals in the Polish legal order.

As far as the first of the distinguished terms is concerned, it is important that it is clearly referred, in the word 'other', to the defects (infringements) listed in Article 439 CPC. This provides the basis for the statement that the flagrant nature of the violation should not be determined only by whether it is obvious, undoubted, can be directly stated, but also by the rank of the provision that has been violated.[190] In this sense, obvious violations of procedural law provisions that are of fundamental importance for the correct identification and resolution of the issue of criminal liability of the accused can be regarded as flagrant. Such importance should undoubtedly be attributed to provisions expressing procedural principles or guarantees. In the case of substantive law infringements, to the category of 'flagrant' belong, in accordance with an assumed assumption, those that concern the basic regulations on criminal responsibility and legal qualification of an act. A flagrant violation of law occurs not only when a procedural body can be

[186] Supreme Court Judgment, 19 March 1977, II KZ 55/77, OSNKW 1977, nos 4–5, pos 46.

[187] Supreme Court Decision, 2 March 2022, III KK 19/22, Lex no 3405894.

[188] Errors in establishing facts may only indirectly justify overturning the contested decision if they are, in essence, a result of violation of procedural law: Supreme Court Judgment, 21 May 1996, IV CCN 4/96, unpublished.

[189] Supreme Court Judgment, 18 February 2010, II CC 14/10, Lex no 583770.

[190] See Świecki (n 20) 530–31; Supreme Court Judgment, 18 March 2015, III CC 442/14, Lex no 1729284; Supreme Court Judgment, 8 October 2009, V CC 99/09, OSNKW 2010, no 3, pos 26.

accused of such a violation (it is charged to this body), but also when a flagrant violation of rights or interests results from objective reasons, independent of this body.[191] The second of the terms making up the structure of the grounds for a cassation appeal in question involves the requirement that a specific violation could have had a significant impact on the content of the ruling. According to the prevailing view in the case law, this requirement is met if it is possible to prove that the contested decision would have been materially different from the one that was made, had it not been for the flagrant violation of law.[192]

The previous findings were devoted to the presentation of grounds for cassation in their positive formulation provided for in Article 523 § 1, first sentence of the CPC. These grounds are also normatively clarified by their regulation from the negative side through a statutory specification of what may not constitute grounds for cassation. Of fundamental importance in this regard is the provision contained in the second sentence of Article 523 § 1 CPC, according to which a cassation appeal may not be filed only due to the penalty being disproportionate. The only exception in this regard concerns the Prosecutor General, who in cases of felonies may file a cassation appeal only due to the disproportionality of the penalty (Article 523 § 1a CPC). The exclusion of this possibility in the case of parties does not completely exclude the raising of the disproportionality of the punishment. What is important is that it should be accompanied by an objection of violations of procedural law or substantive law provisions, which *in concreto* could have had a significant impact on the content of the decision on penalty.[193] A different type of negative regulation of cassation grounds results from the reference, within the scope of the regulation of cassation proceedings, to the accordingly application of the provisions regulating appeal proceedings (Article 518 CPC). Based on this, it should be stated that – in connection with the content of Article 447 § 6 CPC – the grounds for cassation cannot be based exclusively on the objections, the consideration of which is possible in the procedure of correcting the judgment (Article 105 CPC), in the procedure of supplementing or modifying the judgment to the extent of the decisions set out in Article 420 CPC, or in the procedure of supplementing or modifying the decision on costs (Article 626 CPC).

Within the framework of the regulation of cassation appeals and the procedure for bringing them, two significantly different courses can be distinguished. One is initiated by a cassation appeal of a party. The second is initiated by a cassation complaint of special entities, which include the General Public Prosecutor, the Commissioner for Human Rights (Rzecznik Praw Obywatelskich) and the Ombudsperson for Children, who has the right to a cassation appeal, if the issuance of final a ruling infringed the rights of a child (Article 521 § 2 CPC). The key points of each of these courses will be presented below. Before doing so, however, it must be emphasised that with respect to the rights of the parties and the cassation proceedings, the above-mentioned application of the rules governing the appeal proceedings to the cassation must also be borne in mind.

[191] Supreme Court Judgment, 6 September 1996, II CCN 71/96, OSNKW 1997, nos 1–2, pos 14; Supreme Court Judgment, 28 March 2002, I KZP 8/02, OSNKW 2002, nos 5–6, pos 33.

[192] Supreme Court Judgment, 18 March 2003, IV CCN 332/00, OSNwSK 2003, no 1, pos 574; Supreme Court Judgment, 15 November 2007, II CC 62/07, Lex no 346221.

[193] Supreme Court Judgment, 3 November 1999, IV CCN 206/99, OSNKW 2000, nos 1–2, pos 15.

The parties may file a cassation appeal in principle against a final and binding (valid) judgment of the appellate court concluding proceedings.[194] This means that they are not entitled to lodge a cassation appeal either against a ruling in the form of decision of the appellate court or against a judgment that has become final and binding in the court of first instance, even if it concludes the proceedings.[195] As an exception, parties may file a cassation appeal against final decisions of the appellate court on discontinuance of the proceedings and application of a protective measure specified in Article 93a CC, eg therapy, addiction therapy, placement in a psychiatric facility (Article 519 CC). The requirement that a cassation appeal may only be lodged against judgments ending the proceedings excludes the possibility to lodge a cassation appeal against the judgment of the appellate court reversing the appealed verdict and referring the case for re-examination,[196] as in such a case the content of the judgment is, in fact, the order to continue the proceedings. It is inadmissible to file a cassation appeal only against the statement of reasons of the judgment of the appellate court (*argumentum ex* Article 519, second sentence CPC).

The parties' right to cassation from final judgments of the appellate court ending the proceedings is subject to a number of limitations. First and foremost, it cannot be used by a party if it has not previously appealed against the judgment of the court of first instance.[197] The *ratio legis* of this restriction is to eliminate situations in which a party would use a cassation appeal in place of an ordinary appeal and inaugurate an ordinary instance control. It does not apply if a judgment in the appellate instance is amended to the disadvantage of a party who did not file an appeal, and if violations specified in Article 439 § 1 CPC are raised in the cassation.[198] A separate group is constituted by object-related limitations on lodging a cassation appeal by the parties, connected with the direction of this extraordinary appeal measure. They concern only the proceedings, the subject of which is the settlement of the issue of criminal liability of the accused.[199] According to Article 523 § 2 CPC, a cassation appeal to the advantage (to the benefit of the accused) may be filed only if the accused is sentenced for a criminal or fiscal offence for a penalty of imprisonment without a conditional suspension of its execution. This provision means that a cassation appeal in favour of a party is inadmissible, first, if the sentence of imprisonment has been conditionally suspended, and second, if a lighter punishment has been imposed, such as an autonomous fine, or the proceedings have been conditionally discontinued. This solution is undoubtedly aimed at limiting the number of cassation appeals filed by the parties. However, one can see a certain danger connected with it, consisting in a reduced care of the appellate court about the content of the judgment, and especially its justification, in cases in which a conditional suspension of the adjudicated imprisonment sentence is finally applied, which excludes cassation

[194] Supreme Court Resolution, 24 July 2001, I KZP 15/01, OSNKW 2001, nos 9–10, pos 74.
[195] Marszał and Zagrodnik (n 1) 768–69.
[196] Such a judgment may be appealed against by the appellate court, which is discussed in the next section.
[197] Supreme Court Judgment, 17 March 2011, III KK 352/10, Lex no 794160; Supreme Court Decision, 26 September 2012, V KK 119/12, Lex no 1226777.
[198] Supreme Court Decision, 31 January 2001, V KZ 1/01, Lex no 51829; Supreme Court Judgment, 2 December 2015, III KK 287/15, OSNKW 2016, no 2, pos 15.
[199] Supreme Court Judgment, 24 July 2001, I KZP 15/01, OSNKW 2001, nos 9–10, pos 74.

control of the judgment.[200] Under Article 523 § 3 CPC a cassation to the disadvantage of the accused may be filed only in the case of the acquittal of accused or the discontinuance of the proceedings. It follows from this provision that it is not possible for a party to file a cassation for the purpose of a more severe punishment. The presented limitations related to the direction of the cassation appeal also do not apply to violations of Article 439 of the CPC.

The right of the parties to file a cassation appeal is subject to a time limit of 30 days, running from the date of service of the ruling with statement of reasons.[201] Filing a cassation appeal should be preceded by filing a motion requesting the service of a reasoned ruling. A motion requesting the service of the ruling with the statement of reasons shall be filed with the court which rendered the ruling within a final time limit of seven days from the date of the ruling's announcement, and if the Act provides for serving the ruling, as of the date of its service (Article 524 § 1, second sentence CPC).[202] The procedural effects of the filing of such a motion are also triggered by the filing of a cassation within the prescribed seven-day period (Article 524 § 1, third sentence, in conjunction with Article 445 § 2 CPC). Apart from such a case, the absence of a motion requesting the service of the ruling of the appellate court with a statement of reasons excludes the possibility of filing a cassation appeal by a party. Specific requirements for a cassation appeal from party include the obligation to have it drawn up and signed by a solicitor, a legal counsel or a counsel of the General Counsel to the Republic of Poland (compulsory representation by a lawyer – Article 526 § 2 CPC) and the obligation to pay a fee for the cassation appeal, unless the party is exempted from this obligation (Article 527 CPC).[203] The cassation must also be accompanied by an adequate number of copies for the opposing parties (Article 446 § 2 in conjunction with Article 518 and *argumentum ex* Article 530 § 1 CPC).[204] The filing of a cassation appeal by the parties takes place via the appellate court (Article 525 § 1 CPC).

The subject of the cassation appeal is more broadly defined in the case of the aforementioned special entities. According to Article 521 CPC, the General Public Prosecutor, the Commissioner for Human Rights and the Ombudsperson for Children may file a cassation appeal against any final and binding court ruling concluding proceedings. It follows that they may file a cassation appeal also against the judgment of the court of first instance, if in that instance it acquired the attribute of validity, as well as against final court ruling in the form of decisions, if they end the proceedings, eg final and binding decisions to discontinue criminal proceedings or to uphold the prosecutor's decision to discontinue the pre-trial proceedings. These entities file a cassation directly to the Supreme Court (Article 525 § 2 CPC) and are not bound by the time limit set for

[200] Supreme Court Decision, 2 February 2001, V KKN 550/00, Lex no 48292.

[201] Świecki (n 20) vol II, 549.

[202] See also Supreme Court Resolution, 9 June 2006, I KZP 10/06, OSNKW 2006, nos 7–8, pos 65.

[203] It should be noted that under the cited provision a person deprived of liberty shall not pay a fee when filing a cassation appeal. The fee shall be payable only if the cassation appeal is left unheard or dismissed (Article 527 § 2 CPC). The fee shall be refunded to the party who paid it, if the cassation appeal is granted, even in part, or if it is withdrawn (Article 527 § 4 CPC).

[204] Supreme Court Decision, 8 November 2000, II KZ 129/00, OSNKW 2001, nos 1–2, pos 11; R Kmiecik, 'Glosa do postanowienia Sądu Najwyższego z dnia 20 października 1998 r' (1999) III KZ 109/98, OSP no 3, pos 67.

the parties (Article 524 § 2 CPC). In terms of the broadly defined right of special entities to file a cassation appeal, the following exclusions regarding the filing or granting of a cassation appeal are of significance:

1. No cassation appeal may be lodged against a ruling rendered by the Supreme Court in a hearing of a cassation appeal – prohibition of super cassation (Article 539 CPC).[205]
2. A cassation appeal concerning the same accused and the same ruling may be brought only once by each person entitled to do so (Article 522 CPC).[206]
3. A cassation appeal to the disadvantage of the accused shall not be accepted after a year has passed from the date on which the ruling became final (Article 524 § 3 CPC).[207]

Although theoretically these exclusions also refer to the parties to the proceedings, in practice their importance becomes apparent within the course of cassation proceedings, the impetus for which is the cassation of special subjects. The parties may initiate a cassation by special entities, requesting it both when their cassation is inadmissible, eg due to the limitations arising from Article 523 §§ 2 and 3 CPC, or the time limit for filing it has expired, and when their cassation has not had the intended effect.[208]

Regardless of who files the cassation, this must be done in written form. It must therefore comply with the general requirements for a pleading set out in Article 119 § 1 CPC. The specific requirements for the content of a cassation appeal include the indication of the appealed sattlements of the appellate court (the scope of the appeal), specification the nature of the alleged violation, the indication by the appellant of what he/she demands, ie the formulation of the cassation requests, and the statement of reasons for the cassation appeal (Article 427 §§ 1 and 2 in connection with Articles 518 and 526 § 1 CPC).

If the cassation is filed by a party, the president of the appellate court reviews it in terms of the admissibility of the cassation, the observance of the time limit for filing the cassation, the legitimacy to appeal and the fulfilment of the formal requirements of the cassation. If the outcome of this control is positive, or if the formal deficiencies of the cassation, eg the lack of the fee or compulsory representation by a lawyer, are successfully remedied, the president of the appellate court (the chair of the appellate division) issues an order of acceptance of the cassation, initiating the preliminary cassation proceedings (*postępowanie okołokasacyjne*),[209] serves copies of the cassation to the parties other than the appellant and sends the file to the cassation court without delay; however, in the case of a cassation that has not been filed by a prosecutor, this occurs after receiving his/her written response to the cassation (Article 530 § 1 CPC). The order of acceptance of the cassation appeal is not subject to complaint. However, its correctness is indirectly subject to the control of the Supreme Court, which issues a decision to leave the cassation appeal unheard if it is found that it is inadmissible, was filed by an

[205] Supreme Court Decision, 12 December 2003, II KZ 45/03, OSNwSK 2003, no 1, pos 2698.
[206] Supreme Court Decision, 9 March 2022, III KZ 7/22, Lex no 3409439.
[207] Marszał and Zagrodnik (n 1) 771.
[208] Supreme Court Judgment, 8 October 2002, III KKN 119/01, OSNKW 2003, nos 1–2, pos 17.
[209] Supreme Court Decision, 28 April 2003, III KZ 3/03, Lex no 78399.

unauthorised entity or out of time, or does not meet the formal requirements, as well as if it finds that the cassation appeal has been accepted as a result of a groundless restitution of a time limit (Article 531 § 1 CPC).[210]

The indicated preliminary cassation procedure is a manifestation of a kind of written adversarialism related to the examination of the cassation, which acquires particular significance in those cases where the examination of this complaint takes place in a session.[211] It is based on the prosecutor's obligation to file an answer to the cassation appeal. If the public prosecutor's finding that the appeal is not manifestly unfounded, a copy of the written answer of the public prosecutor to the cassation appeal shall be served by the court on the other parties, their defence counsels and attorneys (Article 530 § 4 CPC). Considering a cassation appeal to be manifestly unfounded, the public prosecutor shall send a copy of the answer to the cassation appeal to the other parties, their defence counsels and attorneys, who within fourteen days of receiving the answer of the public prosecutor may present their position to the court in writing. Although the law does not provide for an obligation to file an answer to the cassation appeal from the public prosecutor, the parties and their defence counsels are entitled to file such an answer (Article 428 § 2 in conjunction with Article 518 CPC).

The primary forum for the Supreme Court to hear a cassation appeal is the trial (*argumentum ex* Article 535 § 1 CPC).[212] The principle of examining the cassation appeal at a trial is subject to exceptions in three groups of cases, namely if the Supreme Court rejects of a cassation as obviously groundless (Article 535 § 3 CPC), upholds it in its entirety if it is manifestly justified (Article 535 § 5 CPC) or finds of an absolute reason for reversion of the ruling set out in Article 439 § 1 CPC (Article 439 § 1 *in principio* in conjunction with Article 518 CPC). It should be noted that a cassation appeal filed pursuant to Article 521 CPC shall be examined by the Supreme Court at a trial (Article 535 § 4 CPC). This does not apply only if the cassation appeal filed in favour of a party is upheld in its entirety if it is manifestly justified.[213]

The regulation of the cassation trial is essentially based on the accordingly application of the provisions governing the course of the appeal trial (Article 518 CPC) and – based on the 'further' reference provided for in Article 458 CPC – the provisions for which original area of regulation is the course of the main trial. However, it would be erroneous to believe on this basis that in cassation proceedings, as in the case of a main trial or appeal trial, it is permissible to take evidence on the merits, which would allow, inter alia, the cassation court to make its own findings of fact in the case. With reference to the findings already made in connection with the grounds for cassation, it should be emphasised at this point that the cassation control is carried out only from the perspective of verifying violations of law, to the exclusion of reviewing the correctness of factual findings.[214] It cannot constitute a renewed appellate review,

[210] Supreme Court Decision, 21 May 2020, IV KZ 17/20, Lex no 3214956.

[211] W Grzeszczyk, *Kasacja w sprawach karnych* (Warsaw, Ministerstwo Sprawiedliwości. Departament Kadr i Szkolenia, 2001) 219.

[212] Zabłocki (n 99) 588.

[213] Supreme Court Judgment, 4 November 2021, I KK 115/21, Lex no 3330724.

[214] Supreme Court Judgment, 6 September 1996, II KKN 63/96, OSNKW 1997, nos 1–2, pos 11.

'third instance',[215] which would serve once again to verify the correctness of the assessment of evidence or the legitimacy of factual findings.[216] On the other hand, the cassation court should verify whether in connection with making factual findings the courts adjudicating at both instances did not commit a flagrant violation of procedural rules, which could have affected factual findings, and consequently, the content of the judgment. In this respect, however, it is not the factual findings themselves that are subject to review, but the manner in which they were made.[217] The above comments entitle us to conclude that the scope of evidence proceedings in the course of the cassation trial is in fact determined by the limits of the cassation court's examination of the case, in particular through the objections raised. Evidentiary proceedings at the cassation trial are therefore admissible within the limits justified by the need to confirm or exclude the objections of a flagrant violation of law raised in the cassation, or a violation of law, which is taken into account ex officio.[218] This excludes, in principle, the examination at the cassation hearing of evidence on the merits of the case on which the factual findings underlying the ruling on the issue of criminal responsibility of the accused subject to the cassation appeal are based.

With regard to the main trial, the question of the participation of a person deprived of liberty in the trial is regulated in an autonomous manner. The rule is that it is not brought to the cassation trial. An exception to this is when the President of the Supreme Court, or the Supreme Court, considers the presence of such a person at the cassation trial necessary (Article 535 § 2 CPC). The participation of the prosecutor in the cassation trial is mandatory. The participation of the defence counsel is also mandatory in cases of mandatory defence as illustrated earlier (see chapter three), as set out in Articles 79 and 80 (Article 450 in conjunction with Article 518 CPC).

Having heard the case, the Supreme Court shall dismiss the cassation appeal or reverse the appealed ruling in whole or in part (Article 537 § 1 CPC).[219] According to Article 537 § 2, the Supreme Court, when reversing a contested ruling, shall refer the case to the court having jurisdiction over it for re-examination or shall discontinue the proceedings; when the conviction is found to be manifestly unjust, the Supreme Court shall acquit the accused. A judgment of the appellate court shall not be reversed due to the fact that its statement of reasons does not meet the requirements set out in applicable regulations (Article 537a CPC).

Complaints Against Appellate Court Judgments

A complaint against a judgment of the court of appeal only serves to challenge an appellate court judgment revoking a judgment of the court of first instance and referring the

[215] Supreme Court Decision, 20 April 2011, II KK 78/11, Lex no 847135; Supreme Court Decision, 22 August 2013, II KK 190/13, Lex no 1352411; S Zabłocki, 'Przegląd orzecznictwa Sądu najwyższego – Izba Karna' (1997) *Pal* nos 7–8, 180.

[216] Supreme Court Judgment, 20 April 2011, II CC 78/11, Lex no 847135.

[217] Supreme Court Judgment, 6 September 1996, II CCN 63/96, OSNWK 1997, nos 1–2, pos 11.

[218] Supreme Court Judgment, 3 April 1997, III CCN 170/96, OSNKW 1997, nos 7–8, pos 69.

[219] Supreme Court Decision, 29 April 2022, III KZ 21/22, Lex no 3414698.

case for reconsideration (revocation judgment, a so-called cassation judgment – *wyrok kasatoryjny*). As has been mentioned previously, this is a judgment that has the attribute of validity in the full meaning only in the formal aspect connected with the lack of possibility to challenge it by means of ordinary legal remedies.[220] At the level of substantive validity, a revocation judgment has an effect of validity only to the extent to which it decides on the appeal filed against the judgment of the court of first instance, for in this respect its issuing results in inadmissibility of re-examination of the appeal in the appellate instance. The *ratio legis* of the institution of complaint against the judgment of the appellate court is to ensure eliminating groundless revocations of judgments in the appellate instance, which result in referring the cases for re-examination in the first instance.[221] The idea is to speed up the criminal process.[222] In relation to the complaint, it is sometimes said to cause a 'freezing effect' in the area of jurisdiction of appellate courts by exerting a psychological influence on judges of these courts, to restrain their possible inclination to issue revocation judgments.[223]

With regard to the complaint against a revocation judgment of the appellate court, as was the case with the cassation, the law defines its grounds, ie the categories of defects because of which it may be brought. According to Article 539a § 3 CPC a complaint may be filed exclusively due to an infringement of Article 437 or due to the violations indicated in Article 439 § 1.[224]

In the case of an infringement of Article 437 CPC, it is in fact a violation of the norm expressed in § 2 of this provision, which sets out the grounds for issuing revocation rulings in the appellate instance. Such violations consist, first of all, in issuing a judgment revoking the appealed verdict of the court of first instance and referring the case for re-examination, despite the fact that none of the grounds for issuing such a judgment, listed in Article 437 § 2, second sentence CPC, existed.[225] It should be pointed out here that in accordance with this provision, issuance of a revocation judgment may take place only in the situations indicated in Article 439 § 1 CPC (absolute reasons for reversal) or Article 454 CPC (*ne peius* rules), or if it is necessary to carry out the entire judicial examination again. In addition to an erroneous finding of one of the mentioned circumstances, a violation of Article 437 § 2 CPC may consist in the appellate court issuing a revocation judgment on grounds other than those specified in the second sentence of Article 437 § 2 CPC. It also occurs when the court issued a revocation judgment even though it should have discontinued the proceedings due to the occurrence of a procedural obstacle, eg the statute of limitations on criminality, following the revocation of the appealed judgment.[226]

[220] cf Steinborn (n 184, 2017) 418–19; Steinborn (n 184, 2011) 83–84.

[221] Supreme Court Judgment, 27 July 2017, IV KS 2/17, OSNKW 2018, no 5, pos 35; Supreme Court Resolution, 14 September 2017, I KZP 9/17, OSNKW 2017, no 10, pos 59.

[222] Supreme Court Judgment, 7 April 2022, III KS 20/22, Lex no 3392042.

[223] A Lach, 'Skarga na wyrok sądu odwoławczego' in A Lach (ed), *Postępowanie karne po nowelizacji z dnia 11 marca 2016 r* (Warsaw, Wolters Kluwer, 2017) 261.

[224] Supreme Court Judgment, 13 April 2022, I KS 3/22, Lex no 3392041; Supreme Court Decision, 1 April 2022, I KS 7/22, Lex no 3418416; A Sakowicz, 'Zakres kontroli dokonywanej przez Sąd Najwyższy przy rozpoznaniu skargi na wyrok kasatoryjny sądu odwoławczego' (2018) *BSP* no 1, 15860.

[225] Supreme Court Decision, 10 November 2021, III KS 23/21, Lex no 3315422.

[226] Supreme Court Decision, 30 September 2021 r, III KS 17/21, Lex no 3322020.

The second category of violations on which a complaint against a cassation judgment of an appellate court may be based are the most serious infringement of a mainly procedural nature, listed in Article 439 § 1 CPC, which has already been cited several times and discussed earlier. At first sight, one could wonder about the sense of distinguishing the grounds for complaint referring to the invoked provision, since this provision also appears in the context of the first of the distinguished grounds. However, it can be seen that in the latter case it is a question of verifying the correctness of the finding of the absolute reasons of appeal set out in Article 439 § 1 CPC by the appellate court in relation to the judgment and proceedings before the court of first instance, whereas as an autonomous ground of complaint provided for in Article 539a § 3 *in fine* CPC, this provision refers directly to the judgment of the appellate court setting aside the judgment of the court of first instance and referring the case for re-examination. In this way, the point is to verify the cassation judgment of the appellate court in terms of the violations specified in Article 439 § 1 CPC and to eliminate situations in which the basis for continuation of the criminal trial and re-examination of the case would be a judgment of the appellate court affected by gross violations listed in the indicated provision.

The right to file a complaint against a cassation judgment of the appellate court is vested in the parties (Article 539a § 1 CPC). The time limit for filing a complaint is seven days and runs from the date of service of the cassation judgment of the appellate court together with a statement of reasons (Article 539b § 1, first sentence CPC).[227] It is a final time limit (*argumentum ex* Article 122 § 2 CPC), and therefore may be reinstated if failure to comply with it is due to reasons beyond the control of the party.[228] As a rule, filing a complaint should be preceded by a motion for serving the appellate court ruling with a statement of reasons.[229] Such a motion should be filed with the appellate court within seven days of the announcement of the judgment by that court, and if the law provides for delivery of the judgment, from the date of its delivery (Article 524 § 1, second sentence, in connection with Article 539b § 1, second sentence CPC). The same consequences as filing a motion for service of a cassation judgment of the appellate court with a statement of reasons is caused by filing a complaint against such judgment before the final time limit for filing the indicated motion.

A complaint against a judgment of the appellate court setting aside a first-instance judgment and referring the case back for re-examination must be made in writing (Article 428 § 1 in conjunction with Article 539f CPC). In addition to the general requirements for a pleading (Article 119 § 1 CPC), a specific requirement as to its content arises from the obligation to specify the nature of the alleged violation (Article 526 § 1 in conjunction with Article 539f CPC). This means that the complaint must contain an allegation, the content of which, in accordance with the findings made earlier concerning its grounds, should raise an infringement of Article 437 § 2 CPC (eg in conjunction with Article 439 § 1(10) and Article 439 § 2 or in conjunction with Article 454 § 1 CPC) or a violation specified in Article 439 § 1 CPC. A cassation judgment of the appellate court may be complained against in whole or in part (Article 539a § 2 CPC). The formal requirements for a complaint against a revocation judgment of a court of

[227] Supreme Court Decision, 21 September 2018, III KS 25/18, OSNKW 2018, no 12, pos 80.
[228] Supreme Court Judgment, 29 May 2012, III KK 87/12, Lex no 1212370.
[229] Świecki (n 20) vol II, 642–42.

appeal, which do not concern its content, include that the complaint be drawn up and signed by a solicitor, a legal adviser or an adviser to the Prosecutor General's Office of the Republic of Poland (compulsory representation by a lawyer; Article 526 § 2 in conjunction with Article 539f CPC) and that a fee be paid.[230] It is also a formal requirement that the appropriate number of duplicates for the other parties shall be enclosed with a complaint (Article 539c § 1 CPC).[231]

Following the filing of the complaint with the appeal court that issued the contested revocation judgment, the president of that court (chairman of the appeal division) carries out a review of the complaint in terms of the admissibility of the complaint, compliance with the time limit for filing it, the legitimacy to file the complaint and the fulfilment of the formal requirements, including whether it is based on reasons indicated in Article 539a § 3 CPC (Article 530 § 2 in conjunction with Article 539f CPC).[232] If the outcome of this check is positive, or if the complaint has been efficiently corrected following a request to remedy defects under Article 120 § 1 CPC, the president of the appellate court issues an order accepting the complaint and serving copies of the complaint on the other parties with an instruction on the right to file a written response to the complaint within seven days of service of the copy (Article 539c § 2, first sentence CPC).[233] After the expiry of this time limit, the president of the court should immediately order the file to be sent to the Supreme Court. If, however, after the complaint and the files are received by the Supreme Court, the Court finds that the complaint is inadmissible, was filed by an unauthorised entity or out of time or does not meet the formal requirements, or finds that the acceptance of the complaint was due to the groundless restitution of a time limit, it issues a decision to leave the complaint unheard (Article 531 § 1 in conjunction with Article 539f CPC). Such a decision indirectly indicates that the order accepting the complaint against the judgment of the court of appeal is defective. If the Supreme Court determines that the complaint has defects of a removable nature and that steps to remedy the defects have not been conducted in the appellate court, it should return the case file to the appellate court to take steps to remedy the defects (Article 531 § 2 in conjunction with Article 539f CPC).

The Supreme Court shall consider a complaint in a session without the participation of the parties (Article 539e § 1 CPC). As a result of considering the complaint against appellate court judgments, the Supreme Court may either reject the complaint or uphold it. Rejection of the complaint takes the form of a decision. If the complaint is upheld, the contested cassation judgment is revoked and the case is referred back to the appellate court. A judgment is required in this case (Article 539e § 1 CPC). It is worth noting that the Supreme Court in the proceedings in question may not, as a consequence of revoking the appealed judgment of the appellate court, discontinue the proceedings, even if it notices a violation justifying such a secondary decision, eg under Article 439 § 1(9) CPC (*argumentum a contrario ex* Article 539e § 2 CPC).[234]

[230] See also Supreme Court Decision, 10 April 2014, SDI 10/14, Lex no 1459165; Świecki (n 20) vol II, 626.
[231] Supreme Court Judgment, 8 November 2000, II KZ 129/00, OSNKW 2001, no 1–2, pos 11.
[232] Świecki (n 20) vol II, 625–26.
[233] Supreme Court Decision, 26 June 2019, V KZ 24/19, Lex no 2692767.
[234] cf Supreme Court Judgment, 28 July 2021, V KS 20/21, Lex no 3395866; Supreme Court Judgment, 26 October 2017, V KS 9/17, OSNKW 2018, no 2, pos 14.

Renewal of Proceedings

A motion for renewal of proceedings, because this is the form of an extraordinary appeal measure, serves the purpose of eliminating from legal circulation final (valid) court rulings that end the proceedings, that are affected by the most serious defects, due to which the ruling cannot stand, because it is detrimental to the interests of justice. In its traditional form, the renewal of proceedings concerned situations in which after issuing the final judgment new facts or evidence came to light indicating that an innocent person had been convicted, or that the judgment was based on false evidence. Currently, the grounds for renewal of proceedings are more broadly defined. They are regulated in Articles 540, 540a and 542 § 3 CPC. The grounds specified in these provisions constitute a closed catalogue. The exceptional character of the renewal of proceedings determines the strict interpretation of these provisions.[235]

There are two modes of renewal of proceedings concluded by a final court ruling: upon request and ex officio.[236] Different grounds (reasons) for renewal are assigned to these modes. The easiest way to illustrate this is to note that renewal of proceedings ex officio is applicable only in the case of revealing one of the repeatedly indicated violations, listed in Article 439 § 1 CPC (Article 542 § 3 CPC). These infringements constitute a *iunctim* between cassation and renewal of proceedings concluded by a final court decision. This is confirmed in Article 542 § 4 CPC, from which it follows that the renewal of proceedings for the reasons listed in Article 439 § 1 CPC may not take place if they were subject to examination under the cassation procedure.

The main group of reasons for renewal of proceedings upon request is included in Article 540 CPC. This provision gives rise to the following three grounds for renewal:

1. *ex delicto* (Article 540 § 1 point 1 CPC);[237]
2. *de novis* (Article 540 § 1 point 2 CPC);
3. other grounds (Article 540 §§ 2 and 3 CPC).[238]

The *ex delicto* ground allows for the renewal of proceedings both in favour and against the accused. Renewal of proceedings *ex delicto* may take place if, in connection with the proceedings, a criminal offence has been committed, and there is a good reason to believe that it might have affected the contents of such a ruling (Article 540 § 1(1) CPC).[239] It is not only the crime of giving false testimony or bribery. The renewal may result from the commission of any other crime in connection with the proceedings, eg unlawful threats against witnesses or members of the judiciary, issuing a ruling with a certain content for personal gain, taking part in beating a witness, creating false evidence or obliterating traces of a crime. For the renewal of proceedings it is sufficient to have a reasonable suspicion (good reasons to believe) that a certain offence might have affected

[235] Supreme Court Judgment, 21 October 2008, IV KO 59/08, OSNwSK 2008, no 1, pos 2069.

[236] Supreme Court Decision, 20 May 2010, V KO 47/10, OSNKW 2010, no 8, pos 73; Appeal Court Decision in Katowice, 11 December 1998, II AKo 350/98, OSA 1999, no 6, pos 47. See also Supreme Court Judgment, 9 October 2018, III KO 106/18, Lex no 2572697.

[237] Doda and Gaberle (n 69) 526; Zabłocki (n 99) 593.

[238] Świecki (n 20) vol II, 674–75.

[239] Hofmański, Sadzik and Zgryzek (n 88) 303.

the contents of the final ruling.[240] According to Article 541 § 1 CPC, the fact that an offence has been committed must be established by a final convicting judgment, unless such a ruling cannot be issued for any of the reasons listed in Article 17 § 1 points 3–11 or Article 22 CPC, ie due to the legal or factual obstacles specified in these provisions.[241] In the case of a final conviction, the court examining the motion for renewal of proceedings (renewal court) does not have the power to independently examine whether the crime attributed to a certain person was actually committed.[242] In this respect, it is bound by the content of the final conviction. The motion for the renewal of the judicial proceedings shall indicate the convicting judgment or the ruling issued in criminal proceedings stating that the convicting judgment could not be rendered (Article 541 § 2 CPC).

The *de novis* ground, also referred to as *propter nova*, allows proceedings to be renewed only in favour of the accused. It consists in the possibility of renewal of proceedings if after the ruling has been issued, new facts or evidence come to light, which indicate that:

1. the sentenced person has not committed the act, or their act does not constitute a criminal offence or does not carried any penalty;
2. the sentenced person has been sentenced for another crime carrying a more severe penalty, or material circumstances obligating the extraordinary mitigation of punishment have not been duly considered, or material circumstances contributing to the aggravation of the penalty have been incorrectly relied upon;
3. the court has discontinued or conditionally discontinued the proceedings, relying on an incorrect assumption that the accused committed the alleged crime (Article 540 § 1 point 2 CPC).

The term 'new evidence' includes in its scope both new sources of evidence (eg new witnesses or new documents) and new means of proof (eg new testimony or explanations), even if the latter are derived from sources of evidence that were previously known to the parties or the court.[243] New facts are generally established by new evidence.[244] Thus, they will not usually constitute an independent ground for *propter nova* renewal, but will be indicated in addition to the new evidence from which they arise. Sometimes, however, certain facts do not require proof, such as facts covered by common notoriety. Thus, if, sticking to the example given, a certain fact becomes common knowledge after the final conclusion of the court proceedings, it is subject to qualification as a 'new fact' that may lead to the renewal of proceedings.[245] '*Nova*' are new facts or evidence that, prior to the final ruling, were not known not only to the court but also to the party lodging request for renewal (*noviter reperta*). They provide grounds for renewal of court proceedings only if they indicate one of the defects listed above. New facts or evidence

[240] Supreme Court Decision, 5 December 2012, III KO 28/12, OSNKW 2013, no 1, pos 10; Supreme Court Decision, 9 October 2012, III KO 41/12, Lex no 1220886.

[241] Supreme Court Decision, 7 July 1978, I KZ 52/78, OSNKW 1978, no 9, pos 107.

[242] Supreme Court Judgment, 7 July 1978, I KZ 52/78, OSNKW 1978, no 9, pos 107.

[243] Supreme Court Judgment, 5 March 1982, II KZ 30/82, OSNKW 1982, no 6, pos 36.

[244] Supreme Court Decision, 10 November 1992, II KRN 197/92, OSNKW 1993, nos 1–2, pos 10; Zabłocki (n 99) 657.

[245] Supreme Court Judgment, 10 November 1992, II KRN 197/92, OSNKW 1993, nos 1–2, pos 10.

are not grounds *de novis* if they did not cause one of these consequences and only indicate, for example, that the accused was given an excessively severe punishment, and this is not accompanied by a change in legal classification.

Another group of grounds for renewal are *propter decreta* grounds. According to Article 540 §§ 2 and 3 CPC, the proceedings shall be renewed:

1. for the benefit of a party if the Constitutional Court (the Constitutional Tribunal) adjudicates on the non-compliance with the Constitution, a ratified international agreement, or the statute, of the legal provision based on which the ruling was issued; the renewal may not take place to the disadvantage of the accused;
2. for the benefit of the accused, when such a need results from a decision of an international authority acting under the provisions of an international agreement which has been ratified by the Republic of Poland.[246]

Complementary to the grounds for renewal presented so far are the grounds *propter machinationem*, set out in Article 540a, and *propter in absentia*, regulated in Article 540b CPC. According to the first of these provisions, court proceedings concluded by a final ruling may be renewed if:

1. the sentenced person to whom provisions of Article 60 §§ 3 or 4 CC or of Article 36 § 3 of the Criminal Fiscal Code has been applied did not confirm in the criminal proceedings the information disclosed by them;
2. the circumstance defined in Article 11 § 3 CPC occurs.

The ground indicated in point (1) gives the possibility to draw negative procedural consequences against a disloyal accused, having the status of a so-called 'small crown witness', who, having obtained certain benefits resulting from a conviction with the application of extraordinary mitigation of penalty or conditional suspension of the enforcement of the imposed penalty due to disclosing to a law enforcement authority important information concerning, for example, persons cooperating in the commission of a criminal or fiscal offence and the circumstances of its commission, then breaks the agreement underlying the milder conviction by failing to confirm the disclosed earlier information.[247] As for the second point, it is about the possibility of renewal proceedings as a consequence of revoking or substantially amending a final judgment which, due to the amount or type of sentence imposed therein, made it inadvisable to conduct proceedings against the convicted person in a case of misdemeanour subject to imprisonment for up to five years and gave the basis for its 'absorptive' discontinuance (Article 11 §§ 1 and 3 CPC).[248] Taking into account the presented circumstances resulting in the possibility of renewal of proceedings under Article 540a CPC, it seems quite obvious that renewal on the basis of them may take place only to the disadvantage of the accused, and it is up to the prosecutor to make a motion in this regard. In these cases, renewal is facultative, ie it may or may not take place.

[246] See further M Wąsek-Wiaderek in P Wiliński (ed), *System Prawa Karnego Procesowego*, vol III: *Zasady procesu karnego, cz 2* (Warsaw, Wolters Kluwer, 2014) 1352 et seq; Supreme Court Judgment, 17 August 2011, II KO 72/10, OSNKW 2011, no 10, pos 92.

[247] Hofmański, Sadzik and Zgryzek (n 88) 318–19.

[248] ibid 322.

According to Article 540b § 1 CPC, court proceedings concluded with a final ruling may be renewed upon a motion of the accused, filed within a final time limit of one month as of the date on which the accused became aware of the ruling issued with regard to them, provided that the case was heard with the accused being absent as no notification of the date of the session or trial was served on them or where it was served otherwise than personally, if the accused proves that they had no information on the date of the session or trial and was not aware of the possibility of a ruling being issued with them being absent (*propter in absentia*).[249] This solution is aimed at strengthening the guarantees of the right of defence of the accused, in particular in the aspect of providing him with the possibility of exercising the rights arising from participation in the examination of the case and the right to appeal the decision ending the proceedings.

A motion for the renewal of proceedings terminated by a final court ruling may be filed primarily by the parties (Article 542 § 1 CPC). In principle, by means of a motion for renewal proceedings, the party may contest the resolutions or findings only if they are prejudicial to their rights or interests (Article 425 § 3 in conjunction with Article 545 § 1 CPC). This limitation does not apply to the public prosecutor, who may file a motion against as well as in favour of the convicted person (Article 425 § 4 in conjunction with Article 545 § 1 CPC). If the sentenced person has died, a request for renewal of the proceedings for their benefit may be submitted by their closest relative by blood or affinity (Article 542 § 2 CPC). The renewal of proceeding to the benefit of the accused shall not be prevented by the execution of a penalty, expungement, act of clemency or any circumstances excluding prosecution or substantiating the suspension of the proceedings (Article 529 in conjunction with Article 545 § 1 CPC).

The motion for the renewal of proceedings must be in writing and must therefore comply with the general conditions for a pleading set out in Article 119 § 1 CPC. In principle, the CPC does not set out specific requirements that should be met by the content of such a motion. An exception concerns the obligation, already signalled above, to indicate in a motion based *ex delicto* the convicting judgment establishing the commission of an offence which was connected to the proceedings covered by the motion for renewal or the ruling stating that the convicting judgment could not be rendered (Article 541 § 2 CPC). It can be said that, in the case of any motion for renewal,

[249] In addition, it may be noted that the possibility of reopening the proceedings is excluded in the event of one of the circumstances regulated in Art 540b § 2 CPC, which constitute negative grounds for reopening the proceedings at the request of the accused. The first of these circumstances is that the defendant is served with the notice of the date of the trial or hearing in accordance with the rules of service of notices and decisions set out in Art 133 § 2, Art 136 § 1 and Art 139 § 1 CPC. It follows from this reference to the provisions mentioned at the end especially that the renewal of the proceedings at the request of the defendant cannot take place if the notice or the decision may be deemed to have been served as a consequence of non-receipt of the letter despite being served twice (fiction of personal service – Art 133 § 2 CPC) where the non-delivery is due to a refusal to accept the letter (Art 136 § CPC) or due to the fact that the notification or the decision has been sent to an address of the defendant which is not up to date, where he has failed to inform of a change of residence or of his residential address also due to imprisonment and also to an outdated post office box (Art 139 § 1 CPC). The second circumstance excluding the renewal of the proceedings at the request of the accused pursuant to Art 540b § 1 CPC is the attendance of the defence counsel at the trial or the hearing at which the case has been tried despite the absence of the accused person due to the lack of service of the notice of the hearing or service otherwise than personally.

its content is decided by the purpose that guides its filing.[250] First of all, the content of the motion should be to indicate and to prove one of the grounds for renewal of the proceedings. Moreover, the application should specify the applicant's demand as to the expected decision of the court adjudicating on the renewal of proceedings. The motion may concern the whole or part of a final judgment or order (Article 425 § 2, first sentence, in conjunction with Article 545 § 1 CPC). If a motion for the renewal of proceedings is not filed by the public prosecutor, it shall be drawn up and signed by a solicitor, a legal counsel or a counsel of the General Prosecutor of the Republic of Poland. Other formal requirements include payment of a fee for the application and attaching the appropriate number of copies for the opposing parties. The motion for the renewal of proceedings may be withdrawn with the effect of leaving it unheard (Article 432 in conjunction with Article 545 § 1 CPC).

The question as to whether proceedings shall be renewed shall be resolved by the regional court, and the question of renewing the proceedings concluded by a ruling of the regional court shall be resolved by the appellate court. The court shall adjudicate in a panel of three judges (Article 544 § 1 CPC). The question as to whether proceedings concluded by a ruling rendered by an appellate court or the Supreme Court shall be renewed shall be resolved by the Supreme Court in a panel of three judges (Article 544 § 2 CPC).[251]

Before the ruling is issued, the court may order a verification of the facts, which shall carried out by the court on its own or by the judge appointed from the adjudicative panel for this purpose, or by a court requested by the way of legal assistance (Article 546 CPC).[252] The function of the fact-finding is only to make it probable that one of the grounds for renewal exists in relation to the proceedings covered by the motion for renewal, eg new evidence presented by the defence counsel which indicates that the convicted person did not commit the crimes.[253] The parties have the right to participate in these verifying actions, and therefore should be notified of their time and place. The session, which is the forum for the court's ruling on the question of renewal of proceedings, is generally held without the participation of the parties. However, the president of the court or the court may decide to recognise the motion of renewal with the participation of the parties (Article 544 § 3 CPC).

The following rulings may be made as a result of the filing of a motion for renewal of proceedings:[254]

1. Leaving the application unheard when the renewal is inadmissible, if the motion has been filed by an unauthorised person or if the formal defects of the motion have not been remedied within the seven-day period set for their remedy (Article 430 § 1 in conjunction with Article 545 § 1 CPC).[255] Leaving the motion unheard shall

[250] See also M Ciukas, 'Domniemanie niewinności w postępowaniu wznowieniowym' (2010), *Prok i Pr* no 6, 65 et seq.; Supreme Court Decision, 17 November 2010, II KO 37/10, OSNwSK 2010, no 1, pos 2273.
[251] Supreme Court Decision, 20 January 2022, II DO 64/21, Lex no 3359133.
[252] Supreme Court Decision, 8 December 2021, V KO 78/21, Lex no 3326817.
[253] Supreme Court Decision, 25 February 2021, V KO 31/20, Lex no 3123925.
[254] Supreme Court Decision, 11 June 2015, IV KO 22/15, OSNKW 2015, no 11, pos 93.
[255] See also Supreme Court Decision, 16 December 2004, IV KZ 57/04, OSNwSK 2004, no 1, pos 2417.

be decided by the court by means of a decision; this decision may be subject of complaint, unless it has been issued by an appellate court or the Supreme Court (Article 547 § 1 CPC).[256]

2. Dismissal of the motion for renewal the proceedings. This ruling is a consequence of the finding that there are no grounds for renewal the proceedings;[257] it takes the form of a decision, which is also subject to complaint, unless the Supreme Court or a court of appeal has ruled (Article 547 § 1 CPC).[258]
3. A decision on the renewal of proceedings may take two forms:
   - Set aside the judgment under appeal and refer the case back to the court of competent jurisdiction for re-examination (Article 547(2), first sentence CPC). Such a decision is the rule in cases where the motion for renewal is granted; this decision shall not be subject to any appeal measures (Article 547 § 2, second sentence CPC).[259] If the proceedings have been renewed pursuant to a motion for the benefit of the accused, and if they are conducted after the death of the accused, or if a reason occurs for suspending the proceedings, the president of the court shall designate an ex officio defence counsel to defend the rights of the accused, unless the moving party itself has already appointed a defence counsel (Article 548 CPC).
   - Set aside the contested decision and acquit the accused or discontinue the proceedings (Article 547 § 3 CPC).[260] The court may acquit the accused by a judgment, only provided that – according to the newly disclosed facts or evidence – their conviction was manifestly unjust, so the conviction is strikingly defective. The court decides on acquittal or discontinuation in the form of a judgment. A judgment acquitting the accused or discontinuing the proceedings shall be subject to appeal, unless the judgment was issued by the Supreme Court (Article 547 § 3 second sentence and § 4 CPC).[261]

[256] Supreme Court Decision, 25 September 2013, III KK 231/13, OSNKW 2013, no 12, pos 103.
[257] Supreme Court Decision, 12 April 2001, III KO 53/99, OSNKW 2001, nos 7–8, pos 67.
[258] Supreme Court Decision, 21 October 2010, V KZ 64/10, OSNwSK 2010, no 1, pos 2066.
[259] Supreme Court Judgment, 6 October 2006, II KO 46/06, Lex no 202151.
[260] Supreme Court Judgment, 16 April 2021, V KA 1/20, OSNK 2021, no 8, pos 33.
[261] Supreme Court Judgment, 8 December 2020, II KA 1/20, OSNK 2021, no 2, pos 6.

INDEX

www.ingramcontent.com/pod-product-compliance
Ingram Content Group UK Ltd.
Pitfield, Milton Keynes, MK11 3LW, UK
UKHW020235290926
15470UKWH00002B/552

9 781509 950775